North Korea's Cities

Industrial facilities, internal structures and typification

Rainer Dormels

Jimoondang
85 Gwanginsa-gil, Paju-si, Gyeonggi-do, 413-756, Korea
82 Donhwamun-ro, Jongno-gu, Seoul, 110-360, Korea
Phone: 82-2-743-3096 E-mail: edit@jimoon.co.kr
82-2-743-3192~3 E-mail: sale@jimoon.co.kr
Fax: 82-2-743-0227, 82-2-742-4657
Homepage: www.jimoon.co.kr

The National Library of Korea Cataloging-in-Publication (CIP)
North Korea's Cities - Industrial facilities, internal structures and typification / By Rainer Dormels
ISBN 978-89-6297-167-5 93340 330.911-KDC5 301.095193-DDC21 CIP2014019129

Printed in Korea

This work was supported by the Academy of Korean Studies (KSPS) Grant funded by the Korean Government (MOE) (AKS-2011-BAA-2105)

Acknowledgements

The present work analyses 27 cities of the DPR Korea in the context of two quantitative studies. Of primary importance in this context is the equipment of cities with industrial companies as well as the internal structure of the cities. Further descriptions not only serve the purpose of making the script less monotonous but also provide a better understanding of the quantitative study. My wish to write a geographical work on North Korea has existed since the early 1990s, when I studied in Korea. Since then, I began to regularly collect relevant essays and monographs and I also began to assemble statistics regarding North Korean industrial companies. Over the course of years, statistics grew more extensive and after my appointment to professorship in Vienna I was in particular supported by Ji-young Choi in terms of the statistics of industrial companies. Whenever I found time in the course of my other duties, I worked on the publication on the geography of North Korea. Eventually, I decided to limit my research to the cities of the DPR Korea. These studies were intensified after I was able to form a group of academics who were supported by the Academy of Korean Studies (KSPS) grant funded by the Korean Government (MOE) (AKS-2011-BAA-2105) in the context of their Core University Program for Korean Studies (CUPKS) since 2011. This support first and foremost enabled the completion and publication of the present work. Numerous people contributed to the completion of this publication. At this point I would like to express my sincere thanks to Yen Nguyen and Krisztián Pál Kaszás, who made the numerous figures. Furthermore, Lena Edlinger, Cathi Hlawacek, Marianne Jung, Chanmi Na, Sabrina Obenaus, Daniela Olivier, Ada Patterer, Wolfgang Pirkfellner and Hanna Shin were helpful with various tasks such as proof-reading, translating from the original German version to English and other duties. The pictures were taken during my two travels to North Korea in the years of 2006 and 2012. Also I want to thank our proofreaders Mike Dirks and Christopher M. Doll. My gratitude is furthermore dedicated to director Lim, Sam Gyu of Jimoondang Publishing Co. for the inclusion in their program, the proof-reading, the in-design, and the printing, etc. Last but certainly not least, I would like to express sincere thanks to my wife Sung Eun, who accompanied me during my extensive and time-consuming project with her patience and sacrifice. May this book contribute to the provision of new information in regards to the treated object of research!

Vienna, April 2014
Rainer Dormels

Contents

IV. Profiles of the cities of DPR Korea

I. Introduction

I.1. Overview of topics, objectives and methods

The present study, which deals with the cities of North Korea, approaches the research topic from three different angles. One of the angles is of a qualitative nature and the remaining two are quantitative.

The first approach deals with the facilities of the cities, especially with industrial plants. In 1996 the Sanŏpyŏn'guwŏn[1] (Korea Institute for Industrial Economics & Trade)[2] issued a manual on North Korean companies in the mining sector and industry[3] which introduces and lists North Korean power plants, mines and industrial companies divided by sectors. This piqued my curiosity with regard to the geographical distribution of the sites for the listed industrial companies and I started, based on this manual, to create a list of the industrial companies sorted by cities and counties. Over time, other literature and sources that could be used as a basis for a study of the geographical distribution of locations of North Korean industrial companies appeared. In the present research, five sources that list North Korean industrial companies are analyzed from a statistical point of view, whereby first the cities and counties, in which the facilities are located, are ascertained. Developed on the basis of such data, not only statements about which cities are more equipped with industrial plants than others should be made, but also information about the importance of the individual cities for the industrial development of the country should be found.

The second methodological approach is used to study the structure of the cities of North Korea. The analysis of the data on changes in the administrative divisions within the cities, answers to the questions about the extension or reduction of the urban area and the

1 The Romanization follows the usage of the Romanization in North Korean publications, as it is used in "DPR Korean 2008 Population Census." The Romanization used there can be seen as a variant of the McCune-Reischauer Romanization, but consonant assimilations are less considered. In other words, aspects of transliteration are more intensified. For example Paekma instead of Paengma, Masikryŏng instead of Masingnyŏng. In provinces, cities, counties and districts, diacritical marks are omitted as in "DPR Korea 2008 Population Census." And the city "Kim Chaek" is written in the present work in derogation from "Census" as a single word "Kimchaek." Diacritical marks in political paroles are also omitted, for example: Chollima instead of Chŏllima, Songun instead of Sŏn'gun. Furthermore, for personal names of the North Korean ruling family Kim as well as for dynasty names, for example: Joson instead of Josŏn, Koryo instead of Koryŏ, Koguryo instead of Koguryŏ.

2 Hereafter referred to as: KIET.

3 Authors: Yi Sang-chik, Choe Sin-rim, Yi Sŏk-ki.

development of centers within the city are to be found.[4]

The third approach concerns itself with the elaboration of particular characteristics of the cities. Overviews on the geography of Korea, which also have a regional section, that includes North Korea,[5] also devote only a few lines to North Korean cities. This piqued my curiosity already in the 1980s for the cities in the north of the Korean peninsula and I began to collect information on the cities of North Korea from a variety of sources. This information was initially very sparse, but over time more and more overviews and encyclopedias were published in North as well as in South Korea, but also research and journalistic reports, which provided information about North Korean cities. Of course, the current information situation on North Korean cities is overall fragmentary, thus a comprehensive urban geography is not possible and merely some mosaic-like aspects can be considered. The present publication therefore is not trying to gather as much information about the cities of North Korea as possible, but information is offered which either has a useful relevance for the typification of the cities and for the elaboration of specific characteristics or which can be used for the interpretation and explanation of the results of the quantitative research approaches of the present study.

In summary it can be said that due to the fact that access to the area of research and the sources is subject to strong restrictions, the present research does not attempt to present a comprehensive geography of the 27 North Korean cities. However, the study, following the three above presented approaches, is limited to the following substantial focal points:

- Elaboration of particular characteristics of the cities (heuristic classification of the cities),
- Growth and urbanization processes of the individual cities,
- Interrelations between the cities (population shares, quota of companies).

The presentation of the results is divided into two. First, results with regard to interrelations between the cities (population shares, numbers of factories, etc.) are presented. Secondly, each of the 27 cities will be granted a separate chapter, where results are presented from all three approaches.

With regard to the regional administrative divisions, the present study is broadly

4 Parts of the research within the second methodological approach are based on a previous project supported by the Academy of Korean Studies which consists of the making of hybrid maps and a research about the inner structure of North Korean cities (Grant Number AKS-2007-R 10). But the results are published here for the first time. The 20-volume Joson-hyangtho-taebakkwa (Encyclopedia of North Korean Geography and Culture) was used as a source, which was published in 2003 by the Institute for Peace Affairs (hereafter referred to as IPA). For more information on the methodology see chapter IV.1.

5 For example Kang Sŏk-o (1984), Jŏng Jang-ho (1986) and Im Tŏk-sun (1992).

based on the data published in IPA (2003). However, subsequent changes of the city area of Pyongyang and the restoration of the provincial-level city Nampho[6] and other major changes in city areas were taken into account.[7] Authentic information about changes in the urban areas of Pyonyang and Nampho are shown in the yearbooks Joson-jungang-nyŏn'gam 2010 and 2011.

Furthermore, data from the Kwangmyŏng-paekkwa-sajŏn 8[8] (2009) were used and compared with the data from IPA. Important information about changes of the regional administrative units is also provided in the "DPR Korea 2008 Population Census" and the Toro-jidochŏp (2009).[9]

I.2. Previous research and sources about the cities of North Korea

Scientific papers on North Korean cities, the North Korean city planning or the North Korean system of cities are rare. The most comprehensive overview of urban systems and city planning in North Korea is provided by Kim Wŏn (1998), in a monograph on the socialist city planning, in which the 5th Chapter (pp. 211-312) deals with North Korea. Research on urban planning in North Korea was offered in the doctoral thesis of Kim Hyŏn-su (1994), in which the capital, Pyongyang, is in the focus. In Im Tong-u (2011) various city planning aspects of Pyongyang are dealt with. An overview of the urban planning in North Korea is also provided by a book chapter by Kim Ki-ho (2006). Various essays in a book of the Taehan-thomok-hakhoe (Korean Society of Civil Engineers) (2009) also deal with topics related to urban and regional development in North Korea. An overview of urban development processes in North Korea was provided by Jo/Adler (2002).

A project was carried out at the Institute for Far Eastern Studies at the Kyŏngnam University, in which the North Korean cities of Chongjin, Sinuiju and Hyesan were the main focus. This was mainly done on the basis of surveys of North Korean refugees. However, it is all about an urban sociological project that deals with politics, economy, society, issues of women's rights and urbanization processes, especially in the above

6 The data in Yonhap News Agency Pukhan-yŏn'gam 2011 regarding the administrative divisions are similar to those in IPA of 2003, with the only difference that 2011 Pukhanyŏn'gam shows the recent changes in the size of Pyongyang and Nampho. This suggests that the data in IPA in general seem to reflect the latest knowledge available in South Korea.

7 Relevant deviations from the data in IPA (2003) can be stated based on new sources not only for Pyongyang and Nampho but also for Anju and Kaesong.

8 Hereafter referred to as PSC-8.

9 Hereafter referred to as JC.

mentioned regional cities.[10] For this particular research focus Choe Wan-gyu (2004b) and Jang Se-hun (2006a, b) are especially relevant.

Historical aspects of cities in the DPRK are the subject of a research project at the Tongguk University. The first results are an anthology of Pukhan-tosisa-yŏn'guthim (2013), which focuses on methodological questions about the study of the history of North Korean cities as well as a monograph with explanation of sources dealing with the cities of Hamhung and Phyongsong by Ko Yu-hwan/Pak Hŭi-jin (2013).

Essentially based on the "DPR Korea 2008 Population Census," Kim Tu-sŏp, Choe Min-ja, Jŏn Kwang-hŭi, Yi Sam-sŏk and Kim Hyŏng-sŏk (2011) analyze in the seventh chapter of their book North Korea's population and also aspects of urbanization.

Recently the view of North Korean cities, however, is limited to the capital or the capital region: Yi Ki-sŏk (2008), Schinz/Dege (1990), Springer (2003).

Herl (2004) provides an overview of the urban geography of North Korea issued by Palka/Galgano (United States Military Academy at West Point).

With the aim of "development potentials of the growth poles" in terms of defining Korean unification, Yi Sang-jun/Kim Chŏn-kyu/Pak Se-hun/Sin Hye-won (2011 and 2012)[11] investigated the cities of Nampho, Sinuiju, Rason, Chongjin and Wonsan with the help of modern GIS technology and through interviews of refugees from North Korea.

Yi Ki-sŏk's aim (2001) is a systematic, clear presentation based on the latest available data as information for teachers in Korean elementary and middle schools. In the framework of these presentations inter alia the administrative subdivision of North Korea, the population of North Korea and North Korea's cities are treated in separate sections. Additionally it introduces areas within North Korea, which are identified for intensive cooperation with foreign and South Korean partners (Rajin-Sonbong, Kumgangsan, Sinpho, Nampho and Kaesong).

The Organizing Committee of the 29th International Geographical Congress (2000) provides one chapter each on the region of Pyongyang-Nampho and on the development program for the Tumen region. Furthermore, a number of other papers that refer to selected cities of North Korea were published.

Other important sources are geographical overviews and area studies. The most important source on the historical aspects of the development of cities, especially during the period of the Japanese occupation, is the standard work, released in 1945, by the German geographer Lautensach (1945). In 1951 a geography of Korea was published by the Russian geographer Saitschikow, which also includes North Korea and was also pub-

10 The project has resulted so far in several essays, pamphlets and in the following four monographs: Choe Wan-kyu (ed.) (2004a, 2006, 2007), Ku Kap-u et.al. (2008).

11 Hereafter referred to as Yi Sang-jun et. al. (2011) or Yi Sang-jun et. al. (2012).

lished in 1958 in a German version.

Incomplete however, as already mentioned, is the information about the cities of North Korea in South Korean overviews on the geography of Korea. North Korea was for a long time in South Korea only a topic of anti-communistic education. It was only after the onset of the "Northern Policy" under the government of President Roh Tae-woo (1988-1993), that it was possible to write in an open manner about North Korea, with seemingly harmless topics such as linguistics, cultural goods and regional geographical and touristic representations taking precedence. Therefore the most popular scientific papers published in the 90s were created from the pens of journalists, who wanted to introduce to the South Koreans, the regions of their country, the latter couldn't visit.

Ko Thae-u (1992) and Pae Ki-chan (1994) depict the various provinces of the DPRK in separate chapters. The central points of Ko are the administrative division, landscapes and cultural heritage as well as the specifics of each county and city. Also Paek Ki-chan (1994) shows great interest in the administrative units. However, his chapters on individual provinces are more problem-oriented and contain strong criticisms on the policies of the DPRK.

The Chosun Ilbo daily news paper published between 18.9.1995 and 12.2.1996 a thirteen-part series, in which journalists of the political department at about a third of a page presented a North Korean city or county. These articles are based partly on basic information, which can be found in encyclopedias and on the other hand testimonies of refugees from these regions are used.

Detailed information is also provided by the five-part picture book series by the South Korean Han'guk-munwŏn (1995) on the occasion of the fiftieth anniversary of the division of the country. Here, detailed information about administrative division, topography, climate, attractions, and about the trade of the individual counties and cities are portrayed. A lot of this information stems from the lexicon "Paekkwa-jŏnsŏ," which was published in North Korea from 1982 to 1984, whose details were usually accepted without critical questions.

In 2003, the Encyclopedia of North Korean geography and culture was published, which was jointly released by the Kwahak-paekkwa-sajŏn chulphansa (North Korea) and by the Phyŏngwa-munje-yŏn'gusŏ (The Institute for Peace Affairs, Republic of Korea) (IPA 2003). This lexicon includes a lot of information on history, physical geography, industry and the culture of the cities. Information of which content would be problematic for one of the two Koreas have been expressed as one-sided or were just omitted. Also ratings or a differentiation of the information according to their importance is missing in this encyclopedic work. It is largely based on various reference works that were published in North Korea.

In 1990, a 30 volume overall presentation of the geography of the DPR Korea, Joson-jiri-jŏnsŏ,[12] have been published in North Korea of which 20 volumes deal with various

12 Hereafter referred to as KJY.

fields of the geography of North Korea, the remaining ten deal with individual regions. The information reflects the standard of knowledge until the mid-1990s.

I.3. Basic information on provinces and cities in North Korea

I.3.1. Changes in the boundaries of the provinces

The Democratic People's Republic of Korea (DPRK) or North Korea lies in Northeast Asia between 36° and 43° north latitude and 124° and 130° east longitude.

According to official data of the Central (North) Korean News Agency, Korea has a total area of 223,370 km², of which 5,907 km² are taken by islands. North Korea's area is with its 123,138 km² slightly larger than South Korea (Republic of Korea) with 100,232 km² (Joson-jungang-thongsinsa 2005, 1).

The southern border of the DPRK with the Republic of Korea forms the DMZ (demilitarized zone), which is in total 4 km wide and 248 km long. To the north runs a 1,360 km long border with the People's Republic of China, whilst the border with Russia is only 17.2 km long in the Northeast. In the west and east, North Korea is surrounded by sea. The total coastline is 2,495 km (Korea Annual 2003, 700).

Although Korea had been a victim of Japanese imperialism, it was divided in 1945 on the 38th Latitude into an American and a Soviet zone of influence. Two U.S. officers received the task of developing a plan for the division of Korea on the night of 10th August to 11th August 1945. They were given half an hour for this task. The 38th Latitude was chosen, because it divides Korea into two roughly equal halves, and because the capital Seoul thus became part of the American zone of occupation (Kindermann 1994, 51).

The border between North and South Korea thus was changed as a result of the Korean War on June 25th 1950, the battle lines quickly changed and almost all of Korea was captured once by the North Korean People's Army and once under the UN mandate of the alliance of South Korea and the U.S. Army.

After 1945, the new authorities in the DPR Korea had criticized that the original administrative division of the country was created, with its multi-level management system with regard to the objectives of Japanese imperialism, for the centralization of the country.

In particular, the lowermost units (*ri*) would be too small compared to the excessively large provinces and counties. Furthermore, the administrative places in the provinces and districts were often not located in the center of the areas concerned, but at the seashore, on railway lines, along main roads, in places, which created favorable conditions for the exploitation of the country by the Japanese.

With the territorial reform in December 1952, many new districts were created by dividing larger counties into smaller ones for example from 98 counties 168 counties were created, and the other way around from 10,120 *ri* 3,658 *ri* were created (Kim Yong-jae 2004, 44).

The territorial reform of December 1952 transformed the four-stage administrative system into a three-stage system. Under the new system, the provinces (*do*) consist of cities (*si*) and counties (*kun*). The cities are divided into districts (*dong*) and rural units (*ri*). The counties consist of an administrative center (*up*), rural units (*ri*) and working-class districts (*rodongjagu*).[13]

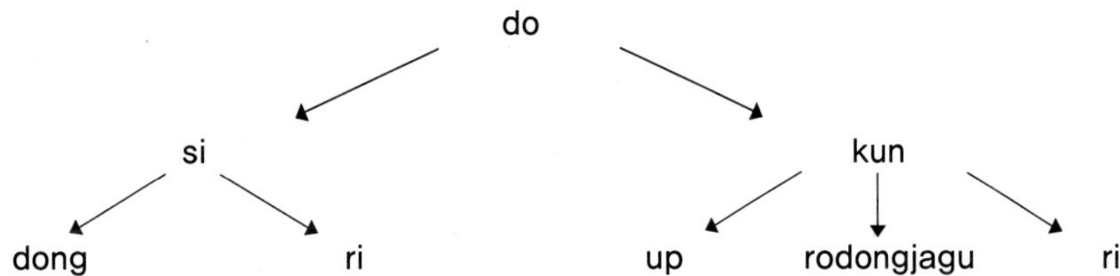

Figure I.-1. Regional administrative structure (provinces) of the DPRK since 1952

The structure of cities that are independent from provinces (*jikhalsi/thukpyolsi*) is similar:

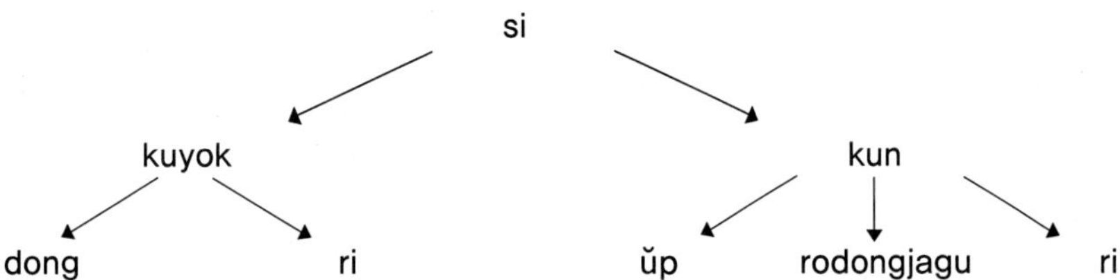

Figure I.-2. Regional administrative structure (jikhalsi/thukpyolsi) of the DPRK since 1952

Since the division of Korea, the DPRK conducted a number of changes in terms of administrative space planning.

At the provincial level, the following significant changes have been made over time:

13 The Korean names are in the following as a rule preferred for regional units, but diacritical marks are omitted: *up* instead of *ŭp*, *kuyok* instead of *kuyŏk*, *thukpyolsi* instead of *thŭkpyŏlsi*, *myon* instead of *myŏn*.

1. Formation of Kangwon Province (North)

September 1946: Kangwon Province, which was divided by the 38th Latitude, was increased to the North around the Wonsan area, in explanation around parts of the provinces Hamnam and Kyonggi, and got provincial status, so that presently a province of Kangwon exists in North Korea as well as in South Korea. Wonsan became capital of this province.

2. Formation of two new provinces (Jagang, Ryanggang) in the mountainous North

31.1.1949: The new province Jagang was formed out of the *kun* of Kanggye, Jasong, Huchang, Wiwon, Chosan and Huichon (formerly Phyongbuk Province) and Jangjin (partly) (formerly province Hamnam)

30.10. 1954: The province Ryanggang was newly formed out of the city of Hyesan-si (formerly Hambuk Province) and ten *kun.*[14]

3. Division of Hwanghae Province

30.10. 1954: The province Hwanghae is divided into Hwangnam (South-Hwanghae) and Hwangbuk (North-Hwanghae).

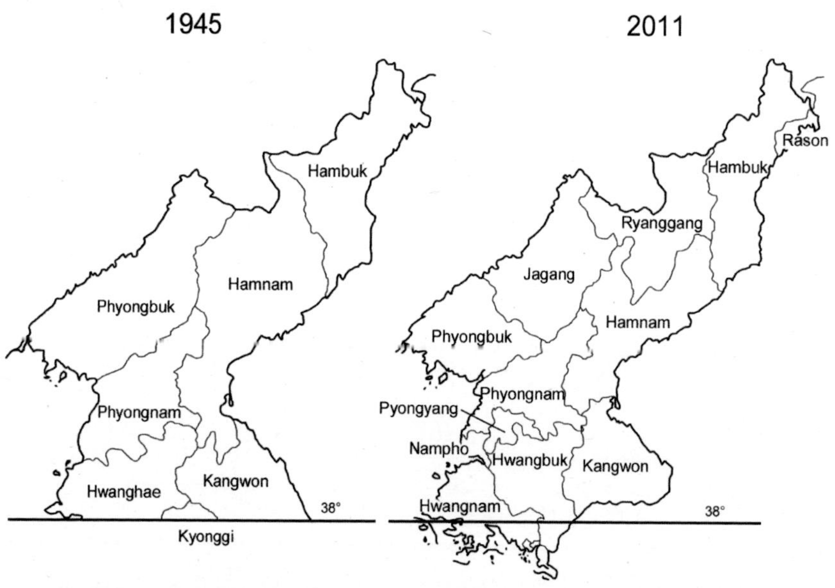

Figure I.-3. Administrative structure of North Korea in 1945 and 2011[15]

14 Inter alia following changes were made later on:
15.1.1965: Pujon-kun (formerly Ryanggang-do) becomes part of Hamgyong-namdo
7.8.1978: A part of Hamgyong-namdo becomes part of Taehungdan-kun (Ryanggang-do)

15 The provinces are in the following mostly designated as shown in Fig. I.3.-3 (with the omission of diacritical marks). These are partly abbreviated versions of the names: Hambuk–Hamgyong-bukto; Hamnam–Hamgyong-namdo; Phyongbuk–Phyongan-pukto; Phyongnam–Phyongan-namdo; Hwangbuk–Hwanghae-pukto; Hwangnam–Hwanghae-namdo.

I.3.2. Formation, development and resolution of the province independent cities

Some cities are managed directly from the central province and are thus independent from the province. Currently these are Pyongyang, Nampho and Rason. Other cities such as Kaesong, Hamhung and Chongjin had temporarily occupied a province independent status, but have since lost this status.

The names of the province independent cities in Korean literature are inconsistent. Sometimes they are called *jikhalsi* and at other times *thukpyolsi*. North Korean sources depict that until recently all the province independent cities were defined as *jikhalsi*. The fact that Rason is referred to as *thukpyolsi* from early 2010 is also confirmed by North Korean sources. According to South Korean sources, Nampho was in 2010 also a *thukpyolsi* and it is stated in the Yonhap Yearbook, that Pyongyang was renamed in September 2004 to a *thukpyolsi*. Nevertheless, Pyongyang is in the following page still identified as *jikhalsi*.

The capital, Pyongyang (formerly part of the Phyongnam Province), has had provincial status since September 1946. Over time (for example in 1959, 1960, 1963, 1972, 1984, 1995), the city area has increased. In recent years, however, there was a reduction of the urban area of Pyongyang. First, a *kuyok* and three *kun* of the metropolitan area of Pyongyang were removed and assigned to the Hwangbuk Province.[16] Thereafter, Kangnam-kun again became a part of Pyongyang.[17]

The city Nampho was established in the year of 1950 as part of the Phyongnam Province. In December 1979, Nampho was then connected with Taean-si and Ryonggang-kun into a *jikhalsi*. Nampho again in January 2004 became a part of the Phyongnam Province. Only the former *kuyok* of Hanggu and Waudo remain in the city area. Nampho was awarded the title of *thukpyolsi* and the other *kuyok* of Taean, Kangso, Chollima of the city became a *kun* and, additionally together with Ryonggang-kun became a part of the Phyongnam Province. In 2011, however Nampho is again a province independent city with all its parts, which it in 2004, in addition with Onchon-kun (formerly Phyongnam).

Rason consists of the former Rajin-si and the Sonbong-kun. Rajin-Sonbong was formed in September 1993 into a *jikhalsi*. In August 2000, it was renamed Rason-jikhalsi.[18]

16 See Joson-jungang-thongsinsa (Korean Central Yearbook) 2010 (map).

17 See Joson-jungang-thongsinsa (Korean Central Yearbook) 2011 (map).

18 The details about the status of Rason are inconsistent. Rason is on the one hand denominated in KCNA on August 15th 2001, May 23th 2003, September 11th 2006, May 5th 2008 and also on June 29th 2011 as a part of Hambuk, also according to IPA-2 (2003, 511) Rason is also from 2004 again part of Hambuk and the "DPR Korea 2008 Population Census" classifies Rason as a part of Hambuk. In the map at the beginning of the North

In the beginning of 2010, Rason became a *thukpyolsi.*

Kaesong is located in the south from the 38th Latitude and thus was from 1945 until the Korean War part of South Korea. During the Korean War the city became a part of North Korea. In the Mid-1950s,[19] Kaesong-si was connected to Kaephung-kun and Phanmun-kun and became a province independent city. Then, Jangphung-kun also became a part of the Kaesong-jikhalsi in March 1960. In November 2002, in relation to the establishment of the Kaesong Industrial Region, changes in the regional administration were also made. As a consequence, Kaesong lost its province independent status. Phanmun-kun was divided and dissolved into Kaephung-kun and Kaesong-si. The remaining administrative units, Kaesong-si and Kaephung-kun and Jangphung-kun became independently from each other part of the Hwangbuk Province.[20]

The East Sea cities of Hamhung (Hamnam) and Chongjin (Hambuk) became province independent cities on December 10th 1960, however in 1970, both were reintegrated into their respective provinces. Chongjin however was unified in November 1977 with Musan-kun and Kyongsong-kun and again formed a *jikhalsi*, until it lost its status on February 8th 1985, whereby Kyongsong and Musan again were separated from Chongjin and became *kun* of the Hambuk Province.

I.3.3. Backgrounds of the administrative transformations

The reasons for the establishment of new provinces and *jikhalsi* vary depending on the period of time.

After 1945 and in the 1950s, administrative measures were carried out with regard to the new situation of the division of the country and in order to overcome the consequences of the Japanese rule over Korea. Pyongyang became, similar to Seoul in South Korea, a province independent city. The division of Korea had cut the provinces of Kangwon and Kyonggi. The northern part of Kangwon had no cities, so that Wonsan and the surrounding area were integrated into Kangwon. Kaesong is located south of the 38th Latitude and was originally part of the Republic of Korea. However, boundary changes as a result of the Korean War brought the city into the DPR Korea. Kaesong and the surrounding area

Korean yearbook Joson-jungang-nyŏn'gam, Rajin and Sonbong are classified as part of Hambuk until 1996. Between 1997 and 2001 Rajin-Sonbong and since 2002 until 2012 Rason under its new name is portrayed as a province independent city, while in the same map between 2004 and 2009 Nampho and Kaesong are part of Phyongnam and Hwanghae Province. The latter can be used as proof that Rason has not lost its status as province independent city, in contrary to Nampho and Kaesong in 2004.

19 According to IPA-2 (2003, 433) in June 1957, other sources mention the year 1955.

20 In the meantime, the city of Kaesong has been expanded again around the area of Kaephung.

were thus a special area under the direct control of the state. In the division of the southern province of Hwanghae in Hwangbuk and of Hwangnam, it is sometimes assumed, that the goal would be to increase the number of provinces, in order to come up with a similar number of provinces such as in South Korea.

Because the coastal regions of North Korea have been more developed than other areas in the country under the Japanese rule, the highlands provinces of Jagang and Ryanggang were established in 1949 and 1954.

From the 1960s to the mid-1980s the two northern East Sea cities Hamhung and Chongjin were temporarily *jikhalsi*. Both are centers of heavy industry. On the other hand, the establishment of *jikhalsi* in the east of the country can also be interpreted as a symbol of the desire for a regional balance between the west of the country with its capital Pyongyang and the East. Regionalist tensions between Phyongan-do and Hamgyong-do should be prevented. In the recent administrative changes at the provincial level, economic developments, albeit in different ways, have exerted influence. In principle, administrative changes at the provincial level and special economic zones can be distinguished. The Kaesong-kongŏp-jigu and the Kŭmgangsan-kwan'gwang-jigu are special economic zones that have been created independently from the administrative regional division of the country into provinces and *jikhalsi/thukpyolsi*. The establishment of special economic regions has certainly had an impact on the official administrative division of the DPR Korea. What ought to be mentioned here is the creation of Rason-Sonbong-jikhalsi (now Rason-thukpyolsi). Conversely however, together with the creation of Kaesong-kongŏp-jigu, Kaesong-jikhalsi was abolished. Kaesong was under the direct administration of the state for a long time. This was due to the strong military presence in the city lying on the DMZ. With the establishment of the Kaesong-kongŏp-jigu and the gain of tourism to Kaesong, the military presence was reduced in the city, so the city is no longer be administrated by the head office directly, but became part of the Hwangbuk province.[21]

The upgrade of Nampho indicates a strengthening of the promotion of the capital region, while the reduction of Pyongyang means, that now the number of privileged capital residents was reduced, which again reduced state expenditure, and those affected, who were no longer citizens of Pyongyang were dissatisfied by this.

21 Interview with a person in charge in Kaesong 2006.

II. North Korean cities

II.1. The location of North Korean cities and their physical-geographical factors

If one tries to determine the distribution of North Korean cities within geographic regions, it should be noted, that there have been several attempts to accomplish such a subdivision (see Jŏng Jang-ho, 1986, 342-349). By considering the simplest regional classification by

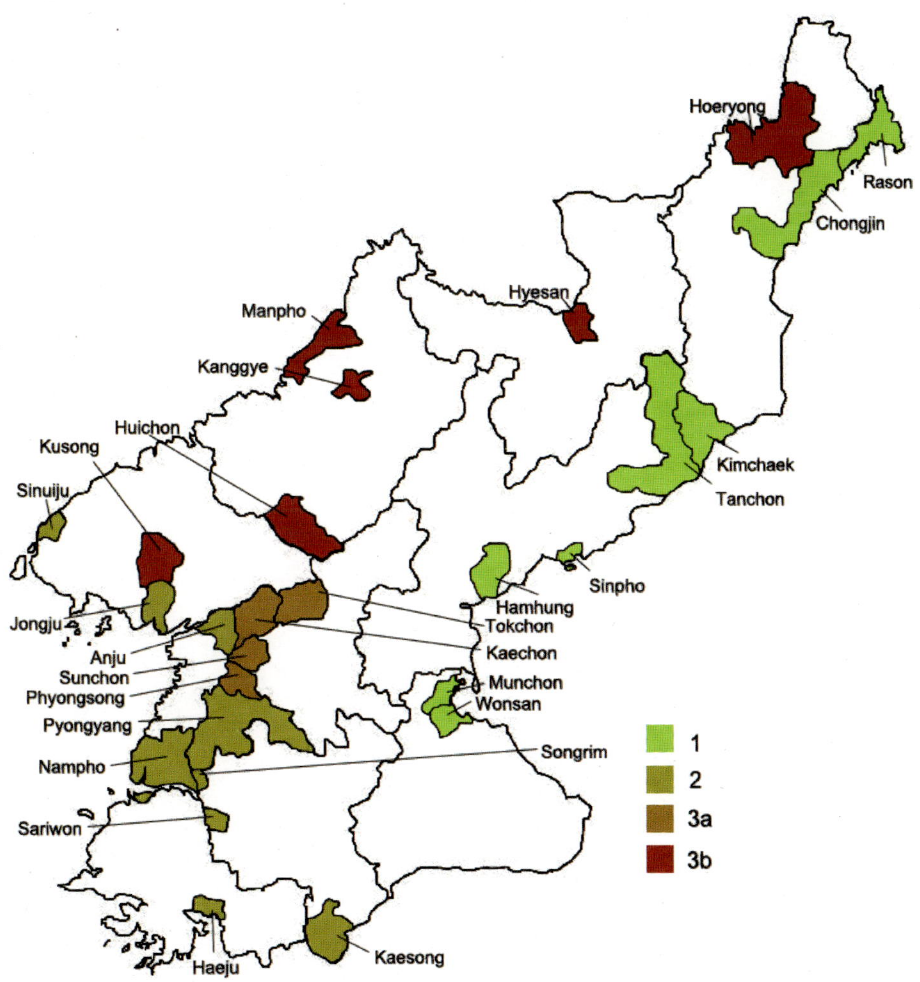

Figure II-1. North Korean cities divided according to types of landscape (Legend: 1 Northeastern coastal district; 2 Northwest Coast District/Western plains, 3a Central hills of Hwangphyong; 3b Plateaus and highlands)

Saitschikow (1958), we are able to ascertain that there are eight North Korean cities in the "northeastern coastal district": Rason, Chongjin, Kimchaek, Tanchon, Sinpho, Hamhung, Munchon, Wonsan.

In the northwestern coastal district and the Western plains, there are nine cities: Sinuiju, Jongju, Anju, Pyongyang, Nampho, Songrim, Sariwon, Haeju (Northwestern coast district) and Kaesong (Western plains).

Ten of 27 North Korean cities are located in the "North Korean mountain district." Four

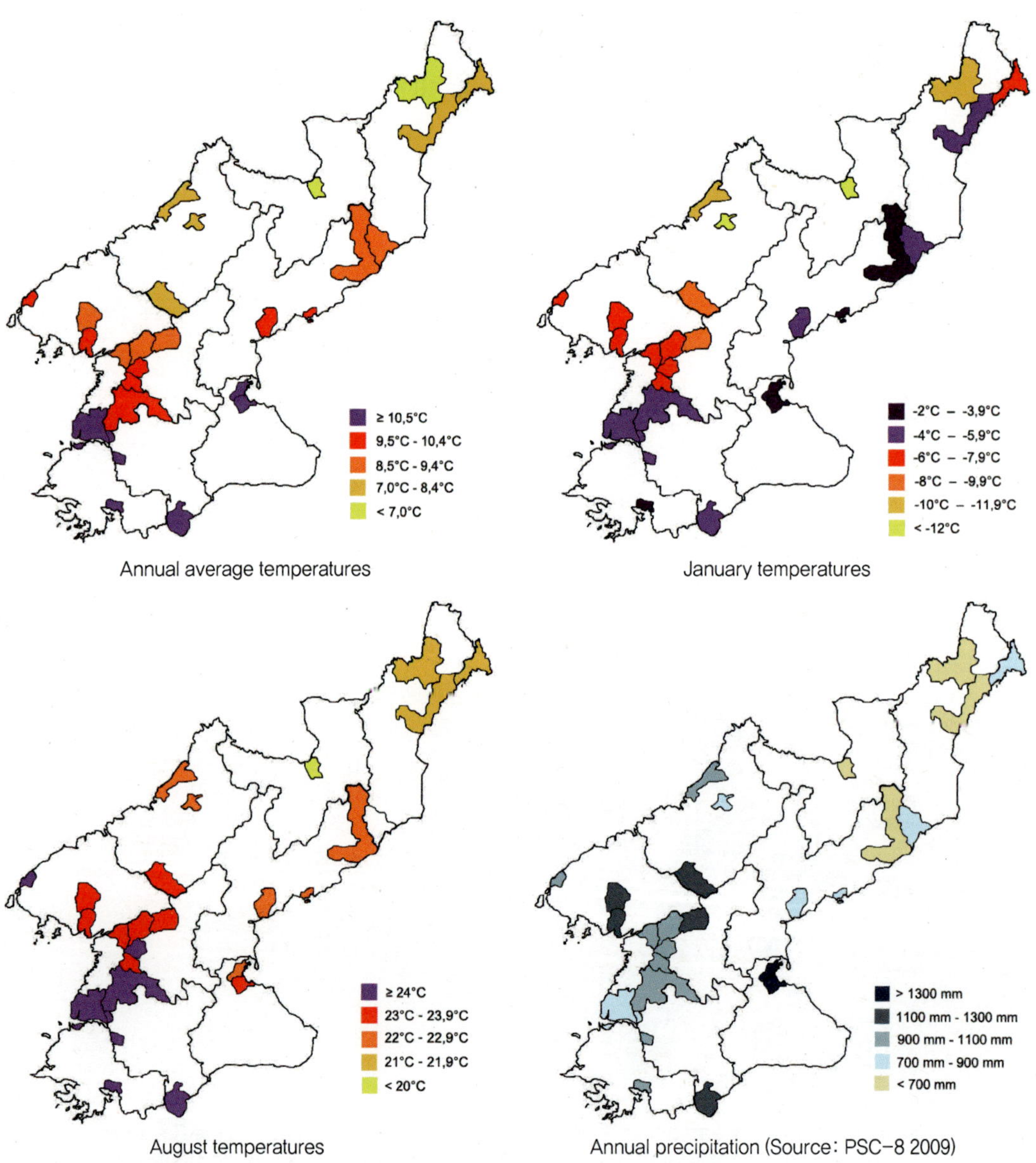

Figure II-2. North Korean cities and climate data (temperature and precipitation)

of these are located in an area that is named "the central hill country of Hwangphyong" by Kang Sŏk-o (1984, 119): Tokchon, Kaechon, Sunchon, Pyongsong. These cities lie practically at the threshold between the plains of the Yellow Sea and the mountains. Four cities are located on the high plains in the far North of the country: Kanggye, Huichon, Manpho (Jagang high plain) and Hyesan (Kaema-high plain); Kusong is located in the West of the plateau region in "the highlands of Phyongbuk" and Hoeryong is located east of it on the mountain range of Hamgyong.

For many older cities in the DPR Korea, its coastal location is defining. However, cities were later also added in a landlocked situation and a threshold location.

In view of climatic conditions, it can be stated that the differences in temperature between the warmer south and the colder north are much more pronounced in winter than in summer. The temperatures in winter are relatively mild on the east coast and extremely cold in the far north. Conversely, the West is a bit warmer than the East in summer. The West has also more precipitation than the North East.

II.2. Distance from the capital

Another possible criterion for the categorization of cities is their distance from the capital. Especially in states like North Korea, where the country's infrastructure is not yet fully developed, the distance to the capital plays an important role. Seven North Korean cities are located at a distance of less than 100 km away from the capital Pyongyang, whereby in each case the city center is taken into account (JC 2009):

- Phyongsong (31 km), Nampho (53 km), Sunchon (53 km), Songrim (55 km), Sariwon (66 km), Anju (69 km) and Kaechon (95 km).

Of these cities, Phyongsong, Nampho and Songrim border on the city of Pyongyang.
Nine cities are located at a distance of 100 km to 225 km from the capital:

- Jongju (121 km), Tokchon (137 km), Haeju (140 km), Kusong (159 km), Huichon (165 km), Kaesong (191 km), Wonsan (208 km), Munchon (220 km), Sinuiju (225 km).

Among these nine cities, Kaesong and Wonsan are cities that are effortlessly reachable from Pyongyang within one afternoon due to the presence of a highway and are popular tourist destinations. The train from Pyongyang to Sinuiju takes just a little bit more than five hours.

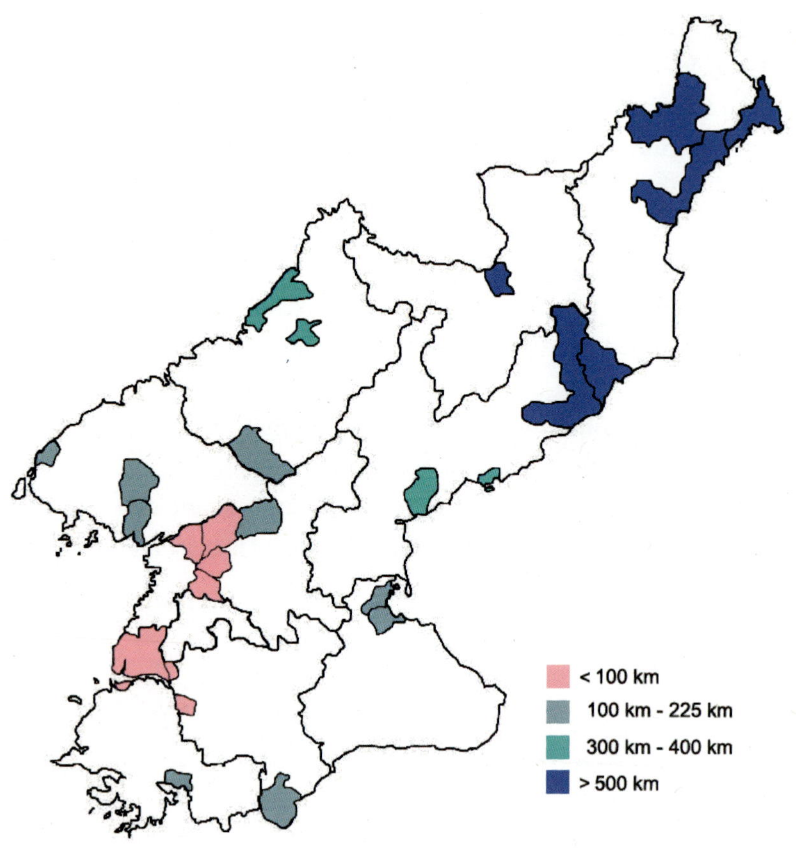

Figure II-3. The distance of North Korean cities from the capital Pyongyang

A little bit deeper inland or further north on the east sea coast, there are four cities that are located between 300 km and 400 km away from Pyongyang:

Kanggye (303 km), Hamhung (318 km), Manpho (359 km), Sinpho (391 km).

Furthest from the capital, there are six cities located in the northeast of Korea as follows:

Tanchon (523 km), Kimchaek (576 km), Hyesan (623 km), Chongjin (754 km), Hoeryong (841 km), Rason (852 km).

II.3. The development of the modern Korean city network

This classification of North Korean cities according to the date of their appointment to a city is limited to the time since the annexation of Korea by Japan.[1]

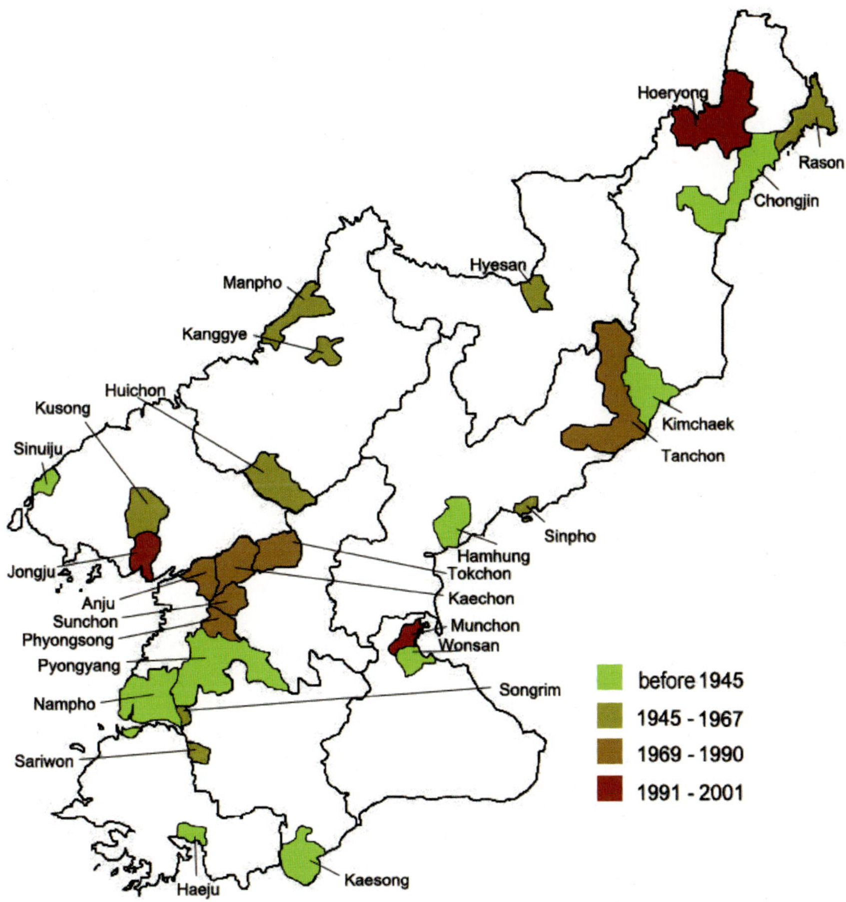

Figure II-4. Cities of North Korea and the date of appointment to the city[2]

II.3.1. Phase 1: The colonial urban system (1910–1945)

The development of the urban system in North Korea at the time of the Japanese colonial rule was inspired by the development of railways and the opening of the ports.

1 To historical aspects of North Korea's cities see Yun Jŏng-sŏp (1987), Kim Chŏl-su (2005) and Chae Thae-hyŏng (2010).

2 Cities, which no longer exist nowadays (Hungnam, Taean) are not shown in the map. The city areas shown in the map are the most recent ones.

The development therefore took place on the west and the east coast. In 1914, this was followed by the introduction of the Japanese *fu* 府 or *pu*-system in Korea, whereby twelve pu were established in the whole of Korea. Five of them are now located in the area of North Korea:

Pyongyang	
Jinnampho (now: Nampho)	
Wonsan	now: provincial capital of Kangwon
Chongjin	now: provincial capital of Hambuk
Sinuiju	now: provincial capital of Phyongbuk

In the 30s and in the first half of the 40s, five more cities were added: three cities on the east coast (Hamhung, Sŏngjin and Rajin) as well as the former capital Kaesong and Haeju in the South.

Hamhung (1930)	now: provincial capital of Hamnam
Kaesong (1930)	Hwangbuk
Rajin (1936-1949)	
Haeju (1938)	now: provincial capital of Hwangnam
Sŏngjin (now: Kimchaek) (1943)	Hambuk

II.3.2. Phase 2: The development of inland cities (1945–1967)

In 1947, the Hwangbuk Province was established. At the same time Sariwon became a city and its provincial capital. In the same year, Songrim, an industrial satellite city of Pyongyang, was founded so that until 1950, the year of the outbreak of the Korean War, two cities were founded in Hwangbuk. Hungnam became a city in 1949 and became part of the city of Hamhung in 1960. Kanggye emerged as the capital of the newly founded province of Jagang.

Ranam (1945-1960)	Hambuk, now part of Chongjin
Sariwon (1947)	provincial capital of Hwangbuk
Songrim (1947)	Hwangbuk
Hungnam (1949-1960)	Hamnam
Kanggye (1949)	provincial capital of Jagang

Thus—except Pyongsong—all provincial capitals in the DPR Korea were founded until 1954. After the Korean War until 1967, two cities emerged on the east coast (Sinpho,

Rajin) and four in the inland (Hyesan, Manpho, Huichon, Kusong).

Hyesan (1954)	provincial capital of Ryanggang
Sinpho (1960)	Hamnam
Manpho (1967)	Jagang
Huichon (1967)	Jagang
Kusong (1967)	Phyongbuk
Rajin (1967)	(today part of Rason)

II.3.3. Phase 3: Development of the capital region around Pyongyang (1969-1990)

Between 1969 and 1990 a city formation was conducted in Phyongnam. Among the seven cities, that emerged here, six are located in the Phyongnam region and one in Hamnam.

Phyongsong (1969)	provincial capital of Phyongnam
Taean (1978-1983)	(today part of Nampho)
Tanchon (1982)	Hamnam
Sunchon (1983)	Phyongnam
Tokchon (1986)	Phyongnam
Anju (1987)	Phyongnam
Kaechon (1990)	Phyongnam

II.3.4. Phase 4: Creation of cities in the periphery as a regional balance (1991-2001)

If we take a look at the cities, which have emerged in the 90s, one has the impression that their creation would have been a political objective to accomplish a regional balance in the urban network.

Munchon (1991)	Kangwon
Hoeryong (1991)	Hambuk
Jongju (1994)	Phyongbuk
Hungnam (2001-2005)	Hamnam

In summary, it is clear that in the 1940s and 1950s North Korea first established capitals for the new provinces of Hwangbuk, Jagang, Ryanggang as well as two cities of heavy industry (Songrim, Hungnam). In the 1960s, five cities emerged in peripheral areas (east sea coast, northern inland), and in addition Phyongsong, Pyongyangs satellite town, was founded as a science city and as a provincial capital of Phyongnam. The result of the only city foundation in the 1970s, Taean (as part of Nampho-jikhalsi), had only existed for half a decade though. In 1982, the mining town of Tanchon was founded. Up to this point, you can see a desire for a balanced regional development of the country as a strategy behind the practice of the appointment to a city. In 1983-1990, the aim of the upgrading of four *kun* of the Phyongnam Province to a city was the goal of the concentration of development of the region south of the capital Pyongyang. In the further course of the 1990s, some small towns were founded in peripheral areas. Since 1995 there has been no new foundation of a city anymore, a result, which has lasted until today.

II.4. Classification according to population, area size, and shares in "urban" population

Now the North Korean cities are classified in view to their population numbers. If you want to divide the 27 North Korean cities in large cities, medium-sized cities and small cities, it is important to note that there are different definitions. If you follow earlier definitions, which serve as a basis until today in the German administration, cities from 100,000 inhabitants would be deemed as large cities. This would mean that all North Korean cities would be classified as large cities. In the regional development planning, a new definition is often used, in which cities with 50,000 to 250,000 inhabitants are called medium-sized cities (Schmidt-Lauber inter alia). Heineberg (2006, 77) refers to large cities of medium order of magnitude, if there are 200,000 to 500,000 inhabitants. Therefore, 13 of the 27 North Korean cities would be defined as (large) medium-sized city. All other cities would be large cities, whereby ten of them due to its population of less than 500,000 inhabitants could be considered as small city, three as large cities and Pyongyang as the only (small) metropolis. According to the definition of Heineberg we have 13 medium-sized cities as well as ten smaller and four large cities.

The following table follows the data of the "DPR Korea 2008 Population Census," only the values for Pyongyang and Nampho were changed in accordance with the administrative changes that took place after 2008. The population of Pyongyang has been reduced as a result of the restructuring of 3,255,288 inhabitants down to 7.9%, while Nampho with originally 366,815 inhabitants became by the incorporations now almost a city with over a million inhabitants.

According to the figures of the "DPR Korea 2008 Population Census," about 46.4% of the population is registered within the boundaries of the 27 North Korean cities. Compared to South Korea, where an urbanization rate of around 90% is mentioned, this is very little. A policy of inhibiting the growth of cities, and a lower economic growth have been the decisive factors here.

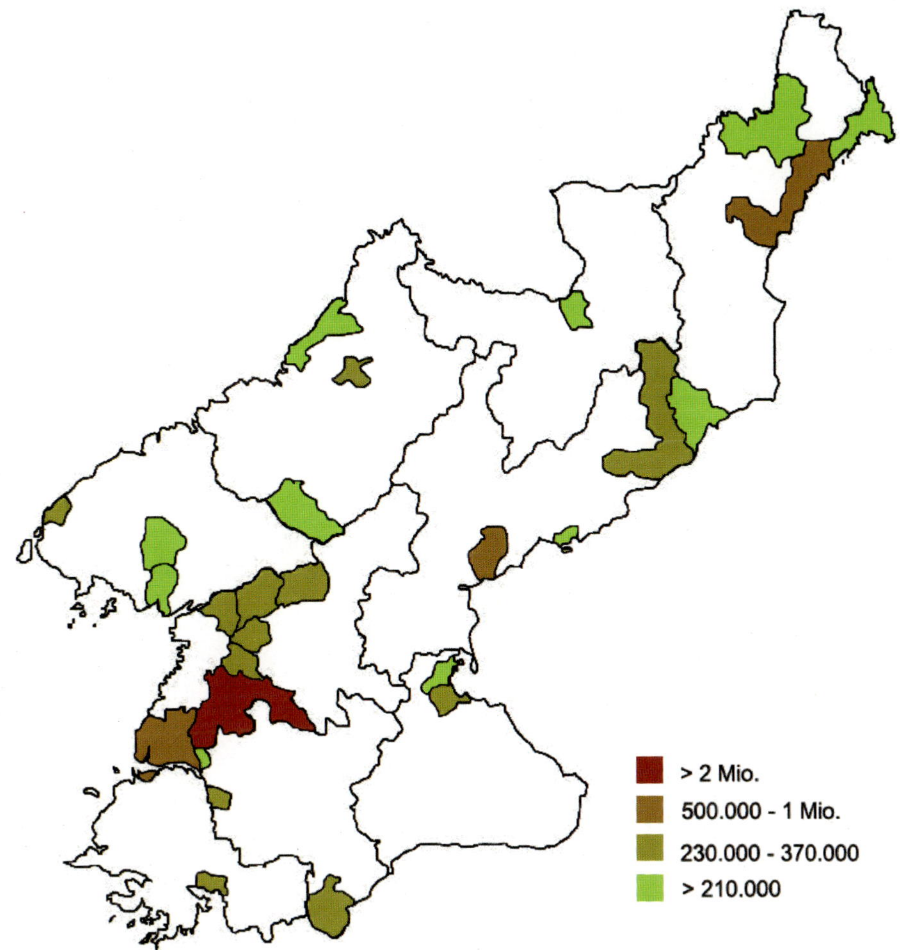

Figure II–5. Population of the North Korean cities

Despite these changes, Pyongyang still has more than three times as many inhabitants as the second largest city, Nampho, in terms of population. Pyongyang also has a larger population than the provinces with the exception of Phyongnam and Hamnam. Except for Pyongyang and Nampho, only the east coast cities Hamhung and Chongjin each have a population of over 500,000.

Table II-1. Large cities

Pyongyang	2,999,466	12.8%	1
Nampho	983,660	4.2%	2
Hamhung	768,551	3.3%	3
Chongjin	667,929	2.9%	4

Wonsan, Sinuiju and the mining town of Tanchon have around 350,000 inhabitants. Also Nampho would fall into this category without the incorporations. While the two largest cities are located in the west of the country, four of the next five largest cities are located on the east coast and in addition there is the north-western border city of Sinuiju.

Table II-2. Large medium-sized cities

Wonsan	363,127	1.6%	5
Sinuiju	359,341	1.5%	6
Tanchon	345,875	1.5%	7

Kaechon, Kaesong, Sariwon, Sunchon and Phyongsong have around 300,000 inhabitants. Haeju, Kanggye, Anju and Tokchon have around 250,000 inhabitants. Among the 16 largest cities in the country, there are two province independent cities (Pyongyang and Nampho) and another city that has long held the status of a province independent city (Kaesong). Eight cities are provincial capitals. Four of the five other cities are located in the Phyongnam Province (Kaechon, Sunchon, Anju, Tokchon).

Table II-3. Small medium-sized cities

Kaechon	319,554	1.4%	8
Kaesong	308,440	1.3%	9
Sariwon	307,764	1.3%	10
Sunchon	297,317	1.3%	11
Phyongsong	284,386	1.2%	12
Haeju	273,300	1.2%	13
Kanggye	251,971	1.1%	14
Anju	240,117	1	15
Tokchon	237,133	1	16

The cities Kimchaek, Rason, Kusong, Hyesan and Jongju have around 200,000 inhabitants. Huichon, Hoeryong and Sinpho have around 150,000 inhabitants.

Table II-4. Large small cities

Kimchaek	207,299	0.9%	17
Rason	196,954	0.8%	18
Kusong	196,515	0.8%	19
Hyesan	192,680	0.8%	20
Jongju	189,742	0.8%	21
Huichon	168,180	0.7%	22
Hoeryong	153,532	0.7%	23
Sinpho	152,759	0.7%	24

The three smallest cities in North Korea are Songrim, Munchon and Manpho. Among the nine smallest cities in the country, five of the six cities are located at a high altitude or in the mountains (Kusong, Hyesan, Huichon, Hoeryong and Manpho). Only Kanggye, one of the mountain towns in the interior of the country has around 250,000 inhabitants.

Table II-5. Small towns

Songrim	128,831	0.6%	25
Munchon	122,934	0.5%	26
Manpho	116,760	0.5%	27

If one were to categorize the cities of North Korea by size-class, the following classification would be possible by number of inhabitants:[3]

Table II-6. Classification of cities in the DPRK by population

Metropolis	Pyongyang
Large cities	Nampho, Hamhung, Chongjin
Medium-sized cities	Wonsan, Sinuiju, Tanchon, Kaechon, Kaesong, Sariwon, Sunchon, Phyongsong, Haeju, Kanggye, Anju, Tokchon
Small cities	Kimchaek, Rason, Kusong, Hyesan, Jongju, Huichon, Hoeryong, Sinpho, Songrim, Munchon, Manpho

3 The difference between the fourth-largest city (Chongjin) and the fifth-largest city (Wonsan) is more than 300,000 inhabitants. The difference between the smallest medium-sized cities and the largest small cities amounts to nearly 30,000 residents. Since the differences in terms of population are small in the ranking, where middle-sized and small cities are directly sequential, the classification was performed as above. Therefore Kimchaek belongs here to the small cities, even though it has just over 200,000 residents.

With regard to the population number, there are statistics, which allow the recording of changes in population. People had to rely on estimates for a long time. Eberstadt and Banister (1992) published data from the years 1980, 1982, 1986 and 1987, which stem directly from North Korea. The data from "the 1993 DPR Korea Population Census" include the population numbers of North Korea's provincial capitals. Now it would be possible to compare such data with the data of "DPR Korea 2008 Population Census" such as in Kim Tu-sŏp (et.al.) (2011, 180) happened. The changes of the administrative units have also to be taken into account in such a comparison, what unfortunately happens in the rarest of cases.

Somewhat more difficult is the estimation of the surface area of the cities. Here we have the sources IPA (2003) and PSC-8 (2009). However, it is not always clear how up-to-date the specified values are. Both sources show for 17 cities (apart from rounding differences) the same values: Hoeryong, Kimchaek, Chongjin, Tanchon, Sariwon, Songrim, Haeju, Huichon, Manpho, Kanggye, Wonsan, Munchon, Kusong, Jongju, Tokchon, Sunchon, Hamhung. Different values have been indicated in four cities. In the case of Sinuiju and Rason, the difference between the two sources is 10 km^2 or less. In the case of Kaechon, the difference is bigger: 738 km^2 (IPA-3, 2003, 108) and 664,76 km^2 (PSC-8, 2009, 398). The difference in the city of Sinpho was especially great, where IPA (12 2003, 256) indicates 43 km^2 and the PSC-8, (2009, 595) 218.1 km^2. In such cases, the value of the more recent source of PSC-8 was in the present study taken over. In the case of Phyongsong and Anju, the area size of the city was not indicated in IPA, but in PSC-8. Neither IPA nor the PSC-8 has information regarding the area of the city of Hyesan. But here you can find an indication in the Korean Wikipedia, which was taken over under reverse.

In the case of Kaesong, the city region has changed in recent years. Kaesong-si (without *kun*) and the *kun* originally belonging to Kaesong-jikhalsi (Jangphung-kun, Phanmun-kun and Kaephung-kun) are listed separately in the IPA and there is also information on area surfaces. Kaesong-si currently comprises the territories previously occupied by Kaesong-si (without *kun*) and the former Phanmun-kun and Kaephung-kun. By adding the area for these three units in the IPA, the total area of the present city of Kaesong could be calculated. Quite the same applies for Nampho, the PSC-8 could be used here as a source for the addition of the area indication, which now make up the city of Nampho.

More problematic is the calculation of the total area of Pyongyang. In the IPA, an area of 2,629.4 km^2 is indicated. In the meantime, Sangwon-kun, Junghwa-kun and Sungho-kuyok no longer belong to Pyongyang. Subtracting the areas of the two kun, you get a result of 1,907 km^2. However, there are no values for Sungho-kuyok. Thus we can only state that the area of Pyongyang on the basis of the information provided by the IPA is less than 1,907 km^2. To calculate the population density of the city of Pyongyang, the values of the former *kuyok* of Sungho were temporarily taken into account, both in the area as well as in the population.

All values are rounded off to whole numbers.

Table II-7. Total area of cities

	km^2
Tanchon	2,172
Pyongyang	< 1,907
Hoeryong	1,750
Chongjin	1,591
Nampho	1,281
Huichon	984
Kimchaek	854
Kaesong	766
Rason	754
Tokchon	692
Manpho	672
Kaechon	665
Kusong	653
Hamhung	556
Jongju	480
Anju	433
Phyongsong	381
Sunchon	368
Wonsan	314
Munchon	278
Hyesan	277
Kanggye	264
Sinpho	218
Haeju	207
Sinuiju	190
Sariwon	188
Songrim	65

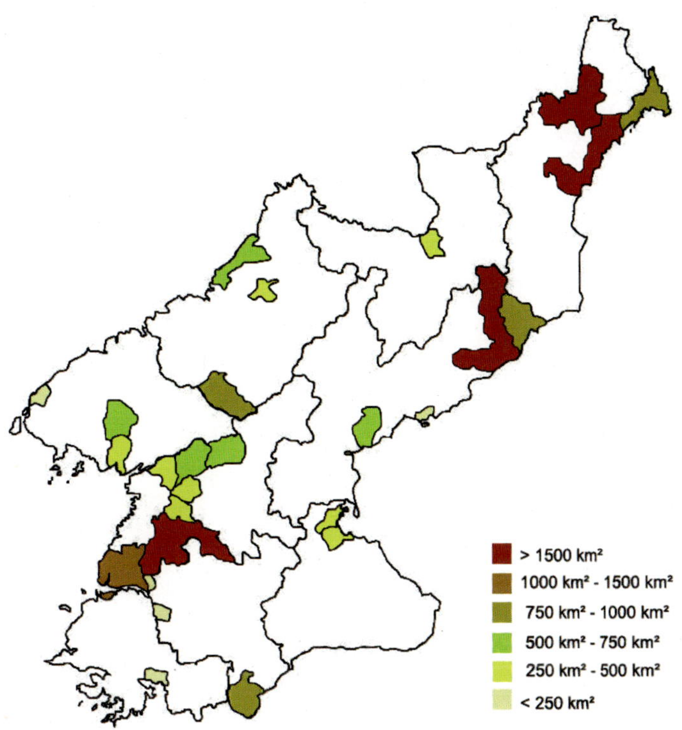

Figure II-6. Total area of cities

Although the above values to the area sizes of the cities are to be regarded with caution, the size of the mining city of Tanchon attracts attention. Including Hoeryong Huichon and Kimchaek, three more cities from Northeast Korea belong to the largest area of the country. Apart from that, among the nine largest cities in terms of area size, there are the three province independent cities Pyongyang, Nampho and Rason as well as two other cities Chongjin and Kaesong, which were province independent in the past. Among the four cities with the lowest area size are three from Hwanghae of the DPR Korea, which is in the south of DPR Korea.

Table II-8. Population density of the North Korean cities

	P/km²
Songrim	1,982
Sinuiju	1,891
Sariwon	1,637
Pyongyang	1,617
Hamhung	1,382
Haeju	1,320
Wonsan	1,156
Kanggye	954
Sunchon	808
Nampho	768
Phyongsong	746
Sinpho	701
Hyesan	696
Anju	555
Kaechon	481
Munchon	442
Chongjin	420
Kaesong	403
Jongju	395
Tokchon	343
Kusong	301
Rason	261
Kimchaek	243
Manpho	174
Huichon	171
Tanchon	159
Hoeryong	88

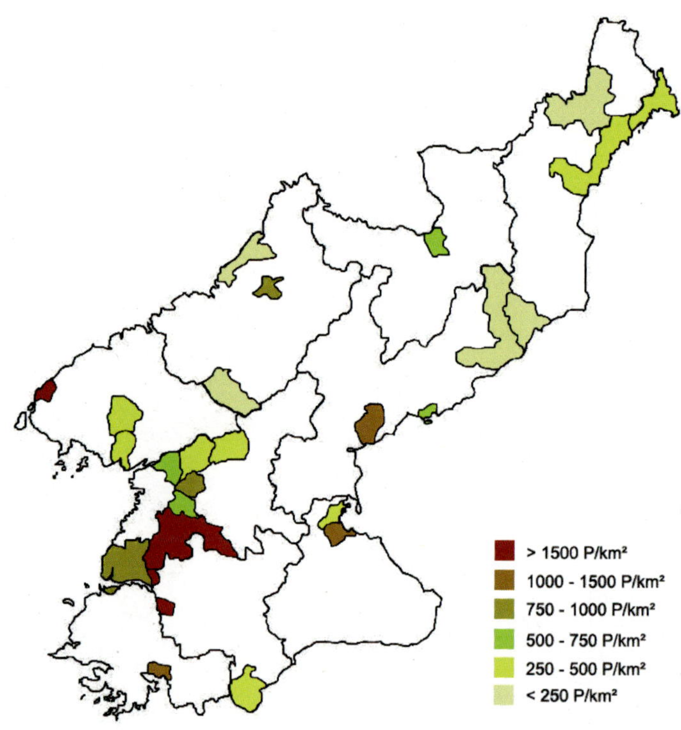

Figure II-7. Population density of the North Korean cities

The three smallest cities in terms of area, Songrim, Sinuiju and Sariwon; are also the ones with the highest population density. They are followed by Pyongyang and Hamhung. The city center of Hamhung is considered to be the most densely populated region in North Korea.

It is to be kept in mind that while dividing the North Korean cities by population and area size, agricultural and forestry usable territory was usually assigned to the cities, in order to come close to the ideology of economic autarchy of the regional units. The extent, to which this was done however, is different and it is therefore useful not only to indicate the population of a city, but also to ascertain the extent of agricultural or forestry used area within the urban areas.

A step in this direction could be the calculation of the rural administrative units ("*ri*") as part of the total number of administrative units.

Table II-9. Ratio of urban administrative units (*dong*, *up*, *rodongjagu*) and rural administrative units (*ri*)[4]

	dong etc../*ri*	%
Kanggye	36/0	100
Chongjin	93/14	87
Hyesan	25/4	86
Sinuiju	50/9	85
Haeju	26/5	84
Hamhung	101/19	84
Pyongyang	287/75	79
Sariwon	31/9	78
Wonsan	45/14	76
Songrim	19/7	73
Sinpho	16/6	73
Tokchon	23/9	72
Kaechon	26/12	68
Nampho	82/49	67
Sunchon	21/ 11	66
Huichon	21/12	64
Phyongsong	21/13	62
Kusong	25/18	58
Kimchaek	23/19	55
Munchon	16/14	53
Tanchon	40/38	51
Anju	21/22	49
Kaesong	31/33	48
Rason	21/13	48
Jongju	14/18	44
Manpho	12/16	43
Hoeryong	19/28	40

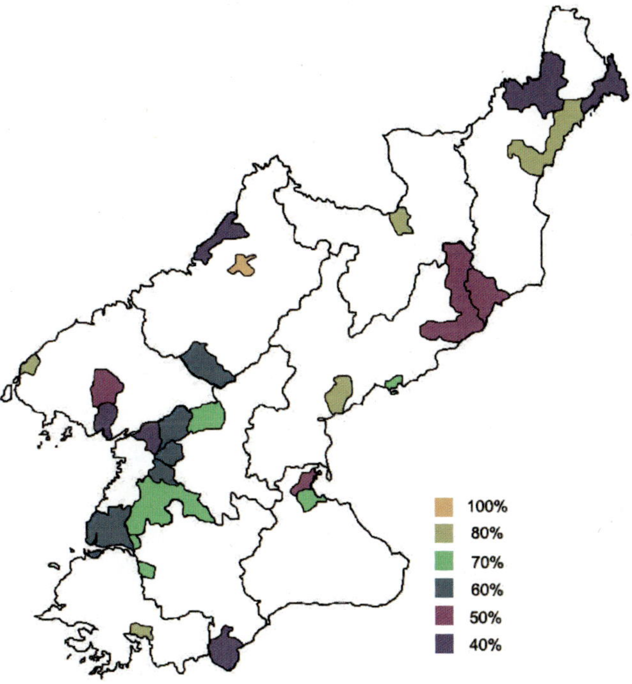

Figure II-8. Ratio of urban administrative units (*dong*, *up*, *rodongjagu*) and rural administrative units (*ri*)

4 The number of *ri* and other administrative units (*dong*, *up*, *rodongjagu*) is based on the information from the IPA. In the following cities, other values were taken from the PSC-8 (in parenthesis are the changes compared to IPA): Kanggye (+2 *dong*, -2 *ri*); Tanchon, Tokchon, Phyongsong (+1 *dong*, -1 *ri*); Sinuiju, Anju (+1 *dong*); Kimchaek (+1 *dong*, -3 *ri*); Rason, Manpho (+1 *dong*, +1 *ri*); Kaechon, Songrim (+1 *ri*).

Another possibility is to use the data of the "DPR Korea 2008 Population Census" (2009) to calculate how high the percentage of the population living in urbanized ("urban") areas is, and how high the percentage of the population living in rural ("rural") areas is.

Table II-10. Ratio of "urban" population and "rural" population

	Urban	Rural
Kanggye	100%	0%
Sinuiju	93%	7%
Chongjin	92.1%	7.9%
Hamhung	91.6%	8.4%
Wonsan	90.5%	9.5%
Hyesan	90.3%	9.7%
Pyongyang	90.1%	9.9%
Tokchon	88.8%	11.2%
Haeju	88.4%	11.6%
Sariwon	88.2%	11.8%
Sinpho	85.7%	14.3%
Sunchon	84.3%	15.7%
Phyongsong	83.2%	16.8%
Kaechon	82.1%	17.9%
Huichon	80.9%	19.1%
Rason	80.4%	19.6%
Kusong	79%	21%
Munchon	75.3%	24.7%
Kimchaek	74.9%	25.1%
Songrim	74.4%	25.6%
Nampho	71.5%	28.5%
Manpho	70.8%	29.2%
Anju	69.8%	30.2%
Tanchon	69.6%	30.4%
Kaesong	62.4%	37.6%
Hoeryong	60.2%	38.8%
Jongju	54.1%	45.9%

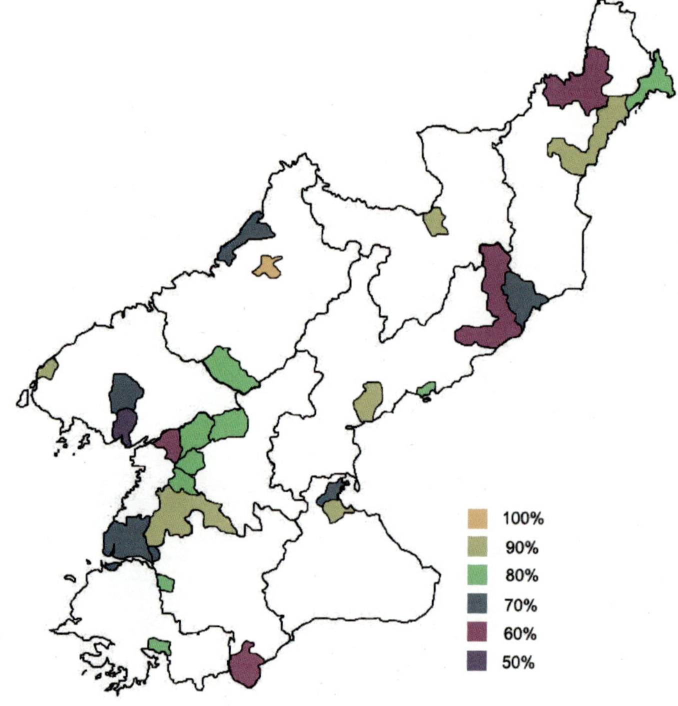

Figure II-9. Ratio of "urban" population and "rural" population

All together, in North Korea according to the numbers of the "DPR Korea 2008 Population Census" (2009) about 60,6% of the North Korean population live in "urban" areas.

If one assumes that the inhabitants living in ri can be distinguished as "rural," one can usually assume that a high proportion of *dong*, *up* and *rodongjagu* is synonymous with a high proportion of urban population. In three cities, however, significant deviations attract attention:

Songrim has a high *dong*-proportion, but a low proportion of urban population.

Also, Nampho has less urban population in regard to the expectation of the percentage of dong.

In Rason, however, the reverse exists: the share of the urban population is greater than expected in view of the *dong*-proportion.

This could be explained by the fact that in the *ri* of the cities of Nampho and Songrim, an intensive farming near the capital city is practiced, while on the other hand, the lower density of *ri* in Rason is due to the mountainous surface area.

In view of the shares of "urban" population, four categories can be distinguished:

Cities with very high "urban" percentage of the population (over 88%): Kanggye, Sinuiju, Chongjin, Hamhung, Wonsan, Hyesan, Pyongyang, Tokchon, Haeju Sariwon

Cities with high "urban" share of the population (between 79 and 86%): Sinpho, Sunchon, Phyongsong, Kaechon, Huichon, Rason, Kusong

Cities with a low "urban" share of population (between 69 and 76%): Munchon, Kimchaek, Songrim, Nampho, Manpho, Anju, Tanchon

Cities with a very low "urban" share of population (between 54 and 63%): Kaesong, Hoeryong, Jongju.

III. Industrial companies in the cities

III.1. Introductory remarks

III.1.1. Special features of the sources

In the 1990s, the first major studies on industrial companies in North Korea were published in South Korea: KOTRA (1995) and KIET (1996). Both sources were concerned with the different industrial sectors of the North Korean industry. A multitude of North Korean industrial company names were mentioned, and partially the administrative regional unit, in which the respective factory was located, was stated. The initial idea of the present research was not to sort the industrial companies of these sources by industrial sectors as has already been done in KOTRA (1995) and KIET (1996), but according to their location (*si* and *kun*), in order to generate a source for purposes of editing regional geographical issues on North Korea.

Over time, more and more sources came along that were suitable for an inventory of industrial companies in North Korea. The work, which was published in 1995 by the KOTRA, was still a small-format book in comparison to its followers, which were published in five-year intervals, always by other South Korean financial institutions: Han'guk-sanŏp-ŭnhaeng (2000), kdb (2005a,b), KOFC (2010).

Even North Korea itself had in the meantime—via Japan—recognized the Internet as a medium and therefore KCNA news for the period from 1998 are available. Because these news reports by the KCNA also mentioned industries, they were another welcomed source for our inventory of the North Korean industrial factories.

A multitude of names of industrial companies were also found in the total 20-volume IPA (2003), this time sorted by region.

Finally, the directory of leading employees of important North Korean institutions and associations (MOU 2012) by the South Korean Ministry of Unification provided another source, since important industrial companies were also recorded in it.

It was not always shown in these sources, where the industrial companies are located. The first task was to collect the names of the industrial companies electronically and—if necessary—to ascertain the locations of the factories. Then, the companies were sorted by location (i.e. by cities and counties). Since the sources differ significantly in structure, separate lists for each source were made, which contain the companies for the North Korean cities and counties. These lists are the basis for the city descriptions in Chapter IV and for the quantitative analysis in the present chapter.

Although it is not possible to determine the number of employees in each industrial plant, these tables give us at least the possibility to determine the number of industrial companies, by using the data given in the sources. The ascertained number of companies through this method is certainly not the complete number of all companies. Each source has made a selection of companies, which were recorded. The procedure for the selection of companies varies depending on the source. This means that the various sources also require different approaches of interpretation. Depending on the nature of the source, the statistics based on them provide different information. Thus, it should be noted that the number of companies, the share of companies in cities and the share of industrial sectors of companies from source to source are different.

Table III-1. Companies in DPRK according to the five sources (in parenthesis: important companies)[1]

	KOFC (2010)	MOU (2012)	IPA (2003)	KCNA (1998–2011)	KIET (1996)
companies (important)	812 (180)	1311 (111)	2401 (578)	668	2480 (761)
share in cities	61.7% (66.7%)	61.9% (72.1%)	23.9% (45.7%)	69.5%	52.7% (67.8%)
share of companies in the light industry of all companies	25.3%	62.6%	48.7%	50%	41.2%
share of heavy industry of all companies	59.1%	26.5%	37.2%	35,1%	49.1%

Because industrial companies in North Korea were deliberately scattered over the country in terms of self-sufficiency of the regional units of the county or municipal level, it is helpful for the purpose of the typification of a city, to consult a source that does not also present small companies in its lists, but a selection of the most important companies of the country. Especially the works that are published by the Korean financial institutions every five years fulfill this purpose. The present research is based on the latest edition from 2010 (KOFC).[4] The share of companies of the heavy industry is particularly high in this source.

In addition, a selection of the most important companies of the country is further presented in the directory 2012 (MOU) by the Ministry of Unification. It lists the names

1 What the individual sources understand by "important companies," is explained in more detail in III.1.2.

2 Only taking in account companies located in cities.

3 Only taking in account companies located in cities.

4 Also companies, which do not appear in the 2010 edition, but appear in the editions of 2000 and 2005, were considered.

of important people of North Korea from all groups of society. However, there are no addresses or phone numbers, let alone e-mail addresses, so that the practical benefit for the majority of citizens would be rather low. The share of light industry companies is particularly high in this source.

Both sources therefore claim to provide the listing of the country's most important companies. They are thus evaluated from this perspective, whereby the former is given priority, because it is intensively dealing with the companies, while the latter is only an enumeration of companies stating the employee in responsible positions.

The 20-volume IPA (2003) examines in an encyclopedic way all cities and counties of North Korea. For each *si*, each *kuyok* and each *kun*, there is a heading for "important factories," where usually up to ten important companies are presented. Furthermore, names of factories are frequently cited in introductory descriptions of the economy of the provinces, *si* and *kun*. Also in the descriptions of the rural *ri*, the most important companies of the *ri* are usually cited, but the most important companies are rarely listed in the descriptions of the *dong*.

However, this does not mean that the companies mentioned in the IPA (2003) in reality belong to the most important in the country. This means, that a result is expected, where companies appear relatively regularly scattered across the country, while in statistics, for example that are based on KOFC (2010) and MOU (2012), which have recorded the most important companies in the country, regions, where the companies are clustered, appear even more strongly. This explains the low proportion of 23.9% of companies in the cities, as shown above in the IPA (2003), which is even lower than the percentage of the population that live in the cities which is 46.4%.

From the data obtained through the analysis of the IPA (2003), it can also be expected, that on the one hand, a city with many *kuyok* and on the other hand cities and counties with many *ri* have especially a lot of companies in the statistics. However, the IPA also has advantages. Since it does not only record industrial companies, but also includes other important companies and as well as important cultural institutions in the *kun* and *si*. Therefore, the IPA (2003) is a useful resource to track quantitative approaches, in order to come closer to a functional typification of the cities.

While the above mentioned three sources are depicted as compiled secondary sources, which are statistically evaluated here, KCNA is a primary source. The Korean Central News Agency (shortly thereafter as: KCNA) is the central state news agency of the DPR Korea and was founded on December 5th 1946. For this research, the archives of the years from 1998 to 2011, which are available on the website http://www.kcna.co.jp/, were examined by companies. The companies, which are here recorded statistically, are companies, which were—for whatever reasons—important enough for the North Korean news agency to mention. For example, the factories that are presented were visited (by Kim Jong-il), praised or had erected mosaics for the glory of the North Korean ruler. The results of the statistical tests to these sources also show most notably which cities have played a major role for the North Korean propaganda in the last decade and where regional priorities of the North Korean economic policies were set.

An intermediate position is occupied by the KIET, which was published in 1996. It is compiled on the one hand, since in it important companies are distinguished from the rest, on the other hand, it is based mainly on companies, which are mentioned in the Rodong-sinmun newspaper.

As the footnotes reveal, the information usually comes from sources from the 1980s and 1990s. It is therefore possible that a not inconsiderable part of the sources listed here do not exist anymore. It is the source with the most listed companies and therefore it can be assumed, that even small and medium-sized factories have been considered.

III.1.2. Approach of presenting the results of research to the industrial companies in the cities

In III.2. to III.6. the results of the analysis of the sources are first presented separately from each other in the order set out above. In III.7. the results from the overall view of all five sources are portrayed.

First, in the presentation of the results of each source, it's all about the total number of the industrial companies in the relevant cities and also about the percentage of all industrial companies that the 27 cities each have, in the investigated sources. In III.2. to III.7. the results of these researches will be shown both in table[5] as well as on a map.[6]

It is easy to foresee, that cities with many inhabitants have more companies than cities with few inhabitants, especially when the differences regarding to the population number are very large. In chapter II.3., the 27 cities in the DPR Korea are divided into a metropolis, three large, twelve medium and eleven small cities. It will be initially assumed hypothetically, that the four largest cities will occupy the front four positions in terms of the number of industrial companies, and that the medium-sized cities are to be found within the first 16 ranks and the small towns will occupy the last eleven ranks. To get a

5 However, since the statistics of the present research are based on five very heterogeneous sources and thus the share of companies, that are located in cities is different according to sources, a different method of presentation of the values in the table for preparing the figures was chosen, which compensates the differences. The percentages given in the tables refer to the share of companies of all companies in the country. However, to ensure uniformity of the figures for all five sources, the share of companies, which are located in a particular city, were calculated for the presentation on the map, by the share of all companies, which are located in all 27 cities. Six categories were then identified, which were used for the illustrations of the results of all five sources equally: category 1 (≥ 5%), category 2 (≥ 4 %, < 5%), category 3 (≥ 3 %, < 4%), category 4 (≥ 2 %, < 3%), category 5 (≥ 1%, < 2%), category 6 (< 1%). All calculations were rounded to a decimal number after the decimal point.

6 See e.g. Table III.2-1/Figure III.2-1.

first overview of which city shows especially many and which city has particularly few factories, exceptions to this assumption will be presented separately in a table.[7]

In order to assess the industrial character of a city in a more effective way, the number of companies is provided in relation with the population.[8] The results of these tests are also presented in a table[9] as well as cartographically.[10] Tables are also produced that provide information about which cities have more and which cities have fewer companies than can be expected when taking the population into account.[11] The values are calculated by the proportion of companies in regards to all companies, which was divided by the proportion of population in ratio to the total population, so that the divisor of smaller cities is correspondingly small and therefore the size of the dividend is stronger reflected in the result than in larger cities. Large cities (including the metropolis Pyongyang), medium-sized cities and small cities (see chapter II.3.) are thus considered separately. It was investigated, which of the smaller towns belong to the front, middle and back nine cities of the 27 cities in the tables.

In a third step, the most important companies are listed. In the sources KOFC (2010), MOU (2012) and KIET (1996), some companies are presented in detail, while others are listed under the heading "other" or mentioned merely in tables or maps. While in the calculation of the above tables, all companies were taken into account, in the section about "important companies," only the in detail described companies are represented. In the IPA (2003), there is for each city (except for the cities divided into *kuyok*), each *kun* and each *kuyok* specifically a heading for "Important companies." In the section "important companies" only the latter are taken into account.

None of the used sources have the ambition or goal to list all companies of the country. The companies that are listed already represent a selection. Therefore, the "important companies" portray another selection within the selection. Especially the

7 See e.g. Table. III.2-2.

8 The percentages of the industrial companies of a city of all companies of the investigated source are thereby divided by the percentage of the urban population in the total population of the DPRK. For clarification, the value 1 thus is subtracted from the obtained number, so that for those cities, whose share of the companies is lower than the proportion of the population, arise a negative number.

9 Similar to the cartographic representation of the shares of the companies in each city, for the figures of the relation between the number of industrial companies to the population, a presentation was chosen, which ensures consistency of the 5 sources used. Therefore, the percentage of companies that are located in the 27 cities was divided by the proportion of total population. (The fact that you take the proportion of the total population as the divisor and not the proportion of the population, that lives in cities, you get in view of a 46.4% share of city residents, an divisor, which is approximately twice as small, so that the quotient is higher, which facilitates the division into categories). For the representation in the map five categories were formed: category1 (≥ 4); category 2 (≥ 3, < 4), category 3 (≥ 2, < 3), category 4 (≥ 1, < 2), category 5 (< 1).

10 S. e.g. Table III.2-3/Figure III.2-2.

11 S. e.g. Table III.2-4 and Table III.2-5.

distribution of these particularly important companies of the country to the cities may be particularly meaningful for statements on industrial facilities of the city concerned, on the other hand it must be kept in mind, that the number of important companies in KOFC (180 important factories) and MOU (111 important companies) are very low, whereby a quantitative analysis may lose its significance.

Finally, it is investigated, which cities are particularly strongly represented in the various industrial sectors. In doing so, a division into four areas is made: light industry, heavy industry, mining and energy, whereby the divisions, which were made by the respective source, were kept due to practical considerations. However, these are different from source to source, so that it can happen, that a company is listed as belonging to the light industry, can also be listed under the heavy industry in a different source. The division of the KOFC source is taken from the version of the year 2010. Heavy industry and light industry are divided here as follows:

- Heavy industry: Defense industry, iron industry, non-iron, nonferrous metal processing industry, mechanical engineering, automotive industry, electrical-, electro technical engineering, shipbuilding, chemical industry, building materials industry.
- Light industry: food industry, textile industry, shoe industry, paper industry

In the section on the defense industry however, a systematic presentation of the most important companies was missing, so that this section was not included in the statistics.

MOU (2012) dedicates the fields of light industry, mining and energy its own subsection. The industries that are mentioned in the other sub-chapters (building materials industry, mechanical engineering, electrical engineering industry, iron industry and shipbuilding, chemical industry) thus belong to the heavy industry.

The allocation to the industrial sectors of the IPA and KCNA sources had of course to be made by myself. Companies, which are mainly active in the consumer goods industry, were understood to be companies of light industry.

In KIET (1996), the companies were divided by industrial sectors in eleven chapters, which are further divided into sub-chapters: I. mining, II. food and tobacco, III. textile, clothing, footwear, IV. timber, pulp, paper, V. chemistry, VI. cement·glass·ceramics; VII primary metal industry; VIII fabricated metal industry · machine equipment; IX. vehicles; X. furniture and miscellaneous; XI. energy. The areas II, III, IV and X belong in the present research to light industry and the areas V, VI, VII, VIII, and IX belong to heavy industry.

III.1.3. Research limitations and possible sources of error

Finally it should be noted that the editing of the above sources is limited, and this fact should be considered in the interpretation of the results. From a too far-reaching interpretation of the data must be warned. Some of these objections are:

- It is not always clear whether the companies that are presented in the sources actually still exist.
- Sometimes one and the same company has different names over time, which means that some companies are repeatedly found in the same sources under different names each.
- It may also occur that different companies have the same name (especially if the companies were named after a date).
- Often the location of the factory cannot be ascertained without doubt.[12]
- Oppinions can vary which companies can be seen as an industrial company and whether they should be included into the lists.[13]

III.2. KOFC (2010)

III.2.1. Total number of companies

Since KOFC (2010) deliberately includes only the most important companies, this source is particularly suited to obtain information about the distribution of the most important industrial companies in North Korea. It is therefore analyzed first. Because of their deliberate restriction on the most important companies, it is the source exhibiting the second lowest number of companies,[14] after the internet source KCNA.

On the other hand, it must be considered that KOFC (2010) has a clear focus on the industrial sectors of the heavy industry. In other words, it is the source of the five studied sources, in which the proportion of companies of light industry in the total number of companies is the slightest and the corresponding proportion of companies of heavy industry is the highest (see chapter III.1.). Based on the analysis of this source it is thus expected, that in terms of the number of companies, the cities with a strong heavy industry are ahead in the rankings.

12 In the present research, an attempt was made to keep the number of companies, which cannot be allotted, as low as possible. It was the easiest way to do so for the IPA (2003), since the factories are ordered by region anyway. With a few exceptions, all companies of a city or county could be assigned. From the source "KCNA," approximately 15% could not be determined, and in the other sources were less than 5% of the sources, which could not be determined.

13 Fisheries, for example, were not included in the lists, since most of them are devoted mainly to fishing. But it may also be that a fishing operation has a processing plant.

14 KOFC lists 812 companies, KCNA lists 668.

Table III.2-1. Total number of companies by cities (Source: KOFC 2010)

	Companies	%	Population %
Pyongyang	118	14.5	12.8
Nampho	35	4.3	4.2
Hamhung	33	4.1	3.3
Chongjin	32	3.9	2.9
Wonsan	27	3.3	1.6
Sinuiju	23	2.8	1.5
Sunchon	18	2.2	1.3
Kaechon	18	2.2	1.4
Haeju	17	2.1	1.2
Sariwon	16	2	1.3
Hoeryong	15	1.8	0.7
Tokchon	15	1.8	1
Kanggye	14	1.7	1.1
Anju	13	1.6	1
Kaesong	13	1.6	1.3
Hyesan	12	1.5	0.8
Tanchon	12	1.5	1.5
Kimchaek	11	1.4	0.9
Huichon	10	1.2	0.7
Manpho	9	1.1	0.5
Munchon	8	1	0.5
Sinpho	7	0.9	0.7
Phyongsong	7	0.9	1.2
Rason	6	0.7	0.8
Jongju	5	0.6	0.8
Kusong	4	0.5	0.8
Songrim	3	0.4	0.6

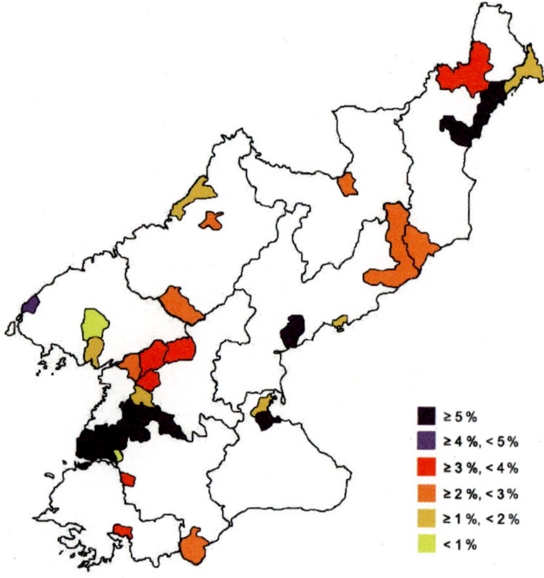

Figure III.2-1. Total number of companies by cities (Source: KOFC 2010)

Regarding the total number of companies in KOFC (2010), the order of the first six cities follows the order of the population. While Pyongyang has about three times as many inhabitants as Nampho, the quotient of the number of companies in both cities is slightly larger with 3.4. Pyongyang is followed by a group of three cities (Nampho, Hamhung, Chongjin), which show approximately equal numbers of companies.[15] This is the group of cities which are classified as large cities in chapter II.3.

15 Three of the 35 companies of Nampho are located in the *kun* of Ryonggang and Onchon.

Since, according to the evaluation of this source, the proportion of the companies in the cities altogether is significantly greater than the proportion of the population, it is likely that this is also the case with the individual cities. Among the four largest cities, the difference between the proportion of companies and the proportion of the population in Pyongyang, Hamhung and Chongjin is still significant, while it is only 0.1 in Nampho.

According to Table III.2-1, while there are four and five companies lying between the 4th and 5th ranks, the 5th and 6th and the 6th and 7th, the difference to the respective city from the 7th rank is at most one company, in terms of the total number of companies, and at rank seven the difference to the respective city, which occupies the respective following ranking in terms of the total number of companies, is at most one company. This is an indication that the companies are distributed relatively evenly among the cities.

In KOFC (2010) the five largest cities of DPR Korea are followed, in terms of the total number of companies with few exceptions, by the medium-sized cities and then the smaller cities.

Table III.2-2. Deviations between population rank and rank number of companies (Source: KOFC 2010)[16]

	Rank 1-4	Rank 5-16	Rank 17-27
Big cities	X	–	–
Medium-sized cities	–	X	Phyongsong, Tanchon
Small cities	–	Hoeryong, Hyesan	X

In the case of Tanchon, the proportion of the companies is at the same level as the proportion of the population, while the proportion is even lower in the small cities of Phyongsong, Rason, Jongju, Kusong and Songrim.

16 In this table the large cities (in terms of population), which are not occupying the ranks of 1-4 in relation to the proportion of companies, the medium-sized cities, which are not occupying the ranks of 5-16 and small cities, that are not ranked at 17-27, are listed.

III.2.2. Total number of companies in relation to population

Table III.2-3. Total number of companies in relation to population (Source: KOFC 2010)

Hoeryong	1.6	1
Manpho	1.2	2
Wonsan	1.1	3
Munchon	1	4
Hyesan	0.9	5
Sinuiju	0.9	6
Tokchon	0.8	7
Haeju	0.8	8
Huichon	0.7	9
Sunchon	0.7	10
Anju	0.6	11
Kaechon	0.6	12
Kimchaek	0.6	13
Kanggye	0.5	14
Sariwon	0.5	15
Chongjin	0.3	16
Sinpho	0.3	17
Hamhung	0.2	18
Kaesong	0.2	19
Pyongyang	0.1	20
Nampho	0	21
Tanchon	0	22
Rason	-0.1	23
Phyongsong	-0.2	24
Jongju	-0.2	25
Songrim	-0.3	26
Kusong	-0.4	27

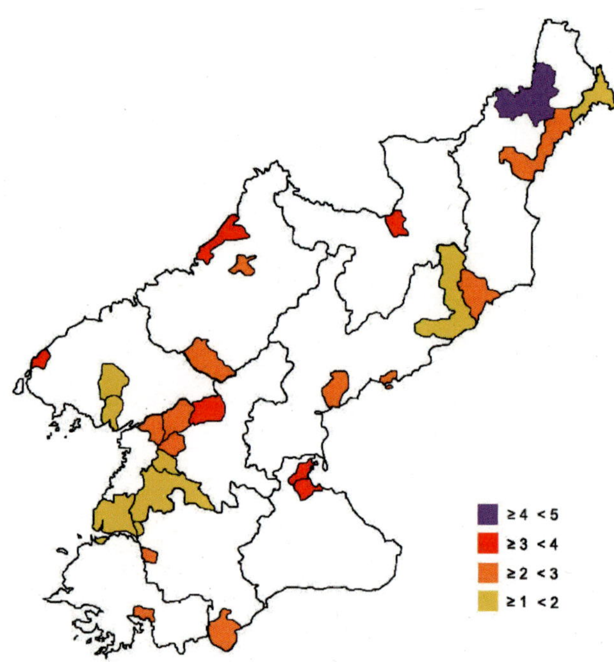

Figure III.2-2. Total number of companies in relation to population (Source: KOFC 2010)

The exceptions shown in table III.2-4. have already demonstrated that the border town to China, Hoeryong, offers more companies than it could be expected when taking into account the population. The analysis of the quotient of companies % and population % makes it clear that, with Manpho and Hyesan, two other border towns in relation to their population number possess numerous companies.

Table III.2-4. Total number of companies in relation to population (Source: KOFC 2010) – Small cities

More companies than expected	Hoeryong (1), Manpho (2), Munchon (4), Hyesan (5), Huichon (9)
Balance: Population-Number of companies	Kimchaek (13), Sinpho (17)
Fewer companies than expected	Rason (23), Jongju (25), Songrim (26), Kusong (27)

Four of the five first-ranked small cities are located in the northern mountainous region. Hoeryong mainly has companies of light industry and mining, while in Manpho, Munchon and Huichon the heavy industry sector dominates. Hyesan displays the same amount of companies of light industry as well as of the heavy industry. If armament companies would have been included in the calculations, Kusong probably would have more companies in this source. Songrim is a small industrial satellite city of Pyongyang with a large iron and steel complex and no other major industrial plants. Also, in Jongju there is a smeltery, otherwise though, Jongju is heavily influenced by agriculture.

The capital Pyongyang (20) and the large cities of Chongjin (16), Hamhung (18) and Nampho (21) are all in the lower middle of the table, which means that they offer fewer companies than expected from the population number.

Among the medium-sized cities, three cities (Wonsan, Sinuiju and Haeju), which are well equipped with both companies of the light industry as well as the heavy industries, have more companies than expected. Tokchon also belongs to the group of the cities with more companies than expected due to its numerous coal mines.

Table III.2.-5. Total number of companies in relation to population (Source: KOFC) – Medium-sized cities

More companies than expected	Wonsan (3), Sinuiju (6), Tokchon (7), Haeju (8)
Balance: Population-Number of companies	Sunchon (10), Anju (11),Kaechon (12), Kanggye (14), Sariwon (15)
Fewer companies than expected	Kaesong (19), Tanchon (22), Phyongsong (24)

Haeju and Hyesan are the only cities of their province respectively. In Kangwon there are only two cities, Wonsan and Munchon. Perhaps the concentration of these provincial centers has led to the fact that they are included in these statistics in the front field. The high proportion of Sinuiju compensates the lower proportions of Kusong and Jongju.

Among the cities with fewer companies than expected in view of the population numbers, there are cities like Kaesong and Tanchon with a relatively low proportion of "urban" population. The mining town Tanchon is also the one city with the largest area size of all North Korean cities. Phyongsong is a small provincial capital, in which a large part of the "urban" population is not working in companies, but in administrative and educational institutions.

III.2.3. Important companies

In KOFC (2010) 180 of the 812 industrial companies are dedicated a separate small chapter. Therefore one can assume that these companies have a special meaning. Consequently it is examined in this research, how these important companies are distributed among the cities of North Korea.

Table III.2.6 shows the number of the most important companies in the seven largest cities of North Korea, as well as the percentage portion of the total number of important companies. The cities were ranked according to their size (according to their number of inhabitants).

Table III.2.-6. Number of important companies in the seven largest cities (Source: KOFC 2010)

	Companies	%
Pyongyang	22	12,2
Nampho	15	8,3
Hamhung	8	4,4
Chongjin	9	5
Wonsan	5	2,8
Sinuiju	5	2,8
Tanchon	6	3,3

All the seven of the largest cities of North Korea have five or more important companies. However, when considering only the most important companies, the quotient between the companies of Pyongyang and Nampho is only 1.5. This means that relatively many important companies are located in Nampho. Among the important companies in Pyongyang are six companies of the light industry, twelve of the heavy industry, one mining company and three power plants. Within the 15 listed companies in Nampho are 14 companies of heavy industry and the "December" Thermal Power Station. These two cities are followed by a group of three cities with eight or nine companies (Sunchon, Chongjin, Hamhung). These cities have an emphasis on heavy industry, whereas Sunchon is also focused on mining.

Among the other cities, Sunchon stands out with its nine important companies; whilst all the remaining cities have none to four major companies. (in parenthesis: the rank according to the size of the city in relation to the population)

Table III.2.-7. Number of important companies in the 20 smallest cities (Source: KOFC 2010)[17]

Companies	
9	Sunchon (11)
4	Anju (15), Kimchaek (17), Manpho (27)
3	Tokchon (16), Rason (18), Kusong (19), Munchon (26)
2	Kaechon (8), Haeju (13), Hyesan (20), Huichon (22), Sinpho (24)
1	Kaesong (9), Sariwon (10), Phyongsong (12), Kanggye (14), Jongju (21), Hoeryong (23), Songrim (25)

Manpho, Munchon, Kimchaek, Rason and Kusong are smaller cities that possess a high number of important companies, when considering their proportion of population.

On the other hand, Hoeryong has a total of 15 companies, but only one of them qualifies as an important company in the source. The medium-sized cities of Sunchon, Tanchon and Anju show in relation to the population many important companies.

In summary, it can be assumed that in Pyongyang the proportion of important companies is even lower than the proportion of the population, while on the other hand in Hamhung, the proportion of important companies is more than twice as high as the proportion of the population. It appears therefore, that Pyongyang has by far most companies, although among them are proportionately less important companies, while conversely in Nampho also compared to Hamhung and Chongjin, which have a similar number of companies, there are many important companies. Furthermore, it is striking that Sariwon has as many important companies as the large cities of Hamhung and Chongjin.

III.2.4. Industries

Overall, if we classify the 812 companies listed in KOFC by industrial sectors, the result will be quite unbalanced. Only 149 (18.3%) belong to the area of light industry; and 399 (49.1%) companies, which is almost half of the total number, are assigned to the heavy industry. 152 (18.7%) companies are mines and the remaining 112 (13,8%) companies are power plants.

501 (61.7%) of the 812 companies are located in cities. In particular, the companies of light industry are concentrated in the cities (127 of 149) (85.2%). And 296 of 400

17 In parenthesis: Rank in terms of population.

companies of the heavy industry are located in cities, which is almost three-quarters of them (74%). In contrast, there are only 49 of the 152 mines (32.2%) and 29 of the 111 power plants (26.1%) located in cities.

Among the identified 180 particularly important companies, 120 (66.7%) of them are located in cities.

The 180 companies are classified as follows into the sectors: light industry (22 companies, of which 21 are in cities), heavy industry (107 companies, of which 79 are in cities), mining (29 companies, of which 10 are in cities) and energy production (22 companies, of which 10 are in cities).

Almost a quarter of the companies of light industry (23.5%) are concentrated in the capital Pyongyang. As cities with a strong light industry focus, Kaesong, Sinuiju, Hoeryong, Wonsan and Haeju show in terms of the number of companies of light industry who line up in the phalanx of the big cities Hamhung, Chongjin Nampho.

Table III.2.-8. Number of companies of light industry in the North Korean cities (Source: KOFC 2010)

Companies (Light industry)	
35	Pyongyang
4-9	Hamhung (9), Kaesong, Sinuiju (8), Hoeryong, Wonsan, Nampho (7), Haeju, Chongjin (6)
2-5	Hyesan (5), Sinpho, Kanggye, Sariwon, Sunchon (4), Anju (3), Rason, Kimchaek (2)
0-1	Kusong, Phyongsong, Munchon, Manpho, Tanchon, Kaechon (1), Huichon, Tokchon, Songrim, Jongju (0)

Of the 22 important companies of light industry, six are in Pyongyang, three in Sinuiju and two each in Sunchon and Hamhung.

Pyongyang is ranked in the front as well in relation to companies of heavy industry with its percentage of 17.5%. In the following places are the three large cities.

The city with the highest number important heavy industries is Nampho (14 companies), only then Pyongyang follows (12 companies). The two other large cities of the country, Hamhung and Chongjin, contain six important companies of heavy industry each. Sunchon, Wonsan and Kimchaek each have four important companies.[18]

18 Still, in Hamhung and Sunchon, one could include each one company, because KOFC (2010) adds the Vinalon

Table III.2.-9. Number of companies of heavy industry in North Korean cities (Source: KOFC 2010)

Companies (Heavy industry)	
70	Pyongyang
21–26	Nampho (26), Hamhung (24), Chongjin (21)
12–15	Sinuiju (15), Wonsan (14), Sariwon (12)
6–10	Sunchon, Haeju (10), Kanggye (9), Kimchaek, Anju, Huichon (8), Munchon (7), Tanchon, Manpho, Phyongsong (6)
2–5	Kaesong, Jongju, Hyesan (5), Tokchon (4), Kaechon, Kusong, Rason, Sinpho, Hoeryong (3), Songrim (2)

Most mining operations (9.2%) are allocated to the city of Kaechon. This is followed by Tokchon, Pyongyang and Hoeryong and then the mining town of Tanchon. Of the six cities that have more than one mining operation four are in the area of Phyongnam (Kaechon, Tokchon, Pyongyang and Sunchon), one in the area of Hambuk (Hoeryong) and finally Tanchon (south of Hambuk).

Table III.2.-10. Number of mines in North Korean cities (Source: KOFC 2010)

Companies (Mining)	
14	Kaechon
7–10	Tokchon (10), Pyongyang (7)
3–5	Hoeryong (5), Tanchon (4), Sunchon (3)
1	Kimchaek, Songrim, Anju, Wonsan, Chongjin, Hyesan

However, in view of the important mines, Tanchon leads with three mines, followed by Sunchon with two mines.

The power plants are widely scattered throughout the country. KOFC (2010) indicates particular attention to the newly built power plants in Wonsan.

Table III.2.-11. Number of power plants in North Korean cities (Source: KOFC 2010)

Companies (Energy)	
4–6	Pyongyang (6), Wonsan (5),Chongjin (4)
2	Manpho, Huichon, Nampho
1	Rason, Tanchon, Anju, Kanggye, Tokchon, Haeju, Sunchon, Hyesan

Complex, which is available in both cities or rather was, into the textile industrial sector and thereby classifies as light industry. In other sources such important companies are allocated to the chemical industry.

Of the more important power plants, three are located in Pyongyang and two in Chongjin.

III.2.5. Conclusion

The number of companies in the capital Pyongyang is not particularly high when measured by the number of inhabitants, especially regarding the share of important companies. This may be because a high proportion of the inhabitants of Pyongyang are not actually involved in the industrial production.

On the other hand, in Pyongyang, compared to other North Korean cities, most of the companies are located by a significant margin. However, this distance is reduced considerably if only the important companies are considered. By the number of important companies of heavy industry, Pyongyang is actually overtaken by Nampho. Except in the big cities with an emphasis on heavy industry such as Chongjin and Hamhung, there are many important companies in Sunchon (heavy industry and mining). Wonsan and Sinuiju are cities that have many companies both in light industry as well as in heavy industry. Typical mining towns are Tanchon, Kaechon and Tokchon.

In comparison to the population, the four border cities to China (Hoeryong, Manpho, Sinuiju and Hyesan) as well as the two cities in Kangwon-do (Wonsan and Munchon) have a lot of companies. On the other hand, the low industrial equipment of the farthest city from Pyongyang, Rason, is obvious.

III.3. MOU (Who's who in North Korean important institutions and organizations 2012)

III.3.1. Total number of companies

An important difference to KOFC (2010) is that in MOU (2012) the proportion of companies in light industry is higher than the proportion of companies in heavy industry.[19] As a result of the analysis it is expected therefore with consideration to the locations of industrial companies that smaller cities or cities with a pronounced strong light industry possess a particularly large number of companies here.

19 62.6% of the companies in the 27 cities are companies of light industry.

Table III.3.-1. Total number of companies by cities (Source: MOU 2012)

	Companies	%	Population %
Pyongyang	238	18.2	12.8
Nampho	71	5.4	4.2
Hamhung	58	4.4	3.3
Sinuiju	34	2.6	1.5
Kaesong	33	2.5	1.3
Chongjin	33	2.5	2.9
Wonsan	31	2.4	1.6
Tanchon	29	2.2	1.5
Sariwon	28	2.1	1.3
Sunchon	27	2.1	1.3
Haeju	25	1.9	1.2
Kaechon	24	1.8	1.4
Kanggye	23	1.8	1.1
Hyesan	22	1.7	0.8
Phyongsong	19	1.4	1.2
Anju	17	1.3	1
Hoeryong	15	1.1	0.7
Tokchon	13	1	1
Rason	12	0.9	0.8
Manpho	11	0.8	0.5
Munchon	10	0.8	0.5
Kimchaek	10	0.8	0.9
Jongju	9	0.7	0.8
Huichon	6	0.5	0.7
Kusong	6	0.5	0.8
Songrim	4	0.3	0.6
Sinpho	3	0.2	0.7

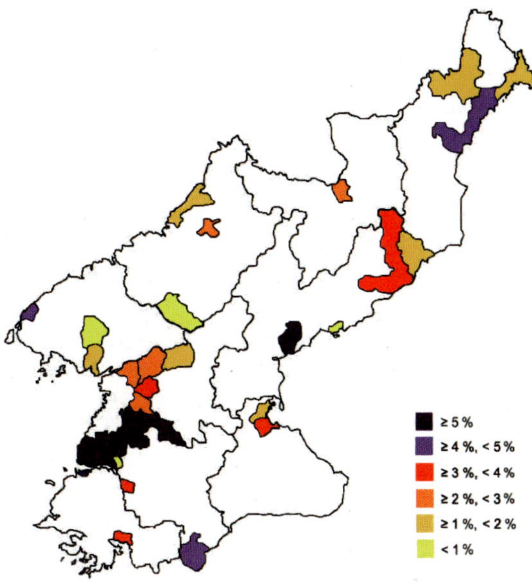

Figure III.3.-1. Total number of companies by cities (Source: MOU 2012)

Most factories are located in the three most populous cities of Pyongyang, Nampho and Hamhung. The proportion of Pyongyang is higher than in KOFC (2010), which is due to the fact that many companies of light industry are located in the capital. Furthermore, it is noticeable, that the difference between Nampho and Hamhung is greater than in KOFC (2010), which is related to the higher number of companies in the light industry in Nampho, but also with the high number of companies of mining. Hamhung in turn has significantly more companies than the cities of Sinuiju, Kaesong and Chongjin; the former both have more or the same number of companies as the 4th largest city Chongjin, because there are more companies in light industry in Sinuiju and Kaesong.

Table III.3.-2. Deviations between population rank and rank number of companies (Source: MOU 2012)

	Rank 1-4	Rank 5-16	Rank 17-27
Big cities	X	Chongjin	-
Medium-sized cities	Sinuiju	X	Tokchon
Small cities	-	Hyesan	X

III.3.2. Total number of companies in relation to population

Table III.3.-3. Total number of companies in relation to population (Source: MOU 2012)

Hyesan	1.1	1
Kaesong	0.9	2
Sinuiju	0.7	3
Kanggye	0.6	4
Sariwon	0.6	5
Sunchon	0.6	6
Manpho	0.6	7
Munchon	0.6	8
Haeju	0.6	9
Hoeryong	0.6	10
Wonsan	0.5	11
Tanchon	0.5	12
Pyongyang	0.4	13
Hamhung	0.3	14
Anju	0.3	15
Nampho	0.3	16
Kaechon	0.3	17
Phyongsong	0.2	18
Rason	0.1	19
Tokchon	0	20
Kimchaek	-0.1	21
Jongju	-0.1	22
Chongjin	-0.1	23
Huichon	-0.3	24
Kusong	-0.4	25
Songrim	-0.5	26
Sinpho	-0.7	27

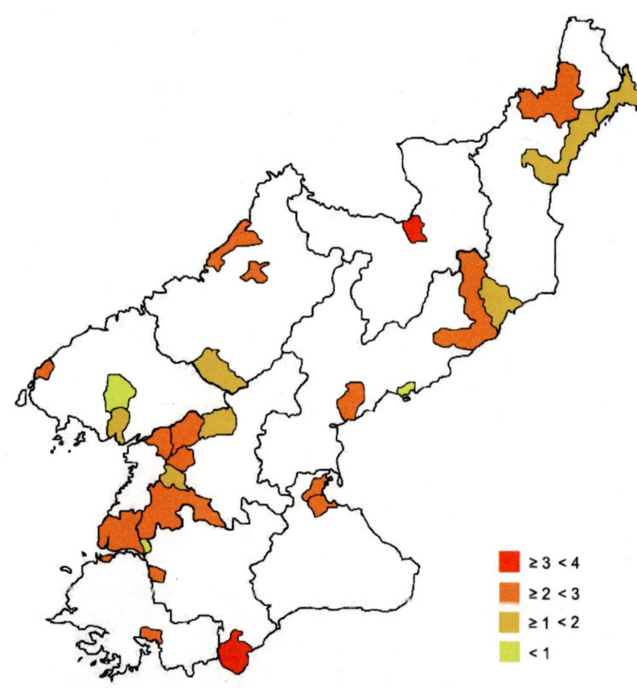

Figure III.3.-2. Total number of companies in relation to population (Source: MOU 2012)

Table III.3.-4. Total number of companies in relation to population (Source: MOU 2012) – Small cities

More companies than expected	Hyesan (1), Manpho (7), Munchon (8)
Balance: Population–Number of companies	Hoeryong (10)
Fewer companies than expected	Rason (19), Kimchaek (21), Jongju (22), Huichon (24), Kusong (25), Songrim (26), Sinpho (27)

It is noticeable that the four small cities with the most companies in relation to the population, namely Hyesan, Manpho, Munchon and Hoeryong, are taking the four first places among the small cities also in the KOFC source.

The capital Pyongyang (13) and the large cities Nampho (16) and Hamhung (14) lie in the middle of the table. Chongjin (23) is in the lower third of the table and has fewer companies than expected from the population.

Table III.3.-5. Total number of companies in relation to population (Source: MOU 2012) –Medium-sized cities

More companies than expected	Kaesong (2), Sinuiju (3), Kanggye (4), Sariwon (5), Sunchon (6), Haeju (7)
Balance: Population–Number of companies	Wonsan (11), Tanchon (12), Anju (15), Kaechon (17), Phyongsong (18)
Fewer companies than expected	Tokchon (20)

In comparison with KOFC (2010), it is mainly noticeable that a lot of companies have been declared for Kaesong. This may be related to the fact that this source includes more companies of light industry than heavy industry and Kaesong has a high number of light industry companies. In contrast, MOU (2012) lists one power plant, one mining company and eight mines, but only three factories for the mining town Tokchon.

III.3.3. Important companies

In contrast to the total number of companies in the MOU (2012), within the important companies group, the companies of the heavy and light industry are clearly in the majority. Only 13 of the 111 classified as important companies belong to the light industry. Thus an approximation to the result of the data analysis in KOFC (2010) can be expected.

In fact, the most important companies are situated in the four largest cities of the country.

Table III.3.-6. Number of important companies in the seven largest cities (Source: MOU 2012)

	Companies	%
Pyongyang	16	14.4
Nampho	8	7.2
Hamhung	7	6.3
Chongjin	7	6.3
Wonsan	3	2.7
Sinuiju	3	2.7
Tanchon	6	5.4

It stands out that, similarly alluded to in KOFC (2010), Sunchon has more important companies than the cities Wonsan and Sinuiju, which have larger populations than Sunchon.

Table III.3.-7. Number of important companies in the 20 smallest cities (Source: MOU 2012)

Number	
5	Sunchon (11)
3	Sariwon (10), Tokchon (16), Kimchaek (17), Hyesan (20)
2	Haeju (13), Anju (15), Huichon (22)
1	Kaechon (8), Kaesong (9), Kanggye (14), Rason (18), Kusong (19), Songrim (25), Manpho (27)
0	Phyongsong (12), Jongju (21), Hoeryong (23), Sinpho (24), Munchon (26)

The small cities of Hyesan, Kimchaek and Huichon have, compared to their population, a particularly large share of factories, which are classified as important. Out of these, only Hyesan had also in regard to all enterprises a high ratio to the population share. In the small cities of Munchon and Hoeryong, there are no important companies according to MOU (2012) although they were high in proportion to their population shares with respect to all companies.

The medium-sized cities of Tanchon, Sunchon and Tokchon have a particularly high share of factories in relation to its population, although Tokchon was in last place within the medium-sized companies in this ranking.

Compared to the total number of companies Kaesong has only few important companies.

III.3.4. Industries

A total of 1,311 companies were included in the statistics of existing studies. It is noticeable that there are especially a lot of companies of light industry in this source. 778 (59.3%) of the companies are referred to as companies of light industry. 195 companies (14.9%) are associated with mining and 40 power plants (3.1% of companies) are listed. The remaining 298 companies (22.7%) are considered as heavy industry, since they aren't listed as light industry in the source. These are from the following sectors: building materials industry (78 companies), the machine building industry (125 companies), the electro-technical industry (28 companies), iron manufacturing/shipbuilding (39 companies) and the chemical industry (29 companies).

811 of the 1,311 companies (61.9%) are located in cities. Slightly higher is the share of companies of light industry, of which 508 of the 778 companies are located in the cities (65.3%). However, the share of heavy industry is larger, 215 of 298 companies are located in cities (72.1%). 73 of 195 mines (37.4%) and 15 of the 40 power plants (37.5%) are located in cities.

80 of the 111 important companies are located in cities. This includes nine of the 13 more significant companies of light industry. 52 of 59 significant companies of heavy industry, nine of the 24 more significant companies of mining and ten of the 15 more important companies of the energy industry.

Also MOU (2012) shows a significant concentration of light industry companies in the capital city. 22.4% of the total companies of light industry are located in Pyongyang. This is followed by the large cities of Nampho and Hamhung. In front of the next big city, Chongjin, Kaesong, Sinuiju and Wonsan as well as Kanggye, Sariwon and Phyongsong are queued.

Table III.3.-8. Number of light industry companies in North Korean cities (Source: MOU 2012)

Number of companies (Light industry)	
175	Pyongyang
29-42	Nampho (42), Hamhung (36), Kaesong (29)
16-23	Sinuiju (23), Wonsan (22), Kanggye, Sariwon, Phyongsong (18) Chongjin (17), Haeju (16)
7-11	Kaechon, Anju (11), Hyesan (10), Hoeryong (9), Tanchon, Manpho, Sunchon (7)
1-5	Kusong, Rason, Munchon (5), Kimchaek, Jongju, Huichon (4), Tokchon, Songrim (2), Sinpho (1)

The nine important companies of light industry are located in Pyongyang (3 companies), Sariwon (2 companies) and Huichon, Hyesan, Kaesong and Sinuiju (each has one company).

In heavy industry the proportion of companies in the capital Pyongyang with 16.6% is a bit smaller than in KOFC (2010). Here again in the following place are the large cities Hamhung, Nampho and Chongjin.

Divided into the individual sectors within heavy industry, the following picture is revealed. Most of the 124 factories in the sector of engineering are located in Pyongyang (26 companies), followed by Nampho (10), Chongjin, Wonsan (7) and Sinuiju (6). Pyongyang (11 companies) additionally leads in the building material industry (78 companies), and is followed by Sunchon (6), Hamhung (5) and Tanchon (4). Five of the 39 companies in the iron manufacture / shipbuilding sector are situated in Nampho, and four each are in Pyongyang, Hamhung, Haeju and Munchon. Hamhung is home to most of the 29 chemical plants (four plants). In Sunchon three are located, in Jongju. The companies of the electro-technical industry sector (with a total of 28 companies) are concentrated in the largest cities of the country: Pyongyang (ten companies), Hamhung (six companies) and Nampho (three companies).

Table III.3.-9. Number of companies of heavy industry in North Korean cities (Source: MOU 2012)

Number of companies (Heavy industry)	
51	Pyongyang
20-22	Hamhung (22), Nampho (20)
7-14	Chongjin (14), Sunchon (11), Sinuiju (10), Wonsan, Haeju (9), Tanchon, Sariwon (8), Hyesan (7)
3-5	Kimchaek, Munchon, Anju (5), Kanggye, Kaesong, Kaechon, Jongju (4), Rason, Manpho (3)
1-2	Sinpho, Huichon (2), Kusong, Tokchon, Songrim, Phyongson, Hoeryong (1)

Nine of the more important heavy industry companies are located in Pyongyang, and seven each in Nampho and Hamhung, as well as five in Chongjin and four in Tanchon.

Tanchon is reported to be the city with the most mines. The following five cities, led by Kaechon and Tokchon, are all located in the mining area Phyongnam.

The power plants are scattered around the country. Four of which are located in Pyongyang, two each in Rason and Chongjin and one each in the cities of Nampho,

Tanchon, Tokchon, Manpho, Sunchon and Anju.

Table III.3.-10. Number of mines in North Korean cities (Source: MOU 2012)

Number of companies (Mining)	
13	Tanchon
8-9	Kaechon, Tokchon (9), Pyongyang, Nampho, Sunchon (8)
5	Hyesan, Hoeryong (5)
1-2	Rason, Sariwon (2), Kimchaek, Songrim,Sinuiju, Jongju (1)

III.3.5. Conclusion

Since MOU (2012) included a significantly higher number of companies of light industry than KOFC (2010), it shows significantly higher proportions for cities with a lot of light industry (Pyongyang, Nampho, Kaesong, Phyongsong). However, the companies in Kaesong and Phyongsong usually belong to the smaller ones. Many important companies are located in the four largest cities as well as in Tanchon and in Sunchon. The investigations of important industries confirm basically the results of the analysis of KOFC (2010).

III.4. IPA (Encyclopedia of North Korean Geography and Culture) (2003)

III.4.1. Total number of companies

IPA (2003) describes all the cities and counties of the country and names the most important companies, in particular the companies that are located in the rural *ri*. Therefore a high share of companies in the periphery are named, which do not belong to the biggest and most important companies of the country. Hence, it is to be expected, that the cities with especially numerous *ri* will show particularly many companies.

Table III.4.-1. Total number of companies by cities (Source: IPA 2003)

	Companies	%	Population %
Pyongyang	139	5.8	12.8
Nampho	81	3.4	4.2
Hamhung	36	1.5	3.3
Kaesong	27	1.1	1.3
Hoeryong	26	1.1	0.7
Chongjin	26	1.1	2.9
Manpho	25	1	0,5
Kaechon	25	1	1.4
Sinuiju	22	0.9	1.5
Wonsan	19	0.8	1.6
Anju	17	0.7	1
Haeju	16	0.7	1.2
Phyongsong	16	0.7	1.2
Tanchon	13	0.5	1.5
Munchon	12	0.5	0.5
Sunchon	11	0.5	1.3
Sariwon	10	0.4	1.3
Hyesan	9	0.4	0.8
Kimchaek	8	0.3	0.9
Jongju	7	0.3	0.8
Kusong	7	0.3	0.8
Tokchon	6	0.2	1
Songrim	4	0.2	0.6
Rason	4	0.2	0.8
Kanggye	4	0.2	1.1
Huichon	3	0.1	0.7
Sinpho	2	0.1	0.7

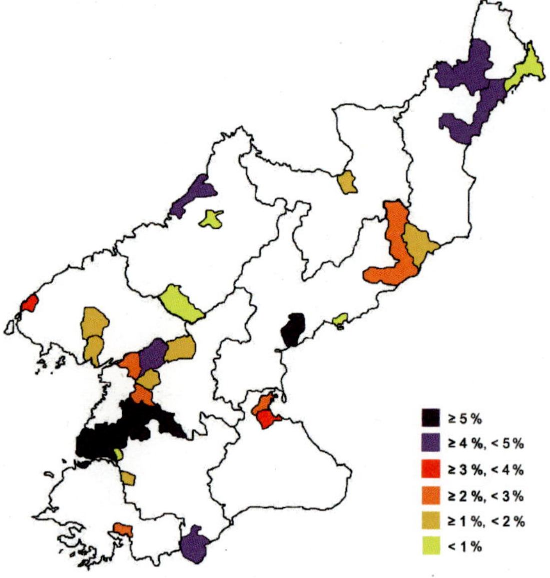

Figure III.4.-1. Total number of companies by cities (Source: IPA 2003)

Therefore it is also possible to explain the strikingly low amount of companies in the capital Pyongyang. In comparison to the cities with the three most populous cities Pyongyang, Nampho, Hamhung also have the most companies.

These cities are followed in the ranking of the most companies by five cities: Kaesong, Manpho, Hoeryong, Chongjin and Kaechon, whereas the small cities of Manpho and Hoeryong stand out. A reason for the high number of companies in both cities is their high number of *ri*. Manpho and Hoeryong are the two cities with the biggest *ri*-share in the administrative units (see. chapter II.3.). Additionally, Manpho has a high number of power plants.

Table III.4.-2. Deviations between population rank and rank number of companies (Source: IPA 2003)

	Rank 1-4	Rank 5-16	Rank 17-27
Big cities	X	Chongjin	-
Medium-sized cities	Kaesong	X	Sariwon, Tokchon, Kanggye
Small cities	-	Hoeryong, Manpho, Munchon	X

IPA (2003) shows very few companies in Kanggye, probably due to the fact that it has also few *ri*.[20]

III.4.2. Total number of companies in relation to population

Table III.4.-3. Total number of companies in relation to population (Source: IPA 2003)

Manpho	1	1
Hoeryong	0.6	2
Munchon	0	3
Kaesong	-0.2	4
Nampho	-0.2	5
Kaechon	-0.3	6
Anju	-0.3	7
Sinuiju	-0.4	8
Haeju	-0.4	9
Phyongsong	-0.4	10
Wonsan	-0.5	11
Hyesan	-0.5	12
Hamhung	-0.5	13
Pyongyang	-0.5	14
Sunchon	-0.6	15
Chongjin	-0.6	16
Jongju	-0.6	17
Kusong	-0.6	18
Tanchon	-0.7	19
Kimchaek	-0.7	20

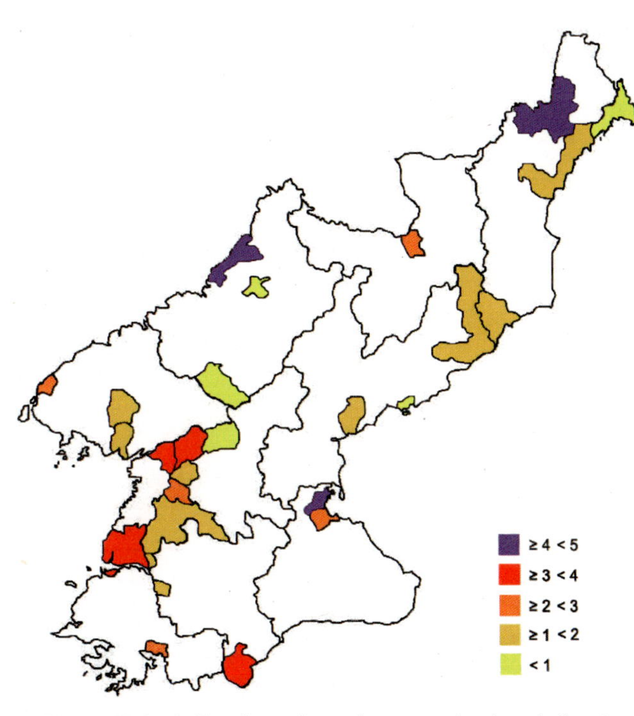

Figure III.4.-2. Total number of companies in relation to population (Source: IPA 2003)

20 According to IPA (2003), Kanggye had two *ri* until 2003, although these have been converted in the interim to *dong*.

Songrim	−0.7	21
Sariwon	−0.7	22
Rason	−0.7	23
Tokchon	−0.8	24
Kanggye	−0.8	25
Huichon	−0.9	26
Sinpho	−0.9	27

It is noticeable that, concerning smaller cities, the same cities lead the rankings in KOFC (2010) and MOU (2012). While in Manpho one can find companies of light industry as well as of heavy industry, Hoeryong primarily has light industry companies and in Munchon there are heavy industry companies.

Table III.4.-4. Total number of companies in relation to population (Source: IPA 2003) – small cities

More companies than expected	Manpho (1), Hoeryong (2), Munchon (3)
Balance: Population – number of companies	Hyesan (11), Kusong (17), Jongju (18)
Less companies than expected	Kimchaek (20), Songrim (21), Rason (23), Huichon (26), Sinpho (27)

Regarding the large cities, Nampho (5) is leading, while Pyongyang (14), Hamhung (13) and Chongjin (16) are in the middle of the ranking.

Table III.4.-5. Total number of the companies in relation to population (Source: IPA 2003) –medium-sized cities

More companies than expected	Kaesong (4), Kaechon (6), Anju (7), Sinuiju (8), Pyongsong (9)
Balance: Population – number of companies	Haeju (10), Wonsan (11), Sunchon (15)
Less companies than expected	Tanchon (19), Sariwon (22), Tokchon (24), Kanggye (25)

Overall, Figure III.4.-2 shows that in the following city groups more companies are located than to be expected from the population:

- four border cities to China (Sinuiju, Manpo, Hyesan, Hoeryong); exception: Rason
- four southern cities (Kaesong, Haeju, Wonsan, Munchon)
- three cities in the conurbation of Pyongyang – Phyongnam: Nampho, Anju, Kaechon

III.4.3. Important companies

In the IPA one can find for every city (*si*), every *kuyok* and every county (*kun*) detailed portrayals of the nature of the land, the history, the economy, and the cultural specific features etc. Within the scope of these representations, the column "important companies" is to be found as well. Here the most important companies of the described administrative unit are introduced. However, these companies are not exclusively industrial companies, but also transport facilities (railway stations, ports), agricultural companies are named here. Nevertheless, for the present quantitative investigation merely the industrial companies are considered (light industry, heavy industry, mining and power plants) to produce

Table III.4.-6. Number of important companies by cities (Source: IPA 2003)

	Companies	%	Population %
Pyongyang	89	15.4	12.8
Nampho	26	4.5	4.2
Wonsan	13	2.2	1.6
Hamhung	12	2.1	3.3
Kaesong	10	1.7	1.3
Chongjin	10	1.7	2.9
Hyesan	9	1.6	0.8
Sunchon	9	1.6	1.3
Sinuiju	9	1.6	1.5
Hoeryong	7	1.2	0.7
Anju	7	1.2	1
Kaechon	7	1.2	1.4
Munchon	6	1	0.5
Jongju	6	1	0.8
Tanchon	6	1	1.5
Haeju	5	0.9	1.2
Phyongsong	5	0.9	1.2
Manpho	4	0.7	0.5
Kusong	4	0.7	0.8
Kimchaek	4	0.7	0.9
Sariwon	4	0.7	1.3
Rason	3	0.5	0.8
Tokchon	3	0.5	1
Kanggye	3	0.5	1.1
Songrim	1	0.2	0.6
Sinpho	1	0.2	0.7
Huichon	1	0.2	0.7

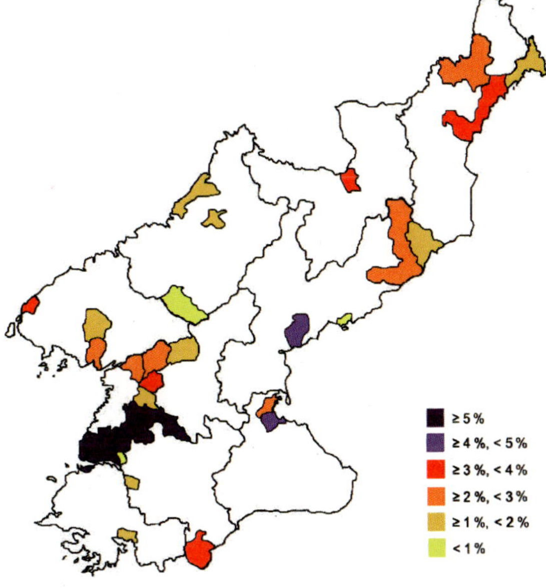

Figure III.4.-3. Number of important companies by cities (Source: IPA 2003)

comparability with the data compiled from the other sources. Therefore, altogether 578 important industrial companies were considered.

The table for all companies shows a very low share for the cities, but the values of the important companies come close to the values of the tables for all companies of the sources of KOFC and MOU. Twelve of the thirteen important companies in Wonsan and nine of the ten important companies in Kaesong are companies of light industry.

Table III.4.-7. Deviations between population rank and rank number of important companies (Source: IPA 2003)

	Rank 1-4	Rank 5-16	Rank 17-27
Big cities	X	Chongjin	-
Middle sized cities	Wonsan	X	Phyongsong, Sariwon, Tokchon, Kanggye
Small cities	-	Hyesan, Hoeryong, Munchon, Jongju	X

Table III.4.-8. Number of important companies in relation to the population (Source: IPA 2003)

Hyesan	1	1
Munchon	1	2
Hoeyrong	0.7	3
Manpho	0.4	4
Wonsan	0.4	5
Kaesong	0.3	6
Jongju	0.3	7
Sunchon	0.2	8
Pyongyang	0.2	9
Anju	0.2	10
Nampho	0.1	11
Sinuiju	0.1	12
Kaechon	-0.1	13
Kusong	-0.1	14
Kimchaek	-0.2	15
Haeju	-0.2	16
Phyongsong	-0.2	17
Tanchon	-0.3	18
Hamhung	-0.4	19
Rason	-0.4	20
Chongjin	-0.4	21

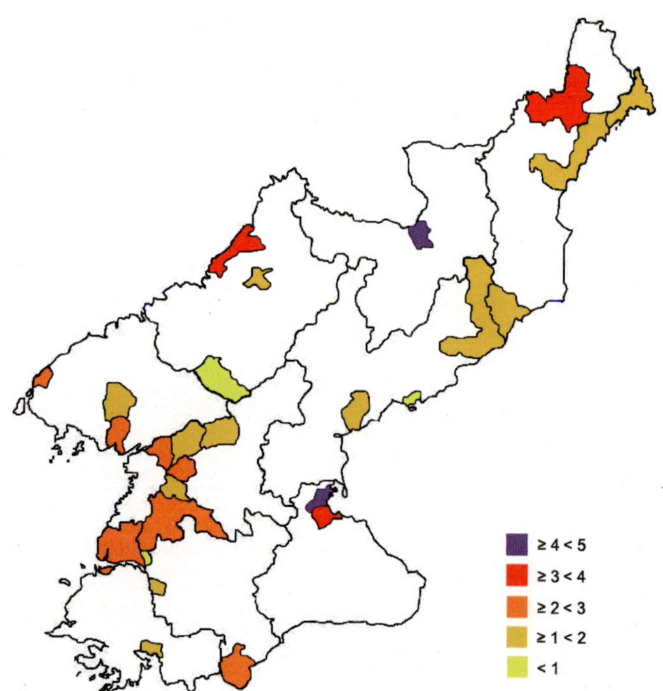

Figure III.4.-4. Number of important companies in relation to the population (Source: IPA 2003)

Sariwon	−0.5	22
Tokchon	−0.5	23
Kanggye	−0.5	24
Songrim	−0.7	25
Sinpho	−0.7	26
Huichon	−0.7	27

It is noticeable, that the first four cities concerning the total number of important companies in relation to population (Hyesan, Munchon, Hoeryong, Manpho) are the same cities that are in the analysis of the sources KOFC and MO that lie ahead among the small cities of North Korea concerning the total number of companies in relation to the population.

The fact that Kaesong is ranked in the forefront, can be explained when regarding that today's city of Kaesong comprises the former city of Kaesong as well as of the former counties of Phanmun and Kaephung, so that here the important companies are formed by adding up three administrative units.

Five of the six companies of the small cities of Munchon and Jongju, which also have more companies than one could assume from its population, are companies of heavy industry. Hyesan and Hoeryong have companies from both industries, just as Manpho, where additionally power plants are located.

Cities that offer more companies than expected from the share of population, are regionally concentrated in the border region to China (Manpho, Hyesan, Hoeryong) as well as in Kangwon province (Wonsan, Munchon).

III.4.4. Industries

When classifying the industries, only the 575 (264) companies that are located in cities were considered. 281 (129) of them are companies of light industry, 213 (110) of them are companies of heavy industry, 61 (13) of them are mines and 20 (12) of them are power plants (in parenthesis: important companies)

Table III.4.-9. Number of companies of light industry in North Korean cities (Source: IPA 2003)

Companies (Light industry)	
73	Pyongyang
42	Nampho
11–22	Kaesong (22), Hamhung (18), Sinuiju (15), Hoeryong (14), Phyongsong, Chongjin (12), Manpho (11)
4–7	Anju, Wonsan (7), Sariwon, Kaechon (6) Hyesan, Haeju (5), Kusong, Sunchon, Munchon (4)
0–3	Kanggye, Songrim (3), Sinpho, Tanchon (2), Huichon, Rason, Jongju, Kimchaek (1), Tokchon (0)

Table III.4.-10. Number of important companies of light industry in North Korean cities (Source: IPA 2003)

Important companies (Light industry)	
58	Pyongyang
8–9	Kaesong (9), Nampho (8)
4–5	Kaechon, Sinuiju, Wonsan, Hyesan (5), Sariwon, Sunchon, Anju, Phyongsong, Hamhung (4)
2–3	Kanggye, Hoeryong (3), Kusong (2)
0–1	Tanchon, Manpho, Munchon, Sinpho, Jongju, Chongjin (1), Kimchaek, Tokchon, Rason, Songrim, Haeju, Huichon (0)

Nevertheless, in the light industry Pyongyang and Nampho dominate by far; concerning the important companies, though, Kaesong overtakes Nampho.

Table III.4.-11. Number of companies of heavy industry in North Korean cities (Source: IPA 2003)

Number of companies (heavy industry)	
32–42	Pyongyang (42), Nampho (32)
18	Hamhung
7–12	Wonsan (12), Chongjin (11), Haeju (10), Manpho (9), Munchon (8), Anju, Sinuiju, Kaechon (7)
4–6	Jongju (6), Kimchaek, Sunchon, Tanchon, Hoeryong (5), Sariwon, Phyongsong (4)
0–3	Tokchon, Kusong, Hyesan, Kaesong (3), Huichon, Rason (2), Songrim (1), Kanggye, Sinpho (0)

Table III.4.-12. Number of important companies of heavy industry in North Korean cities (Source: IPA 2003)

Number of important companies (heavy industry)	
18–22	Pyongyang (22), Nampho (18)
8	Wonsan, Hamhung (8)
4–6	Chongjin (6), Sunchon, Munchon, Jongju, Haeju (5), Sinuiju, Kimchaek (4)
2–3	Hyesan, Anju (3), Kusong, Tanchon, Manpho, Tokchon, Rason (2)
0–1	Phyongsong, Hoeryong, Songrim, Huichon (1), Kaesong, Kaechon, Sariwon, Kanggye, Sinpho (0)

When regarding the companies of heavy industry, it stands out that there are merely three more important companies in Pyongyang than in Nampho.

Table III.4.-13. Number of mines in North Korean cities (Source: IPA 2003)

Number of companies (mining)	
18	Pyongyang
12	Kaechon
5–7	Nampho,Hoeryong (7), Tanchon (5)
1–2	Kaesong, Tokchon, Sunchon, Anju (2), Kimchaek, Chongjin, Haeju, Hyesan (1)

Among those there are 13 important ones: Hoeryong (3), Pyongyang, Tanchon, Kaechon (2), Chongjin, Hyesan, Tokchon, Kaesong (1).

20 power plants are in the cities: Pyongyang 7, Manpho 5, Chongjin 2, Kanggye, Kimchaek, Tanchon, Tokchon, Rason, Anju 1, of which twelve are important: Pyongyang (7), Chongjin (2), Tanchon, Manpho, Rason (1).

III.4.5. Culture

In IPA (2003), for every city, every *kuyok* and every county, important cultural sites and other institutions of cultural significance are introduced in a separate segment (educational institutions, museums, media, ensembles etc.). Altogether 622 institutions are named, of which 474 are located in the 27 cities.

Table III.4.-14. Total number of cultural institutions by cities (Source: IPA 2003)

	Culture	%	Pop. %
Pyongyang	223	35.9	12.8
Nampho	36	5.8	4.2
Hamhung	28	4.5	3.3
Sinuiju	20	3.2	1.5
Wonsan	19	3.1	1.6
Kanggye	16	2.6	1.1
Kaesong	16	2.6	1.3
Haeju	15	2.4	1.2
Sariwon	15	2.4	1.3
Chongjin	14	2.3	2.9
Hyesan	11	1.8	0.8
Phyongsong	11	1,8	1.2
Tanchon	7	1.1	1.5
Sinpho	6	1	0.7
Rason	5	0.8	0.8
Kimchaek	5	0.8	0.9
Sunchon	5	0.8	1.3
Songrim	4	0.6	0.6
Hoeryong	4	0.6	0.7
Jongju	3	0.5	0.8
Tokchon	3	0.5	1
Anju	3	0.5	1
Munchon	2	0.3	0.5
Kusong	2	0.3	0.8
Huichon	1	0.2	0.7
Manpho	0	0	0.5
Kaechon	0	0	1.4

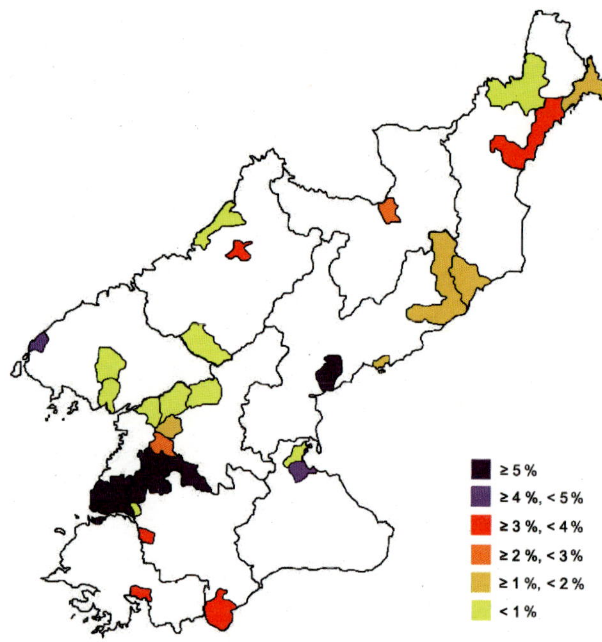

Figure III.4.-5. Total number of cultural institutions by cities (Source: IPA 2003)

Numerous cultural sites are located in the provincial capitals, also in relation to their population. An exception is the capital of Hambuk, Chongjin, with its relatively few cultural sites. Particularly many cultural sites in relation to population are available in Pyongyang, Sinuiju and Kanggye. The first twelve places in the list above are taken exclusively by cities which are province independent (Pyongyang, Nampho) or were until recently (Kaesong) as well as by provincial capitals. Merely the province independent city of Rason, located in the extreme Northeast of the country, has less cultural sites than cities which are not provincial capitals.

Table III.4.-15. Deviations between population rank and rank number of cultural institutions (Source: IPA 2003)

	Rank 1-4	Rank 5-16	Rank 17-27
Big cities	X	Chongjin	-
Middle-sized cities	Sinuiju	X	Sunchon, Tokchon, Anju
Small cities	-	Hyesan, Sinpho, Rason	X

Table III.4.-16. Total number of cultural institutions in relation to population (Source: IPA 2003)

Pyongyang	1.8	1
Kanggye	1.4	2
Hyesan	1.3	3
Sinuiju	1.1	4
Kaesong	1	5
Haeju	1	6
Wonsan	0.9	7
Sariwon	0.8	8
Phyongsong	0.5	9
Sinpho	0.4	10
Nampho	0.4	11
Hamhung	0.4	12
Rason	0	13
Songrim	0	14
Kimchaek	-0.1	15
Hoeryong	-0.1	16
Chongjin	-0.2	17
Tanchon	-0.3	18
Jongju	-0.4	19
Sunchon	-0.4	20
Munchon	-0.4	21
Anju	-0.5	22

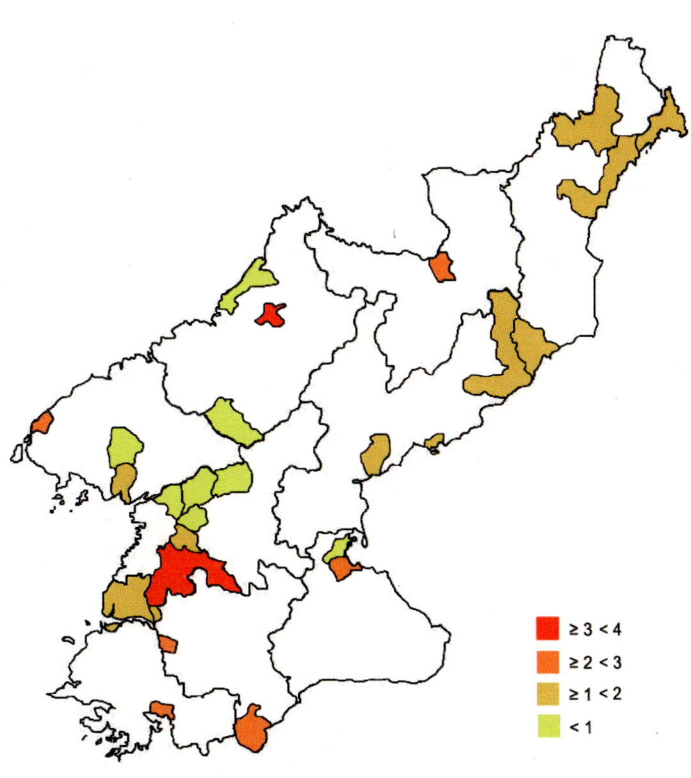

Figure III.4.-6. Total number of cultural institutions in relation to population (Source: IPA 2003)

Tokchon	−0.5	23
Kusong	−0.6	24
Huichon	−0.7	25
Manpho	−1	26
Kaechon	−1	27

When comparing the share of all companies with the share of "culture," the share of "culture" is higher in 22 cities, but not in Hoeryong, Anju, Munchon, Kaechon and Manpho. These cities also have a higher share of important companies in relation to "culture." However, this is followed by the cities: Sunchon, Tokchon, Jongju, Kusong, Huichon.

III.4.6. Conclusions

A specific feature of the IPA (2003) is the fact that it names more companies which are situated in counties (*kun*) than in cities (*si*). Next to the three largest cities, Hoeryong and Manpho also belong to the cities with the most companies. Pyongyang and Nampho dominate in the light industry, whereas concerning the heavy industry Nampho is almost on par with Pyongyang.

Overall, due to the peculiarities of this source, an analysis of the statistics of this source alone is not unproblematic. Nevertheless, it is a source which is very helpful for the qualitative consideration.

III.5. KCNA (1998–2011)

III.5.1. Total number of companies

In the previously analyzed sources (KOFC, MOU, IPA) companies are listed which have been selected through editorial work. In other words, the companies in these sources have been considered as so important that they should be listed in a work dealing with important factories in North Korea. In contrary to the aforementioned sources, the news in the internet-edition of the KCNA is of a more direct source, since the companies have not been edited by the source. Some companies are presented in special articles due to their importance, others are mentioned, because Kim Jong-il has visited them. Yet others employ workers, who received a special honour or a mosaic of Kim Il-sung is put up in a company. Therefore it is to be expected that on the one hand companies of particular importance are named, or companies, which are of special significance for North Korean propaganda.

Table III.5.-1. Total number of companies by cities (Source: KCNA 1998-2011)

	Companies	%	Population %
Pyongyang	177	26.5	12.8
Hamhung	39	5.8	3.3
Nampho	27	4.0	4.2
Kanggye	22	3.3	1.1
Chongjin	21	3.1	2.9
Hyesan	17	2.5	0.8
Wonsan	15	2.2	1.6
Huichon	14	2.1	0.7
Sinuiju	12	1.8	1.5
Tokchon	11	1.6	1
Sunchon	11	1.6	1.3
Sariwon	11	1.6	1.3
Tanchon	11	1.6	1.5
Kaechon	10	1.5	1.4
Anju	9	1.3	1
Haeju	9	1.3	1.2
Manpho	8	1.2	0.5
Rason	7	1	0.8
Kaesong	7	1	1.3
Hoeryong	5	0.7	0.7
Phyongsong	5	0.7	1.2
Jongju	4	0.6	0.8
Kimchaek	4	0.6	0.9
Munchon	3	0.4	0.5
Songrim	2	0.3	0.6
Kusong	2	0.3	0.8
Sinpho	1	0.1	0.7

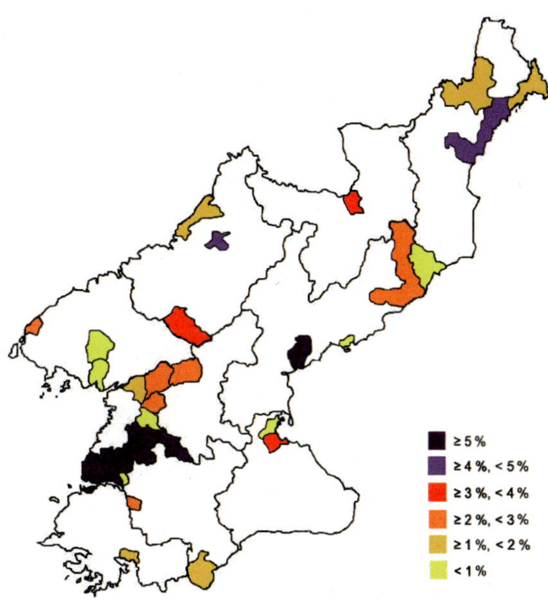

Figure III.5.-1. Total number of companies by cities (Source: KCNA 1998-2011)

The most populous cities Pyongyang, Nampho and Hamhung are on the top of the table, but it is noteworthy that Hamhung has more companies than the more populous Nampho.

Among the cities in terms of the highest number of companies are six, of which three belong to the more populous cities. Chongjin, Wonsan, Sinuiju, but not the other three: Kanggye, Hyesan, Huichon. All latter three are located in the northern interior of the Republic (Jagang-do, Ryanggang-do). Also, Manpho (Jagang-do) is listed with many factories in the KCNA.

Overall, there are more light industry companies than heavy industry companies in this source, but nearly half of the companies of the light industry are situated in the capital Pyongyang.

Because, apart from the light industry companies in Pyongyang, only few companies of the light industry are mentioned in this source, the light industry city of Kaesong is in the lower section of the table.

Table III.5.-2. Deviations between population rank and rank number of companies (Source: KCNA 1998-2011)

	Rank 1-4	Rank 5-16	Rank 17-27
Big cities	X	Chongjin	-
Medium-sized cities	Kanggye	X	Kaesong, Phyongsong
Small cities	-	Hyesan, Huichon	X

Regionally, the cities, which have more companies in relation to the population, are the capital Pyongyang and the four cities of the mountain provinces of Jagang and Ryanggang. The two border towns to China, Manpho and Hyesan, show a similar result according to other sources as well.

III.5.2. Total number of companies in relation to population

Table III.5.-3. Total number of companies in relation to the population (Source: KCNA 1998-2011)

Hyesan	2,1	1
Kanggye	2	2
Huichon	2	3
Manpho	1,4	4
Pyongyang	1,1	5
Hamhung	0,8	6
Tokchon	0,6	7
Wonsan	0,4	8
Anju	0,3	9

Rason	0,3	10
Sariwon	0,2	11
Sunchon	0,2	12
Sinuiju	0,2	13
Haeju	0,1	14
Kaechon	0,1	15
Chongjin	0,1	16
Tanchon	0,1	17
Hoeryong	0	18
Nampho	0	19
Munchon	−0,2	20
Kaesong	−0,2	21
Jongju	−0,2	22
Kimchaek	−0,3	23
Phyongsong	−0,4	24
Songrim	−0,5	25
Kusong	−0,6	26
Sinpho	−0,9	27

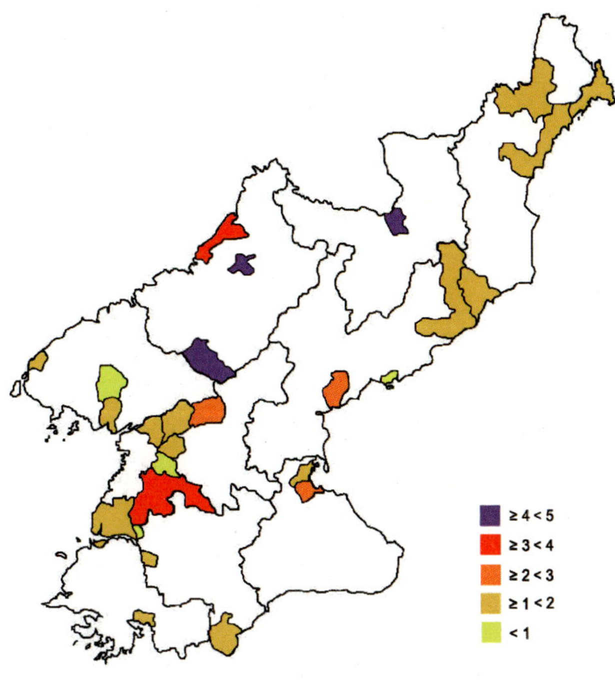

Figure III.5.−2. Total number of companies in relation to the population (Source: KCNA 1998−2011)

It should be noted, that in the previously considered sources in terms of the small cities, Hyesan, Manpho, Hoeryong and Munchon were among the cities in which the most companies are located in relation to the population. However, here Huichon is second and Rason is fourth in terms of the small cities. Due to the slogan "Huichon Tempo" and the Huichon Ryŏnha General Machinery Plant, Huichon has an important propagandistic role, and Rason is a special economic zone of the DPR Korea, for which foreign investors are looked for. However, Hoeryong and Munchon have fewer companies in this source than in previously considered sources.

Table III.5.−4. Total number of companies in relation to the population (Source: KCNA 1998−2011) − Small towns

More companies than expected	Hyesan (1), Huichon (3), Manpho (4)
Balance: Population−Number of companies	Rason (10)
Less companies than expected	Hoeryong (19), Munchon (20), Jongju (22), Kim-chaek (23), Songrim (25), Kusong (26), Sinpho (27)

Among the big cities, Nampho (18) and Chongjin (16) are in the lower middle of the table. However, it should be noted that, in contrary to the previously considered sources, Pyongyang (5) and Hamhung (6) lie in the front section. Here, Pyongyang and Hamhung are industrial representatives of the western half of North Korea (Kwansŏ) and the eastern half of North Korea (Kwanbuk).

Table III.5.-5. Total number of companies in relation to the population (Source: KCNA 1998-2011)- Medium-sized cities

More companies than expected	Kanggye (2), Tokchon (7), Wonsan (8), Anju (9)
Balance: Population-Number of companies	Sariwon (11), Sunchon (12), Sinuiju (13), Haeju (14), Kaechon (15), Tanchon (17)
Less companies than expected	Kaesong (21), Phyongsong (24)

Kanggye, which comes in third place, lies among the medium-sized cities at the top. It can be assumed that this is also due to propagandistic reasons ("Kanggye Spirit"). In Tokchon seven out of the eleven companies are mines.

III.5.3. Important companies

When looking at the results of the KCNA, it was also possible to deduce how often the factories were mentioned in this source; as an important factory is considered to be one that has been found 10 times or more. As a result, there are 43 major companies.

Nine factories have been mentioned more than 25 times: three heavy industry companies from Hamhung: February 8 Vinalon Complex, Ryongsŏng Machine Complex, and Hungnam Fertilizer Complex.

Four more of these nine are heavy industry factories from different cities: Chollima Steel Complex (Nampho), Kim Chaek Iron and Steel Complex (Chongjin), Ragwŏn Machine Complex (Sinuiju), Hwanghae Iron and Steel Complex (Songrim). The factory which has been mentioned the most is the Kim Jong Suk Textile Mill from Pyongyang.

Most of the companies (nine out of twelve) from Pyongyang are light industry factories.

Most of the companies, which are situated in *kun* and had been mentioned ten times or more, are power plants. The most mentioned one of those is the Ryesonggang Hydropower Plant (Thosan-kun, Hwangbuk).

III.5.4. Industries

Among those 43 companies are 14 companies of light industry, 16 of heavy industry, four mines and nine power plants.

Of which 33 are located in cities:

- 12 companies of the light industry: Pyongyang (9), Huichon, Sinuiju, Kanggye (each 1)
- 16 companies of the heavy industry: Nampho (4), Hamhung (3), Pyongyang (2), Huichon, Sinuiju, Chongjin, Kimchaek, Songrim, Anju, Kusong (each 1)
- 3 mining companies: Sunchon (2), Tanchon (1)
- 2 power plants: Pyongyang, Wonsan (each 1)

Out of the 464 considered companies, which are situated in cities, belong

- 232 to the light industry
- 163 to the heavy industry
- 26 to mining and
- 43 to energy.

Table III.5.-6. Number of companies of the light industry in North Korean cities (Source: KCNA 1998-2011)

Companies (light industry)	
111	Pyongyang
12-15	Hamhung (15), Nampho (13), Kanggye (12)
5-9	Sariwon (9), Wonsan (8), Kaesong, Huichon, Hyesan (7), Sinuiju, Chongjin (6), Phyongsong, Rason (5)
2-4	Hoeryong, Haeju (4), Anju (3), Manpho, Kaechon, Sunchon (2)
0-1	Sinpho, Kusong, Jongju, Tokchon (1), Kimchaek, Tanchon, Munchon, Songrim (0)

The dominance of companies of the light industry in the capital, which are mentioned in the KCNA, is notable.

Table III.5.-7. Number of companies of the heavy industry in North Korean cities (Source: KCNA 1998-2011)

Companies (heavy industry)	
52	Pyongyang
23	Hamhung
11	Chongjin, Nampho
4-6	Sinuiju, Kanggye (6), Haeju, Tanchon, Wonsan, Hyesan (5), Kimchaek, Anju, Huichon (4)
0-3	Munchon, Jongju, Manpho, Sunchon (3), Kaechon, Sariwon, Tokchon (2), Kusong, Songrim, Hoeryong, Rason (1), Kaesong, Sinpho, Phyongsong (0)

The dominance of Pyongyang (in the West) on the one hand and of Hamhung (in the East) on the other hand is obvious.

Mining: Tokchon 7, Tanchon 5, Sunchon 4, Kaechon, Hyesan, Pyongyang 3, Nampho 1

Energy: Pyongyang 11, Chongjin, Kanggye 4, Manpho, Kaechon, Huichon 3, Anju, Sunchon, Wonsan, Nampho, Hyesan 2, Songrim, Rason, Tanchon, Tokchon, Hamhung 1.

III.5.5. Conclusion

The capital Pyongyang and the cities in the provinces of Jagang and Ryanggang have a lot of companies in relation to the population. One, therefore, can conclude that especially the new, modern companies, many of them are built with foreign capital and know-how, are situated in the capital. On the other hand, the capital as well as the cities in the mountain provinces have a big symbolic value for the regime and play a significant role for state propaganda. Kanggye is one of the "Eight Scenic Spots in the Songun Era," additionally the "Kanggye spirit" is worshipped, Huichon plays particularly due to the Hydroelectric Power Station Huichon, which has been built with "Huichon Speed," as well as the Huichon Ryŏnha General Machine Factory, a significant role for propaganda.

Also Hamhung as the center of Kwanbuk, the Northeast of the Korean Peninsula, with its three very important companies of heavy industry, is particularly emphasized by the KCNA.

III.6. KIET (Yi Sang-chik, Choe Sin-rim, Yi Sŏk-ki 1996)

III.6.1. Total number of companies

The information in KIET (1996) is based on North Korean sources, mostly in the Rodong Sinmun newspaper. In this point there is a similarity to KCNA. KIET (1996) is the source which lists the most companies. It is therefore to be expected that rather smaller companies are mentioned here. However, it is the oldest source. The data stems mostly from the period before the Great Famine in North Korea in the mid-1990s. Companies of heavy industry have been somewhat more included than companies of light industry.

Table III.6.-1. Total number of companies by cities (Source: KIET 1996)

	Companies	%	Population %
Pyongyang	283	11.4	12.8
Hamhung	126	5.1	3.3
Nampho	115	4.6	4.2
Chongjin	93	3.8	2.9
Kaesong	72	2.9	1.3
Sunchon	60	2.4	1.3
Wonsan	46	1.9	1.6
Haeju	43	1.7	1.2
Kaechon	41	1.7	1.4
Tanchon	39	1.6	1.5
Sinuiju	36	1.5	1.5
Anju	32	1.3	1
Sariwon	32	1.3	1.3
Hyesan	29	1.2	0.8
Rason	29	1.2	0.8
Kanggye	29	1.2	1.1
Kimchaek	25	1	0.9
Hoeryong	24	1	0.7
Manpho	22	0.9	0,5
Tokchon	21	0.8	1
Jongju	20	0.8	0.8
Phyongsong	19	0.8	1.2
Munchon	16	0.6	0.5
Huichon	16	0.6	0.7
Kusong	16	0.6	0.8
Sinpho	13	0.5	0.7
Songrim	11	0.4	0.6

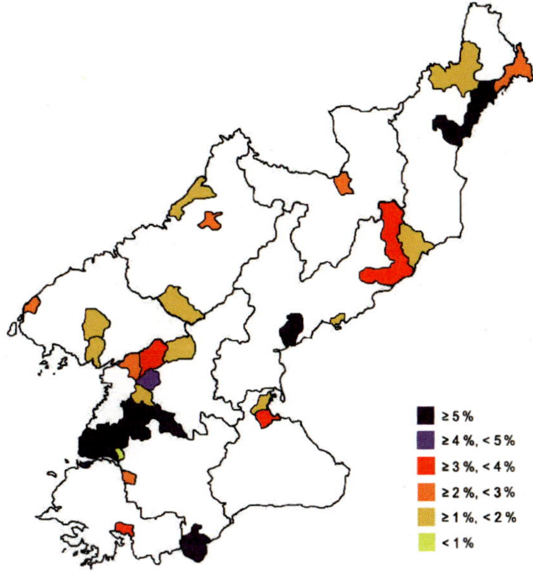

Figure III.6.-1. Total number of companies by cities (Source: KIET 1996)

In Pyongyang, there are slightly more than twice as many companies as in Hamhung. The next six cities follow one another at an interval of at least ten companies. Like within the KCNA source, but unlike the other sources, Hamhung here has more companies than Nampho.

Table III.6.-2. Deviations between population rank and rank number of companies (Source: KIET 1996)

	Rank 1-4	Rank 5-16	Rank 17-27
Big cities	X	-	-
Medium-sized cities	-	X	Tokchon, Phyongsong
Small cities	-	Hyesan, Rason	X

In Pyongyang and Nampho are 18.8% of all industrial companies listed in KOFC. This are more than twice as many as in the two provincial capitals of the Hamgyong provinces Hamhung and Chongjin, where 8% of the industrial companies are located. In MOU the share of the first two cities is even more than three times as large as the share of the latter two (23.5% to 6.9%). In KIET, however, the comparison between the two western cities and the two eastern cities does not fall quite so stark (16.1% to 8.9%). That means that in comparison to the other two sources, KIET (1996) lists more companies which are located in the above mentioned two cities of Hamgyong-region.

III.6.2. Total number of companies in relation to population

Table III.6.-3. Total number of companies in relation to population (Source: KIET 1996)

Kaesong	1.2	1
Sunchon	0.8	2
Manpho	0.8	3
Hamhung	0.5	4
Rason	0.5	5
Hyesan	0.5	6
Hoeryong	0.4	7
Haeju	0.4	8
Chongjin	0.3	9
Anju	0.3	10
Kaechon	0.2	11
Munchon	0.2	12
Wonsan	0.2	13
Kimchaek	0.1	14
Nampho	0.1	15
Kanggye	0.1	16
Tanchon	0.1	17
Sinuiju	0	18
Sariwon	0	19
Jongju	0	20
Pyongyang	−0.1	21
Huichon	−0.1	22
Tokchon	−0.2	23
Kusong	−0.2	24
Sinpho	−0.3	25
Phyongsong	−0.3	26
Songrim	−0.4	27

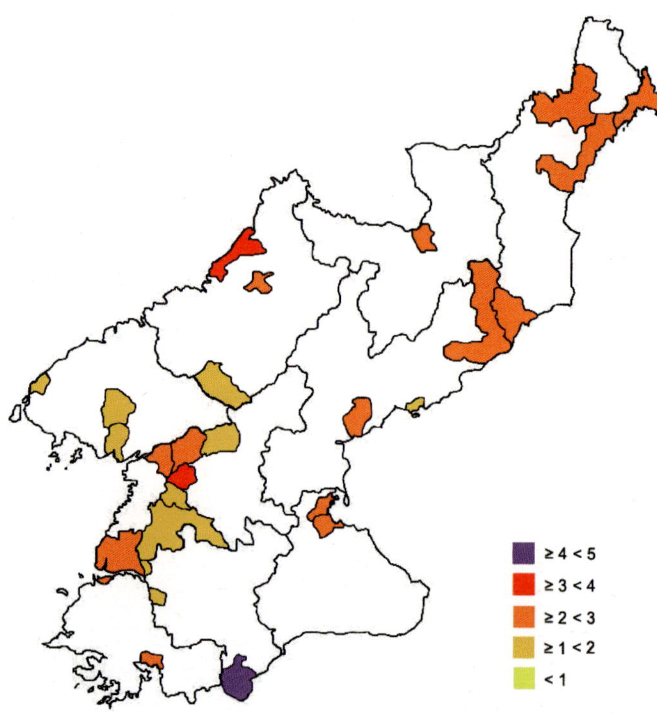

Figure III.6.-2. Total number of companies in relation to population (Source: KIET 1996)

The small cities, in which more companies than expected are located, are the four small cities that lie on the border with China. In contrast to the sources that have previously been investigated, Rason also has more companies than one would expect in view of its population.

Table III.6.-4. Total number of companies in relation to population (Source: KIET 1996) – Small cities

More companies than expected	Manpho (3), Rason (5), Hyesan (6), Hoeryong (7)
Balance: Population–Number of companies	Munchon (12), Kimchaek (14)
Fewer companies than expected	Jongju (20), Huichon (22), Kusong (24), Sinpho (25), Songrim (27)

It is also noticeable, that in this source Hamhung (4) and Chongjin (9) have more companies than one might expect concerning their population. Nampho (15) is ranked in the middle, whereas Pyongyang (21) is ranking lower.

Table III.6.-5. Total number of companies in relation to population (Source KIET 1996) – Medium cities

More companies than expected	Kaesong (1), Sunchon (2), Haeju (8)
Balance: Population–Number of companies	Anju (10),Kaechon (11), Wonsan (13), Kanggye (16), Tanchon (17), Sinuiju (18)
Fewer companies than expected	Sariwon (19), Tokchon (23), Phyongsong (26)

Kaesong and Sunchon are medium-sized cities, which have more companies than expected, and they are also well equipped with companies both of light as well as heavy industry, while there is a prevalence of heavy industry in Haeju.

III.6.3. Important companies

Table III.6.-6. Total number of important companies by cities (Source: KIET 1996)

	Comp.	%	Pop.%
Pyongyang	136	17.9	12.8
Hamhung	47	6.2	3.3
Nampho	45	5.9	4.2
Chongjin	35	4.6	2.9
Sunchon	25	3.3	1.3
Kaesong	24	3.2	1.3
Wonsan	20	2.6	1.6
Sinuiju	19	2.5	1.5

Sariwon	18	2.4	1.3
Anju	14	1.8	1
Tanchon	13	1.7	1.5
Haeju	12	1.6	1.2
Kaechon	12	1.6	1.4
Hyesan	11	1.4	0.8
Tokchon	10	1.3	1
Phyongsong	10	1.3	1.2
Huichon	9	1.2	0.7
Munchon	8	1.1	0.5
Kusong	8	1.1	0.8
Kimchaek	8	1.1	0.9
Kanggye	7	0.9	1.1
Rason	6	0.8	0.8
Hoeryong	5	0.7	0.7
Jongju	5	0.7	0.8
Manpho	4	0.5	0.5
Songrim	3	0.4	0.6
Sinpho	2	0.3	0.7

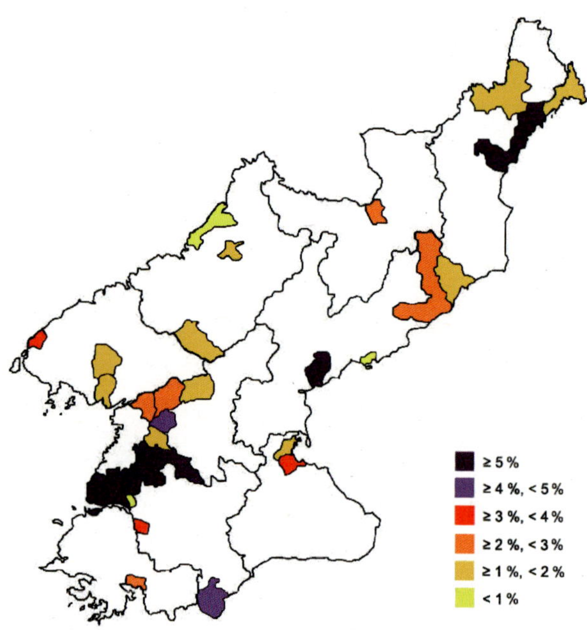

Figure III.6.-3. Total number of important companies by cities (Source: KIET 1996)

Table III.6.-7. Deviations between population rank and rank number of major companies (Source: KIET 1996)

	Rank 1-4	Rank 5-16	Rank 17-27
Big cities	X	-	-
Medium-sized cities	-	X	Kanggye
Small cities	-	Hyesan	X

When comparing the distribution of all companies of North Korean cities with the distribution of the important companies on the North Korean cities, it is noticeable that in the latter, Kaesong is overtaken by Sunchon. Also in KOFC (2010) and MOU (2012), Sunchon had a higher ranking in important companies than in all companies. The same is the case with Sinuiju, Sariwon and Anju. Therefore in these three cities companies are located which belong to the most important in the country.

Table III.6.-8. Total number of important companies in relation to population (Source: KIET 1996)

Sunchon	1.5	1
Kaesong	1.5	2
Munchon	1.2	3
Hamhung	0.9	4
Sariwon	0.8	5
Anju	0.8	6
Hyesan	0.8	7
Huichon	0.7	8
Sinuiju	0.7	9
Wonsan	0.6	10
Chongjin	0.6	11
Nampho	0.4	12
Pyongyang	0.4	13
Kusong	0.4	14
Haeju	0.3	15
Tokchon	0.3	16
Kimchaek	0.2	17
Kaechon	0.1	18
Tanchon	0.1	19
Phyongsong	0.1	20
Rason	0	21
Hoeryong	0	22
Manpho	0	23
Jongju	−0.1	24
Kanggye	−0.2	25
Songrim	−0.3	26
Sinpho	−0.6	27

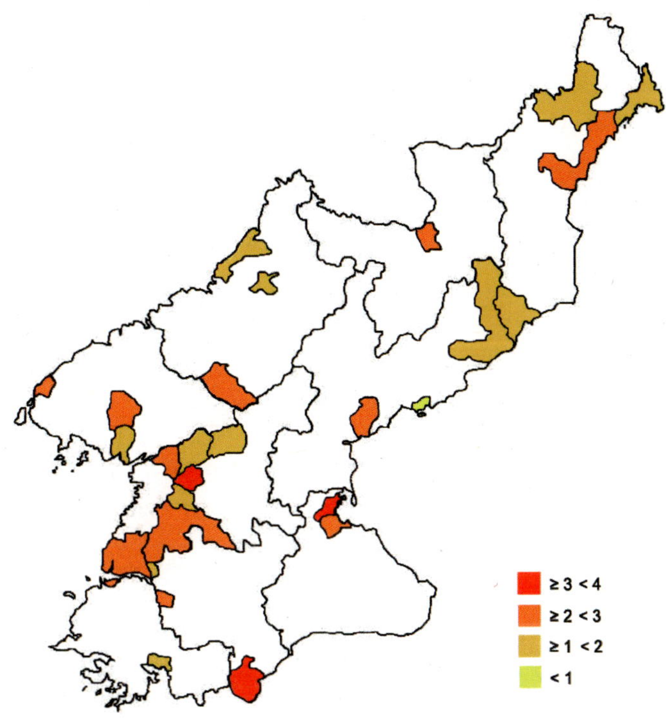

Figure III.6.-4. Total number of important companies in relation to population (Source: KIET 1996)

Table III.6.-9. Number of important companies in relation to population – small cities (Source KIET 1996)

More companies than expected	Munchon (3), Hyesan (7), Huichon (8)
Balance: Population–Number of companies	Kusong (14), Kimchaek (17)
Fewer companies than expected	Rason (21), Hoeryong (22), Manpho (23), Jongju (24), Songrim (26), Sinpho (27)

Taking into account all companies in the cities Manpho, Rason and Hoeryong where more companies are to be expected compared to their population, but when taking into account only the important companies, these cities are found in the lower ranks. This shows that although these cities have numerous factories, most of them are less important ones. Only Hyesan ranks also in the front when also taking into account only the important factories. In Munchon a disproportionately greater number of important companies are located. Also, a large number of the few companies located in Huichon belong in the important category.

The largest cities are ranked either in the front or in the upper middle field: Hamhung (4), Chongjin (11), Nampho (12), Pyongyang (13).

Table III.6.-10. Number of major companies in relation to population-medium-sized cities (Source KIET 1996)

More companies than expected	Sunchon (1), Kaesong (2), Sariwon (5), Anju (6), Sinuiju (9),
Balance: Population-Number of companies	Wonsan (10), Haeju (15), Tokchon (16), Kaechon (18)
Fewer companies than expected	Tanchon (19), Phyongsong (20), Kanggye (25)

Sunchon and Kaesong already belong to the cities with more companies than expected when taking in account all companies. However this is the case of Sariwon, Anju and Sinuiju when taking into account only the important companies.

III.6.4. Industries

A total of 2480 (761) companies are distributed as follows among the various sectors of industry:

- 1081 (230) light industry
- 1016 (414) heavy industry
- 306 (90) mining
- 77 (27) energy

Therefore, the group of light industry companies is similar in size to the group of heavy industry companies. However, when regarding the important companies (number in parenthesis) heavy industry companies are in the majority.

1308 (516) of the companies are located in the 27 cities of North Korea. The proportion of heavy industry companies is higher than the one of the light industry:

- 539 (152) light industry

- 642 (318) heavy industry
- 92 (31) mining
- 35 (15) energy

Table III.6.-11. Number of companies of light industry in North Korean cities (Source: KIET 1996)

Number of companies (Light industry)	
132	Pyongyang
36-44	Hamhung (44), Kaesong (39), Nampho (38), Chongjin (36)
17-21	Sunchon, Wonsan (21), Sinuiju (17)
10-15	Hoeryong, Haeju, Kanggye (15), Anju (14), Kaechon, Tanchon, Sariwon (13), Hyesan (12), Rason (11), Jongju (10)
4-9	Sinpho (9), Kusong, Phyongsong (8), Tokchon, Munchon (7), Kimchaek, Manpho (6), Songrim (5), Huichon (4)

Table III.6.-12. Number of important companies of light industry in North Korean cities (Source: KIET 1996)

Number of important companies (Light industry)	
51	Pyongyang
10-11	Hamhung (11), Kaesong, Nampho (10)
7-8	Chongjin (8), Sinuiju, Wonsan (7)
3-5	Sariwon, Anju, Haeju, Hyesan (5), Sunchon, Phyongsong, Hoeryong (4), Kanggye, Kaechon (3)
0-2	Kusong (2), Kimchaek, Tanchon, Tokchon, Rason, Munchon, Sinpho, Jongju, Huichon (1), Manpho, Songrim (0)

It is clear that light industry companies are centered in Pyongyang, in particular the more important companies. Kaesong shows itself in this source as a city with numerous light industry companies. Furthermore, within the large cities of Hamhung, Nampho and Chongjin numerouslight industry companies are located. These are followed by the medium-sized cities Sunchon, Sinuiju and Wonsan, although the more important companies are located in the latter two cities.

Food · Tobacco

189 (35) i.e. 54,6% (46,7%) of a total of 346 (75) companies, approximately half of them, are located in the *kun* i.e. the counties. Most urban food factories are located in populous cities: Pyongyang 32 (10), Nampho 14 (4), Chongjin 13 (3), Hamhung 13 (1), Kaesong 10 (2), Wonsan 8 (5), Sunchon 8 (0).

Textile • Clothing • Shoes

Of the 418 (104) companies in this industry, 176 (42.1%) of them or rather 23 (22.1%) are located in the *kun*. In the phalanx of the four most populous cities, Kaesong enters, which has a lot of food factories: Pyongyang 67 (28), Kaesong 17 (7), Nampho 17 (7), Chongjin 16(5), Hamhung 16 (5), Sinuiju 11 (4).

Wood • Pulp • Paper

For this industry, a total of 114 (18) companies have been considered, of which 67 (6) or 58,8% (33,3%) are located in the *kun*. Hoeryong 4 (1), which is situated on the Tumen, houses most companies of this industry, after the large cities of Pyongyang 10 (3) and Hamhung 5 (2).

Furniture and Miscellaneous

In this industrial sector about half of the 203 (33) companies are located in the *kun*, namely 110 (14), 54.2% or 42.4%. Kaesong manages to enter into the phalanx of the four largest cities: Pyongyang 23 (10), Hamhung 10 (3), Kaesong 9 (1), Chongjin 6 (0), Nampho 5 (1).

Table III.6.-13. Number of companies of heavy industry in North Korean cities (Source: KIET 1996)

Companies (Heavy industry)	
131	Pyongyang
49-80	Hamhung (80), Nampho (63), Chongjin (49)
25-30	Sunchon (30), Kaesong (28), Haeju, Wonsan (25)
13-19	Sinuiju (19), Tanchon (18), Sariwon (17), Hyesan (15), Kimchaek, Rason (14), Anju, Kanggye (13)
3-11	Kaechon, Huichon (11), Manpho, Jongju, Phyongsong (10), Munchon (9), Kusong (8), Songrim (6), Tokchon, Hoeryong (5), Sinpho (3)

Table III.6.-14. Number of important companies of heavy industry in North Korean cities (Source: KIET 1996)

Important companies (Heavy industry)	
76	Pyongyang
24-35	Hamhung (35), Nampho (32), Chongjin (24)
12-14	Kaesong, Sunchon (14), Sariwon, Wonsan (13), Sinuiju (12)
5-8	Tanchon, Anju, Huichon(8), Munchon, Haeju (7), Kusong, Phyongsong (6), Kimchaek, Hyesan (5)
1-4	Kanggye, Rason, Jongju (4), Kaechon, Tokchon, Songrim (3), Manpho (2), Sinpho, Hoeryong (1)

In addition, Pyongyang is on the top of the heavy industry category, although it does not dominate as much as in light industry. The three large cities of Hamhung, Nampho and Chongjin follow Pyongyang in this respect.

Chemistry

Of the total of 319 (95) companies in this industry, 154 (31), i.e. 48.3% or 32.6% of them are located in the *kun*. The cities with the most chemical plants are Pyongyang 28 (11) and Hamhung 25 (11). Far behind, Nampho 13 (4) and Sunchon 11 (6) follow.

Cement • Glass • Ceramic

A total of 193 (57) companies are allocated to this industry, of which 97 or 24 (50.3% respectively 42.1%) are situated in *kun*. Pyongyang 22 (10) clearly tops the list of cities with the most companies in this industry. Sunchon 11 (4), which already is in the top four of chemical plants, enters into the phalanx of the 3 largest cities. Nampho 10 (3) and Hamhung 7 (4) complete the field of the four cities with the most companies in these industrial sectors.

Primary metal industry

Most of the 45 (30) companies of this industry are located in the cities of North Korea, in the *kun* there are between one and three (6.7% respectively 3.3%) companies. Apart from the mining industry, this is the only one in which there is a city that has more companies than Pyongyang. Most companies are in Chongjin 8 (5). Then, the neighboring towns Pyongyang 6 (5) and Nampho 5 (4) follow.

Fabricated metal industry • machine equipment

Most of the 402 (200) companies in this industry are located in the large cities of the country. In the *kun* only 112 (37) 27.9% respectively. 18.5% are situated: Pyongyang 65 (43), Hamhung 38 (19), Nampho 28 (17), Chongjin 20 (10), Kaesong 14 (10), Wonsan 13 (5), Sariwon 11 (7), Haeju 11 (3), Sinuiju 10 (7).

Vehicles

The 57 (31) companies in this industry are mostly located in the cities of the country. Pyongyang has 10 (7) companies. Pyongyang is followed by Chongjin 7 (4) and Nampho 7 (0) and Hamhung 6 (4). In the *kun* of the country, there are a total of only 8 respectively 3 (14% respectively 9.7%) companies.

Mining

For this industry a total of 306 (90) companies were considered, of which 214 (59), i.e. 69.9% (65.6%) over two-thirds are not in the cities but in the *kun* of the country, most of them in the *kun* of Phyongnam with 40 (14) companies.

Also, the five cities where the most mining operations are located are in Phyongnam or rather they are province-free cities which were in the past a part of Phyongnam: Kaechon 17 (6), Pyongyang 14 (6), Nampho 11 (2), Sunchon 8 (6) and Tokchon 8 (5). Only in sixth place follows Tanchon 6 (3), the famous mining town in the Hamnam Province.

Energy

Also, about half of the 77 (27) power plants are located in the *kun*, namely 42 respectively 12 (54.5% respectively 44.4%). In regards to the cities, Pyongyang 6 (3) is followed by Manpho 5 (2), a city situated on the Yalu, then followed by Chongjin 4 (3), Nampho 3 (1).

III.6.5. Conclusion

Kaesong and Sunchon are the two cities that have the most factories in proportion to the population. Kaesong achieved an above-average number of companies, especially in the sectors of furniture, textiles, machinery, cement and food. In regards to important textile companies, Kaesong is only outnumbered by Pyongyang. Sunchon has an above-average number of cement companies. It is striking that in Sunchon an above-average number of companies classified as important are located, not only the cement industry, but as well as the mining and the chemical industries.

III.7. Overall view

III.7.1. Total number of companies

In this chapter the results of the five sources, which have been analyzed, are summarized. This is done by

- an examination of the results of five individual studies on similarities and deviations
- a comprehensive result presented in the form of a table.

With regard to the total number of companies, the sum was calculated as follows: from all five sources the percentage of companies located in the cities were added up and then divided by five.

Table III.7.-1. Total number of companies by city - percentages of all five sources (only companies located in cities) divided by five

	Companies %	Population %
Pyongyang	27.4	12.8
Nampho	8.9	4.2
Hamhung	7.6	3.3
Chongjin	5.3	2.9
Wonsan	3.8	1.6
Kaesong	3.7	1.3
Sinuiju	3.6	1.5
Sunchon	3.2	1.3
Kaechon	3.2	1.4
Haeju	2.9	1.2
Tanchon	2.7	1.5
Kanggye	2.6	1.1
Sariwon	2.6	1.3
Hyesan	2.5	0.8
Hoeryong	2.4	0.7
Anju	2.4	1
Manpho	2.2	0.5
Tokchon	1.9	1
Phyongsong	1.8	1.2
Huichon	1.5	0.7
Kimchaek	1.5	0.9
Rason	1.4	0.8
Munchon	1.3	0.5
Jongju	1.1	0.8
Kusong	0.9	0.8
Sinpho	0.7	0.7
Songrim	0.6	0.6

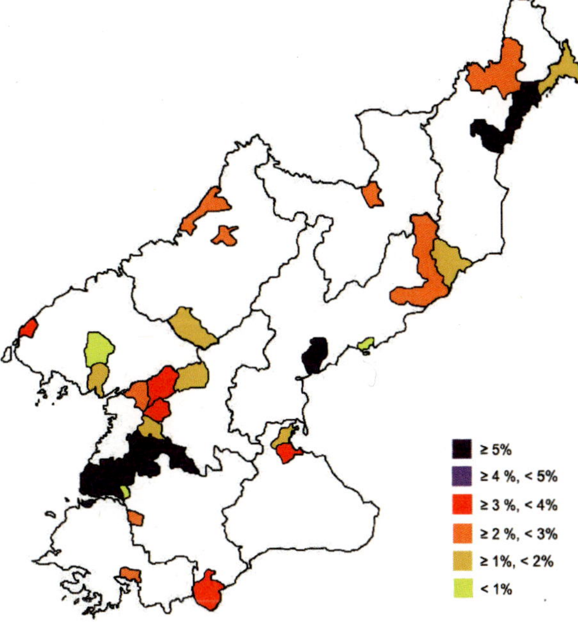

Figure III.7.-1. Total number of companies by city - percentages of all five sources (only companies located in cities) divided by five

With regard to the total number of companies, Pyongyang stands out in all five studies as a frontrunner. The proportion of companies in Pyongyang compared to all companies of DPR Korea varies depending on the source between 5.9% (IPA 2003) and 26.4% (KCNA 1998-2011). If one considered only the companies that are located in the 27 cities in the DPRK, the values for Pyongyang vary between 21.6% (KIET 1996) and 38.4% (KCNA 1998-2011).

The next cities that follow in the table above are the large cities of Nampho, Hamhung and Chongjin. Between them, there is a significant gap, and the gap to the city with the fifth-most companies (Wonsan) is also significant. However, it should be noted that the second largest city Nampho is passed by Hamhung in terms of the total number of companies according to the sources of KCNA and KIET.

Table III.7.-2. Deviations between population rank and rank number of companies (summary of all five sources)

	Rank 1-4	Rank 5-16	Rank 17-27
Big cities	X	-	-
Medium-sized cities	-	X	Tokchon, Phyongsong
Small cities	-	Hoeryong, Hyesan	X

Afterwards, the following twelve positions are usually taken by the twelve medium-sized cities. However, there are exceptions. In the above table, the small cities of Hoeryong and Hyesan rank among the top 16, while the medium-sized cities of Tokchon and Phyongsong are found amongst the lower ranks of the table above as well as in three of the five sources. The three medium-sized cities of Tanchon, Kaesong, Kanggye and Sariwon are also not to be found among the top 16 in each one of the sources. Instead, small cities are found amongst the top 16: Hyesan (four times), Hoeryong (two times), Rason, Manpho, Munchon and Huichon (one time each).

Table III.7.-3. Deviations between population rank and rank number of companies (summary of all five sources)

	Rank 1-4	Rank 5-16	Rank 17-27
Big cities	X	Chongjin (3)	-
Medium-sized cities	Sinuiju, Kaesong, Kanggye (1)	X	Tokchon, Phyongsong (3), Tanchon, Kaesong, Kanggye, Sariwon (1)
Small cities	-	Hyesan (4), Hoeryong (2), Rason, Manpho, Mun-chon, Huichon (1)	X

III.7.2. Total number of companies in relation to population

Signs of a strong polarization can be found in the small cities. Manpho was found in the upper third among all five sources, the same can be said for Hoeryong and Hyesan according to four sources.

Munchon was found three times in the upper and once in the lower third of the ranking. In contrast, Songrim was found in the lower third in all five sources and the same applied to Jongju, Kusong and Sinpho in four sources. Rason was found within three sources at the bottom and according to one source among the top third. A more balanced picture was shown by the cities of Huichon and Kimchaek. The former was found twice in the top and three times in the lower third. Kimchaek was once found in the lower third and otherwise was always in the middle third.

A far more balanced result was shown for the medium-sized cities. With the exception of Tanchon, all cities were once or three times ranked in the first third of the rankings. The large cities were found in most sources with respect to the total number of companies in relation to population in the lower midsection.

To obtain an overall table, the percentages of all five sources (only the companies located in cities) are added up and divided by the total population. To make it comparable with the maps in the previous chapters, this value was then divided by five.

Table III.7.-4. Total number of companies in relation to population – percentage of all five sources (only the companies located in cities) divided total population by five

Manpho	4.4	1
Hoeryong	3.5	2
Hyesan	3.2	3
Kaesong	2.8	4
Munchon	2.7	5
Haeju	2.4	6
Sunchon	2.4	7
Wonsan	2.4	8
Sinuiju	2.4	9
Kanggye	2.4	10
Anju	2.3	11
Hamhung	2.3	12
Kaechon	2.3	13
Pyongyang	2.2	14
Nampho	2.1	15
Huichon	2.1	16
Sariwon	2	17
Tokchon	1.9	18
Chongjin	1.8	19
Tanchon	1.8	20
Rason	1.8	21
Kimchaek	1.7	22
Phyongsong	1.5	23

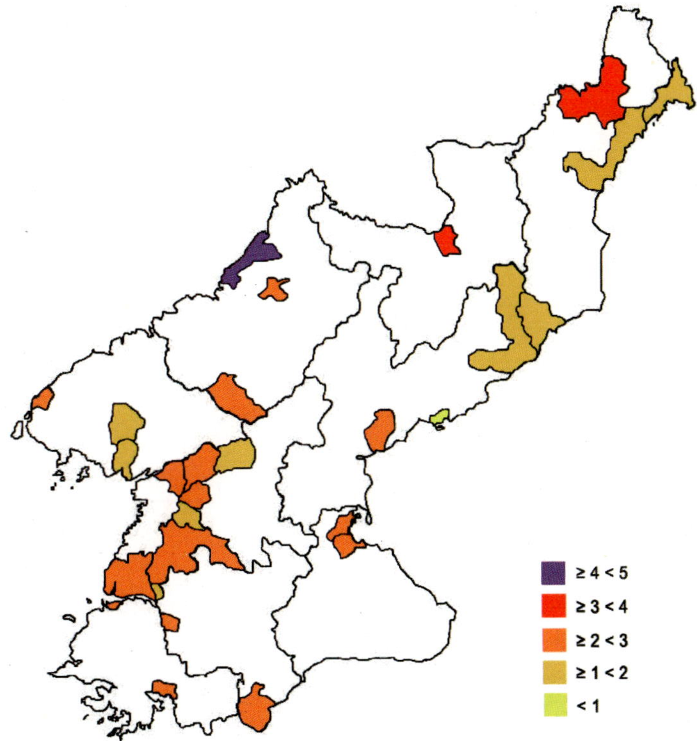

Figure III.7.-2. Total number of companies in relation to population – percentage of all five sources (only the companies located in cities) divided total population by five

Jongju	1.4	24
Kusong	1.1	25
Songrim	1	26
Sinpho	0.9	27

With the exceptions of Manpho and Sinpho, all cities thus show values between one and four. With the exception of five cities (Manpho, Hoeryong Hyesan and Sinpho), all cities show values between one and three. Only two other cities (Haeju, Sunchon) exceed the value of 2.5. This means that the distribution of industrial companies on the cities of the DPR Korea can be stated as quite balanced.

Table III.7.-5. Total number of companies in relation to population size (summary of all five sources) – Small cities

More companies than expected	Manpho (1), Hoeryong (2), Hyesan (3), Munchon (5)
Balance: Population – Number of companies	Huichon (16)
Less companies than expected	Rason (21), Kimchaek (22), Jongju (24), Kusong (25), Songrim (26), Sinpho (27)

Hamhung (12), Pyongyang (14), Nampho (15) and Chongjin (19) are placed in the midfield.

Table III.7.-6. Total number of companies in relation to population (summary of all five sources) –Medium-sized cities

More companies than expected	Kaesong (4), Haeju (6), Sunchon (7), Wonsan (8), Sinuiju (9)
Balance: Population – Number of companies	Kanggye (10), Anju (11), Kaechon (13), Sariwon (17), Tokchon (18)
Less companies than expected	Tanchon (20), Phyongsong (23)

More companies than expected can be found especially in the three small cities, which lie on the border with China, as well as in Kaesong and Munchon.

Less companies than expected are located on the northern East Sea coast (Rason, Chongjin, Tanchon, Kimchaek, Sinpho), also in Phyongbuk (Kusong, Jongju). Furthermore, there are less companies in three cities in the west of the country, which are specialized in certain areas: Tokchon (mining), Phyongsong (administration, education), Songrim (iron and steel works).

III.7.3. Important companies

In the sources some companies were cited as important, and others as less important. Here the procedure was as follows: All companies were included, which appear in at least three sources and appear at least once as an important company.

290 (66.1%) of the as important identified 439 companies are located in cities.

Table III.7.-7. Number of important companies by cities (summary of all five sources)

	Companies	%	Population %
Pyongyang	88	20	12.8
Nampho	27	6.2	4.2
Hamhung	20	46	3.3
Chongjin	16	3.6	2.9
Wonsan	12	2.7	1.6
Sariwon	11	2.5	1.3
Sunchon	10	2.3	1.3
Kaechon	10	2.3	1.4
Sinuiju	10	2.3	1.5
Tokchon	8	1.8	1
Anju	8	1.8	1
Tanchon	8	1.8	1.5
Hyesan	7	1.6	0.8
Haeju	7	1.6	1.2
Kanggye	6	1.4	1.1
Kaesong	6	1.4	1.3
Hoeryong	5	1.1	0.7
Jongju	5	1.1	0.8
Manpho	4	0.9	0.5
Munchon	4	0.9	0.5
Kimchaek	4	0.9	0.9
Phyongsong	4	0.9	1.2
Huichon	3	0.7	0.7
Kusong	2	0.5	0.8
Rason	2	0.5	0.8
Songrim	1	0.2	0.6
Sinpho	1	0.2	0.7

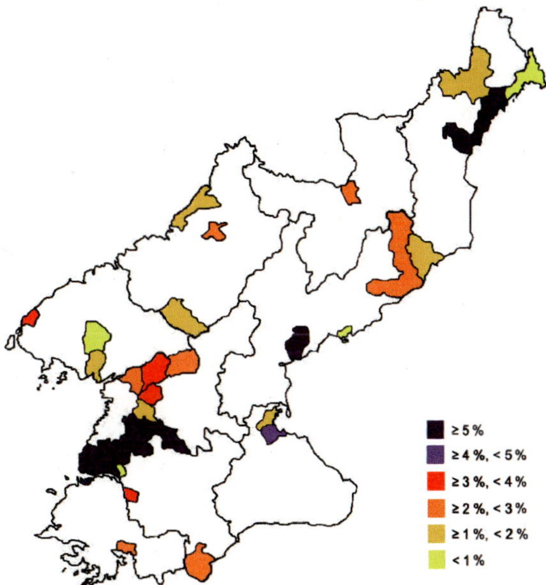

Figure III.7.-3. Number of important companies by cities (summary of all five sources)

Table III.7.-8. Deviations between population rank and rank number of companies (summary of all five sources)

	Rank 1–4	Rank 5–16	Rank 17–27
Major cities	X	–	–
Medium-sized cities	–	X	Phyongsong
Small cities	–	Hyesan	X

Table III.7.-9. Number of major companies in relation to population (summary of all five sources)

Hyesan	1	1
Sariwon	0.9	2
Wonsan	0.8	3
Sunchon	0.8	4
Anju	0.8	5
Tokchon	0.8	6
Munchon	0.8	7
Manpho	0.8	8
Pyongyang	0.6	9
Kaechon	0.6	10
Hoeryong	0.6	11
Sinuiju	0.5	12
Nampho	0.5	13
Hamhung	0.4	14
Jongju	0.4	15
Kanggye	0.3	16
Chongjin	0.3	17
Haeju	0.3	18
Tanchon	0.2	19
Kaesong	0.1	20
Kimchaek	0	21
Huichon	0	22
Phyongsong	−0.2	23
Kusong	−0.4	24
Rason	−0.4	25
Sinpho	−0.7	26
Songrim	−0.7	27

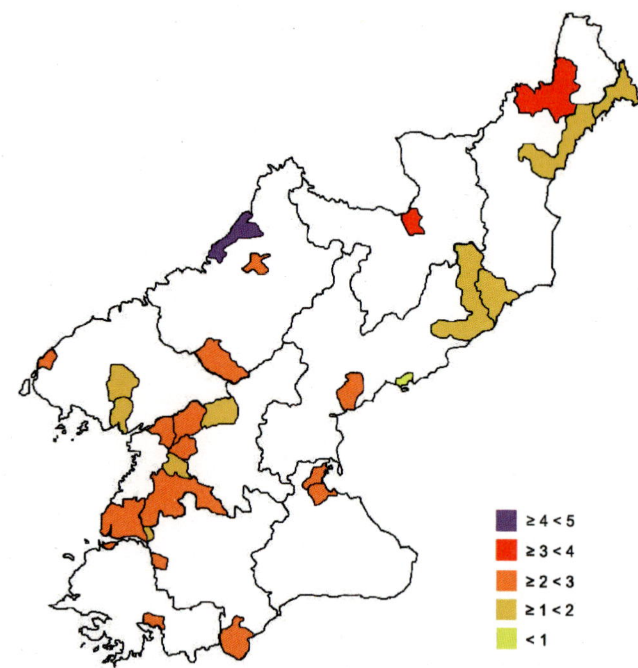

Figure III.7.-4. Number of major companies in relation to population (summary of all five sources)

The small number of important companies in Kaesong in comparison with the number of total companies is remarkable.

III.7.4. Industries

Of the 440 important companies 149 of them (33.9%) belong to light industry, 184 (41.8%) to heavy industry, 77 (17.5%) to mining and 30 (6.8%) to energy industry. Of the 290 important companies that are located in cities, 108 (37.2%) belong to light industry, 184 (50.7%) to heavy industry, 21 (7.2%) to mining and 14 (4.8%) to the energy sector.

The analysis of the five sources revealed that the three largest cities, Pyongyang, Hamhung and Nampho; are at the front of the ranking, in terms of the number of companies in the light industry. They are followed by Kaesong, Sinuiju and Wonsan. Only then, the fourth largest city of Chongjin ranks behind them.

Table III.7.-10. Number of important light industry companies in North Korean cities (summary of all five sources)

Companies (Light industry)	
42	Pyongyang
5–7	Hamhung (7), Sariwon, Kaesong (6), Wonsan, Sinuiju, Nampho (5)
2–4	Hoeryong, Hyesan, Kanggye (4), Chongjin, Sunchon, Kaechon (3), Haeju, Phyongsong, Anju (2)
0–1	Huichon, Jongju, Sinpho, Tanchon, Kusong (1), Songrim, Munchon, Manpho, Rason, Tokchon, Kimchaek (0)

In view of the important companies of light industry, Chongjin ranks even further behind.

In terms of the heavy industry, the four largest cities of Pyongyang, Hamhung, Chongjin and Nampho are dominating. They are followed by Sinuiju, Haeju and Sunchon.

Table III.7.-11. Number of important heavy industry companies in North Korean cities (summary of all five sources)

Companies (Heavy industry)	
38	Pyongyang
11–20	Nampho (20), Hamhung (14), Chongjin (11)
4–7	Wonsan (7), Sariwon, Sinuiju, Haeju, Anju (5), Sunchon, Jongju, Tanchon, Munchon, Kimchaek (4)
0–2	Hyesan, Kanggye, Phyongson, Huichon, Manpho, Tokchon (2), Hoeryong, Kaechon, Kusong, Songrim, Rason (1), Kaesong, Sinpho (0)

Primarily, Kaechon, Tokchon, Tanchon and Pyongyang were found to be the most important mining cities while analyzing the five sources. This applies secondarily for Sunchon, Nampho and Hoeryong. Except for Hoeryong, the mentioned cities are also represented with at least one important company in the mining sector (in parenthesis the number of companies): Kaechon (6), Tokchon (5), Pyongyang (4), Tanchon (3), Sunchon (2) Nampho (1).

Energy facilities are to be found scattered all over the country. This was also revealed by the analysis of the important companies. As far as they are situated in cities, they are located in Pyongyang (4), Chongjin (2), Tokchon, Sunchon, Nampho, Anju, Hyesan, Kanggye, Manpho, Rason (1).

III.7.5. Results

In general it can be noted that apart from a few exceptions larger cities usually have more industrial companies than smaller ones. This can be interpreted as a balanced distribution of companies across the country.

The results of the studies of the different sources show a number of matching points, but they also have deviations. For example in KCNA (1998-2011) the share of industrial facilities in Pyongyang is much higher than in the other sources. This may be related to the fact that this is the latest source and would thus imply that especially in Pyongyang the number of industrial companies in recent years has increased proportionately. On the other hand, many of the companies listed in KCNA (1998-2011) are modern companies of light industry, which are operated in joint venture collaborations, and therefore are awarded special mention by the North Korean news agencies.

In second place after Pyongyang Nampho is ranked according to the evaluation of three sources, and respectively Hamhung according to the evaluation of 2 sources. The latter two sources are sources that directly stem from North Korea (KCNA) or are based on North Korean sources (KIET is based on Rodong Sinmun). There is a chance that companies from Hamhung are mentioned more often in North Korean sources, in order to emphasize the importance of the most important city of Kwanbuk[21] especially.

If only those companies which are located in cities are considered and if we divide the country into 5 regions (Capital region, Phyongnam, Kwanbuk, Phyongbuk/Jagang, South West), the values fluctuate around the proportions of the population. In the source KCNA stronger equipment with industrial companies in the capital region and the region of

21 Kwanbuk means here the regions of Ryanggang, Rason, Hambuk, Hamnam and the North Korean province Kangnam.

Phyongbuk/Jagang is also evident. The sources KOFC (2010) and KIET (1996) show fewer shares of companies in the capital region, instead the Kwanbuk region is better equipped.

Table III-7-12. Groups of cities (shares of companies in the cities of their region – in percent – of all 27 cities of the DPRK (comparison: shares of population in cities in %)

	KOFC (2010)	MOU (2012)	IPA (2003)	KCNA (1998–2011)	KIET (1996)	Population
Pyongyang, Nampo, Songrim	31.2	38.6	39	44.3	31.2	38
Phyongnam	14.2	12.3	13	10	13.5	12.7
Kwanbuk	32.6	27.5	27	26.4	33.5	29.3
Phyongbuk/Jagangdo	13	10.9	11.7	13.3	10.6	11.8
Haeju, Sariwon, Kaesong	9.2	10.7	9.2	5.8	11.2	8.2

Otherwise the sources agree that smaller cities in the far north of the country have a particularly large number of industrial companies in comparison to the population. This demonstrates on one hand the efforts of the North Korean government to promote exactly these regions, but on the other hand, it must be noted that these companies are often small or medium-sized companies so that the statistics can deliver a distorted picture here.

IV. Profiles of the cities of DPR Korea

IV.1. Methodological Remarks

As mentioned in the introduction, the present work approaches the research subject of cities in the DPR Korea using three different methods. On the one hand, special characteristics of the cities have to be ascertained, on the other hand the focus is on growth and urbanization processes of individual cities and furthermore interrelations between cities (population shares, shares in the companies) are discussed. Chapters II and III have already been systematically dealing with the latter point of interest and shown interrelations between cities.The present Chapter IV deals with the individual cities. The results of chapter II and III are now examined to see if and to what extent they are helpful for the typification of the individual cities. Furthermore, chapter IV provides more information on the cities as well as the result of an empirical study on growth, internal structure and urbanization processes of the individual cities.

The city profiles are divided by content into four parts. Part 1 provides an overview, in which tables, in which data from Chapter II on population, area size, etc. for each city, were compiled[1]. It is followed by information on the physical geography and agriculture in each city. The sources that were used are usually the IPA (2003) and PSC-8 (2009). For each city a climatic data table was constructed (based usually on data from PSC-8). In the IPA source you often find in the description of the *ri* information on the proportion of forest area or the cultivable area within the *ri*. On the basis of these details, maps were produced, in which either triangular or square symbols are used. For the cities, where more information on forest area within the *ri* was available, triangular symbols were used, in which the color "green" depicts a forest area share of 100%-67% and the color "blue" a forest area share of 66%-34% and the color "pink" a forest area share of 0%-33%. Percentages are listed next to the icon. If no percentage is listed, but a symbol was placed, this means that although there is no information on the forest area in the IPA, a specification on the proportion of cultivable area exists, so the appropriate color of the icon could be inferred from that data. Therefore, conversely, the color "green" in the square symbols indicates that this *ri* has an acreage share of 0%-33%. The color "blue" refers to an acreage share of 66%-34% and the color "pink" to an acreage share of 100%-67%.

Part 2 of the city profiles focuses on the economy and the equipment of the respective city with industrial companies, but also with cultural institutions. The short overviews

1 To the sources of the data see chapter II.

of the economy of each city are based largely on the IPA (2003) and PSC-8 (2009). An overview of the quantitative research results follows, which has already been demonstrated in Chapter III. Here, however, the results are shown sorted and analyzed by each city. There are usually three tables displayed for each city. All three tables show the results of the five sources that have been analyzed in chapter III separately. Results of chapter "III.7. Overall view" are displayed in the first two tables in the column "Summary."

In the first table of Part 2 ("Ranking") the first number indicates the rank, which the respective city obtained in terms of the number of companies. In parenthesis the number of companies is shown. The second number (in the row "Companies important") represents the rank in terms of the important companies, and in parenthesis according to the number of important companies. The third row "Cultural institutions" indicates the rank each city takes in terms of the number of cultural institutions mentioned in the subsection "culture" of the IPA source. The number in parenthesis refers to the number of cultural institutions.

The numbers of the second table ("Ranking-Total number of companies in relation to population") indicate the rank, which each city scored in terms of the quotient between the proportions of companies and population. The first number refers to the total number of companies, the second to important companies, the third to cultural institutions. Due to the small number of "important companies" in the sources KOFC (2010), MOU (2012) and KCNA (1998-2011), no values were obtained.

Also in the third table ("Specification"), the numbers embody the ranks and the numbers in parenthesis embody the number of companies. The ranks indicate the specialization of the city with regard to light industry, the heavy industry, and the mining and energy sectors. Rank 3 in the light industry sector means, for example, that it is the third highest city specialized in light industry. (In other words: Rank 3 would not mean that it is the third most important city in terms of light industry within the DPR Korea.) The aim of this table is just to find out in which industrial sector each city is specialized. In the ranking numbers were taken into account, which resulted from dividing the number of companies in the sectors of "Light Industry," "Heavy Industry," "Mining" and "Energy" by the total number of industrial companies of the city. An illustration follows that shows the most important companies in the respective city, where especially the important companies, which have been identified as important in chapter III.7.3., were considered. Consequently, all companies have been included that appear in at least three sources and were at least once identified as important.

During the description of the companies the portraying of details, which can be looked up in the KOFC (2010) and IPA (2003), has been avoided. Emphasis was placed, however, on the mention of the total size of the company and the number of employees, in order to assess the fundamental importance of the companies for the individual cities.

Part 3 of the city profiles is dedicated to the presentation of results of a structural analysis of the individual cities. It deals on the one hand with the current distribution of intense built-up districts, the *dong* 洞, within the city area. Thus, following questions were raised regarding the individual cities:

- Are secondary centers definable, aside from the city centre?
- Do the centers have historical antecedents? It was examined here especially, where in the cities, which emerged after 1955; the former administrative seats of a district (*up*) or *rodongjagu* have been situated.

The structural analysis on the other hand is focused on dynamic aspects, where the aim was to find out new information about the urbanization process on individual North Korean cities in detail, and also about the process of urbanization in North Korea in general.

Thus the cities were examined regarding the following questions:

- Has the municipal area been increased or reduced by incorporations or separations?
- Have rural units (*ri* 里) been converted to urban units (*dong* or *rodongjagu*) ("*dong*-formation")? And when and in which parts of the cities have these transformations taken place?
- Has the number of *dong* of a city increased by the splitting of existing *dong* or by restructuring? Here too, an intriguing question exists: when and in which parts of the city have these changes taken place?

For most cities new thematic maps were designed and produced that provide information on incorporations and urbanization processes in the Korean cities.

In the illustrations of the development of the administrative units within the cities, it has to be considered that they always refer to the current city borders. The city borders also always show the situation according to the latest obtainable information from today. This also applies to maps that relate to earlier periods, when the city borders were different than today.

Part 4 provides a final short evaluation. In that part it will be examined—if necessary—to what extent the observations actually prove or not the quantitative results of chapter III.

The cities will be introduced in the following order: Primarily, the cities in the west of the DPR Korea (Kwansŏ) from North to South, then the cities in the East (Kwanbuk) from North to South. Cities, which belong to the same province, will be covered consecutively, whereupon the chapter on the provincial capital will be discussed at first. Therefore, the following sequence is employed: (in parenthesis: the name of the province)

Kanggye, Huichon, Manpho (Jagang);
Sinuiju, Kusong, Jongju (Phyongbuk);
Phyongsong, Anju, Kaechon, Tokchon, Sunchon (Phyongnam);
Pyongyang;
Nampho;
Sariwon, Songrim, Kaesong (Hwangbuk);
Haeju (Hwangnam);
Hyesan (Ryanggang);
Rason;
Chongjin, Hoeryong, Kimchaek (Hambuk);
Hamhung, Tanchon, Sinpho (Hamnam);
Wonsan, Munchon (Kangwon).

IV.2. The Profiles of the 27 cities of DPR Korea

IV.2.1. Kanggye

Capital of the mountainous province of Jagang, which was founded in 1949

The occupation of Korea by Japan promoted especially in the North of Korea the formation and growth of coastal cities. The DPR Korea tried to compensate this development by encouraging the inland regions in particular. One measure in this direction was the formation of the northern mountainous provinces of Jagang and Ryanggang. Kanggye was granted the status of a city (*si*) in 1949, when the province of Jagang was founded and in addition was proclaimed as its provincial capital. It is a medium-sized city according to its population and the only city in DPR Korea that has no rural *ri*. The built-up, urbanized area lies in a narrow, densely populated valley. In regards to its area size, Kanggye is significantly smaller than the other two cities of the Jagang Province (Huichon and Manpho).

Table Kanggye-I. Basic data

Population	251,971 (Rank 14)
Area	263.667 km² (Rank 22)
Population density	954 I./km² (Rank 8)
Administrative units	36 *dong* (100%) (Rank 1)
"Urban" population/"rural" population	100%/0% (Rank 1)

Already in the past: a city of great military importance

Kanggye is located in the northern border area of Korea, which was inhabited for a long time by the Jurchen tribe. The name of "Tokro-gang,"[2] the former name of Jangja-gang, which flows through Kanggye, was dedicated to these earlier times. Therefore, Kanggye became soon a location of great military strategic importance. In 1413, Kanggye gained the status of *tohobu*, an administrative regional center with military functions. In 1436, the city wall of Kanggye was built.[3]

In Korea, Kanggye is known as the home of wild ginseng, bold hunters and beautiful women. The first two statements are due to the fact that Kanggye is located in a forest region—according to North Korean sources, 75.9% of today's urban area is declared as a forest—which is not surprising. The latter statement has its roots in historical narratives. The poet and statesman Jŏng Chŏl (1536-1593) was rumored to have had a romance with the Kisaeng Jin Ok during the period of his exile in Kanggye. A woman named Purang from Kanggye, who lived at the time of King Injo (r. 1623-1649), also gained a legendary status (Ko Thae-u 1992, 208-209). Born into a livestock-breeding family, she rode well and as a child she played war games with boys, where she always was the leader. Disguised as a man, she substituted her ailing father in the military (Yes24.com 2007).

During the time of Japanese rule over Korea, Kanggye became a military base of the occupying power. The North Korean historiography praises the anti-Japanese struggle in Kanggye, which was led by Kim Hyong-jik (1884-1926), the father of Kim Il-sung (PSC-8 2009, 463). Lautensach (1945, 254) talks about a strongly Japanized city that has numerous buildings of the civil administration and the military. He characterizes Kanggye as a main base of Japanese power in North Korea. After 1939, Kanggye became a traffic junction for the transport of goods and tourism due to the opening of the railway line between Sunchon and Manpho (the Manpho-line).

In the Korean War, Kanggye was temporarily the seat of the North Korean government. When they had to leave Pyongyang in October 1950, Sinuiju was temporarily established as the new capital. When enemy troops marched towards Sinuiju, the government relocated to Kanggye (Mossman 1990), where it spent the winter of 1950/51. In an attempt to eliminate the political leadership of the DPR Korea, B-29 bombers of the U.S. Air Force dropped newly developed 12,000 pound bombs (so-called "Tarzan bombs") (Cumings 2004). According to Cumings (2004) stronger bombs were not used until the Iraq War in 2003.

---

2 Tokro is considered as a word from the language of the Jurchen, which is translated as "South" or "Outside." In 1976, the river was renamed.

3 This city wall uses natural boundaries such as the Nam-san in the South, the cliffs of the Puk-chŏn in the North and the cliffs of the Jangja-gang in the West. It was renewed in 1555 and 1739. Its shape is rectangular, and the circumference measures 4,500 m, of which 209 m are still preserved. Their height had amounted to about 4-5 m, although the height of the preserved ruins is 3 m (IPA-7 2003, 59).

The Revolutionary Memorial Jangjasan in Kanggye, which is closely associated with Kim Jong-il, symbolizes the stay of Kim Jong-il in Kanggye. In October 1950, as the KCNA reported on 10.11.2011, he stayed there more than 20 days for the purposes of study and self-training. A special site are the two pine trees, which is said to have been planted by him personally. From the seeds of these two trees, over 27,000 pine trees throughout the country have been planted since 1995.

"World of rivers"

Kanggye is the center of the highlands of the province of Jagang. The city is located west of the Rangnim mountain range and south of the Kangnam mountain range, of which some small chains of mountains branch off in the direction of the city. The built-up urban area became crowded together on a 20 m high rock terrace at the northeastern arc of the Jangja-gang (Lautensach 1945, 254). It lies in a large valley or basin, which is surrounded in the North by the Jabuk-san (835 m), and to the East by a 400 m high hill country, at the western foot of Nam-san (539 m), it is embraced by the Puk-chŏn (in the North) and by Nam-chŏn (in the South), which flow into the Jangja-gang (Kang Sŏk-o 1984, 304). On the shores of the rivers, especially at the Jajang-gang and the Nam-chŏn, small alluvial plains have formed, which are used for growing rice. Apart from that, the agriculture of the suburban vegetable cultivation is emphasized. It is stated that 11.24% of the city area is agricultural acreage (PSC-8 2009, 463).

The Jangja-gang rises in Ryongrim-kun (Jagang-do) on the western edge of the Kwangsŏng- ryŏng and flows in Wiwon-kun Kobo-ri into the Yalu. It is a tributary river of first category of the Yalu, and with 232 km length the largest river of the province.

In addition, there are about ten other rivers in the city area. The city's name is derived from its multitude of rivers (江*kang* means "river," 界 and *kye* means "world"). Apart from mountains that lie on the city boundary of Kanggye, the Taeung-san (1,123 m), which lies in the western part of the urban area, is the highest mountain of the city. The average sea level of the city area is about 300 m, and a continental climate prevails. There is only one city in North Korea, Hyesan, where the winter is much colder than in Kanggye.

Table Kanggye-II. Climate values

Annual average	January temperature	August temperature	Precipitation
7.0℃ (24)	−12.4℃ (26)	22.5℃ (19)	882.7mm (17)

A center of textile and defense industries

Following North Korean depiction, before 1945 this region was a slash-and-burn cultivation area, in which mainly potatoes and millet sprays were grown. After 1945 Kanggye developed into a city of light and heavy industry, where especially the textile industry, engine building and energy industries were developed.[4] Already Saitschikow (1958, 306) describes the favorable location of Kanggye for industrial development and refers to "the existence of copper, zinc, nickel and coal deposits nearby the city." Of great importance is the favorable energy supply situation due to the proximity to several hydroelectric power plants. In numerous media reports outside of DPR Korea, Kanggye is regarded as an important basis for the North Korean defense industry, which is suspected to be located in underground facilities in this inland city.

The results of the quantitative studies on the number of companies show that the ranking of Kanggye here correlated broadly with the ranking regarding the proportion of population (Population: Rank 14, KOFC 13th rank, MOU 13th Rank, KIET 16th Rank, in summary 12th rank.).[5]

Table Kanggye-III. Ranking (in parenthesis: Number of industrial companies or cultural institutions)

Kanggye	KOFC	MOU	IPA	KCNA	KIET	Summary
Companies-total	13 (14)	13 (23)	25 (4)	4 (22)	16 (29)	12
Companies-important	24 (1)	20 (1)	24 (3)		21 (7)	15 (6)
Cultural institutions			6 (16)			

Table Kanggye-IV. Ranking (Total number of companies in relation to population)

Kanggye	KOFC	MOU	IPA	KCNA	KIET	Summary
Companies-total	14	4	25–24–2	2	16–25	10–16

The fact that the news agency of the DPRK, the KCNA, mentions particularly many

4 According to KJY-24 (1990, 520), the share of textile industry, in relation to the total production sum of the industries of Kanggye, was 63% in 1980. Therefore, the share of light industry was 84.7%, the share of heavy industry was 7.3%, the share of energy production 6.1% and lastly the share of mining was 0.5%.

5 The deviation in the IPA source can be explained that in the description of the ri in IPA usually the most important companies of the *ri* were named as well. Therefore it is to be expected that in total that the cities with few ri will show fewer companies in the statistics. At the time of the compilation of the data for the IPA, there were only two *ri* in Kanggye. Now, however, only *dong* and no *ri* exist in Kanggye.

large companies of Kanggye, can be explained due to the propagandistic importance of the city and the numerous visits of Kanggye by Kim Jong-il.

The companies, which are located in Kanggye and listed in the researched sources, are usually not the most important ones. Therefore Kanggye has a lower ranking in regards to the important companies, when the ranking is in relation to what should be expected due to the population share. However, six of the seven companies which are regarded as important companies in at least one source are also mentioned by at least two other sources, so that the number of the as "important" defined companies according to chapter III.7.3., is large enough to allow Kanggye a similar ranking as it holds for the ranking of population share.

Table Kanggye-V. Specification (in parenthesis: Number of industrial companies)

Kanggye	Light Industry	Heavy Industry	Mining	Energy
KOFC	9 (4)	14 (9)	–	9 (1)
MOU	4 (18)	21 (4)	–	6 (1)
IPA	3 (3)	–	–	1 (1)
KCNA	8 (12)	18 (6)	–	7 (4)
KIET	4 (15)	21 (13)	–	9 (1)

Following the results of the statistical analyses, all five sources indicate that Kanggye specializes more on light industry than on heavy industry. However, armaments factories were not considered in these calculations, since they are not listed in the examined sources. In recent years the KCNA reported more frequently of power plants in Kanggye, since after the crisis in the 1990s, DPR Korea relies more on the construction of especially small and medium hydroelectric power plants.

In chapter III.7.3. six important companies (Kanggye General Tractor Plant, Kanggye Precision Machinery Complex, Kanggye Wine Factory, Textile Factory "September," Kanggye Shoe Factory, Kanggye Pencil Factory) were determined for Kanggye.

In 1956, the Kanggye General Tractor Plant began operation. It provides 15HP-strong tractors for the use in mountainous areas. However, in the North Korean media this factory is merely referred to as a tractor factory (KCNA January 23, 1998; April 7, 2011), although in KOFC (2010, 263) it is pointed out that this factory is also called "Factory No. 26" and it is suggested that this factory specializes in munitions as an armaments facility.[6] Various sources mentioned a "No. 26 Factory" that is operated as an arms factory, where apparently 10,000 to 20,000 persons are employed and which is suspected to be located

6 For further information s. kdb (2005b, 147), KIET (1996, 275).

in the southern part of the city.[7] A predecessor of this facility was a factory, which was initially located in Pyongyang and produced firearms. During the Korean War this factory was relocated to Kanggye. By now, it is considered as the headquarter for the North Korean defense industry, whose product range reaches from bullets to chemical weapons (Ju Yung-jung/Yi Yong-su 2010).

Additionally, the production of military goods is assumed in factories such as the Kanggye Precision Machinery Complex and the Textile Factory "September."

In general, the Kanggye Precision Machinery Complex is described as an operation, which produces table clocks and knife tools of all kinds (KIET 1996, 296). In particular, though, Kanggye has a number of important companies of light industry. The Kanggye Pencil Factory provides a wide range of pens, such as crayons, colored pencils, pencils including the pencil brand Samcholli. This company was founded in 1946 (IPA-7 2003, 53).

In North Korea the Kanggye Wine Factory is known for their Inphung liquor and their wine. Mainly raw materials from the region are used. Products of this factory are also exported abroad. In 1956, a certain section from the Kanggye Foodstuff Factory was separated, whereby this liquor factory was launched (IPA-7 2003, 53).[8]

The Textile Factory "September," which is located in Sinmun-dong and Namchŏn-dong, is the basic operation for the textile industry in Kanggye. The name is derived from the fact that Kim Il-sung had given the order to build modern textile factories in the province of Jagang in September 1966. A factory, which was built in the early 1960s, completely burned down in 1967. Afterwards the factory was rebuilt with equipment from the GDR until October 1972. In this factory mainly yarns are produced, which are further processed in other textile factories of the country. The total area size of this building is 65,000 m^2. About 5,000 people are employed by this factory (IPA 2003-7, 53; KOFC 2010, 595).[9] There are numerous other textile industry companies in various parts of the city.

Furthermore, the Kanggye Shoe Factory is mentioned in three of the examined sources (see KIET 1996, 107). Also, frequent mentions in the North Korean media are awarded to the Kanggye Koryo Medicine Factory.[10]

Already in 1937 the construction of the power plant, which is now called Kanggye Youth Power Plant, was started. Initially it was not completed. However, starting from 1958 the construction was then continued and finished in 1964. Subsequently, several extensions and improvements have taken place. The power plant consists of three parts, one of

7 According to Future Korea (2004) the "No. 26 Factory" is located in Namchŏn-dong, and according to Nuclear Threat Initiative (NTI) (n.d. a) in Konggui-dong. See also Bermudez Jr. (2001, 284).

8 See also KIET (1996, 71).

9 For further information see also KIET (1996, 75)

10 E.g. KCNA 18th December 2011.

them is located in the city of Kanggye (No. 3) (Yŏnphung-dong) and two in the Janggang-kun (No. 1 in the Oil-rodongjagu; No. 2 in Sŭngbang-rodongjagu) (KOFC 2010, 147).

Kanggye is a traffic junction in the North of the country. Through Kanggye the Manpho line runs between Sunchon and Manpho, which was opened in 1939. It is about 300 km long. Kanggye is located about 250 km from Sunchon and 50 km from Manpho. From Kanggye the Kanggye-line branches off towards Ryangrim (57 km distance). Commuter trains operate between Kanggye and Ssangbang. Roads leading from Kanggye to the principal up of the province.

Cultural center of the province

Particularly developed in Kanggye is the centrality in terms of cultural institutions. In addition to numerous universities and other educational institutions, there are also museums as well as press and radio facilities and other cultural facilities located in the capital of the province of Jagang.

The landmark of the city is the Inphung Pavilion at the estuary of the Puk-chŏn into the Jangja-gang. To the East and North from there, there are additional historical sites, memorials and public spaces. The Inphung Pavilion was built in 1472 as part of the fortification around Kanggye, which burned down in 1663 and was rebuilt in 1680. The Korea Inphung Trading Company as well as the famous spirituous beverage Inphung-sul from Kanggye bear the name of the Pavilion (IPA 2003-7, 60).

Another important historic building in Kanggye is a government office that was built in 1663 and rebuilt in 1888. During the Korean War this Kanggye government office was destroyed again and rebuilt (KCNA August 8, 2000).

Near the Inphung Pavilion bronze statues of the former leaders Kim Il-sung and Kim Jong-il have been erected.[11]

The Yŏnphung Revolutionary Site is located at the place where Kim Il-sung stayed during the Korean War in December 1950 and where he led a cabinet meeting.

The "Spirit of Kanggye (Kanggye Spirit)"

In January 1998, Kim Jong-il evoked the so-called "Spirit of Kanggye (Kanggye Spirit)," the spirit of defending socialism, since particularly the people of Jagang had to suffer from

11 On 11th October 2011, the two statues were unveiled. Previously, only the statue of Kim Il-sung was there.

the difficulties of the "Arduous March. “Today, the "Bright Lights on the Jangja River” belong to the “Eight Scenic Spots in the Songun Era.”

Expansion of the urban area in the years 1952, 1963, 1967 and 1995 in a northern direction

Kanggye is the capital of the Jagang Province, which was founded in January 1949 from six *kun* of the Phyongbuk Province and from one part of a *kun* of the Hamnam Province. In December 1949, the provincial capital of Kanggye-si was formed from the Kanggye-myon of Kanggye-kun, whilst from the rest of the Kanggye-kun (*6 myon*) the Janggang-kun was formed.

In the years of 1952, 1963, 1967 and 1995, the area of Kanggye-si was extended with parts of Janggang-kun (in the Northeast) and Sijujng-kun (in the Northwest). In 1952, parts of the Kongbuk-myon (Janggang-kun) came to Kanggye-si and formed Hyangro-ri, Tuhŭng-ri, Konggui-ri and Kongin-ri. In March 1961, Hŭngju-ri (Sijung-kun) was added to Kanggye-si and became a *dong*. In October 1967, a part of Changphyŏng-ri (Janggang-kun) came to the city of Kanggye and formed with a part of Koyŏn-dong the Kogye-dong, which was renamed in February 1976 to Jangja-dong. In December 1995, two of the *ri* of Sijung-kun came to Kanggye-si (Uijin-ri; Ssangsin-ri-ri, in 1998 renamed to Sinhŭng-ri).

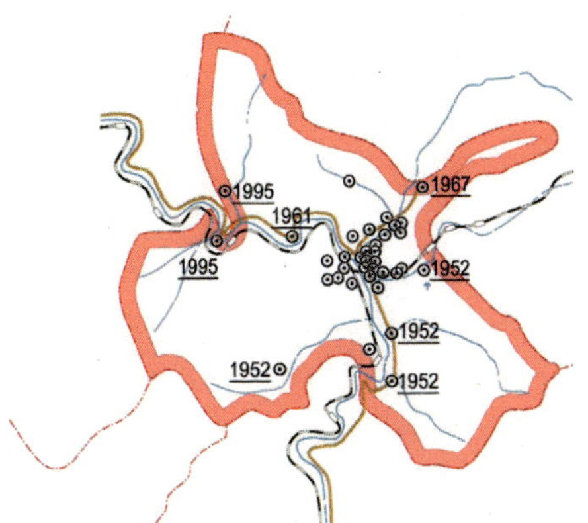

Figure Kanggye-I. Incorporations

Active development of the inner city until the 1960s and early 1980s, afterwards urbanization of the peripheral

In 1955, Kanggye had 21 *dong*, from 1957 to 1961 though nine new *dong* were established, whilst five others were dissolved due to the consolidation with other *dong*. Thus, Kanggye possessed 25 *dong* in 1961.

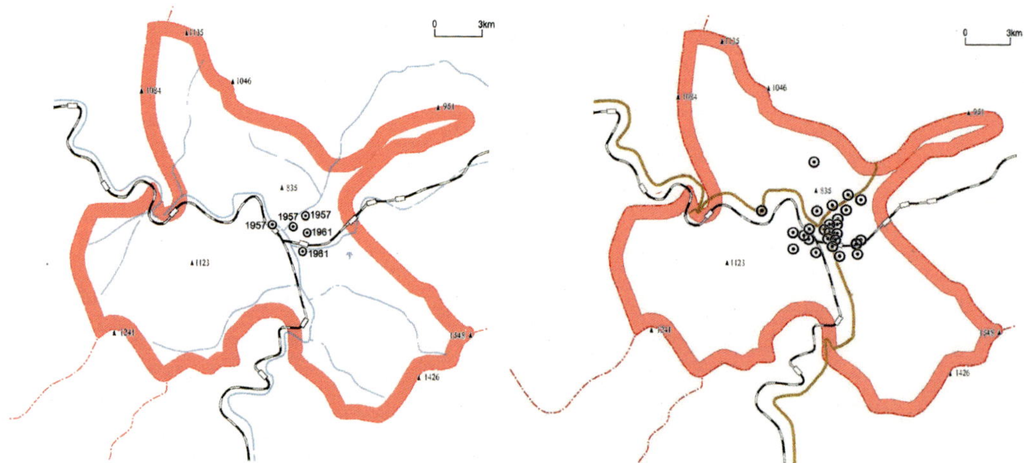

Figure Kanggye-II. Dissolved *dong*

Figure Kanggye-III. *Dong* in 1961

Furthermore, between 1967 and 1999, nine new *dong* were created. Thereby, in a total of five cases, a new *dong* was created by splitting from existing *dong* in 1967 and 1981. This suggests an increase in population and respectively an increase of construction of new housing units in the town center on these two points in time.

But the peripherally located *ri* also got an intense urban character, which was the reason to upgrade them gradually into *dong*. In 1967, 1981 and 1995, a *dong* in the south of the municipal area was affected, whilst in 1999 a *dong* in the west of the municipal area was affected by this phenomenon. The two remaining *ri* of the city lie in the west and southwest of the city. In IPA-7 (2003),[12] they are still presented as *ri*, although the PSC-8 (2009, 463) described Kanggye as a city consisting of 36 *dong* and no *ri*.

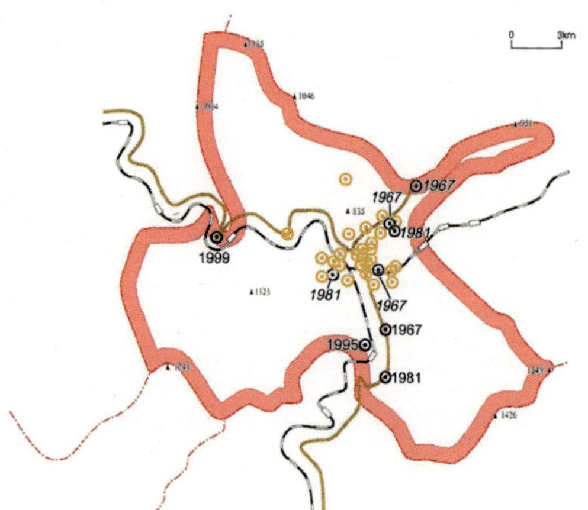

Figure Kanggye-IV. *Dong* in 1999 (displayed with the current city borders)

Functional spatially the downtown of Kanggye could be roughly divided as follows:

Centrally located in the North at the confluence of the Jangja-gang and the Pukchŏn is the administrative and political center with the statues of both Kims and the Inphung Park in the East and with the railway station in the West of the Jangja-gang. Within the center of the city there are companies of light industry, although most companies of the textile industry can be found in East Kanggye. Most companies of mechanical engineering focus on three

12 According to IPA-7 (2003) Kanggye consisted of 34 *dong* and 2 *ri*.

regions on the edge of downtown: in the West (Sosan-dong, Naeryong-dong), in the South (Konggui-dong, Sŏkhyŏn-dong) or in the Northeast (Jangja-dong, Yŏnju-dong, Koyŏng1-dong) (KJY-24 1990, 520-521).

Statistics

Up 1931-1946

	Dong-Formation	*Dong*-Splitting
1955 (21)	21	-
1957 (20)	-	2/-3
1961 (25)	3	4/-2
1967 (29)	1	3
1981 (32)	1	2
1995 (33)	1	-
1999 (34)	1	-

Kanggye – a symbol for "the spirit of defending socialism" in North Korean propaganda

Kanggye is located in the center of the Jagang-plateau in the valley of the Jangja-gang. In the time of the occupation of Korea by Japan, Kanggye was a main base of Japanese power in North Korea. In 1949, Kanggye became capital of the newly founded Jagang Province. In the course of the promotion of inland cities, the industry of the city, especially the arms industry, was expanded. From 1998, the "Spirit of Kanggye" (Kanggye spirit), "the spirit of defending socialism" is propagated throughout the country.

The results of statistical surveys show that the light industry plays a more important role than heavy industry in Kanggye. In fact, the textile industry actually has in Kanggye a dominant role. Although companies of light industry of Kanggye as well as the Kanggye Wine Factory have a good reputation, it is assumed that there are numerous arms factories situated in the city, which is located in the inner country, and that due to reasons of confidentiality there are no official announcements thereof. The Kanggye General Tractor Factory is probably the largest company of the city with its numerous employees.

Kanggye is the only city in DPR Korea, which shows no rural *ri*. After the reconstruction period after the Korean War, urbanization thrusts can be identified by the emergence of new *dong* in 1967 (four new *dong*) and in 1981 (three new *dong*). Two new *dong* each were developed in the 1990s and after 2002.

A densely built-up center can be ascertained, and there are also smaller settlements in the valleys of Jangja-gang and its tributaries.

IV.2.2. Huichon

Gate to the plateau of the province of Jagang

Energy scarcity and the backwardness of their industrial companies are two of the main obstacles in a pathway to the recovery and to the development of the North Korean economy. In North Korean propaganda, Huichon is a symbol of the overcoming of these problems. Due to "Huichon Speed," dams for hydroelectric power stations were constructed in Huichon from 2009 and the Huichon Ryŏnha General Machinery Plant is regarded as an embodiment of North Korean state-of-the-art technology due to the CNC-Technology that is employed in this plant.

Huichon is located at the southern tip of the province of Jagang, which was founded in 1949. In 1967 it was appointed to a city. Based on the number of inhabitants, it is one of the small cities of DPR Korea, but the area size, which belongs administratively to the municipal area, is relatively large. Due to the location near the northern border of the Koryo kingdom and the location of the pass, military camps were set up in this region, already in the Koryo as well as in the Joson period.

Table Huichon-I. Basic data

Population	168.180 (Rank 22)
Area	984 km² (Rank 6)
Population density	171 I./km² (Rank 25)
Administrative units	21 *dong*/12 *ri* (64%) (Rank 16)
"Urban" population/"rural" population	80.9%/19.1% (Rank 15)

Huichon, which is located between Chŏngchŏn-gang and Huichon-gang, had developed into a market as gate to the plateau of Jagang Province, where agricultural products from the surrounding area as well as products from the plateau region had been traded. Due to the construction of important mechanical engineering companies, Huichon developed rapidly after the Korean War into an intermountain city (Kang Sŏk-o 1984, 305).

Even today, Huichon belongs to one of the relatively easily accessible cities of the DPR Korea. The city is situated at the Manpho-Railwayline, which connects Sunchon with Manpho. On this railroad Huichon is located closer to cities in the southern neighbouring province of Phyonnam (Sunchon 109.8 km, Kaechon 70.9 km) than to other cities of its own province of Jagang (Kanggye 140.8 km, Manpho 190.1 km). Concerning the traffic, Huichon is very well connected with Pyongyang. There is a 146 km long motorway between Pyongyang and Hyangsan, and from Hyangsan there are still another 21 km to the center of Huichon (JC 2009, 31).

Urban development in typical basin area

Huichon evolved in a basin, which is limited in the northwest by the Jŏgyuryŏng mountain range and in the Southeast by the Myohyang mountain range. In the latter, even the highest altitudes of the municipal area are reached, where the Myohyang-san (1,909 m), the Indal-san (1,693 m), the Chŏnkhwae-san (1,929 m) as well as the Mudong-san (1,762 m) form the southeastern border. Between the Indal-san and the Chŏnkhwae-san lies the Tasŏt-ryŏng (784 m), through which the road leads to Nyongwon. The road between Hyangsan and Huichon leads through the Wŏllim-kogae (161 m) into the basin of Huichon. In the northwest the Maehwa-san (932 m) protrudes on the border to the Songwon-kun. Towards the Southwest the basin is open.

The largest area of the overbuilt municipal area is located inside the basin of Huichon. It has a west-east-extension of 11 km, a north-south-extension of 10 km and is situated at 140 m above sea level. The basin is a result of tectonic subsidence and subsequent erosion activity of the Chŏngchŏn-gang and its tributary rivers. Vast plains have not been sculpted, only merely smaller erosion surfaces in the valleys of the rivers can be found. The biggest surface was sculpted where the Chŏngchŏn-gang and the Huichon-gang flow together (PSC-8 2009, 455). The Chŏngchŏng-gang runs southeast of the overbuilt urban area, where various rivers converge.

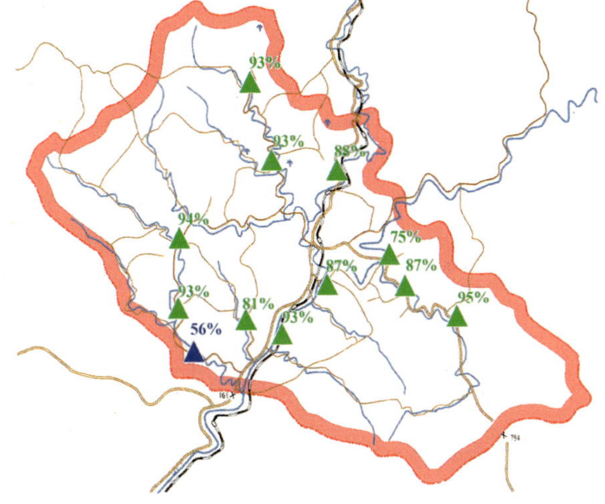

Figure Huichon-I. Forest area in the *ri*

Table Huichon-II. Climate values

Annual average	January temperature	August temperature	Precipitation
8.4℃ (21)	-9.0℃ (23)	23.2℃ (14)	1,190.50 mm (6)

The municipal area is very mountainous. The land classified as forest amounts to 85% of the total area of the city. The land in the *ri* is mainly used as forest area. Forestry has a great significance in Huichon, inter alia: for the provision of mining timber.

Where agricultural cultivation is possible, it is operated at 75% in dry land farming.

The Jagang Province was particularly affected by the famine in the 1990s in North Korea. A UNICEF delegation visited Huichon on 4th April 1997 and found severe malnutrition in children (Unicef Österreich 1997).

In the northern part of the municipal area several mineral springs are located, of which the most important one, Kwadae, is situated 17 km in a north-western direction from the railway station of Huichon.

Most important city of machine construction in the DPR Korea

During the Japanese occupation, Huichon was heavily shaped agriculturally. In the early 1950s, during and shortly after the Korean War, they began to build a significant mechanical engineering industry. The biggest machine tools factory as well as the biggest precision machine factory of North Korea is situated in Huichon. Other important industrial sectors are inter alia: the textile and clothing industry, the glass industry, the pottery as well as the food processing. Additionally hydroelectric power stations have been constructed in and near Huichon.

Table Huichon-III. Ranking (in parenthesis: number of industrial companies or respectively cultural institutions)

Huichon	KOFC	MOU	IPA	KCNA	KIET	Summary
Companies-total	19 (10)	24 (6)	26 (3)	8 (14)	24 (16)	20
Companies-important	17 (2)	13 (2)	27 (1)		17 (9)	23 (3)
Cultural institutions			25 (1)			

The ranking of Huichon in terms of the number of companies is similar to the rank in terms of population (Rank 22). Only the KCNA names for Huichon a lot more companies, which is related to the importance of Huichon for the North Korean propaganda as well as due to the frequent visits of Kim Jong-il.

Table Huichon-IV. Ranking – Total number of companies in relation to population

Huichon	KOFC	MOU	IPA	KCNA	KIET	Summary
Companies-total	9	24	26–27–25	3	22–8	16–22

Table Huichon-V. Specification

Huichon	Light Industry	Heavy Industry	Mining	Energy
KOFC	–	4 (8)	–	2 (2)
MOU	8 (4)	9 (2)	–	–
IPA	19 (1)	2 (2)	–	–
KCNA	10 (7)	17 (4)	–	5 (3)
KIET	26 (4)	1 (11)	11 (1)	–

Statistically, Huichon exhibits according to three sources a specialization of heavy industry rather than of light industry, although the reverse is the case according to two other sources. Of course, one must consider that there are two significant machine construction companies in Huichon, which are crucial for the industrial structure of the city.[13] KCNA and KOFC, two of the most current sources, also emphasize the importance of Huichon for the energy sector of the country.

In chapter III.7.3. three important companies were determined for Huichon, the two machine construction companies Huichon Ryŏnha General Machinery Plant and Huichon Precision Machinery Factory (Factory February 26) as well as Huichon Silk Mill.

An important role for North Korean propaganda has the Huichon Ryŏnha General Machinery Plant (formerly known as Huichon General Machine Factory). During the year 2010 the factory got this new name. It is the largest machine tool factory in the country and, and is proclaimed by the North Korean propaganda as "a model plant of machine-building industry in the 21st century" (Pyongyang Times 11.2.2012, 6). Particular pride is taken in the production of CNC (Computerized Numerical Control) machine tools, which are equipped with the Juche-based CNC technology.

The construction of the factory, which is situated in Jŏnphyŏng-dong, began in 1951, i.e. during the Korean War. In 1954 the first machines were produced with Czechoslovakian help (KOTRA 1995, 122). The factory is considered a "mother factory" for the machine tool factories of North Korea and is considered as a model company for other machine tool factories in the country. Due to the first Six-Year-Plan (1971-1976), the factory was of great importance in the early 1970s. The factory employs 7.000 people and has the size of 1.070.000 m² (KOFC 2010, 252). The factory is located 6 km from Huichon's railway station.

The precision machine factory of Huichon is the largest of its kind in the country. Covering an area of 150.000 m² (KOFC 2010, 255), approximately 3,000 people are

13 According to KJY-24 (1990, 596-570) had the mechanical engineering in Huichon in 1954 a share in the industrial production of 66.6%, in 1960 it was 77.8%, in 1970 87.8% and 70.9% in 1983.

employed. According to the representation in KOFC (2010, 255), the factory was built in 1953 with Czechoslovakian help and expanded in 2008.[14]

The silk factory of Huichon (Huichon Silk Mill) is situated on the banks of Chŏngchŏn-gang and began on 5th September 1988 with its production. Mainly cocoons from northwest of Korea are processed.

In parts of the Youth Electric Complex (Chŏngnyŏn Electric Appliance Complex) presumably armaments are produced.

In the Technical University of Huichon, technicians are particularly trained in the field of mechanical engineering. A predecessor of this educational institution was the University of Telecommunications of Pyongyang, which had been founded in 1959. In 1965 the latter moved to Huichon Jŏnsin-dong and was thus named University of Telecommunication of Huichon. In 1969 it got its present name.

"Huichon Speed"–The power plant construction as a symbol for the ascent to the great and powerful nation

In 2009, the slogan "Huichon Speed" was issued in North Korea. This refers to a mobilization measure which was also described as "a new Chollima speed" and thus reminiscent of the mobilization measure in the construction after the Korean War. As explained by the KCNA on 17th November 2009, "Huichon Speed" is based "on the revolutionary soldier spirit." The occasion of the proclamation of the slogan "Huichon Speed" is the construction of the Huichon Power Station on the headwaters of the Chŏngchŏn-gang. The construction should have been completed by the 100th anniversary of Kim Il-sung. Kim Jong-il has inspected the site eight times and punctual for the North Korean anniversary, in April 2012, the completion of the power block I and II was announced, whereby the hydroelectric power station of Huichon was finished. Through this not only the power supply for the capital Pyongyang was improved, but the hydroelectric power stations also have the function to protect the area of the arable land of the Chŏngchŏn-gang from flooding. The construction began in 2001; the capacity of the power plant is estimated at about 300,000 kilowatts (RKI 7.4.2012). It would thus be the largest power plant of North Korea, which was built in the past 20 years. According to the Pyongyang Times, specifically the dams have been built with great speed: "The dams which had been considered to take over ten years were built in less than two years" (Pyongyang Times 11.2.2012, 6).

14 After representation in KJY-24 (1990, 570), the plant was first built in 1951 as a factory for car accessories and began its production in 1952. In 1954, it was then specialized and extended to the construction of precision machines.

The capitals of the northern neighbour-*kun* of Songwon and Tongsin were once part of Huichon-si

The Huichon-kun emerged in 1952, and it included one *up* and 22 *ri*. In 1954, a part of Ryujung-ri was added to Huichon-up. In the same year Jŏnphyŏng-ri developed into rodongjagu. In 1967 Huichon was awarded the status of a city.

Twice, in 1981 and 1990, the city has been reduced in size in favour of the neighbouring northern counties. In 1981 Myŏngmun-ri as well as Yangji-ri were added to Songwon-kun and Chŏngun-ri to Tongsin-kun. Myŏngmun-ri was then turned into a new up of the Songwon-kun in 1987. In 1990 Chŏngun-ri was combined with a part of Chŏngsang-ri (Huichon-si) and thus formed the new Tongsin-up (Tongsin-kun). The new *up* of Songwon-kun and Tongsin-kun are therefore located on the edge of their kun, but both are on the Manpho-railway line.

Three new *dong* in the mid 90s

When becoming a city in 1967, the new up was split up into nine *dong* and the Jŏnphyŏng-rodongjagu into three *dong*. At the same time, five new *dong* were created from *ri*.

Figure Huichon-II shows the 17 *dong* from 1967 (displayed with the current city borders).

The five new *dong*, which emerged from the former *ri*, are located at the edge of the former *up* or respectively the former *rodongjagu*. It is noticeable, that three new *dong* (Jinsin-dong, Phungsan-dong, Sinhŭng-dong), have emerged north of the former *up* where previously Jisin-ri was located.

Figure Huichon-II. 17 *dong* (1967)

Between 1981 and 1995, four *dong* were added. As a result of the splitting from existing *dong*, Chuphyŏng2-dong and in 1995 Chŏngnyŏn-dong were created in 1981, both in the region of the former Jŏnphyŏng-rodongjagu, where the Huichon Ryŏnha General Machine Factory is located. In 1994, Chŏngha-ri as well as

Figure Huichon-III. 21 *dong* (1995)

Kalhyŏn-ri in the northeast of the city each were established as a *dong*.

According to KJY-24 (1990, 577), there are three regions in Huichon in which the proportion of workers of the population is particularly high, namely the regions of Jŏnphyŏng, Phungsan and Chuphyŏng. Based on this information and the above analysis, it can be concluded that Jŏnphyŏng region is meant to be the northern part of the former working class district of Jŏnphyŏng, which had been established in 1954. The region of Phungsan refers to three new *dong* in the North of the former *up*, which had emerged from Jisin-ri in 1967 at the same time as the city founding of Huichon Furthermore, the region of Chuphyŏng refers to the southern part of the former Jŏnphyŏng-rodongjagu. Here, new *dong* emerged in 1981 and 1995 due to the splitting of already existing *dong*.

Statistics

Urbanized areas before the founding of the city (*up* and *rodongjagu*)

1952-1967 Huichon-up (1)
1954-1967 Jŏnphyŏng-rodongjagu (2)

	Dong-Formation	*Dong*-Splitting
1967 (17)	5	(10)
1981 (18)	-	1
1994 (20)	2	-
1995 (21)	-	1

Huichon – City with two centers and two important companies

Huichon has been known since the 1950s as a city of mechanical engineering. The largest machine tool factory and the largest precision machinery factory of the country are located here. Although numerous industrial companies of other sectors were settled in Huichon over time, the two engineering factories form the backbone of the industry of Huichon. Recently, the city of Huichon plays an important role for the energy supply of the country. Hydroelectric power plants were built in a very short time, so that the term "Huichon Speed" was coined. Thus, the Huichon Ryŏnha General Machine Factory and the hydroelectric power stations of Huichon became the flagship of the North Korean propaganda.

The overbuilt urban area of the town center of Huichon can be divided into an area in the South, the former *up* and into an area in the Northwest, the former Jŏnphyŏng-rodongjagu. Through both areas runs a broad central street, where high-rise residential buildings as well as public facilities are situated, in the South is the Namchŏn street and in the North the Chuphyŏng street.[15] The first area includes the railway station and adjacent in the west of the station is Jŏnsin-dong, where the Technical University of Huichon is located. Within this area lies on the western side of Huichon-gang the Huichon Precision Machinery Factory. A second center has formed near the Ryŏnha machine factory, where the Kim Il-sung statue and building for the worship of the "eternal president" and the Huichon hotel as well as the stadium of Huichon are located.

IV.2.3. Manpho

Settlement at the Korean – Chinese border

Manpho is located 5 km east of the Chinese city of Jian (226,583 inhabitants) and is connected with the latter by a railroad bridge (Yi Oh-hŭi 2011, 158-159). During the Joson period, there was an important fortification that assured protection of the country in the North. Many ships that moved along the Yalu stopped here. It is assumed that the name of this city is derived from this background (Man: ten thousand, numerous; Pho: harbor).

In regards to its population, Manpho is the smallest among the 27 cities of the DPR Korea. Although the city has a large area by comparison, which is the reason why only Hoeryong shows a smaller number in terms of share of *dong* in relation to all administration units.

15 cf. KJY-24 (1990, 577).

Table Manpho-I. Basic data[16]

Population	116,760 (Rank 27)
Area	672.379 km² (Rank 11)
Population density	174 I./km² (Rank 24)
Administrative units	12 *dong*/16 *ri* (43%) (Rank 26)
"Urban" population/"rural" population	70.8%/29.2% (Rank 22)

Situated on the Yalu, the area around Manpho was important in terms of the protection against attackers from the North. Hence, in the beginning of the Joson period a fortification made out of stone was built in Manpho and in 1416 a military camp, a *jin*, was established. Relating to the construction of the fortification, several pavilions such as the Segŏm-Pavilion and the Mangmi-Pavilion were erected. The latter was restored in the second half of the 19th century and is thus still retained. Over 1,000 soldiers were based in Manpho-jin, as well as one interpreter for the communication with the Yurchen, who had command over their language. Manpho-jin was the starting point of one of the most important bonfire systems during the Joson period. Starting from Yŏdundae in Manpho, the signals were passed over to Uiju, Anju, Pyongyang and Kaesong towards Hansong (Seoul) (Corian Clio 2012).

Due to its characteristics as a border town, a customs office or border [frontier] guards was built during the Japanese occupation. Anti-Japanese brigades who operated in Manchuria attacked the city several times. In 1937 a railroad bridge was laid over the Yalu as part of the Japanese transport system, in order to command Manchuria. When Manpho became the terminal station of the Manpho line, the city changed into an important traffic junction. This railroad line was built since 1931 and completed in 1939. Mainly logs that arrived as rafts from the Wŏnchang-Jasong region at the headwater of Yalu were sawed here and transported to the consumption areas by train. Consequently, Manpho developed into an important collection point for wood (encykorea.aks.manphojin, n.d.).

During the Korean War, the route over Jian towards Manpho was one of four important roads over which the Chinese People's Army crossed the border between PR China and DPR Korea.[17]

16 The IPA states 26 administrative units (11 *dong* and 15 *ri*), while the PSC-8 (2009, 464) claims 28 administrative units (12 *dong* and 16 *ri*). The *ri* that is mentioned in PSC but missing in IPA is Phosang-ri.

17 As for the other three routes, the Chinese troupes operated in Sinuiju, Sakju and Junggangjin (IMHC, n.d.).

Lowlands at the middle reaches of the Yalu

The city area developed in a NE-SW elongated direction and is situated at the middle reaches of the Yalu. It predominantly consists of low mountains and thus belongs to the lowest located regions of the Jagang Province. In the northeast and the east where mountains that emanate from the Kangnam mountain range and the Rangrim mountain range give natural protection to Manpho, the terrain is a little bit higher and in the western direction towards the Yalu it becomes gradually lower. In the northeast the Wŏlgi-bong (1,254 m) and in the east the Pŏmbawi-san (1,373 m) arise each as the highest peaks. At the riverside of the Yalu and the Kŏnpho-gang, the Kosan-terrain and the Kŏnha have formed, which belong to the three biggest of the Jagang Province. The deepest position of the city is located in the Namsang-ri (165 m). In the northeast and the southeast, karst landscapes have formed. As can be seen in Figure Manpho-II, the urbanized parts of the city are concentrated in the middle of the city area. Along the Kŏnpho-chŏn in the east of the city are many *ri*.

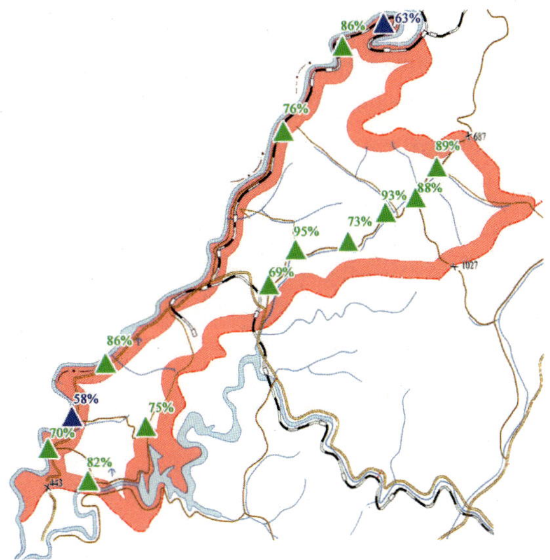

Figure Manpho-I. Forest area in the *ri*

Table Manpho-II. Climate values

Annual average	January temperature	August temperature	Precipitation
7.4℃ (23)	−11.6℃ (25)	22.5℃ (20)	908.8 mm (15)

Hoar-frost falls starting in the beginning of October until the beginning of May (IPA-7 2003, 90).

About 7.5% of the city area is used agriculturally. From this percentage, 67% fall onto cereal (mainly corn and rice) and around 23% onto vegetables (i.e. Chinese cabbage, radish).

Silkworm cocoons are bred in the Manpho Silk Cocoon Farm, which then are sent to various silk factories (such as the Huichon Silk Factory) as basic material (IPA-7 2003, 92).

From a Sawing Site to a Tire–and Rubber–Manufacturer

In addition to the Manpho railroad line, the fact that many power plants such as the Unbong Power Plant (Jasong-kun) were located in the city and in its neighborhood was important for the development of the city's economy. In Manpho there are the power plants Jajanggang, Songhak, Songha, Tŭnggong 1 and Tŭnggong 2. On this basis, industrial companies that produce tires, textiles, machines, food, building materials, and chemical products have developed.

The North Korean KJY-24 (1990, 543) demonstrates the change of the economic structure of the city until the mid-80s.

Table Manpho–III. Proportion of value added of important industrial sectors in Manpho 1946–1986

	1946	1960	1965	1970	1980	1986
Energy industry	–	0,1	5,5	0,6	7,1	18,3
Machinery construction	–	2,5	15,3	5,1	5,5	8,9
Timber industry	100	74,1	15,6	9,5	3,3	1,2
Textile/Food/Basic commodity	–	19,7	50,1	21,2	18,8	22
Rubber	–	–	–	56,4	55,1	39,2

Source: KJY-24 (1990, 543).

At first, the forest industry dominated. Since the mid-50s, though, the light industry was developed. After the construction of the Aprokgang Tire Factory, which was completed at the end of the 60s, it dominated the economy of the city. Since the 80s the hydroelectric power plants of the city are of great importance. Consequentially, the relevance of the forest industry nosedived.

Hence, the Aprokgang Tire Factory is of major importance for the city. In the companies of mechanical engineering, construction machines used in forestry and agriculture, fine mechanical devices and basic commodities (sewing machines, children's bicycles) are produced. Also of high relevance are the Manpho Cement Factory, the Manpho Material Factory and the Manpho Chemical Factory.

Furthermore, there are numerous textile manufactories, factories of food industry, and factories producing daily goods, which are of local relevance.

Table Manpho-IV. Ranking (in parenthesis: number of companies or of cultural institutions)

Manpho	KOFC	MOU	IPA	KCNA	KIET	Summary
Companies-total	20 (9)	20 (11)	7 (25)	17 (8)	19 (22)	17
Companies-important	9 (4)	16 (1)	18 (4)		25 (4)	19 (4)
Cultural institutions			26 (0)			

Apart from the IPA source, Manpho is ranked in regards to the number of companies between rank 17 and 20, although it is the city with the lowest population in DPR Korea. However, there is no source that claims more than four important industrial companies for Manpho.

Table Manpho-V. Ranking (Total number of companies in relation to population)

Manpho	KOFC	MOU	IPA	KCNA	KIET	Summary
Companies – total	2	7	1 - 4 - 26	4	3 – 23	1 - 8

Manpho shows a high number of industrial companies compared to its population. All sources indicate that Manpho ranks in terms of the ratio between companies and the ratio of population among the first six cities. In total, Manpho is in this ranking even at first place.

Table Manpho-VI. Specification (in parenthesis: number of companies)

Manpho	Light Industry	Heavy Industry	Mining	Energy
KOFC	21 (1)	10 (6)	–	1 (2)
MOU	12 (7)	17 (3)	–	2 (1)
IPA	15 (11)	17 (9)	–	3 (5)
KCNA	19 (2)	13 (3)	–	2 (3)
KIET	25 (6)	20 (10)	15 (1)	1 (5)

In three of the five sources Manpho seems to focus more heavily on heavy and chemical industry than on light industry. However, two sources indicate the other way around. Although the statistics do not give a consistent picture, there can be no doubt that given the relevance of the Aprokgang Tire Factory, the industry in Manpho is very much influenced by heavy industry. However, all five sources indicate the importance of the energy sector for the city.

In chapter III.7.3. four companies were identified as important: Aprokgang Tire Factory, Manpho Cement (8.2.) Factory, Manpho Chemical Factory, and Jajanggang Power Plant. Thus, we speak about three companies related to the heavy and chemical industry and one that is related to the energy sector.

At the Aprokgang Tire Factory[18] in Pyŏlo-dong not only tires are produced but also other products made out of rubber. The factory was built from 1966 onwards and put into operation in 1968 under the name Chollima Tire Factory. It bears the current name since 1974[19]. It is the largest tire factory of DPR Korea. The fact that various facilities for employees such as a medical center, a cultural center and an academy belong to this factory, indicates this to be an important factory (IPA 7 2003, 93; KOFC 2010, 390-391).

The Manpho Cement Factory is located close to the Yalu in the northeastern part of the city (about 3 km away from the city center) and has a total area of 430.000 m^2. The construction of this factory started in 1978 within the context of the second Seven Year Plan (1978-1984) and ended in 1982. An expansion of the factory was completed in 1991. Parts of the technology and the equipment come from Romania. A branch terminal line of the Unbong-railroad line (between Manpho and Unbong) runs until the factory. The chalkstone that is processed here is produced in the 2 km distant north-eastern located Chagaphyŏng Mine. The coal is derived from the Mine 2.8. Youth (Phyongnam). The cement that is produced here is important for the construction of power plants nearby, but is also used in other parts of the country (KOFC 2010, 431-433).

The Manpho Chemical Factory is located in Pyŏlo-dong and its construction was completed in 1978. About 2.000 people are employed here. Basic chemistry products such as nitrogen, nitric acid, and sulfuric acid are produced in this factory (KOFC 2010, 372).

The Jajanggang Power Plant is situated in Yŏnha-ri at the Jajanggang lake. During the Japanese Occupation the construction work for the power plant started, however, it remained unfinished. In 1956, though, constructions resumed with Soviet help and the power plant is in operation since 1959. Together with the Suphung Power Plant and the Kanggye Youth Power Plant, it belongs to one energy network who powers all parts of the country (IPA-7 2003, 93; KOFC 2010, 146).

On 12th September, 2009, KCNA reported on a visit of Kim Jong-il at the Manpho Unhwa Factory in which manufacturing is based on the CNC system.

18 Aprokgang (often written as Amnokgang as well) is the Korean term for the Yalu.

19 In 1973 the Chollima Tire Factory in Nampho came into operation; this is how homonymy was prevented.

Rail junction at the northern border of DPR Korea

At the rail station "Youth" Manpho, which connects the city to China, the approximately 300 km long Manpho-railway line ends. It connects the city with the two other cities of the Jagang Province, the provincial capital, Kanggye, and Huichon as well as with the cities of the Phyongnam Province: Kaechon and Sunchon. The rail station "Youth" Manpho is on the one hand a notable station for passenger service, on the other hand coal, fertilizer, etc., which are used in the industries as well as in agriculture of the city Manpho, are transported to this station. Manpho is a little more than 50 km distant from the provincial capital Kanggye. This railway line was built during the Japanese Occupation, starting in 1931 and completed in 1939. The purpose of the construction of this line was the promotion of the wood industry since there had been large forest supplies in this area (Ko Thae-u 1992, 213). Until 1980 the line was electrified. Moreover, Manpho is connected with the neighboring province of Ryanggang through the 252 km long Hyesan-Manpho-"Youth"-line. It was released in 1988 for transportation.

The river port of Manpho is located in Kangan-dong, which connects Manpho over the Yalu with Wiwon and Unbong (IPA-7 2003, 92-93).

Manpho does not seem to have a central function in terms of culture. IPA does not indicate cultural institutions in this city. For the North Korean historiography of importance is the Kosanjin Revolutionary Site, where Kim Il-sung stayed during the Korean War (1950 - 1953) from 8th November to 18th December in 1950.

Since the city founding in 1967, there haven't been any new *dong* for about 40 years

Manpho was granted the status of a city (*si*) in October 1967. In January 1949, the Jagang Province was newly created and at that time Manpho was a *kun* of this province. Area changes arose as a result of enlarge- ments or decreases at the expense or for the benefit of the neighboring Sijung-kun in the south. In 1952 Manpho-kun consisted of one up and 22 ri. In the same year Kŏnphyŏng-ri became Haebang-rodongjagu.

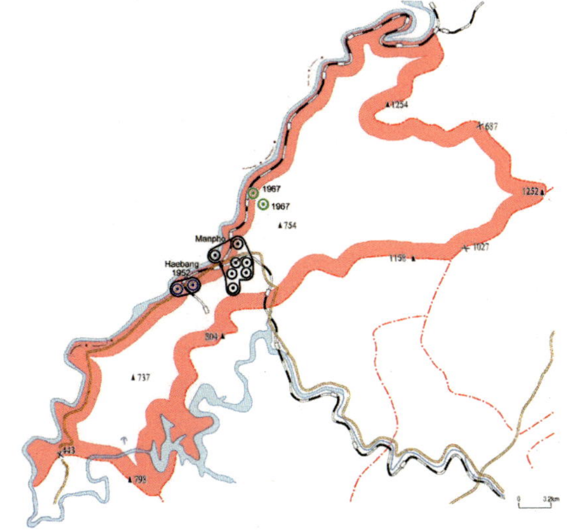

Figure Manpho-II. *Dong* in Manpho

When Manpho was promoted to city in 1967, Manpho-up was divided into seven *dong* (Kogae-dong, Kunmak-dong, Kangan-dong, Segŏm-dong, Saemmul-dong, Ponghwa-dong, Kwanmun-dong). From one part of Haebang-rodongjagu emerged Kuo-dong, the other part together with Pyŏlo-ri became Pyŏlo-dong. Munak-dong and Saemaŭl-dong was developed from Munak-ri. Sibridong-ri emerged from one part of Yŏnpho-ri in the North of the city.

Thus, eleven of twelve *dong* of Manpho emerged already at the city-founding in October 1967. After that time IPA-7 (2003, 87) does not indicate any new developed *dong* and no enlargement of the municipal area. Only the PSC-8 (2009, 464) points out the existence of twelve *dong* without elaborating details.

Three urbanized regions of Manpho

The urbanized area of Manpho is distributed over three regions that are located at the banks of the Yalu:

- the former *up* in the center;
- the former Haebang-rodongjagu south-western of the center (the Aprokgang Tire Factory and the Manpho Chemical Factory are located here);
- the newly developed *dong* that developed from Munak-ri in 1967: Munak and Saemaŭl north-western of the center (the Manpho Cement Factory is located in this region)

Urbanized regions before the city founding (*up* and *rodongjagu*)
1942-1946, 1952-1967 Manpho-up
1952-1967 Haebang-rodongjagu (2)

	Dong-Formation	*Dong*-Splitting
1967 (11)	2	(7)

Manpho – Economic development area for agriculture, tourism and trade

Manpho, the city with the smallest population number among the 27 cities of the DPR Korea, has a very beneficial situation in regards to energy supply. The city has the largest tire factory of the DPR Korea, an important chemical factory and a notable cement factory. The tire factory and the chemical factory are located only a small distance south-west from the city center in the former Haebang-rodongjagu. The chemical factory is located approximately three km away north-west of the city center so that industries that bring along the biggest environmental problems are erected a certain distance to the biggest residential zones. Development potential is offered through the closeness to China with which Manpho is connected through a railway bridge. The graves from the Koguryo period are important sights located on the Chinese banks of the Yalu. The number of tourists that enter DPR Korea from China via Jian and Manpho shows an upward trend since 2000. Already since 1988, Jian was announced as a special economic zone and this resulted in positive outcomes for the border trade. There are plans to establish a trade zone at the North Korean Yalu Island of Pyŏldŭng-do (Yi Oh-hŭi 2011, 158-159). In 2013, Manpho was designated as one of 14 new locations for an economic development area, whereas the points of focus lie in the promotion of agriculture, tourism, and trade.

IV.2.4. Sinuiju

The "New Uiju"

Sinuiju is the largest border town of the DPR Korea to China. It is the most important location to enter North Korea through ground transportation. Due to Sinuiju's position, the city would have had a high potential for special economic areas. However, the physical-geographical circumstances narrow the potential down.

Sinuiju is the capital of the province of Phyongbuk and, according to the number of inhabitants, one of the largest cities of the DPR Korea, though, according to the area size, one of the smallest. Only Songrim is more densely populated than Sinuiju. Therefore it comes as no surprise, that there is hardly any space for economic areas in Sinuiju.

Table Sinuiju-I. Basic data

Population	359,341 (Rank 6)
Area	190 km² (Rank 25)
Population density	1,891 I./km² (Rank 2)
Administrative units	50 *dong*/9 *ri* (85%) (Rank 4)
"Urban" population / "rural" population	93%/7% (Rank 2)

Sinuiju is situated about 40 km above the mouth of the Yalu, approximately in the northwest of the province, directly near the Chinese border. Sinuiju originated in connection to the construction of a railway line due to Japanese authorities, which should have crossed from the Southeast to the northwest of Korea. The construction of this railroad was related to the Russo-Japanese War (1904 - 1904). The railroad contained the route between Seoul, the capital, and Pusan, the south-eastern seaport city, the Kyongbu-line; and the Kyongui-line, which should have connected the capital with Uiju in the northwest. It was planned to connect this route to the Manchurian railroad network by means of the construction of a railroad bridge above the Yalu.

In 1904 the Provisional Military Railroad Authority was established by the Japanese government and within the framework of the metalling, the construction of the north-western part of the rail from Kwaksan to Uiju (235 km) commenced. The most complex problem was the matter of the location of the bridge, which was to be constructed above the Yalu.

A potential position was located near a river crossing close to the settlement of Uiju, where a river isle was located. This region was also used by delegations of the Korean Joson empire as well as by the Chinese Ch'ing empire, who had crossed the Yalu. Another proposal suggested building the bridge over the Yalu about 20 km downstream, where it would push against the Manchurian side upon the county of Antung (today: Dandong). In April 1905 it was decided to implement the latter proposal. The background of this decision was the co-occurring construction of the route from Antung to Mukden (today: Shenyang). On the flooded wetlands of the Yalu, beneath the hills of Chukmyŏn-san, where the Korean ground was reached by the 947 m long bridge, a new city was systematically built. This city was called Sinuiju—"the New Uiju."

When the bridge over the Yalu was finished in 1911, the connection to the Manchurian railway was accomplished, which was the reason of an enormous development process in Sinuiju as well as in Antung. Sinuiju is an important junction, not only for ground transportation. It also developed as a point of departure for maritime traffic on the headwaters of the Yalu. 1923 the capital of Phyongbuk Province was relocated from Uiju to Sinuiju, through which the city became not only the politic, but also the economic center of north-western Korea (Yun Jŏng-sŏp 1987, 128-130).

However, a major harbour could not be developed in Sinuiju. Since the Yalu is frozen during winter, the harbour of Sinuiju is restricted to being open for only half a year. In addition, the tides are big and the accumulation of earth and sand is very strong. The water depth is irregular, since the flow center of the Yalu tilts itself towards the Chinese waterside. When the harbour was opened in 1900, ships of the 1,000 t-class were able to dock, afterwards ships of the 500 t class were able to come in and out. Therefore, the demand for a replacement harbour rose, which was the reason for building the Tasado harbour (Ryongchon-kun) (Kang Sŏk-o 1984, 307-308).

Theoretically Sinuiju is connected with European rail network due to the railway bridge, which can also be used by motor vehicles. The belligerent conflicts during the Korean War have prevented this connection, though. The international traffic to Beijing was only possible from 1954, and from 1964 it was made possible with electric locomotives.

China, amongst others, was instrumental with the setup of the city of Sinuiju after the Korean War. Until 1958 Chinese troops were stationed in Sinuiju, who had built about 100,000 apartments in the city center, while Bulgaria built a hospital in Sinuiju (Jang Sehun 2006b, 470).

City in flood-prone position

Sinuiju is located only a few meters above sea level. In the South and Southeast of the city, the terrain is a bit higher, though. The municipal area consists of an alluvial plain in the lower reaches of the Yalu, of hills from the East and the South, and of islands in the North.

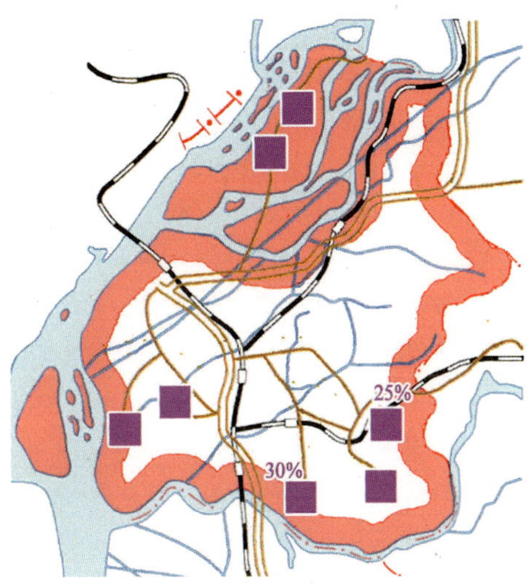

Figure Sinuiju-I. Agricultural land in the *ri*

Sinuiju was built in the midst of meadows and swamps during the Japanese occupation. Since the built-up area lies deeper than the Yalu, it was surrounded by an approximately 3 m high dike at this time. Therefore, Sinuiju is highly prone to flood.

96.7% of the city area consists of elevations at an altitude of 100 m, 3% at an altitude between 100 m-200 m and only 0.3% rises above sea level of 200 m (IPA-5 2003, 73).

Important rivers of this city are the Yalu (Aprok-gang, Amnok-gang), which constitutes the border to China, the Samgyo-chŏn, which forms the boundary to Ryongchon-kun and the Yŏha-chŏn, which is a subsidiary stream of the Samgyo-chŏn.

Table Sinuiju-II. Climate values

Annual average	January temperature	August temperature	Precipitation
9.6℃ (14)	-6.8℃ (17)	24.0℃ (7)	1,001.5 mm (13)

The climate is continental; however it is subject to maritime influence.

The forest accounts for 8% of the city area, wherein pine is strongly represented. Agricultural field cultivation area (vegetables, grains and fruit) makes up 55% of the city, of which more than 30% are located on the banks of the Yalu and the Samgyo-chŏn. The animal husbandry, especially chicken farms and pig farms in Sŏnsang-dong as well as the duck farm in Handan-ri on the island of Wihwa, play an important role (IPA-5 2003, 75). Additionally, fishing companies are located in Sinuiju. In the city there are also coal deposits (PSC-8 2009, 432).

Important location for the light industry of DPR Korea

Due to the forest wealth of the upper running tracks of the Yalu, which was one of the external reasons for the Russo-Japanese War (Lautensach 1945, 242), Sinuiju was in the early days the location for collection and distribution of wood. Therefore, lumbermills and industries, which processed wood, for example the manufacture of paper, pulp and matches were developed. With the construction of the Suphung power plant and the opening of the Manpho- and Hyesan- railway lines, the system of wood transport was changed. The Suphung power plant also provided the necessary energy for the establishment of the industry. Consequently, starting from the textile industry, all kinds of industries were established in Sinuiju, which now developed itself into an industrial city. (Kang Sŏk-o 1984, 308). Especially in the northern and southern peripheral regions of the former urban area, industrial companies such as a shipyard, textile mills, soap factories and pharmaceutical companies emerged (Saitschikow 1958, 323).

The most important industrial sectors for Sinuiju were the sectors of mechanical engineering, chemical industry and the light industry (textile, shoes, food, consumer durables) (IPA-5 2003, 74-75). Sinuiju is one of the most significant locations for the light industry in the DPR Korea (PSC-8 2009, 432).

Table Sinuiju-III. Ranking (in parenthesis: number of industrial companies or cultural institutions)

Sinuiju	KOFC	MOU	IPA	KCNA	KIET	Summary
Companies-total	6 (23)	4 (34)	9 (22)	9 (12)	11 (36)	7
Companies-important	7 (5)	11 (3)	9 (9)		8 (19)	9 (10)
Cultural institution			4 (20)			

Table Sinuiju-IV. Ranking (Total number of companies in relation to population)

Sinuiju	KOFC	MOU	IPA	KCNA	KIET	Summary
Companies-total	6	3	8–12–4	13	18–9	9–12

The ranking in terms of the number of companies coincides broadly, on the whole, with the rank in terms of the population (Rank 6). When evaluating the MOU source, Sinuiju has a better ranking, since MOU has included a lot of light industry companies. On the other hand, Sinuiju has an especially bad ranking during the evaluation of the KIET source, since their focus is on heavy industry.

Table Sinuiju-V. Specification (in parenthesis: number of companies)

Sinuiju	Light Industry	Heavy Industry	Mining	Energy
KOFC	6 (8)	13 (15)	–	–
MOU	7 (23)	11 (10)	14 (1)	–
IPA	6 (15)	19 (7)	–	–
KCNA	10 (6)	7 (6)	–	–
KIET	7 (17)	10 (19)	–	–

It is clear that Sinuiju is a city, in which light industry plays a significant role. On the other hand, in the KCNA source numerous factories in the field of mechanical engineering are presented.

In chapter III.7.3. ten companies have been identified as important: Rakwŏn Machine Complex, Factory 9th August (Sinuiju Mining Machine Factory), Sinuiju Spinning Machine Factory, Sinuiju Chemical Fibre Complex, Sinuiju Enamel Ware Factory, Sinuiju Cosmetics Factory, Sinuiju Shoes Factory, Sinuiju Footwear Factory, Sinuiju Textile Factory, Sinuiju Family Goods Factory.

One of the biggest machine factories of North Korea is the Rakwŏn Machine Complex in the South of the city. Mainly different kinds of excavators are produced here, as well as equipment like centrifuges and generators. The Samgyo-chŏn,[20] which supplies the industrial water, flows in the South of the Complex. The factory has a good transport connection, since it is situated near a two-lane paved road as well as a railway between Sinuiju and Pyongyang. The Rakwŏn Machine Complex employs about 4,500 workers and operates on an area of 93,000 m^2. During the Japanese occupation this company was only a small repair shop for agricultural machines (KOFC 2010, 257). The factory began its production again on September 1945 under the name of Sinuiju Machine Plant (since 1947 Rakwŏn Machine Plant) and produced different agricultural machines (IPA-5 2003, 76-77). During the Korean War it was converted into a munitions factory. In 1952 the reconstruction and enlargement of the factory, which was destroyed during the Korean War, commenced.

20 The 129 km long Samgyo-chŏn, a tributary of the Yalu, forms the Southern boundary of Sinuiju-si to Ryongchon-kun and then flows into the Phihyon-kun.

Figure Sinuiju-II. Rakwŏn Machine Complex (2012)

Figure Sinuiju-III. Rakwŏn Machine Complex (view from Samgyo-chŏn) (2012)

In the Factory 9th August (Sinuiju Mining Machine Factory), which is located in the Ryŏngsang-dong district, mining machines of all kinds (high-speed excavators, rotation excavators, loaders, drills and wagons) are produced. 3,000 employees[21] work on an area of 143,000 m^2.

The Sinuiju Spinning Machine Factory is one of the five major machine factories of the province. The factory was extended in the second half of the 80s.[22]

The Sinuiju Chemical Fibre Complex is located in the northeast of the rail station of Sinuiju in the district of Pangjik-dong[23] and has an area of 490,000 m^2. The sector for paper making, the branch factory for the manufacture of caustic soda, the chemical factory Tongrim, the chemical factory Sinuiju and the factory for dyeing equipment Sinuiju are subordinately organized under the Sinuiju Chemical Fiber Complex.

The United Chemical Fibre Factory Sinuiju emerged in 1919 from the Japanese Fuji Paper Company as the Chosen Paper Factory (annual capacity of 1,000 t), in order to manufacture pulp. 1921 it was incorporated into the Oji Paper Company and expanded. After the Korean takeover of the factory, several expansions were carried out, which resulted in the beginning of the production of newspaper and paper for school books. The destruction during the Korean War was followed by the reconstruction. In 1955 the production was resumed. The raw materials for the pulp produced in this factory were used from reeds in the reed fields of the mouth of the Yalu (Pidan-sŏm, Ryongchon-kun) and from rice straw of the Western agricultural belt along the Green Sea from the city of Jongju, as well as from corn stalks. Salt originates from the salt works from the West coast area, and caustic soda, produced by electrolysis, is needed for the production of chemical fibres and of paper. Electric energy is drawn from the Suphung Power Plant.[24]

21 KOFC 2010, 259; also KIET 1996, 266-267.

22 For more informations: KIET 1996, 287-288.

23 Chosun Ilbo 13November 13, 1995; KOFC (2010, 587) claims that it is located in Majŏn-dong.

24 Han'guk-sanop-ŭnhaeng 2000, 242-244 and 428-429; KOFC 2010, 587-589.

The Sinuiju Enamel Ware Factory was built in the 50s and is the largest small hardware producer of the DPRK with its multiple departments and a branch factory. 130 varieties of enamelled small metal hardware is produced in this factory, i.e. cutlery, crockery, cups, buckets, pots, pans and basins (Choe Sŏn-yŏng 2001). In the year of 2003 the factory was modernised (KCNA 17th September 2003). The factory also produces for export.

The Sinuiju Cosmetics Factory was built between 1945 and 1950 (KJY-23 1990, 438)[25] and originally was located in the center of the city. It produced soap, paper soap, tooth paste, crèmes and body perfume. In approximately 1990 the factory was modernised and expanded in 1995 (KIET 1996, 171). During a visit by Kim Jong-Il in June 1999, the relocation of the factory to South-Sinuiju was ordered by him. The new location was situated about 5 km from the city center, where an industrial area was planned. In January 2001 the factory was completed on the new site with departments for soap, tooth paste and cosmetics (Kim Tu-hwan 2003). In January 2004 a department for the production of boxes and other packaging was added. The cosmetics factory Sinuiju is now considered as the largest cosmetics factory of the DPRK. In November 2004 North Korean media reported that the production under sterile conditions was now possible. The products of Sinuiju are immensely popular in the DPRK and compete with the products of the cosmetics factory Pyongyang. The products made in Sinuiju under the name of "Nŏ-wa na" (You and Me) are intended for the export of the product line. Meanwhile the products are also distributed and sold within the DPRK under the product name of "Pŏmhyanggi" (spring scent).

Figure Sinuiju-IV. Sinuiju Textile Factory (2012)

Figure Sinuiju-V. Pomhyanggi-Products from Sinujiu from a Hotel in Wonsan (2012)

In the Sinuiju Shoes Factory mainly boots, which are sold in the whole province of Phyongbuk, are produced.

25 Quoted after Jŏng Ŭn-i (2012).

The Sinuiju Footwear Factory is actually the largest shoe factory of the DPRK, because it has an annual capacity of 20 million of produced shoes. Mostly textile/cloth shoes are mass-produced here. The manufactured sports shoes, work shoes, rubber boots, PVC shoes, basketball shoes and simple cloth sports shoes are also partially exported. This factory was built already during the Japanese colonial rule. In 1982 16% of the North Korean shoe production could be allocated to this very factory. In April 1992 a special part of the factory responsible for the production of exporting products was finished (KOFC 2010, 608). This factory with its 4,000 employees has its very own energy department generating steam from coal, which is necessary to provide the factory with energy (KIET 1996, 110). In 2009 and 2010 the factory was further modernised (KOFC 2010, 608). According to the statements made by refugees from North Korea, the sports shoes made by the factory have an excellent reputation for footwear. There are 3,500 persons, who are employed by the Sinuiju Textile Factory, working in an area of 154,000 m^2. The factory was built in August 1945 as stated by the (South) Korean commerce bank, and was put in operation in 1947. However, the facilities were destroyed during the Korean War. After the reconstruction, the factory resumed its operation in July 1959.[26] Afterwards, several extensions of the factory were made. It was announced in 1983 that only local raw material would be used. The factory is supplied with staple fibres by the United Chemical Fibre Factory Sinuiju, although energy is provided by in-house thermal power plant. The internally produced yarn is not only used for the in-house subsequent process to cloth, but additionally is supplying small and medium-sized textile companies.

The Sinuiju Family Goods Factory was founded in 1969. In this factory aluminium and resin, amongst other things, are produced in order to manufacture a variety of products for domestic use (IPA-5 2003, 77).

Apart from the companies that were identified as important in Chapter III.7.3, there are certainly numerous other companies in Sinuiju that will be presented here.

In the Factory 4th March communication cables are manufactured. In April 2002 the factory was expanded with a modern production line. This production line, the official newspaper of the Central Committee of the Workers' Party of Korea, the Rodong Sinmun, notably singles out on 1st July 2002, is capable to produce thin insulated wire, as well as thin insulated wire consisting of several strands (Yonhap News Agency 2011). Furthermore, this factory, which is also regarded as an armament factory, produces annually approximately 150,000 pairs of white rubber gloves.[27]

In the factory September General Iron Enterprises annually 96,000 tons of low-grade

26 Han'guk-sanop-ŭnhaeng 2000, 407. According to other data, which are based on an article by the North Korean Rodong Sinmun, the Factory supposedly was built in August 1959 (KIET 1996, 76).

27 Han'guk-sanop-ŭnhaeng 2000, 450.

steel (*samhwachŏl*),[28] 90,000 tons of steel and 90,000 rolled steel is produced.[29] The factory is named after the event when Kim Il-sung supposedly visited in September 1970 and determined the location for the industrial plant. Additionally, it is rumoured that an electric furnace was introduced. The steel factory was modernised with the help of scientists of the Technical University Kim Chaek from the capital Pyongyang (KCNA January 13, 2005).

The Sinuiju Streptomycin[30] Factory is a special factory for antibiotics, in which, amongst other things, the antibiotic-containing ointment Terramycin, medicine for injections etc. are produced.[31]

The Sinuiju Pulp Factory is located in Sinuiju Sumun-dong and is approximately 5,000 m². It was built in September 1949 in order to manufacture rice paper. Starting from 1956 the artificial silk paper production commenced. In 1971 hemp and flax was processed and cigarette paper and packaging papers for food products was produced. As a general rule, reed from the river mouth of the Yalu, corn stalks and rice straw are used as raw materials. The artificial silk pulp is delivered to the Textile Factory Sinuiju, but the sulfuric pulp is necessary for the in-house paper production. Furthermore, the binder material serves use in the briquette and pavement production. The quality of the products is likely to be similar to the paper production department of the United Chemical Factory Sinuiju. The fact that the same machines are used for different kinds of paper might have a negative impact on the quality of the products.[32]

In addition, the Korea Amnokgang Trading Corporation has a registered office in Sinuiju. This determination was handed over in 1977. Assigned to this factory are the export products bases for coloured metal, non-metal, reed processing, marine and agricultural products, clothing, electronic accessories and decorative buckles in Sinuiju and surrounding areas. One focus of its activities lies in the trade with the border areas of the PR China.[33]

Sinuiju special economic zone

North Korea surprised the world by establishing a capitalistic "Special Administrative Region of Sinuiju" in September 2002. This region was supposed to develop itself into an international center for finance, trade, IT industry, modern science, entertainment

28 It is 90-95% steel, since anthracite was used at its smelting. When using coke, 97% steel would be created.

29 Han'guk-sanop-ŭnhaeng 2000, 57.

30 Streptomyzin is an active ingredient, which is obtained from soil microbes and is used for the production of most antibiotics for the human and veterinary medicine as well as for agriculture.

31 Han'guk-sanop-ŭnhaeng 2000, 247.

32 Han'guk-sanop-ŭnhaeng 2000, 430.

33 Naenara: „Korean Trading Company Amnokgang" http://www.naenara.com.kp/de/realtrade/?company+5+4

and tourism. For this purpose, it was planned that the region should receive a largely autonomous government until 31st December 2052. In this manner, the issuance of passports and currency was planned as well. Even their own flag was already designed: with peony on a blue background. Similarities with Hong Kong were probably not unintentional. Official languages were supposed to be Chinese, Korean and English.

Obviously the setup of the economic zone was supposed to be more consistent than the failed attempt in Rajin-Sonbong. As governor—it was highly unusual—a foreigner, Yang Bin, was appointed, who was a 39-year-old Dutch with Chinese origin. According to Forbes, he was, at the time of his planned appointment as governor, the second-richest Chinese in the world.

North Korea is by all means interested in the establishment of special economic zones. However the country is not interested in external political influences. Easily definable peripheral positions seem to be best suited for conducting international experiments from the view of North Korean rulers. While there is enough industrial water and energy from the Water Plant Suphung, the port itself seems to be very small and the rest of the infrastructure is weakly developed. Based on the bad infrastructure, the construction of an industrial complex was rejected by the South Korean Hyundai group.

Shortly after his appointment as governor, Yang Bin announced that several hundred thousand current inhabitants of the 132 km² area were to be dispelled and that a three meter high wall was to be built. Immediately rumours circulated that especially the districts in the North of the city, Apgang-dong, Ponbu-dong, Yŏkjŏn-dong, Chaeha-dong; would be affected by the resettlement to undetermined locations or to South-Sinuiju.[34]

According to a study by KOTRA, it was expected that the investments in this North Korean city would be made by the Chinese and overseas-Chinese, and less made by "Western" companies. Investments of "Western" companies were scheduled as recently as in four to five years later, when improvements in the infrastructure and the business environment would be significantly visible (Yoo, Cheong-mo 2002).

However, things turned out to be quite different than expected. Already in the beginning of October 2002, Chinese security authorities arrested Yang Bin in Shenyang. He was accused with tax evasion and illegal business practices by the Chinese. Later, Yang Bin was sentenced to 14 years in prison.

At a later time Julie Sa, who was the daughter of two Chinese parents, although born in South Korea, where she also grew up, but later emigrated to California, was under discussion as a potential governor. But by the end of 2014 the media announced that the North Koreans had proclaimed the end of the project of the Special Zone Sinŭiju.

What were the reasons for this rapid failure?

34 Kukmin Ilbo September 30, 2002, http://www.kmib.co.kr/html/kmview/2002/0930/091874442311121400.html

Above all, the project was not sufficiently coordinated with China. This initially was pointed out by the reasons that lie with the person of Yang Bin. China possibly had concerns that Sinuiju could become a gambling hell for the Chinese, in which crime and money laundering could rise from. In particular, Sinuiju could have been a pesky competitor in regards to investments for the region of North Eastern China.

Since 2009, though, the development of the Sinuiju special economic zone has been put back on the agenda and under debate, due to an agreement with China concerning the islands of Wihwa and Hwanggŭmphyŏng, in order to develop these areas as joint free trade zones. Also, China has reached an agreement with North Korea over the construction of the new Yalu River Highway Bridge Tong 2010). In 2010 the construction began, and 2014 is supposed to be the year of completion. The new bridge is located approximately 12-13 km downstream from the existing "Korea-China Friendship Bridge," near Hwanggŭmphyŏng, and connects the Dandong New City Zone Guomenwan Exhibition Center with Sinuiju.

On 12.3.2011 the Hwanggŭmpyŏng and Wihwa Island Economic Zone Law was enacted by North Korea, however negotiations between China and Korea are still running and not finished. Most concretely seem to be the considerations regarding Hwanggŭmphyŏng, which is the southern island from the two. An industry specialised on trade and information, tourism and culture as well as a modern agriculture and processing industry, is planned there. It is also planned that there once should be up to 300,000 North Koreans working there (KBS World Radio 2011).

Another area near Sinuiju, which is considered in the plan for the construction of special economic regions, is the area around Taegyedo, where extensive land reclamation was carried out.

Sinuiju is the final destination of the railway line between Pyongyang and Sinuiju. From here, there are rail connections available to China. The rail station "Sinuiju Youth" was built in 1905 as part of the construction of the railway line from Seoul to Sinuiju. This station is the border station for trains to and from Beijing. Both passengers as well as cargo are transported. In the rail station South-Sinuiju, which also lies on the route between Pyongyang and Sinuiju, the Tŏkhyŏn-Line (South-Sinuiju – Uiju – Tŏkhyŏn) and the Paekma-Line (South-Sinuiju – Phihyon – Yomju) fork off. Major roads lead from Sinuiju to the direction of Pyongyang, Uiju and Phihyon. From Sinuiju there are 236 km to Pyongyang.

In the second half of the 2000s, a new wide road between Old-Sinuiju and the Southern boundary of the city was built (Figure Sinuiju-VI and Figure Sinuiju-VII).

Figure Sinuiju-VI. Nam-Sinuiju 2006

Figure Sinuiju-VII. Nam-Sinuiju 2012

Through the port of Sinuiju cargo ships go to the islands located in the lower course of the Yalu and as far as Ryongampho, Pidan-sŏm, Cholsan, Jongju, Nampho and Haeju on the coast of the Yellow Sea. Through the upper course of the Yalu, cargo-and passenger ships come from and go to Uiju, Okkang and Chongsong. Passenger ships are also used as inner-city transportation.

Center of education and culture in the northwest of the DPR Korea

Sinuiju was formerly and is nowadays a city of education. There are numerous secondary educational establishments. Several colleges are specialised in the areas of industry and teacher training. Additionally there are colleges for agriculture, for medicine, for military studies and for the party cadre training. A research institute is concerned with chemical fibres. Furthermore, there are a considerable number of cultural institutions, which is customary for a capital of a province. On the whole, Sinuiju has the fourth-most cultural institutions in all North Korean cities as stated by a table in the IPA (2003) (Table Sinuiju-III).

The ten party members of Rakwŏn

The Rakwŏn Machine Complex is the largest company of the city. The word Rakwŏn has a special ring in Korea, since it has the meaning of "paradise." The Rakwŏn Machine Complex therefore was material for the propaganda stories of Sin Pho-hyang and the "Ten Party Members of Rakwŏn." These were, so according to the narrative, working in the cast iron division of the Rakwŏn Machine Factory (the former name of the company) during the Korean War. At the end of June 1952, Kim Il-sung took part in a plenary meeting of his party cell to discuss the preliminary work for the construction after the War. Sin Pho-hyang, one of the workers, remembered during this conversation that Japanese imperialism had indeed destroyed everything; however it also had been possible to rebuild everything in two to three years. Consequentially, the same should be possible after the cessation of the War. Thus, Kim Il-sung should not be too worried. Kim Il-sung was quite impressed by this assurance according to this narrative. Therefore, he could not forget the words spoken by Sin Pho-hyang (Verlag für Fremdsprachige Literatur 2001, 233). As shown in the above, the ten Party members from Rakwŏn are always remembered, especially when it comes to conjuring the "revolutionary spirit of the independent reconstruction," like for example in the official New Year's message of the DPRK in the year of 2000.

Capital of the province of Phyongbuk

The capital of Phyongbuk Province was initially Uiju. Sinuiju, though, was administratively a part of Uiju. In the administrative reform of 1913 Uiju was put together with Sinuiju, however. Sinuiju thus became the capital of the province and in 1923 the provincial administrative building was relocated to Sinuiju. In 1914 Sinuiju was officially declared as a city (*pu*, since 1947 *si*). In 1939 at the expense of Uiju-kun, Sinuiju's urban area was enlarged. In the reorganizations in the 50s Sinuiju again lost areas, in 1952 to the *kun* of Uiju and Ryongchŏn, in 1954 nine *ri* came to the newly founded Kwangsŏng-kun. In 1989 Sinuiju was divided into three *kuyok* (Nam, Kwangmyŏng, Kangan), although they were abolished again in November 1991.

High population density in Old-Sinuiju

The city was laid out in a checkerboard pattern. At the Yalu, where rafts were cut from the logs from the forest regions of the North, large wood processing factories were created. In 1938 the population of Sinuiju had grown to 52,384 inhabitants, of whom 16% were Japanese and 12% Chinese (Lautensach 1945, 246). The population groups lived in different quarters; there was a Japanese street where today the district of Sinwŏn-dong exists, and a Chinese street, where today the district of Namsŏ-dong and Namha-dong lie (Yi Yo-sep 2002). The Koreans lived in the remaining other districts. In 1945 the city had approximately 120,000 inhabitants. Majŏn-dong, located somewhere east from the rail station, was first considered as the residence of the especially poor population groups early in the 40s.

Sinuiju was victim of heavy bombing by the US war planes during the Korean War. General Douglas MacArthur had ordered the formation of a wasteland between the front and the Korean-Chinese border. On 8th November 1950, therefore, 79 B-29 550-ton incendiaries landed on Sinuiju with the goal of erasing the city from the map (Cumings 2004, 2).

The enormous efforts that were necessary for the reconstruction are thus apparent to building the legend around Sin Pho-hyang and the ten Party members of the Machine Factory Rakwon.

The city center of Sinuiju is completely overpopulated. Already in the 50s Saitschikow (1958, 322) wrote that the lack of a suitable ground for the city was the reason why the city was designed in a compact structure and that the 127,000 inhabitants had to find space in an area of little more than 2 km^2. There were no large parks and gardens in the city. Every patch of ground was occupied with apartment buildings that were allocated in rectangular areas. Straight roads with multi-storey buildings occupied the banks of the river. In the northern and southern fringes of the city several industrial companies had been established.

The provincial capital of Phyongbuk, Sinuiju, is the liveliest city within the DPR Korea. Correspondent with the status as a border town, a vibrant trade and many local changes in the population exist. This is the location, where foreign culture fastest penetrates. Since the 1980s the most famous market in Sinuiju is the Chaeha Market. It was reported, though, that this market vanished in the 1990s (Chosun Ilbo November 13, 1995).

Satellite images from the 2000s, however, indicated that there was a growth relating to this market from 2002 until 2011. Then, in 2012 the market vanished. A new large market was built at the southern border of Old-Sinuiju (North Korean Economy Watch 2013).

The provincial headquarters of the Workers' Party is located in Ponbu-dong, where a lot of cadres of the provincial headquarters of the Party are concentrated. The provincial administrative committee also is in Sinwŏn-dong, where also the high cadre of the provincial administration live. In addition, except special exceptions, most of the cadre lives in the city, but the factually powerful live concentrated in Kwanmun-dong, Kŭnhwa-dong and Yŏkjŏn-dong. The apartment buildings of the provincial cadre are separated from the houses of the population of Sinuiju by a wall (NK Chosun.com 2003).

In 1975 a 3rd class hotel with 53 rooms was built. It is located in Kwanmun-dong and is mostly used by the Chinese. It is situated five minutes by car away from the customs office.

Old-Sinuiju, Nam-Sinuiju, Yŏnha: three urbanized areas

The urbanized areas of Sinuiju are divided roughly into three areas:

Old-Sinuiju, or North-Sinuiju. This is the original Sinuiju, which was protected by dams.

Nam-Sinuiju, or South-Sinuiju, the area south from Old Sinuiju, especially around the former Rakwŏn-rodongjagu and the former Kwangsŏng-up.

The area of the former Yŏnha-rodongjagu in the Northeast of the city.

Incorporations in 1961, 1963 and 1989

After Sinuiju was reduced in size in the 50s, it came to incorporations in the 60s as well as in 1989:

- In 1961 Sangan-ri and Hadan-ri (both in Uiju-kun), as well as Majŏn-ri and Sŏnsang-ri (both in Kwangsŏng-kun) were incorporated into the city
- In 1963 Kwangsŏng-kun was dissolved and, except for Samsang-ri, was integrated into Sinuiju-si. Kwangsŏng-up (1954), Rakwŏn-rodongjagu (1957) and eleven *ri* were affected by this change.
- In 1989 the incorporations of parts of Uiju-kun, which were incorporated as Yŏnha-dong to Sinuiju-si, were made, as well as the incorporation of Tajiri (Uiju-kun).

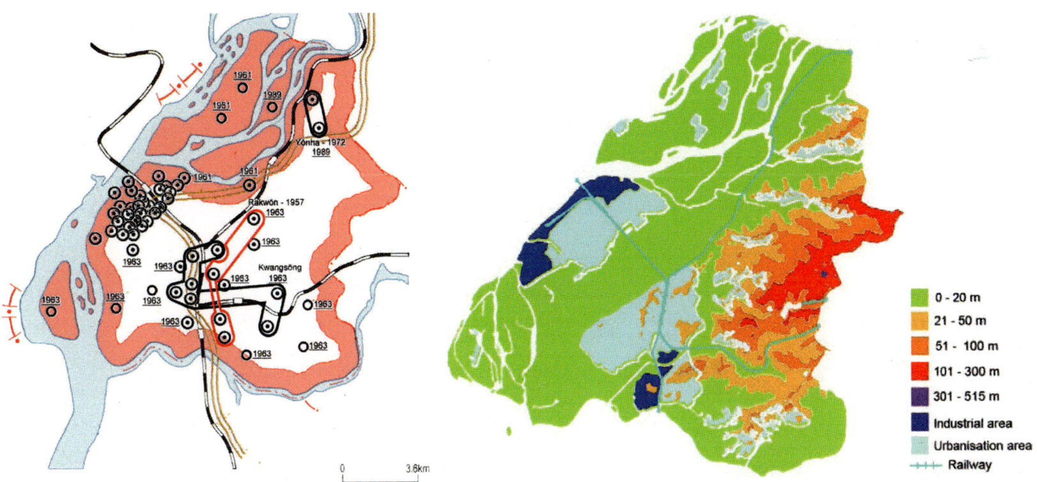

Figure Sinuiju-VIII. Incorporations

Figure Sinuiju-IX. Urbanization and industrial area as well as topography (Source: Yi Sang-jun et.al. 2011, 75, 83)

Urbanization process in Sinuiju

In 1955 31 *dong* were founded in the city of Sinuiju, which were reduced to 25 in the course of the restructuring of the city of Sinuiju. Additionally, Kwangsŏng-ŭp, which was founded in 1954, and the in 1957 founded Rakwŏn-rodongjagu (Kwangsŏng-kun), are part of the city of Sinuiju. Both are located nowadays within the city borders of Sinuiju.

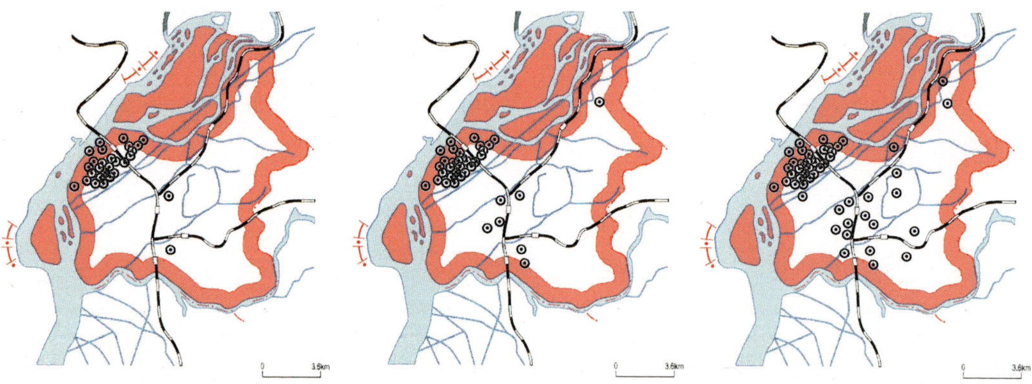

Figure Sinuiju-X. *Dong* 1961 **Figure Sinuiju-XI.** *Dong* 1976 **Figure Sinuiju-XII.** *Dong* 1994

In 1963 Kwangsŏng-up is divided into three *dong*, and Rakwŏn-rodongjagu becomes a *dong*. Sinphung-dong is added to Majŏn-ri, which therefore simultaneously is ascending to Majŏn-dong.

In 1967 due to the splitting four new *dong* were established, three of which are located in Old- Sinuiju, one in the South.

In 1972 Yŏnha-rodongjagu emerges. In 1976 Rakchŏng separates itself from Rakwŏn-dong.

In 1989 five new *dong* come into existence from the former *ri* located in the South of Old- Sinuiju. At the same time, Rakchŏng-dong and Rakwŏn-dong are divided in two *dong* each.

Three new *dong* each emerge from the separation of existing *dong* in 1990 and in 1994. Four of them are located south from Old-Sinuiju, and one within Old-Sinuiju. Another result from the separation is Yŏnha-dong, which emerged from Yŏnha-rodongjagu.

Table Sinuiju-VI. Number of *dong* in the regions of Old-Sinuiju, Nam-Sinuiju and Yŏnha

	Old-Sinuiju	South, (Southeast)	Yŏnha
1955	31	2	–
1957	29	3	
1961	25	3	–
1963	25	5	–
1967	26	8	–
1972	26	8	1
1976	26	9	1
1989	26	16	1
1990	27	18	1
1994	27	20	2

Table Sinuiju-VI. shows the distribution of *dong* (*up*, *rodongjagu*) within Sinuiju in today's border.

The Development of Nam-Sinuiju since the end of the 1980s

It is clear that the administrative structure within Old-Sinuiju was consolidated already around 1961, and between 1961 and 1994, only two new *dong* were created through the separation from another *dong*.

The development outside the old city, which was surrounded by a dam, was much livelier. In 1955 only one *dong*, Sinphung-dong in the Southeast, which was incorporated in 1963 into Majŏn-dong, existed beyond the old city center of Sinuiju. In addition Kwangsŏng-up, which is the administrative headquarter of Kwangsŏng-kun, was incorporated into the city of Sinuiju in 1963. In 1957 Rakwŏn-rodongjagu was founded. In 1963 Kwangsŏng-up was divided into three *dong*. The first signs of development in the South of Sinuiju are exhibited by the newly emerged *dong* in the years of 1967 and 1976.

Figure Sinuiju-XIII. Sinuiju (2012)

Figure Sinuiju-XIV. Nam-Sinuiju (2012)

Far-reaching changes have become apparent then since the end of the 80s. The North Korean government had promoted a program for the development of Nam-Sinuiju (South-Sinuiju).

Due to the constant threat of flood for Sinuiju, it was built in the 80s 5 km away from Sinuiju, on a slightly higher terrain in Nam-Sinuiju. There have been several factories already in this region, for example the Rakwŏn Machine Complex.

Originally it was planned to relocate urban functions from Old-Sinuiju to Nam-Sinuiju. However, only the construction of living areas was implemented. The construction of the living areas though was problematic due to the presence of the existing industrial facilities. (Jang Se-Hun 2006b, 491-492).

Statistics

Therefore in 2002 Sinuiju consisted of 49 *dong* and nine *ri*. The PSC-8 (2009), however, recorded 50 *dong* and nine *ri*, without giving any indications to the *dong*.

	Dong-Formation	*Dong*-Splitting	
1955 (33)	32	-	external 1
1957 (32)	1	-2	external 2
1961 (28)	-	-7/3	external 2
1963 (30)	-	(2)	
1967 (34)	-	4	
1972 (35)	1	-	external 1
1976 (36)	-	1	external 1
1989 (43)	5	2	
1990 (46)	-	3	
1994 (49)	-	3	

Sinuiju – Korea's Door to the Eurasian Mainland

Sinuiju is the capital of the province of Phyongan-bukto. The city is located 40 km above the mouth of the Yalu and at only 6 m above sea level, which is the reason for the latent danger of flood catastrophes. Sinuiju owes its existence to the construction of the railway line from Seoul to here, which was finished in 1905. The Japanese put the distance in this way that the route didn't cross Uiju, but a swamp area in the West, so that the line crossed the Yalu. The final destination on Korean soil was named "New Uiju," thus Sinuiju, by the Japanese. In September 2002 North Korea surprised the world, when it announced the establishment of a capitalistic "Special Administrative Region Sinuiju." This should have been developed as an international center for finance, trade, IT industry, modern science, entertainment and tourism. However, the project was stopped when the designated governor, Yang Bin, a Dutch with Chinese origins, was arrested by the Chinese authorities. At this time the negotiations for Chinese-Korean cooperation for the development of the islands of Hwanggŭmphyŏng and Wihwa are under way. A special potential of Sinuiju for Korea lies in the possible expansion of its functions as a door to the Eurasian mainland.

From 1989 to 1994 the number of *dong* in the South has more than doubled, while

Old Sinuiju almost stagnated.

IV.2.5. Kusong

One of the Kangdong Six Garrison Settlements from the Koryo era

Kusong is located in the center of the Phyongbuk Province. In 1967 the appointment as a city (*si*) was made. Already in the Koryo era a fortified wall was built. After the Korean War an intermountain industrial location was created in the city, especially due to the construction of the Machine Tool Factory. Kusong is one of the smallest cities of the DPR Korea due to its population size, although it is the largest city according to area size of the Phyongbuk Province.

Table Kusong-I. Basic data

Population	196,515 (Rank 19)
Area	653 km² (Rank 13)
Population density	301 I./km² (Rank21)
Administrative units	25 *dong*/18 *ri* (58%) (Rank 18)
"Urban" population / "rural" population	79%/21% (Rank 17)

During the time of the Koryo king Kwangjong (949-975) Korea tried to extend its empire to the Yalu, which resulted into conflicts with the neighbouring Khitan. The latter tried to manage an invasion into Koryo. However, Sŏ Hŭi was able to persuade the Khitan to retreat, who also were in conflicts with Sung China. This was accomplished, because for the Khitan this country wasn't important due to the Jurchen, who lived there. After this retreat of the Khitan, Koryo built six Kangdong Garrison Settlements (east of the River). One of them was Kuju, the current Kusong. Therefore in 994 the fortification of Kuju was built (Lee, Ki-baik 1984, 125). Parts of the fortress are still preserved and are nowadays the most important attractions of the city. The South Gate, which is the largest and most important of the four gates of the wall, was restored several times as

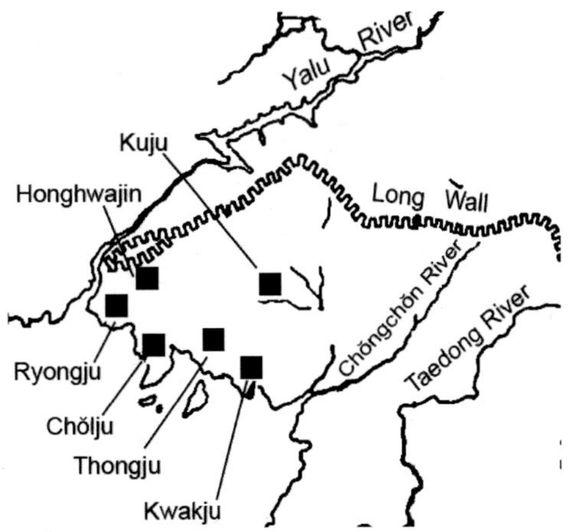

Figure Kusong-I. Kangdong Six Garrison Settlements (based on Lee, Ki-baik 1984, 127 and subsequently modified)

well as rebuilt. The current gate dates back to the build-up in 1836. However, the gate was destroyed during the Korean War, and then reconstructed in 1979.

Typical basin position

Kusong has evolved within a typical valley. The city center is located in the middle of the municipal area within the Kusong-basin position. It is an erosion basin, in which at first the softer granite layers were eroded out. The basin is almost identical with the catchment area of the Chŏngbang-gang and the city area of Kusong. Not only the Chŏngbang-gang, but also its tributary river, the Tongmun-chŏn, is of great importance. The basin has an East-West extension of 21 m, a North-South extension of 30 m and therefore has an oval shape (IPA-5 2003, 112). The Southern part of the basin is also called Panghyŏn-level. Consequently this region offers especially good conditions for agriculture.

The peripheral parts of the municipal area consist mostly of hilly and mountainous country. In the western margin of the city, the Chŏnma mountain chain spreads out in the direction of North-South and here there are also the high mountains of Chŏngryong-san (920 m), which is the highest mountain of the city, and the Kilsang-san (594 m). The more you go into the center of the city, the flatter the land is. The rivers of the city all flow into the Chŏnbang-gang and are short. The Chŏnbang-gang rises from the North of Kusong on Chasu pass. It flows in the North-Eastern parts of Thaechon-up into the Taeryŏng-gang, is 57.2 km long, and also famous for its clear and clean water. On the Chŏnbang-gang and in its influence area, there are reservoirs, for example the Phungsan reservoir, the Choyang reservoir, the Tŏksang reservoir. These reservoirs water the Panghyŏn plain (Kusong-si) and the Andŭre plain (Thaechon-kun). They have a great importance for the water supply of this region.

The 38 km long Talchŏn-gang rises from the foot of the Kilsang-san in the Southwest of the city region and flows through Jŏngju into the Yellow Sea. The Talchŏn-gang is the water source for the reservoirs of the Phungmyŏng and thus has an important role for the irrigation of Jŏngju.

Table Kusong-II. Climate values

Annual average	January temperature	August temperature	Precipitation
9.1°C (18)	-7.6°C (21)	23.6°C (13)	1,290.9 mm (3)

Kusong is one of the rainiest areas of North Korea. 62% of the city area is accounted by forests.

The agricultural cultivable land is 22.6% of the municipal area. Livestock farming is also represented. The Chicken Farm Kusong is nationally famous. Fruit cultivation also exists, especially apples, pears, peaches and other fruits, mostly grown in the South and in the West of the city. Furthermore, the silk worm breeding has developed. Another special culture is the development of beekeeping in Namhŭng-ri, Ryongphung-ri, Namsan,ri, Chŏngsong-ri, Wonjin-ri, Unyang-dong and Taean-ri.

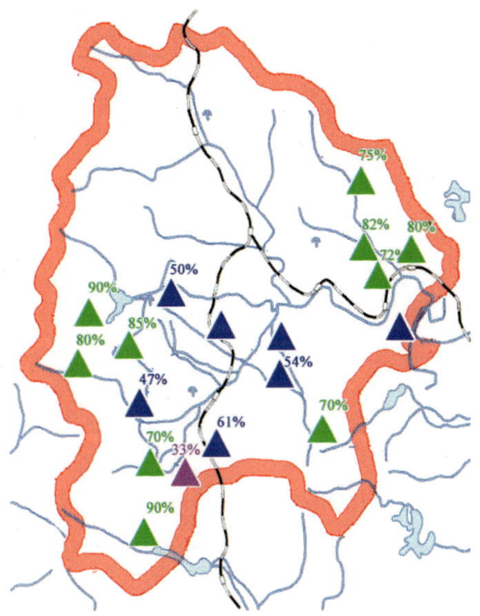

Figure Kusong-II. Forest area in the *ri*

Mechanical Engineering and Textile Industry

In the period of the Japanese occupation the technical craftsmanship of flax and hemp dominated this area (IPA-5 2003, 113). Before 1945 Kusong was also known for its Kusong and Samsŏng Goldmines (Ko Thae-u 1992, 174). Basic industries are the mechanical engineering industry and the textile industry. Therefore, important products are lathes, different drilling machines and suit material. In the regional factories groceries, articles of everyday use, paper, pharmaceuticals, etc. are produced. Widely known are the iron products, for example a lot of iron products like motorised mills, fans, bicycles, as well as school supplies, resin products and wood products.

Table Kusong-III. Ranking (in parenthesis: number of industrial companies or cultural institutions)

Kusong	KOFC	MOU	IPA	KCNA	KIET	Total
Companies-total	26 (4)	25 (6)	20 (7)	26 (2)	25 (16)	25
Companies-important	13 (3)	18 (1)	19 (4)		19 (8)	24 (2)
Cultural institutions			24 (2)			

Table Kusong-IV. Ranking (Total number of companies in relation to population)

Kusong	KOFC	MOU	IPA	KCNA	KIET	Total
Companies – total	27	25	18–14–24	26	24–14	25–24

In all sources Kusong is recognised as a city, which has a small number of companies, in comparison with its population. However, armament industries, which are assumed to be located in Kusong, are not included in the sources.

Table Kusong-V. Specification (in parenthesis: number of companies)

Kusong	Light Industry	Heavy Industry	Mining	Energy
KOFC	12 (1)	5 (3)	–	–
MOU	3 (5)	22 (1)	–	–
IPA	8 (4)	11 (3)	–	–
KCNA	10 (1)	7 (1)	–	–
KIET	5 (8)	14 (8)	–	–

On grounds of these statistics, it is not possible to draw a decision whether the industrial structure of Kusong shows an obvious specialisation on heavy industry or on light industry. However, due to the importance of the Machine Tool Factory and the assumed armament factories on the city grounds, a stronger presence of heavy industry in the city can be proclaimed.

In chapter III.7.3 two important companies were determined for Kanggye. The "3rd April" General Factory (Kusong Machine Tool Factory) in Namsan-dong, Kusong-si (total area of 500.00 m^2, and 5,800 employees) (Yonhap News 2001) is the second largest machine tool factory of North Korea, after the United Machine Tool Factories Huichon. Famous for the production of machine tools of the Kusong series, it was built in 1954 with Hungarian technical assistance in accordance with the 3-Year-Plan between 1954 and 1956 and with the prematurely fulfilled 5-Year-Plan between 1957 and 1960. The first part was finished in 1959 (annual production capacity of approximately 1,000 machines) and therefore advanced to the base of mechanical engineering in the DPRK. In the early days though mostly multifunctional, simple machines were produced, afterwards SV-18, MV-280 and FO-32 lathes and drill press were produced.[35]

The Kusong Textile Factory, in which cotton is produced, was founded in 1951. It is situated in Pangjik-dong. In 1978, a section for dyeing was set up and the factory was expanded with more sectors. With chemical fibres one can produce underwear, socks and other products (IPA 5 2003, 115).

The IPA counts four important factories—other than the above named, they are the Kusong Machine Factory, which is in production since 1985 and produces devices used in mining, and the Kusong Medicine Factory, which specialises itself in natural health supplements and tonics.

Additionally, the existence of armament factories in the north and south of Kusong is assumed.[36]

35 S. IPA-5 (2003, 115-116); KIET (1996, 246-248); KOFC (2010, 252-253).

36 "According to Im Young-sun, a defector from North Korea and former leader of guard platoon in the Military

The most important higher educational institutions of the city are dedicated to the schooling of technical young talents: Kusong Technical University, founded in 1960 and Kusong Machine College, founded in 1956 (IPA-5 2003, 116).

Transportation center in Phyongbuk

Kusong is the transportation center in the heart of Phongbuk. The Phyongbuk railway line between Jongju and Chongsu (Sakju-kun) runs through the urban area. In Jongju the Phyongbuk line encounters the main line to Sinuiju and Pyongyang. It connects the sub centers of Panghyŏng (in the South) and Paekun (in the North) with the center of the city. The railway station Jongju is 41.2 km far from the railway station of Kusong. In the latter station the Phalwŏn line (Kusŏng – Phalwŏn, Nyongbyon-kun) goes off. Roadway connections are available to the *kun* in the proximity, for example Taekwan-kun, Jongju-si, Thaechon-kun, Chonma-kun, Sonchon-kun.

After the elevation to a city in 1967, there is no enlargement of the urban area

Kusong-si emerged in 1967 from Kusong-kun. Kusong-up originated in 1952, and in 1954 two *rodongjagu* were founded (Chahŭng-rodongjagu in the North, Panghyŏn-rodongjagu in the South), and simultaneously the administrative seat of the county (*up*) was enlarged. Kusong-kun was slightly enlarged between 1952 and 1967 (once in 1961). After the city founding, there were no more enlargements.

1967, enlargement of central Kusong; 1976/1984: enlargement of the sub centers

In 1967 the *up* was divided into ten *dong*. At the same time, six new *dong* were constructed from the *ri*, which are located on the fringe of the city center, and two from the North and four from the South of the city.

Construction Bureau of the People's Armed Forces Ministry, North Korea has deployed missiles at a long-range missile base in Paekun-ri [Paegun], Kusong County, North Pyong-an Province, which was completed in 1986" (U.S. Government Printing Office 1997, 12). In Kusong. Paekun-dong exists, which developed from the division of AB Chahŭng, during the urbanisation of Kusong.

Furthermore, Wikimapia lists the „7th Machine Industry Bureau Aircraft Parts Factory," located near the Phanghyŏn Airbase. "This facility is subordinate to the Second Economic Committee and is linked to the Panghyon Airbase. It was completed in 1986 to manufacture parts for MiG-15 and MiG-17. It also completed construction of MiG-29 aircraft from kits. It has primarily produced helicopters and modified the Air Force fleet for missile deliver and communications."

The two *rodongjagu*, which were founded in 1954, remained after the city founding in 1967. In 1974 each *rodongjagu* was converted into a *dong*. Over time, the area was split in two, which occurred in a parallel manner: since 1976 the region of the former *rodongjagu* was divided into two *dong* each, since 1985 into four *dong* each. This suggests that central Kusong has strongly developed up until 1967, and after that the development of the two sub centers was driven forward.

In 1985 the surrounding area of Unyang-ri, which is located near the airbase,[37] was made into a *dong*.

One center and two sub centers

The 25 *dong* of the city can be geographically divided into three groups:

1. the city center, including the industrial area in the middle
2. the Panghyŏn region in the South of the urban area (rice fields and military)
3. the Paekun healing water region in the North of the urban area

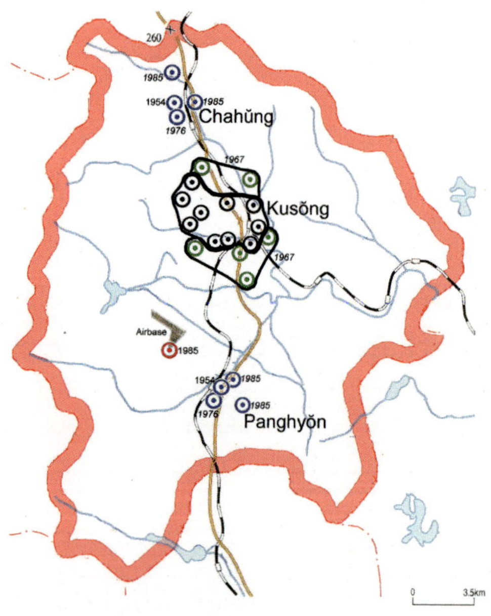

Figure Kusong-III. *Dong*

37 Panghyŏn Airbase was completed in 1986 to manufacture parts for MiG-15 and MiG-17. It also completed construction of MiG-29 aircraft from kits. It has primarily produced helicopters and modified the Air Force fleet for missile deliver and communications."

Statistics

	Dong-Formation	*Dong*-Splitting
1952 (1)	*up*	-
1954 (3)	2 *rodongjagu*	-
1967 (18)	6	(9)
1976 (20)	-	2
1985 (25)	1	4

Kusong – Traffic junction and location of machine construction in the mountainous country of Phyongbuk

Kusong is located in the mountainous region of Phyongbuk on the right bank of Chŏnbang-gang, one of the tributary rivers of Taeryŏng-gang. The city became a traffic junction that is connected to Thaechon and Sakju. It was the collection space for agricultural products of the plains of the surroundings and has developed into a location of mechanical engineering after 1954. Of greater importance is the "3rd April" General Factory (Kusong Machine Tool Factory). Apart from that, Kusong has little industrial companies. In the South of the urban area, though, there is a military airport, near which armament factories are situated.

There is a clear division of development centers within Kusong, namely around the former *up* and the two former *rodongjagu*. After the city founding in 1967 new *dong* only emerged in the years of 1976 and 1985 and only within the regions of the two former *rodongjagu*.

IV.2.6. Jongju

Fortified city during the Joson period

Jongju is an important traffic junction on the way between the capital Pyongyang and the border city of Sinuiju. As a fortified city, Jongju was highly relevant in terms of military strategy. With the highest share of "rural" population among all cities of the DPR Korea, it is the most agriculturally characterized city of the country. Jongju was not designated as a city (*si*) until 1994.

Table Jongju-I. Basic data

Population	189,742 (Rank 21)
Area	480 km² (Rank15)
Population density	395 I./km² (Rank 19)
Administrative units	14 *dong*/18 *ri* (44%) (Rank 25)
"Urban" population/"rural" population	54.1%/45.9% (Rank 27)

During the Joson period, in the middle of the 15th century, a city wall in Jongju was made of soil, and then replaced with stone between 1714 and 1715, which was repeatedly rebuilt and refurbished. The city wall is located south of the Jangtae-san. Towards the West and East, the wall is built on the mountain's ridge and in between lies an almost oval plain. On the southern side of the wall are two gates. The remains of the wall are still maintained (IPA-5 2003, 227).

When an insurgency against the discrimination of the population living in the Phyongan-Province was countered, the insurgents entrenched themselves in the fortified city of Jongju. In 1812, the leader of the rebellion was murdered and the rebellion broke down.

During the Korean War Jongju also played a military strategic role, when Jongju served as a marching-through-area for the South Korean as well as UN troops heading to the North as well as a marching-through-area for Chinese troops on their way southwards. Also nowadays, the army of the DPRK has several emplacements at the sea coast of Jongju.

Famous for rice but also for specialized crops such as chestnuts, fruits, tobacco

Jongju is located in the lowlands on the west coast of the Phyongbuk Province and borders in the northwest on Kusong-si. The city region consists predominantly of flat terrain or downs. The highest elevations are situated at the borders of the municipal area like the Simwŏn-san (566 m) in the East at the border of Kwaksan-kun and the Puldang-san (426 m) in the North at the border of Kusong-si. Between the mouth of the 38 km long Talchhŏn-gang and offshore islands broad areas of land spread out, which was extracted from the sea through impoldering.

For a long time the Talchŏn-gang was popular as a relaxation resort due to its clear water and fine sand (Chosun Ilbo October 23, 1995). The surrounding of the Pongmyŏng-reservoir is also adapted for leisure space. The Pongmyŏng-reservoir (ca. 2 km²) dams the headwater of the Talchŏn-gang, which has its origin at Kilsang-san (in the South of Kusong-si). It is an important source of water in the Yalu-irrigation system. Amongst others, also carp are raised here (IPA-5 2003, 173).

In the North of the municipal area the 38.9 km long Changsuthan-gang rises, which has a drainage area of 145 km². It is dammed in the headwater, which forms the ca. 2 km² big Unjon-reservoir at the eastern border of the municipal area towards Unjon-kun and contributes largely to the raise of the Unjon-terrain.

The forest covers 42% of the municipal area and where oaks as well as pines are strongly represented.

This region is in regards to agriculture one of the most important locations of this province. The arable land is 40% of the municipal area. Important cereals are amongst others rice, corn, and millet, whereas rice accounts for 70% and corn for 25% of the harvested crop amount. Already since the Japanese occupation, rice from the Jongju-terrain is widely known for its delicious taste. In the 70s rich harvest still could be reaped, however due to soil acidification and scarcity of fertilizer, the cereal amount shows gradually a negative trend line. Fruits that are mainly raised in Jongju are apples, pears, peaches, and plums. So-called Jongju-royal-chestnuts, which can also be found in Kwaksan-kun and Sonchon-kun, are still well known. Everywhere in the city chestnut trees are to be seen and in the summer, the unique smell of chestnut flowers stings one's nose. Tobacco is also raised, although there is no tobacco factory in Jongju. The harvested leafs are amongst others processed further in factories in Sonchon and Ryongsong. Recently, in order to attain currency, silkworm cocoons and peppermint are also raised in Jongju (Chosun Ilbo October 23, 1995).

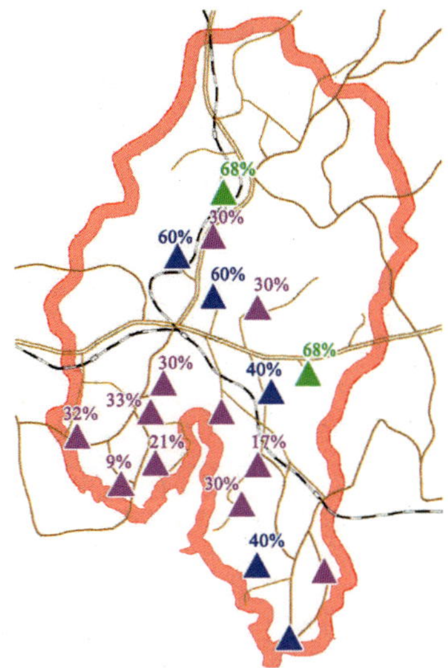

Figure Jongju-I. Forest area in the *ri*

Table Jongju-II. Climate values

Annual average	January temperature	August temperature	Precipitation
9.6℃ (13)	−6.6℃ (15)	23.8℃ (12)	1,127.2 mm (7)

On the Ae-do island, which is more than 10 km away from Ilhae-ri at the southern coast of the municipal area, as well as at the sea coast fisheries are operated on a small scale. Approximately 3,000 people live on Ae-do (Chosun Ilbo October 23, 1995). On Ae-do there can be found the Jongju Fishery Station, which was founded in 1961, is located. Other than fishery, seashells are cultivated here and there are also other facilities where seafood is manufactured (IPA-5 2003, 175).

One specialty of the city is piglets from the northern Ryongpho.

Phyongbuk Smeltery and numerous factories relevant to agriculture

Important industrial sectors of this city are amongst others metalworking, machine engineering (especially manufacturing and reparation of agricultural vehicles and machines) as well as the food, textile, chemical, and pharmaceutical industries. Conserved fruits and other further processed fruit products are regarded as specialty of the city (IPA-5 2003, 74).

Table Jongju-III. Ranking (in parenthesis: total number of companies or cultural institutions)

Jongju	KOFC	MOU	IPA	KCNA	KIET	Summary
Companies-total	25 (5)	23 (9)	20 (7)	22 (4)	21 (20)	24
Companies-important	23 (1)	26 (0)	14 (6)		24 (5)	18 (5)
Cultural institutions			20 (3)			

Table Jongju-IV. Ranking (Total number of companies in relation to population)

Jongju	KOFC	MOU	IPA	KCNA	KIET	Summary
Companies-total	25	22	17-7-19	22	20-24	24-15

Jongju has fewer companies than it could have been expected in regards to its population. However, this is not surprising due to the agricultural orientation of the city. Comparatively high, though, is the number of important companies.

Table Jongju-V. Specification (in parenthesis: total number of companies)

Jongju	Light Industry	Heavy Industry	Mining	Energy
KOFC	-	1 (5)	-	-
MOU	21 (4)	4 (4)	10 (1)	-
IPA	25 (1)	1 (6)	-	-
KCNA	19 (1)	3 (3)	-	-
KIET	5 (10)	14 (10)	-	-

Almost every source implies for this city a distinct specialization towards heavy industry.

In chapter III.7.3. five companies are regarded as important for this city: Phyongbuk Smeltery, October 30 Factory "October 30" (Jongju Bearing Factory), Jongju Tractor Accessory Factory, Jongju Microelement Perphosphoric Acid Lime Fertilizer Factory and the Jongju Export Garment Factory.

The Phyongbuk Smeltery is of great importance for the foreign exchange revenue of North Korea (Chosun Ilbo October 23, 1995). Mainly gold, silver, and copper are smelted (KOFC 2010, 242), but also phosphate fertilizer etc. is produced here. The smeltery is located 800 m southeast of the train station in Wŏlyang-ri at the riverside of Talchŏn-gang. In total 2,300 people are employed there (KOFC 2010, 238). The total area size is about 264,000 m^2 (KOFC 2010, 238) or 388,400 m^2 (IPA-5 2003, 175). The construction work started in August 1979. In 1983 the first stage was completed and so it went into operation, in 1991 another part of the smeltery was finished. In 2009 in some parts of the building restoration and renovation work was carried out. The smeltery benefits from the favorable transport-geographical position of Jongju, since the railway line from Pyongyang to Sinuiju and the Phyongbuk-line as well as the road from Kaesong to Sinuiju pass through the city. The smeltery is connected to the rail network with a branch terminal line. The smeltery obtains electrical energy out of the Chŏngchŏngang Thermal Power Plant (Pakchon-kun). The raw materials that are to be processed are most commonly brought from nearby (KOFC 2010, 239).

The factory "October 30" (Jongju bearing factory), which was set into operation in 1979 is also of importance.

Many companies in Jongju are related to agriculture. For example, the Jongju Tractor Accessory Factory, which produces not only tractor accessories but also many other machines that are used in agriculture. The total area of the factory amounts to 116,000 m^2 (KOFC 2010, 264). In Jongju there are also other factories that produce or repair farm machineries. In the Jongju Microelement Perphosphoric Acid Lime Fertilizer Factory mainly phosphate fertilizer is produced.

The Jongju Export Garment Factory has a total area of 11,500 m^2 and is in production since 1993. On orders from foreign countries, various garments are manufactured here. Amongst others, those articles are exported to Southeast Asia, Germany, Austria, and many other countries (IPA-5 2003, 175).

Apples, pears, peaches, and plums that are harvested in Jongju are mainly processed to tins in fruit processing factories. Those factories are completely financed by the group of overseas Koreans in Japan. However, it is said that since sugar is missing in recent times, many products are spoiled (Chosun Ilbo October 23, 1995).

The Factory No. 25 mainly produces vaccines against hemorrhagic fever (yellow fever) and paratyphoid fever (KOFC 2010, 389).

Other than that, one of four big deposits of rare-earth that exist in DPR Korea is in Jongju. It is located in the North of the municipal area close to Kohyŏn-dong. Already in 1961 it was discovered, but until now only small amounts of zirconium were mined. Rare-earth is not yet promoted (Nam Mun-hŭi 2012).

Traffic center at the northern Yellow sea coast

Jongju is located 105 km away from the provincial capital Sinuiju and has developed to a transport interchange in the place where the Phyongbuk-line, which has been opened in 1939 and connects Jongju to Chŏngsu (Sakju-kun), branches off from the main rail line towards Sinuiju and Pyongyang. The road, which connects Sinuiju and Pyongyang, goes through the municipal area. Northwards goes a road to Kusong-si, a turnoff goes to Taechŏn-kun. This state road towards Kusong, which is not tarred, goes over the dike of Talchŏn-gang over Taekwan-kun and Sakju-kun and further to Sakju-kun, which is located at the riverside of the Yalu.

In the South there is maritime traffic among others towards Cholsan-peninsula and Sinmi island (Sonchon-kun).

Jongju Youth Gymnasium – a landmark of the city

The Jongju Youth Gymnasium was opened in 1986, has a total area of 7,450 m² and has three floors. In the first and second floor are the spectator seats, which can hold 3,500 persons. For travelers, it is sort of a landmark of the city Jongju, because it is clearly visible from a train.

Figure Jongju–II. Youth Gymnasium (2006)

Figure Jongju–III. Building of a house (2006)

Figure Jongju–IV. Region west of the train station (2012)

Figure Jongju-V. Region east of the train station (2012)

Home of pioneers – from writers to cult founders

Traditionally, Jongju is considered home of many scholars. During the Joson period the number of people from this city, who passed the state exam, was especially high. Before 1945 Jongju was regarded as "city of pioneers" or "city of personalities," since various leaders of different fields came from this city. Its position between China and Seoul was a reason why this region came relatively early into contact with Christianity. In particular due to the influence of the Christian Osan-school, which was founded in 1907, Jongju was considered to be a region of high education and sophisticated mentality. People born in Jongju or Osan Elementary School-attendees were among others writers such as Yi Kwang-su (1892-1950) and Kim So-wŏl (1902-1934). Also the painter Yi Jungsŏp (1916-1956) and the philosopher Ham Sŏk-hŏn (1901-1989), who was considered as "the Korean Ghandi," attended the Osan Elementary School.

As a 14-year-old the founder of the Unification Church, Moon Sun Myung (1920-2012), attended the Osan Elementary School for one year. Moon was born in 1920 in Jongju as the fifth child of eight. Later, Moon visited DPR Korea and was welcomed by Kim Il-sung in 1991. After that, Moon acquired two big hotels in the capital Pyongjang. Furthermore, the government gave its consent to the Unification Church to build a pilgrimage site in Jongju. Where the Osan Elementary School once was located as well as in Sŏju-dong, there are secondary educational institutions with focus on agricultural disciplines (Chosun Ilbo October 23, 1995; IPA-5 2003, 176).

Internal structure such as the one in a rural county

In 1952 the then Jongju-kun was narrowed by splitting off a part in the West in order to rebuild the Kwaksan-kun. In the East a part was split off to found the Unjon-kun. The

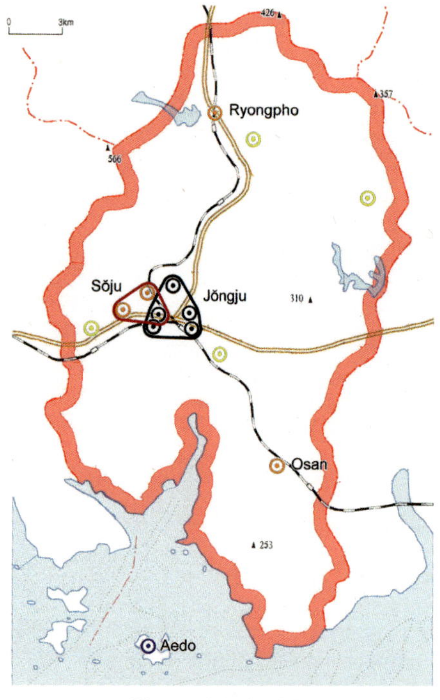

Figure Jongju-VI.

remaining Jongju-kun was designated as city in August 1994.

When Jongju-kun was appointed to a city in 1994, next to the administration center, four *rodongjagu* exist. The oldest of them was the Aedo-rodongjagu which was founded in 1953 on the same-named island. Approximately 3,000 people there live off fishing. The other three *rodongjagu* were built in 1992. Due to the location of the *rodongjagu* and the former *up*, three development poles are identifiable within the municipal area:

1. Center (former up and Sŏju)

The city is dominated by a center, which is located where the former administrative center of the county and the former *rodongjagu* Sŏju has been situated. Within and around the center of rural Jongju the most important industries of the city are localized.

2. Ryonghpo

The northern part is with the former laborers' district Ryongpho, which is locate to the East of Pongmyŏng-reservoir, which is the second development pole of the city. In the Ryongpho region and neighboring Kohyŏn deposits of rare-earth and other natural resources are located. The breeding of piglets in Ryongho has a good reputation.

3. Osan

The third development pole is Osan-dong, which is located in the South of the city with its fruit plants. Osan is known for the Christian Osan Elementary School founded in 1909, which was attended by many prominent Koreans. Today, it is an agricultural college.

At the same time as of the city founding in 1994, *up* and *rodongjagu* were divided into different *dong*. Further four *dong* emerged due to the conversion of *ri*. In the Southwest of the city center, Sangdang-dong and southeastern Sinchŏn-dong were founded. Kohyŏn-dong is located in the East of Ryŏngpho and Oryong-dong at the eastern border also in the North of the municipal area.

Jŏngju (1994) 14 *dong*

	Dong-Formation	*Dong*-Splitting
1952 (1)	*up*	
1953 (2)	1 *rodongjagu*	
1992 (5)	3 *rodongjagu*	
1994 (14)	4	(5)

Jongju – Agricultural center at the coastal flatland

Jongju is a small rural town in the flatland of the Yellow Sea coast. An important factor for the city growth is its beneficial position in terms of traffic between central Korea and the crossing to China in the northwestern part of the peninsula. Jongju has historic importance because of the city fortification and the Christian Osan Elementary School. The most important industry is the Phyongbuk Smeltery, whose construction work started in 1979.

IV.2.7. Phyongsong

Established as a city of science

Phyongsong is a new town located north of the capital Pyongyang and is the administrative center of the Phyongnam Province. Phyongsong was founded as a city of science in the 1960s. However, in 1995 the southern part of the city, in which *inter alia* the Academy of Natural Sciences is situated, became part of Pyongyang. Phyongsong remained as the center of education for young professionals of various sectors in the region, however it also evolved more and more into a place for wholesale marketing of imported goods from China. Yet in the course of economic policies in 2009, the wholesale market of Phyongsong was also closed.

Table Phyongsong-I. Basic data

Population	284,386 (Rank 12)
Area	381 km² (Rank 17)
Population density	746,4 I./km² (Rank 11)
Administrative units	21 *dong*/13 *ri* (62%) (Rank 17)
"Urban" population/"rural" population	83.2%/16.8% (Rank 13)

In all the categories of the above table, Phyongsong takes a middle position among the 27 cities in the DPRK (between rank 11 and rank 17).

It is stated that Phyongsong was founded in the 1960s as a city of science. Since it is reported that Kim Il-sung gave instructions to look for a suitable site for a science city near Pyongyang in 1960. Eventually, Kim Il-sung himself declared the area as suitable when he walked around Sain-ri, in Sunchon city in October 1964. He has also arranged the incorporation of surrounding areas for the foundation of a new city, which he then even appointed as a provincial capital. It is said that the name of "Phyongsong" was personally given by Kim Il-sung (Chosun Ilbo January 8, 1996). Phyongsong means "fortress guarding the capital Pyongyang" and consists of the first two syllables of the words Pyongyang (平壤) and Sŏngsae (城塞) (Fortress) (IPA 3 2003, 48).

After the Academy of Sciences was founded, many research institutes have been established under the auspices of the College of Natural Sciences and Phyongsong gradually began to adopt characteristics of a scientific research city. The main research and teaching institutions, such as the Academy of Natural Sciences, and Natural Sciences University, were located in a special science district in the south of Phyongsong. Between this district and the rest of the city a significant social gap developed. While the residents of the science district enjoyed a standard of living such as the population of Pyongyang did, the remaining residents suffered under a standard of living, which was common to other provincial cities of North Korea (Chosun Ilbo January 8, 1996). In 1995 a separation of both parts of the city was carried out and the southern part now forms the Unjong-kuyok of Pyongyang.

Hilly land east of the Taedong-gang

Phyongsong is located in the basin of the Taedong-gang (according to the classification of landscapes by Lautensach 1945) in the hilly land of Phyongan-namdo (Kang Sŏk-o 1984) or at the threshold between the northwestern coastal district and the North Korean mountain district (Saitschikow 1956). In the municipal area, low to moderate topographic highs are usually achieved. More than half of the municipal area lies at an altitude of 100 to 200 m above sea level.

Located in the west of the city is the Chŏngryŏng-san, as part of the Chŏngryŏng mountain range, with its height of 547m as the highest elevation. In the southeastern area of the city Phyongsong subsides more and more. Overall, about 53% of the total area of the city is declared as mountains and forests. The most important plains in Phyongsong are the Kangdong plain and the Chasan plain. The former is crossed by the Taedong-gang, which in turn forms the eastern border of the city. The Chasan plain extends to the northern boundary of the area of Phyongsong and is traversed by tributary rivers of the Taedong-gang. Northwest of this plain is the Taebongsan water reservoir, the largest in the municipal area. Popular as a place of excursions for the inhabitants of Phyongsong is the water reservoir in the southwest of the urban area in Sangcha-dong.

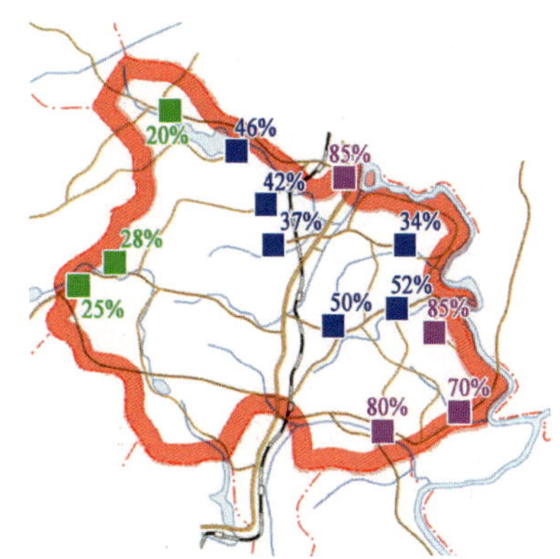

Figure Phyongsong-I. Agricultural land in the *ri*

The agriculture of Phyongsong is of major importance as well. Especially the cultivation of fruits such as apples, pears and peaches was promoted lately. 28% of the total area of Phyongsong mainly serves as fields for rice, corn and soybeans. Other important vegetables in the region are radish, Chinese cabbage and spinach. A flagship business is the Paeksong co-op farm, in which sometimes even foreign ambassadors "assist" (KCNA 4.6.2005).

Table Phyongsong-II. Climate data

Annual average	January temperature	August temperature	Precipitation
9.7°C (10)	−6.6°C (14)	23.9°C (9)	1,091 mm (8)

Light industry and military vehicles

The main industries of the city are the light industry and the automotive engineering industry. In terms of light industry, the production of daily goods plays a predominant role. There are bigger factories for the production of synthetic leather, rubber bands and watches located in the city. On a regional basis, in addition to daily goods, gemstones are processed. The vehicle engineering industry is also significant, since numerous kinds of cars are produced. Furthermore, textiles and foodstuff are produced in the city, which are not only sold nationwide but are even exported (PSC-8 2009, 396).

Table Phyongsong-III. Ranking (in parenthesis: number of industrial companies or cultural institutions)

Phyongsong	KOFC	MOU	IPA	KCNA	KIET	Summary
Companies-Total	23 (7)	15 (19)	13 (16)	21 (5)	22 (19)	19
Companies-Important	25 (1)	27 (0)	17 (5)		16 (10)	22 (4)
Cultural institutions			12 (11)			

Table Phyongsong-IV. Ranking (Total number of companies in relation to population)

Phyongsong	KOFC	MOU	IPA	KCNA	KIET	Summary
Companies – Total	24	18	10–17–9	24	26–20	23–23

The number of industrial companies is lower than one would expect in relation to population.

Table Phyongsong-V. Specification (in parenthesis: number of industrial companies)

Phyongsong	Light Industry	Heavy Industry	Mining	Energy
KOFC	19 (1)	3 (6)	–	–
MOU	1 (18)	27 (1)	–	–
IPA	3 (12)	22 (4)	–	–
KCNA	1 (5)	–	–	–
KIET	13 (8)	12 (10)	–	4 (1)

Phyongsong is clearly specialized in light industry. When the KOFC and KIET sources convey a different picture, this is due to the fact that industries that produce commodities such as watches have been filed in these sources in the section of machine construction and thus formally are assigned to heavy industry.

In chapter III.7.3. four important companies have been identified for Phyongsong: The Phyongsong rubber band factory, the Phyongsong factory for agricultural machines, the Moranbong watch factory and the Phyongsong factory for synthetic leather goods. The main factory in Phyongsong however is the Phyongsong automobile factory (Factory March 16). This factory is being distinguished between a "new factory" and an "old factory" and is located in Kuwŏl-dong.[38] 2.7 km northeast of the factory is the train station Ponghak. East of the factory there is a paved road leading to Pyongyang and Sunchon. An area of 248,000 m^2 belongs to the factory and approximately 7,000 to 8,000 workers are employed there. In 1974, the factory was expanded. The military jeeps Kaengsaeng 69 and Kaengsaeng 69 Na as well as Thaebaeksan trucks are produced here. The construction of 6-ton and 10-ton trucks were reported for 1999 and 2004. Armored cars are also produced here. The main suppliers for the automotive factory in terms of iron products are, the huts

38 According to the Chosun Ilbo of 8.1.1996: the factory is presented as an automobile plant of Thaebaeksan, located in Paesan-dong. If this was correct, this factory would then no longer be located in the urban area of Phyongsong, due to the separation of Paesan-dong to Pyongyang in 1995. In the IPA this factory neither is found in the volume of Phyongyang (chapter Unjong-kuyok) nor in the presentation of the city of Phyongsong. However in the PSC-8 (2009, 396) vehicle manufacturing is recorded in the description of Phyongsong.

of Kimchaek and Songjin, and in terms of nonferrous metal products the metallurgical factory Puryong (kdb 2005b, 205-206) is mentioned. There is evidence that there is also a "Taebaeksan 96" truck assembling plant in Phyongsong since 2007, which was built by the Russian automobile manufacturer KamAZ (NKEW 2008).

According to Chosun Ilbo (January 8, 1996), apart from the Moranbong watch factory, mainly local factories of smaller size exist in Phyongsong. The Moranbong-watch factory was built in the mid-70s (completed in 1978) with plant parts entirely imported from Switzerland, producing watches with mainsprings and also semi-automatic watches (Chosun Ilbo 8.1.1996). This factory employs about 600 people; the annual productivity is 400,000 watches (kdb 2005b, 129).

Training center for professionals in the region

Although the important research and teaching institutions, for which Phyongsong was famous for, are located in Pyongyang now due to territorial reforms, there are still a number of relevant institutions, in particular in the scientific and technical field, left in the city of Phyongsong.

The National Mineral Resources Survey Team is a research institute, which specially engages in the study of mineral deposits. It was built in January 1955 and is according to IPA considered as one of the most important companies of the city. Among important institutions in the field of research and teaching, the city offers next to the Research Institute for Technical Microbiology following universities, the following as well:

- Phyongsong Technical University
- Phyongsong Teacher training College
- Phyongsong School of hard coal mining
- Phyongsong University of Veterinary and Livestock
- Phyongsong Medical University (IPA-3 2003, 53-55)
- Phyongsong University of Arts (KCNA 11.12. 2009)
- Phyongsong College of Education

The provincial capital Phyongsong is considered as a training city for professionals from the entire region, starting from doctors and teachers in the mountain villages in Yangdok and Maengsang to technicians in the large factories of Kaechon and Sunchon (Kŭmsu-kangsan 2002, 36).

In the north of the city, the revolutionary memorial of Paeksong in Paeksong-ri is located. The Kim Il-Sung University was temporarily moved during the Korean War from March 1952 to that location. The site is a destination for locals and occasionally also for foreigners (KCNA April 23, 2002). In 2008, a martyr cemetery was completed in Phyongsong, where anti-Japanese fighters, "working class heroes," local party officials and functionaries are buried (KCNA December 30, 2008). In Phyongsong there is also a newly built stadium where mass gymnastics are demonstrated (KCNA October 20, 2005).

An important cultural and historical site in Phyongsong is the Buddhist temple Anguk-sa in Ponghak-dong, on Pongnin Mountain, in the central west of the municipal area. It was originally founded in 503 at the time of the Koryo dynasty, and rebuilt in 1419 and again in 1785. Most of the surviving buildings date back to the time of the last reconstruction.

Phyongsong as handling site for Chinese goods

With increasing trade activities between North Korea and China, Phyongsong developed into a new handling site for goods of all kinds, which mainly find their way into the country through Sinuiju. An important market for imported goods is the capital Pyongyang. However, in order to have access to the capital, a special travel permit is required, so that many traders are only able to reach Phyongsong, where they resell their goods. However, the trade with other regions of North Korea was often accomplished via Phyongsong as well. Traders from the southern Sariwon, Haeju and Nampho often came to Phyongsong to stock up their goods. It is also technically efficient to transport goods across Phyongsong in the East Sea Cities of Wonsan and Hamhung instead of bringing them directly to the east coast from Sinuiju (Kim, Min Se 2007). Initially the North Korean government had actively supported this market in order to improve the situation of supply in the country. Allegedly, the market of Phyongsong had 30,000 - 40,000 stalls (Korea Herald September 21, 2009).

In connection with the currency reform of 2009, it became public that the central market in Phyongsong, which had factually functioned as a wholesale market, had been closed down. The success of the major markets had probably consequences for the government, which the government assumedly saw as a threat or negative influence. The government feared capitalistic influence and the growing power of the operators of the markets. Thus, the wholesale market in Phyongsong was closed; and supposedly two smaller markets were built in the neighborhood (Korea Herald September 21, 2009). The way and manner of how the market activities in this city develop is considered as a barometer of how far the North Korean authorities generally allow market activities (Pak In-ho 2010).

Development of the city of Phyongsong and changes in the urban area

The foundation of Phyongsong proceeded in two stages. In January 1965, initially Phyongsong-kun was formed and in December 1969, the appointment to a city followed. Phyongsong-kun was formed of parts of Sunchon-kun (three *ri*), the Pyongyang-si (parts of one *dong* and one *ri*) and the Sunan-kun (one *ri*).

Between 1967 and 1974, the area of Phyongsong-kun or respectively Phyongsong-si was extended. Starting with the splitting of the science district in 1995, Phyongsong had to cede territory to the capital Pyongyang in the mid-1990s. In the 1960s and 1970s Phyongsong was enlarged three times by a total of 14 *ri* - of them 12 *ri* from Sunchon-kun:

- 1967: four *ri* from Sunchon-kun, and two *ri* from Kangdong-kun,
- 1972: two *ri* from Sunchŏn-kun and
- 1974: again six *ri* from Sunchŏn-kun were added.

To a great extent, Phyongsong can be seen as having emerged from the county of Sunchon.

In 1995, the science district in the south of Phyongsong split off from Phyongsong, together with the Academy of Natural Sciences and the Natural Sciences Academy, when two *dong* (Toksan-dong and Paesan-dong) and parts of two other *dong* of Phyongsong formed the new Unjong-kuyok (the "district of benevolent affection") of the capital Pyongyang.

Afterwards the area of Phyongsong was further reduced, even though not as significant as in 1995:

- In 1999 one *ri* (Kyŏngsin-ri) was added to Kangdong-kun (Pyongyang-si) and
- In 2000, a part of a *dong* (Songryŏng-dong) was added to Unjong-kuyok (IPA 1 2003, 37).

Figure–Phyongsong II shows the outline of the present Phyongsong-si; the small map (on the right) added the boundary lines of Unjong-kuyok (Pyongyangsi), which was part of Phyongsong until 1995, and also the boundary lines of the Kyŏngsin-ri, which was part of Phyongsong until 1999. The smaller map thus shows the outline of Phyongsong between 1974 and 1995. The larger map shows the current *ri* and *dong* (2002). Units that are located in areas that were incorporated after the founding of Phyongsong-kun are characterized by the year of incorporation.

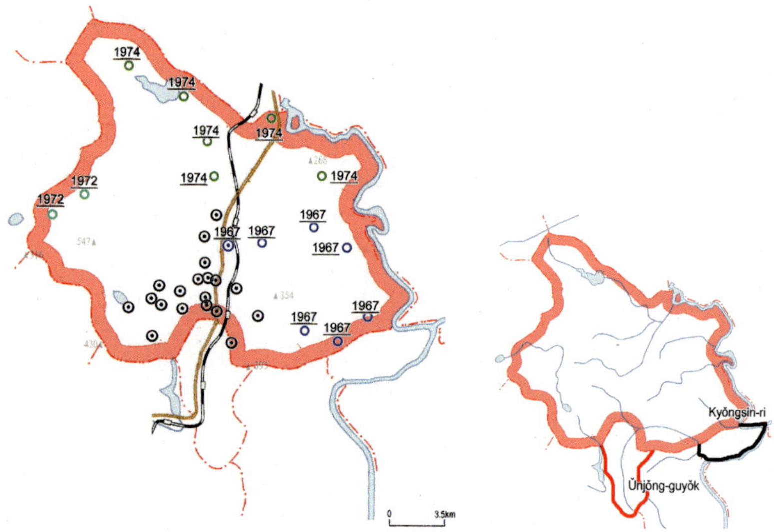

Figure Phyongsong-II. Incorporations

The city center of Phyongsong is located in the old Sain-ri of the Sunchon-kun, and extends to the west from the train station of Phyongsong, directly in the north of the capital Pyongyang.

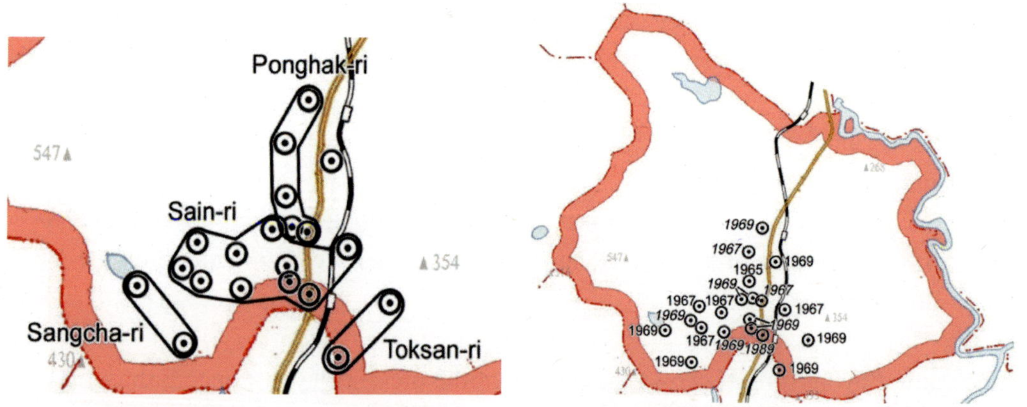

Figure Phyongsong-III. Representation of the *dong* that derive from the same *ri*

Figure Phyongsong-IV. Origin of *dong*

19 of the 20 *dong* of Phyongsong have already been created in the 1960s. Only Yŏkjŏn-dong ("the district before the station"), which had been split off in 1989 from Jungdŏk-dong, was formed later, which suggests that Phyongsong grew especially in the area around the railway station.

Two settlement guidelines

The urbanized area of Phyongsong is largely situated in the southwest of the city, following two guidelines:

The valley of the Phyongsong-chŏn, which runs from the train station towards the West. Along the banks of the Phyongsong-chŏn, there are residential towers and public buildings located. A special feature of Phyongsong is that the city along the Phyongsong-chŏn has developed between the mountain ranges as an elongated strip (Kŭmsu-kangsan 2002, 36).

The railway and highway, which run from Phyongyang towards Sunchon in a northern direction, including the western valleys. The main road runs, coming from Pyongyang, towards an impressive three-part complex of buildings, leading into a road coming from the Phyongsang Station, which then passes the Kim Jong-suk Middle School No. 1 and the Phyongsong Synthetic Leather Factory in the direction of Ponghak.

Although, no side roads derive from the route between Phyongsong station and Rason, the railway station forecourt is relatively large. Since the entry permit to Pyongyang is controlled at Phyongsong station, many people have to get off here. At the train station of Phyongsong some kind of customs office has therefore developed. While in the east of the station fields are located, in the West a 5 km long line of houses have developed in the valley of Phyongsong-chŏn. The Pyongyang train station is 42.5 km far from Phyongsong station. 6.3 km south of the station Phyongsong a second station exists in the city, the Ponghak Station.

Statistics

Phyongsong consists, according to IPA-3 in 2002, of 20 *dong*[39] *and 13 ri*. Ten of the *dong* originated from the fact that a *ri* was appointed to a *dong*. The remaining ten *dong* originated from the fact that existing *dong* had been divided.[40]

	Dong-Formation	*Dong*-Splitting
1965 (1)	1	-
1967 (7)	4	2
1969 (19)	5	7
1989 (20)	-	1

39 According to the PSC-8 (2009, 395) the number of *dong* became larger with 21, but the number of the 13 *ri* remains the same.

40 Sometimes there are mixed forms. In the below statistics spitted *dong* are treated, which have emerged in the same year only of one or more *ri*, as if *ri* have been appointed to *dong*.

Phyongsong – Provincial capital with educational institutions and little industry

Phyongsong is a satellite city of Pyongyang with its numerous educational institutions. As the capital of the Phyongnam Province, the city provides numerous administrative institutions. Therefore, this city shows, in relation to other North Korean cities with a similar population, less industrial companies. However, there are a number of light industry companies and one large car factory. After the appointment as a city, there are hardly any growth impulses that can be recognized through *dong*-analysis. The development of market activities in Phyongsong is considered as indicator for the opening of the North Korean economy to market economy activities.

IV.2.8. Anju

A city with a long tradition as an administrative and military center

Anju is a city with a long tradition on the lower reaches of the Chŏngchŏn-gang, one of the four major rivers of North Korea. It is located at an old road for delegations that has exceeded the river. Originally the craft of Anju was based on the processing of agricultural products. In the 1970s, Anju became an industrial location due to the construction of a large chemical company. In 1987, Anju became a city (*si*).

Due to the population as well as the area size, Anju is ranked in the middle between the 27 cities of the DPR Korea. Numerous *ri* testify that large areas of the city have a rural character.

Table Anju–I. Basic data

Population	240,117 (Rank 15)
Area	433 km² (Rank 16)
Population density	555 I./km² (Rank 14)
Administrative divisions	21 *dong*/22 *ri* (49%) (Rank 22)
"Urban" population/"rural" population	69.8%/30.2% (Rank 23)

Anju is a walled town, which developed on the road from the South towards Uiju, and also developed into an important market town. The fact that Anju was of great administrative and military importance at the beginning of the Joson period and as well as in the Koryo period, is evidenced by the fact that the name of the Phyongan Province is composed of the initial syllables of the cities Pyongyang and Anju. The city walls of Anju consist of three parts, the inner wall, the outer wall and the new wall. The inner wall was built in the Koguryo period, the outer wall at the beginning of the Joson time and the new wall in the 17th century.

The inner wall, which was constructed during the Koguryo period, was built west of the Kadu-san, and the Chŏngchŏn-gang in the North serves as a natural moat and it is located on the high bank of the river. The wall has an oval shape and a diameter of 2,280 m. The wall uses mountain ridges, high banks of the river and hills of the plateau. Remnants of the wall have been preserved. The Paeksang pavilion is located northwest of the wall. It was first built in the Koryo period. When the city wall was completed in the Joson period, the Paeksang pavilion was reerected. During the Korean War it was destroyed by the air raid of the U.S. Air Force and rebuilt in 1977 (Kondŭre Mandŭre 2005; IPA 3 2003, 289-290). Another tourist attraction is the Chilsŏng Park with its lake and the seven artificial islands, symbolizing the zodiac sign of the Great Bear. On one of these islands is the Chilsŏng Pavilion (Jong, Song Il 2011, 126).

Flood endangered downtown

The urban area can be roughly divided into two physical regions. On the one hand, in the north and northwest of the city, the flat land is located in the valley of the Chŏngchŏn-gang and in the West are the Western Korean Coast Lowlands. This location, in the flat country, and the closeness of the city center to the Chŏngchŏn-gang signify a special flood hazard for the city.

However, the south of the urban area is occupied by highland, which is a part of the Myohyang mountain range. With 534 m, the Madu-san is the highest elevation within the municipal area. Additional to the Chŏngchŏn-gang, which flows through the north of the city, the backed-up Yŏnphung-ho on the border to Kaechon is an important source for the water supply of Anju. It is also promoted as a tourist attraction by the name of "sea in mountain" (Jong, Song Il 2011, 125).

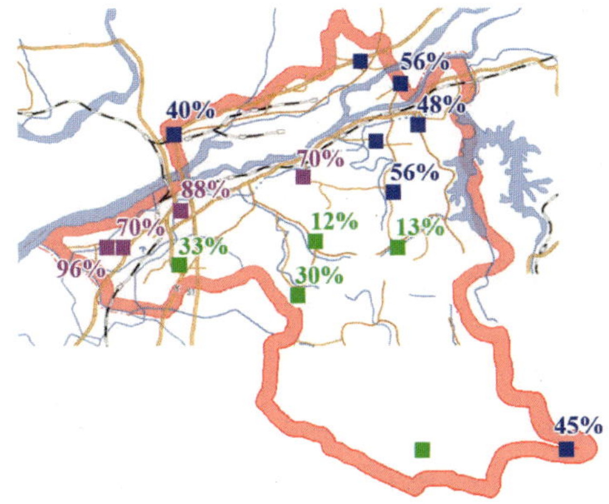

Figure Anju-I. Agricultural land in the *ri*

Table Anju-II. Climate values

Annual average	January temperature	August temperature	Precipitation
9.4℃ (15)	-7.3℃ (18)	23.8℃ (11)	1.013 mm (11)

The agriculture of Anju primarily focuses on the production of grain, which mostly is rice and corn. Yet, in order to supply the urban population, the production of vegetables (Chinese cabbage, radish, spinach, and cucumber), fruits (pears, apples, peaches, grapes) and meat is brought forward as well. Pigs, ducks and chicken are kept in intensive livestock farms. The seat of the authority, which is responsible for the irrigation systems within the Phyongnam Province, is located in Anju. It was installed in 1956 (IPA-3 2003, 287).

Development into an industrial city after the construction of the Namhŭng Youth Chemical Complex in the 1970s

Until the liberation from the Japanese occupation, there were exclusively weaving mills and breweries in this region. In the mid 1970s, Anju developed into a "new industrial city." The main industries of Anju are the chemical industry, as well as the power generation and mechanical engineering industries. A special feature of the industrial structure is the 94% high proportion of the total industrial production of large companies that are financed from the state budget. IPA-3 (2003, 286) mentions here the Namhŭng Youth Chemical Complex, the Chŏngchŏngang Thermal Power Plant, the Anju Telecommunication Machine Factory, the September 28 Machine Factory, the Anju Tractor Accessory Factory, the Anju Silicate Brick Factory, the Silk Factory Anju, the Anju Export Garnment Factory and the Ryongwŏn Mine.

Furthermore, there are also companies in the city that are funded by the municipal city, which mainly produce textiles, daily goods, food, medicine and furs.

This city is surrounded by major coal mines. Within the urban area, there are mines of iron, lead, graphite and limestone.

Table Anju-III. Ranking (in parenthesis: number of industrial companies or cultural institutions)

Anju	KOFC	MOU	IPA	KCNA	KIET	Summary
Ranks	14 (13)	16 (17)	11 (17)	15 (9)	12 (32)	16
Important	11 (4)	14 (2)	11 (7)		10 (14)	11 (8)
Culture			22 (3)			

Table Anju-IV. Ranking (Total number of companies in relation to population)

Anju	KOFC	MOU	IPA	KCNA	KIET	Summary
Ranks	11	15	7-10-22	9	10-6	11-5

The ranking of the number of companies is similar to the ranking of the population. However, Anju achieved a higher ranking in the number of important companies, which is reflected by the high number of state-funded large-scale companies.

Table Anju-V. Specification (in parenthesis: number of industrial companies)

Anju	Light Industry	Heavy Industry	Mining	Energy
KOFC	14 (3)	15 (8)	9 (1)	8 (1)
MOU	9 (11)	11 (5)	–	5 (1)
IPA	16 (7)	13 (7)	8 (2)	8 (1)
KCNA	17 (3)	11 (4)	–	4 (2)
KIET	11 (14)	22 (13)	11 (2)	2 (3)

A significant specialization on heavy or light industry cannot be ascertained. Both areas are represented in Anju with several important companies.

In chapter III.7.3. eight companies were identified as important for Anju: Namhŭng Youth Chemical Complex, Anju Anillon Spinning Mill, Anju Silicate Brick Factory, September 28 Machine Factory (former Anju Trailed Farm Machine Factory), Anju Telecommunication Machine Factory, Anju Silk Factory, Factory No. 121 (Anju Paper Factory), Chŏngchŏngang Thermal Power Plant.

The Namhŭng Youth Chemical Complex is one of the most important petrochemical factories in the western region of North Korea. 1974, the year of the commencement of the Chemical Combine Namhŭng, is considered as the hour of birth of Anju as an industrial city. In 1976, they already began with the production. At the company, which is located in Namhŭng-dong, various chemicals such as urea fertilizer, polyethylene, acrylonitrile and polypropylene are produced. In this company even a Technical University exists, which is used for the training of technicians in the chemical field. It was built in August 1976. Also the Anju Anilon Spinning Mill is assigned to the Namhŭng Youth Chemical Complex and operates since October 1987. Primarily staple fibers are produced there (IPA-3, 2003, 284-285). When the Anilon Spinning Mill was built, professionals from the GDR were employed, and the machines came from the VEB Textima project Karl-Marx-Stadt. The oil, which was processed in Anju, came from the Soviet Union and China. In the combine 10,000 people were employed. For these people and for the workers in the coal mines in the neighborhood, new homes were built (Becker 1988, 48-49).

The Anju Silicate Brick Factory is in operation since 1986. The area size of the property is 300,000 m² (IPA-3 2003, 285). At the September 28 Machine Factory, a wide range of pumps for mining, irrigation of fields, for the use in factories or on building lots are produced (IPA-3 2003, 284). The Anju Silk Factory is located in Namhŭng-dong and mainly produces artificial silk and pure silk. Also silk scarves and ties for men are produced (IPA-3 2003, 284). The Factory No. 121 was established in 1980. Here, pulp as well as various paper products are produced (art paper, cardboard, newsprint, toilet paper etc.), but also soaps and alcohol (IPA-3 2003, 287).

The Chŏngchŏngang Thermal Power Plant burns coal from nearby mines and supply companies in the region such as the Namhŭng Youth Chemical Complex with energy. The construction started in 1971 with Chinese technical assistance and, in 1976 (power plant 1) and 1977 (power plants 2-4), was completed (KOFC 2010, 155).

In 1975, shortly after the construction of the Namhŭng Youth Chemical Complex, the Anju Hotel with a capacity of about 800 people, the Anju department store and the restaurant Anju Chilsŏnggak with a capacity of approximately 400 people were built hotel in Anju-up (IPA-3 2003, 284-287).

Three urbanized areas before the city founding in 1987

The current urban area of Anju can initially be divided into two parts, the northern densely populated part of the city of Anju and the southern, mountainous part, which was created in 1997 as Ungok-jigu consisting of seven *ri* of the city of Anju and one *ri* of the city Sunchon, although the latter in the meantime became a part of the city of Anju.

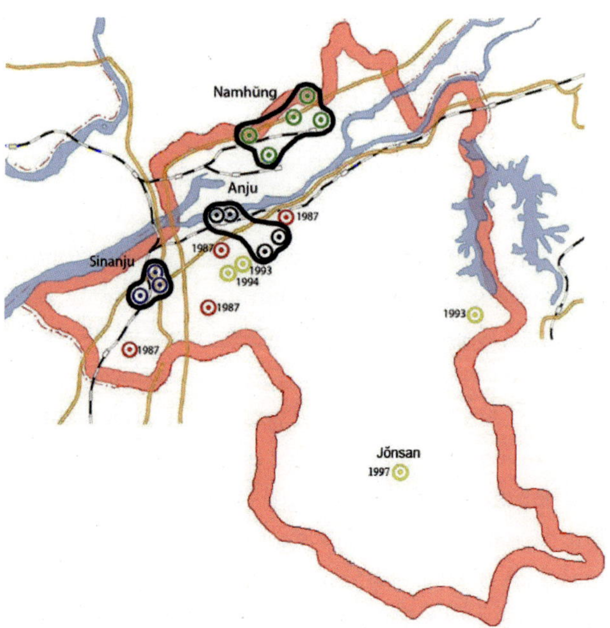

Figure Anju-II. *Up*, *rodongjagu* and *dong*

The southern part of the county demonstrated three clearly separated centers, even before Anju was appointed to a city in 1987:

1. the administrative center of the county (Anju-up)
2. Sinanju ("New-Anju")
3. the *rodongjagu* of Namhŭng.

The old road, which has been used by diplomats between Pyongyang and Uiju, had crossed the Chŏngchŏn-gang in the walled city of Anju. Anju has developed into an important trading center. However, the railway line from Seoul to Sinuiju went past the town. On this line, therefore, the "New" Anju, Sinanju, developed. Anju stagnated and Sinanju prepared itself to surpass Anju. According to Lautensach (1945, 253), the newly founded Sinanju had 13,029 inhabitants due to vigorous growth, whilst Anju had 18,284 inhabitants. On the other hand, in 1974 in a *rodongjagu*, in Pakchon-kun, located in the north of Anju, the Namhŭng Youth Chemical Complex was built. In 1980 the *rodongjagu* was added into the Anju-kun. Thus, the Anju-kun possessed together with the *up* and the two *rodongjagu* three urbanized areas. However, the development of new *dong* near the former *up* between 1987 and 1994 shows, that against expectations, which were entertained prior to 1945, the area around the old *up* of the *kun* became more developed than Sinanju. Thereby Anju/Sinanju had a different development than Uiju/Sinanju.

When Anju-kun was upgraded into a city (*si*) in 1987, the *up* and the two *rodongjagu* Sinanju and Namhŭng were divided into a total of twelve *dong*. Moreover, four new *dong* were created by the splitting from *ri* or the transformation of *ri*:

1. Anju-up

The former administrative center of Anju-kun, Anju-up, was split, at the same time as the designation of Anju into a city, into three *dong*: Tŭngbangsan-dong, Namchon-dong, Chilsŏng-dong. The rest was combined with Ryŏngyŏn-ri to Ryŏnyŏn-dong. These four *dong* are located in the center of the city. A tourist attraction is the Paeksang Pavilion in Tŭngbangsan-dong. In this *dong* modern apartment buildings have been built (Commie Travel). In Chilsŏng-dong the Chilsŏng Park with its pond is located, on whose edge the Anju-Chilsŏnggak restaurant was built. Also the Anju department store is in Chilsŏng-dong.

2. Sinanju

In 1952, Wŏnhŭng-ri emerged from three *ri* of the Sinanju-myon due the abolition of the *myon*. In 1963 the Wŏnhŭng-ri was formed as Sinanju-rodongjagu.

When Anju was granted a status as a city (*si*), Sinanju-rodongjagu on the one hand was divided into Sinwŏn-dong and Wŏnhŭng-dong, although the remainder, with parts of the Songhak-ri, formed the Yŏkjŏn-dong. These three *dong* lie in the west of the city around the "Youth" Sinanju station in Yŏkjŏn-dong, where the Kaechon line (between Sinanju and Kaechon), which has been opened in 1915, splits from the Phyongui line (between Pyongyang and Uiju), which is the name used in North Korea to designate the main railway line of the country. In Sinwŏn-dong, the Sinanju Textile Factory is located.

Sinanju became a victim of violent US-bomber attacks during the Korean War, due to the railway bridges over the Chŏngchŏng-gang.

Figure Anju-III. Sinanju (2012)

Figure Anju-IV. Sinanju station (2012)

Figure Anju-V. Sinanju (North) (2012)

3. Namhŭng in the north of the city

In 1972 the Tŏksŏng-rodongjagu was founded within Pakchon-kun, which is situated in the northern border to Anju-kun, from Tŏksŏng-ri, as well as parts of Ryonghŭng-ri and Namhŭng-ri. In 1980 it merged with the Anju-kun and was renamed Namhŭng-rodongjagu. When the city was founded the *rodongjagu* was divided into five *dong* (Namphyŏng-dong, Kubong-dong, Namhŭng-dong, Tŏksŏng-dong and Toksan-dong). The *dong* are located near the short railway branch line that is the Kubong line, which branches off from the main line eastwards, bifurcates into two parts and ends within the urban area of Anju. In this area the stations of Namhŭng, East Namhŭng, Kubongsan, and Chŏnghwaryŏk and the factories "Youth" Namhŭng Chemical Combine, and the Anjus Acrylic Spinning Company, the Anju Silk Weaving Company, the Paper Mill "No. 121" and the power plant Chŏngchŏngang are located.

4. New *dong*-formations in the course of the city founding

In addition to the twelve *dong* that emerged from the *up* and the two *rodongjagu*, four additional *dong* arose during the city founding. Two of them emerged close to the old *up*: Chŏngchŏngang-dong as a split-off of Wŏnphung-ri east of the city center, and Phungnyŏn-dong, which is a split-off of Misang-ri, southwest of the city center.

Two other *dong* originated in the southwest of the municipal area: Changsong-ri turned into Changsong-dong and in the southwest corner of the city Chŏngsong-ri became Chŏngsong-dong.

Changes after the city founding

Overall, Anju had thus 16 *dong* at the time of the foundation of the city. In 1993 and 1994 three more *dong* that were converted from *ri* were added: in 1993 Songam-dong and Misang-dong, in 1994 Munbong-dong.

1. Urbanization of the center in the South-Southwest direction

Misang-dong and Munbong-dong lie south of the old *up* and north of Changsong-dong. Therefore an expansion of the urbanized area of Anju from the city center towards the South-Southwest is ascertained.

2. Reduction of the municipal area in favor to Kaechon

Songam-dong is located in the outer southeast of the municipal area of Anju on the border to the city of Kaechon. In 1997, they reduced the municipal area of Anju when part of Songam-dong (Anju-si) was formed into Ryongwŏn-dong of Kaechon-si.

3. The formation of the Ungok-jigu in 1997

Seven *ri* south of the city (Ryongbok-ri, Ryongdam-ri, Ryongjŏn-ri, Junhŭng-ri, Ripsŏk-ri,

Panryong-ri, Kuryong-ri) together with Sinhŭng-ri (Sunchon-si) form the Ungok-Chigu, an area with a status on the level of a *kun*. The working-class district of Jŏnsan is formed from parts of Ryongbok-ri and Junghŭng-ri. This Ungok-jigu is presented on new maps as part of the city of Anju.[41]

Statistics

Urbanized areas before the city founding (*up* and *rodongjagu*)

1939-1949, 1952-1987 Anju-up (1)

1963-1987 Sinanju-rodongjagu (2)

1972-1987 Namhŭng-rodongjagu (first Tŏksŏng-rodongjagu, 1980 renamed Namhŭng-rodongjagu) (3)

	Dong-formation	*Dong*-splitting
1987 (16)	4	(9)
1993 (18)	2	-
1994 (19)	1	-

Anju – a city with different historical roots

If you genetically divide the North Korean cities roughly into three groups, the first group includes cities, which were an administrative center already before the influence of the Japanese in the Joson-time, the second group includes cities that have been established by the Japanese or whose foundation is attributed to measures of Japanese participants, and the third group contains those cities that were founded after 1945 by the DPR Korea.

Therefore, it is possible to divide the urbanized regions of Anju into three areas, which can be assigned to each of the three groups described above. The city center of Anju is genetically traced back to a fortified old town. Sinanju owes its existence to the fact that the railway line from Seoul to Sinuiju had left Anju located in the East, and in the 1970s, Namhŭng was built from the ground up.

41 Even the DPR Korea 2008 Population Census (2009) and PSC-8 (2009) do not call the Ungok-jigu a separate administrative unit. According to IPA-3 (2003) and IPA-4 (2003), Anju has 19 *dong* and 14 *ri*, and the Ungok-jigu consists of one *ku* (*rodongjagu*) and eight *ri*. According to PSC-8 (2009, 397), Anju (obviously without Ungok-jigu) has 20 *dong* and 14 *ri*.

Whenever the region is ravaged by floods, the city on the Chŏngchŏn-gang always makes the headlines. The oil import dependency of the city due to the high importance of the Namhŭng Youth Chemical Complex must have become a serious problem for the city due to the changes in the foreign policy conditions.

IV.2.9. Kaechon

City with a tradition of craftsmanship and trade

Coal is the main energy source of the DPR Korea. The decline in coal production was an important cause of the economic crisis in the 1990s. The slight improvement of its economic situation in the 2000s is also due to the improvement of the DPRK's coal production.

One of the most important issues to the North Korean leadership in the field of economic policy is their "coal policy," in explanation: the question of how much coal should be exported and in which inland sectors coal should be used. This context has a great influence on typical mining cities such as Kaechon. Kaechon belongs to a group of five cities north to the capital Pyongyang in the Phyongnam Province. All of these cities have been appointed a city status between 1969 and 1990. Located in the West from Kaechon is Anju, whilst on the East there is Tokchon and in the South Sunchon.

Table Kaechon-I. Basic data[42]

Population	319,554 (Rank 8)
Area	664.76 km² (Rank 12)
Population density	481 I./ km² (Rank 15)
Administrative units	26 *dong*/12 *ri* (68%) (Rank 13)
"Urban" population / "rural" population	82.1%/17.9% (Rank 14)

Among the cities that neither have a province independent status nor are a provincial capital, Kaechon is, after Taechon, the city with the second largest population in the DPRK. After the foundation of the Koryo dynasty (918-1392) by Thaejo Wang Kŏn (r. 918-943), fortified military camps were established in various parts of the Northwest. One of such fortifications was set in Masan in 930 and named Ansu-jin, which was an

42 Number of population according to the Central Bureau of Statistics (2009, 20); area size and administrative units according to PSC-8 (2009, 398). According to the IPA 3 (2003, 109) Kaechon had eleven *ri*; Jayang-ri is new.

important military installation in the North of Korea. In this region, there was fierce fighting with both the Khitan and later with the Mongols. At times, the region fell into the rule of the Mongol Yuan dynasty.

There were a number of changes to Kaechon's name, in 1080 to Ryŏngju, in 1217 to Ikju and in the 14th Century to Kaeju. When the region became part of the Phyongan Province in 1413, Kaeju was appointed to a county and therefore named Kaechon (Yi Wŏn-sun 1991, 599-600). Based on the rich mineral resources, iron crafts developed in Kaechon after the 17th century, which boosted trade activities. Kaechon thus developed into a city of craftsmanship and trade (Chae Thae-hyŏng-2010, 233-235). Prior to 1945, the region around Kaechon was mainly economically characterized by mining, craftsmanship and agriculture.

During the Japanese occupation, coal (especially from the mines of Joyang, Kaechon and Pongchŏn in the East and North of the city) and iron ore was extracted and brought to Japan. After 1945, Kaechon became a major industrial city on the basis of its resources and the construction of broad industrial sectors. The most important industrial sectors were coal mining, metal mining, metal and engineering industry.

City between the rivers

The downtown of Kaechon has formed on the foot of a mountain north to Kaechon-chŏn. The urban area is situated between the major rivers of Chŏngchŏn-gang in the North and Taedong-gang in the South. The location probably is also the reason for the name of the city. Kae (介) means "in between." Later, the Chinese character for the first syllable 介 was replaced with the homonymous syllable 价, meaning: good or virtuous (IPA-3 2003, 108).

The present name, Kaechon, originated from 1413, when names of cities with lower administrational status, were changed in terms of their final syllable, from "*ju*" to "*chon*" (川 river, stream) or to "*san*" (山 mountain). Consequentially, the name Kaeju was changed to Kaechon (Chae Thae-hyŏng 2010, 188-194).

The highest regions of the municipal area are located in the east, south and at the western border, where the foothills of the Myohyang mountain range extend. The region flattens gradually into the Kaechon-plain in the northwestern area. The highest elevations of the city are located on the eastern border of the city, the Paekthap-san (1,199 m) and the Jeil-bong (1,190 m). In the east, south and northwest, plains and caves have formed due to limestone. In the West, hilly plains extend, and this is also the area, where the main agricultural crops are grown. 53% of the city is below 200 m above sea level, 17% over 500 m above sea level.

From the east and the south of the city 17 rivers that have a length of more than 5 km flow into the Chŏngchŏn-gang. Correlatively to the numerous water resources, there are also numerous reservoirs. The water is primarily used for agricultural irrigation and as industrial water.

Kaechon is one of the cities that is counted as one of the coldest in January, although it is one the warmest in August.

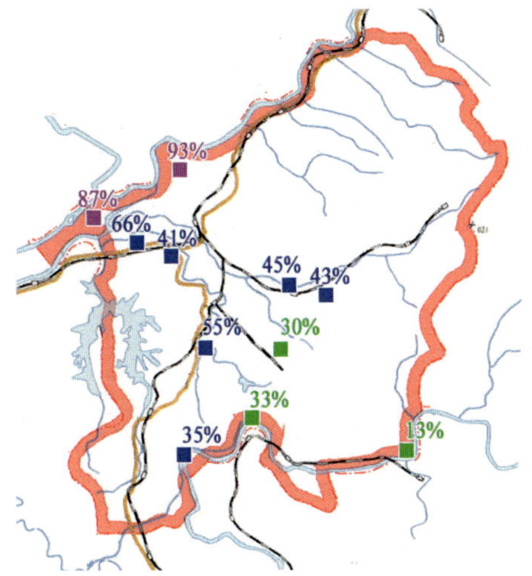

Figure Kaechon-I. Agricultural land in the *ri*

Table Kaechon-II. Climate values

Annual average	January temperature	August temperature	Precipitation
9,4℃ (16)	−7,4℃ (20)	23,9℃ (10)	1.066,7 mm (10)

Mountains and forests amount to 61% of the total area of the city. Mainly oaks, larches and pines can be found. Approximately 21% of the total area is usable for agriculture, of which 19.6% is used for wet rice agriculture, 66.9% for dry land farming and 5.3% for mulberry cultivation that is used for silkworm rearing. The most important crop is corn. Though, an important special product of this region is tobacco, of which half is exported. In terms of fruits, apples, pears and peaches, are counted to the main products.

Besides agriculture, animal husbandry is also important in Kaechon. Important farms are the Chicken Farm Kaechon and the Duck Farm Kaechon. The first was put into operation in 1968 and specializes in the production of eggs for the city population. The latter is one of the largest duck farms for the production of duck meat in North Korea and is located in Kuŭp-ri in the middle of the urban area (IPA-3 2003, 116-117). The Compound Feed Factory Kaechon, which was founded in 1965, has supra-regional significance. Animal feeding stuff and veterinary medicine from Kaechon is also supplied to other parts of the province Phyongan-namdo.

A town specialized in mining

During the Japanese occupation, mainly coal and iron ore was extracted and manual work was conducted in Kaechon and its vicinity. Agriculture accounted for the major part of the economy. After the establishment of the government of the DPRK, the mining industry continued to operate whereas the production of coal accounts for a large proportion. In Kaechon, there are also many factories which produce food, pharmaceuticals, textiles and garments. Additionally cement, bricks or slaked lime are produced in Kaechon.

Table Kaechon-III. Ranking (in parenthesis: number of industrial companies or cultural institutions)

Kaechon	KOFC	MOU	IPA	KCNA	KIET	Summary
Total number of companies	8 (18)	12 (24)	8 (25)	14 (10)	9 (41)	9
Important companies	20 (2)	22 (1)	12 (7)		13 (12)	8 (10)
Cultural institutions			27 (0)			

Table Kaechon-IV. Ranking (Total number of companies in relation population)

Kaechon	KOFC	MOU	IPA	KCNA	KIET	Summary
Total number of companies	12	17	6-13-27	15	11-18	13-10

In the ranking concerning the number of companies, Kaechon ranks lower than in the ranking in view of population number (rank 8). There are few important companies. Six of the ten important companies in chapter III.7–overall view are mines. In the IPA no important cultural institution were accounted for Kaechon.

Table Kaechon-V. Specification (in parenthesis: number of industrial companies)

Kaechon	Light Industry	Heavy Industry	Mining	Energy
KOFC	23 (1)	27 (3)	1 (14)	-
MOU	19 (11)	22 (4)	3 (9)	-
IPA	23 (6)	21 (7)	1 (12)	-
KCNA	21 (2)	20 (2)	4 (3)	3 (3)
KIET	24 (13)	24 (11)	1 (17)	-

In chapter III.7.3. ten companies were identified as important for Kaechon, of which six are mines: Kaechon Area Coal Mining Complex, Pongchŏn Coal Mine, Joyang Coal

Mine, Kaechon Coal Mine, Chŏndong Mine, Ryongwŏn Mine. The remaining four important companies are the Kaechon Export Clothing Factory, Kaechon Pig Iron Factory, Kaechon Disabled Soldiers Music Instruments Factory and Kaechon Paper Factory.

The most important industrial sector in Kaechon is coal mining. More than 30% of the coal reserves of Northern Phyongnam are located in Kaechon, primarily in the North (Jajak-dong, Jŏnjin-dong, Ramjŏn-dong, Sambong-dong, Pukwŏn-dong) and the East (Aril-dong Joyang-dong) of the city. 81.3% of the coal mines are under the control of the central administration and 18.7% of them are small and medium-sized mines that are subject to the regional administration. In Kaechon, seven coal mines are subjected to the central administration (IPA-3 2003, 115): in the North the coal mines Ramjŏn, Kaechon and Pongchŏn, in the East the coal mines Joyang and Sinrip (Aril-dong), in the Southeast the coal mine Mujindae (Mukbang-dong) and in the Northwest, the coal mine Sinsŏng. Furthermore, there are also more than 100 small and medium-sized mines that are subject to the regional administration.

There are also other natural resources in Kaechon: iron ore, lead, kyanite, graphite, limestone. Regarding the iron, two mines are of importance: Chŏndong (Ryongjin-dong, South of the city center) and Ryongdam (North of the city). It is about brown iron ore (limenit) that has a good quality with a fe content of 50-60%. In addition, the Kaechon area is nationwide the region with the highest concentration of graphite. In particular the Wŏnri Mine (Pukwŏn-dong) has to be mentioned at this point. Lead and zinc are extracted in the Sŭngchang Mine. Limestone deposits are in Ryongjin-dong south of the city center, and kyanite deposits are available in the two mines of Ramjŏn and Sambong in the North of the city.

Other important industrial companies of the city are either metal processing factories, such as the Kaechon Pig Iron Factory or the Kaechon Silumin Factory that manufactures aluminum products or machinery for mining usage, such as the Workshop for Exploration Machinery Kaechon and the machine factory Kaechon.

Among the companies of light industry, which warrant a mention, are the Kaechon Export Clothing Factory, which has been founded in 1958, and the Kaechon Food Factory, which was established for the processing of meat, seafood and vegetable products in the early 1980s and which also produces soft drinks and beer since the 1990s. Furthermore, the Kaechon Disabled Soldiers Music Instruments Factory with a specialization in brass and woodwind instruments, as well as the Kaechon Paper Factory (IPA-3 2003, 116-117).

In addition, there are reports that Syria ordered rocket engines that were made at "January 8th Factory" in Kaechon (Futurekorea 2004).

Transportation hub in northwestern Korea

Kaechon is a transportation hub in the western part of North Korea and an important seat of the railway administration of North Korea (Kaechon Railway Administration). The Manpho railway line runs through Kaechon from north to south connecting Kaechon with Manpho and Huichon in the north as well as with Sunchon in the south. Splitting from this line at the Kaechon station are the Kaechon line which leads to Anju as well as the Joyang Coal line. From Chŏndong station, which is situated south of the Kaechon station at the Manpho Line, another branch line leads to the limestone quarries in Ryongdae-dong. The Taegŏn-line between Unsan (Unsan-kun) and Pongchang (Pukchang-kun) crosses the southern part of Kaechon. The distance from Kaechon to the provincial capital Phyongsong is 66km.

Starting point for the Kaechon-Lake Thaesong Waterway

The 150 km long Kaechon-Lake Waterway, which was built between November 1999 and October 2002 runs from Taegak-ri (in the south of Kaechon) through Sunchon-si, Sukchon-kun, Phyonwon-kun and Chungsan-kun to Lake Thaesong (Kangso-kun). As a multi-purpose facility, it serves as agricultural irrigation, but is also used to generate electricity as well as for flood protection. The Taegak Youth Dam which was built within the framework of the project is also a sightseeing place for tourists. The project was financially supported by the OPEC (Chong Yong-su 2002).

Between 1952 and 1969 ten *rodongjagu* developed, in 1990 Kaechon became a city (*si*).

In August 1990 Kaechon became a city (*si*). Between 1952 and 1969 a total of ten *rodongjagu* developed in the area of today's Kaechon. In 1990, during the transformation of Kaechon-kun to Kaechon-si Kaechon-up and the *rodongjagu* were regrouped to *dong*.

From 1990, only four *dong* originated from *ri*

During the city's founding, three new *dong* (Namchŏn-dong, Sŭngchang-dong, Ryongdae-dong) were constructed from parts of *ri*. Another "new" *dong* is the result of the single incorporation of Kaechon-si: in 1997 a part of Songam-dong (Anju-si) was incorporated and renamed to Ryongwŏn-dong. Songam-dong, formerly a *ri*, had been designated as *dong* in 1993.

A splitting of *dong* did not take place after Kaechon became a city.

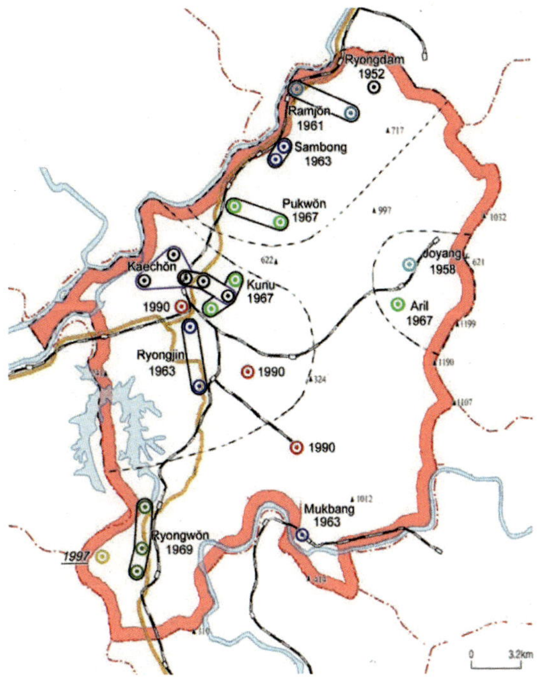

Figure Kaechon-II. Kaechon-up and the former *rodongjagu*

Structure of the urbanized areas of the city of Kaechon

The urbanized areas of Kaechon-si can be divided into five regions as follows:

1. Center (Northwest)

In the Northwest of the city the city center of Kaechon is located. Situated there are the former Kaechon-up, the former Kunu-rodongjagu and Ryongjin-rodongjagu and the in 1990 developed Namchŏn-dong and Sŭngchang-dong. In Sinsong-dong, north of the railway station of Kaechŏn, there is a coal mine. In Kunu-dong there is a co-op farm. The area of the former Ryongjin-rodongjagu is located near the Chŏndong station, here are the Chŏndong Mines, where iron carbonate is extracted. In Ryongjin-dong (in the South of the former *rodongjagu*) limestone is mined. There is a mine in Sŭngchang-dong which is south of the city center.

2. Northern region

In the North of the municipal area, the *rodongjagu* Ryongdam, Ramjŏn, Sambong and Pukwŏn were located. The areas in the far North, including the former *rodongjagu* Ryŏngdam and Ramjŏn, form the Ramjŏn mine region. When Kaechon city was founded, Ramjŏn-dong developed out of Ryongdam-rodongjagu, whilst Jajak-dong and Jŏnjin-dong were formed out of Ramjŏn-rodongjagu. In 1967 areas had been transferred from the Ramjŏn-rodongjagu into the Ryongdam-rodongjagu and vice versa. From the Ramjŏn mine region coal and iron ore are extracted. Major production sites are the Ramjŏn Coal Mine, the Ramjŏn Mine and the Kaechon Mine.

From Sambong-rodongjagu, Pongchŏn-dong and Sambong-dong were formed in 1990. In this area the Pongchŏn Coal Mine and Sambong Mine are located. The Pukwŏn-rodongjagu was divided into Inhŭng-dong and the Pokwŏn-dong. The Wŏnri Mine is located there, where graphite is extracted. Also located in this area are the Wŏnri Mineral Spring and affiliated relaxation resorts.

3. Eastern region

The *rodongjagu* of Joyang and Aril both became a *dong* in 1990. Important is the Joyang Coal Mine and the Sinrip Coal Mine, which is located in Aril-dong.

4. Southeast

In the southeast of the city the former Mukbang-rodongjagu and the in 1990 developed Ryongdae-dong (1990) are situated. Mukbang-rodongjagu became a *dong* during the city founding. In this area the Mujindae Coal Mine and the Mukbang Mineral Springs are located. Mukbang is located on the Taegŏn railway line between Unsan (Unsan-kun) and Taegŏn (Sunchon-si) to Pongchang. Until 1984 Pongchang-ri was still part of the Kaechon-kun, but afterwards it was counted to Pukchang-kun. However, Mukbang has no direct rail link to the center of Kaechon. In Ryongdae-dong limestone is conveyed for the Silicate Brick Factory Anju. A railway branch line was built to Chŏndong station, in order to transport the limestone to Anju. In the far Southeast of the urban area the internment camp of Kaechon is located.

5. Southwest

In the southwest of the city is the former Ryongwŏn-rodongjagu, which was dissolved in 1990 into Sŏnam-dong, Kagam-dong and Ryongam-dong, as well as into the in 1997 newly created Ryŏngwŏn-dong. In this area the Ryŏngwŏn Mine is located. In Ryŏngam-dong, there are two reservoirs, as well as the Songam Cave. The latter is praised in the issues 2/2006 and 4/2010 of the quarterly North Korean journal "Foreign Trade" as a tourist attraction along with 70 or respectively more than 100 attractions. According to the North Korean news agency KCNA (July 3, 2004), only a few years ago the cave has been rediscovered. Visits by Kim Jong-il were reported for March 1996 and April 2002.

Statistics

Urbanized areas before the city founding (*up* and *rodongjagu*)

1939-1949, 1952-1990 Kaechon-up (1)
1952-1990 Ryongdam-rodongjagu (2)
1958-1990 Joyang-rodongjagu (3)
1961-1990 Ramjŏn-rodongjagu (4)
1963-1990 Sambong-rodongjagu (5)
1963-1990 Ryongjin-rodongjagu (6)
1963-1990 Mukbang-rodongjagu (7)
1967-1990 Pukwŏn-rodongjagu (8)
1967-1990 Kunu-rodongjagu (9)
1967-1990 Aril-rodongjagu (10)
1969-1990 Ryongwŏn-rodongjagu (11)

	Dong-Formation	*Dong*-Splitting
1990 (25)	3	(11)
1997 (26)	-	1

Conclusion: three *dong* were formed due to upgrading the former *ri* during the city foundation.

Enlargement of the municipal area in 1997 by the incorporation of Ryongwŏn-dong, which was split from a *dong* in the city of Anju.

Kaechon – numerous former *rodongjagu* with its mining villages

Kaechon mainly is recognized and famous as a result of coal and iron ore mining. The mining goes back to the time of the Japanese occupation. Numerous *rodongjagu*, which had been set up until the city founding in 1990, indicate the natural resources of the urban area.

Both, the statistics and other sources, have identified Kaechon as a typical mining town. The high number of *rodongjagu*, which were located in Kaechon-kun previous to the city founding, is also a sign of numerous mines in the urban area. Culturally Kaechon does not hold any central function, although it is a major traffic junction in northwestern Korea.

IV.2.10. Tokchon

City of automobile industry and mining situated at a reservoir

Tokchon is a mountainous mining town. It is situated east of the city of Kaechon on the northern border of the Phyongnam Province. The city became known due to the Sŭngri ("victory") Motor Plant, one of the few vehicle factories in the DPRK. There are further numerous coal pits within the city, from which coal is used *inter alia* in the Pukchang Thermal Power Complex (in the Pukchang-rodongjagu, Pukchang-kun). Starting with the coal mines of Tokchon, Chenam and Hyŏngbong, there are six big coal pits in the city (IPA-3 2003, 189). In 1939 the Pyongdok-railway line was built, in order to dispatch the coal of the northern Phyongnam-coal field. This connects the coal-mining areas of Kujang-kun (Phyongbuk) and Tokchon with Pyongyang. In connection with the mining, the mechanical engineering was developed. The most important factory in this sector is the Mining Machine Complex in Osan-dong, in Tokchon. Furthermore, there are factories for the textile production and the food production. In 1982 the Kŭmsŏng lake originated from the damming of the upper reaches of the Taedong-gang, whereby wide parts of the area of Tokchon were flooded.

Table Tokchon-I. Basic data

Population	237,133 (Rank 16)
Area	692 km² (Rank 10)
Population density	343 I./km² (Rank 20)
Administrative units	23 *dong*/9 *ri* (72%) (Rank 12)
"Urban" population/"rural" population	88.8%/11.2% (Rank 8)

Among the cities that neither are province independent nor are a provincial capital, Tokchon is the city with the highest share of urban population among the cities of the DPRK.

Tokchon is situated in a region, which had an important military strategic role when Koryo was moving forward towards the North. In the year of 947 the Tŏksŏng-Camp was founded in today's municipal area. In 1001 the town was named Tŏkju. Then in 1413 the Tŏkchŏn-kun was founded. The construction of the car factory in the 1950s provided stimulation for the growth of Tokchon.

Only 9% of agricultural land

The municipal area is situated in the internal mountainous countryside and exists mainly of low to medium-height mountains. From the edge to the center of the city, the height of the terrain reduces gradually.

The Myohyang mountain range extends in the North and the West, which also marks the border to the Kujang-kun and to Kaechon. Here, medium-sized mountains are elevated, such as the Ryongmun-san (1,180 m) and the Paektap-san (1,199 m). In the South on the border to Pukchang-kun, the Jangan-mountain range is located with the highest elevation of the city, the Jangan-san (1,250 m). In the east of the city, erosion activities in the limestone area of the Taedong-gang and of its tributary, Siryang-gang, as well as the tectonic movements have built the Tokchon basin and the Chŏngsong basin. In this area, there are many limestone caves to be found (IPA-3 2003, 186). The Kŭmsŏng lake was developed due to the damming of the upper reaches of the Taedong-gang in 1982.

Table Tokchon-II. Climate values

Annual average	January temperature	August temperatures	Precipitation
8.8℃ (20)	-8,4℃ (22)	23.2℃ (15)	1,202.3 mm (5)

In comparison to other towns of the Phyongnam Province, relatively a lot of rain falls in Tokchon, and the temperatures are a little lower as well.

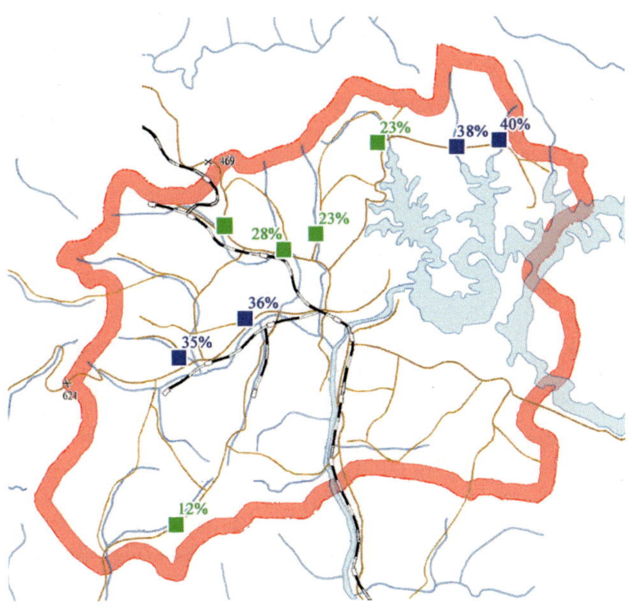

Figure Tokchon-I. Agricultural land in the *ri*

The cultivable area accounts for merely 9% of the municipal area, from which 54.9% is used for the growing of grain (primarily maize) and 34.2% for the growing of vegetables. Also the animal husbandry is an important component of the economy of Tokchon. Mulberry trees are an important special crop for the production of cocoons (IPA-3 2003, 189).

Mining and the Sŭngri Motor Plant

Kaechon is famous for its automotive industry. The city has numerous factories in the industrial sectors of mechanical engineering, in which machines are produced for mining, machine accessories, transformers and other machines, as well. Mining plays an important role in Tokchon. There are dozens of mines and the coal, which is mined from it, is mostly used in the Pukchang Thermal Power Complex, which is in the neighboring county. Silk weaving and textile industry also has tradition here. Moreover, food, kitchen utensils, daily goods, paper, furniture and clothes are produced.

Table Tokchon-III. Ranking (in parenthesis: number of industrial companies or cultural institutions)

Tokchon	KOFC	MOU	IPA	KCNA	KIET	Summary
Companies-total	12 (15)	18 (13)	22 (6)	10 (11)	20 (21)	18
Companies-important	15 (3)	9 (3)	23 (3)		15 (10)	10 (8)
Cultural institutions			21 (3)			

Table Tokchon-IV. Ranking (Total number of companies in relation to population)

Tokchon	KOFC	MOU	IPA	KCNA	KIET	Summary
Companies – total	7	20	24-23-23	7	23 – 16	18 – 6

In the ranking of the number of companies, Kaechon oscillates, depending on the source, around the ranking of the number of inhabitants. However, the number of important companies (which is mentioned in chapter. III.7.3) is comparably high on account of the mining companies.

In Kaechon an unequivocal specialization on the mining industry is ascertained. Therefore, the heavy industry generally has a stronger position than the light industry in the city.

Table Tokchon-V. Specification (in parenthesis: number of industrial companies)

Tokchon	Light Industry	Heavy Industry	Mining	Energy
KOFC	–	25 (4)	2 (10)	10 (1)
MOU	27 (2)	25 (1)	1 (9)	3 (1)
IPA	–	7 (3)	3 (2)	4 (1)
KCNA	23 (1)	22 (2)	1 (7)	12 (1)
KIET	21 (7)	25 (5)	2 (8)	6 (1)

In chapter III.7.3. eight companies were determined as important for Tokchon: one of the companies is in the sector of motor vehicle construction, one in the sector of mechanical engineering, five in the sector of mining and one in the sector of power production: Sŭngri Motor Plant, Tokchon Coal Mining Machine Complex, Tokchon Area Coal Mining Complex, Tokchon Coal Mine, Wŏlbong Coal Mine, Jangan Coal mine, Jenam Coal Mine and the Taedonggang Power Station.

The Sŭngri Motor Complex, which lies on the edge of the Sŭngri-san, is considered as the largest car producing factory in the DPRK with its 25,000 employees and a size of 600,000 m². Parts of the factory are subterranean, so that the production can continue even in the case of an evacuation. Tokchon is linked to Pyongyang with a railway line. The factory is 500m away from the railway station of Tokchon, which is a distance that is bridged by a spur runway (KOFC 2010, 271). In 1952 the construction began and in 1956 it was finished under the name of Tokchon Motor Factory[43] (IPA-3 2003, 189). In the beginning the factory only produced car accessories. In November 1958, a model in the style of the Soviet 2.5 Tonners GAZ-51,[44] the "Sŭngri-58"-truck, was produced. During the time of the first Seven-Year-Plan (1961-1970, including a three year extension) the range of products was extended. Now, besides trucks, passenger cars and jeeps are produced as well (KOFC 2010, 271). The factory was renamed to Sŭngri (victory) Engine Factory in 1975. In the 1980s the approximate production was between 6,000 to 7,000 vehicles and sank to 150 vehicles in 1996 (Kim, Mi-young 2002).

The Tokchon Coal Mining Machine Complex is located in Osan-dong and is connected to the railway network with a spur runway. Here coal carriages, production lines and other utensils for coal mines are produced (IPA-3 2003, 189). The complex covers a total area of 50,000 m² (KOFC 2010, 260).

In the municipal area other companies are to be found, for example in the sector of machine construction such as the Tokchon Machine Accessory Factory and the Tokchon

43 "Some of the facilities were built by the Chinese as a logistical base during the Korean War (1950-53)" (Kim, Mi-young 2002).

44 "Since the 1950s, North Korea's auto industry has persistently relied on 'anatomy plan drawing'-a practice of disassembling foreign-made car models and drawing their parts design one by one." (Kim, Mi-young 2002).

Machine Repair Kongjang. Additionally, the light industry is represented in Kaechon. The most important companies of light industry are the Tokchon Textile Factory, the Tokchon Silk Factory and the Tokchon Basic Foodstuff Factory (IPA-3 2003, 188).

The Tokchon Area Coal Mining Complex has an important function for the extraction of anthracite in the northern Phyongnam coal field. Six big and 40 middle-sized to small coal mines are subordinated to the complex. The coal is, *inter alia*, delivered to the Pukchang Thermal Power Station.

The Taedonggang Power Station was established by damming the upper reaches of the Taedong-gang, through which the Kŭmsŏng Lake was created. In 1972 enquiries were made, however difficulties arose, so that a group of experts from Yugoslavia was sent. Then in 1973 the construction started and in 1983 it was concluded. In November 1986 a delegation of Siemens has visited the power station, in order to negotiate the modernization of the plant (KOFC 2010, 148).

For the education of specialists four big technical training centers can be found in Tokchon which either are specialized in the construction of vehicles or in mining. The advanced technical college for construction of vehicles, the Tokchon Technical University (established in 1960, and is specialized in the construction of vehicles), the Toksong Technical University and the Hyŏngbong Technical University (established in 1979, Factory affiliated with of the Tokchon Coal Mine).

Tokchon is connected with the capital by the Pyongdok- Railway line (between Pyongyang and Kujang over Tokchon). The Sŏchang line leads to the west of the city from the Tokchon railway station. From the west of the city one is able to reach a country road over the Alil pass to the neighboring town Kaechon. On the Kŭmsŏng lake cargo boats and passenger ships go to the district Nŏngwon. The distance between the city centers of the cities of Tokchon and Kaechon is 42 km. The provincial capital of Pyongsong is 104 km away (IPA-3 2003, 189) from Tokchon.

Until the city founding eight *rodongjagu* existed

In 1952 Tokchon-kun was founded with one *up* and 22 *ri*. In October 1954 Samhŭng-ri (Pukchang-kun) was added. Between 1958 and 1967 five *rodongjagu* have been founded:

- Jangsang-rodongjagu (1958) (Tokchon Coal Mine),
- Hyŏngbong-rodongjagu (1963),
- Chŏngsong-rodongjagu (1963),
- Jangan-rodongjagu (1967), in October 1981 renamed to Namdŏk-rodongjagu,
- Jenam-rodongjagu (1967).

In June 1981 the following were established:

- the Sangdŏk-rodongjagu (Sŏchang Coal Mine) and
- the Sinsŏng-rodongjagu (Tŏksŏng Coal Mine).

At the same time Osan-rodongjagu (Tokchon Coal Mining Machine Complex) was split off from Chŏngsong-rodongjagu.

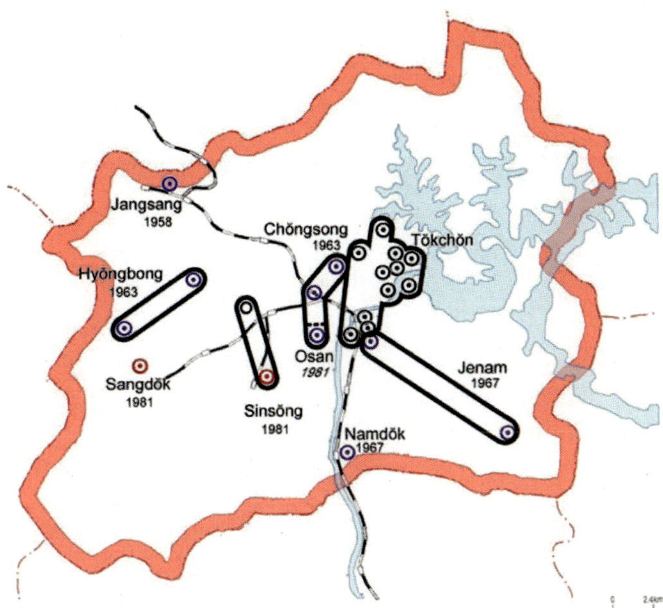

Figure Tokchon-II. *Dong* and former *rodongjagu*

In connection with the construction of the Kŭmsŏng-ho, which originated in 1982 due to the damming of the upper reaches of the Taedong-gang; Tokchon-up was increased in July 1982 and at the same time Namyang-ri received the remaining rests of three *ri*.

No changes after the designation as a city in 1986

In June 1986 Tŏkchŏn was designated as a city. The *up* was split in eleven *dong*, whilst eight *rodongjagu* are split up into *dong* and *ri*.

The IPA-3 (2003, 183) does not mention any new *dong* and no incorporations[45] after the Tokchon was designated as a city.

45 There was probably a slight change in the 2000s. According to IPA-3 (2003, 183) Tokchon consists of 22 *dong* and ten *ri*, according to PSC-8 (2009, 389) of 23 *dong* and nine *ri*.

Statistics

1952, 1 *up*
1958, 1 *up*, 1 *rodongjagu*
1963, 1 *up*, 3 *rodongjagu*
1967, 1 *up*, 5 *rodongjagu*
1981, 1 *up*, 8 *rodongjagu* (of which one by splitting)
1986, 22 *dong*, 10 *ri*

Tokchon – Many former working-class districts, a typical mining town with a car construction facility

Tokchon is an important mining town. Similar as in the case of Kaechon, there were numerous *rodongjagu* before Tokchon became a city. The automotive industry has a major importance for this city as well, although it had to suffer a slump in production. In the 1970s a reservoir lake was artificially built, which has flooded several former agricultural settlements.

IV.2.11. Sunchon

A new industrial city

Sunchon is located south of city of Kaechon and north of the city of Phyongsong. Before the Korean War Sunchon was still dominated by agriculture. The city is one of the areas that have been newly established as an industrial area after the war when the transformation of Sunchon started. Based on the rich limestone and coal reserves, the emergence of small and large mines and factories began. In particular, the production of cement has a great significance for the city. Sunchon is a traffic junction and with the establishment of the Sunchon Vinalon Complex in the 1980s many citizens from all areas moved here and thus Sunchon became the face of a large city (Chosun Ilbo September 25, 1995). However, Vinalon hasn't been produced in Sunchon for a long time.

Table Sunchon-I. Basic Data

Population	297,317 (Rank 11)
Area	368 km² (Rank 18)
Population density	808 I./km² (Rank 9)
Administrative units	21 *dong*/11 *ri* (66%) (Rank 15)
"Urban" population / "rural" population	84.3%/15.7% (Rank 12)

Basin of the Taedong-gang in the central hilly terrain of Phyongnam

Sunchon is located within the central hilly terrain of Phyongnam in the basin of the Taedong-gang, whose middle reaches flows through the city. The center of the city area is occupied from North to South by the Sunchon Basin. Starting from there, the area to the East and West is gradually getting higher. The greatest heights are in the urban area in the Northeast due to the Chŏnsŏng mountain range (Sakkat-bong 878 m; Kama-bong 414 m). In the West, the city has a share in the eastern decrease of the Chŏngryong mountain range with the Kuksa-bong (344 m), the Toun-san (441 m) and the Sindŏk-san (358 m) (IPA-3 2003, 234).

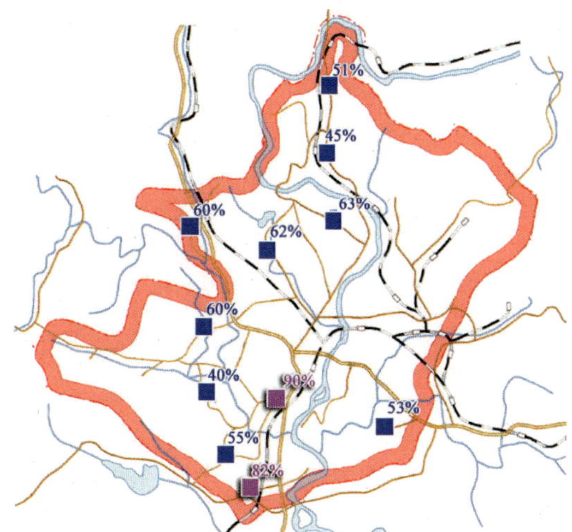

Figure Sunchon-I. Agricultural land in the *ri*

Table Sunchon-II. Climate values

Annual average	January temperature	August temperature	Precipitation
9.7℃ (12)	−6.7℃ (16)	24.0℃ (8)	1,011.8 mm (12)

The cultivable area accounts for approximately one third of the municipal area. It is located near Taedong-gang and Kŭmchŏn-gang.

Significant cement production and a former Vinalon factory

The region has developed into a modern industrial area since the end of the Second World War. The most important industrial sector is the building material industry. The chemical industry is a sector with a relatively long history and it primarily deals with the processing of natural resources such as limestone. In the 1980s, the construction of the Sunchon Vinalon Complex brought attention to the city. Furthermore, the pharmaceutical industry, the machine construction, the shoe industry and the food industry play a major role. Additionally, there are important mines located in Sunchon. There, coal and limestone are produced.

Table Sunchon-III. Ranking (in parenthesis: number of industrial companies or cultural institutions)

Sunchon	KOFC	MOU	IPA	KCNA	KIET	Summary
Companies-total	7 (18)	10 (27)	16 (11)	11 (11)	6 (60)	8
Companies-important	3 (9)	6 (5)	8 (9)		5 (25)	7 (10)
Cultural Institutions			17 (5)			

Table Sunchon-IV. Ranking (Total number of companies in relation to population)

Sunchon	KOFC	MOU	IPA	KCNA	KIET	Summary
Companies–total	10	6	15–8–20	12	2–1	7–4

Sunchon's rank is usually higher in terms of numbers of companies than in the ranking of population. Table Sunchon-III especially shows that the city is home to many important industrial companies.

Table Sunchon-V. Specification (in parenthesis: number of industrial companies)

Sunchon	Light Industry	Heavy Industry	Mining	Energy
KOFC	15 (4)	18 (10)	6 (3)	13 (1)
MOU	25 (7)	6 (11)	5 (8)	7 (1)
IPA	18 (4)	10 (5)	5 (2)	–
KCNA	22 (2)	18 (3)	3 (4)	8 (2)
KIET	18 (21)	14 (30)	6 (8)	13 (1)

A specialization on heavy industries is obvious as well as the fact that a variety of industries are located in the city.

In chapter III.7.3. ten companies were identified as important for Sunchon. Among them there are companies of heavy industry, light industry, mining and the energy production: Sunchon Cement Complex Sunchon Vinalon Complex, Sunchon Calcium Cyanamide Fertilizer Factory, Sunchon Pharmaceutical Factory, September 25 Machine Factory (Sunchon Tractor Factory), Textile Factory Sunchon, Sunchon Shoe Factory, Sunchon Area Coal Mining Complex, 2.8. Jik-dong Youth Coal Mine, Sunchon Thermal Power Station.

The Sunchon Cement Complex is one of the largest modern companies of the DPR Korea regarding the area size and the production capacity. The total area of the factory is 880,000 m^2. The factory is located in a hilly area about seven km east of the city center of Sunchon, near limestone and coal mines. In 1973 North Korea signed a contract for the furnishing of a cement factory was imported by the Japanese company Mitsui (80%) and the Danish company FLSmith (20%). The production started in 1977, when the first part of the factory was completed. Other parts of the factory were completed in 1978 and 1979. The company receives limestone through a conveyer belt from the Sŏngsang Mine that is located 12 km away. The coal for firing the lime kilns is provided by the Jikdong Youth Coal Mine. Between 1995 and 1997 a 6.3 km long conveyer belt between the two companies was built. Gypsum *inter alia* was imported from China. The Ponghwa Chemical Factory (Paekma-rodongjagu, Phihyon-kun, Phyongbuk) provides heavy oil. The Pyongyang Thermal Power Station supplies electric power. Kraft paper, though, has to be imported. The produced cement is also exported abroad, and the transport is carried out across Nampho harbor (KOFC 2010, 417-420).

The Sunchon Vinalon Complex, which is situated east of the Taedonggang, was built in the 1980s on the Ryŏnpho plain (Kangan-dong) and became a symbol of the city. This industrial park was built on a site of 14 km^2 (Chosun Ilbo September 25, 1995) and began its operation in 1989 and produced various chemicals such as vinalon, methanol and fertilizers (IPA-3 2003, 237). However, since a long time vinalon hasn't been produced anymore in this factory. The KCNA had reported about the Sunchon Vinalon Complex until 1999, but has stopped since then. Since 2012, the KCNA has reported about a Sunchon Chemical Complex, which is possibly a successor company of the Vinalon Complex.

The Sunchon Calcium Cyanamide Fertilizer Factory was founded in 1940 by a predecessor of Mitsubishi Chemical Industries Limited. During the Korean War it was destroyed and after the reconstruction of the factory in 1954 it has resumed production. On a total area of 300,000 m^2 approximately 1,200 workers are employed. Calcium cyanamide fertilizer and carbide are mainly produced. The limestone is provided by the 14 km distant Sŏngsang Mine, the coal is provided by the 17.5 km distant Pongchang Coal Mine (Pukchang-kun). Energy is drawn from the Pukchang Thermal Power Complex (KOFC 2010, 384-385).

The Sunchon Pharmaceutical Factory has been in operation since 1958. Various antibiotics and injection solutions and synthetic medicines are manufactured here (IPA-3 2003, 238). In the September 25 Machine Factory (Sunchon Tractor Factory) smaller tractors are manufactured. This factory has been in operation since 1969 (IPA-3 2003, 236-237). In the sector of light industry in particular, the Sunchon Textile Factory that was built in the 1970s specializes in boots, and the Sunchon Shoe Factory, which was built in the early 1980s, and the Sunchon Children Footwear Factory (IPA-3 2003, 237-239) are to be named.

The Sunchon Area Coal Mining Complex has been developed since 1972 and founded in 1977. Several mines in Sunchon and in the county of Unsan are assigned to this complex. Among the most important ones is the 2.8. Jik-dong Youth Coal Mine (KOFC 2010, 472-474). The Sunchon Thermal Power Station was built with Chinese assistance. It serves as a power supply for industrial companies as well as for the private consumption in the city of Sunchon. It was built in 1984, on the site of the Sunchon Vinalon Complex. In 1987 the first generator was connected to the grid, which was followed by the generators 2 to 4 in 1988. Between 1989 and 1994 there were explosions that destroyed parts of the facilities. In 1998, the repair work was probably completed. Coal from the Northern Phyongnam coal field (KOFC 2010, 156-157) is being burned in this power plant.

To support the industry, there are universities and colleges in Sunchon that educate in the fields of chemistry, fertilizers, cement and silicates. In addition, the city is home to a research institute for antibiotics.

Sunchon is an important traffic junction. The Pyongra railway line between Pyongyang and Rajin runs through this city. Sunchon is about 58 km away from Pyongyang and about 22 km from the provincial capital Phyongsong. In the direction of northeast this line also connects Sunchon with the cities of Hamhung, Tanchon, Kimchaek and Chongjin. From Sunchon the Manpho-line bifurcates and reaches the 300 km distant border town of Manpho at the Yalu across Huichon and Kanggye.

Also, the river transport has been improved. While in October 1980 in Tongam-ri (since 1983 Tongam-dong), a sluice was built at the Taedong-gang, the cement, coal, chemical fertilizer producing Sunchon was connected by a canal with the areas on the lower reaches of the Taedonggang, where corn is produced (Chosun Ilbo September 25, 1995).

Urban development at the Taedong-gang as well as mining and a cement factory in the east of the city

In 1943 Sunchon had become an *up*, although it was downgraded back to a *myon* by the end of the Japanese colonial periode. As a result of a local government reform of 1952, Sunchon became an *up* again. In 1974, the neighboring Unsan-kun was dissolved and almost the whole county became part of Sunchon-kun. In 1965, 1967 and 1974 large parts from Sunchon-kun were assigned to the newly established Phyongsong-kun. Then, in 1983 Sunchon-si was founded.

Figure Sunchon-II shows that the urbanized area of Sunchon can be divided into four major regions:

1. Old city center: west of the Taedong-gang

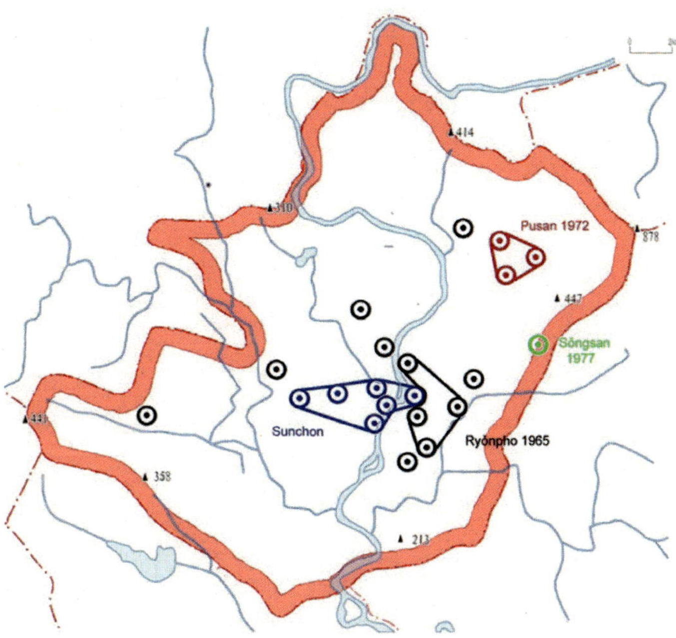

Figure Sunchon-II. *Dong* and former *rodongjagu* at the time of the city founding

2. New Ryŏnpho: *inter alia* Sunchon Vinalon Complex (built in the 1980s)
3. Mining region of Jik-dong (former Pusan-rodongjagu)
4. Osa-dong (former Sŏngsan-rodongjagu)

West of the Taedong-gang, the Sunchon station as well as educational institutions are located as well as the Ri Su-bok Sunchon-Chemical College. In Ryŏnpho, on the eastern side of the river, the Sunchon Vinalon Complex was built in the 1980s. Within the mining region of the former Pusan-rodongjagu especially the coal mining industry in Jik-dong, which also promotes coal for export, (KCNA June 30, 2003) is worth a mention. Also there is a ceramics factory in Jik-dong. The Sunchon Cement Complex (construction 1973-1979) is located in the area of the former Songsan-rodongjagu.

Reduction of the municipal area in favor of Unsan-kun and Ungok-jigu

In January 1992, Unsan-kun was re-formed, therefore large parts of Sunchon-si were incorporated in that *kun*. However, already in December 1992 Unsan gave back two *dong* (Puhung-dong and Jik-dong), in explanation the former Pusan-rodongjagu, and in 1995 Unsan-kun incorporates two *dong* from Sunchon-si.

The balance is that six *dong* in the east of Sunchon-si are located in areas that have

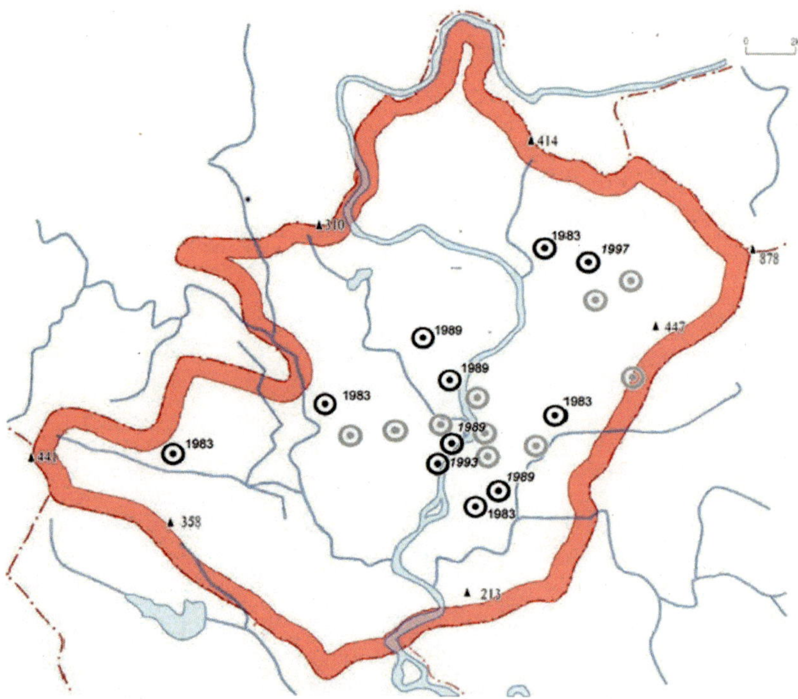

Figure Sunchon-III. *Dong*, which originated in 1983 or later

been still part of Unsan-kun before 1974. In 1997 Sinhŭng-ri has been incorporated into Ungok-jigu, which has been founded in 1997.

Figure Sunchon-III makes it clear that five of the six *dong*, which originated between 1989 and 1997, are located near the Sunchon Vinalon Complex. Therefore, in 1989 Kangpho-dong and Sŏksu-dong emerged from Kangpho-ri, where settlements were built (Chosun Ilbo September 25, 1995) for the employees of the Vinalon Complex. The creation of Saemaŭl-dong, from parts of Jik-dong and Puhŭng-dong in 1997, can probably be interpreted as a sign of the intensification of coal mining in this region, especially since the KCNA reported between 1998 and 2003 on several occasions about the coal mining in Jik-dong (KCNA January 8, 1998; October 26, 1998, July 1, 2003).

Statistics

Urbanized areas before the city founding (*up* and *rodongjagu*)

1952: Sunchon-up (1)

1965: Ryŏngpho-rodongjagu (2)

1972 Pusan-rodongjagu (3)
1977: Sŏngsan-rodongjagu (4)

	Dong-Formation	*Dong*-Splitting
1983 (15)	5	(6)
1989 (19)	2	2
1993 (20)	-	1
1997 (21)	-	1

The numbers refer to the current municipal area.

Sunchon – Industrial city with a variety of companies from different industrial sectors

Sunchon is a new industrial city, which has a variety of important companies from various industries. Thus statistically the ranking of the number of companies in the city is above the ranking on the population. The old city center is located west of the Taedong-gang. On the east side the supposedly prestigious Sunchon Vinalon Complex was built, which operated only for a short time. The environmental impairing Sunchon Cement Complex is located a few kilometers from the city center.

The construction of the Sunchon Vinalon Complexes was crucial for the development of the city. After the 1980s there was little growth.

IV.2.12. Pyongyang

IV.2.12. 1. Overview

The historical center in the northwest of Korea

Pyongyang is the capital of the Democratic People's Republic of Korea and dominates the northwestern part of Korea since the past. As capital of empires, such as the Koguryo Empire, as well as secondary capital and as a provincial capital, Pyongyang has a long tradition as an administrative center.

Table Pyongyang-I. Basic data

Population	2,999,466 (Rank 1)
Area	< 1,907 km² (Rank 2)
Population density	1,617 I./km² (Rank 4)
Administrative units	287 *dong*/75 *ri* (79%) (Rank 7)
"Urban" population / "rural" population	90.1%/9.9% (Rank 7)

Pyongyang arose at "a place where river and hills offered protection" (McCune 1980, 45). The fact that the Taedong-gang, where the city emerged, was navigable up to Pyongyang and offered the possibility to cross the river added to the geographical favorable location (Dege 1991, 21).

Before relocating the capital of Koguryo in the year 586 to where the present-day center of Pyongyang is, the seat of government was established at two different places close by, in the third century once northeast of the modern-day Pyongyang, where a walled town was built, and finally when the construction of the Anhak palace, on the foot of the Taesŏng-san in the year 413, led to the beginning of the relocation of the capital. The relocation from Kuknaesŏng to Pyongyang eventually took place in the year 427. The reason why the capital was moved to the present day location was because of its secure location. A system of city walls was built that utilized the natural environment especially the hills such as the Moran-bong (Dege 1991, 21).

Figure Pyongyang-I. *Kuyok* and *kun*[47]

46 Pyongyang consists of 18 *kuyok* and two *kun* (Kangnam and Kangdong).

Pyongyang lies in the middle of the Taedonggang basin, which is comprised of a plain in the West and of low hills in the eastern part. Pyongyang is located in a region, where wet rice cultivation plays an important role. Furthermore, numerous cultivable areas for vegetables, specialized fruit farms and big animal husbandry farms are located in the municipal area.

Table Pyongyang-II. Climate values

Annual average	January temperature	August temperature	Precipitation
10.2℃ (8)	-5.9℃ (13)	24.2℃ (4)	939.8 mm (14)

Largest industrial city of the DPRK

In pre-modern times Pyongyang was famous for its craftsmanship. Up until the modern period, there was a multitude of sericulture in the city and a big scale cotton production. From 1890 Japan started to mine coal in the east part of the city. Light industry companies such as sock factories, breweries and mills were also built during the Japanese colonial era. Nowadays Pyongyang is the largest industrial city of DPRK with a focus on specialized mechanical engineering (transport, precision instruments etc.). But most notably was the construction of a consumption oriented light industry.

Table Pyongyang-III. Ranking (in parenthesis: number of industrial companies or cultural institutions)

Pyongyang	KOFC	MOU	IPA	KCNA	KIET	Summary
Ranks	1 (118)	1 (238)	1 (139)	1 (177)	1 (283)	1
Major	1 (22)	1 (16)	1 (89)		1 (136)	1 (88)
Culture			1 (223)			

Table Pyongyang-IV. Ranking (Total number of companies in relation to population)

Pyongyang	KOFC	MOU	IPA	KCNA	KIET	Summary
Rank	20	13	14-9-1	5	21-13	14-9

Table Pyongyang-V. Specification (in parenthesis: number of industrial companies)

Pyongyang	Light Industry	Heavy Industry	Mining	Energy
KOFC	8 (35)	16 (70)	10 (7)	14 (6)
MOU	5 (175)	20 (51)	13 (8)	9 (4)
IPA	12 (72)	20 (42)	6 (18)	9 (7)
KCNA	7 (111)	15 (52)	7 (3)	15 (11)
KIET	8 (133)	19 (130)	14 (14)	12 (6)

Compared to other North Korean cities, Pyongyang has by far the largest amount of companies. However, according to most sources the number of companies in relation to the population is not particularly high, especially considering the share of the important companies. A main reason for this might be that a large part of the inhabitants of Pyongyang is not actually involved in the production. The share of companies in Pyongyang in relation to all companies of DPRK is higher in the MOU source than in the KOFC source, which can be traced back mainly due to the many light industry companies in Pyongyang. The share of industrial companies in the KCNA source is also by far higher than in the other sources. This might be because this source is the most recent one amongst them, which would mean that in the last few years, especially in Pyongyang, the number of industrial companies increased at least proportionally. The companies mentioned by the KCNA source are on the other hand mostly modern light industry companies, which are operated through joint ventures and are therefore particularly often mentioned by the North Korean news agency.

In chapter III.7.3. 88 companies were determined to be of importance[47] for Pyongyang: Pyongyang Aeguk Knitted Goods Factory, Pyongyang Children's Clothing Factory, Pyongyang Changgwang Clothing Factory, Pyongyang Beer Factory, Pyongyang Vegetable Processing Factory [Jung 5]; October 5th Automation Instrument Factory, Taedonggang Battery Factory, Pyongyang Food Packing Materials Factory, Pyongyang Children's Foodstuff Processing Factory, March 26th Factory (Pyongyang Electro Cable Factory), Moranbong Automation Instrument Factory, Pyongyang Garment (Clothing) Factory, Pyongyang Shoes Factory, Pyongyang Slag Prefab Parts Factory, Kim Jong Suk Pyongyang Silk Mill, Pyongyang Construction Machine Factory, Pyongyang Integrated Circuit Factory, Pyongyang Communication Machine Factory, Phyongchon Daily Necessities Factory, Pyongyang Thermal Power Complex, Pyongyang Bearing Factory [Phyongchon 16]; Aeguk Moran Garment Factory [Moranbong 1]; Pothonggang Footwear Factory (former Pyongyang Vinyl Chloride Shoes Factory), Pyongyang Children Knitted Goods Factory, Pyongyang Knitting Needle Factory, Pothonggang Electric Appliances Factory [Pothonggang 4]; Pyongyang Wood Products Factory, West Pyongyang Bearing Factory, Pyongyang Rolling Stock Factory, Kim Jong Thae Electric Locomotive Complex, Pyongyang Trolley Bus Factory [Sosong 5]; Taesong Ceramic Factory, Pyongyang Cosmeticts Factory [Taesong 2]; Aeguk Garment Factory „Choi Jong Rak," Pyongyang Coal Mining Machine Plant [Taedonggang 2]; Kyŏngryŏn Aeguk Carbonated Drink Factory, Tongdaewon Garment Factory, Moranbong Joint Venture Company, Pyongyang Footware Factory, East Pyongyang Square Steel Factory [Tongdaewon 5]; Pyongyang Steel Works, Pyongyang Rubber Factory, Pyongyang Cornstarch Factory, Pyongyang Essential Foodstuff Factory, Kim Jong Suk Pyongyang Textile Mill, Pyongyang Textile Machine Factory, Pyongyang Songyo Knitted

47 The names placed in the square brackets are *kuyok* or *kun*, in which the companies reside. The number after the name shows the number of companies of the relevant *kuyok* or respectively *kun*.

Goods Factory, Pyongyang Elevator Factory, Pyonyang Essential Goods Factory,Pyongyang Pharmaceutical Factory, Pyongyang General Lighting Appliances Factory, Pyongyang Daily Necessities Factory, Pyongyang Shoe Mould Factory, East Pyongyang Machine Factory, Pyongyang Bulb Factory [Songyo 15]; Taehung Unjong Wood Processing Factory [Unjong 1]; Maram Assorted Feed Factory, Pyongyang Precision Machine Factory (March 25th Factory), September 18th Factory (Ryongsŏng Bearing Factory), Ryongsong Meat Processing Factory [Ryongsong 4]; Sŏpho Railway Machine Factory [Hyongjesan 1]; Mangyongdae Machine Tool Factory, Mang'gyongdae Roentgen Factory, Pyongyang Film Factory, Pyongyang Wheat Flour Processing Factory, Man'gyongdae Aeguk Aluminium Sash Factory, Man'gyongdae Disabled Soldiers' Fountain Pen Factory, Ryuwon Footwear Factory, Pyongyang Rice Mill [Man'gyongdae 8]; Taedonggang TV Set Factory, Taedonggang Beer Factory, Mirim Concrete Block Factory [Sadong 3]; Saenal Electronic Applications Factory, Pyongyang Building-materials Factory [Ryokpho 2]; East Pyongyang Power Station, Pyongyang Metal Building-materials Factory, Pyongyang Chemical Building-materials Factory, July 28th Ceramic Factory, Rakrang Paper Factory, Aeguk Preventive Medicine Factory, Pyongyang

Table Pyongyang-VI. Population and important companies in the *kuyok* and *kun* of Pyongyang

	Population	IPA important	Important companies III.7.3.	Quotient population (%)/ companies; IPA-important
Jung (Central)	131,333 (4.4%)	4 (4.4%)	5 (5.7%)	1-1.3
Phyongchon	181,142 (6%)	12 (13.3%)	16 (18.2%)	2.2-3
Moranbong	143,404 (4.8%)	3 (3.3%)	1 (1.1%)	0.7-0.2
Pothonggang	105,180 (3.5%)	3 (3.3%)	4 (4.5%)	0.9-1.4
Sosong	147,138 (4.9%)	3 (3.3%)	5 (5.7%)	0.7-1.2
Taesong	115,739 (3.9%)	9 (10%)	2 (2.3%)	2.6-0.6
Taedonggang	207,081 (6.9%)	3 (3.3%)	2 (2.3%)	0.5-0.3
Tongdaewon	143,561(4.8%)	5 (5.6%)	5 (5.7%)	1.2-1.2
Sonkyo	148,209 (4.9%)	12 (13.3%)	15 (17%)	2.7-3.5
Samsok	62,790 (2.1%)	1 (1.1%)	0	0.5-0
Unjong	47,569 (1.6%)	1 (1.1%)	1 (1.1%)	0.7-0.7
Ryongsong	195,891 (6.5%)	3 (3.3%)	4 (4.5%)	0.5-0.7
Sunan	91,791 (3.1%)	0	0	0-0
Hyongjesan	160,032 (5.3%)	2 (2.2%)	1 (1.1%)	0.4-0.2
Mangyongdae	321,690 (10.7%)	8 (8.9%)	8 (9.1%)	0.8-0.9
Sadong	140,869 (4.7%)	6 (6.7%)	3 (3.4%)	1.4-0.7
Ryokpho	82,548 (2.8%)	1 (1.1%)	2 (2.3%)	0.4-0.8
Rakrang	282,681 (9.4%)	10 (11.1%)	8 (9.1%)	1.2-1
Kangdong	221,539 (7.4%)	3 (3.3%)	6 (6.8%)	0.4-0.9
Kangnam	69,279 (2.3%)	1 (1.1%)	0	0.5-0
	2,999,466	90	88	

Leather Factory, Rakrang Disabled Soldiers' Essential Plastic Goods Factory [Rakrang 8]; Kangdong Area Coal Mining Complex, Hŭkryŏng Coal Mine, Namgang Power Plant, Tŏksan Coal Mine, Kangdong Coal Mine, Mirim Floodgate Power Plant [Kangdong 6].

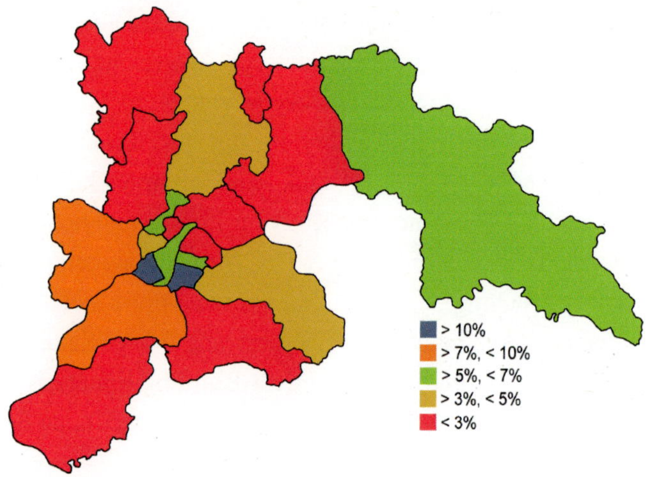

Figure Pyongyang-II. Share of important companies according to III.7.3

The *kuyok* with the most industrial companies in Pyongyang are Phyongchon and Sonkyo in the southern part of the city center, which are followed by Mangyongdae and Rakrang that are located in the Southwest. Among the nine companies that are mentioned in IPA and are located in the Taesong-kuyok, four are small power plants.

The most populous *kuyok* are Mangyongdae and Rakrang, where new high rise residential blocks were built.

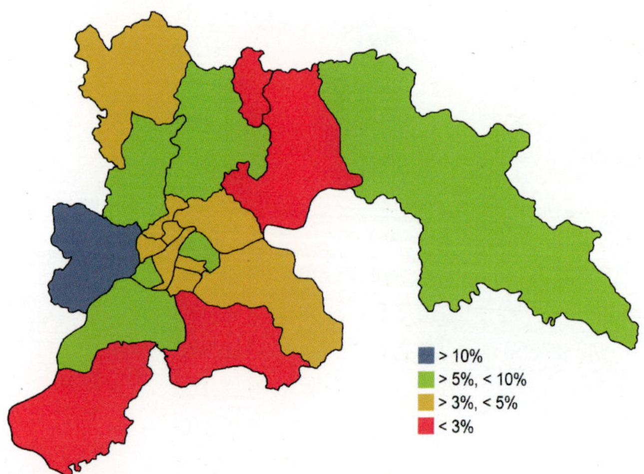

Figure Pyongyang-III. Share of population

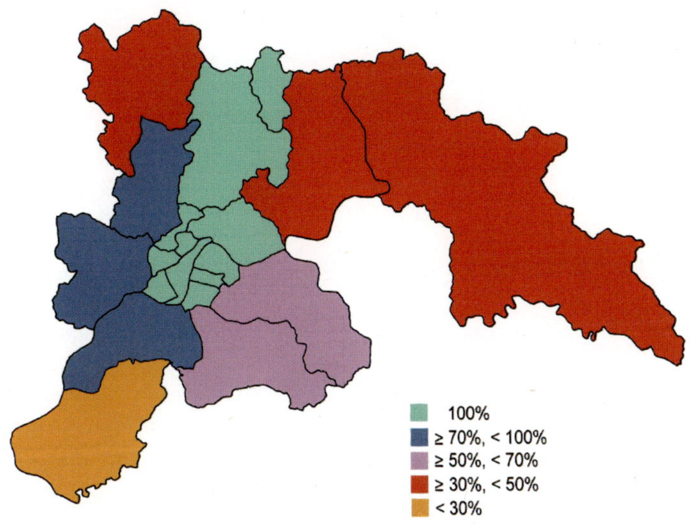

Figure Pyongyang-IV. Percentage of "urban" population

Table Pyongyang-VII. Ratio of urbanized administrative units to rural units as well as the ratio of "urban" to "rural" population (Sources for data: DPR Korea 2008 Population Census, data for 1986: Yi Ki-sŏk 2008, 27)

	Dong/ri	Share *dong*%	Urban (difference to 1986)	Rural
Jung (Central)	21/0	100%	100%	0%
Phyongchon	17/0	100%	100%	0%
Moranbong	17/0	100%	100%	0%
Pothonggang	15/0	100%	100%	0%
Sosong	15/0	100%	100%	0%
Taesong	15/0	100%	100% (+3.3%)	0%
Taedonggang	25/0	100%	100%	0%
Tongdaewon	18/0	100%	100%	0%
Sonkyo	21/0	100%	100%	0%
Samsok	4/7	36.4%	50.6% (+3.1%)	49.4%
Unjong	4/0	100%	100%	0%
Ryongsong	15/0	100%	100% (+3.6%)	0%
Sunan	5/9	35.7%	48.2% (+6.7%)	51.8%
Hyongjesan	15/3	83.3%	91.1% (+11.7%)	8.9%
Mangyongdae	29/2	93.5%	98.2% (+6.4%)	1.8%
Sadong	13/6	68.4%	71.9% (+2%)	28.1%
Ryokpho	6/6	50%	73.8% (+9.6%)	26.2%
Rakrang	21/9	70%	90.4% (+21.1%)	9.6%
Kangdong	1 Up, 9 Ku/15	40%	72.4% (−1.1%)	27.6%
Kangnam	1 Up/18	5.3%	27.8% (+4.1%)	72.2%

Among the 18 *kuyok* of Pyongyang, there are merely *dong* and no *ri* only in eleven of the 18 *kuyok*. In the *kuyok* of Samsok and Sunan around half of its inhabitants live in rural *ri*. Kangdong-kun is characterized by its coal mines and therefore has a high rate of urban inhabitants, while Kangnam-kun is ruralized.

Changes of the bigger administrative regional units in Pyongyang

In September 1946 Pyongyang became a city with province-independent status. In July 1948 the urban area was further extended. In December 1952 the *kuyok*-system was introduced. Pyongyang then consisted of five *kuyok*, in which 92 *ri* existed (of which 21 are rural *ri*). In February 1955 the inner-city *ri* were regrouped to *dong*. The outcome of this administrative restructuring was five *kuyok* (Central, East, West, South, and North), in which there are 67 *dong* and 13 *ri*. In April 1957 parts of two *ri* of the Taedong-kun (Phyongnam Province) were incorporated, which created two new *dong* in the West-kuyok. After some more inner-city restructuring in April and June of 1957, Pyongyang consisted of five *kuyok* with 109 *dong* and 14 *ri*. In June 1958 parts of the West-and the North-kuyok form the Taesong-kuyok.

In September 1959 five new *kuyok* were formed. The existing ones were partly renamed. In October 1960 parts of the *kun* of Kangdong, Taedong, Sunan were incorporated and seven new *kuyok* were formed. In May 1963 three *kun* were added to Pyongyang-si, so it consisted of 18 *kuyok* and three *kun*. At the same time as well as in January 1965, there were changes in the *kuyok*. In March 1996 parts of Taedong-kun came to Jung-kuyok. In October 1966 a large scale administrative regroupment was performed, consequentially many new *dong* and *ri* emerged. In April 1972 Sunan-kun was upgraded to Sunan-kuyok. Through regrouping in November 1972 a lot of new *dong* emerged. In 1979 Pyongyang consisted of 19 *kuyok* and three *kun* with 228 *dong*, 110 *ri* and 3 *up*. In December 1979 the *kuyok* of Jung and Ŏisŏng were combined to form the Jung-kuyok. In October 1981 Taedonggang-kuyok is split whereby the Munsu-kuyok emerged. In June 1982, in relation with the construction of the residential district of Munsu, the Tongmun-dong is split up in ten *dong*. In March 1983 Munsu-kuyok is combined with the Taedonggang-kuyok. At the same time Kangdong-kun becomes a part of the municipal area of Pyongyang. In May 1995 parts of the city of Phyongsong, where the Academy of Science is located, form the Unjong-kuyok of Pyongyang-si. In November 1995 parts of Paewŏn-rodongjagu (Songchon-kun) were added to Kangdong-kun and parts of Yonsan-kun (Hwangbuk Province) to Sangwon-kun. In December 1999 Kyŏngsin-ri (Phyongsong-si) was given to Kangdong-kun. In December 2000 parts of Songryŏng-dong (Phyongsong-si) came to Kwangmyŏng-dong (Unjong-kuyok). The map of Korea in the Korean Central Yearbook of 2010 shows Sungho-kuyok as well as Kangnam-kun, Junghwa-kun and Sangwon-kun as part of the Hwangnam Province. The 2011 Korean Central Yearbook map shows Kangnam-kun again as part of Pyongyang. From this time onwards Pyongyang consists of 18 *kuyok* and two *kun*.

Table Pyongyang-VIII. Number of *kuyok* and *kun* in Pyongyang

December 1952	5 *kuyok*
June 1958	6 *kuyok*
September 1959	11 *kuyok*
October 1960	18 *kuyok*
May 1963	18 *kuyok*, 3 *kun*
April 1972	19 *kuyok*, 3 *kun*
December 1979	18 *kuyok*, 3 *kun*
October 1981	19 *kuyok*, 3 *kun*
March 1983	18 *kuyok*, 4 *kun*
May 1995	19 *kuyok*, 4 *kun*
2010	18 *kuyok*, 1 *kun*
2011	18 *kuyok*, 2 *kun*

In the following examination of the 18 *kuyok* and two *kun* of Pyongyang, the city area is divided into an area west to the Taedong-gang and east to the Taedong-gang. In addition we distinguish the inner-city districts from the city outskirts. Inner-city districts west to the Taedong-gang include Moranbong, Pothonggang, Sosong and Taesong, and the inner-city districts east to the Taedong-gang are Taedonggang, Tongdaewon and Sonkyo. Western outskirts are Samsok, Unjong, Ryongsong, Sunan, Hyongjesan, Mangyongdae and the outskirts east to the Taedong-gang are the *kuyok* of Sadong, Ryokpho and Rakrang as well as the *kun* of Kangdong and Kangnam.

IV.2.12. 2. Downtown districts west of the Taedong-gang

Jung-kuyok – the center of the capital

The Jung-kuyok (central district) is the political and administrative center of the capital. Around the Kim Il-sung Square, which lies centrally at the banks of the Taedong-gang, the Grand People's Study House, the Ministry of Foreign Affairs, the KWP Party headquarters, the Korean Central History Museum, the Korean Art Gallery, the Ministry of Foreign Trade and the Cabinet Secretariat are situated. North of the Kim Il-sung Square is the Grand Monument Mansudae *inter alia* with the bronze statues of Kim Il-sung and Kim Jong-il.

Numerous high-rise residential blocks are located in Jung-kuyok. Along the Chollima Road, which runs from Phyongchon-kuyok in the northwest of the Jung-kuyok and ends at the Pothong Gate, numerous residential high-rise apartments were built in 1970. The Changwang Street is located north of the station. In 1985 thousands of high-rise residential blocks were completed here. Near the Kim Il-sung Square and the Mansudae monument, modern high high-rise residential blocks of Changjŏn Street are located, which were completed in 2012.

Important offices of the tourism sector such as the in 1953 founded Korea International Travel Company (KITC) are located here as well. North of the train station is the Koryo Hotel, which was completed in 1985. The islands of Rŭngra and Yanggak in the Taedong-gang also belong to the Jung-kuyok. On the former the May Day Stadium that seats 150,000 people is situated and the Rungra People's Pleasure Ground, which was opened in 2012, with a dolphinarium, is there as well. On the island of Yanggak the Yanggakdo hotel is situated.

Figure Pyongyang-V. Changjŏn-street (2012)

Figure Pyongyang-VI. Kim Il-sung Square (2012)

Since numerous representative buildings as well as buildings for administrative purposes were built in Jung-kuyok, the industrial importance of this *kuyok* decreased. The five companies of this *kuyok*, which were identified as important companies according to Chap. III.7.3., are solely light industry companies. Among these are three companies of the textile industry: Pyongyang Aeguk Knitted Goods Factory, which began its production in 1971 and lies at the foot of the Changgwang-san, in Sŏchang-dong; the Pyongyang Children's Clothing Factory, which was built between 1973 and 1974 at the Changgwang road, and the Pyongyang Changgwang Clothing Factory, which has been founded in 1970.

That the residential functions have been abandoned at the expense of representational buildings etc., is underlined by the fact that seven *dong* "disappeared" in the area of today's Jung-kuyok. In 1959 the first merger of two *dong* occurred in the extreme north of the *kuyok* where the Moranbong Park was built in the same year (in Moranbong-kuyok two additional *dong* "disappeared" in 1960 for the same reason). The merger of the Changjŏn-dong with the Mansu-dong in 1972 coincides with the period of the opening of the Mansudae Grand Monument. The remaining "disappeared" *dong* are located in the northern part of the *kuyok*. The emergence of new *dong* is limited to the period between 1957 and 1967.

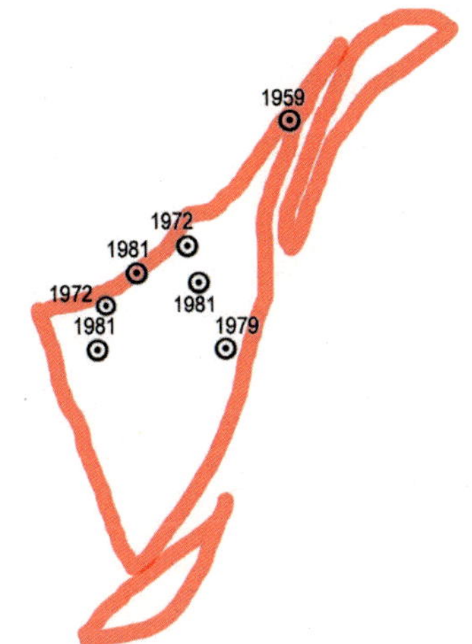

Figure Pyongyang-VII. Vanished *dong* (Jung)

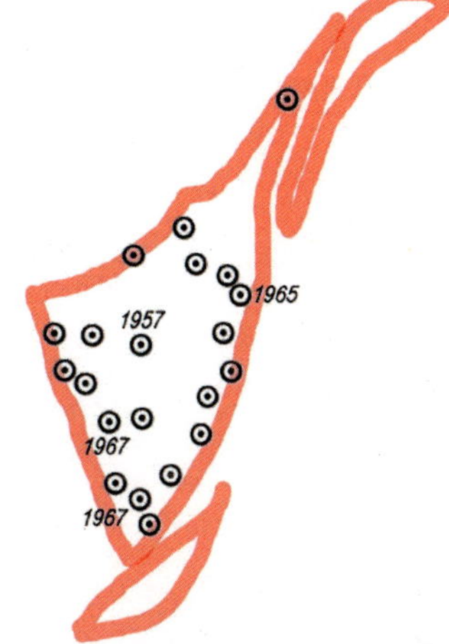

Figure Pyongyang-VIII. *Dong* in Jung-kuyok

Statistics Jung-kuyok (21 *dong*)

Year (*dong* total)	new *dong*
1955 (24)	
1957 (25)	1
1959 (24)	-1
1965 (25)	1
1967 (27)	2
1972 (25)	-2
1979 (24)	-1
1981 (21)	-3

Phyongchon-kuyok – the *kuyok* with most of the industrial companies

This *kuyok* is located southwest of the railway line through Pyongyang that separates it from the Jung-kuyok. In this *kuyok* a variety of industrial companies including the Pyongyang Thermal Power Complex are situated. The Chollima road runs through this *kuyok*. Foreign visitors are often brought to the Mansudae Art Studio and School. At the foot of the Pothong-gang at the Ansan Bridge, the Pothonggang Hotel, which was opened in 1972, is located. Major universities in this *kuyok* are the Pyongyang Jong Chol-Ku University of Commerce and the Pyongyang University of the Printing Industrial Arts.

Figure Pyongyang-IX. Pyongchon-kuyok (2012)

The Pyongchon-kuyok is the *kuyok* of Pyongyang with most of the important industrial companies. The October 5th Automation Instrument Factory went into operation in 1954 (IPA 2003-1, 442-443) and has a total area of 280,000 m^2 (KOFC 2010, 306-307). The Moranbong Automation Instrument Factory started operations in 1983 (IPA 2003-1, 442). Both factories are located within the industrial zone of the Phyongchon district. The Taedonggang Battery Factory is located in Jŏngphyŏng-dong. It was built in 1975 with Soviet aid and put into operation in 1982. In 1987 the company was expanded by using Soviet equipment. The total area amounts to 165,000 m^2, where 4,500 workers are employed (KOFC 2010, 304). In the March 26th Factory in Jŏngphyŏng-dong a variety of cables are manufactured (IPA 2003-1, 442). It is the largest electric cable factory in the DPR Korea, where 4,000 workers are employed on a total area of 116,000 m^2. The construction of the factory began in 1959 with the help of the Czechoslovakia, and the production began in 1962 (KOFC 2010, 303-304). In the Pyongyang Slag Prefab Parts Factory in Jŏngphyŏng-dong (chemical) building material is produced (IPA 2003-1, 443). It is in operation since 1975.

The Mansudae Windasia Joint Venture Company produces jewelry for women (rings, necklaces etc.). Production started in 1994; since 1997 in collaboration with the Japanese company Windasia (IPA 2003-1, 442). The Pyongyang Shoes Factory in Ponghak-dong manufactures leather shoes for men, women and children (IPA 2003-1, 443). It was built as part of the six-year economic plan (1971-1976). In the second half of the 1990s toll processing contracts with foreign companies were signed, but nowadays the production was switched back to satisfy domestic needs again (KOFC 2010, 609).

The Kim Jong Suk Pyongyang Silk Mill was founded in 1926 (IPA 2003-1, 443). It is located in Haeun-dong and has a total operating area of 120,000 m² and approximately 3,000 workers. "Kim Jong Suk" was attached to the factory name in 2009 (KOFC 2010, 598-599). The Pyongyang Men's Clothing Factory in Ansan-dong was built as part of the six-year economic plan (1971-1976). Construction began in 1971, and the operation started in 1976 (IPA 2003-1, 443). In the Pyongyang Children's Foodstuff Processing Factory, which was built in 1992, food such as soy milk is produced (IPA 2003-1, 443).

The Pyongyang Thermal Power Complex in Saemaŭl-dong was built between 1961 and 1970 with Soviet aid and supplies the cities of Pyongyang, Nampho and Songrim with energy (IPA 2003-1, 444). It is the first thermal power plant of the DPR Korea, which was built for industrial purposes. It is also used to supply the population with heating. Construction began in 1961. However, when Soviet aid was stopped in August 1964, the construction was delayed. The first parts of the power plant, though, went into operation in 1965. The power plant burns coal from the northern Phyongnam-coal region (Region of Sunchon, Tokchon, Kaechon) and from the coal field of the Kangdong region.

Statistics Pyongchon-kuyok (17 *dong*)

Year (*dong* total)	new *dong*
1955 (5)	
1957 (6)	1
1961 (7)	1
1963 (11)	4
1967 (13)	2
1972 (15)	2
1989 (17)	2

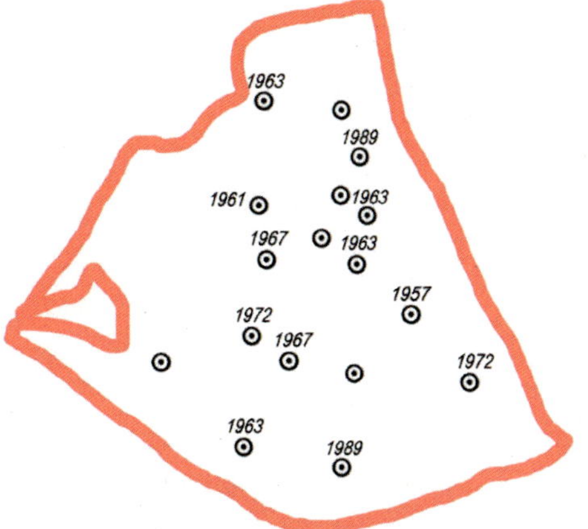

Figure Pyongyang-X. *Dong* in the Pyongchon-kuyok

Most *dong* ermerged between 1963 and 1972. The two newly in 1989 established *dong* are the ones of most recent date within the *kuyok* within the downtown area west of the Taedong-gang.

Moranbong-kuyok – Parks and the Arch of Triumph

The Moranbong-kuyok lies northwest at the foot of Moran-bong. It lies just west of the Taedong-gang and north of the central Jung-kuyok. In this *kuyok* the Triumphal Arch (Kaesŏn-mun) is situated and within the Moranbong park is the Kim Il-sung stadium and the Kaesŏn Youth Park. In this area are the main radio and television stations of the country as well.

In Moranbong-kuyok, there are some industrial companies of the light industry. The Moranbong General Foodstuff Factory was built in 1982 and produces amongst others biscuits (IPA 1 2003, 224). The Aeguk Moran Garment Factory was built in 1987 and expanded in 1989 (IPA-1 2003, 225). In the Pyongyang Moran Disabled Soldiers' Music Instruments Factory mainly string instruments made of wood are produced. This company was already founded in 1973, but in 1987 a new building was constructed for it (IPA 1 2003, 225).

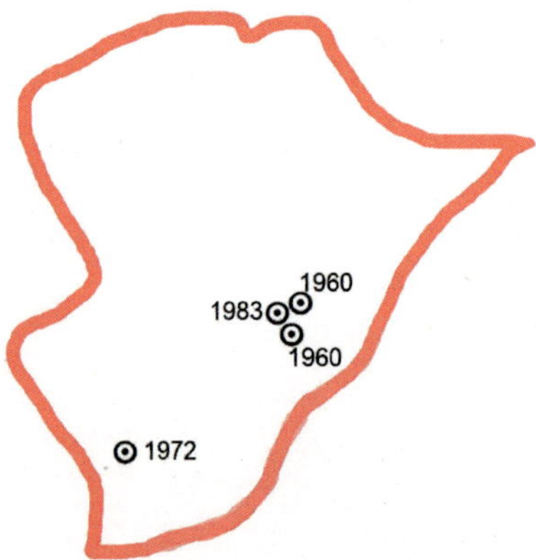

Figure Pyongyang-XI. Vanished *dong* (Moranbong)

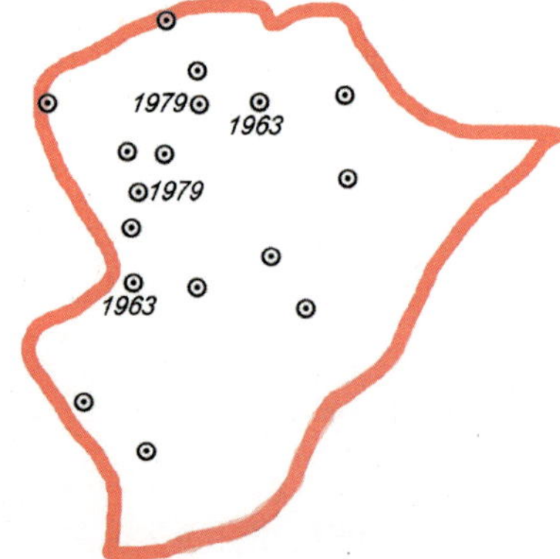

Figure Pyongyang-XII. *Dong* in Moranbong-kuyok

It is noticeable that between 1960-1983 four *dong* "vanished" due to mergers. Three of them were located in the east of the *kuyok*, in the area near the riverbank of the Taedong-gang, where today the Moranbong Park is located. The "vanishing" of the *dong* testifies that the residential areas close to the riverbank, including the old kisaeng district, were eliminated and major parks were built instead.

On the other hand four *dong* emerged in 1963 and 1979 in the center and in the west of the *kuyok*.

Year (*dong* total)	new *dong*
1955 (17)	
1960 (15)	-2
1963 (17)	2
1972 (16)	-1
1979 (18)	2
1983 (17)	-1

Pothonggang-kuyok – Ryugyong hotel and residential complex for the executive

The railway line from Pyongyang station towards Sinuiju runs through the Pothong-kuyok in South-North direction. Ten of 15 *dong* of the *kuyok* are east of the railway line. The southern part of this eastern part is occupied by the Ponghwa Street, the most important street of the *kuyok*. This approximately 1,900 m long road was built from 1958 to 1959 in the time of "Pyongyang speed." In the northeast the Ryugyŏng Hotel is situated. In the western part of the *kuyok* lies south the Pothonggang station and north of it, on a foothill, the DPR Korea Executive Housing Complex Rakwŏn and the Headquarter of the National Defense Commission.

Figure Pyongyang-XIII. Ryugyŏng-Hotel (2012)

Figure Pyongyang-XIV. Subway station Hwanggŭmbŏl (2012)

The Pothonggang Yeung Hoi Joint Venture Company is a partnership between the North Korea-based Pothonggang Co and the Hong Kong-based Lida Trade Co, which launched in October 2000. It produces instant noodles (IPA-1 2003, 240). The Jangsu

(Longevity) Koryo Medicine Export Factory was founded in 1972 (IPA-1 2003, 240-241). Pothonggang Footwear Factory (former Pyongyang Vinyl Chlorides Shoes Factory) is situated in Rakwŏn-dong (IPA-1 2003, 241).

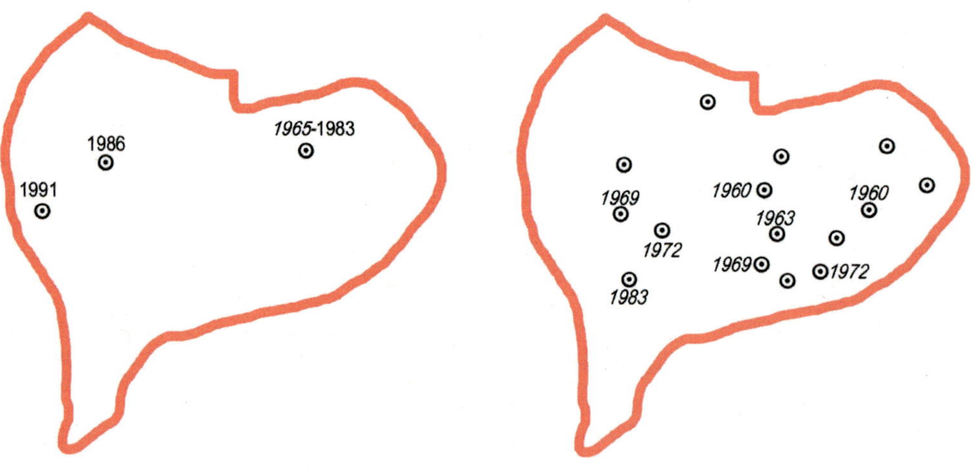

Figure Pyongyang-XV. Vanished *dong* (Pothonggang)

Figure Pyongyang-XVI. *Dong* in Pothonggang-kuyok

The *dong* which has vanished in 1983 was situated near the Ryugyŏng Hotel, whose construction began in 1987. The two *dong* that disappeared in 1986 and 1991 were located in the west of the *kuyok*.

Statistics Pothonggang-kuyok (15 *dong*)

1955 (9)	
1960 (11)	2
1963 (12)	1
1965 (13)	1
1969 (15)	2
1972 (17)	2
1983 (17)	-1/1
1986 (16)	-1
1991 (15)	-1

Sosong-kuyok – Location of Kim Jong Thae Electric Locomotive Complexes

The Sosong-kuyok consists of a western part - with the region around West Pyongyang Station. West of the station, in Namgyo-dong, the Kim Jong Thae Electric Locomotive

Complex is situated. East of the station, an area adjoins that is divided into six dong. The area of the *kuyok* then narrows in the center, where the Pyongyang Trolley Bus Factory is located in Sŏkbong-dong. In the center of the eastern part of the *kuyok* the Exhibition of the Three Revolution is situated.

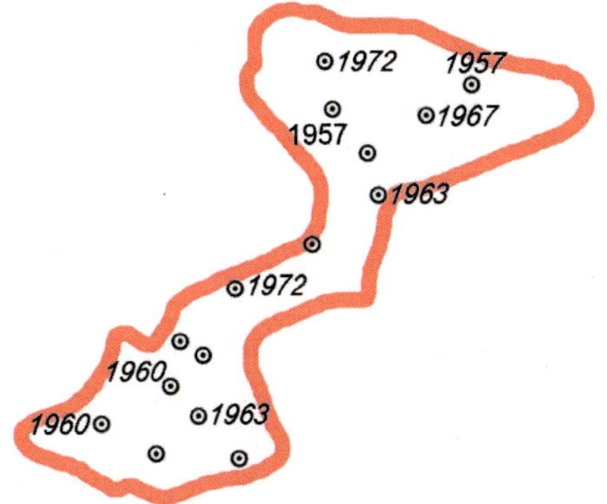

Figure Pyongyang-XVII. *Dong* in Sosong-kuyok (2012)

Figure Pyongyang-XVIII. Inhung-street (right: Hyŏksin subway station) (2012)

In the Kim Jong Thae Electric Locomotive Complex a variety of passenger trains is produced. The company was founded in 1930. The Pyongyang Trolley Bus Factory amounts to a total area of 63,000 m² where approximately 5,000 people are employed (KOFC 2010, 275).

The Pyongyang Plastic Building Materials Factory started its operation in 1963 and produces any types of plastic pipes (IPA-1 2003, 301). The Pyongyang Wood Products Factory was established in 1960. The Joson Myŏngsim Trade Company, which was not included in the statistics of industrial companies due to its designation as a trading company, produces according to IPA-1 (2003, 300-301) various kinds of honey. All three companies are located in Sŏchŏn-dong directly in the east from the West railway station.

Statistics Sosong-kuyok (15 *dong*)

	Dong-Formation	*Dong*-Splitting
1955 (6)		
1957 (8)	2	-
1960 (10)	-	2
1963 (12)	-	2
1967 (13)	-	1
1972 (15)	-	2

After 1972, no administrative changes were made any more in this *kuyok*.

Taesong-kuyok – urbanized West, Taesong-san in the East

The Taesong-kuyok consists of a narrow densely populated western part and a wider sparsely populated eastern part.

Through the western part runs the Kŭmsŏng road, south of it the Kim Il-sung University and the Kŭmsusan Palace of the Sun as well as the mausoleum of Kim Il-sung are located. The Pyongyang University of Foreign Languages is situated within the residential area north of Kŭmsŏng-road. In the East lies the Taesong-san and at its foot the Revolutionary Martyrs Cemetery, the Pyongyang Central Zoo, the Folk Park and other facilities.

Figure Pyongyang-XIX. Zoo (2006)

Figure Pyongyang-XX. Ryongbuk Middle School (2012)

In the IPA nine important companies are mentioned: four power plants and five companies of the light industry. The Taesongsan Small Size Power Plant 1-4 were all constructed in 1990 (IPA-1 2003, 89-90).

In the Taesong Ceramic Factory mainly structural ceramics are produced (IPA-1 2003, 90). In the Taesong Pharmaceutical Factory, which produces since 1974 in Kosan-dong in the eastern part of the district, especially products for external use are made (IPA-1 2003, 90). The Ryongbok General Foodstuff Factory in Ryongbuk-dong manufactures mainly sauces and seasoning. The Pyongyang Secondary Education Book Printing Factory in Misan2-dong was built in 1977 and began its operation in 1978. According to IPA-1 (2003, 90) a Pyongyang Cosmetics factory is located in Taesong-kuyok as well, which manufactures creams, soaps etc. since 1957.

Figure Pyongyang-XXI. Vanished *dong* (Taesong)

Figure Pyongyang-XXII. *Dong* in Taesong-kuyok

Statistices Taesong-kuyok (15 *dong*)

	Dong-Formation	*Dong*-Splitting
1955 (9)		
1960 (11)	2	0
1963 (13)	0	2
1967 (14)	0	1
1972 (17)	0	3
1979 (16)	0	-1
1983 (15)	0	-1

Both mergers were made in the west of the *kuyok*.

IV.2.12. 3. Inner city district east to the Taedong-gang

Taedonggang-kuyok – Munsu-Street and embassy area

The Taedong-gang runs around the Taedonggang-kuyok in the west and in the north. It was founded in 1960. In 1981 the western part was separated and formed the Munsu-kuyok, which was again incorporated in the Taedonggang-kuyok in 1983. In this *kuyok* there are many broad streets with residential houses and public institutions. The in 1983 built Munsu-street runs in the South-North direction. In this street the Pyongyang airport used to be as well. The south border of the *kuyok* is marked by the Tongdaewon-Street, which runs from the West to the East. From this street, the Taehak-street runs in the northeast direction.

Within this *kuyok* the Pyongyang Maternity Hospital is located, which is often shown to foreigners, as well as the East-Pyongyang theatre, the Pyongyang University of International Studies, the University of Economics (in Ueam-dong), the University of Music and Dance and numerous other universities, the embassy area as well as the Korean Workers' Party Monument.

Figure Pyongyang-XXIII. Taedonggang-kuyok (2012)

The Aeguk Garment Factory "Choi Jong Rak," which has been named after an overseas Korean, is located on Munsu-Street. There, they produce men's apparel for export. The Korea Ten Thousand Years Health General Company was founded in 1982. They produce traditional Korean pharmaceuticals (Koryo medicine). In the Pyongyang Instant Noodle Factory the Taedonggang Instant Noodles are produced (IPA-1 2003, 76). The Achim Panda Computer Joint Venture Company which has been founded in 2002 is located in Tapje-dong, where the electronics companies called "Achim (morning) and China's Nanjing Panda Electronics. Co. cooperate. According to KOFC (2010, 260) the Pyongyang Coal Mining Machine Factory is located in Taesang-dong. The factory which has been built in 1954 employs 3,000 workers on a total area of 64,000 m².

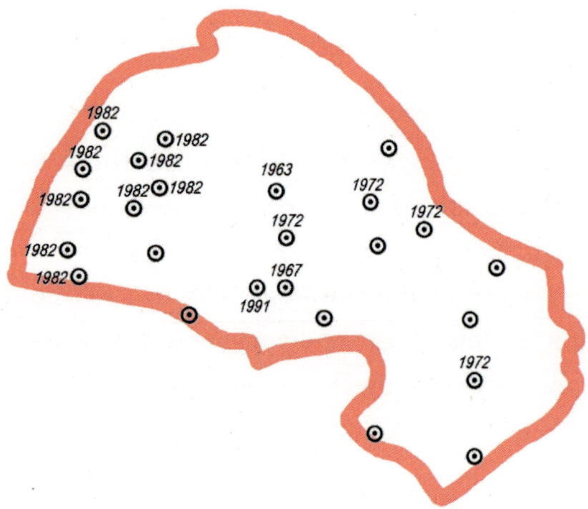

Figure Pyongyang-XXIV. *Dong* in Taedonggang-kuyok

On the territory of today's Taedonggang-kuyok nine *dong* existed in the year 1955. Until 1991 16 other *dong* were formed by separation from already existing *dong*, two to three new *dong* emerged consequentially in every decade, with the exception of the early 1980s, when the construction of new residential houses on the newly built Munsu street and along the Taedonggang banks was the reason for the formation of numerous new *dong*.

Year (*dong* total)	new *dong*
1955 (9)	
1963 (10)	1
1967 (11)	1
1972 (15)	4
1982 (24)	9
1991 (25)	1

It is possible to divide the *kuyok* into three areas. In 1981 the *kuyok* was divided for a short period, in the West the Munsu-kuyok emerged. The part that also belonged to the Taedonggang-kuyok between 1981 and 1983 is called "East" in the table below. The part that belonged to the Munsu-kuyok between 1981 and 1983 is subdivided in the "West," which include the area around the Munsu-street and the Taedonggang banks, while the remaining parts of the former Munsu-kuyok are classified as "Center."

Table Pyongyang-IX. *Dong* in Taedonggang-kuyok

	East	Center	West
1955 (9)	6	3	–
1963 (10)	6	4	–
1967 (11)	6	5	–
1972 (14)	8	6	–
1981 (15)	9	6	–
1982 (24)	9	6	9
1991 (25)	9	7	9

It is clearly noticeable that the developmental pole lies in the western part of the *kuyok*.

Tongdaewon-kuyok – the *kuyok* east to the Juche Tower

Tongdaewon-kuyok is located directly south from Taedonggang-kuyok. Since 1982 the Juche Tower is located there in the Tongdaewon-kuyok. In Tongdaewon-kuyok several research and educational facilities, like the Kim Il-sung High Level Party University, the Kŭmsŏng University of Politics, the Kim Hyong Jik University of Education, the Pyongyang University of Dramatic and Cinematic Arts, the Pyongjang University of Physical Education and others, are located.

On the territory of today's Tongdaewon-kuyok nine *dong* in 1955 were situated. Until 1972 nine others emerged due to separations from already existing *dong*. It can be noticed that IPA-1 (2003, 110) does not mention any new *dong* in the period after 1972.

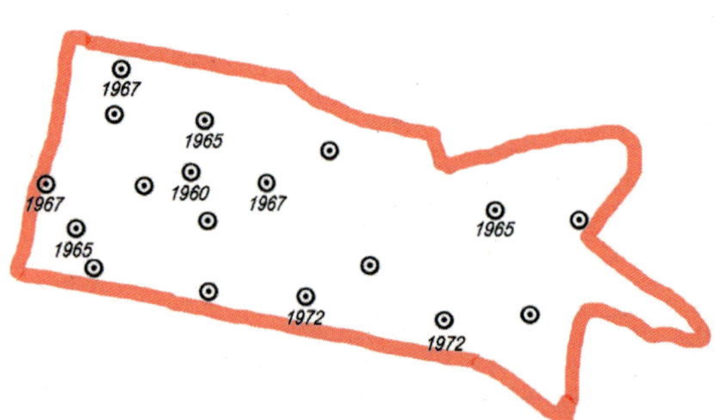

Figure Pyongyang-XXV. *Dong* in Tongdaewon-kuyok

Figure Pyongyang-XXVI. Tongdaewon-kuyok (2012)

Year (*dong* total)	new *dong*
1955 (9)	
1960 (10)	1
1965 (13)	3
1967 (16)	3
1972 (18)	3

The eastern part of the *kuyok* is hilly including the 82 m high Munsu-bong.

Table Pyongyang-X. *Dong* in Tongdaewon-kuyok

	West	East
1955 (9)	6	3
1960 (10)	7	3
1965 (13)	9	4
1967 (16)	12	4
1972 (18)	12	6

The West and the area around Munsu-bong both doubled their amount of *dong*. In the West no new *dong* emerged after the 1960s.

The Kyŏngryŏn Aeguk Carbonated Drink Factory was established in 1961 as Raengchŏn Cider Factory. In 1982 the factory, which is located at the bottom of the Munsu-bong, that produces cold soft drinks, was renamed to its current name. The beginnings of the Educational Books Printing Factory as a print shop can be traced back to 1946, and the company operates as a factory since 1948. Textbooks of all kinds, starting from the primer for kindergartens to university textbooks are printed there. The Tongdaewon Garment Factory is located at Tongsin2-dong. The Moranbong Joint Venture

Company was part of the Tongdaewon Garment Factory and is operating as an independent factory since 1987. The Pyongyang Footwear Factory is situated in Samma2-dong, in the eastern part of the district. Its predecessor used to be a factory that produced galoshes since 1921. However, the factory on its current place was built in 1958. Throughout the years the factory constantly increased its range of products (IPA-1 2003, 111; KOFC 2010, 609).

Songyo-kuyok – Industrial area in East-Pyongyang

The Chŏngnyŏn-street which has been built in 1958 that merges into the Munsu-street in the North runs through the western part of Songyo-kuyok. Located in this *kuyok*, there are many factories of the light industry sector that produce steel ware, rubber, cereal products, other food, textile, textile machines, elevators, medicine, lighting appliance etc. Songyu-kuyŏk also consists of a western part and a hilly eastern part.

On the territory of today's Songyo-kuyok ten *dong* existed in the year 1955. Until 1972 eleven more emerged due to separations from already existing *dong*.

On the southern border to Rakrang-kuyok the Mujin-chŏn runs into the Taedong-gang. One of its tributary streams separates the Songyo-kuyok in a western and an eastern part.

The central street in the western part is the Chŏngnyŏn-street that runs from North to South. Between this street and the Taedong-gang large factories are lined up in the southern part of this district. For example: the Pyongyang Rubber Factory, the Pyongyang Textile Machine Factory, the Kim Jong Suk Pyongyang Textile Mill, the Phyongun-Jungsong Joint Venture Corporation. In the South lies Taedonggang station.

The eastern border of this district runs along the Phyŏngdŏk-son railway line from Kujang to Tokchon.

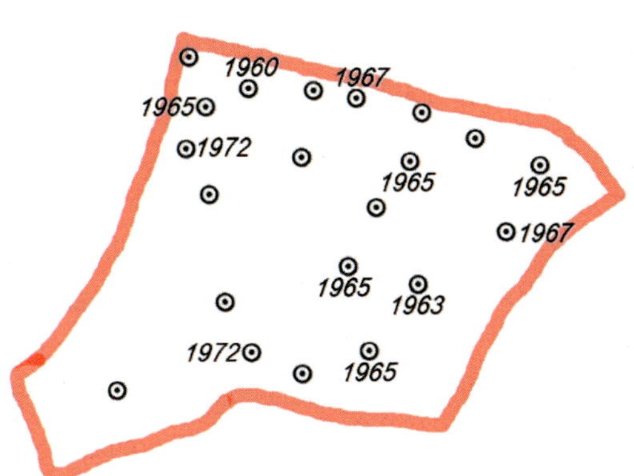

Figure Pyongyang-XXVII. *Dong* in Sonkyo-kuyok

Figure Pyongyang-XXVIII. Sonkyo-kuyok (2012)

Year (*dong* total)	new *dong*
1955 (10)	
1960 (11)	1
1963 (12)	1
1965 (17)	5
1967 (19)	2
1972 (21)	2

Table Pyongyang-XI. *Dong* in Sonkyo-kuyok

	West	East
1955 (10)	5	5
1960 (11)	6	5
1963 (12)	6	6
1965 (17)	7	10
1967 (19)	8	11
1972 (21)	9	12

The "East" possibly had a stronger development than the "West." In the year 1965 alone, five new *dong* emerged. This might be, because the majority of the factories developed close to the rail lines in the east and southeast of the *kuyok*. Even here there are no administrative changes shown after 1972.

After Pyongchon-kuyok, Sonkyo-kuyok is Pyongyang's *kuyok* housing most of the industrial companies.

The most important and largest factory of this district is the Kim Jong Suk Pyongyang Textile Mill. Other factories of this *kuyok*, such as the Pyongyang Textile Machine Factory and the Songyo Knitted Goods Factory, emerged as former subsidiaries of this company.

The Kim Jong Suk Pyongyang Textile Mill has a total area of 1,300,000 m² with 10,000 employees. Commencement of construction was in 1949, in 1950 the factory was completed, however it was destroyed during the Korean War. Starting from 1954 the factory was rebuilt and relaunched. In 1955 a paint factory was built with Soviet help. Later on, additional enhancements followed (KOFC 2010, 592). In 2011 the Pyongyang Textile Mill was named Kim Jong Suk Pyongyang Textile Mill. The Pyongyang Textile Machine Factory was established in 1952 as a subsidiary of the Pyongyang Textile Mill, but became an independent factory in 1956 (IPA-1 2003, 310-311). The Pyongyang Textile Tools Factory was part of the Pyongyang Textile Machine Factory and became independent in 1959. The total area is 58,000 m² (IPA-1 2003, 311). Pyongyang Songyo Knitted Goods Factory, which produces knitwear for adults and kids, was separated from the Pyongyang Textile Mill and became independent in 1963 (IPA-1 2003, 311).

Pyongyang Steel Works is located in Utme-dong in the east of the district. The factory was built in 1971 and started its production in 1973. The total area is 140,000 m² (IPA-1 2003, 310). The Pyongyang Rubber Factory was established in 1920. Within the scope of the second Seven-Year-Plan (1978-1984) huge enhancements were undertaken (IPA-1 2003, 310). Up until 1945 the Pyongyang Elevator Factory was a small repair shop. Starting from 1971 it became a main factory for the production of elevators. Also valves etc. are built there (IPA-1 2003, 311). The Pyongyang General Lighting Appliances Factory was established in 1946 and has a total area of 120,000 m². In the same year the Pyongyang Pharmaceutical Factory was established (IPA-1 2003, 312).

The Pyongyang Cornstarch Factory produces food made of corn. This factory was built in 1931 by an American company, but was taken over by Mitsubishi in 1937 (IPA-1 2003, 310). Pyongyang Essential Foodstuff Factory's predecessor is a factory built in 1933. They produce sauces and oil (soy sauce, soybean paste etc.) (IPA-1 2003, 310). The Pyongyang Essential Goods Factory produces bags, raincoats, hairpins etc. The factory was established in 1947 (IPA-1 2003, 311-312).

The Phyongun-Jungsong Joint Venture Corporation has started the automobile assembly in 2011. It is a cooperation between the Guidance Bureau of Passenger Transport (Pyongyang) and China Dandong China-DPRK Border Trading Co Ltd. The total area is larger than 10,000 m². "It produces Kumgangsan-brand buses with 19 to 50 seats and Chonmalli-brand 0.5 to 15 ton trucks" (Pyongyang Times October 8, 2011).

IV.2.12. 4. City suburbs west of the Taedong-gang

Samsok-kuyok – *Kuyok* with large agricultural companies

The Samsong-kuyok is the most northeastern *kuyok* of Pyongyang, west from the Taedong-gang. It consists of four *dong* and seven *ri*, although all *dong* are located in the southern part of the *kuyok*. The northwest of the *kuyok* is occupied by the southern part of the Chŏngryong mountain range, where the Kuksa-bong (444 m) marks the border for Unjong-kuyok and Ryongsong-kuyok and the Paekjuk-san (393 m) marks the border to Unjong-kuyok. The eastern border is formed by the Taedong-gang, in which the Todŏk-ri,where the in 1983 completed Ponghwa Barrage is situated, on the border to Kangdong-kun is located (IPA-1 2003, 275). In the southeast of the *kuyok*, where the Taedong-gang meanders towards East, a domicile of the leadership of the DPRK is suspected.

In Samsok-kuyok a number of specialized agricultural companies are situated, especially the Taedonggang Combined Fruit Farm in the east of the *kuyok*. Examples of intensive animal husbandry are the Kwangdŏk Pig Farm in the north of the *kuyok*, as well as the Wŏnsin General Poultry Farm, the Wŏnsin Chicken Farm and the Todŏk Duck Farm.

Due to the excellent location, according to the *feng shui* philosophy, between mountains and rivers, there are a number of historical tombs within the *kuyok*.

The IPA merely stated one single industrial company of this *kuyok* as an important company: the Samsok Stevia Refining Factory. It is a food factory, which cleans, extracts and refines stevia (sugar leaf) on a total area of 25,000 m² since 1981. This illustrates the economic structure, which is very highly aligned to the agriculture of this *kuyok*.

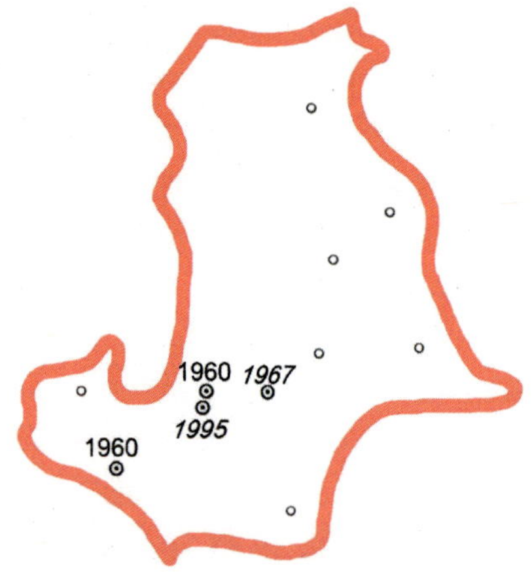

Figure Pyongyang-XXIX. *Dong* and *ri* in Samsok-kuyok

Statistics Samsok-kuyok (4 *dong*, 7 *ri*)

	Dong-Formation	*Dong*-Splitting
1960 (2)	2	-
1967 (3)	-	1
1995 (4)	-	1

Twice (in 1967 and in 1995) new *dong* were created in the center of the *kuyok* by splitting from Sŏngmun-dong, thereby suggesting a growth in population during this time. Between 1986 and 2008, the proportion of the urban population of Samsok-kuyok grew by 3.1% to 50.6%.

Unjong-kuyok – the science district

Until 1995 Unjong was still a part of Phyonsong-si. Phyongsong itself had been founded in the 1960s as a city of science. Numerous research institutions, above all the Academy of Natural Sciences, were built here. However in 1995, the southern part of the city of Phyongsong, the part where the Academy is located, was reorganized as Unjong-kuyok of the city of Pyongyang. Consequentially two *dong* (Tŏksan-dong, Paesan-dong) and parts of two other *dong* of Phyongsong-si became part of the newly founded Unjong-kuyok (the "district of the benevolent affection") of Pyongyang-si.

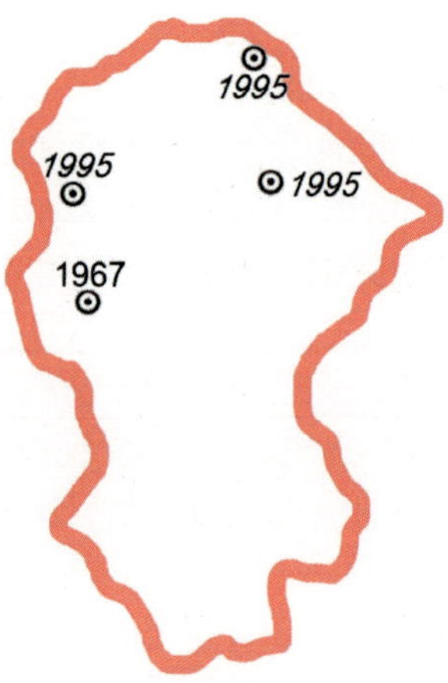

Figure Pyongyang-XXX. *Dong* in Unjong-kuyok

The Taehŭng Unjong Wood Processing Factory, which produced a wide range of furniture, is the only industrial company that is listed in IPA as an important company for this district. It has a total area of 6,600 m² (IPA-1 2003, 390-391).

Statistics Unjong-kuyok (4 *dong*)

	Dong-Formation	*Dong*-Splitting
196 7(1)	1	-
199 5(4)	-	3

The *dong* are situated in the north of the *kuyok*, near the city of Phyongsong.

Ryongsong-kuyok at the foot of the Chŏngryong mountain range

The *kuyok* hosts a multitude of educational and research institutions with a focus on agriculture. A housing estate of the ruling elite should be located in this *kuyok*. The east of the *kuyok* is occupied by a part of the Chŏngryong mountain range.

Large agricultural companies are the Ryongsong Quail Farm, the Ryongsong Chicken Farm, which was built in 1966, and the Pyongyang Greenhouse Farm, which was built in 1971 and is specialized in greenhouse vegetables.

Additionally, the three industrial companies, which are listed in the IPA as important companies, are connected with the agriculture: the Maram Assorted Feed Factory started with its operation in 1968 (IPA-1 2003, 170), the Moranbong Kimchi Factory in Hwasŏng-dong has a total area of 2,500,000 m² and processes vegetables from the Agricultural Association Operation Hwasŏng (IPA-1 2003, 170-171). The Ryongsong Meat Processing Factory started its operations in 1956 and processes apart from meat also fish, soybeans, fruit, etc. (IPA 1 2003, 170).

The KOFC (2010, 256) also mentions the Pyongyang Precision Machine Factory (March 25th Factory) as an important company, which is located in Ryongsong-kuyok with 3,500 workers. In 1959, it went into operation, in 1960 a Bearing division with Chinese assistance was built.

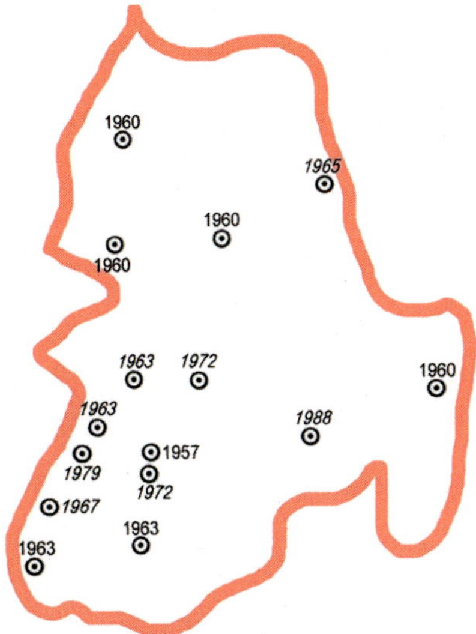

Figure Pyongyang-XXXI. *Dong* in Ryongsong-kuyok

The September 18th Factory (Ryongsong Bearing Factory) is referred to in KIET (1996, 297-298) as one of the leading Bearing factories of the DPRK. It was built with the help of the Soviet Union, the first construction stage was completed in 1984 and the second construction stage in 1986. The operating area is specified with multiple 10,000 m².

Statistics Ryongsong-kuyok (15 *dong*)

	Dong-Formation	*Dong*-Splitting
1957 (1)	1 *rodongjagu*	-
1960 (5)	4	-
1963 (9)	2	2
1965 (10)	-	1
1967 (11)	-	1
1972 (13)	-	2
1979 (14)	-	1
1988 (15)	-	1

Sunan-kuyok – *Kuyok* with the International Airport of Pyongyang

In Sunan-kuyok the Pyongyang Sunan International Airport is located. Thus the *kuyok* is also the seat of various logistics companies and airlines, starting with the Air Koryo. Apart from that, the *kuyok* is rather influenced by agriculture. Specialized companies in the *kuyok* are the Pyongyang Ostrich Farm and the Sunan Fruit Farm. Important industrial companies for this *kuyok* are neither listed in IPA nor KOFC.

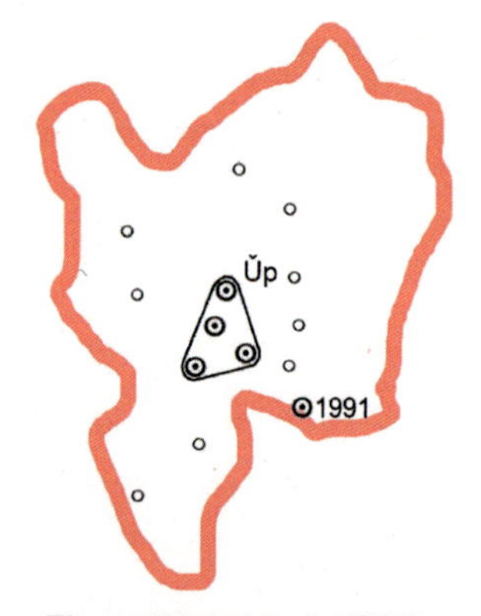

Figure Pyongyang-XXXII.
Dong and *ri* in Sunan-kuyok

Statistics Sunan-kuyok (5 *dong*, 9 *ri*) (until 1972 Sunan-kun)

	Dong-Formation	*Dong*-Splitting
1952(1)	1 *up*	-
1972 (4)	-	(3)
1991 (5)	1	- (1991/2)

The county was transferred into a *kuyok* in 1972. In doing so, the *up* was divided into four *dong*. Later in 1991, in the south of the *kuyok* Taeyang-dong was founded.

Hyongjesan-kuyok – *Kuyok* with the second highest increase in the rate of urbanization since 1986

Important facilities in Hyongjesan-kuyok are the Korea Film Studios and the Pyongyang

University of Railways. The Hyongjesan Export Knitted Goods Factory, which went into operation in 1982, is located in Sŏson-dong. It produces knitwear for men and women that are also exported (IPA-1 2003, 451-452). Other important companies of the *kuyok* are the Pyongyang Cinema Film Copy Factory, founded in 1948 and the Sopho Railway Machine Factory. There are also chicken farms in the *kuyok* (Hadan Chicken Farm, Sŏpho Chicken Farm) and a research institute founded in 1965 for Poultry Science.

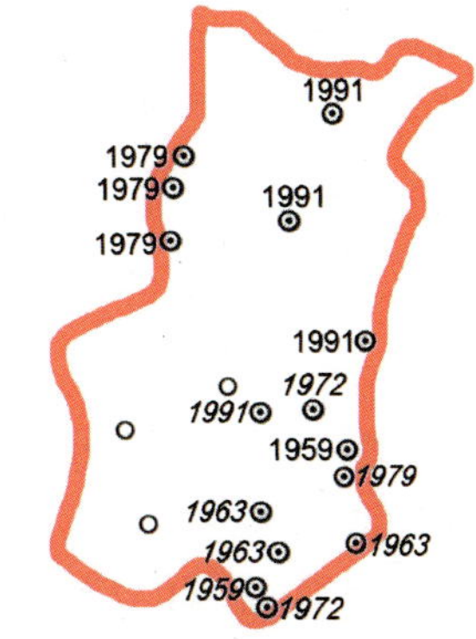

Figure Pyongyang-XXXIII. *Dong* and *ri* in Hyongjesan-kuyok

Statistics Hyongjesan-kuyok (15 *dong*, 3 *ri*);

	Dong-Formation	*Dong*-Splitting
1959 (2)	2	
1963 (5)	-	3
1972 (7)	-	2
1979 (11)	3	1
1991 (15)	3	1

More recent are the *dong* in the northern half of the *kuyok*. The three *dong*, located in the northwest, were established in 1979. In 1991, three new *dong* were founded in the northeast of the *kuyok*. Between 1986 and 2008, the percentage of urban population in Samsok-kuyok grew from 11.7% to 91.1%, this is the second highest increase of a *kuyok* of Pyongyang within this period of time after the Rakrang-kuyok.

Mangyongdae-kuyok – Kwangbok residental area and Chŏngchun Sport Village

In the center of this *kuyok* the Ryonggak-san (292 m) rises. The eastern boundary is formed by the Pothong-gang, the southern border by the Taedong-gang. In the southwestern border the Taebo-san (372 m) rises. The main settlement areas are located east of the Ryonggak-san in Kwangbok Street, where high rise residential blocks, shops and businesses are lined up. The Kwangbok residential district with 30,000 apartments was built in 1989. This is crossed by Chŏngchun Street, where numerous sports facilities are located. The construction of the Kwangbok Street and the sports facilities are connected with the 13th World Festival of Youth and Students (WFYS), which was held from 1-8 July 1989. West of the Chŏngchun street is the Mangyongdae-dong, where the Kim Il-sung Military University is located, the birthplace of Kim Il-sung as well as an amusement park. Agricultural specialized companies in the *kuyok* are the Mangyongdae Chicken Farm, the

Ryongbok Pig Ranch and Chilgol Farm Fish Breeding Ground.

The Mangyongdae Machine Tool Factory is located between the railway line from Pyongyang to Nampho and the road between Pyongyang and the Taedong-up. It was founded in 1959 by the merger of three production cooperatives. On a total area of 66,100 m^2 3,000 workers are employed (IPA 1 2003, 193; KOFC 2010, 253). The Manggyongdae Roentgen Factory in Tangsang-dong manufactures medical devices. It was built from 1971 and went into operation in 1973. The total area is 11,000 m^2 (IPA-1 2003, 193-194). The Pyongyang Piano Joint Venture Company on Kwangbok Street is a cooperation between companies from the DPRK and Austria.

The Pyongyang Film Factory was built in 1981 and started its business in 1985. It has a total area of 23,000 m^2 (IPA-1 2003, 195). The Pyongyang Aluminum Goods Factory manufactures kitchen utensils. It has a total area of 50,000 m^2 (IPA-1 2003, 195). The Mangyongdae Disabled Soldiers' Fountain Pen Factory is located on Kwangbok Street. They started operating in 1952 and now have a size of 30,000 m^2 (IPA-1 2003, 194). The Ryuwon Footwear Factory produces sports shoes (KOTC 2010, 610).

The construction of the Pyongyang Wheat Flour Processing Factory in Samhŭng-dong began in 1976. It has a total area of 120,000 m^2 (IPA-1 2003, 194-195). The Pyongyang Rice Mill started its production in 1982 and has a total area of 190,000 m^2 (IPA-1 2003, 195). The Kwangbok Street Kimchi Factory was built in 1992 and went into operation in 1994. The total area is 35,000 m^2 (IPA-1 2003, 193).

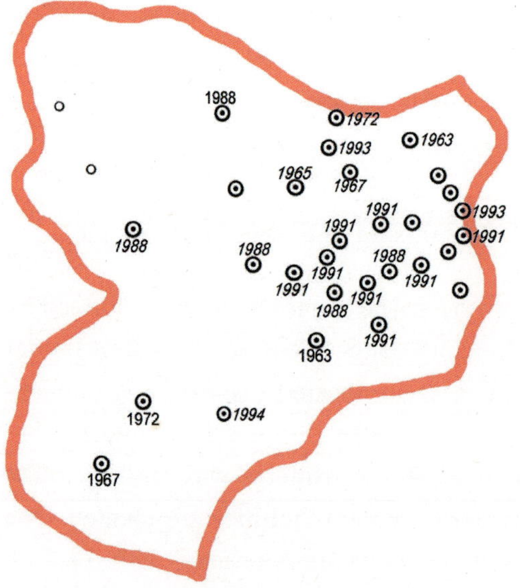

Figure Pyongyang-XXXIV. *Dong* and *ri* in Mangyongdae-kuyok

Statistics Mangyongdae-kuyok (29 *dong*, 2 *ri*) West

	Dong-Formation	*Dong*-Splitting
1952 (1)	1 *up*	-
1955 (6)	5	-
1963 (8)	1	1
1965 (9)	-	1
1967 (11)	1	1
1972 (13)	1	1
1988 (18)	1	4
1991 (26)	-	8
1993 (28)	-	2
199 4(29)	-	1

IV.2.12. 5. City suburbs east of the Taedong-gang

Sadong-kuyok – concentration of the population in the north of the *kuyok*

The population of the *kuyok* is concentrated on the Mirim-plain in the North.

The Taedonggang Beer Factory uses the facilities of a British brewery, which was closed in 2000. Since 2002 they produce in Pyongyang, where German brewing technology is also used.

The Taedonggang TV Set Factory in Samgol-dong is the first and largest TV factory of the DPR Korea. It was built in the beginning of 1974 with Romanian help and operation started in 1980. The total area amounts to 670,000 m². In 2001 TVs for the South Korean LG Group were assembled here (IPA-1 2003, 252-253; KOFC 2010, 307-308). The Mirim Concrete Block Factory is located near the Mirim Barrage. It was built in the early 1950s and contributed to the rebuilding of the city after the Korean War. Later it provided a great service in the construction of residential streets and the residential districts Maxima, Munsu, Kwangbok, Rakwŏn and Thongil (IPA-1 2003, 253).

In the Sadong General Foodstuff Factory kimchi, pastries and fruit drinks are manufactured. The district has a long tradition of producing fur in Songhwa2-dong. The manufactured goods are also exported to Europe (IPA-1 2003, 253).

A specialized agriculture company in the Sadong-kuyok is the Pyongyang Pig Farm.

Statistics Sadong-kuyok (13 *dong*, 6 *ri*)

	Dong-Formation	*Dong*-Splitting
1955 (1)	1	-
1963 (3)	2	-
1965 (4)	1	-
1967 (6)	2	-
1972 (8)	1	1
1974 (9)	-	1
1983 (10)	-	1
1991 (12)	-	2
1994 (13)	1	-

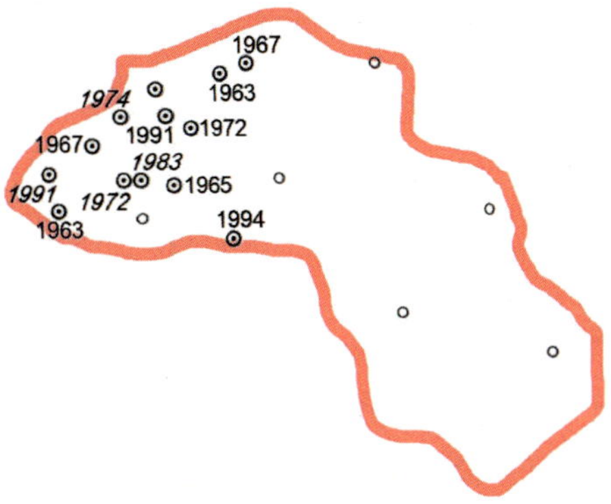

Figure Pyongyang-XXXV. *Dong* and *ri* in the Sadong-kuyok

Ryokpho-kuyok – agricultural *kuyok* in the south of Pyongyang

Residential areas of this *kuyok* are found in the North and in the center.

The IPA mentions a number of companies of agriculture that are located here, but only one factory, the Saenal Electronic Applications Factory which was built in 1986. KOFC

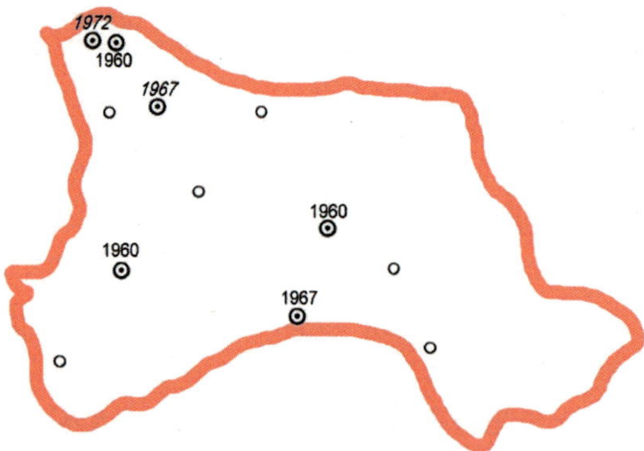

Figure Pyongyang-XXXVI. *Dong* and *ri* in the Ryokpho-kuyok

(2010, 448) states that the Pyongyang Building Materials Factor construction started in 2003 and was completed in 2007. It produces tile, sanitary ceramics, artificial marble etc.

In the Ryokpho Ranch, which was established in 1954, pork and milk are produced. In the Pyongyang Fruit Farm, which was built in 1952, apples, pears, peaches and grapes are mainly cultivated. The September 27th Chicken Farm was built in 2001 (IPA-1 2003, 149-150). Within the district numerous historical tombs are situated, such as those for King Tongmyŏng in Ryongsan-ri.

Statistics Ryokpho-kuyok (6 *dong*, 6 *ri*)

	Dong-Formation	*Dong*-Splitting
1960 (3)	3	-
1967 (5)	2	-
1972 (6)	-	1

Between 1986 and 2008 the share of urban population in Ryokpho-kuyok grew by 9.6% to 73.8%.

Rakrang-kuyok–*Kuyok* with the latest high rise residential block neighborhood

The population is concentrated in the north of the district, where in the second half of the 1980s until 1993 tens of thousands of apartments in the Thongil residential district were completed. In the south of the district the Pyongyang-plain is located, which stretches across Kangnam County and is an important rice-growing region for supplying the population of the capital. A specialized company in the district is the Tudan Duck Farm. In the district numerous historical tombs in particular from the Koguryo period are situated. A major sight of the district is the Monument of Reunification. Pyongyang University of Science and Technology (PUST) which was opened in 2010 is located in the Rakrang-kuyok, which is the first privately financed educational institution of the DPR Korea.

Figure Pyongyang-XXXVII. Rakrang-kuyok (2012)

Figure Pyongyang-XXXVIII. Monument to the Three-Point Charter for National Reunification (2012)

The East Pyongyang Power Station in Rakrang-dong was built with the help of the Soviet Union between 1989 and 1991, in order to provide electricity and heat supply for the Rakwŏn residential area that was still under construction at that time. In 2002 extensions of the power plant were made with the support of OPEC (KOFC 2010, 155-156).

In Rakrang-kuyok are numerous factories that produce building materials. The Pyongyang Metal building materials factory is located in the Jŏngo-dong region at the eastern edge of the district. Here, among other things, bathtubs, handles, heaters are produced. In the 1970s, the business was expanded (IPA-1 2003, 125). In s Pyongyang August 17th Structural Elements Factory, which was built in 1986 and started its operation in 1991 on a total area of 112,000 m², door and window frames and electrical equipment are manufactured (IPA-1 2003, 126). The Pyongyang Chemical Building Materials Factory manufactures waterproof paper, fiber tubes, roofing tiles, and antiseptic liquids. It was founded in 1960 as the Pyongyang Ceramic Factory and produced building blocks and bricks amongst other things. In the early 1970s the production changed to chemical building materials. The factory processes asbestos from the Sŭngri Chemical Factory (Rason), dolomite from Kimchaek and Phyongsong and white cement from the Sŭnghori Cement Factory (Sungho-kun, Hwangbuk Province) (IPA-1 2003, 126).

The Rakyŏn Joint Corporation manufactures polystyrene (EPS), which is used for packing fragile goods or as thermal insulation plates (IPA-1 2003, 125). Also calm worms and inedible shell fish as bait are made here (KCNA November 11, 2003). The Rakrang Paper Factory was founded in 1959. After several expansions, it has a total area of 28,000 m². The Meari Sound Equipment Company is located on Thongil Street. It is the best known manufacturer of audio equipment such as microphones, amplifiers etc. in the DPR Korea. The company was founded in 1948 and reorganized in 1991. The Aeguk

Preventive Medicine Factory was founded in 1993. The total area amounts to 19,500 m². The Pyongyang Leather Factory is located in the region Jŏngo-dong and has a total area of 96,900 m². This company, whose construction started in 1972, went into operation in 1974, and produces leather which is used for further processing *inter alia* in footwear factories (IPA 1 2003, 125).

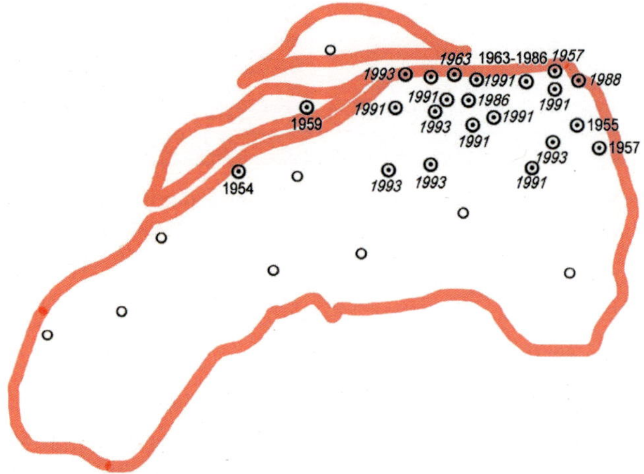

Figure Pyongyang–XXXIX. *Dong* and *ri* in the Rakrang-kuyok

Statistics Rakrang-kuyok (21 *dong*, 9 *ri*)

	Dong-Formation	*Dong*-Splitting
1954 (1)	1 *rodongjagu*	-
1955 (2)	1	-
1957 (4)	1	1
1959 (5)	1	-
1963 (7)	2	-
1986 (7)	-	-1/1
1988 (8)	-	1
1991 (16)	-	8
1993 (21)	-	5

In the 1950s and 1960s several *ri* have been converted into *dong*, in the 1980s and 1990s existing *dong* were split and thereby new *dong* came into being.

Between 1986 and 2008 the share of urban population in Rakrang-kuyok grew by 21.1% to 90.4%

Kangdong-kun – Location of significant coal mines

Except for the west, the terrain of the district is mountainous. Most *rodongjagu* focus on the western half of the *kun*, where the Kangdong Area Coal Mining Complex is located. Only the Namgang-rodongjagu is located in the extreme Southeast. The most significant sight of the *kun* is the alleged Tomb of King Tan'gun.

Important companies in the *kun* are the Kangdong Area Coal Mining Complex among others of which are the Hŭkryŏng Coal Mine, the Tŏksan Coal Mine and the Kangdong Coal Mine.

Of further importance are the hydroelectric power stations of the *kun*, such as the Namgang Power Plant that was built between 1989 and 1993 in the South of the *kun*, which dams up the water of the Nam-gang, a tributary of the Taedong-gang, and the Mirim Floodgate Power Plant.

In Kubin-ri an agricultural farm is located, specializing in the breeding of goats.

In Kandong-up are a couple of factories that manufacture machines, food, essential goods, clothing, and building materials. In Kobi-rodongjagu are several factories that produce building materials, chemical goods and bricks.

Major coal-fired power plants are the Hŭkryŏng Coal Mine (Hŭkryŏng-rodongjagu), Kobi Coal Mine, Kandong Coal Mine (Kobi-rodongjagu), Taeri Coal Mine (Taeri-rodongjagu) Songga Coal Mine Toksan Coal Mine, Jangrim Coal Mine, Phyongsan Coal Mine (Songga-rodongjagu), Hari Coal Mine (Hari-rodongjagu) and Samdŭng Coal Mine (Samdŭng-ri).

Kangdong-kun is composed of one up, nine *rodongjagu* and 15 *ri*.

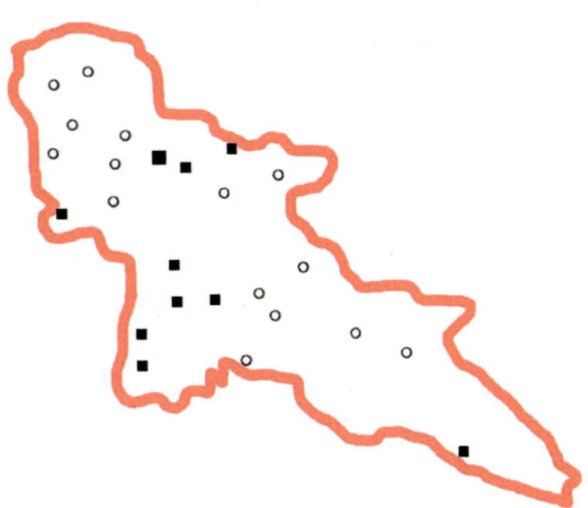

Figure Pyongyang-XL. *Up*, *rodongjagu* and *ri* in Kangdong-kun

Statistics Kangdong-kun
1952 (2) *up*, Hŭgryŏng-rodongjagu
1963 (3) Hari-rodongjagu
1967 (6) Kobi-rodongjagu, Songga-rodongjagu, Taeri-rodongjagu
1989 (7) Namgang-rodongjagu
1993 (10) Hari-rodongjagu was split and consequentially Sangri-rodongjagu was formed. Hŭgryŏng-rodongjagu was

split and thus Sokchu-rodongjagu was formed.
Songga -rodongjagu was split and Ryŏngnam-rodongjagu was formed

Kangnam-kun – rice producer for the capital's population

This county lies in the south of the Pyongyang plain and is a major rice producer. Even fish are caught and cultivated in Kangnam County. In Ryonpho-ri on the Taedong-gang is a fishing cooperative, while in Majong-ri and Sinŭng-ri fish breeding farms were established. In Kangnam-up wich has been founded in 1952 several factories are located that manufacture clothing, agricultural equipment, food and medicine. In Koŭp-ri a cement factory can be found that manufactures vehicle accessories, in Ryonggok-ri.

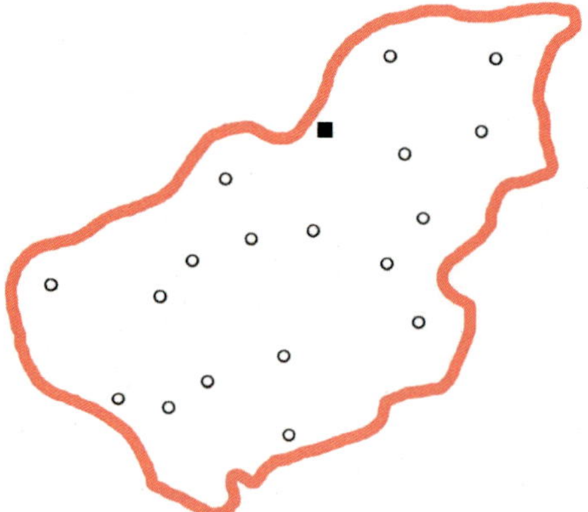

Figure Pyongyang-XLI. *Up* and *ri* in the Kangnam-kun

Kangnam-kun is composed of one *up* and 18 *ri*.

IV.2.12. 6. Summary: Administrative changes in the *kuyok* and kun of Pyongyang

Between 1957 and 1995, 190 new *dong* emerged in Pyongyang. More than half of the new *dong* in the inner city area and about 35% of the new *dong* in the outskirts areas emerged in the 1960s. In the 1970s, the number of new *dong* in the inner city area was higher than in the outskirts, in the 1990s it is *vice versa*.

Table Pyongyang-XII. New *dong* in the regions of Pyongyang

	Inner City (West)	Inner City (East)	Outskirts (West)	Outskirts (East)	
1950s	4 (8.9%)	–	3 (4.8%)	3 (6.5%)	10 (5.3%)
1960s	27 (60%)	18 (48.6%)	22 (35.5%)	16 (34.8%)	83 (43.7%)
1970s	11 (24.4%)	9 (24.3%)	11 (17.7%)	4 (8.7%)	35 (18.4%)
1980s	3 (6.7%)	9 (24.3%)	6 (9.7%)	4 (8.7%)	22 (11.6%)
1990s	–	1 (2.7%)	20 (32.3%)	19 (41.3%)	40 (21.1%)
	45	37	62	46	190

Administrative changes not only lead to new *dong* being formed, it also happens that existing *dong* will be merged with another *dong* and thus disappear. So there are also periods, in which the number of *dong* in a *kuyok* does not increase, but decreases. Compared to most other cities of North Korea the phenomena of vanishing *dong* are relatively frequent in Pyongyang. Also, in other cities *dong* only have disappeared until 1972, but this phenomenon is, however, observed mainly in Pyongyang. According to present calculations based on the source IPA-I a total of 17 *dong* disappeared in Pyongyang between 1959 and 1991. Of these, 16 are located in the inner city area west of the Taedong-gang and one in Rakrang (city suburbs east of the Taedong-gang).

Table Pyongyang-XIII. Vanished *dong*

	Jung	Moranbong	Pothonggang	Taesong	Rakrang	
1959	1					1
1960		2				2
1972	2	1				3
1979	1			1		2
1981	3					3
1983		1	1	1		3
1986			1		1	2
1991			1			1
	7	4	3	2	1	17

Mergers of *dong* can be interpreted as an indication that in this region residential areas have disappeared in favor of areas for other use. This is identifiable especially in the inner-city districts, especially in Jung-kuyok, where residential and economic functions were displaced by the construction of squares, representational buildings, parks and so on. This causes a reduction of the residential population and leads thereby to a reduction of the *dong*, where large-scale changes in the existing buildings can be made relatively fast or later on. An example of the fast disappearance of *dong* in the context of constructional transformation is the reduction of *dong* in the Moranbong Park area, where in the years of 1959 and 1960, at the time of the creation of the park, a total of three *dong* disappeared in the Jung-and Moranbong-kuyok.

The number of new *dong* in the 1980s is comparatively low. An exception is the Taedonggang-kuyok (inner city districts east of the Taedong-gang), where in 1983 the residential area Munsu was completed with 17,000 apartments (Verlag für Fremdsprachige Literatur 1995, 83).

In the city suburbs west of the Taedong-gang almost as many *dong* emerged in the 1990s as in the 1960s. Eleven of the 20 new *dong* were established in the 1990s in

Mangyongdae-kuyok, where the Kwangbok residential area was completed with more than 30,000 apartments in 1989 (Verlag für Fremdsprachige Literatur 1995, 83). Four new *dong* emerged in 1991 in the central and northern part of the Hyongjesan-kuyok, three of them due to the transformation of *ri* to *dong*, whereby the proportion of the urban population in this *kuyok* grew between 1986 and 2008 by 11.7%.

In the city suburbs east of the Taedong-gang the total number of emerged *dong* in the 1990s surpasses the number of emerged *dong* in the 1960s. This is due to the establishment of the Thongil residential area in Rakrang-kuyok, which was completed in 1993 and includes tens of thousands of apartments (Verlag für Fremdsprachige Literatur 1995, 83). The Rakrang-kuyok is also the *kuyok* with the highest increase in the proportion of urban population among the *kuyok* of Pyongyang between 1986 and 2008 (plus 21.1%).

IV.2.13. Nampho

Port of Pyongyang – Second largest city of the DPR Korea

Nampho is the port of the capital Pyongyang and thus the largest trading port of North Korea on the Yellow Sea Coast. Further characterizations of the city are "industrial center of the Phyongan-Hwanghae region" and "location for stacking rice and seafood on the Northwest Coast" (Chosun Ilbo January 15, 1996). The development of the city, which was initially called Jinnampho, began in 1897 with the admission as an international treaty port by the Korean government. After the independence of Korea from Japanese rule, the syllable Jin (stock) was removed from the name, since it is reminiscent of the colonial heritage as a port of entry for the Japanese during the Sino-Japanese War (IPA-2 2003, 22-23).

Table Nampho-I. Basic data

Population	983,660 (Rank 2)
Area	1281 km² (Rank 5)
Population density	768 I./km² (Rank 10)
Administrative units	82 *dong*/49 *ri* (67%) (Rank 14)
"Urban" population/"rural" population	71.5%/28.5% (Rank 21)

The municipal area of Nampho changed several times in the course of time. In 1979 Nampho became a city with provincial status, thus independent from the Phyongnam Province, which apart from Nampho itself included Taean-si and Ryonggang-kun. In 1983 the city was composed of five *kuyok* and one *kun*. In 2004, however, Nampho again became a part of the Phyongnam Province, but the city area included only the two southernmost *kuyok*. In 2010 Nampho was then detached from the Phyongnam Province and contains again all the parts, which were a part of the municipal area already before 2004 and additionally the Onchon-kun on the Yellow Sea coast. Thus, Nampho became the second largest city in terms of population of the DPR Korea.

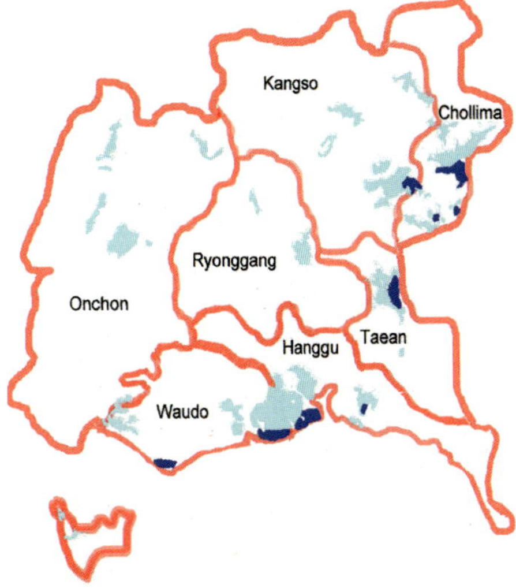

Figure Nampho-I. Urbanised areas (light-blue) and industrial areas (dark blue); (Source Yi Sang-jun et.al. 2011, 52)

The seaport of the Taedonggang-Basin, Jinnampho, was during the first Sino-Japanese War (1894-1895) a small fishing village (Lautensach 1945, 264). Since this war, the port of Jinnampho was a military supply base for the Japanese army (Hŏ U-gung 2007, 102). In 1897 Jinnampho was approved by the Korean government as an international treaty port. The population of Jinnampho grew, the urban area expanded and industrial plants were established. By 1934, Jinnampho had grown into the third largest port of Korea (after Pusan and Inchon) (Lautensach 1945, 264). Factories for the processing of agricultural products and mineral resources originated in the vicinity of the port, from which the goods were then shipped to Japan.

On the basis of the steel industry the machine construction and the shipbuilding industry developed after 1945. Other commercial sectors such as the glass industry made Nampho into a major industrial city. Also the port grew further with the capital Pyongyang in the back.

In May 1981, on the occasion of a visit by Kim Il-sung in Nampho a plan was drawn up, which summarizes three goals:

Nampho as a gateway of the capital Pyongyang and as its biggest satellite town is to be developed into an international port city, which is often visited by foreigners,

Nampho is to be further developed as the largest trading port in the DPR Korea and its export volume is to be increased,

Nampho is expected to develop into the largest industrial region in the west of the DPR Korea, with a concentration to be made on heavy industry (iron production, smelting plants, machine construction, building material production) (Kim Wŏn 1998, 245).

City on the lower reaches of the Taedong-gang

Nampho is located on the lower reaches of the Taedong-gang. Jinnampho developed between bays on the north side of the estuary of the Taedong-gang at the blunt end of a rocky headland (Lautensach 1945, 264), the southern part of the Osŏk-mountain range. In the west of the town center is the Yŏndae-san (98 m), the Wŏn-san (109 m), the Myŏnghyŏp-san (35 m) as well as the Ma-san and in the east with the Handu-san (61m) some low elevations. The tides in Nampho are strongly distinctive. In 1915 land was filled between the built-up city and the Pibal island and the islands of Pibal and Kadŏk were artificially connected with the mainland (Kim Ryŏn-ok 1991, 405).

Within the Osŏk-mountain range in the south are with the Osŏk-san (566m) and the Kuksa-bong (506 m) also the highest elevations of the current municipal area. Apart from this mountain range mostly alluvial and erosional plains predominate. Especially at Samhwa-chŏn and at Sŏchŏn-gang wide plains have formed. Approximately 82% of the city is 50 m below sea level (Yi Sang-jun et.al. 2011, 42). In front of the city are numerous islands such as Cho-do and Ori-sŏm. On the coast of the Yellow Sea territory was recovered, which is now used for agriculture. There are also, in particular in the area around the Kwangryang bay, numerous plants for sea salt production.

Table Nampo–II. Climate values

Annual average	January temperature	August temperature	Precipitation
10.5°C (6)	−4.8°C (9)	24.2°C (5)	837.4 mm (19)

The southern location in comparison to other cities of the DPR Korea causes relatively high temperatures in January in Nampho, the western location for high August temperatures. Rainfall in Nampho in nationwide comparison is low. Only on the east coast are cities, where the annual rainfall is less than in Nampho.

Since the city is situated on the west coast and in the basin of the Taedong-gang, it is well suited for the cultivation of cereals, with wet rice cultivation playing an important part. Therefore, measures of irrigation like the establishment of the Kiyang Region Irrigation Management Office (Kangso) in 1959 have an important role. It is situated in Chŏngsan-ri (Kangso-kuyok) and its task is the ensuring of the water resources of the Thaesŏng-Lake as well as the water supply for the agriculture in the Kiyang region (IPA-2 2003, 47). The Kiyang No. 1 Pumping Station (Chollima-kuyok) with a size of 13,500 m^2, pumps for this purpose water from the Taedong-gang in the Thaesŏng-Lake (IPA-2 2003, 139). Another Pumping Station, the Kiyang No. 2 Pumping Station, is situated in Kangso and has a size of 78,000 m^2. The Pumps for both stations were established in the Rakwŏn

Machine Factory in Sinuiju (IPA-2 2003, 47). In order to supply the urban population with meat, milk and eggs, large farms with intensive livestock farming were established, like the Nampho Chicken Farm, the Nampho Pig Farm, the Kangso Chicken Farm which was founded in 1967 in Janmjin-ri (IPA-2 2003, 46), the Kangso Pig Farm which was founded in 1970 (IPA-2 2003, 46-47) as well as the Taean Chicken Farm. In Taean-kuyok Taejŏng-ri numerous dairy cows are kept (IPA-2 2003, 35). Also the fruit cultivation in the urban area was very much extended. The most important fruits are apples, peaches, pears, grapes as well as persimmons. The rearing of silkworm cocoons in Nampho was also extended (IPA-2 2003, 35).

In Nampho are the fishing and fish cultures of particular importance. Important fish farms are located in Onchon County on the Yellow Sea Coast and Waudo-kuyok Ryŏngnam-ri, where the number of fisheries has increased strongly after the construction of the West Sea Barrage (IPA-2 2003, 35). Important is also the salt production in the plants Kwangryangman, Kuisŏng, Kŭmsŏng and Unha (Onchon-kun). The first two have already been built during the Japanese rule (Kwangryangman: at the beginning of the 1900s, Kuisŏng: in the 1920s) (IPA-4 2003, 340-341).

Major heavy industry companies in the Pyongyang-Nampho-Corridor

Nampho is an important site for key industries as well as the light industry. The four most significant companies of the city are the Chollima Steel Complex, the Taean Heavy Machine Complex, the Kŭmsŏng Tractor Plant and the Taean Friendship Glass Factory. The most important branches of the city are the metal industry (important huts for iron and iron compounds, like the Chollima Steel Complex, April 13th. Iron Works and the May 18th Forging Factory, which went into operation in 1989, are located in Chollima-kuyok), the machine construction, the mining industry (hard coal in Kangso, granite in the district Ryonggang and in Ryongwon-ri and in Mayong-rodongjagu, Onchon-kun), the chemical industry, the building material industry (sheet glass, ceramics, building stone, cement) and the light industry (fabrics, daily goods, food, shoes, paper) (IPA-2 2003, 31-35). In addition, the car factory Pyonghwa Motors is located in Nampho.

Table Nampho-III. Ranking (in parenthesis: number of industrial companies or cultural institutions)

Nampho	KOFC	MOU	IPA	KCNA	KIET	Summary
Companies-total	2 (35)	2 (71)	2 (81)	3 (27)	3 (115)	2
Companies-important	2 (15)	2 (8)	2 (26)		3 (45)	2 (27)
Cultural institutions			2 (36)			

Table Nampho-IV. Ranking (total number of companies in relation to population)

Nampho	KOFC	MOU	IPA	KCNA	KIET	Summary
Companies-total	21	16	5-11-11	19	15-12	15-13

It has already been determined by consideration of the sources that Nampho is the second most populous city in the DPR Korea, according to the evaluation of three sources the city is in in second place and according to the evaluation of two other sources behind Hamhung in third place. KCNA is a North Korean source and the information in KIET is based on the North Korean daily paper Rodong Sinmun. Perhaps companies from Hamhung are more frequently mentioned in North Korean sources to emphasize the significance of the most important city of Northeast Korea.

Table Nampho-V. Specification (in parenthesis: industrial companies)

Nampho	Light Industry	Heavy Industry	Mining	Energy
KOFC	16 (7)	7 (26)	-	12 (2)
MOU	15 (42)	15 (20)	9 (8)	10 (1)
IPA	11 (42)	15 (32)	10 (7)	-
KCNA	13 (13)	12 (11)	6 (1)	14 (2)
KIET	23 (38)	6 (63)	7 (11)	11 (3)

Table Nampho-V shows, that the city has numerous companies from different industrial sectors. In addition to companies of the heavy industry, the city is also home to numerous companies of the light industry. However, the major companies belong in the vast majority to branches of the heavy industry.

In chapter III.7.3. 27 companies were identified as important, of which twelve are situated in Old-Nampho: the Nampho Shipbuilding Complex, the Nampho Ship Factory, the Nampho Ship Repair Factory, the September 10th Ship Repair Factory, the West Sea Ship Repair Factory, the Nampho Telecommunication Machine Factory, the Nampho Dye Factory, the Nampho Children's Medicine Factory, the Nampho Glass Complex, the Nampho Disabled Soldiers' Footwear Factory, the Nampho General Smeltery as well as the Nampho Electrode Factory. Eleven are located in the *kuyok* Kanso, Chollima and Taean: the Kŭmsŏng Tractor Factory, the Kangso Knitting Mill, the Kangso Footwear Factory (Kangso), the Chollima Steel Complex, the April 13th Iron Works, the Kangsŏn Automation Equipment Factory, the Taedonggang Tile Factory, the December Thermal Power Station (Chollima), the Taean Heavy Machine Complex, the Taedonggang Electric Appliances Factory, the Taedonggang and the Taean Friendship Glass Factory as well as four in the *kun*: the Ryonggang Electric Machine Factory, the Ryonggang Generator Factory, the Ryonggang Granite Mine and the Onchon Sindok Spring Water Factory.

Most of the important companies are situated in the two southern *kuyok* of Old-Nampho.[48] In Nampho are important shipyards, starting with the Nampho Shipbuilding Complex, which is the most significant shipyard on the Yellow Sea coast. It has a total area of 273,000 m^2 and 7,000 employees. The Nampho Ship Factory, the Nampho Ship Repair Factory and the September 10th Ship Repair Factory are organisationally subordinate to it. Before 1945 mainly ships were repaired here. Afterwards the complex was expanded into a shipyard, which manufactures numerous types of ships (KOFC 2010, 319-322). The West Sea Ship Repair Factory is situated in the Waudo-kuyok.

The Nampho Telecommunication Machine Factory has a factory area of 23,000 m^2 and employs 3,000 workers. In 1947 it began the production of telephones, in 1962 the production of radios and in 1964 the production of televisions. Nowadays, it has a wide product range (IPA-2 2003, 164). *Inter alia* probably also radar installations for military use are produced (KOFC 2010, 308).

The Nampho Dye Factory started its operation in 1965 and manufactures apart from colours, a variety of chemical products (IPA-2 2003, 34).

The Nampho Children's Medicine Factory started its operation in 1966. Here, mainly multivitamin supplements as well as amino acid supplements for children are produced (IPA-2 2003, 162-163).

A spectacular project is the joint venture of the South Korean Pyonghwa Motors, which is owned by the Unification Church in North Korea. A contract was signed in 2000 and in 2002 a factory, 2 km away from the port was completed in Nampho. Workers "there completed partially built cars, in a form called knockdown kits, that were imported from manufacturers in Italy" (Fiat) and China (Ramstadt 2012). In a total area of 1,000,000 m^2 340 people are working (KOFC 2010, 273). As part of restructuring after the death of the church founder in 2012, the management of Pyonghwa Motors was transferred to North Korea (Kim Sŏk-jong 2013).

Apart from that there are numerous companies of light industry in the two southern parts of Nampho, such as the Nampho Disabled Soldiers' Footwear Factory, the Nampho Knitted Goods Factory and the Nampho Foodstuff Factory. In the Nampho Knitted Goods Factory textiles for adults and children are produced. Main products of this factory are underwear, sweaters, bonnets and workout clothes. The factory was built in the 1970's with the support of the Pyongyang Textile Factory (IPA-2 2003, 164-165). The Nampho Foodstuff Factory is situated in Waudo-kuyok and is specialized in the manufacturing of products from sea products. The goods produced here are distributed throughout the whole

48 This refers to the two *kuyok* Hanggu and Waudo. Unless otherwise noted, are the companies located in Hanggu-kuyok.

country and are also exported. In 1986, a four-storey modern production building was completed (IPA-2 2003, 111-113).

The Nampho General Smeltery was located in Hadaedu-dong, Hanggu-kuyok. It was built between 1913 and 1915 and was a significant company of the non-ferrous metal smelting. Also chemicals were produced here (IPA-2 2003, 163-164). The Nampho Electrode Factory was located in Jungdae-dong. It has already been established at the time of the Japanese occupation and has manufactured furnishings for Smeltries (IPA-2 2003, 163). Both plants were torn down as port extension works (KOFC 2010, 110).

The Nampho Glass Complex was situated in Ryusa-dong, Hanggu-kuyok. Commodities were the abundant deposits of sand from the neighbouring Kumipho and Monggŭmpho (district Ryongyon). After the reconstruction after the Korean War, it was expanded to the leading glass manufacturer of the DPR Korea (IPA-2 2003, 163). In 2000 the factory was demolished due to its backwardness and from an environmental consideration (KOFC 2010, 441).

After the Nampo General Smeltery and the Nampho Glass Complex were torn down and the Taean Friendship Glass Factory was built, the four most important companies of Nampho are now in the area between Old-Nampho and Pyongyang, in the "Nampho-Pyongyang-Corridor" (Roussin/Ducruet 2010). In addition to the glass factory the Taean Heavy Machine Complex (also in the Taean-kuyok), the Chollima Steel Complex (in the Collima-kuyok) and the Kŭmsŏng General Tractor Factory (in the Kangso-kuyok) belong to the four most important companies of Nampho.

The Taean Heavy Machine Complex is situated in Taean-dong, in the *kuyok* of the same name. It produces electrical installations and special facilities. Before 1945, it was a simple iron foundry. As from 1945 initially small agricultural tools were produced. In 1948 electric motors and transformers were added. The electric motors played a major role in the construction of an irrigation network for the agriculture of the DPR Korea (IPA-2, 2003, 93-94). In 1954 the plant was supported by the PR China and in 1986 by the UNDP (KOFC 2010, 297). Between 1975 and 1980 the plant was converted for the production of heavy machinery. In 30 departments 10,000 employees work and produce mainly for domestic consumption[49] (Grabowsky 1985, 28). The Taean Heavy Machine Complex is situated on the banks of the Taedong-gang, on the four-lane highway between Pyongyang and Nampho and near the Phyongnam railway line. 14,000 people work on 1,130,000 m^2. In this company machines are produced, which are used in hydroelectric power stations and in other big manufacturing plants in the DPR Korea (KOFC 2010, 296-298). In 2004, within the Taean Heavy Machine Complex, the Taean Meccamidi (TM) joint-

49 Grabowski (1985, 28), who had travelled in North Korea in the 1980's, explains that 5% of the production, according to the plant manager, would be exported, namely transformers and motors to Bulgaria, China, Thailand and India.

venture company, a French-North Korean cooperation, which employs approximately 100 workers, was established. This joint venture is specialized in the production of 1 to 50 M watts hydraulic power plant generator. With this numerous small and medium hydraulic power plants are to be equipped throughout the country (Roussin/Ducruet 2010, 14).

The Taedonggang Electric Appliances Factory began its operation in 1973. It manufactures electric power facilities like transformers and switchboards, which are used in the whole country (IPA-2, 2003, 93). The Nampho Electric Machine Factory, which is also located in the Taean-kuyok, manufactures electric domestic appliances like ventilators, small electric motors, transformers of all kinds, which are distributed throughout the whole country. Before its restoration and expansion in the 1980s, it was a small repair workshop for electrical appliances (IPA-2, 2003, 92).

The Taean Friendship Glass Factory is the largest glass factory in the DPR Korea. It was built with financial and technical support from the PR China. The start of construction was in July 2004, the completion was celebrated on October 9th 2005 on the 60th anniversary of the founding of the Worker's Party of Korea. The total size of the factory plant is 293,000 m². The factory is located on the banks of the Taedong-gang on the road between Pyongyang and Nampho. Electrical energy is drawn from the East Pyongyang Thermical Power Plant. Products of the factory are also exported to Russia and China (KOFC 2010, 440-441).

Important huts for iron and iron compounds, such as the Chollima Steel Complex, April 13th Iron Works and the May 18th Forging Factory, which became operational in 1989, are situated in the Chollima-kuyok. The Chollima Steel Complex is an important center for metallurgy in North Korea. Its former name is Kangsŏn Steel Works. In 1936 the works was founded and after 1945 it expanded more and more and other companies were allocated to it, so it evolved into a large complex. In 2007, factory facilities from China were assembled. The total size of the works is 2,740,000 m², 13,000 persons are employed there (IPA-2, 2003, 139-140; KOFC 2010, 208-210).

The April 13th Iron Works (Posan Iron Works) are situated in Posan-dong and produce iron from iron ore and coal from the environment exclusively for further processing in the Chollima Steel Complex (IPA-2, 2003, 139). The works became operational in 1969 and have 5,000 employees (KOFC 2010, 212-213). Besides, in the Chollima-kuyok the machine construction (Kangsŏn Automation Equipment Factory), the production of building material (Taedonggang Tile Factory) as well as the generation of energy (December Thermal Power Station) is represented by major companies.

The Kŭmsŏng General Tractor Factory is situated in Kiyang-dong, Kangso-kuyok and is a leading producer of tractors of the DPR Korea. Before 1945 the Japanese company Asahi produced light metal products here. From 1946, chemical products like caustic soda and bleaching powder were produced here made from salt. After the Korean War smaller agricultural equipment under various corporate designations were manufactured. In 1956 the company was named Pyongyang Farm Machine Factory and started with the construction of tractors in 1958. The renaming to Kŭmsŏng Tractor Factory took place in 1973, and the company bears the name Kŭmsŏng General Tractor Factory (IPA-2 2003, 47-48) since 1985. Here, the red-painted tractors are built, which are used everywhere in North Korean agriculture (Dege 1991, 76).

Otherwise, companies of the light industry that are important, such as the Kangso Knitting Mill, which was a production cooperative in the 1950s and moved to Chŏngsan-ri in 1957, are located in the Kangso-kuyok. In 1966 the transformation into a factory took place. It mainly produces sportswear and underwear (IPA-2 2003, 47). The Kangso Footwear Factory sprang into action in the beginning of the 1980s and manufactures mainly boots, shoes for workers and sports shoes (IPA-2 2003, 47). In the 1990s the Kangso Ceramic Factory came on stream[50] (KCNA June 2, 2010). After the economic crisis in the 1990s, also in particular small and medium-sized coal-fired power stations were opened in the Kangso-kuyok.

In Ryonggang-up, the county capital, a factory for electrotechnical objects like generators, transformers and technical ceramics as well as a factory for agricultural gadgets like rise transplanting machines and threshing machines is situated (IPA-2 2003, 196). In both *kun* of Nampho-Si, Ryonggang and Onchon, are factories, which bottle Spring Water. In the Ryonghyo-ri (Ryonggang-kun) also granite is mined.

To support the industrial activities in the city are various universities and research institutes in Nampho with a focus on engineering, agriculture, fisheries, pedagogy and politics, which are partially affiliated with the big companies.

Largest port in the country and a good transport link to the neighbouring capital

Nampho has the largest international cargo port of the DPR Korea. The construction of the port served Japanese strategic purposes. In 1978 the port was extended with the help of the Soviet Union (KOFC 2010, 110). According to an assessment by Hŏ U-gung (2007, 102) one can observe concrete extensions and specializations of the docks until the 1970s. From this time on, however, the tempo of the extensions came to a standstill. However, an improvement of the situation brought the building of the West Sea Dam in 1986, which lead to a deepening of the gutter of the Taedong-gang and now is supposed to enable the

50 Roussin/Ducruet (2010, 14) report about a Ceramic Factory in the Nampho-Pyongyang-Corridor that works "with Italian origin equipments".

shipping to Sunchon and Tokchon (Hŏ U-gung 2007, 102-103). In 2000, the Nampho Smeltery and the Nampho Electrode Factory were torn down, in order to build a place for a container port, which was built between 2002 and 2005 (KOFC 2010, 110; KCNA December 13, 2005).

The West Sea Barrage system on the lower reaches of the Taedong-gang was inaugurated in June 1986. Within five years they had cordoned off the sea in a width of 8 km. The locks can be passed by ships up to 50,000 tons. Over the swing bridge on the lock basin lead a railway line, a highway and a walkway. The pent-up water in the basin is used for irrigation also of marsh land as well as for drinking-water and industrial water. In connection with the construction of the West Sea Barrage System, several other locks (e.g. Mirim Barrage and Ponghwa Barrage) were built on the Taedong-gang (Jo/An 2002, 157-161).

There are two motorways between Pyongyang and Nampho. One was built in 1978 and leads through Kangsŏn and Taean, it is 44 km long, has a width of 15 m and four-lanes. It is mainly used for industrial purposes. Important companies in the Pyongyang-Nampho-Corridor are situated on this street. The other motorway was built from 1998 and completed in 2000, which leads from the Kwangbok Street in Pyongyang through the Kangso-kuyok, the Ryonggang-kun in the Hanggu-kuyok over the Chŏngnyŏn Bridge (Youth Bridge). It is 46.3 km long, has a width of 64 m (of which 48 meters are road) and 12 lanes. It is called "Youth Hero Motorway" (Hwang Man-ik/Yi Ki-sŏk 2005, 136; KCNA November 13, 2010).

The Phyongnam rail road leads from Pyongyang over Kangsŏn, Kangso and Ryonggang to Nampho. There are numerous branch lines. From Nampho a line leads to Onchon.

Due to its location near the capital Pyongyang, the city of Nampho has always been a preferred location for foreign or South Korean investors in North Korea. The South Korean group Daewoo signed a joint venture contract with the North Korean company Samchŏlli in 1995. The National Industry Cooperation, which was founded through this, runs a textile plant in Nampho and exports shirts, bags and jackets to Japan and Europe (Yoon, Suh-kyung 2000). In 2002, a car factory was built due to the joint venture with the South Korean company Pyonghwa Motors. Among the 14 Economic Development Zones of the DPR Korea, which were named in 2013, is also the Waudo Export Goods Processing Zone.

In addition to the West Sea Barrage the KCNA (August 16, 2012) considers the Pyongyang Golf Course, the Ryonggang Hot Spring Center and the three old tombs in Kangso-kuyok and the tomb in Tokhung-Ri as important attractions in Nampho. The Koguryo Tombs were inscribed on the World Heritage List in June 2004. Numerous of those are in the area of Nampho-si. In September 1973, an athletes' village with a stadium, sports halls, a swimming pool and an ice rink was created on the banks of Samhwa-chŏn (Pae Ki-chan 1994, 59).

Nampho – region of localization of political propaganda

In Nampho one finds concentrated places, which play an important role in the political propaganda of the DPR Korea. The Taean machine work is described as the "symbol of the industrialization by itself" (Grabowsky 1985, 28). When Kim Il-sung inspected the Taean heavy machine work in Taean-si (now Nampho-si Taean-kuyok) in 1961, he presented instead of the previous method of the management of factories and companies through the plant manager, the so-called Taean Work System, which intends a collective management by a party committee.

In Kangso-kuyok is the agricultural collective Chŏngsan, where Kim Il-sung presented the "Spirit of Chŏngsan-ri" and the "Method of Chŏngsan-ri," according to which the management should take the specific circumstances into consideration on the spot concerning the solution of problems. Foreign observers were given the impression that, in accordance with the Chŏngsan-ri method, a lot of questions about the agricultural organisation were not centrally settled, but decentralized in the counties and cooperatives[51] (Grabowsky 1985, 28-32).

Also the Kangsŏn Steel Mill (today's name: Chollima Steel Mill), where the Chollima Movement, North Korea's first mobilization campaign is located, is situated in the Chollima-kuyok (Chosun Ilbo January 15, 1996). In 1956 there was a lack of materials and financial resources, also the domestic as well as the foreign political situation was very strained. Kim Il-sung therefore requested at the plenary session of the central committee of the Workers' Party of Korea in December 1956, an early fulfilment of the Five-Year-Plan, which was planned from 1957. After the plenary session Kim Il-sung visited the steel mill Kangsŏn and clearly defined his ideas (Jo/An 2002, 120-123). The campaign was named Chollima (Thousand-Mile-Horse). Later also the factory as well as the district, in which it is located, were named after the movement.

The Twin Cities Nampho (from 1950)/Taean (1978–1983)

In 1950, the city of Nampho was established, which was divided into 27 *ri*. There were large rearrangements in 1952. Afterwards Nampho consisted of 16 *dong* and seven *ri*, and in 1960, Nampho consisted of 15 *dong* and eight *ri*.

In March of 1978 the neighbouring Taean-si was established, but existed only until 1983.

In December of 1979 Nampho-si, Taean-si and Ryonggang-kun form Nampho-jikhalsi. The former Nampho-si turns simultaneously into the Nampho-kuyok, which

51 About the Chŏngsan-ri Method see KCNA 8.2.2002.

consists of 26 *dong*.

In 1983, the Nampho-kuyok was divided into the Hanggu-kuyok and the Waudo-kuyok; Taean-si is divided into the three *kuyok* Kangso, Taean and Chollima. Nampho now consists of Ryonggang-kun and five *kuyok*:

Hanggu-kuyok: 15 *dong*, 5 *ri*
Waudo-kuyok: 14 *dong*, 4 *ri*
Kangso-kuyok: 12 *dong*, 7 *ri*
Taean-kuyok: 8 *dong*
Chollima-kuyok: 13 *dong*, 2 *ri*

On 9th January 2004 Nampho-jikhalsi is dissolved and the area is assigned to the Phyongnam Province. The former *kuyok* of Hanggu and Waudo form the Nampho-tukkupsi, the other three *kuyok* (Taean, Kangso, Chollima) are each converted into a *kun*, also the Ryonggang-kun is part of the Phyongnam Province.

When in 2010 Nampho again was detached from the Phyongnam Province, all parts were again re-assigned to the again province-independent city, which already before 2004 belonged to the municipal area as well as additionally the Onchon-kun (previously Phyongnam Province).

In the analysis of the urbanization processes, the municipal area of Nampho shall now be looked at divided into three areas:

Old-Nampho: Hanggu-kuyok and Waudo-kuyok
Old-Taean (Pyongyang-Nampho-Corridor): Taean-kuyok, Chollima-kuyok and Kangso-kuyok
Ryonggang-kun and Onchon-kun

1963, 1974 and 1984 Enhancement of Old-Nampho

In Old-Nampho two main streets were extended in the 1970s, the main street of Hanggu, the Yurisŏn Street, which was completed in September 1973 and which runs from Hanggu-dong to the entrance of the Nampho sports complex and the Waudo Street from the Samhwachŏn Bridge to the salt extraction plant Nampho in the West of the *kuyok*. Dege (1991, 76) observed, that Nampho by the accumulation of the lower Taedong-gang became a city of islands, which had to be connected to each other by dams and bridges. On one of these islands is the Hanggu-Hotel which is also visited by foreigners.

Old-Nampho, that is to say, the former *kuyok* of Hanggu (H) and Waudo (U), has been expanded five times since 1950. In 1963, two *ri* from the Onchon-kun and three *ri* from Ryonggang-kun, in 1974 another three *ri* from Onchon-kun and in 1984 another three *ri* from Ryonggang-kun were incorporated. Then, in 1988, one *ri* from Unryul-kun (Hwangnam Province) was added to the municipal area and in 1996 the Chodo island, which previously was a *ri* of Kwail-kun (Hwangnam Province), was incorporated.

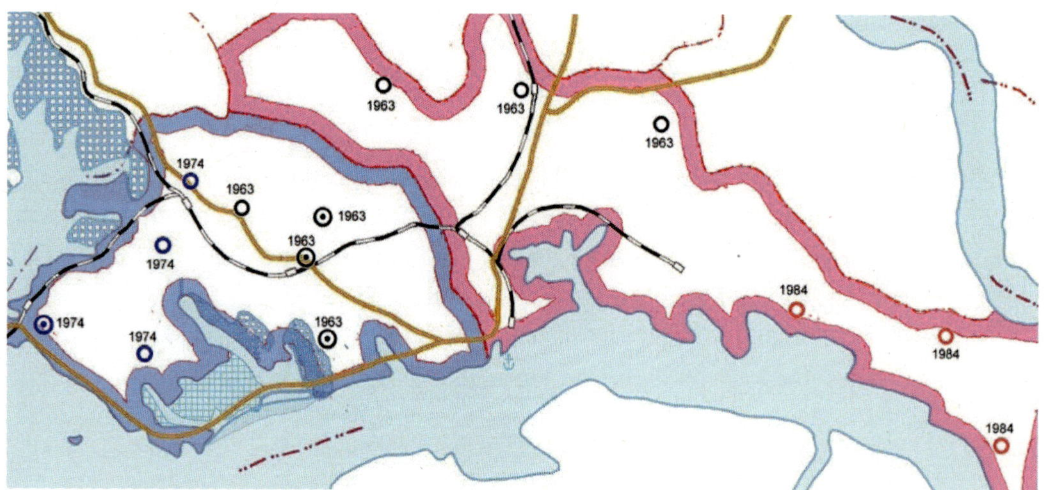

Figure Nampho-II. Old-Nampho – incorporations

Phases of urban development in Old-Nampho

In 1955 out of the 36 *dong* that existed in 2002, eleven *dong* are located in today's municipial area of Nampho, of which seven are in the former Waudo-kuyok (in the West) and four in the former Hanggu-kuyok (in the East).

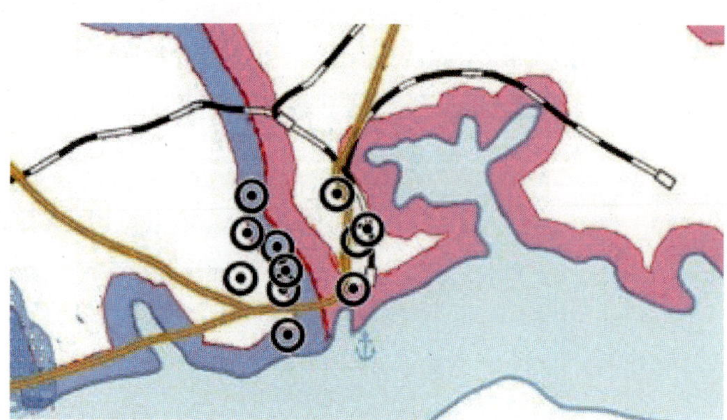

Figure Nampho-III. 1955 – 11 *dong* in Old-Nampho

In the 1960s, between 1960 and 1967, 16 new *dong* were added, twelve of them by splittings from already existing *dong*. Five new *dong* originated in the western Waudo, eleven in the eastern Hanggu.

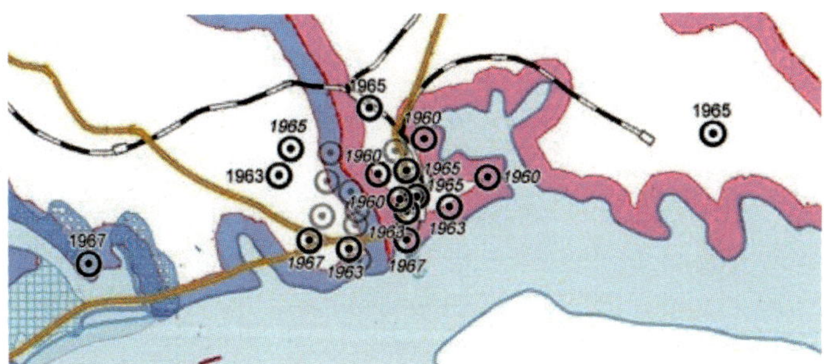

Figure Nampho-IV. 1960s-16 new *dong* in Old-Nampho

After 1967, only nine new *dong* were established in Nampho, three of them between 1977 and 1988. In the 24 years between 1968 and 1992 thus only three new *dong* were established within today's municipal border of Nampho. Only in the 1990's there was a stimulation. Six *dong* were established between 1993 and 1999.

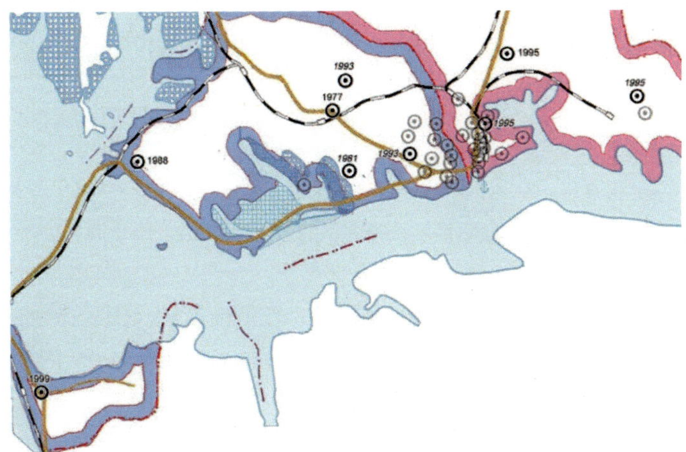

Figure Nampho-V. New *dong* in Old-Nampho after 1967

The first eleven *dong* that existed in 1955 in the municipal area of today's Nampho were all located within the area of the city center. In the 1960s this city center was strongly compacted. 14 of the 16 new *dong* of the 1960s are situated in the city center. Conversely, seven of the nine *dong*, which emerged from 1977, are outside of the city center. Therefore, concerning the development of Old-Nampho, one can conclude that until the second half of the 1960s, in particular urbanization processes through the development of the city center took place and from the mid-70s also an increasing in the urbanization of settlements outside the city center can be determined.

The following table shows the number of *dong* differentiated by the former *kuyok*:

Table Nampho-VI. Number of *dong* in Waudo and Hanggu between 1955 and 1999

	Waudo (West)	Hanggu (East)
1955 (11)	7	4
1960 (15)	7	8
1963 (19)	9	10
1965 (24)	10	14
1967 (27)	12	15
1977 (28)	13	15
1981 (29)	14	15
1988 (30)	15	15
1993 (32)	17	15
1995 (35)	17	18
1999 (36)	18	18

If one compares the developments in the West (Waudo) with those in the East (Hanggu), three phases can be distinguished:

from 1960 until 1967: development of the city center with increased development in the East

from 1977 until 1993: development of the areas outside the center in the West

around 1995: development of the areas outside the center in the East

In particular the construction of the in 1986 finished West Sea Barrage might have been of great significance for the developments in the west of the city (Waudo).

Statistics: Nampho Waudo-kuyok and Hanggu-kuyok (altogether 36 *dong*)

1955 (11 *dong*)

	Dong-Formation	*Dong*-Splitting
1960 (15)	-	4
1963 (19)	1	3
1965 (24)	2	3
1967 (27)	1	2

1977 (28)	1	-
1981 (29)	-	1
1988 (30)	1	-
1993 (32)	-	2
1995 (35)	1	2
1999 (36)	1	-

Old-Taean

The three *kuyok* of Kangso, Taean and Chollima have emerged in 1983 from Taean-si, which emerged in 1978 from Kangso county and from parts of Ryonggang, namely Taean-rodongja, Taejong-ri, parts of Sŏngam-ri (Namyang village) and parts of Ripsong-ri (Ripsok village).

Prior to the formation of the city of Taean, the following *up* and *rodongjagu* existed in this area since 1952 :

1952 (1 *up*, 2 *rodongjagu*): Kangso-up, Kiyang-rodongjagu, Kangsŏn-rodongjagu
1956 (1 *up*, 1 *rodongjagu*): Kangso-up, Kangsŏn-rodongjagu (the original Kangso-up was downgraded to Tŏkhŭng-ri, Kiyang-rodongjagu and Thanpho-ri became the new *up*.)
1957 (1 *up*, 2 *rodongjagu*): Kangso-up, Kangsŏn-rodongjagu, Taean-rodongjagu
1969 (1 *up*, 3 *rodongjagu*): Kangso-up, Kangsŏn-rodongjagu, Taean-rodongjagu, Posan-rodongjagu

When Taean-si was formed in 1978, Kangso-up and the three *rodongjagu* were divided as follows into 31 *dong*, so that Taean-si consisted of 31 *dong* and ten *ri*:

Kangso-up (10): Segil-dong. Sanŏp-dong, Saemmul-dong, Kiyang-dong, Munhwa-dong, Rakwŏn-dong, Pongsang-dong, Kisan-dong, Sŏhak-dong, Thanpho-dong
Taean-rodongjagu (6): Tŏksŏng-dong, Chungsŏng-dong, Kŭmsan-dong, Oksu-dong, Taean-dong, Ŭndŏk-dong
Posan-rodongjagu (4): Namsan-dong, Munchŏn-dong, Posan-dong, Kwanpho-dong,
Kangsŏn-rodongjagu (11): Ponghwa-dong, Sangbong-dong, Yŏkjŏn-dong, Phogu-dong, Ssari-dong, Chŏnjin-dong, Chŏnnae-dong, Saegori, Jung-dong, Talma-dong, Wonjŏng-dong

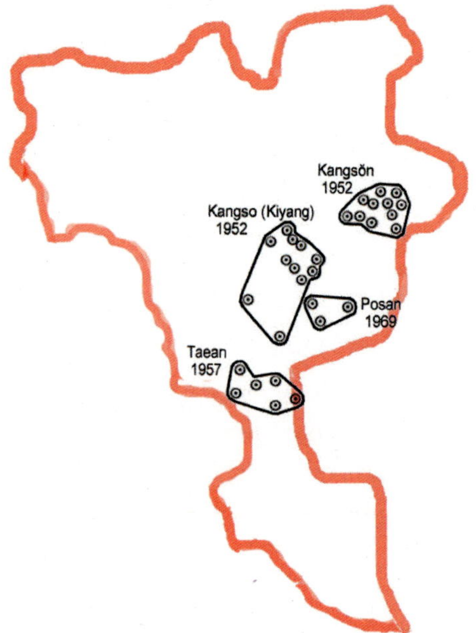

Figure Nampho-VI. *Up* and *rodongjagu* in Old-Taean

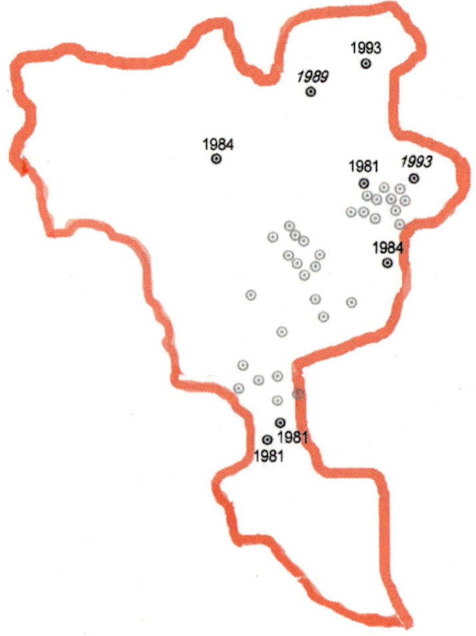

Figure Nampho-VII. New *dong* in Old-Taean between 1981 and 1993

In 1979 Taean-si was then removed from the Phyongnam Province and became part of Nampho-jikhalsi.

In 1981, three new *dong* were established that resulted from rearrangements from *ri*: from Taejŏng-ri Taejŏng-dong and Saemaul-dong are formed and from parts of three different *ri* Jŏnjin-dong arises, so that Taean-si, before its dissolution in 1983 consisted of 34 *dong* and 9 *ri*. These are split up into the three now emerging *kuyok* of Nampho:

Kangso-kuyon now consists of ten *dong*, which emerged from the division of Kangso-up, two of four *dong* (Namsan-dong and Kwanpho-dong), which emerged from the Posan-rodongjagu, the in 1981 newly emerged Jŏnjin-dong as well as eight *ri*. Kwanpho-dong however, was in 1984 assigned in the Chollima-kuyok.

Already at the formation of Chollima-kuyok it consists of 13 *dong* and one *ri*, wherein among those *dong* are the eleven, which emerged from the Kangsŏn-rodongjagu as well as the other two of the four *dong* (Posan-dong, Munchŏn-dong).

Eight *dong* were allocated to the Taean-kuyok, namely those six, which emerged from the Taean-rodongjagu as well as the two Saemaul-dong and Taejŏng-dong established in 1981.

After the formation of the *kuyok* they lightly change their size. After the Chollima-kuyok got awarded a part of Kwanpho-dong already in 1983, in 1984 Kwanpho-dong and Kochang-ri were assigned from Kangso-kuyok to the Chollima-kuyok, in the same year three *ri* from Ryonggang county were added in the Taean-kuyok. In 1987 Taebosan-ri from

Taedong-kun was added to the Kangso-kuyok, in the same year the Kangso-kuyok was extended at the expense of the Chollima-kuyok, by the adding of a part of Kochang-ri. In 1989 Taebosan-ri was added from the Kangso-kuyok to the Chollima-kuyok. Except for the inclusion of Taebosan-ri (today's Taebosan-dong), those were changes between parts of the current province-independent city Nampho.

Between 1984 and 2002 five new *dong* emerged in the three *kuyok*. In 1984 Tŏkhŭng-ri (Kangso-kuyok) becomes a *dong*. Pobo-ri (Chollima-kuyok) changes into Kangchŏl-dong.

Through reorganization in 1989 emerges in the Kangso-kuyok from various *ri* and a *dong* a new Sŏgi-dong. By a division of the Wonjŏng-dong (Chollima-kuyok) the new Hwasŏk-dong emerges in 1993; in the same year Taebonsan-ri (Chollima-kuyok) becomes a *dong*. In 2002 the Kangso-kuyok has 14 *dong* and six *ri*, the Chollima-kuyok has 17 *dong* and one *ri* and the Taean-kuyok has eight *dong* and three *ri*. In total are 39 *dong* and ten *ri* in the three *kuyok*.

Statistics (region of the former Taean-si)
1978 31 *dong*
1981 34 *dong* (3 *ri* become a *dong*)
1984 36 *dong* (2 *ri* become a *dong*)
1989 37 *dong* (1 new *dong* due to the splitting from *dong*)
1993 39 *dong* (1 *ri* becomes a *dong*, 1 new *dong* due to the splitting from a *dong*)

Development in the counties (*kun*)

Ryonggang-kun was originally part of the Phyongnam Province. In 1979 it became part of the province-independent city of Nampho, then in 2004 it was again part of Phyongnam, in 2011 again part of Nampho. In 1952 the *kun* consisted of one *up* and 20 *ri*. In the course of time Ryonggang-kun has been reduced several times: in 1963 three *ri* were added to Nampho, in 1978 the Taean-rodongjagu, which emerged in 1957 from Taean-ri, as well as the Taejŏng-ri, parts of Sŏngam-ri and parts of Ripsŏng-ri were added to the newly founded Taean-ri. In 1984 three *ri* were added to the Taean-kuyok and

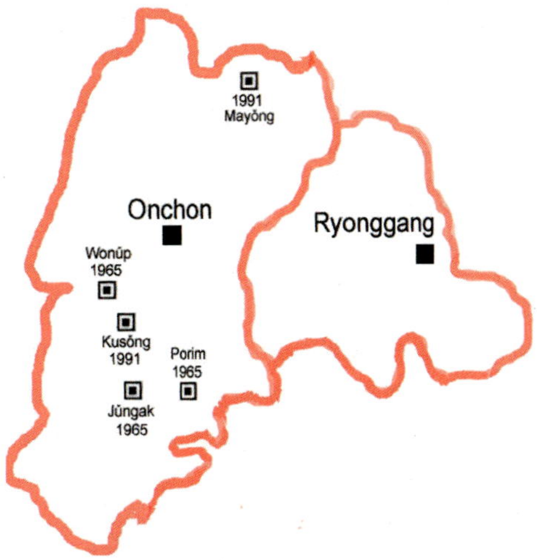

Figure Nampho-VIII. *Up* and *rodongjagu* in Ryonggang-kun and Onchon-kun

also three *ri* to the Hanggu-kuyok, so that the district Ryonggang in 2002 consists of one *up* and ten *ri*.

Onchon-kun was formed in 1952 from parts of the *kun* of Ryonggang and Kangso. It consisted of one *up* and twelve *ri*. In 1958 the county was extended through parts of Jungsan-kun. In 1963 Taedae-ri and Hwado-ri were added to the Nampho-si. In 1965 the *ri* Wonŭp, Jŭngak and Porim each became *rodongjagu*. In 1967 there was a regrouping within the *kun*, also a part of Kangso-kun was added. In 1974 Sogang-ri, Ryongnam-ri and Sinryŏng-ri were added to Nampho. In 1991 parts of Ansŏk-ri were in the northwest of the *kun* connected with land, which was acquired through land reclamation and formed two new *ri* (Undok, Unjong). Kuisŏng-ri and Mayŏng-ri became *rodongjagu*. In 2003 the district thus had one *up*, five *rodongjagu* and 14 *ri*. Since 1952, therefore, there were following *up* and *rodongjagu*:

1952 (1 *up*) Onchon-up

1965 (1 *up*, 3 *rodongjagu*) Onchon-up, Wonŭp-rodongjagu, Jŭngak-rodongjagu, Porim-rodongjagu

1991 (1 *up*, 5 *rodongjagu*) Onchon-up, Wonŭp-rodongjagu, Jŭngak-rodongjagu, Porim-rodongjagu, Kuisŏng-rodongjagu, Mayŏng-rodongjagu

Whereas the Mayŏng-rodongjagu is located in the north of the county and here especially in basalt stones are drilled due to the mining, the other four *rodongjagu* are located in the south of the county, where the large salines are situated.

Nampho – a large potential for foreign investments after Korean Reunification

Through the regional changes in 2010, Nampho became the city with the second largest population of the DPR Korea. Also in terms of the area, through the merging of the Onchon-kun, today's Nampho is as large as never before in history. The fact that now, with Pyongyang and Nampho, two of three province-independent cities are located in the central west of the DPR Korea, stresses the importance the government of the DPR Korea attaches to Nampho and thus the central region in Northwest Korea for the economic development of the country. Due to its proximity to Pyongyang, but also to South Korea, Nampho belongs s to the most popular locations of North Korea for foreign potential investor.[52]

52 In an expert poll by the South Korean Korea Research Institute for Human Settlements (KRIHS) about a suitable location for a "second Kaesong Industrial Region" Nampho was by far named the most. This was followed by Haeju and Pyongyang. (Yi Sang-jun; Kim Chŏn-kyu; Yi Paek-jin 2012, 64).

Nampho can roughly be divided into three conurbations: Old-Nampho, the Pyongyang-Nampho-Corridor (Old Taean) and the agricultural and fishery regions (Ryonggang-kun and Onchon-kun). The demolition of obsolete and environmentally hazardous industrial plants in Old-Nampho in favour of docks illustrates a functional diversification towards the heavy industrial characterized Pyongyang-Nampho-Corridor.

IV.2.14. Sariwon

Traffic center in Hwangbuk

Sariwon is the capital of the Hwangbuk Province and is the area's administrative, economic and cultural center. It is one of the most densely populated cities of the DPR Korea. Only Songrim and Sinuiju have a higher population density.

Table Sariwon-I. Basic data

Population	307,764 (Rank 10)
Area	188 km² (Rank 26)
Population density	1,637 I./km² (Rank 3)
Administrative units	31 *dong*/9 *ri* (78%) (Rank 8)
"Urban" population/"rural" population	88.2%/11.8% (Rank 10)

In the beginning of the Joson dynasty (1392-1910) the important Jabi-pass, which was important for the North-South traffic in Korea was blocked[53] and instead the Tongsŏn-pass, which is located east of the Jŏngbang-san, was used, thus Sariwon fulfilled the function of an important traffic center and expanded. When the Kyongui railway line was commissioned in 1905 and in Sariwon the Haeju line and the Jangyŏn line branched off from it, the character of Sariwon as a traffic junction was further strengthened. When additionally to the good traffic conditions, the industry in Sariwon developed on the basis of the mining of the region, Sariwon constantly became more important and the seat of the district capital was moved from Pongsan to Sariwon in 1912 . Sariwon kept enlarging, in 1929 Sawŏn-myon became Sariwon-myon, in 1939 it became Sariwon-up. At the end of the occupation period Sariwon-up had twelve *ri* and 25 *kun* and complied with more than 50,000 inhabitants the conditions to be appointed to a city. In 1947 Sariwon was separated from Pongsan-kun and appointed to a city (IPA-10 2003, 50). In the Korean War 95% of Sariwon was destroyed.

53 In 1361 Red Turbans forced their way into the pass and blocked it. Since that time, especially the delegations of the Chinese Ming dynasty shunned it (Daum Encyclopedia Jabiryŏng).

Sariwon – endangered by drought

Sariwon developed in the western lowlands of North-Hwanghae on the lower reaches of the Jaeryŏng-gang. In the northeast of the national territory, the western part of the Jŏngban-san mountain range[54] extends with its elevations Jŏngban-san (481 m), Palyang-san (440 m) and Kama-bong (481 m). Jŏngbang-san, which consists of quartzites, and the other mountains in its environment surround the city of Sariwon in the North like a screen and contribute with their steep faces and odd rocks to the beauty of the city.

Figure Sariwon-I. Forest area in the *ri*

The city area decreases in height towards the South and eventually becomes a plateau. In the southwest of the city the Kyŏngam-san (140 m) is located, in the southern periphery the Mia-san (150 m). 82.6% of the municipal area has a height of 100-300 m above sea level.[55]

Table Sariwon-II. Climate values

Annual average	January temperature	August temperature	Precipitation
10.5℃ (7)	-5.1℃ (10)	24.3℃ (3)	901.9 mm (16)

The weather around the time of May to June is very dry and in the past as in the present severe drought damages are not uncommon. The average annual rainfall of 901.9 mm falls more than 52% in summer. The Chŏngbang-chŏn and Sangmae-chŏn rivers are often so dry, that the bare floor turns up except during the period between July to September (Chosun Ilbo February12, 1996).

45% of the municipal area is cultivated land area, of which 40.5% is wet rice cultivation, 35.4% is dry farming and 21.5% is orchards. The most important crops are rice, corn, soybean, wheat, barley and foxtail millet. Also, there are specialized livestock farming like

54 The South Korean geographer Kang Sŏk-o (1984) does not speak of a mountain range, but of the Jŏngbangsan hilly land. According to the North Korean version, the Jŏngbang mountain range is 60 km long, has a width of 6-8 km and has an average height of 420 m. To the highest mountains belong the Puindang-san (659 m), the Jŏnju-san (652 m), the Chŏnnyŏ-bong (657 m), the Kami-bong (481 m) and the Jangbang-san (481 m) (IPA-10 2003, 38).

55 Above 100 m are 6.3%, between 300 and 500 m 11.1%.

the Sariwon Chicken Farm (KCNA December 12, 2008) and a fish farm at the Kilsŏng port. 20.9% of the area of Sariwon is forest, of which 68.2% is pine, 14.6% is oak woods and 11% is acacia forest (IPA-10 2003, 53 and 56). A special product, which made Sariwon famous, are the grapes, which have been cultivated since the 1950's in the fruit tree groves in Torim-do. They are called "Victory-Grapes." Fruit tree groves pears and apples are also cultivated. Wine and jam preserves are manufactured as well (Chosun Ilbo February 12, 1996). The Migok Co-op farm is considered as a model farm, which has the goal "to assimilate the peasantry to the working class and industrialize agriculture rapidly" (KCNA July 6, 2009).[56] Kim Il-sung is said to have visited it 16 times and also Kim Jong-il was seen there often. There is a Revolution Museum and on holidays the museum is often visited by foreign diplomats.

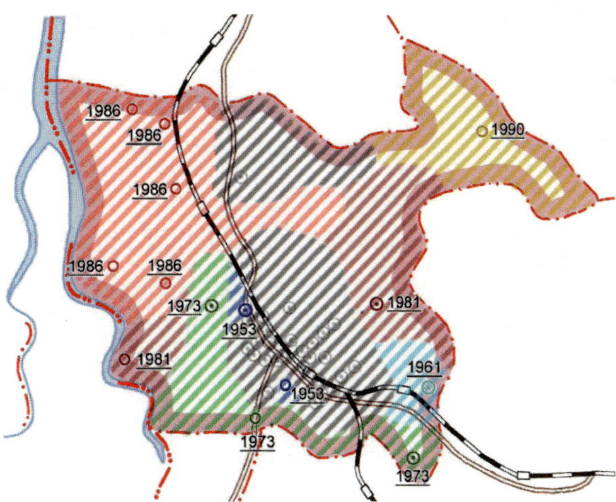

Figure Sariwon-II. Agricultural region in Sariwŏn and incorporated administrative units

Figure Sariwon-II shows, that Sariwon has been extended with agricultural areas in the course of time. Regions, which are close to the city and where vegetables are cultivated in (green marking), adjoin to the urbanized area (gray marking) in the west and in the south. In the West a rice plain extends towards the Jaeryŏng-gang (red marking). In the far Northeast is the mountainous forest region of Sŏngsan-ri (yellow marking) and in the Southeast are the fruit tree groves of Torim-dong (light-blue marking) located.

Sariwon is considered „Home of Magnolia" (Chosun Ilbo February 12, 1996). The city has this attribute not only due to the fact, that one can see magnolia everywhere, not only at Kyŏngam-san, at Sangmae-san and at Chŏngbang-san, but also in parks, at playgrounds, on streets. This is associated with the story, that Kim Il-sung saw magnolias there on a school trip in 1924 for the first time. When he again visited Sariwon around 1964, he saw this flower again and decreed in 1991, that it should be made into the national flower of the DPRK. 50,000 flowers are planted annually in Sariwon and also sent

56 KCNA (July 6, 2009) further explains: "The fields under cultivation have been standardized like a paduk (go) board and unique gravity-fed waterways and many dwelling houses have been constructed across the country to convert the countryside into a socialist fairyland good to live in." Another such model farms are the Sinam Co-op Farm in Ryongchon County, North Phyongan Province, the Chongsan Co-op Farm in Kangso District, Nampho and the Samjigang Co-op Farm in Jaeryong County, South Hwanghae Province and the Tongbong Co-op Farm in Hamju County, South Hamgyong Province. the Unhung Co-op Farm, Thaechon County, North Phyongan Province (KCNA July 6, 2009; February 22, 2013).

to other regions (Chosun Ilbo February 12, 1996).

Center of the textile industry

Based on good traffic conditions in Sariwon, an industry already developed on a modest scale before 1945, starting with the textile industry. Furthermore there were farms, which are linked to agriculture (milling, breweries, manufacturing of agricultural equipment). After 1945, a modern industry was built up, which is related to the fact that the city as a provincial capital was built up into an administrative, economic and cultural center. Nowadays there are also companies for machine construction and metalworking, building materials, fertilizer and for the production of goods for the daily need (school supplies, cultural products, etc.).

Machine construction has a big meaning for the development of equipment for the agriculture (IPA-10 2003, 55-56). Concerning the share of the total output volume of the industry of the city of Sariwon, the textile industry comes by far in first place. This is followed by the food industry, machine construction and the manufacture of goods for the daily use.[57]

Table Sariwon-III. Ranking (in parenthesis: number of industrial companies or cultural institutions)

Sariwon	KOFC	MOU	IPA	KCNA	KIET	Summary
Companies-total	10 (16)	9 (28)	17 (10)	12 (11)	13 (32)	13
Companies-important	26 (1)	10 (3)	21 (4)		9 (18)	6 (11)
Cultural institutions			9 (15)			

Table Sariwon-IV. Ranking (total number of companies in relation to population)

Sariwon	KOFC	MOU	IPA	KCNA	KIET	Summary
Companies–total	15	5	22–22–8	11	19–5	17–2

Table Sariwon-V. Specification (in parenthesis: number of industrial companies)

Sariwon	Light Industry	Heavy Industry	Mining	Energy
KOFC	12 (4)	5 (12)	–	–
MOU	10 (18)	14 (8)	12 (2)	–
IPA	7 (6)	14 (4)	–	–
KCNA	4 (9)	22 (2)	–	–
KIET	15(13)	9 (17)	11 (2)	–

57 According to KJY-26 (1990, 426) there are four branches whose share of production between 1960 and 1984 achieved double-digit figures: (in parenthesis are the figures for 1984) the textile industry (43.3%), the food industry (15.8%), production of goods for the daily use (11%) and machine construction (15.8%).

Sariwon, according to its population is the tenth largest city in the DPR Korea. It is ranked, concerning the number of companies, slightly below the rank in terms of population. However, it looks slightly better in terms of the important companies. Although the light industry is considerably more represented than the heavy industry in Sariwon, the values in table Sariwon-V show that the industry in Sariwon is quite versatile.

In chapter III.7.3. eleven companies were identified as important: Sariwon Textile Factory, Sariwon Export Towel Factory, Sariwon Knitted Goods Factory, Sariwon Footwear Factory, Sariwon Cornstarch Factory, Sariwon Tobacco Factory, Sariwon Mining Machine Factory, Sariwon Tractor Accessory Factory, Sariwon Machine Factory, Sariwon Electric Appliances Factory, Sariwon Potassium Fertilizer Complex.

The total area of the Sariwon Textile Factory is 280,000 m², about 1,000 persons are employed there (KOFC 2010, 594). The operation started already before 1945 under the name Sariwon Silk Mill. It received the current name in September 1945 and started with the production of cloths. In 1970 a spinning was added and in 1974 a dye-works (IPA-10 2003, 57-58). In the Sariwon Export Towel Factory *inter alia* towel cloths, travel towels, sheets, bathrobes etc. for children and adults are produced. The articles produced there are exported as far as Japan and China (IPA-10 2003, 58). The Kyŏngamsan Garment Export Factory manufactures padded clothes and jackets, which are exported to China, Canada, Germany, Switzerland and other countries (KCNA January 7, 2003). The Sariwon Cornstarch Factory is a company which produces *inter alia* corn noodles, potato flour, dextrose, cornstarch syrup, glucose, biscuits, spirits and oil. The potato flour and the cornstarch syrup, which are produced here, are also send to other food factories in other cities for further processing (IPA-10 2003, 57). The Sariwon Tobacco Factory was built in 1969. From dried tobacco leaves cigarettes are produced, which are sold throughout the country (IPA-10 2003, 57).

The Sariwon Potassium Fertilizer Complex is actually located outside the municipal border of Sariwon in the nearby Pongsan-kun (Chosun Ilbo February 12, 1996).[58] The construction of this factory started in September 1986 with Soviet help, in order to liberate the DPR Korea from the import dependency of potash fertilizer, and it was supposed to be completed in 1990. It was a core project of the 3rd Seven-Year-Plan (1987-1993), but it could not be fulfilled, so that a puffer plan (1994-1996) was inserted. It was planned to produce potash fertilizer in this factory from potash feldspar, which was stored in large quantities in Chŏngdan-kun (Hwangnam), at a rate of 510,000t/year (Chosun Ilbo February 12, 1996). The plant was built by military units and can be seen with its two high chimneys from the highway between Pyongyang and Kaesong. After Moscow has pulled itself out of the project, the project stagnated (Quinones 2002, 13) and was probably abandoned later.

58 Probably in Masan-ri, in the Chosun Ilbo there is talk of Madong-ri. In Pongsan-kun however there is no administrative unit Madong-ri. Madong is the name of a village within Masan-ri (IPA-10 2003, 263)

Junction for the rail, road and water traffic – "City on the canal"

Sariwon is a traffic junction, which connects Pyongyang, Kaesong, Haeju, the coast of the West Sea and the inland mountain region. In Sariwon the Korean main railroad line, which runs from Pusan to Sinuiju and the Haeju-Youth-Line fork. Sariwon has three stations Sariwon Youth, Sariwon East and Jŏngbang. It is reported, that at the station Sariwon Youth also intercity buses to Pyongyang are waiting for passengers.

The municipal area is crossed by a highway between Pyongyang and Kaesong. Through the city center leads a state road of the first category to Haeju, which is 75 km away. By car, Sariwon can be reached from Pyongyang in 45 minutes.

Through the Kilsŏng port, Sariwon is connected over the Jaeryŏng-gang and the Taedong-gang with the Songrim port and the region of Pyongyang as well as with the Nampho port.

In February 1954, a canal was built to the city center, which made the water of the Jaeryŏnggang flow to the city center, and on the foothills of the Kyŏngam-san two big lakes were created, which are connected with the canal subterranean. After the construction of the West Sea Barrage in Nampho (1981-1986), the water level of the Taedong-gang, into which the Jaeryŏng-gang flows, increased, the Kilsŏng quay, which is located 4 km west of the city center in Taesŏng-dong, was extended in 1988 for passengers and for cargo and thus the shipping routes to Songrim, Nampho, Pyongyang opened. On this waterway industrial products from Pyongyang and Nampho and agricultural products from the Hwanghae provinces are transported (Chosun Ilbo February 12, 1996).

Provincial center for education, culture and health care

Sariwon has ten universities and colleges. The most well-known are the Agricultural College "Kye Ŭngsang,"[59] the University of Medicine "Kang Kŏn,"[60] the Geology University Sariwon, the Koryo Medicine University Sariwon as well as the three pedagogical colleges. A major research facility is the Institute of Cattle Owning. Sariwon also has institutions, which are typical for a provincial capital like a library, an arts center, a mask theater, a cinema, a sports field, a museum of history and a radio station. Also, the Art Ensemble of the province North-Hwanghae has its seat in Sariwon. There are ten hospitals and other medical institutions like the People's Hospital of the province North-Hwanghae. In Sariwon is also one of three prisons, of whose existence a delegation of Amnesty International was officially

59 It was founded in 1959 as Agricultural University Sariwon and in 1990 named after the geneticist Kye Ŭngsang.

60 It was founded in 1971 as Medical University and was named in 1990 after the general chief of staff, who died in the Korean War.

informed in April/May 1995.

Tourism areas: Jŏngbang-san and Kyŏngam – "Folk Custom Street"

The area on the foothills of the Kyŏngnam-san was a popular recreation area for Koreans in the past and lately was extended as a touristic destination for foreigners. The canal itself is suitable for boat games and strolls. Of outstanding landscape are the Kyŏngnam lakes, which are connected through a subterranean waterway with the canal and the Kyŏngnam pavilion, which dates back to the 15th century. In addition to Kyŏngnam-san, spring water, a fairground, a zoo and an artificial waterfall are named as popular destinations of Korean tourists (Chosun Ilbo February 12, 1996). Opened for foreign tourists is the newly designed "Folk Custom Street" on Kyŏngam-san and its foothill. Pavilions, houses in traditional Korean style, the Kyŏngamsan hotel, restaurants and exhibit goods related to Korean culture and history were put up there (KCNA November 24, 2005).

A special tourist attraction within the municipal borders of Sariwon offers the Jŏngbang-san in the north of the city with its mountain fortress made of stone. The mountain fortress of Jŏngbang was built in the Koryo period, it forms a circle with a wall length of 12 km and is 5-6 m, in some parts up to 10 m high. It was part of the fortification for the city Pyongyang, which is situated 48 km north. A sight is the southern gate off the fortress. The amusement park Jŏngbang is 1 km away from this gate. Within the mountain fortress is the famous Sŏngbul temple, which was built in 898. It was often visited by school classes on class outings. According to the Chosun Ilbo, approximately in 1988, a summer residence of Kim Il-sung was set up, at the entrance of the mountain fortress Jŏngbang guards were positioned and one could only walk until the playground (amusement park) (Chosun Ilbo February 12, 1996).

Newcomers with a "good reputation"

Since Sariwon has about 300,000 inhabitants, the ratio of locals and people from other regions is 6 to 4. Because a lot of residents of Sariwon have left to the South after the Korean War, a considerable number of remaining inhabitants were driven out to northern regions and instead people from the Hamgyong and Phyongan provinces with a "good reputation" were settled here. Thus, newcomers often have better opportunities to hold a public office. However, collisions between newcomers and locals have not often been reported. The cause is said to be the gentle disposition of the people from the Hwanghae provinces (Chosun Ilbo 12, 1996).

A statue for Kang Kŏn

In honour of the general chief of staff Kang Kŏn (1918-1950), who died during the Korean War, a statue was erected in Sariwon on the 20th anniversary of the Korean Workers' Party in 1968. Also a street, named after him, was built. At the Kangkŏn street the Sariwŏn Hotel, the Sariwon Department Store, the „Kang Kŏn" Medical University and the „Kang Kŏn" University Hospital are located.

International associations

There are a number of foreign relief organizations, which were active in Sariwon or still are. The activities are often related to the children's hospital of Sariwon and the orphanage of Sariwon.[61]

In addition to the foreign relief organizations and tourists, who visit the Jŏngbang-san or the tourism streets around the Kyŏngam-san, Sariwon has contact with other countries trough the twin towns of Székesfehérvár (Hungary) and Lahore (Pakistan) as well as the Agricultural Cooperative Jŏngbang, which has the name affix "DPRK-Mongolian Friendship" and is regularly visited by members of the Mongolian embassy. Foreign diplomats are lead to the agricultural cooperative Migok, an example cooperative of the country.

"Residential buildings higher than the buildings of the administration"

In Puk4-dong ten 24-storey high rise residential blocks catch one's eye. These might be related with the "Order on the Spot" by Kim Il-sung. Since the elevators do not work, one has to go up to the 24th storey and the coal for the heating will be pulled up with a roller (Chosun Ilbo 12, 1996). In North Korean propaganda, Kim Il-sung is praised because in March 1970 he ordered the construction of high rise residential blocks for workers in Sariwon, which are higher than the buildings of the organs of power.

Administrative, economic and cultural center of the province North-Hwanghae City since 1947, since then incorporations (six times)

In 1947 Sariwon was detached from Pongsan-kun and became a city (*si*). It consisted of twelve *ri*. In December 1952 the *ri* were regrouped and Sinchang-ri was initially added to

61 Among the relief organizations that were active in Sariwon are ADRA (Adventist Development and Relief Agency) and HBAid (Hungarian Baptist Aid).

Pongsan-kun. After that, the municipal area was expanded five times at the expense of Pongsan-kun (1953, 1961, 1973, 1981, 1986) and once at the expense of Yonthan-kun:

In December 1953, Kyŏngam-ri (from parts of Pongsan-kun) and Sangha-ri (from parts of Pongsan-kun and Unpha-kun) were expanded. Kwangsŏng-ri and Kuryong-ri were created from other parts, which are incorporated from the Pongsan-kun.

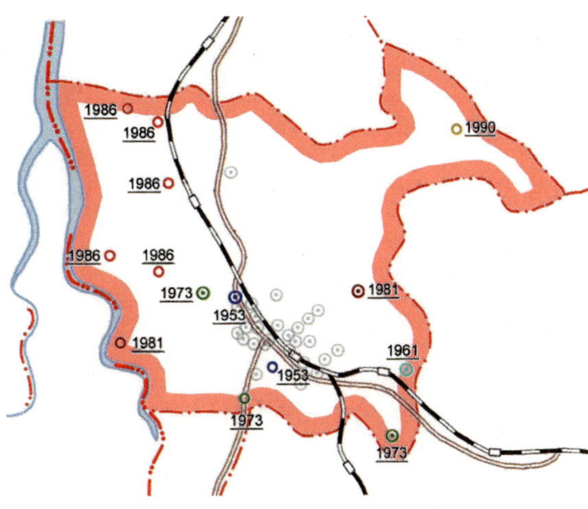

Figure Sariwon–III. Incorporations

In 1961 parts of Sŏngsan-ri and parts of Torim-ri (both Pongsan-kun) form the new Torim-ri, which got incorporated into Sariwon.

In March 1973 two *ri* (Migok-ri and Mangŭm-ri) and the Ŏsu-rodongjagu from the Pongsan-kun are added. In 1981, with Sinchang-ri and Haesŏ-ri, two more *ri* from the Pongsan-kun are added, in October 1986 with Taeryong-ri, Munhyŏn-ri, Pongŭi-ri, Sŏnjŏng-ri and Jŏngbang-ri five more.

In December 1990 Sŏngsan-ri from Yonthan-kun is added to Sariwon-kun.

Common administrative regrouping in the second half of the 50s

In 1955 twelve *dong* were made from five *ri*. All are situated in the city center of Sariwon. Apart from that the Ŏsu-rodongjagu, which already became a *rodongjagu* in 1953 and a *dong* in 1974, is located in the present municipal area of Sariwon since 1973.

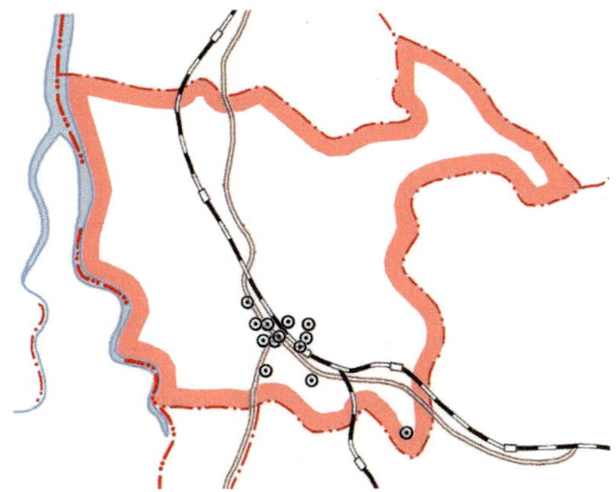
Figure Sariwon–IV. 1955 13 *dong*

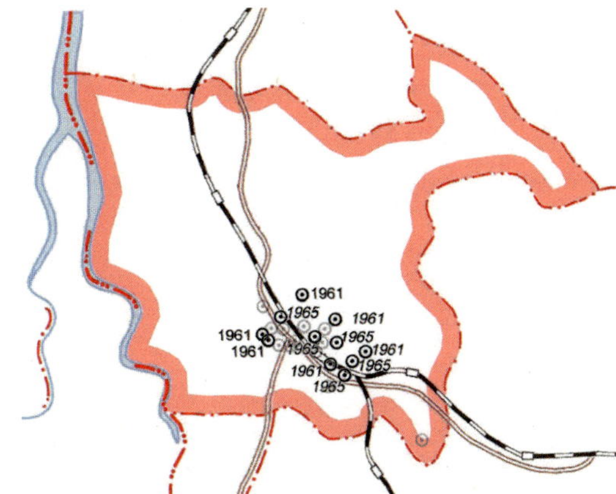

Figure Sariwon–V. New *dong* 1961 and 1965

In 1956 there were further re-groupings, which led to the divisions of the centrally situated Sangmae-ri into Ogang-ri, Chŏlsan-dong and Sangmae-dong. Due to further regroupings in June 1957 the number of *dong* within Sariwon was reduced through mergings to eleven. In February 1959 Sinyang-ri, which is situated on the southern outskirts of Central-Sariwon, became a *dong*.

The map of Sariwon-IV shows the location of the twelve *dong* of Sariwon-si from 1955 and Ŏsu-dong. The current municipal borders are shown, so that the Ŏsu-rodongjagu in the East appears within the municipal borders.

The 60s: Enhancement of the city center

In March 1961 Kyŏngam-dong, which is situated on the southern outskirts of Central-Sariwon, became a *ri* again. At the same time six new *dong* were created, three by the separation from already existing *dong*, whilst three *ri* were formed to *dong*. These new *dong* indicate a growth of the city center to the Southeast, Southwest and to the North.

In January 1965 there were again regroupings, five new *dong* were added. Two of them are situated in the center of the city, further three indicate an expansion of the city center towards Southeast.

1981 and 1991: new *dong* also offside the municipal area

In the 70's no new *dong* were created. Then, in 1981 three *ri* become *dong*, Kyŏngam-ri, which was already a *dong* between 1955 and 1961; Kwangsŏng-ri, which is located on the northwest rim of Central-Sariwon and which was incorporated in 1953, and Torim-ri in the Southeast of the municipal area, a part of the city of Sariwon since 1961.

In 1991 five new *dong* were created in the North of the city.

Figure Sariwon-VI. New *dong* 1981 and 1991

Structure of the city of Sariwon

Due to the distribution of the *dong*, three regions with an urbanised character within the city Sariwon can be identified:

1. The center with the administrative functions of the city as a provincial capital and important factories like the textile factory in the southeast of the municipal area
2. The Jŏngbang area with the Sŏngbul temple and the research institute for cattle owning in Sŏngmun-dong (in the North of the municipal area)
3. East-Sariwon with Torim-dong and Ŏsu-dong. In Torim-dong there is an orchard and a grain processing factory. From 1953 until 1974 Ŏsu-dong was *rodongjagu*.

All three centers developed around the railways stations of the city.

KJY-26 (1990, 426) mentions four large industry regions for the city of Sariwon, of which three are situated within the center. These three regions are (in parenthesis the region's share of the total number of industrial employees of Sariwon in 1983):

- the Sanŏp region in the East: (56.8%)[62],
- the Taesŏng region in the West (19.2%)[63] and
- the Wonju-Chŏlsan region in the North (1.9%).

The fourth region, mentioned in KJY-26 (1990, 426), is the Torim-Ŏsu region on the southeast border of the city (7.8%), other regions (14.2%)

The northeast of the municipal area is occupied by the Jŏngbang mountain range, in the west of the city center are rural areas with dry farming for the urban vegetable supply, and further in the West are large areas of wet rice cultivation.

Statistics

In 2002 Sariwon consisted of 31 *dong* and nine *ri*.

	Dong-Formation	*Dong*-Splitting
1955 (13)	13	-
1956 (15)	2	-

62 Here are *inter alia* the Sariwon Textile Factory, the Sariwon Tractor Accessory Factory and the Sariwon Knitted Goods Factory.

63 Here are *inter alia* the Kyŏngamsan Ŭnha Garnment Factory.

1957 (12)	-	-3
1959 (13)	1	-
1961 (18)	-1/3	3
1965 (23)	-	5
1981 (26)	3	-
1991 (31)	3	2

Sariwon – city on the way between Pyongyang and Seoul

Sariwon is conveniently situated for public transport between Pyongyang and Kaesong. It is a provincial capital and a rural industrial town concentrating on textile industry. In several stages, in particular in 1986, agricultural areas were incorporated into the municipal area. Nevertheless, Sariwon is one of the cities with a high proportion of urban population and is one of the most densely populated cities of the DPR Korea. In North Korean geographical descriptions, Sariwon has been called a satellite town of Pyongyang.

Due to its location between the capitals of the two Koreas in the case of a reunification Sariwon has quite good development potential.

IV.2.15. Songrim

Kyomipho – the port of Kenji

Songrim is an industrial satellite town in the lower reaches of the Taedong-gang, south of the capital Pyongyang. It lies to the east of the Taedong-gang towards the Nampho-si and borders directly to the south on Pyongyang. Songrim is famous for the Hwanghae Iron and Steel Complex. Songrim was originally a remote village, but as a result of the establishment of the ironwork it has developed rapidly to an iron city. The water depth, which allows ship traffic of the Taedong-gang, and the establishment of the Songrim railway line (from Hwangju to Songrim) in 1908, the favorable traffic binding of the town as well as the plentiful availability of industrial water were positive location factors for the development of the ironwork.

Table Songrim-I. Basic data

Population	128,831 (Rank 25)
Area	65 km² (Rank 27)
Population density	1,982 I./km² (Rank 1)
Administrative units	19 *dong*/7 *ri* (73,1%) (Rank 10)
"Urban" population/"rural" population	74.4 %/25.6% (rank 20)

Until 1947, the name of Songrim was still Kyŏmipho, the "harbor of Kenji." A name that stems from a Japanese given name. When the Japanese military searched for a landing field for the preparation of the Japanese-Chinese war in the 1880s, they founded the landing field at today's Songrim. Therefore the town was named after the responsible commander Watanabe Kenji 渡邊兼二, Kenji Port (Kenjiho, Korean reading: Kyŏmipho). Because the surname was too common, the given name was chosen. After the construction of the ironworks in 1914, Songrim has developed with giant strides to a town of iron smelting. In 1950 Songrim had 50,000 inhabitants. 30,000 bombs alone fell during the Korean War on the ironworks.

The town lies on the eastern shore of the Taedong-gang and in its wide elevation level therefore predominantly consists of plains. In the East, however, it becomes a little bit hilly. The highest elevation is in the east of Masan-ri, situated at Songrim-san (187 m), which is assigned to the Wŏlbong mountain range.

On the shores of the Hwangju-chŏn (in the South) and the Maesang-chŏn (in the North) (tributaries of the Taedong-gang) were piled up to the Tangsan field, the Sŏkthan field, the Sinryang field, the Sinsŏng field, the Masan field and the Sŏsong field. After 1945 reservoirs were built.

Floods are a common danger in wide parts of the city, although floods are dammed by the construction of the west sea floodgate in Nampho and other preventive measures. (IPA-10 2003, 98).

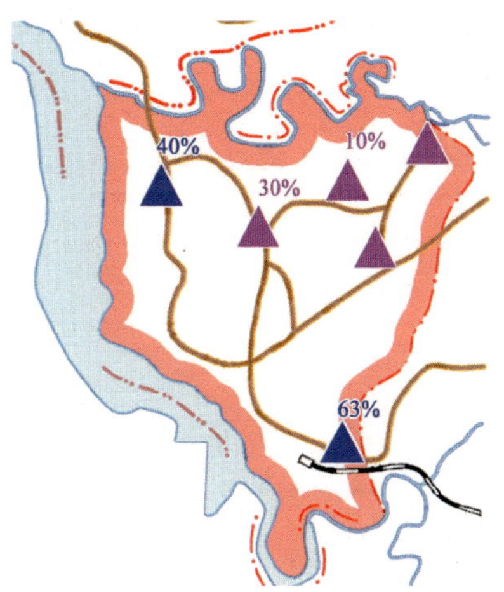

Figure Songrim-I. Forest area in the *ri*

Table Songrim-II. Climate values

Annual average	January temperature	August temperature	Precipitation
10.6℃ (5)	−5.2℃ (11)	24.5℃ (2)	869.7 mm (18)

36% of the city area is agricultural land, 38% of which are used for wet rice agriculture, 48% for dry field agriculture and 10% for fruit cultures (apples, peaches, pears). Sinryang-ri in the southeast corner of the town has a forest portion of 63%, with Sŏsong-ri in the northwest corner the forest area is 40%, with the neighboring Masan-ri at 30%, with remaining three *ri* in the Northeast the forest portion lies around 10%. Rice, maize, soy beans and vegetables are important agricultural products of the town. Chicken farms are in Tangsan-ri and Masan-ri directly to the north of the city center. Tangsan-ri, which lies in 2 km from the city center, is also an important vegetable producer of the town. The terrace cultivation is supported by numerous pumps and miles long irrigation lines. Approximately 70 different vegetables are cultivated through irrigation agriculture. (IPA-10 2003, 108). An important vegetable service area of the Hwanghae Iron and Steel Complex is distant Sŏkthan-ri in the north-east corner of the city, 5 km from the municipal area.

Songrim – the town of the Hwanghae Iron and Steel Complex

The specific feature of the industrial structure of Songrim is the dominance of a company, the Hwanghae Iron and Steel Complex. As per KJY-26 (1990, 444) 85.2% of the industrial production, 54% of the industrial employees and 85.7% of the industrial company surface falls on this complex. However, most other companies of the town are also in direct or indirect connection with the iron complex, if it is as a supplier, or as a food producer for the employees of the factory.

Table Songrim-III. Ranking (in parenthesis: number of the industrial companies or cultural facilities)

Songrim	KOFC	MOU	IPA	KCNA	KIET	Summary
Companies-total	27 (3)	26 (4)	23 (4)	25 (2)	27 (11)	27
Companies-important	21 (1)	17 (1)	25 (1)		26 (3)	26 (1)
Cultural facilities			18 (4)			

Table Songrim-IV. Ranking (total number of companies in relation to population)

Songrim	KOFC	MOU	IPA	KCNA	KIET	Summary
Companies – total	26	26	21 – 25–14	25	27 – 26	26 – 27

Table Songrim-V. Specification (in parenthesis: number of industrial companies)

Songrim	Light Industry	Heavy Industry	Mining	Energy
KOFC	–	10 (2)	4 (1)	–
MOU	17 (2)	18 (1)	6 (1)	–
IPA	3 (3)	22 (1)	–	–
KCNA	–	7 (1)	–	1 (1)
KIET	10 (5)	7 (6)	–	–

Thus the Hwanghae Iron and Steel Complex is the only company of the city, which was determined as important in chapter III.7.3.

The Hwanghae Iron and Steel Complex is situated in Songsan-dong on the shore of the Taedong-gang. This ironwork is, after the Kim Chaek Iron and Steel Complex in Chongjin, the second largest one of the DPRK. It gets its iron ores from the mines of Songrim, Unryul, Jaeryong, Thaethan and Tŏkwŏn. Northeast, 1.7 km away from the complex, the railway station Songrim is situated. The two-lane unpaved street to Hwangju is 2.5 km away. Large ships cannot dock onto the Taedong-gang, however since the complex lies within the industrial region of Pyongyang, an organic interaction is possible between the different iron works. The energy is sourced from its own power station, or from the power station Pyongyang. Coal comes from mines of the regions of Anju and Kangso, limestone from the mines Sŭngho-ri, Sindŏk, Songrim. On a company surface of 3,300,000 m^2 10,000 people are employed.

Because the factory possesses relatively modern equipment, it is also shown to foreign delegations (KOFC 2010, 201).

The Mitsubishi Company had examined iron works in the area of the Hwanghae Province from 1912 and starting from 1913 it established a temporary department for the construction of the ironworks. Then in 1917 the construction of the work was started: the first ironworks on the Korean peninsula and in 1918 the production began. This Mistubishi iron work was later renamed into Kyŏmipho- or Kenjiho iron work. The iron works were built approximately 13 km from Hwangju-up in a fishing village on the tributary of the Taedong-gang. Because the iron ore pits lie in Jaeryong, Unryul and nearby Anak (and Hasŏng), Songrim is a favorable place to supply the ironworks with the iron ores obtained from here. Also the overland transport is very favorable; the connecting Songrim line (built in 1908) from Hwangju to Songrim, is connected with the mainline of Seoul to Sinuiju. The Taedong-gang supplies the utility water and therefore there are good natural conditions for the arrangement of an industrial complex. In the ironworks raw iron was produced for military purposes and was brought to Japan. The factory was rebuilt after the retreat of the Japanese in 1947. During the Korean War the iron work was strongly damaged and in 1958, after the reconstruction work was concluded, the production was resumed again. In particular in the 80s it came to enlargements and modernizations. Today the ironwork, which carries in the meanwhile the name Hwanghae Iron and Steel Complex has developed to the basis on the iron production with different departments. Once the Hwanghae Iron and Steel Complex occupied 18,000 people with approximately 120,000 inhabitants in town and generated one quarter of the national annual steel production. In 1994 the production stopped, after the coke imports from China stopped and the local coal deliveries dried up. In 2002 a conversion was carried out, in order to be able to use local anthracite coal instead of the coke that would have to be imported (KOFC 2010, 201-205; IPA-10 2003, 99).

The port of Songrim on the shore of the Taedong-gang is one of eight trading ports of North Korea and, besides Nampho and Haeju, one of three on the Yellow Sea coast. It lies 40 km from Pyongyang and was used during the Russian-Japanese war by the Japanese as a landing strip for materials, among other things for the construction of rails, and has grown bit by bit, when new iron ores were found. The port of Songrim was declared a trading port in 1975, however, the function of the port is mostly for the Hwanghae Iron and Steel Complex. The water depth is described as 11 m. There are three quays: one for commodities, one for raw material delivery for the Hwanghae ironworks and one for the import of crude oil from Chinese Darien (KOFC 2010, 115). The port of Songrim also is famously known for the fact that rice auxiliary deliveries from South Korea are extinguished.

In the town there are several educational institutions and cultural facilities, which exist to a large part in connection with the ironworks. The University of Technology of Songrim was founded in 1960 to educate the workers of the Hwanghae Iron and Steel Complex and other factories. Its predecessor is the industrial college of Kyŏmipho. In 1961 a research institute was founded in Songrim for fuel chemistry.

The day-care center "Children's Palace Songrim" was built on the edge of the Songrim-san, in particular for the care of toddlers of the workers of the ironworks Hwanghae. It can accommodate 1,500 toddlers (up to kindergarten age). Predecessors date back to 1948, and when in 1957 the factory increased, the day-care center was also developed. In 1973 a new building was built and the day-care center was renamed to "Songrim Children's Palace." (IPA-10 2003, 100-102).

In 1969 the North Korean authorities began to build in a test phase "apartment blocks in the style of Songrim" to save costs for building materials. (Pae Ki-chan 1994, 136). An important measure was that above all building materials from the respective region were mainly used. Also units of factory workers should help with the building of a house. This application of wide parts of the population in the construction of houses, admittedly needed a simplification of the realization of the building of a house (Jang Se-hun 2006b, 480). The model, tested in Songrim, was applied later on also in many other towns of the country (Pae Ki-chan 1994, 136).

In 1947 city foundation, in 1954 slight reduction of the city's territory

In 1914 Ryongbok-ri (county of Hwangju) was converted into three *ri*, Kyŏmipho, Tong-Kyŏmipho and Sŏ-Kyŏmipho. Then in 1938 three *ri* were merged to Kyŏmipho-up, so that the county of Hwangju had now two *up*, because Hwangju-myon had been appointed at the same time also to *up*.

In 1947 Kyŏmipho-up was combined with Songrim-myon to the city of Songrim.

Thus due the foundation of the city of Songrim in 1947, 28 *ri* were established, of which some were combined in 1952.

In 1954, when the province of North-Hwanghae was founded, the Songrim-si was reduced slightly in favor of the Hwangju-kun.[64] For the time afterwards IPA-10 (2003) describes no enlargement or reduction of Songrim-si.

1957: Twelve *dong* on the Taedong-gang shore are combined into five *dong*

Then in 1955 15 *ri* were converted into *dong*. Now 15 *dong* and seven *ri* originated. Twelve of these *dong* were located on the shore of the Taedong-gang, where now Songsan-dong, Wŏlbong-dong and Sinhŭng-dong lie. This is the area with the iron work and the port of Songrim. Two *dong* were in the center of the city (Ungok-dong and Chŏlsan-dong) and one in the southeast of Songrim (Unha-dong).

Then in 1957 twelve *dong* on the Taedong-gang shore were regrouped to five *dong* now. In 1958 Unha-dong became Sinryang-ri; in the west of the city two new *dong* originated (Oryu-dong and Tongsong-dong). These were the only *dong*, which have not originated from splitting off of already existing *dong* after 1955. Then in 1961, five new *dong* originated by separating from already existing *dong*, four of which are situated in the city center, one in the east of the municipal area.

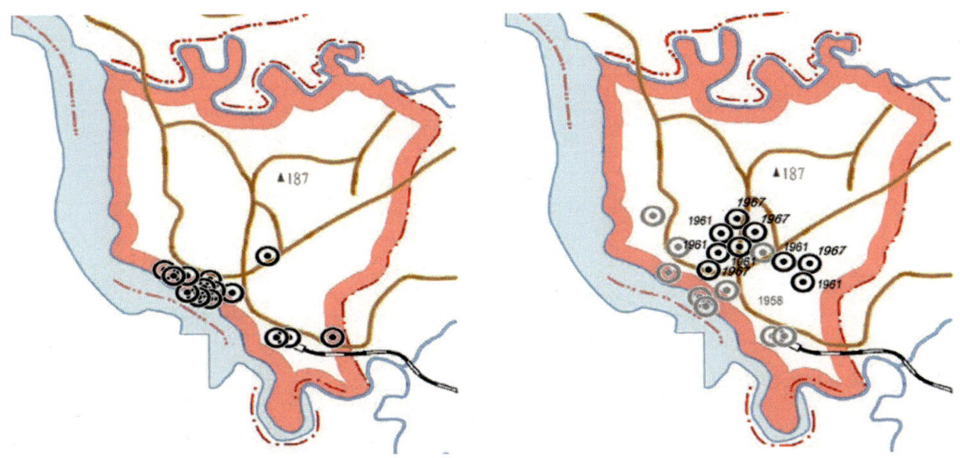

Figure Songrim-II. *Dong* (1955)

Figure Songrim-III. *Dong* (1967)

The comparison of the distribution of *dong* between 1955 and 1961 makes clear that in the time of the reconstruction of the iron works until 1958, there have been numerous administrative changes. One could put up the hypothesis that on the Taedong-gang shore the housing developments (and with it the *dong*) have disappeared in favor of factory and port arrangements and later new housing developments have originated above all in the

64 A part of Sinryang-ri came to Samjŏn-ri (Hwangju-kun).

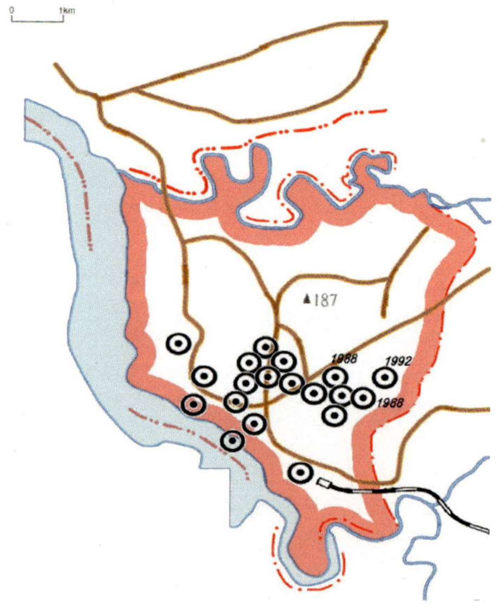

Figure Songrim-IV. *Dong* (1992)

center of the town.

The changes in 1967 go in the same direction as the changes in 1961. From four new *dong* three lie in the center and one in the East.

In the 1970s there are no administrative changes. The changes in 1988 and 1992 show two trends.

1. In 1988 as well in 1992 the number of *dong* situated on the Taedong-gang shore decreases around one *dong* in each year as a result of merging of *dong*.
2. In the east of the city two new *dong* originate in 1988, in 1992 another *dong* originates.

Dong (divided by the location within the city)

	Total	Shore	Center	Southeast	West	East
1955	15	12	2	1	–	–
1957	8	5	2	1	–	–
1958	9	5	2	–	2	–
1961	14	5	6	–	2	1
1967	18	5	9	–	2	2
1988	19	4	9	–	2	4
1992	19	3	9	–	2	5

The following trends appear:

Industrial removal on the Taedong-gang shore in the 50s and in the 80s/90s

In the second half of the 1950s, the number of *dong* on the Taedong-gang shore dramatically decreased. It stands in connection with the reconstruction of the Hwanghae Iron and Steel Complex. Residential areas disappeared in favor of port- and industrial facilities. Between 1988 and 1992 the number of *dong* on the Taedong-gang shore further decreases. Here other interior works in the hut or in the port were possibly carried out.

Removal of residential districts in the center of the city in the 1960s

Between 1961 and 1967 the number of *dong* increased in the city center of Songrim from two to nine. This shows an increase of residential districts in the city center.

From the 1960s and strengthened in 1988/92: "New life" in the East of the city

In the 1960s the first two *dong* in the east of the town originated. In 1988 and 1992 the number of *dong* increased in the east to five, of which *dong* with the names Sae-sallim "new life" 1-4 exist. These names already provide information that these *dong* will be new residential areas.

Statistics

	Dong-Formation	*Dong*-Splitting
1955 (15 *dong*)	15	-
1957 (8 *dong*)	-	-7
1958 (9 *dong*)	-1/2	-
1961 (14 *dong*)	-	5
1967 (18 *dong*)	-	4
1988 (19 *dong*)	-	-1/2
1992 (19 *dong*)	-	-1/1

Songrim – Industrial satellite town of Pyongyang

Songrim is dominated by one single company, thus the Hwanghae Iron and Steel Complex. Under changing development conditions this concentration on heavy industries could lead to big challenges for the economic situation of the city.

With the aim to contribute to the necessary diversification of the city's economic structure, the North Korean government in 2013 named the Songrim Export Goods Processing Zone as one of 14 new planned economic development zones of the DPRK.

IV.2.16. Kaesong

Former capital of the Koryo dynasty

Kaesong is the former capital of the Koryo dynasty (918-1392). The city is situated in the west of the country near the DMZ. Because the city lies south of the 38th degree of latitude, it was granted to South Korea after 1945. However, the Korean War (1950-1953) resulted in the fact that Kaesong became a part of the DPR Korea. In 2002 a special economic zone, in which South Korean investors employ North Korean workers, was established in Kaesong.

Table Kaesong-I. Basic data

Population	308,440 (Rank 9)
Area	766 km^2 (Rank 8)
Population density	403 I./km^2 (Rank 18)
Administrative units	31 *dong*/33 *ri* (48%) (Rank 23)
"Urban" population/"rural" population	62.4%/37.6% (Rank 25)

Kaesong was chosen to be a capital already in 901 under the name Songak, when the unfaithful Silla Prince Kungye had brought wide areas of Kangwon, Kyonggi and Hwanghae in central Korea under his control and declared the state "Later Koguryo." Subsequently he built a new capital in Chŏrwŏn and later proclaimed the State of Majin, later Thaebong. At last the ruler was hunted by his own generals from the throne and was killed on the run. The latter generals supported Wan Kŏn, who came from the area of Songak. He founded in 918 the State of Koryo (918-1392), and built in 919 the capital of Songak, today's Kaesong (Lee, Ki-baek 1984, 99-100). The city was established in a basin, which has Songak-san in the North and looks at the Ryong-san. It is not only the home region of the ruler, but also the nature from geomantic considerations that is described as ideal for the construction of a capital. Kaesong was called a "City of the Geomancy" on account of the excellent situation. The starting point of these geomantic considerations was the Manwŏldae, where the royal palace is situated (Yun Jŏng-sŏp 1987, 48). There are numerous discourses about the geomancy of the city Kaesong.[65]

Then under the Joson dynasty (1392-1910) the capital was shifted in 1396 to Hanyang, today's Seoul. The inhabitants of Kaesong therefore were at a distance from the political power and from administrative positions. Consequentially many turned to trade.

65 Yoon, Hong-key's (2006, 241) theory on the high number of discourses on the geomancy of Kaesong is as follows: "Kaesong's geomantic conditions were interpreted and modified to serve the Wang family in establishing, legitimizing, and maintaining their power".

After the 18th century traders from Kaesong began with the cultivation of ginseng, which became an important commercial product from this region (Kang, Man-gil 1982, 89).

The municipal area is in the western coastal lowland. Merely the south part of the Ahobiryong mountain range rises in the direction of southwest pulling into the city. The Ryesŏng-gang limits the city in the West, the Han-gang in the Southwest and the Rimjin-gang in the Southeast. Important mountains in the city are the Moji-san (778 m), the Songak-san (490 m), the Jinbong-san (310 m), the Kunjang-san (277 m), the Tusŏk-san (415 m) and the Hani-san (219 m) (PSC-8 2009, 645).

Table Kaesong-II. Climate Values

Annual avarage	January temperature	August temperature	Precipitation
10.7℃ (3)	-4.1℃ (7)	24.2℃ (6)	1,264.9 mm (4)

In Kaesong's agriculture primarily grain is cultivated, although there is also livestock breeding, fruit cultivation and the sericulture.

Dominance of light industry

In the following considerations as well as in the statistics the companies of the Kaesong Industrial region are not considered. In Kaesong, industrial sectors of light industry rule, in particular the textile industry, but also the food sector.[66] A specialty of Kaesong is the "Koryo Ginseng," also alcoholic beverages made from ginseng are produced. Furthermore oils, different chili pastes, vegetable products etc., are produced.

Table Kaesong-III. Ranking (in parenthesis: number of the industrial companies or cultural institutions)

Kaesong	KOFC	MOU	IPA	KCNA	KIET	Summary
Companies-total	15 (13)	5 (33)	4 (27)	19 (7)	5 (72)	6
Companies-important	27 (1)	21 (1)	5 (10)		6 (24)	16 (6)
Cultural institutions			7 (16)			

66 According to KJY-26 (1990, 810) the food industry had a share of 80% of the city's total industry production in 1953. In 1984 the food production was down to 15.4%, and the textile industry grew to a 40%.

Table Kaesong-IV. Ranking (Total number of the companies in relation to population)

Kaesong	KOFC	MOU	IPA	KCNA	KIET	Summary
Companies–total	19	2	4–6–5	21	1–2	4–20

In the ranking of the number of the companies Kaesong, the city with ninth-most inhabitants of the DPRK, has bad ratings in both KOFC and KCNA, although Kaesong has especially good ratings in the other sources. The former sources are both sources with the smallest number of companies. I.e. Kaesong has good ratings when a lot of companies are mentioned. This is a hint for the fact that in Kaesong a lot of companies exist, but they are not among the important ones.

Table Kaesong-V. Specification (In parenthesis: number of industrial companies)

Kaesong	Light Industry	Heavy Industry	Mining	Energy
KOFC	1 (8)	24 (5)	–	–
MOU	2 (29)	24 (4)	–	–
IPA	2 (22)	25 (3)	11 (2)	–
KCNA	1 (7)	–	–	–
KIET	3 (39)	23 (28)	17 (3)	10 (2)

Table Kaesong-V shows the unequivocal specialization of Kaesong on light industry. From chapter III.7.3. there are important companies, five belong to the textile industry and one produces essential goods: Kaesong Textile Factory, Kaesong Sewing Thread Factory, Kaesong Knitting Goods Factory, Kaesong Garment Factory, Kaesong Aeguk Garment Factory, Kaesong Essential Plastic Goods Factory.

The Kaesong Textile Factory was established in 1952, is located in Pangjik-dong and produces grid-pattern cloth (IPA-2 2003, 253). The Kaesong Garment Factory is situated in Kwanhun-dong and was opened in 1957 (KJY-26 1990, 810). The Jannansan Export Garment Factory began in 1957 as a co-operative and was established in 1973 as a factory (IPA-2 2003, 254).

The Kaesong General Foodstuff Factory in Ryonghŭng-dong was established at the time of the Six-Year-Plan (1971-1976). Main products of this factory are soy paste, oils, soy sauce and processed vegetable products and meat products (IPA-2 2003, 253-254).

The Kaesong Koryo Insamsul Factory was founded in 1952 as a spirit factory. After the factory received its current name in 1961, alcoholic beverages from ginseng were produced which were also exported to foreign countries, (IPA-2 2003, 252-253). In the Kaesong Porcelain Goods Factory in Pangjik-dong different goods are produced of porcelain and glass, such as vases, ashtrays and dishes (IPA-2 2003, 253). The Kaesong Essential

Plastic Goods Factory is located in Unhak-dong and was established in 1973 and produces different articles of vinyl, such as mackintoshes, shoes or bags (IPA-2 2003, 253).

There are universities in Kaesong for the party cadre as well as for the departments of art, light industry and educational theory. Furthermore, there are cultural institutions such as a radio station, an artist's group, a newspaper, museums etc.

The Kaesong industrial region

Start of the construction of the Kaesong Industrial region was in 2003, and in 2005 the official opening took place. In April 2013 the work stopped at times. At that time 123 companies operated in the Kaesong Industrial region, 53,000 people from North Korea and 800 people from South Korea were employed and produced[67] "everything from clothing and electronics to chemicals and metals" (Cronin 2012, 6). A specific feature of this special economic zone is that it also was continued even after "May 24 2010, [when] all commerce outside of Kaesong was shut down completely" (Cronin 2012, 14).

Moreover, the creation of an economic development zone was announced in 2013 for top technology in Kaesong.

Unesco world heritage

Above all Kaesong is also town with a big touristic potential. In 2013 several places of interest of the city of Kaesong were enrolled as a Unesco world heritage site. Among them are parts of the town wall, the Manwoldae Palace, the Namdaemun (South gate), the Koryo Sŏnggyungwan and several mausoleums and graves (tombs).

The city of Kaesong is an important traffic junction. The discontinuous railway line between Pusan and Sinuiju crosses the city. Also, there is a highway between Pyongyang and Kaesong.

67 The initial plan actually had included a larger size of the industrial park: „The original master plan negotiated by Hyundai Asan and the North Korean government included a 10-square-mile industrial park incorporating residential housing and all of the commercial enterprises typically found in a town. The first phase was planned to encompass more than 800 acres, house some 300 companies with 70.000 workers and be completed by 2007. Phase two would add another 1,225 acres, 700 companies and 130,000 employees and was set to be finished by 2009. The third phase would add nearly 3,000 acres, 1,000 more companies and 150,000 more workers, and would be finished in 2012. Fully occupied, the complex would occupy over 5,000 acres, include 2,000 South Korean businesses, employ more than 350,000 North Koreans and produce $20 billion in annual revenue" (Cronin 2012, 6).

Figure Kaesong-I. View from Janam-dong to Janam-san with the Kim Il-sung Statue (2006)

Figure Kaesong-II. South Gate (2006)

Figure Kaesong-III. Highway of Pyongyang to Kaesong (2006)

Figure Kaesong-IV. Journey of the workers to Kaesong Industrial region (2006)

Kaesong – once part of South Korea

Kaesong is situated south of the 38th degree of latitude and was after the separation of Korea part of South Korea. Due to border movements as a result of the Korean War (1950 - 1953) Kaesong became part of North Korea.

From 1957 to 2003 Kaesong had a province-independent special status. The city had an area of 1,308,634 km², the number of inhabitants is estimated at just 400,000. Kaesong is 78 km away of Seoul and it is less than 12km to the internal Korean border at Phanmunjŏm.

In 2002 a special economic zone, in which South Korean investors employ North Koreans, was established in Kaesong.

Kaesong was granted city (*pu*) status in October 1930. As a part of South Korea it became in 1949 a city (*si*) of Kyonggi Province. After the city had become part of North Korea in the course of the Korean War, the Kaesong-jigu was founded in December 1952. In June 1957 Kaesong-jikhalsi was founded. Kaesong-jikhalsi consists of Kaesong city in a narrower sense as well as of the counties of Kaephung and Phanmun and from 1960 also the county of Jangphung.

2002: Formation of the economic zone Kaesong; in 2003: Kaesong is incorporated into the Hwangbuk Province

In November, 2002 the special economic zone of Kaesong was formed. Until then the province-independent city of Kaesong, consisted of four parts:

- Kaesong-si (in a narrower sense),
- Kaephung-kun,
- Phanmun-kun and
- Jangphung-kun.

In 2002 numerous reorganizations took place, through which the area of the city Kaesong is increased in the narrower sense due to the splitting of the county of Phanmun, whose parts were divided to the city of Kaesong and the county of Kaephung. In June 2003, Kaesong becomes a normal city and was merged into province Hwangbuk like the counties of Kaephung and Jangphun. Then in September 2005, the Kaephung-kun was added to Kaesong. A North Korean map from 2009 (JC 2009, 50-51) shows Kaesong as city that consists of the areas, which existed before the reorganizations in November 2002 of Kaesong-si (in a narrower sense) and the counties of Kaephung and Phanmun. Jangphung however remains a county of the province Hwangbuk.

If we therefore count the areas, which belonged to the four parts of the province-independent city of Kaesong before the reorganization In 2002, Kaesong consisted therefore in the course of time roughly seen of the following parts:

Table Kaesong-VI. Changes in the size of the municipal area of Kaesong

Districts (as of 2002)	Kaesong (in the narrower sense)	Kaephung	Phanmun	Jangphung
1952	X	X	X	
1954	X			
1955	X	X	X	
1960	X	X	X	X
2003	X		partly	
2005	X	X	X	

If we look therefore at Kaesong as an area in the borders of three units: the city of Kaesong (in the narrower sense), the counties of Kaephung and Phanmun (state of 2002), we can register following changes outgoing from the current municipal area (state, map from 2009, changes of borders within areas which belong to the city of Kaesong are not registered)

- In 1958 a part of Sŏam-ri (Jangphung-kun) joins the county of Phanmun.
- In March, 1961 Kaephung-kun was extended by Ryohyŏn-ri (Kumchon-kun, Hwangbuk).
- Also in 1961 Jangphung-kun handed over three *ri* (Ryonghŭng-ri, Samgŏ-ri and Sansŏng-ri) to the Kaesong-si (in the narrower sense).
- In 2002 Sŏnjŏk-ri (Phanmun-kun) is added to Jangphung-kun. However, on the map from the Toro-jidochŏp from 2009 (JC 2009, 50-51) the area is shown again as a part of Kaesong-si.

Statistics

In 1957 Koryŏ-dong was split up and Haeun-dong was created. Suchang-dong came to Naman-dong and rose in it. In 1958 Sŏhŭng-dong rose into Naman-dong, from a part of Tŏkam-ri Posŏn-dong was created. In 1959 a *dong* originated from Unhak-ri. In 1961 Songhak-dong originated from a splitting from Manwŏl-dong.

	Dong-Formation	*Dong*-Splitting
1955 (14)		
1957 (14)	-	1/-1
1958 (14)	1	-1
1959 (15)	1	-
1961 (16)	-	1
1967 (20)	-	4
1983 (23)	2	1
1988 (25)	1	1
1993 (26)	-	1
1994 (27)	1	-

Structure

In the area of today's Kaesong 14 *dong* (and, in addition, Phanmun-up,[68] which later has been renamed to Pongdong-ri, and in addition, Kaephung-up) exist since 1955. Twelve of these *dong* are situated in the south or in the west of the Janam-san. Therefore, the area south and west of the Janam-san can be seen as the old part of the city.

Between 1957 and 1961 four new *dong* originated (two of it due the splitting from already existing *dong*). Both split *dong* lie in the southwestern edge of the old city center, the two *dong* which were created by the change of former *ri,* are situated in the east of the city center (Unhak-dong in the Southeast, Posŏn-dong in the Northeast). Inside of the city center three *dong* were centralized in 1957/1958 to one.[69]

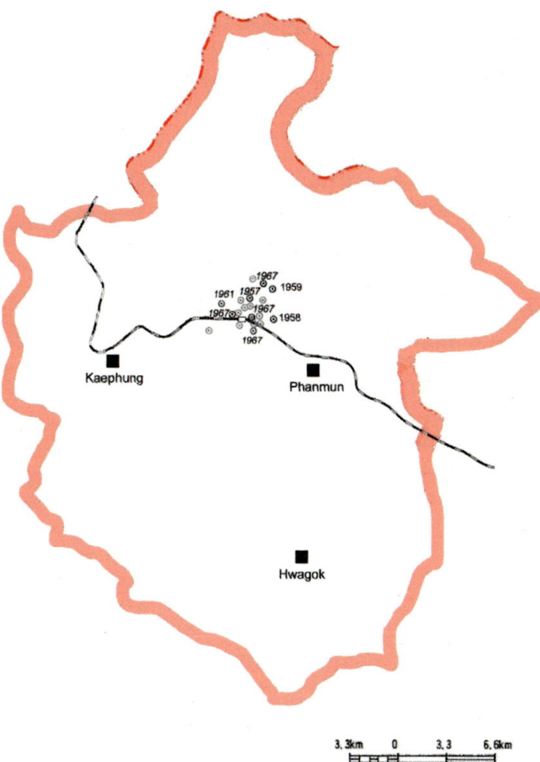

Figure Kaesong-V. *Dong* (1967)

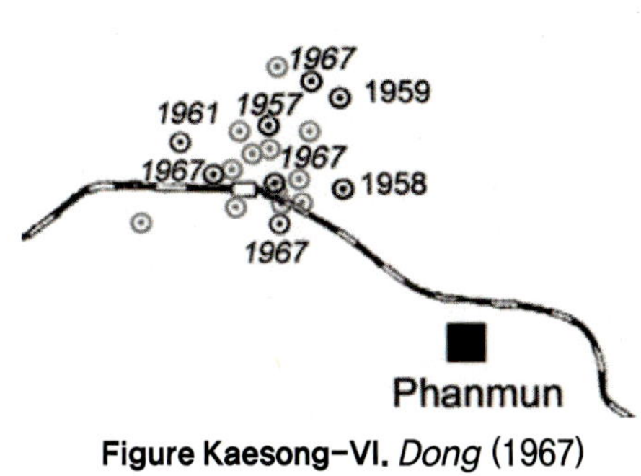

Figure Kaesong-VI. *Dong* (1967)

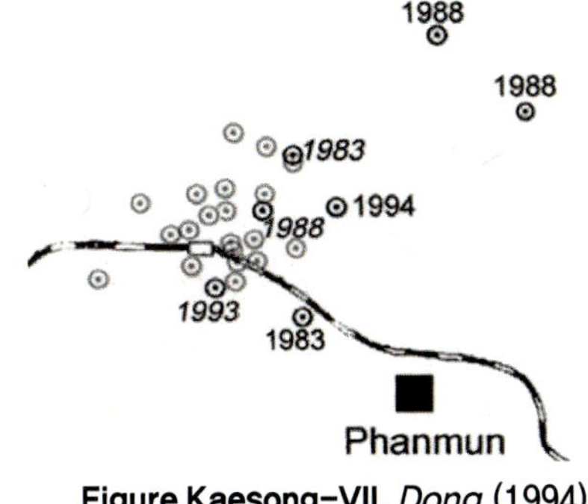

Figure Kaesong-VII. *Dong* (1994)

68 In 1953 the administrative center of the county of Phanmun had moved. From the former Phanmun-up Sangdo-ri was created and Pongdong-ri became the new Phanmun-up.

69 In 1957 Koryŏ-dong was split and Haeun-dong originated. Suchang-dong was transferred into Naman-dong. In 1958 Sŏhŭng-dong was swallowed by Naman-dong, a part of Tŏkam-ri turned into Posŏn-dong. In 1959 Unhak-ri was made a dong. 1960 a part of Manwŏl-dong was cut off and transferred to Songhak-dong. 1961 Songhak-dong originated out of a splitting of Manwŏl-dong.

Four *dong* originated in 1967 due to the splitting from other *dong*. Three (Yŏkjŏn-dong, Nammun-dong and Namsan-dong) lie in the center area south or west of the Janam mountain. One *dong* (Pusan) lies southeast of the city center.

Moreover, in 1967 Hwagok-ri (Phanmun-kun) became a working-class district, but again turned into a *ri* in 1977.

In the 70s no new *dong* developed. Between 1983 and 1994 seven *dong* originated. Four of them lie east of the city center, one south of the city center and two in the periphery east of the city. The latter two settlements show very regular settlement forms in the satellite picture. In Ŭndok-dong[70] there are large chicken and duck farms. In Ryonghŭng-dong, which became a *dong* in 1988, there is the Ryŏngthong temple, which was rebuilt with South Korean help and whose reconstruction was finished in 2005.

Kaesong – City in the middle of the Korean peninsula with big developing potential

The proximity to South Korea led to the fact that in Kaesong no strategically important companies of heavy industry were developed.

New city developments can be ascertained in the periods from 1957 to 1967 and from 1983 to 1994 above all in the east and in the south of the city. Until the start of construction of the Kaesong Industrial region in 2003 and the related opening of the city for the tourism, Kaesong was a city strongly characterized by the military. The original plans for the Kaesong Industrial region which have only partially been implemented indicate the big developing potential of this city.

IV.2.17. Haeju

An important city in the Koryo and Joson era

The port city of Haeju has been several times under consideration as a possible site for a special economic zone due to its proximity to South Korea. The capital of the Hwangnam Province has a great strategic military importance and is located directly near the maritime border between the two Koreas. The industry of the city is characterized by smelters, agricultural engineering and a cement factory. Furthermore, Haeju has a touristic potential. Haeju is one of the geographically smallest cities of the DPR Korea.

70 In 1983 a part of Jonjae-ri (Phanmun-kun) was incorporated into Kaesong-si (in a narrower sense). From this part the Ŭndŏk-dong was newly formed. (IPA-2, 2003 gives different information, according to page 247, this incorporation took place in 1983, according to page 294 and page 421 in 1988.)

Table Haeju-I. Basic data

Population	273,300 (Rank 13)
Area	207 km² (Rank 24)
Population density	1,320 I./km² (Rank 6)
Administrative units	26 *dong*/5 *ri* (84%) (Rank 5)
"Urban" population/"rural" population	88.4%/11.6% (Rank 9)

Already in the Koryo and Joson period, Haeju was an important strategic traffic point between Pyongyang, Kaesong and Seoul. Consequently, a lot of relicts of the old times exist in the downtown area of the city. When Korea was divided into twelve *mok* 牧 in 983, Haeju-mok was one of them. At the end of the Joson period, Haeju belonged along with Seoul, Pyongjang, Jonju and Kaesong to one of the five largest cities of the country. The Suyang mountain fortress dates back to the Koguryo period. The city wall of Haeju was built in 1291, and restored in 1555 and 1591, as well as rebuilt in 1747 (Panzercho 2012).

The fact that in 1906 the railway line between Seoul and Sinuiju was far from Haeju, due to Namchon, and placed in Sinmak, initially had a negative effect on the development of the city. However, already in the period of the Japanese occupation, narrow gauge railways towards Haeju were built. After 1945, the railway network was then further expanded around Haeju. In the period of the Japanese occupation, the port of Haeju was expanded between 1928 and 1932 and used for the removal of rice and natural resources from Korea to Japan.

In 1938 Haeju was designated as a city. After 1945, light and heavy industry were settled in this area.

Important guidelines for the development of the city Haeju were formulated in 1976:

The development of Haeju into a resort town, in which there would be cure and medical treatment services

as well as the enlargement of the port and the promotion of Haeju as an international port city and

the active development of Haeju into a center of light industry and agriculture (Kim Wŏn 1998, 247-248).

A city between sea and mountains

Characteristic of Haeju is its location between the sea and mountains. In front of Haeju, Kyonggi bay has developed with numerous islands. From the ground and the climate, Haeju is actually balanced. Haeju is, in terms of traditional Korean standards, geographically well situated on a river, the Kwangsŏk-chŏn, whereby a built-up urban area on the opposite

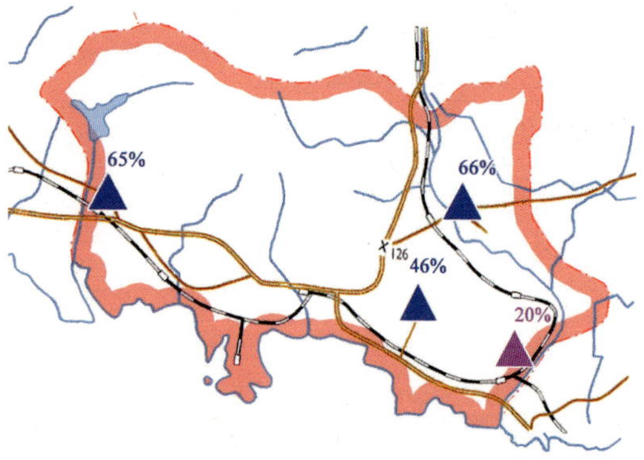

Figure Haeju-I. Forest area in the *ri*

northern Suyang-san (899 m) and the Jangdae-san (685 m) is leant against, and the Namsan (122 m) is opposite. From Haeju the Ryongdang peninsula protrudes into the Haeju bay and opposite is the Jinpho peninsula, so that between these two islands lies only a narrow neck. The region around the Suyang-san was proclaimed as a natural reserve by the North Korean authorities. Of the total area more than 90% are hills and ridges, which are located below sea level of 200 m.

The Kwangsŏk-chŏn flows through the city, from the North towards Southeast, and east of the Ryongdang peninsula it flows into the sea. On its banks in the region of Kwangha-dong, Kwangsŏk-dong, Haechŏng-dong; the Kwangsŏk-chŏn-park was established.

The average annual temperatures as well as the August temperatures are the highest of all cities of the DPR Korea. The strong wind that blows here is very characteristic for this city.

Table Haeju-II. Climate values

Annual average	January temperature	August temperature	Precipitation
11.1℃ (1)	−3.4℃ (4)	24.5℃ (1)	1,080.80 mm (9)

The forest makes up 42% of the total area of the city. In Chakchŏn-ri, there are a lot of freshwater fish hatcheries. The pear is considered to be a speciality of this city.

Smelters, cement factory and manufacture of agricultural machinery

Among the most important industrial companies of Haeju are the agricultural equipment factory, a cement factory, two cabins and a glass plate factory, However, Haeju also has a fishing port and is a naval base of North Korea. Haeju is located in the south of the country, far away from the power plants in the North. Thus, there are major problems due to the lack of power supply.

Table Haeju-III. Ranking (in parenthesis: number of industrial factories or cultural institutions)

Haeju	KOFC	MOU	IPA	KCNA	KIET	Summary
Companies-total	9 (17)	11 (25)	12 (16)	16 (9)	8 (43)	10
Companies-important	19 (2)	15(2)	16 (5)		12 (12)	14 (7)
Cultural institutions			8 (15)			

Table Haeju-IV. Ranking (Total number of companies in relation to population)

Haeju	KOFC	MOU	IPA	KCNA	KIET	Summary
Companies – total	8	9	9–17–6	14	8–15	6–18

Nowadays Haeju is better positioned in the number of companies ranking than in the population ranking (Rank 13). However, most companies of Haeju are not among the most significant ones of the country.

Table Haeju-V. Specification (in parenthesis: number of industrial companies)

Haeju	Light Industry	Heavy Industry	Mining	Energy
KOFC	5 (6)	17 (10)	–	11 (1)
MOU	11 (16)	8 (9)	–	–
IPA	21 (5)	5 (10)	12 (1)	–
KCNA	14 (4)	5 (5)	–	–
KIET	20 (15)	3 (25)	18 (1)	7 (2)

Except in KOFC, Haeju shows a specialization on heavy industry, where smelters and agricultural manufacturing play an important role.

In chapter III.7.3. seven companies are identified as important: the Haeju October 13th Youth Smeltery, the Haeju Smeltery, the Haeju Trailed Farm Machine Factory, the Haeju Cement Factory, the Haeju Plate Glass Factory, the Haeju Knitted Goods Factory and the Haeju Shoe Factory.

The Haeju October 13th Youth Smeltery is located in Sŏkmi-dong and has a total area of 390,000 m². Here, lead ore is melted. The smelting furnace and the electrolysis plant were introduced by the Japanese company Tojo (KOFC 2010, 237). In 1982 the construction of the plant was started and in 1985 the building was completed (IPA-8 2003, 73). The Haeju Smeltery dates back to the period of the Japanese occupation. For example,

Superphosphate, sulfuric acid and copper are melted here. It is located in Ryongdang-dong and has a plant area of 94,000 m² (KOFC 2010, 237).

The Haeju Trailed Farm Machine Factory has a plant area of 110,000 m² (IPA-8 2003, 72) and manufactures rice combines, threshers, trailers, rice-seedling trans planters, other farm machines and various kinds of farm machine accessories. It was founded in October 1958. The products are also used in other provinces of the country (KCNA September 29, 2005).

The Haeju Cement Factory is located in Ryongdang-dong and was built in 1936 by the Japanese company Ube Cement Production Ltd. The total plant area is 500,000 m². It is located about 1 km away from the port of Haeju. The cement which is produced here is also exported to Southeast Asia and China (KOFC 2010, 425).

In the Haeju Plate Glass Factory, a wide variety of glass bottles and glass products are produced for everyday life. Sand of Kumipho and Manggŭmpho is processed here (IPA-8 2003, 73).

The most important light industry companies in Haeju are the Haeju Knitted Goods Factory and the Haeju Shoe Factory.

The planned Haeju Special Economic Zone

Haeju was considered as the ideal location for a special economic zone for a long time. In the late 1990s Hyundai and North Korea agreed in principle to build an industrial complex in the DPR Korea. Kim Jong-il wished Sinuiju to be the site for the new industrial complex.

Hyundai preferred Haeju, Nampho and Sinuiju were their second and third choices. Specifically, in September 1999 a “Plan for Industrial Complex Development” was prepared by Hyundai, which showed Kangryong-kun located in the Southwest of Haeju as a prospective site. However, these plans were responded to by rejection and incomprehension in North Korea, since Haeju was also a strategically sensitive naval port. Additionally, this region is known as a military zone, in which even farming is prohibited and where there is neither water nor electricity. In 2000 the location of Kaesong for an Industrial Complex was agreed on (Lim, Eul-chul 2007, 9-24).

In 2007 the leaders of the two Koreas, Roh Moo-Hyun and Kim Jong-il, agreed at their most recent summit meeting to develop the North Korean port of Haeju together into a special economic zone. It was to be centered around the Haeju port. In the 2nd South-North Korean Summit Joint statement it was read: “The South and the North have agreed to create a “special peace and cooperation zone in the West Sea” encompassing Haeju and vicinity in a bid to proactively push ahead with the creation of a joint fishing zone and maritime peace zone, establishment of a special economic zone, utilization of Haeju harbor, passage of civilian vessels via direct routes in Haeju and the joint use of the Han River estuary" (Institute for Far East Studies 2007). Plans envisaged a size of 16,500,000 m^2. Additionally, the port of Haeju should have been extended. The estimated cost of over 4.5 billion US$ was mentioned. An economic agreement between South Korea and North Korea was planned, which should have allowed a trade between the port of Haeju and the port of Inchon, located 20 km from the former. At the end of 2007 the South Korean government announced the plan of establishing and launching an international investment fund for the development of the North Korean Haeju port (RKI October 31, 2007). Also planned was "a business hub covering a wide array of industries, from fisheries to manufacturing. The Haeju project and the Kaesong Industrial Complex should be complementary to each other" (Ko, Kyong-tae 2007). However, ultimately the Haeju project was refused by the DPR Korea due to the strategic importance of Haeju port to the North Korean Navy. One major problem was the controversial dispute over the North Limit Line in the Yellow Sea.

Disputed maritime border between North and South Korea

When the inter-Korean Armistice Agreement was signed on May 27th 1953, the United Nations Command (UNC) and the army of the DPRK established a Military Demarcation Line (MDL) in the country. In regards to the islands, an agreement was found as well. Due to the superiority of the naval forces of the UN troops, practically all significant islands of the Korean peninsula were in their power. Since the military defense of the Northern islands was not possible, all islands north of the 38th latitude came into North Korean influence, according to the ceasefire agreement. Five islands,[71] which were directly in front of the coast of the North Korean province Hwanghae however were located south of the 38th latitude, were consequently awarded to South Korea.

Conflicts occurred in regards to the question of the affiliation of the sea. In the East, this was not a problem due to the natural extension of the MDL to the sea, which was recognized by both sides. It was however more difficult in terms of the situation on the west side, which was rich with islands. The former UNC Commander Mark Wayne Clarke highlighted the current "Northern Limit Line" (NLL) on 30th August 1953 and notified the DPRK later about this "sea border." This boundary is located between the North Korean mainland and those five islands, which are south from the 38th latitude.

For a long time the DPR Korea did not answer this proposal, which was the reason why South Korea and the UNC assumed that the DPR Korea would accept this draft.

71 The talked about islands are: Yŏnphyŏng island (7.4 km^2), Paegnyŏng (47 km^2), Taechŏng (25 km^2), Sochŏng (6 km^2) and U (0.2 km^2) (Sin Hyo-hŏn 2006, 18). Nowadays, about 15,000 people live on the largest island of Paekryŏng, of which several thousands are marine soldiers.

However, from December 1973 the DPR Korea rejected the NLL. Although it was recognized that the five islands were under the power of the US, the DPR Korea designed a new maritime border and declared that the South Korean ships could only pass through the waters around these islands with permission. From this point on, both countries are accusing each other of intrusion into their territorial waters.

The reason for the North Koreans concerns are obvious. For one, there are strategic military reasons, since the South Koreans expanded the Paegnyong island into a naval base and thus this embodies a threat to the many North Korean naval bases on the Yellow sea coast. Additionally, the NLL complicates the journey of North Korean ships, for example, from Haeju to China. Furthermore the NLL is located in an area with rich fishing grounds (Choe Yŏng-jae 1999). On September 2nd 1999 the DPRK announced their version of an "Inter-Korean MDL in the West Sea (Yellow Sea)." This is basically an extension of the boundaries between the provinces of Kyonggi in the South and the Hwanghae provinces in the North.

On March 23th 2000 three zones were built by the North Koreans around the five islands, which are according to the North Koreans, in the military power of the US, although within the waters of North Korea. Furthermore, two sea routes were established, which should facilitate the access to the islands Paegryong, Taechŏng and Sochŏng (zone 1) and to the Yŏngphyŏng islands (zone 2).

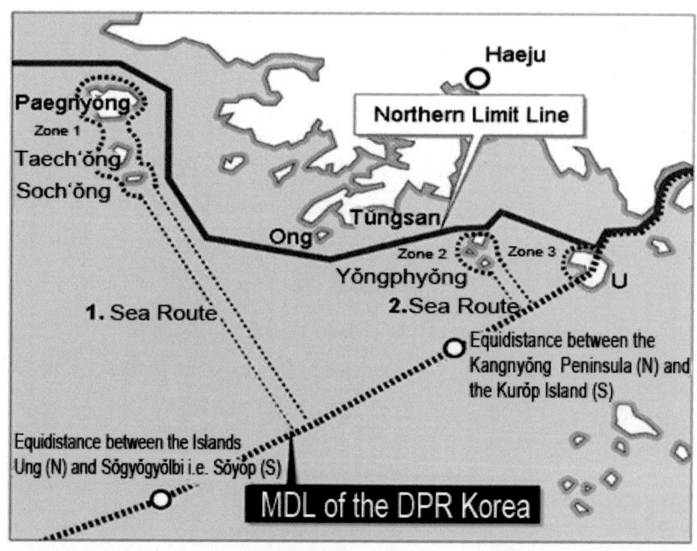

Figure Haeju-II. NLL and MDL, which is proclaimed by the DPRK

The NLL thus was proclaimed as annulled. South Korea and the UNC, however, insist on the validity of the NLL as the *de facto* maritime border, until a new maritime MDL is determined by a Joint Military Commission in a cease-fire agreement. The different views on the maritime border between the two Koreas are a constant source of conflict.

Haeju as a touristic and cultural center

Haeju is open to foreigners. A major attraction is the Puyong Pavilion in Puyong-dong, which originates from the 16th century. It was destroyed during the Korean War and restored in 2003.

The Suyang-san is known for its waterfalls that plunge 128 m, as well as due to the Suyang fortress. On the Suyang-san an amusement park is located for the population of the city.

In Hakhyŏn-dong the remains of the in 937 built Kwangjo Temple are located.

Haeju is also a cultural centre of the province of Hwangnam. There are several universities in the fields of agriculture, teacher training, engineering and medicine.

Developments of the city after 1945 and development centers

In 1961 and 1965 the city area has been increased by the rural countryside. Two *ri* each from neighbouring *kun* were incorporated into the city of Haeju.

The development of the city of Haeju was focused on the city centre. The Ryongdang peninsula, the area of Yŏnha in the West and the region of Hakyŏn, which was incorporated in 1965, are further development centres of the city.

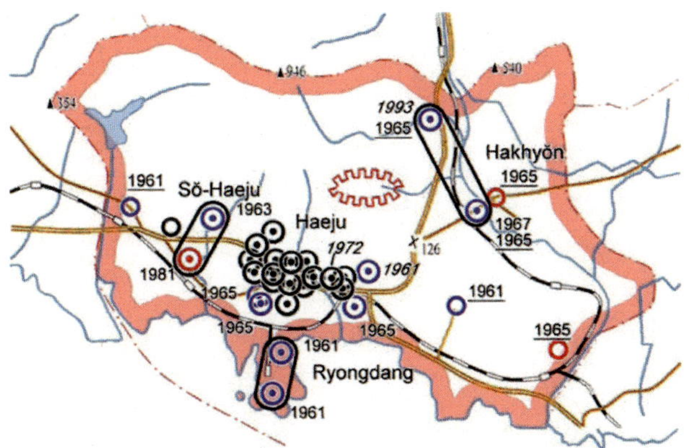

Figure Haeju–III. *Dong* and *ri* of Haeju[73]

72 Figure-Haeju III shows in the middle the Suyang-san fortress. Underlined years indicate that the relevant municipal unit was incorporated in the year in question into Haeju. Cursively written years placed next to the *dong* that have arisen in the year in question, by splitting from other *dong*. The other year figures next to the *dong* are the years, in which the *ri* were elevated to a *dong*.

1. City center

15 of the 26 *dong* of the city already existed in 1957 and are all located in the city center. Two other *dong* within the center originated in 1961 (Taegok-dong[73]) and in 1972 (Sansŏng-dong) by splitting from existing *dong*.

In 1965, three *ri* of Haeju-si were made into *dong*, which adjoin the south of the city center: Sokmi and Kyŏlsŏng in the Southwest and Sŏkchŏn in the Southeast. 20 of the 26 *dong* of Haeju are therefore focused in the centre of the city.

2. Ryongdang peninsula (port)

The city's port is located in the south of the Ryongdang peninsula. In 1961 Ryongdang-ri was divided into the two *dong* of Ryongdang and Sŏae. On the Ryongdang peninsula several industrial plants are located, for example the Haeju October 13th Youth Smeltery, the Haeju Cement Factory and the Haeju Fertilizer Factory.

Between the port and the city centre, there are several areas used for agriculture as well as probably for military purposes.

3. West (So)-Haeju (Yŏnha, Ŭppha)

In the west of the city area, Yŏnyang-ri developed into Yŏnha-dong in 1963 and into a growth pole. Because of the expansion of the inner city area of Haeju in the western direction, this has already almost been merged with the downtown area. Recent settlements have developed in the southwest of Yŏnha, where Ŭppha-ri was made into a *dong* in 1981. In 1993 Yŏnyang-ri was newly formed from parts of Yŏnha-dong and Ŭppha-dong.

Sinwang-ri, which adjoins in the East, was incorporated in 1961 from the neighbouring Pyoksong-kun. In 1968 the Singwang Reservoir was built in the North.

4. Hakhyŏn

In the northeast of the municipal area, Hakyŏn-dong, which is separated from the city center through hills, has developed into another settlement area. In 1967 this *dong* was established from a splitting from Jakchŏn-ri. In Hakyŏn there is a dairy farm. In 1993 the eastern part of the *dong* was split into Yanji-dong.

This whole eastern part of the city Haeju, Jakchŏn-ri (from which later Hakhyŏn-dong and Yangji-dong emerged) and Jangbang-ri, was incorporated only in 1965 from Chongdan-kun. Yŏngyang-ri, which adjoins in the Southeast, joined the city Haeju in 1961.

73 Taegok-dong is located in the Northeast of the city centre. Here, the significant Haeju Trailed Farm Machine Factory is located.

Statistics

Haeju 26 *dong*, 5 *ri*; 1955 17 *dong*

	Dong-Formation	*Dong*-Splitting
1955 (17)		
1957 (15)	-	-2
1961 (18)	2	1
1963 (19)	1	-
1965 (22)	3	-
1967 (23)	1	-
1972 (24)	-	1
1981 (25)	1	-
1993 (26)	-	1

Haeju – high potential for development after reunification

Currently Haeju is located in the south-western tip of the country and thus has major energy problems. The port function is severely limited due to the NNL sea border with South Korea. Haeju has developed as a provincial capital into a cultural center, which is also open for foreign visitors. Among other touristic attractions are the Puyong pavilion as well as the waterfalls of Suyang-san. However, there are only few significant industrial plants, albeit the economical and touristic potential is large, in case of an approach or a reunification with South Korea.

From the 1970s, one *dong* was established per decade.

IV.2.18. Hyesan

Border town to China and gate to Paektusan

Hyesan is the capital of the Ryanggang Province which has been founded in 1954. It is located on the Chinese border and is connected with China since 1986 with a bridge over the border river of Yalu. Hyesan therefore is known for trade with China. Hyesan is also known for the "Youth" Copper Mine, which is operated by a joint venture company consisting of partners from the DPR Korea and China. Additionally, the construction of the Power Plant Samsu between 2004 and 2007 was the occasion for numerous comments in the media. The memorial of the victory of the Battle of Pochonbo is a landmark of the city, which is located centrally in Hyemyŏng-dong and was built in 1967.

City of forestry

Already since the time of the Japanese occupation the most important industry of the area was forestry. Hyesan was a gathering place for logs, which came from the surrounding region. From there the logs were transferred to the paper mills of Kilju, Sinuiju and Songjin (today: Kimchaek). For this reason Hyesan is, compared to other cities in its periphery, well connected with roads. In 1937 the railway to Kilju was completed, in order to transport logs to Japan. In 1936 a bridge was built over the Yalu. Lautensach (1945, 229) referred to Hyesan as the most important settlement of the Kaema highlands. In 1982 Hyesan was portrayed by Campbell as a tiny hamlet, however already in 1936 Hyesan developed to a settlement with 11,795 inhabitants. Lautensach (1945, 229) expedites that there are wooden buildings of the gendarmerie and police, of the post office, as well as some Japanese department stores in the purely Japanese built center. Not far from the road to Kapsan the higher modern brick buildings of the barracks, hospital and the forest authority are towering. The bordering parts of the city consist of Korean village houses.

With the other cities and counties on the border to China, Hyesan is connected by roads (Ko Thae-u 1991, 297-298). In the 1970s the forest inventories were depleted. Herbs, mountain vegetables, hops and skins are now the typical products from the forests around Hyesan.

Table Hyesan-I. Basic data

Population	192,680 (Rank 20)
Area	277 km² (Rank 21)
Population density	696 I./km² (Rank 13)
Administrative units	25 *dong*/4 *ri* (86%) (Rank 3)
"Urban" population/"rural" population	90.3%/9.7% (Rank 6)

Hyesan is one of the smallest cities of North Korea, in terms of population as well as-area size. The *dong*, in which over 90% of the population live, are concentrated in the Northern border of the city. This suggests a very high population density in the urbanised areas of Hyesan.

Situated in a basin on the upper Yalu

Hyesan is located in a cup-shaped widening of the upper valley of the Yalu, which has been dispelled in thin-plate gray shale and gray-white tuffs, dense just above the mouth of the Hŏchŏn-gang (Lautensach 1945, 229). Hyesan is 715 m above sea level, therefore Hyesan is the highest located city of North Korea (Jong Song Il 2011, 99). In the northeast of the municipal area, there is a high plateau, which was formed by lava flows from Paektusan, on the east and southern boundary of the municipal area high mountains protrude and in the West the Hŏchŏn-gang flows. Approximately three-quarters of the municipal area (74%) consists of forest area (Yi Ok-hŭi 2011, 160/IPA-16 2003, 88).

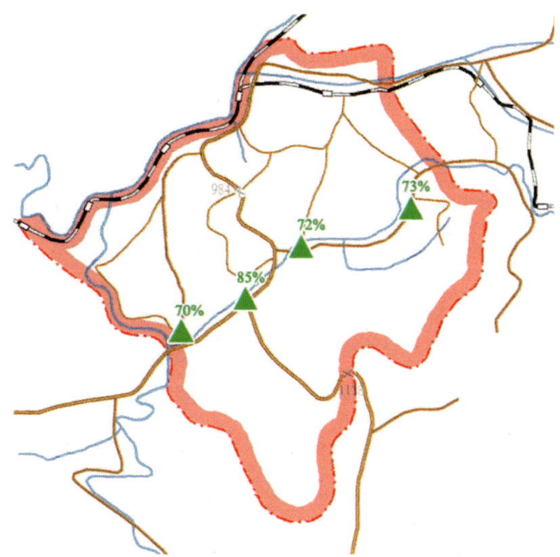

Figure Hyesan-I. Forest area in the four *ri* of the city of Hyesan

The agricultural land is 18% of the total city area. Mostly vegetables are cultivated (radish, Chinese cabbage, spinach, peppers, etc.). Regarding cereals, mostly corn, beans, rice plants, wheat and others are planted. In the intra-mountain basin, agriculture is operated as well, partly even in small scale on a private basis. In the animal husbandry, there are dairy and chicken farms.

Table: Hyesan-II. Climate values

Annual average	January temperature	August temperature	Precipitation
3.6℃ (27)	−16.6℃ (27)	19.8℃ (27)	583 mm (26)

The continental character of the climate is clearly ascertained. Due to the altitude, the summer is not very hot. Freezing weather, however, starts already in late September and continues through until May.

City with a high number of factories

Major industrial sectors in Hyesan are the copper mining industry, the wood processing industry in the region of Wiyŏn, the machine construction, the clothing and footwear industry, ironware industry and the production of Humer ears (concrete tubes from spiral spun concrete). As a cultivating product, next to their blueberries, the hops from Hyesan is famous, with which beer is brewed with all over North Korea, including in Hyesan itself.

Table Hyesan-III. Ranking (in parenthesis: number of industrial companies or cultural institutions)

Hyesan	KOFC	MOU	IPA	KCNA	KIET	Summary
Companies-total	16 (12)	14 (22)	18 (9)	6 (17)	14 (29)	14
Companies-important	18 (2)	7 (3)	7 (9)		14 (11)	13 (7)
Cultural institutions			11 (11)			

Table Hyesan-IV. Ranking (Total number of companies in relation to population)

Hyesan	KOFC	MOU	IPA	KCNA	KIET	Summary
Companies – total	5	1	12-1-3	1	6-7	3-1

In terms of population Hyesan occupies rank 20. However, in regards to Hyesan's equipment the city is better placed in all categories. In view of the quotient between the shares on the total number of companies and the share on the population, Hyesan is usually in the foremost places. Hyesan shows itself in regards to this quantitative evaluation of the statistics as a strongly developed industrial city.

Table Hyesan-V. Specification (in parenthesis: number of industrial companies)

Huichon	Light Industry	Heavy Industry	Mining	Energy
KOFC	4 (5)	23 (5)	8 (1)	6 (1)
MOU	20 (10)	10 (7)	7 (5)	–
IPA	9 (5)	18 (3)	9 (1)	–
KCNA	15 (7)	16 (5)	5 (3)	11 (2)
KIET	14 (12)	13 (15)	9 (2)	–

When considering the specification, it is striking that Hyesan specializes more in light industry, than in heavy industry. Also, the mining industry in Hyesan is listed in all five sources.

To check the above quantitative results, the most important companies of the city are now looked upon at. In chapter III.7.3. seven important companies were identified for Hyesan: the Hyesan Footwear Factory, the Wiwon Sawmill, the May 8th Forestry Machinery Factory, the Hyesan Paper Factory, the Hyesan Textile Factory, the Hyesan Blueberries Processing Factory and the Hyesan Youth Mine.

A copper mine, a company of mechanical engineering, and five companies of light industry are also included.

The May 8th Forestry Machinery Factory is a base for the production of forestry equipment (chain saws, wood processing plants etc...), which, as IPA-16 (2003, 90) explains, was built on the instructions of Kim Il-sung on 8th May 1958. The products of this factory are delivered to forestry bases in the whole country.

Two of the five light industry associated companies of Hyesan are wood-processing factories, the Wiwon Sawmill and the Hyesan Paper Factory. The Wiwon Sawmill has been operating since 1954. Here a wide range of products are made of wood (for example wardrobes), but also vegetable material (tannins). The area of the factory land is 200,000 m^2 (IPA-16 2003, 90).

A speciality of the region is products made from blueberries, which are picked from the mountains in and around Hyesan. The products of the Hyesan Blueberries Processing Factory (including alcoholic drinks, juices) satisfy not only the needs of the entire province of Ryanggang, but are also sold nationwide and additionally exported abroad.

In the Hyesan Textile Factory threads and fabrics are made from chemical fibers (Vinalon and staple fibers). It was built in 1963. In the beginning, between 1979 and 1980, the factory was redesigned, so that it began to produce fabrics from the chemical fibres.

The Hyesan Footwear Factory is specialised in the manufacture of shoes made from injecting moulding plastic.

Hyesan Youth Copper Mine as an example for cooperation with China

The proximity to China is significant *inter alia* due to joint economic activities between the two countries. An example of such cooperation is the Hyesan Youth Mine. It is the copper mine with the largest copper inventories in Asia with its existing stocks of 160 million tons (SNKECSA 2011, 73). It initially only had regional importance, until it was expanded to a copper mine in the late 1960s (IPA-16 2003, 91). On 19th September 2011 the implementation of the operation of the mine through the Hyesan-China Joint Venture Mineral Company was formally started. This company was established already on 1st November 2007 by the Wanxiang Resources Limited Company (China) and the Ministry of Mining Industries (DPRK) with the goal to produce and sell copper (North Korea Leadership Watch 2011).

In recent times, it is tried to attract investors from Changbai for joint ventures in Hyesan (Kim, Kwang Jin, 2012).

The construction of the Samsu Hydroelectric Power Station

A great change within the municipal area of Hyesan was brought by the construction of the Samsu-Hydroelectric Power Station. The beginning of construction was celebrated in May 2004 (KCNA 7.5.2004), and in May 2007 the completion arrived. The dam was built at the confluence of the Unchon-gang and the Hochon-gang, on the border between the city of Hyesan and the county of Samsu. As capacity, 50,000 kW were provided by the North Koreans. 30,000 workers were mobilised. KCNA (May 7, 2004) specified as a goal the solution to the electricity sustenance problem around the area of Paektusan, especially in Samjiyon-kun (KCNA August 3, 2006), in which there are numerous national memorials. Additionally, the new artificial lake should contribute to the enhancement of the landscape of the city of Hyesan and the county of Samsu. Thus, the lake could also be a touristic destination especially for visitors from China (Mok Yong-jae 2012). On the other hand, the construction of the hydroelectric power station is blamed for a flood of the copper mine "Youth" Hyesan (Jŏng Thae-wŏn 2007).

Provincial capital with appropriate cultural facilities

As the capital of Ryonggang Province, there are numerous cultural institutions in Hyesan, starting from universities and research institutions, which specialise in medicine, education, agriculture, mining, forestry and wood chemistry. Also, press organs such as the daily newspaper "Ryanggang" and the radio station Hyesan are represented in the city.

Border trade with China and its effects

The economic standstill of North Korea, which has been increasingly evident since the 1980s, increased the importance of exports from China. Chinese Goods arrived through the neighbouring region of Changbai through Hyesan into the country. Hyesan, after Sinuiju, is the second largest border city to China of North Korea. Thus it became a goods turnover location, from which the goods would be transported to Sinuiju, Hamhung, Pyongyang and even to Sariwon. Therefore, the standard of living in Hyesan was comparatively considered as high, which was the reason that the term "Libya Hyesan"[74] was born (Yi Ok-Hŭi 2011, 159-162).

Opposite of Hyesan on the Chinese side the large community of Changbai, part of the

74 In North Korea workers were sent to Libya in the 1980s. They lived better than people, who worked in the USSR. Libya was considered as a symbol of richness (Yi Ok-hŭi 2011, 185).

Autonomous County of Changbai of the Koreans (Jilin Province), is located. Hyesan and Changbai are connected by the Changbai-Hyesan International Bridge. The bridge was built in 1936, however it was destroyed several times and also rebuilt. The existing bridge dates back to the renovation in 1985. The bridge is 148 m long and 9 m wide (Baidu n.d.).

When it does not rain, there are many locations in Hyesan, in which the Yalu has a width of less than 30 m. In the winter, a thick ice layer emerges, which enables the easy transition to the Chinese riverside. Therefore, in the early times Hyesan was a city, which was used for smuggling and escaping from North Korea.

Also, Hyesan as a border town is known for its residents, who are confronted with information from abroad comparatively often. In response, the North Korean state apparatus employed strengthened controls and military missions. Especially the famine in the 1990s worsened the situation. Escape, smuggling and discontent with the regime was boldly registered in Hyesan. Therefore, the North Korean government responded with far-reaching purges that began in 1997 and peaked in 1999. South Korean Media speak of arrests, deportations, executions and other killings of citizens of the city of Hyesan (Kang Chŏl-hwan, 2011).[75]

Hyesan – the basis for the Paektusan tourism

Hyesan is also a starting point for tourism to Paektusan, especially for Chinese tourists. On the program is the Monument of the Victorious Battle of Pochonbo, the College of Education Kim Jong-suk, as well as a performance at the University of the Arts (Mok Yong-chae 2012). The 38.7 m high Ponchobo Monument plays a major role for North Korean propaganda as a reminder of the battle led by Kim Il-sung on 4th June 1937 in the anti-Japanese struggle. The most important historic landmark of the city is the Kwaegung Pavilion. It served as the south gate of the fortification of Hyesan-jin, which was built as a defence for the protection against invaders from the North, at the beginning of the Joson time in the year of 1421 as a replacement and restoration of an older fortress. From this pavilion a beautiful view of the Yalu exists (VNC Asia Travel n.d./Jong Song Il 2011, 100). An important place of remembrance for the population is the in 1959 built and in 1965 expanded cemetery of heroes in Hyesan (KCNA 6.12.2002).

1954: city foundation – capital of Ryanggang Province

In 1934 Hyesan became an *up* within the Kapsan-kun. In 1942 Hyesan-kun was newly

75 As well: Yi Jŏng-hun (2001).

established. After the liberation, Hyesan was again a *myon* and in the course of a large-scale administrative transformation it became an *up* again in 1952.

In 1954 Hyesan-si was founded from the *up*, the Wiyŏnpho-rodongjagu and three *ri* of the Hyesan-kun; however from the rest of the *kun* Unhung-kun was formed. Hyesan-up was split into six *dong* and one *ri*; Wiyŏnpho-rodongjagu in one *dong* and two *ri*. The latter three *ri* were made into a *dong* in 1955.

1961 – Expansion of the city around the rural areas

After becoming a city, incorporations were made in 1954 and 1961. The incorporation of 1954 covered the west of the city, where a portion of Jungun-ri (Samsu-kun) was merged with Chungdong (Hyesan-kun). In 1961 Jungun-ri was split completely. One part, together with Chungdong-ri, formed Kanggu-dong (Hyesan-si), the other part was added to Phosŏng-ri (since 1991: Phosŏng-rodongjagu) (Samsu-kun).

Additionally in 1961, five *ri* were added to the city of Hyesan. All four *ri* of the city of Hyesan and Komsan-dong, which emerged in 1981 from Osichŏn-ri, came to the city in 1961.

Developments and structure

The old market of Hyesan was located in what is now Hyegang-dong, north of the "Youth" Hyesan railway station, where today the Market road (Jang-road) is located.

In 1957 Hyejang-dong was incorporated into Hyegang-dong. In 1961, the *dong* have been separated again. Additionally, in 1957 Yŏnphung-dong originated in the north-eastern region of the former Wiyŏnpho-rodongjagu by splitting-off from Wiyŏn-dong.

Figure Hyesan-II shows the location of the ten *dong* in 1957, four *dong* of them, which emerged from Wiyŏnpho-rodongjagu, are located in the East; however the former *up* lies in the West.

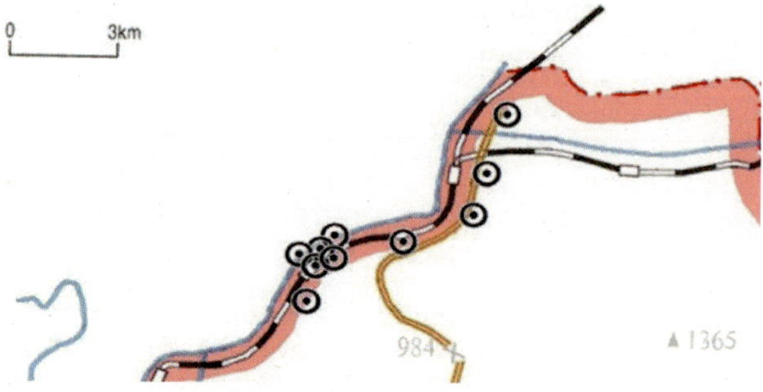

Figure Hyesan-II. The ten *dong* in 1957

In the 1960es, ten new *dong* emerged (figure Hyesan-III).

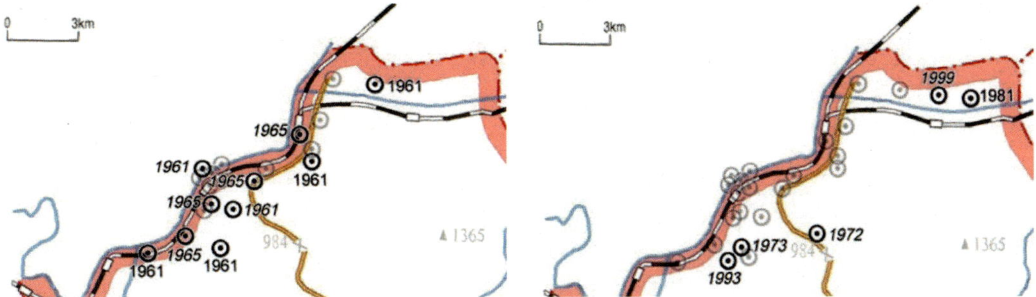

Figure Hyesan-III. The *dong*, which emerged in the 1960s.

Figure Hyesan-IV. *Dong*, which emerged since 1972.

Clear city expansions are seen in the south and southwest of the center.

Since 1972, five new *dong* originated (figure Hyesan-IV).

As growth centers beyond the two centers (Hyesan, Wiyŏn) are the regions south from the city center as well as the regions on the northern border to the municipal area.

Figure Hyesan-V gives an overview of the entire municipal area as well as the current *dong* of the city. Even the former Hyesan-up as well as the former *rodongjagu* of Wiyonpho is shown.

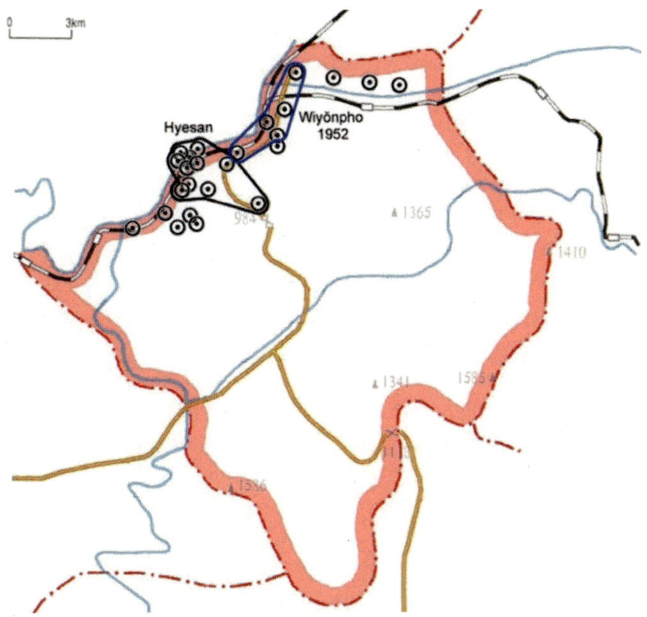

Figure Hyesan-V. *Dong* in the city of Hyesan

Statistics

Urbanized areas before the city foundation (*up* and *rodongjagu*)

1952-1954 Hyesan-up

1952-1954 Wiyŏnpho-rodongjagu

	Dong-Formation	*Dong*-Splitting
1954 (7)	-	(5)
1955 (10)	(3)	-
1957 (10)	-	1/-1
1961 (16)	4	2
1965 (20)	-	4
1972 (21)	-	1
1973 (22)	-	1
1981 (23)	1	-
1993 (24)	-	1
1999 (25)	-	1

Incorporations

1954: + Part of Jungun-ri (Samsu-kun)

1961 *ri* of Unhŭng-kun; + part of Jungun-ri (Samsu-kun)

Hyesan – border city with a considerable number of middle and small factories

From the statistics about Hyesan, it is noticed that the city has especially a lot of factories, in comparison to its population, and that it occupies top positions in the relevant tables. How can this phenomenon be explained? One can notice that Hyesan has a considerable number of factories for its area size, that these factories are partially known nationwide due to their specialisations, albeit they are not the largest factories in the country. The qualitative analysis thus relativizes the quantitative result with regard to the importance of Hyesan as an industrial city.

Furthermore, the population of the city of Hyesan is mostly concentrated in the valley of the Yalu. This high population density in a limited part of the municipal area embodies the fact, that in the statistics the ratio of industrial companies is high compared to the population. From the latter statistical finding, it cannot be concluded that Hyesan is a city that is particularly strongly affected industrially. A large part of the most important industrial companies are in a relationship with the forest economy. With the objective of stimulation and differentiation of the economic structure of the city on the Korean-Chinese border, Hyesan was appointed in 2013 as one of the 14 new locations for an economic development zone of the DPR Korea.

IV.2.19. Rason

City in the northeast corner of the DPR Korea

Rason is situated near the East Sea on the border of the DPRK to China and Russia and was created as a merger of Rajin-si with Sonbong-kun to Rajin-Songbong-si in 1993. In 2000 Rajin-Sonbong was renamed Rason. In the period of Japanese rule over Korea, ports were created in Rajin and Sonbong. Rajin-Songbong Free Economic and Trade Zone was proclaimed in December 1991 and was the first free trade zone of the DPR Korea. Since the late 2000s increased activities to improve the infrastructure in the city of Rason have been observed, which are connected to investments from China and Russia.

Table Rason-I. Basic data

Population	196,954 (Rank 18)
Area	754 km² (Rank 9)
Population density	261 I./km² (Rank 22)
Administrative units	21 *dong*/13 *ri* (48%) (Rank 24)
"Urban" population/"rural" population	80.4%/19.6% (Rank 16)

Sonbong, which was still called Unggi until 1981, is the northernmost port, which has developed 25 km south of the Tumen mouth in Songbon Bay, which is a part of Josan Bay. Since it is a sunken bay, the water is deep. The bay is surrounded in the East, North and West by mountains and faces the sea in the South. Originally it was a remote village. The port operated since 1909, but initially had only local significance (Saitschikow 1958, 268). The opening of the port to international trade in 1912 and the opening of the Tumen line (Hoeryong-Unggi) in 1933 initiated a rapid development. Together with Chongjin, the Unggi port should serve the transport between Japan and Northeast China. In 1926 an extensive remodeling work on the port took place. For a further expansion of the ports, the port bays of Chongjin and Unggi proved to be both too small. A new port base for the Japanese was thus created in 1932 in Rajin Bay, 35 km south of the mouth of the Tumen (Saitschikow 1958, 269).

Rajin is surrounded in the East, North and West on three sides by mountains. In front of the city, there are the two islands, Taecho-do and Socho-do, thus forming a natural wharf. The inside of the bay is wide, the water deep and despite its northern location, the bay does not freeze in winter, so that a natural port was able to be built here. After the construction of the port, the population increased rapidly, and the city experienced an amazing development (Kang Sŏk-o 1984, 339). At the same time Rajin also became the location of one of the major Japanese naval bases in North Korea close to Soviet border (Saitschikow 1958, 269).

After the Korean War Rajin lost its function as a trading port and was used as a naval port, as location for shipyards and as a fishing base. The construction of the Sŭngri Chemical Complex in 1968 changed the industrial structure of the town radically. Also Unggi, which had developed at the end of the period of Japanese occupation as a gateway to North Manchuria, lost these conditions as a result of the Second World War and the hinterland was limited to the catchment area of the Tumen. The development of the ports of Chongjin and Rajin led to stagnation too.

The northern foothills of the Hamgyong mountain range run north of the city in northwestern direction. Narrow, long plains are between the mountains and the coast, in which Rajin and Sonbong have developed. The rivers are thus very short, apart from the border river in the north, the Tumen. Important mountains are the Songjin-san (1.146 m), the Poroji-bong (819 m) and Kwangdae-tŏk (638 m) near Sonbong. The coast has several bays, of which the Josan Bay and the Rajin-bay are the most important. From the offshore islands, Taecho-do is the largest with an area of approximately 4.3 km^2.

Table Rason-II. Climate values

Annual average	January temperature	August temperature	Precipitation
7.0℃ (25)	-7.3℃ (19)	21.2℃ (25)	793.5 mm (21)

Because of the sea and the relatively small built-up urban area, the climate of this city is greatly influenced by the sea. In summer and spring it is often very foggy and in winter, a strong northwest wind blows.

Under Japanese rule a Japanese military base was situated in Rajin, from where agricultural products were transported to Japan. Especially a lot of millet was cultivated. Dry farming was used on more than 85% of the cultivatable land in the urban area. An important product is potatoes. The livestock sector plays an important role as well. Milk or milk products such as butter are famous products of Rason. The fishing industry is of great importance. Fishery stations emerged in Rajin and Sonbong.

Change in the economic structure by the construction of Sŭngri Chemical Complex

Important industrial sectors of Rason are the chemical industry (processing of crude oil), energy production, the mechanical engineering (ship repairs, production of agricultural machinery) and wood processing (production of railway sleepers). But also food, medicine, clothing, paper, furniture, cement and other products are produced in Rason.

In 1970, the fishing took another 60% of the production of the industry in Rajin. This changed after the Sŭngri Chemical Complex and the June 16th Thermal Power Station were built. In 1980, the chemical industry took up for 63% (1983: 67.5%) and the energy sector accounted for 12% (1983: 12%). The share of the fishery fell to 12.4% (1980) and 9.4% (1983) (KJY-29, 1990, 545).

Table Rason-III. Ranking (in parenthesis: number of industrial companies or cultural institutions)

Rason	KOFC	MOU	IPA	KCNA	KIET	Summary
Companies-total	24 (6)	19 (12)	24 (4)	18 (7)	15 (29)	22
Companies-important	14 (3)	19 (1)	22 (3)		22 (6)	25 (2)
Cultural institutions			15 (5)			

Table Rason-IV. Ranking (total number of companies in relation to population)

Rason	KOFC	MOU	IPA	KCNA	KIET	Summary
Companies – total	23	19	23-20-13	10	5-21	21-25

In the ranking about the number of companies, Rason is usually ranked behind its population rank (rank 18). In particular, there are hardly any important companies in the city.

Table Rason-V. Specification (in parenthesis: number of industrial companies)

Rason	Light Industry	Heavy Industry	Mining	Energy
KOFC	7 (2)	20 (3)	–	4 (1)
MOU	22 (5)	18 (3)	8 (2)	1 (2)
IPA	22 (1)	7 (2)	–	1 (1)
KCNA	6 (5)	24 (1)	–	9 (1)
KIET	17 (11)	17 (14)	9 (2)	3 (2)

A specialization on light or heavy industry cannot be deduced from Table Rason-V. In chapter III.7.3. however, only one company has been identified as important for Rason, namely the Sŭngri Chemical Complex.

The construction of this facility began in June 1968 with Soviet assistance. The first phase was completed in September 1973, the second in 1976 (KOFC 2010, 378-379). Oil was delivered from the Soviet Union. On one hand railway was used, which crosses the border at the Tumangang-rodongjagu, on the other hand crude oil was imported via the Sonbong harbor, where a pipeline to the plant was built. Important products of the factory are benzene, paraffin, petrol, naphtha, diesel, crude oil, heavy oil, among others. It was delivered to the Namhŭng Youth Chemical Complex, other chemical factories around the country, the transport industry and the June 16th Thermal Power Station, which was built in August 1973 (KJY-29 1990, 545-546). In the 1990s, the crude oil supplies from Russia were stopped. Afterwards, even oil from Iran had been processed, but the foreign exchange crisis of North Korea in mid-1994 also stopped this import (KOFC 2010, 380). After the Agreed Framework between The United States of America and the Democratic People's Republic of Korea was signed on October 21, 1994, a joint venture between a North Korean company and the U.S. Stanton Asian Development Company was founded in 1995, with the aim of restarting the production of the petrochemical plant and the power plant (Kim Roi 2006). Ultimately, the negotiations were not successful and were canceled at the outbreak of the so-called second North Korean crisis in 2002. However, in the context of Toll-processing procedures the Sŭngri Chemical Complex resumed its production, where crude oil from the Yemen and Oman (1997), China (1998), Russia (1999) and Hong Kong (1999) was processed (KOFC 2010, 380-381). In June 2013 a Mongolian oil trading and refining company, called HBOil JSC, started a new trial, which is said to have acquired 20 percent of the Sŭngri refinery for $10 million. It is expected that the plant will run again after one year. Crude oil is delivered from Mongolia, the refined products go back to Mongolia (Kohn/Humber 2013).

In connection with the construction of the Sŭngri Chemical Complex, the June 16th Thermal Power Station was built with Soviet aid as well, which burns the produced heavy oil and provides on the other hand the Chemical Complex with electrical energy. The construction was started in 1968. Facilities were imported from the Soviet Union and the Federal Republic of Germany (Kraftwerk Union). A part of the power plant was completed in 1973, another in 1977. Between 1995 and 2002, the plant was supplied with heavy oil from KEDO (Korean Peninsula Energy Development Organization), which had been established in the context of the Agreed Framework in Geneva (KOFC 2010, 154-155).

The Rason Taehŭng Trading Corporation is an example for a new company, which is a fishing company with fishing operations and processing plants. It was commissioned in 2002 and is located in Sinha-dong on the beach near the Changjin Bay. Facilities for freezing and drying of seafood amongst others are situated on a total area of 96,680 m^2. Products from shrimp or crabs are also exported to Japan, Russia and other countries (IPA-2 2003, 453).

Rason Economic Special Zone

In December 1991 North Korea had proclaimed the Rajin - Songbong Free Economic and Trade Zone. This was part of a funded project by the UNDP (United Nations Development Program) called "Tumen River Area Development Program (TRADP)." Since it was the first special economic zone of the DPRK, the euphoria was great. There were talks about a "Golden Triangle," which included parts of northeastern Korea as well as the neighboring states of Russia and China. However the investments in this region, which was distant from the capital Pyongyang and whose infrastructural was barely developed, did not meet expectations. Hotels, banks, trading companies and a casino, which had to be closed after Chinese officials had gambled public money away, dominated the headlines about this region for a long time. Thus, the project, in which both Koreas, China, Russia and Mongolia were involved, was interrupted, since the withdrawal of North Korea in November 2009 (RKI February 24, 2010).

However, over time, Russia and the PR China showed stronger interest in the traffic geographical advantages of the nearly ice-free ports in winter. In 2008 Russia secured a 50-year right to use the quay No. 3 of the port of Rajin. The 54-km-long railway between Rajin and Russia's Khasan was restored with the aim of exporting coal from Russia via Rajin (RKI September 26, 2013). After the extension of the road between Wŏnjŏng-ri, on the border to China, was recently completed, extracted coal in Hunchun was transported via Rajin to the southern regions of China (Shanghai) (RKI January 20, 2012). On this highway a ride between Hunchun and Rason takes about an hour (RKI May 12, 2011). Furthermore, China also acquired a ten-year lease right for the first quay of the port of Rajin in March 2010 (RKI June 14, 2011).

Later it also received 50-year rights for the piers 4.5 and 6 (RKI May 12, 2011). The background of China's activities in Rason is also a development plan of northeastern China, through which the economic development should be encouraged in the cities of Changchun, Jilin and Tumen. By connecting this region with a population of eleven million people, with Rason and the Russian city of Vladivostok, a direct access to the East Sea coast would be created (RKI May 12, 2011). Also China and North Korea agreed on China supplying the Special Economic Zone of Rason with electric power (RKI September 13, 2011).

Meanwhile Rason has developed into a city, in which more than 150 joint venture companies operate, who cooperate with partners from China, Japan, Russia and Canada among others (Chosun Ilbo November 12, 2013).

Rajin-City from 1936-1949

Rason is a fusion of Rajin-si and Sonbong-kun, which was called Unggi-kun up to the year 1981. Rajin was already a city (*pu/si*) between 1936 and 1949. In 1949 it became a *kun.*

1967-1993: Rajin-si, for a few months Unggi (Sonbong) is already part of the city

In August 1967 a part of Rajin-kun and Unggi-kun formed Rajin-si; seven *ri* of the Rajin-kun came to the Puryong-kuyok of Chongjin-si. In October 1967 Rajin-si was split and the Unggi-kun emerged again.

But the former *up* of Unggi-kun initially remained in Rajin-si. Hongŭi-ri was at first the new Unggi-up. In November 1967, however Hongŭi was converted to *ri* again and Unsang-ri became Unggi-up. In 1968 Ungsang was converted *ri* again and four *dong* (Sanghyŏn, Junghyŏn, Hahyŏn, Songphyŏng) and a part of the Paekhak1-dong of Rajin-si are formed into Unggi-kun. Thus the old Unggi-up was practically restored again like before the unification of Rajin-si. In the progress of these transformations, parts of Paekhak1-dong and Paekhak2-dong were added to Unggi-kun from Rajin-si, as Paekhak-ri and as well as Chŏlju-ri.

In 1973 Rajin was divided into three *kuyok*; the *kuyok*-system was again abolished in 1974. In 1981 Unggi-kun was renamed to Sonbong-kun.

1993 Rajin-Sonbong-jikhalsi; 2000 Rason-jikhalsi; 2010 Rason-thukbyolsi

In 1993, Rajin-Sonbong emerges as *jikhalsi.* Rajin-si became Rajin-kuyok and Sonbong became *kun* of the newly formed city. In 2000 Rajin-Sonbong was reformed to Rason-jikhalsi. Rajin-kuyok and Sonbong-kun disappeared. In 2010 Rason finally became *thukbyolsi.*

Urban expansion, reductions

Twice, in 1967 and 1993, Rajin was reduced in favor of the neighboring southern Chongjin:

- In 1960, the Rajin-kun had been extended by five *ri* from the Puryong-kun. In August 1967 as Rajin-si was formed, these five *ri* and two more from Rajin were added to Chongjin.
- In 1993, seven *dong* and two *ri* came from Rajin-si to Chongjin-si. One of these *ri*

(Muchang-ri) came back to Rajin-Sonbong-si in 1955.

Also in 1993, three *ri* of Undok-kun (Wŏnjŏng-ri, Hahoe-ri-ri Hayŏphyŏng) merged with Sonbong-kun, in the same year Chŏlju-ri of Sonbong came to Undok-kun.

Structure

The following information applies only to areas of Rason, which are still today parts of its urban area. Areas that are now within the city border of Chongjin, are not listed.

At the foundation of the city in 1967, Rajin-up was divided into seven *dong* (Namsan, Tongmyong, Sinan, Anhwa, Yŏkjŏn, Jigyŏng, Changphyŏng). The emerging Sinhŭng-rodongjagu was divided into two *dong* (Sinhŭng, Chŏnggye) in 1961. Anju-rodongjagu, which had also been set up in 1961, was converted to Anju-dong.

In 1967, Unggi-up was divided into four *dong* (Sanghyŏn, Songphyŏng, Junghyŏn, Hahyŏn). At the same time Paekhak1-dong, Pakehak2-dong and the Tumangang-rodongjagu (*dong* since 2000) emerged.

When Unggi-up was re-formed in 1968, even parts of Paekhak1-dong were added, and the rest of Paekhak1-dong became Paekhak-ri. Paekhak2-dong was divided to Paekhak-ri (Unggi-kun) and the newly formed Kwan'gok-dong (Rajin-si).

In 2000, Unggi—in the meantime renamed Sonbong—was then divided again into the four above-mentioned *dong*.

Neglecting the redissolution of Sonbong-up in four *dong* in 2000, only four new *dong* emerged within the present urban area of Rason since the 70s until 2003:

- When the city of Rajin switched to the *kuyok* system in 1973, numerous rearrangements of administrative units were made. In the course of this, Sinhae-dong and Yuhyŏn-dong were newly formed.
- In 1981 Ungsang-ri (Sonbong-kun) was formed to a *rodongjagu* (*dong* since 2000).
- In 2000 Haebang-dong arises from a partition of Anju-dong.

On Figure Rason-I you can see that the center of Rajin consists of the former *up* and two adjacent *rodongjagu* (Anju, Sinhŭng), which were formed in 1961. The splitting of the eastern Haebang-dong from Anju-dong within the former Anju-rodongjagu however occurred later in 2000. North and South at some distance to the city center, Sinhae-dong and Yuhyŏn-dong developed. Both became *dong* in 1973.

Four *dong* in the former Sonbong-kun originate from the former Sonbong-up. This region forms the second center within Rason-si. In the North the former Ungsang-

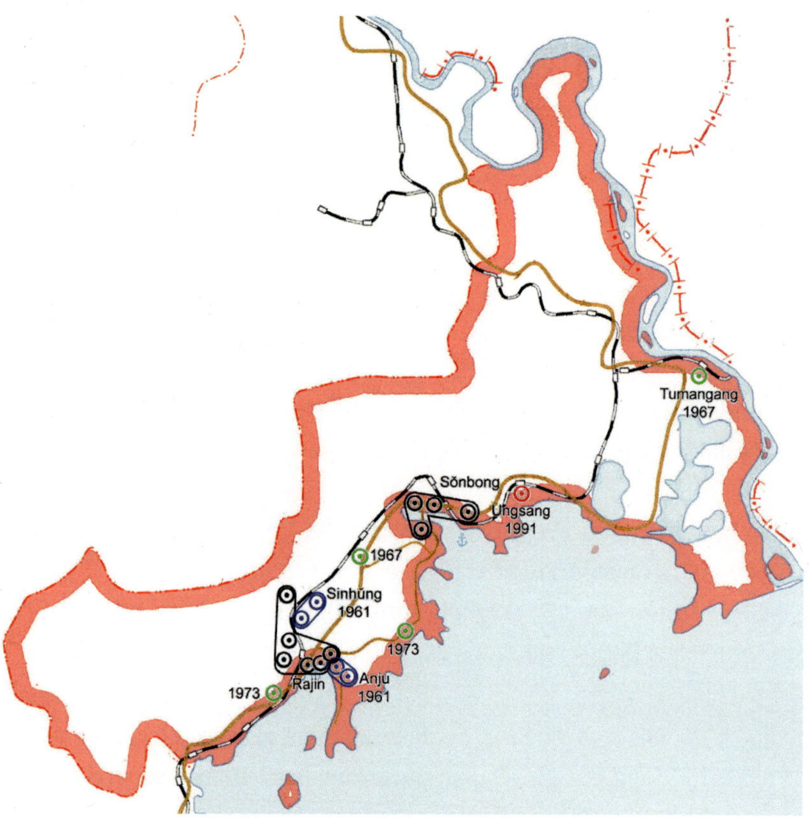

Figure Rason-I. *Dong* and former *rodongjagu*

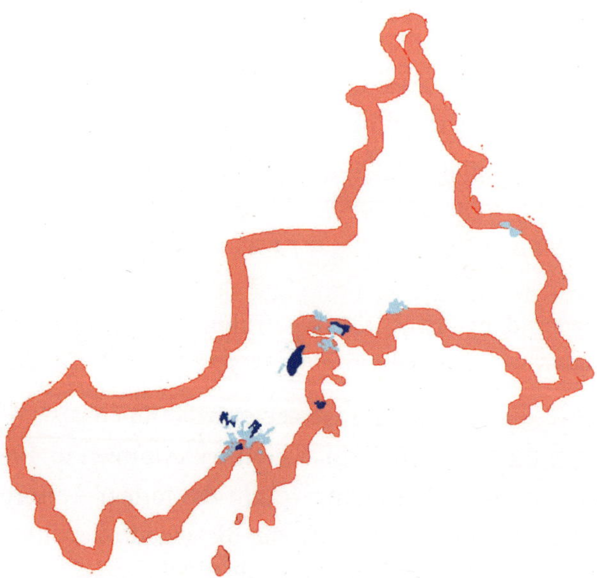

Figure Rason-II. Urbanized areas (light blue) and industrial areas (dark blue)
(Source: Yi Sang-jun et. al. 2012, 42)

rodongjagu is situated and in the very North the former Tumangang-rodongjagu.

The Sŭngri Chemical Complex in Kwan'gok-dong was built *quasi* in the middle of the two centers of Rajin and Sonbong.

The map in Yi Sang-jun et. al (2012, 42) was developed by using GIS methods and it confirms the results of the above analysis. Figure Rason-I and Figure Rason-II show six major built up areas within the city of Rason. These are - from North to South - the former Tumangang-rodongjagu, the former Unsang-rodongjagu, the former Sonbong-up, Kwangok-dong (Sŭngri Chemical Complex), which was founded in 1968, Shinhae-dong, which was established on the coast in 1973 (Rason Taehŭng Trading Corporation, which was put into operation in 2002 is located there) and the core of the former Rajin-kun (with the *up*, the former *rodongjagu* of Sinhŭng and Anju, both founded in 1961, and the 1973 established Yuhyŏn-dong).

Statistics

Urbanized areas prior to city foundation (*up* and *rodongjagu*)

1952 - 1967 Rajin-up (1)
1952 - 1967, 1968-2000 Unggi-up (since 1981 Sonbong-up) see above (2)
1961 - 1967 Sinhŭng-rodongjagu (3)
1961 - 1967 Anju-rodongjagu (4)

	Dong-Formation	*Dong*-splitting
1967 (17)	2 *dong*, 1 *rodongjagu*	(10)
1967 (18)	1 *up*	-
1967 (18)	-1 *up*/1 *up*	-
1968 (13)	-1 *up*	-4 *up*-formation
1973 (15)	2	-
1981 (16)	1 *rodongjagu*	-
2000 (20)	-	4, (3 of them because of *up*-separation)

Adjusted, without taking into account the multiple displacement of up of Sonbong-kun:

	Dong-Formation	*Dong*-splitting
1967 (17)	2, (1)	(10)
1968 (16)	-	-1

1973 (18)	2	-
1981 (19)	(1)	-
2000 (20)	-	1

Rason – Ports near the new Chinese economic development zones

The two ports Rajin and Sonbong had already been developed under Japanese rule in Korea. After 1945, the geopolitical conditions changed and the two ports stagnated. Fishing dominated the economic structure in the region Rajin-Sonbong up to the 1970s, until the Sŭngri Chemical Complex was completed.

The proclamation of the Rajin-Songbong Free Economic and Trade Zone in December 1991 aroused only moderate interest from potential investors. The region was too far away from the capital Pyongyang and the infrastructure was underdeveloped. Additionally, there were more reasons why a financial engagement in the DPR Korea seemed problematic. The location of the port of Rajin and Sonbong recently led to greater engagements of the neighboring states of Russia and China. Investments, especially in the ports and their infrastructure, have been made. For the PR China, the port of Rajin is of importance to the development of the region Changchun-Jilin-Tumen.

IV.2.20. Chongjin

Port and industrial city established under Japanese rule

Chongjin is the capital of Hambuk Province and one of the four North Korean cities with more than 500,000 inhabitants. It is a city of nonferrous metal smelting. The port was built at the time of Japanese rule over Korea.

Table Chongjin-I. Basic data

Population	667,929 (Rank 4)
Area	1,591 km² (Rank 4)
Population density	420 I./km² (Rank 17)
Administrative units	93 *dong* / 14 *ri* (87%) (Rank 2)
"Urban" population / "rural" population	92.1%/7.9% (Rank 3)

At first Chongjin was nothing more than a small fishing village, which was developed close to a foothill within the county of Puryong. In the First Sino-Japanese War (1904-1905) Chongjin was used as a landing place for military equipment of the Japanese, and during that time the village counted around 100 houses. During this war, the Japanese promoted a supply route for its military in 1905: a 90 km long railway line from Chongjin to Hoeryong, which was completed in 1906. In 1907, the 17 km long railway line to Ranam was completed. Also in 1907 Chongjin, including the county of Puryong, was appointed city status. In 1908 the port was opened for international trade. There were several reasons for the Japanese to open the port so quickly. Chongjin was an important port for the transportation of timber and other products from the forest areas of North Korea and Manchuria, and for the transport of fishery products. In particular, the port of Chongjin was of major strategic military importance as a supply route for the Japanese into the North. Already in 1907 a large military base in Ranam was built. In this context, the port of Chongjin was essential as a landing place for any goods. In addition, the advantageous natural conditions, due to the depth of the sea and the natural protection from winds by Ssangyŏn-san and Chŏnma-san in the North, encouraged the construction of a port (Yun Jŏng-sŏp, 1987, 127-128).

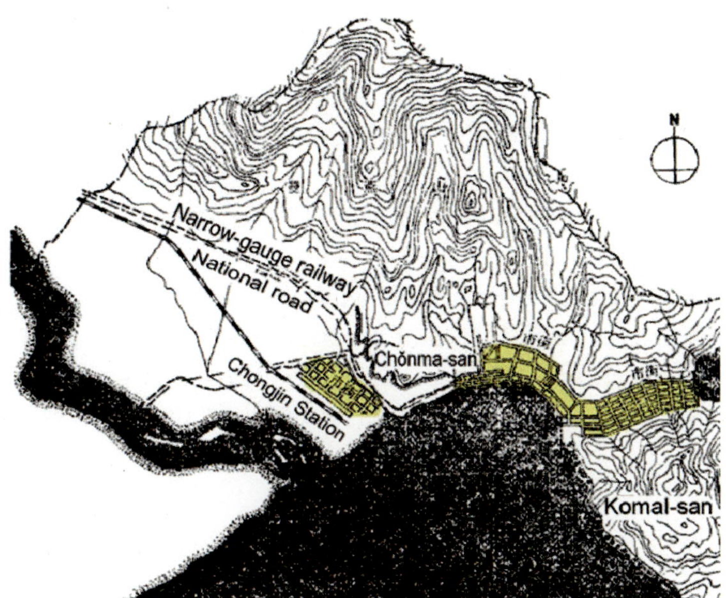

Figure Chongjin-I. Chongjin around 1915 (Source: Yun Jŏng-sŏp 1987, 128)

Figure Chongjin-I shows the built-up urban area of 1915. It becomes clear that the oldest parts of the city are located in regions that are now part of Sinan-kuyok (in the East, the built-up areas at the foothill north of the 183 m high Komal-san) and today's Phohang-kuyok (in the West, the built-up areas between the Chŏnma-san and the station). The built-up urban area gradually expanded westward toward the Susŏng plain. Factory suburbs, formed in the wide, flat river valley of the Susŏng-chŏn[76], which almost reached Ranan, which is located 17km south of Chongjin,

The development of Chongjin was accelerated by the connection to the Korean rail network (1928) and by the opening of the railway line to Changchun (1933) (Lautensach 1945, 203).

Table Chongjin-II. Population development according to Lautensach (1945, 203)

Chongjin	Inhabitants
1913	8,000
1928	23,407
1938	72,353

Chongjin developed into one major fish landing site. And it developed into an industrial city as well:

- ores from the region Musan were processed in the ironworks,
- due to the timber resources of the hinterland an artificial silk factory was built,
- several mills processed Manchurian soybeans into oil and press cake,
- fish processing companies emerged, which produced fish oil, fish meal, oil sardines and other canned fish[77] (Lautensach 1945, 203-204)

The construction of the Japanese military town Ranam south of Chongjin had already started in 1907. In 1923 Ranam became the seat of the Provincial Administration of Hamgyong-pukto[78]. In 1943 Ranam became part of Chongjin-pu. In 1945, there were several restructurings, in which Chongjin was divided and the Ranam-si created. Ranam

76 The Susŏng-chŏn flows through the structured valley between the Hamgyong mountain range and the Hoeryong hills and flows at Ŏhang-dong (Sunam-kuyok) into the sea. In the vicinity of the water mouth, the Susŏng plain has formed.

77 Lautensach emphasizes the fact that Chongjin was expanded to an industrial city in contrast to Rajin and Unggi, which can be proved by the fact that in Rajin 76% of the turnover of the transit goods are from Manchuria, while the share in Chongjin is only at 21% (Lautensach 1945, 204).

78 From 1884 to 1923 Kyongsong was the site of the provincial administration of Hambuk. But this Kyongsong is not the same site as the present Kyongsong-up. In the course of extensive regional reorganization in 1952, Juŭl became the new administrative center of Kyongsong-kun and consequently was renamed Kyongsong-up, on the other hand the current Kyongsong-up, which was located at the northern edge of the redesigned district, became Sŭngam-ri, and was converted in 1963 to the Sŭngam-rodongjagu of Kyongsong-kun (IPA 2003-14, 312, 318).

remained a city (*si*) until 1960, when it again was merged with Chongjin as Ranam-kuyok.

To support the reconstruction of the city after the Korean War, Poland sent experts to Chongjin for city planning. They were involved in the development of a master plan for Chongjin, in which the two cities of Chongjin and Ranam should be connected. Other countries also helped with the reconstruction. Romania and Czechoslovakia both were involved in the construction of Ranam Pharmaceutical Factory and the Chongjin Central Hospital. Disagreements came up between the Koreans and Poles during the reconstruction of Chongjin, so that the Poles finally returned home[79] (Jang Se-hun 2006b, 469-471).

City development in the plain of Susŏng-chŏn

The city area consists mainly of medium-high and low mountains, except for the foothills of the Hamgyŏng mountain chain that runs northwest of the city and are occupied by the sea coast and floodplains as well. The most mountainous *kuyok* of the city are Puyun, Chongam, Songphong, and Sinam. In Puyun there are several of mountains over 1,000 m, and the Kosŏng-san (1,754 m) is the highest mountain in the city. The largest plain in the city is the Susŏng-plain (90 km^2). At the borders of the triangular alluvial plain at the East Sea border, where Susŏng-chŏn flows through in many arms, Chongjin and Ranam have developed.

The climatic and topographic conditions for agriculture are bad, which narrows down rice cultivation. Therefore, grain must be supplied from other provinces in the southwest of the country, which is not unproblematic due to lack of fuel and deficient infrastructure. As an industrial city, Chongjin was therefore particularly affected by the famine in the 1990s, which even motivated an American journalist to choose Chongjin as the setting for a novel.[80]

Of special noteworthiness is the Majŏn Deer Farm in Majŏn-dong (Chongam-kuyok). They focus on the manufacturing of products made from deer antlers. Set up in 1955, this farm was the first that had specialized in the breeding of deer (IPA-14 2003, 68). And fishing is of importance. The Chongjin Fishery station is the most important company

79 The differences of opinion are related to the construction of apartment buildings in low-lying areas. In the plains, where the urbanized area lies, experience has shown a risk of flooding in heavy rain due to the low-lying terrain. The Polish experts had thus advised that it would be better instead of building without protective measures a one-storied house, to increase the ground to above sea level and then build four- to five-storey multi-family houses. But since materials and capital was missing and the housing shortage grew, the North Korean authorities have reviewed these proposals as beyond reality and rejected these proposals after several years of debate and pursued a strategy of constructing living room to distribute rapidly and in large quantities to the population. As a result, when it rains, in parts of the *kuyok* Phohang and Sinam water flows back up from the sewers and it comes to flooding (Jang Se-hun 2006b, 502).

80 Demick (2009).

within the city in this industry. Especially the sardine fishing has a long tradition in Chongjin.

Table Chongjin-III. Climate values

Annual average	January temperature	August temperature	Precipitation
8.1°C (22)	−5.5°C (12)	21.5°C (24)	594 mm (25)

The temperature values shows that Chongjin counts as one of the coldest cities in the country, although the winters are relatively mild.

"City of Iron"

The most important industrial sector of the city is iron smelting[81]. The Kim Chaek Iron and Steel Complex enjoys nationwide recognition. Other important industrial sectors are the shipbuilding industry as well as the chemical and electrical industry. Furthermore, building materials such as bricks, cement and flat glass are manufactured in Chongjin. The light industry is represented by food factories in each *kuyok*, textile factories and factories for essential goods. There are also several mines in Ranam-kuyok. Major mining products from Chongjin are nickel and limestone amongst others.

Table Chongjin-IV. Ranking (in parenthesis: number of industrial establishments or cultural institutions)

Chongjin	KOFC	MOU	IPA	KCNA	KIET	Summary
Companies-total	4 (32)	6 (33)	6 (26)	5 (21)	4 (93)	4
Companies-important	4 (9)	3 (7)	6 (10)		4 (35)	4 (16)
Cultural in-stitutions			10 (14)			

Table Chongjin-V. Ranking (Total number of industrial companies in relation to population)

Chongjin	KOFC	MOU	IPA	KCNA	KIET	Summary
Companies – total	17	23	16–21–17	16	9 –11	19–17

81 According to North Korean information (KJY-29, 1990, 488) the mining industry was with 17.7% of the total production output the city's most important industry in 1949, followed by food manufacturing (13.2%), metallurgy (11.1%) and the chemical industry (10.5%). In 1960, the metallurgy was already the most important industry with 20.8% followed by the chemical industry (14.2%) and engineering industry (13.3%). The light industry was of considerable importance too (food industry 10.7%, textiles 11.3%). 1985 the metallurgy then took a dominant position with 47.8%, followed by mining (10.4%) and the machinery industry (9.8%).

Table Chongjin-VI. Specification (in parenthesis: number of industrial companies)

Chongjin	Light Industry	Heavy Industry	Mining	Energy
KOFC	17 (6)	12 (21)	12 (1)	5 (4)
MOU	16 (17)	5 (14)	–	4 (2)
IPA	14 (12)	12 (11)	13 (1)	6 (2)
KCNA	18 (6)	6 (11)	–	6 (4)
KIET	16 (36)	11 (49)	16 (4)	8 (4)

According to the industrial companies ranking, Chongjin (667,929 inhabitants) is in three of the five investigated sources behind cities that have much smaller population. In the MOU, where relatively many companies of light industry are included, it is surpassed by the light industrial cities of Sinuiju (359,341 inhabitants) and Kaesong (308,440 inhabitants); in the IPA by Kaesong and in the KCNA by Kanggye (251,971 inhabitants), a city that plays a major role for the state propaganda of North Korea ("Kanggye spirit"). In sources that include relatively many heavy industry companies, Chongjin came in fourth place in the industrial companies ranking as well as in the population ranking. Also Table Chongjin-V makes it clear that Chongjin is a city of heavy industry.

In chapter III.7.3. 16 companies were identified as important for Chongjin, including three plants of the metallurgy: the Kim Chaek Iron and Steel Complex, the Chongjin Structural Steel Works and the Chongjin Steel Works. Mechanical Engineering is represented with six factories: the Ranam Coal Mining Machine Complex, the Chongjin Machine Tool Factory, the Chongjin Tractor Accessory Factory, the Hambuk Shipbuilding Complex (Chongjin Shipbuilding Factory), the Chongjin Railway Factory and the Chongjin Bus Factory. Furthermore there are the Kangdŏk Refractory Factory, the Chongjin Chemical Fiber Factory, the Ranam Pharmaceutical Factory and the light industry establishments Chongjin Oil Factory and Chongjin Footwear Factory. These are completed by the power plants March 17th Hydro-Power Station and Chongjin Thermal Power Station.

The most famous company of the city and most important plant of iron metallurgy in the DPR Korea is the Kim Chaek Iron and Steel Complex. It is located in Sabong-dong (Songphyong-kuyok) and processes iron ore from the 100 km distant Musan Mine. Raw water is supplied by the Susŏng-chŏn. The plant is connected through branch terminal lines to the railway network, so that the factory is connected by the Wŏlla-line with Rason and Kimchaek and by the Hamgyong-line with Hoeryong. Maritime transport of raw materials and products is handled through the port of Chongjin. Above all, there are other factories of the sectors of shipbuilding and mining engineering close by, which process the products of the Complex.

The Kim Chaek Iron and Steel Complex has a total area of 4,300,000 m^2. The number of employees is said to be about 50,000. To the complex belong, *inter alia,* the Chongjin

Iron Works, the Chongam Mine and Jungdo Mine that provide limestone, as well as the Kangdŏk Refractory Factory. The original name of the Complex was Chongjin Iron Works, and was renamed in 1951 to Kim Chaek Iron Works. This plant was built between 1938 and 1942 by the Japanese company Mitsubishi. During the Korean War, the smelting was suspended and the plant manufactured armaments. Starting in 1954, the blast furnaces went back into operation again (IPA 14, 2003, 67-68; KOFC 2010, 195-201). In 1974, the company had grown from a simple iron hut to an industrial complex with numerous departments and received its present name. In 1984 the Kim Chaek Iron and Steel Complex took up 43% of the total production output of Chongjin-si. In the same year the complex employed 27.3 % of all industrial workers in the city (KJY-29, 1990, 489).

Shortage of materials and fuel have certainly led the Kim Chaek Iron and Steel Complex to be unable to operate properly, which led due to crosslinking with other numerous companies in the region that almost every factory and company in Chongjin fell into a kind of hibernation (Im, Jeong Jin 2011). Also, due to the fact that crude oil and coke had to be imported, they now also smelt with local anthracite. The result is of course a lower quality steel and is officially known as "Juche steel" and called the result of the autonomy consciousness of Koreans.

The Chongjin Iron Works are located in the Phohang district on the coast. Raw water is supplied by the Susŏng-chŏn. Covering an area of 900,000 m², approximately 8,000 persons are employed. The factory was built in 1939, from 1940 on the first blast furnaces that were manufactured in Japan were used. The company was constantly expanded over time (KOFC 2010, 210-212).

The Ranam Coal Mining Machine Complex is a leading company for the production of mining equipment in the DPR Korea. On a total area of 100,000 m² approximately 4,000 persons are employed. The company was built in the 1950s and was expanded in 1961 (IPA-14 2003, 68; KOFC 2010, 259). The Chongjin Machine Tool Factory is located in Chongam-kuyok. The total area is 360,000 m². The factory employs 950 persons. It was built in 1958. Lathes and drill machines are manufactured and distributed nationwide (IPA-14 2003, 69-70; KOFC 2010, 255). As an embodiment of the "Kanggye spirit," a parole to hang on during the 1990s at the time of acute famine in the DPR Korea, which was officially sugarcoated as "arduous march," the "torchlight of Ranam" was introduced in 2001. The behavior of the workers of Ranam Coal Mining Machine Complex is described as exemplary. "The workers and officials of the complex settled the very urgent problems of fuel and raw materials on their own efforts during the 'arduous march' and the forced march to produce good quality steel. They also manufactured up-to-date equipment requiring high technology by introducing a new engineering method and built two factories while ensuring the production of modern mining equipment" (KCNA December 4, 2001)[82].

82 KCNA (May 24, 2002) citing Rodong Sinmun explains the importance of the torch of Ranam: "This torch represents a torch of revolution in the new century as it fully embodies the intense loyalty to the leader, the

The Hambuk Shipbuilding Complex (Chongjin Shipbuilding Factory) with an area of 597,000 m² and 7,500 employees is next to the companies in Nampho and Rajin one of the three largest shipyards in the DPR Korea. It was built in 1937 and was re-established in 1954 after the devastation of the Korean War with the help of the Soviet Union (IPA-14 2003, 70-71; KOFC 2010, 323-324). The Chongjin Bus Factory, situated on a total area of 82,000 m² with 1,300 employees, manufactures the buses that operate in rural areas of the DPR Korea. Sine 1992 trams are produced there as well. (IPA-14 2003, 70; KOFC 2010, 274-275).

The Chongjin Chemical Fiber Factory is located in Songphyong-kuyok and has an area of 1,000,000 m². It is the largest manufacturer of rayon yarn in the DPR Korea. The factory was built between 1933 and 1938 (IPA-14 2003, 70; KOFC 2010, 586-587). The Ranam Pharmaceutical Factory was founded in 1949. During the Korean War, this factory changed their location often, until it was re-established again in 1955 to its present location. They produce, *inter alia*, disinfectants and vitamins (IPA-14 2003, 68).

The March 17th Hydro-Power Station is located in the Puyun-kuyok. The construction started in 1959 with Chinese help. After construction was halted, in 1967 they went back to build a dam and a power plant was completed each in the years of 1972, 1976 and 1982 (KOFC 2010, 138-139). The Chongjin Thermal Power Station was built with Soviet help with the goal of power supply for the Kim Chaek Iron and Steel Complex, as well as to supply the population of Chongjin with heating. Originally, the construction started in 1974, but was interrupted, so they officially began construction work in November 1980. In 1984 the first two, and in 1986 the third generator was completed. The power plant burns coal from the northern coal field of Hambuk and provides power to the Kim Chaek Iron and Steel Complex, as well as other industrial plants in the north of the DPR Korea (IPA-14 2003, 70; KOFC 2010, 156).

The second largest port of the DPR Korea – Investments from China and Russia

The port of Chongjin is the second largest of the DPR Korea and the largest on the North Korean East Sea coast. It was already opened in 1908 by Japan and was a typical military port. In 1974, the port facilities were reinforced and since 1983 the PR China started to use this port for its trade with Japan. The port is divided into a western and an eastern harbor, the eastern harbor is used for trade, while the western harbor is used by the Kim Chaek Iron and Steel Complex. Since the port is connected by a broad gauge railway line with Russia, it is well suited for the shipment of goods from the northern neighbor. In 2010, the PRC and the DPR Korea have agreed on a restoration of the railway line between Tumen

core of the Kanggye spirit. … The torch calls on the people to meet the requirements of the Kanggye spirit for boldly breaking through difficulties by their own efforts, believing in their own strength."

and Chongjin, which should be conducive to the export of Chinese goods over Chongjin (KOFC 2010, 112-113; 115). Similar to the case of the Port of Rajin, Russians and Chinese also compete in Chongjin for the right of use of the port. After Russia allegedly should have already been granted such rights, Yanbian Haihua Group, which is a private Chinese developer, signed a contract with a North Korean firm to jointly manage and use two piers of Chongjin port for the next 30 years on 1st September 2012.

After giving the rights to use two piers of the Port of Chongjin to a Chinese company, plans for a special economic zone in Chongjin were discussed. Such projects should have existed since 2003, in which it is planned to subdivide Chongjin and Nam-Chongjin into two regions. The provincial administration for Hambuk, which is currently in the *kuyok* of Phohang and Sinam, is to be moved to the Ranam-kuyok. The Chongjin Special Economic Zone is planned to consist of the Sunam-kuyok and the northern Phohang-kuyok, Chongam-kuyok and Sinam-kuyok, whilst the south of the Susŏng-chŏn, which is located in Songphyong-kuyok, and Ranam-kuyok shall be summarized as Nam-Chongjin and not be included in the zone (Choi Song-min 2012).

Cultural capital of Hambuk

The capital of Hambuk is also its cultural center. There are numerous universities in the municipal area, which specialize in engineering, mining and metallurgy, agriculture, medicine, education and politics. The city is home to a radio station, a newspaper and an artist group representing the Hambuk Province.

Chongjin–"North Korea's Fashion Capital"

Chongjin is the port at which the first ship with Korean returnees from Japan came in 1959, and even now many Koreans, who returned from Japan, still live here. Also might the fact, that many people flocked here from different regions due to the large industrial plants since the time of Japanese rule, is a reason for why the city's residents are reputed to be open to new ideas. Therefore Chongjin also got the reputation as the leading city in North Korea in the field of what is "trendy." Shorts in skirts already appeared in the 1980s, in the 1990s even disco pants were "in style" (Chosun Ilbo September 18, 1995). More recent reports of Chongjin confirm the reputation of the city as "North Korea's Fashion Capital." Used clothes arrive in large packages by ship via the port of Chongjin from Japan to North Korea. Among them are many clothes that are in fashion in Japan and South Korea. Particularly many residents of the city travel to China to stay afloat through petty trade and take fashion trends and clothing into the country. While the residents of Pyongyang wear these foreign fashionable clothes usually only at home, because control is supposedly more strict in Pyongyang, the reservation of the residents and the control willingness of the authorities in Chongjin are probably less strong (newfocusintl 2013).

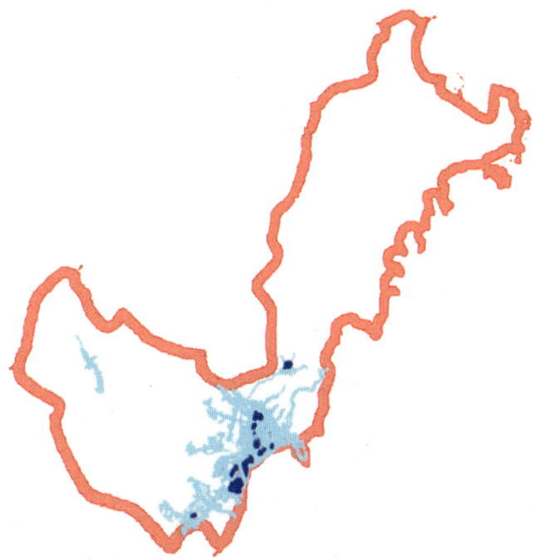

Figure Chongjin-II. Urbanized areas (light-blue) and industrial areas (dark blue); (Source Yi Sang-jun et.al. 2012, 71)

A city divided in *kuyok*

Chongjin, a city since 1913, consists of 93 *dong* and 14 *ri*, which are divided into seven *kuyok*. Since 1960 the *kuyok*-system was introduced. At the same time Ranam-si was incorporated. Twice, between 1963-1970 and 1977-1985 Chongjin was a city with special status with a level of a province. Also, the size of the urban area was frequently changed. The urban area was enlarged twice at the expense of the *up* or the city of Rajin: seven *ri* in 1967, and seven *dong* were incorporated between 1993 and 1995.

Chongjin consisted of six to eight *kuyok* since 1960. Permanent *kuyok* of Chongjin have been: Sinam, Chongam, Phohang, Sunam, Songphyong and Ranam. Between 1977 and 1985 the Kyongsong-kun and Musan-kun were still part of the city. Puryong-kun, which is known for its metallurgy (silicon ore, chromium-iron), was as Puryong-kuyok twice a part of Chongjin between 1960-1970, and 1972-1985.

The other changes in the number of *kuyok* are due to fact that Puyun-kuyok arose only 1970 by splitting off of Ranam-kuyok, and that it became part of the Ranam-kuyok again for a short term between 1993 and 1994.

Table Chongjin-VII. Chongjin-Number of *kuyok* and *kun* with special consideration to the regions of Puyun and Puryong

Year	Status	*kuyok*	Puyun	Puryong	*kun*
1960	*si*	7	part of Ranam	*kuyok*	
1963	*jikhalsi*	7	part of Ranam	*kuyok*	
1970	*si*	7	*kuyok*		
1972	*si*	8	*kuyok*	*kuyok*	
1977	*jikhalsi*	8	*kuyok*	*kuyok*	2
July 1985	*si*	8	*kuyok*	*kuyok*	
Dec. 1985	*si*	7	*kuyok*		
1993	*si*	6	part of Ranam		
1994	*si*	7	*kuyok*		

The division of the city into *kuyok* invites contemplation about the changes in the structure of the city on a *kuyok*-level. Unfortunately not all *dong* are shown on the map in the IPA, so a detailed analysis like with the other cities is not possible.

Developments in the individual *kuyok*

In the following, the three central *kuyok* of Sinan, Phohang and Sunan are examined first, then the Songphyong-kuyok that connects the old Chongjin with Ranam. After that we focus on Ranam including Puyun, which lies southwest from the "actual" Chongjin and finally the largest *kuyok* by area, the Chongam-kuyok.

City center

The Sinam-kuyok (10 *dong*) consisted at the time of its founding in 1960 of nine *dong* and two *ri*. In 1985 these two *ri* merged to become a *dong*.

The Phohang-kuyok (14 *dong*), in which the eastern port of Chongjin is located, was founded in 1960 of the three *dong* of Namgang, Namhyang and Minju, although the latter was divided into the three *dong* of Chŏngsong, Suwŏn and Subuk, so that the *kuyok* consisted of five *dong*. In 1963, the *dong* of Namgang and Suwŏn were divided into two parts each and the *dong* Chŏngsong and Subok into three parts each. Pukhyang-dong was separated from Namhyang-dong. In 1967 Namgang3-dong emerged from parts of Namgang2-dong and Chŏngsong1-dong. In 1972 Sanŏp-dong emerged from parts of the neighboring Chongam-kuyok, where many factories are located. Sanŏp-dong became part of the Phohang-kuyok. Therefore, 13 of 14 *dong* of Phohang-kuyok go back to three *dong* formed in 1955, which were split in 1960, 1963 and 1967.

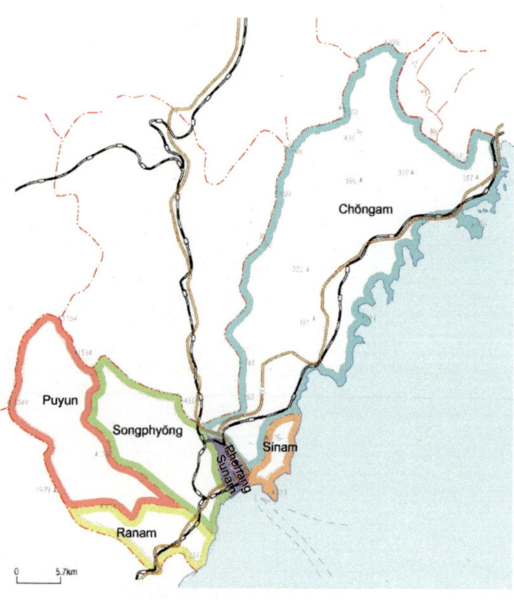

Figure Chongjin-III. *Kuyok*

The Sunam-kuyok (9 *dong*) was founded in 1960 out of five *dong*, another was created by splitting off simultaneously with the establishment of the *kuyok*. Three other *dong* emerged by separation in 1963.

30 of 33 *dong* of the three central *kuyok* of Chongjin thus already existed in 1963.

Ranam

In the south of the city the Ranam-kuyok (19 *dong*, 2 *ri*) and the Puyun-kuyok (seven *dong*, one *ri*) are situated, which were still parts of Ranam-si until 1960.

In 1945 Chongjin was divided and Ranam became city, until it became again part of Chongjin in 1960. After several reclassifications in 1945 (16 *dong*; 10 *dong*, 6 *ri*), in 1949 (15 *dong*) and in 1952 (13 *ri*), the city consisted of six *dong* and seven *ri* in 1955. In 1960 Ranam became a *kuyok* of Chongjin-si. Two *ri* are put together, Puyun-ri was upgraded to a *dong*. As a result Ranam-kuyok now had seven *dong* and five *ri*. 1963 Rahŭng-dong is divided into two parts. In 1970 Puyun-kuyok was formed out of Puyun-dong and Ŏyu-ri and is split off from Ranam-kuyok. This split-off still exists today and was only reversed for a short period (1993-1994). In 1978 and 1987, Ranam-kuyok was slightly enlarged. In 1978, five new *dong* are formed out of *ri*. In 1987 and 1991 each three new *dong* arose by splitting off from the other *dong*. In 1999 Hoehyang-ri became a *dong*.

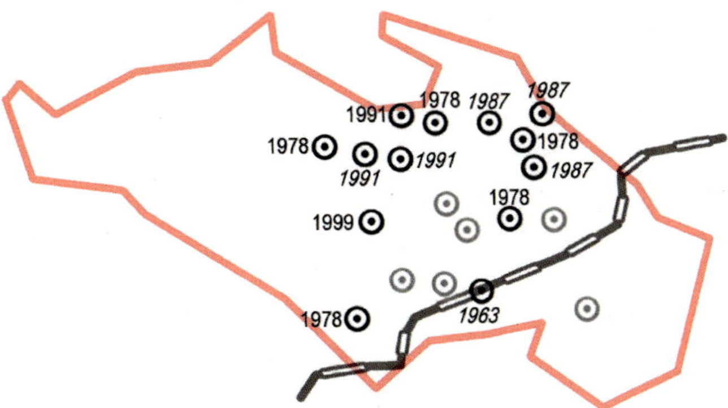

Figure Chongjin-IV. Ranam

Particularly noticeable is the rise of the new *dong* between 1978 and 1991. This coincides with the planned expansion of the Nam-Chongjin region (South-Chongjin). When talking in the context of the region Nam-Chongjin, the partially hilly area north of the former garrison town of the Japanese is understood. The employees of the Kim Chaek Iron and Steel Complex in Songphyong-kuyok who lived near their place of work, were exposed to the emissions from the operation to a large extent. This is the reason why they wanted to create industrial residential centers since the early 1970s, in areas where not so many factories are. Therefore, the development plan for Nam-Chongjin in 1976 was set up. With the mobilization of experts and the acquiring of building materials from around the country, homes for 1,500 families were built in less than a year, with a small park, green spaces, service facilities and so on. However after that no further assistance was provided by the headquarters. The number of homes built proved to be only a drop in the ocean. In 1983 a plan to expand Chongjin into a modern city of heavy industry existed and 5,000 apartments should have been built in Nam-Chongjin. But since only the city was in charge, they lacked the financial resources from the headquarters. It is assumed that in the second half of the 1980s the construction project came to a halt (Jang Se-hun 2006b, 489). It apparently was worse from the 1990s. Residents of high-rise buildings left and the city turned into a necropolis i.e. a Ghost Town. Reasons for this development were heating problems of the apartments; they were lacking elevators as well as facilities for the basic needs for the residents. The situation was worsened by famine and the economic crisis in North Korea in the 1990s (Jang Se-hun 2006b, 491).

Puyun

Puyun is known for its nickel deposits. In 1960 Puyun-ri became a *dong* of Ranam-kuyok, In 1967 it became Puyun-rodongjagu. In 1970 the *rodongjagu* was divided into six *dong* and together with Oyun-ri, Puyun-kuyok, at the same time Ayan-ri was split from Ŏyun-ri. In 1985 Ayang-ri became a *dong*. Ayang-dong was located in the farthest South of the *kuyok*, while all other *dong* of Puyun-kuyok are lined up on a street in the North. 1993 Puyun-kuyok was dissolved and was moved to Ranam-kuyok. In that process Puyun-rodongjagu was formed again from all the *dong* of the *kuyok* (i.e. including Ayang-dong). 1994 Puyun-kuyok was formed again of Puyun-rodongjagu and Oyu-ri as before, the *rodongjagu* was again divided into seven *dong*.

Area between Chongjin center and Ranam

The Songphyong-kuyok (13 *dong*, 5 *ri*) was founded in 1960 from three *dong*, four *ri* of Chongjin city and the *up* and three *ri* from Puryong-kun. The *up* became *dong*, simultaneously two new *dong* became in to being by splitting existing *dong* and two other *dong* have been founded by upgrading *ri* to *dong*. In 1963 three new *dong* were created by splitting and in 1972 and 1987 one each.

Chongam – the area between Chongjin center and Rason

The Chongam-kuyok (21 *dong*, 6 *ri*) was founded in 1960 out of six *dong* of Chongjin-si and two *ri* of Puryong-kun. In 1963 three new *dong* arose by splitting, in 1967 one by upgrading a *ri* and one by splitting from another *dong*. In 1992 three *ri* were upgraded to *dong*. The area of the *kuyok* was increased twice: in 1972 seven *ri* of the Puryong-kun were included. In 1993 seven *dong* and two *ri* from Rajin-si were included: Raksan (*rodongjagu* since 1952), Samhae (*rodongjagu* since 1972), Kwanhae (*dong* since 1973), Pangjin, Rijin and Rasŏk (all three *rodongjagu* since 1973), Rochang (*dong* since 1991) and Muchang-ri which became part of Rajin-Sonbong-si in 1995, and Sŏ-ri. The five *rodongjagu* had all been converted to *dong* in 1974.

Statistical Summary: from the 1970s on almost all new *dong* in Ranam and Chongam

Table Chongjin-VII shows the founding of new *dong* in each *kuyok*. The second column shows how many *dong* existed prior to the establishment of the *kuyok*. The other columns indicate how many *dong* arose, the first number by *dong* establishment, the second by *dong*-splitting. The Puyun-rodongjagu was divided in six *dong* 1970, therefore, the number "5" has been put in brackets and the subdivision was not counted in the statistics.

Table Chongjin-VIII. *Dong*-Formation in the individual *kuyok*

kuyok	existing	1960–1967	1970–1978	1985–1987	1991–1999	Total
Sinam	9 of 10			1 : –		1 : – (1)
Phohang	3 of 14	– : 10	– : 1			– : 11 (11)
Sunan	5 of 9	– : 4				– : 4 (4)
Ranam	6 of 19	– : 1	5 : –	– : 3	1 : 3	6 : 7 (13)
Puyun	0 of 7	1 : –	– : (5)	1 : –		2 : – (2+5)
Sŏngphung	4 of 13	2 : 5	– : 1	– : 1		2 : 7 (9)
Chŏngam	7 of 21	1 : 4	5 : –		4 : –	10 : 4 (14)
	34 of 93	4 : 24 (28)	10 : 2 (12)	2 : 4 (6)	5 : 3 (8)	21:33 (54)

Table Chongjin-IX. Number of *dong* in the individual *kuyok*

kuyok	1955	1960–1967	1970–1978	1985–1987	1991–1999	Increase
Sinam	9	9	9	10	10	11%
Phohang	3	13	14	14	14	367%
Sunan	5	9	9	9	9	80%
Ranam	6	7	12	15	19	217%
Puyun	0	1	6	7	7	–
Sŏngphung	4	11	12	13	13	225%
Chŏngam	7	12	17	17	21	200%
	34	62	79	85	93	174%

Half of all *dong* (14 of 28), which newly emerged in the 1960s, are situated in the city center, in particular in Phohang. A quarter of the new *dong* of the 1960s is located in Songphung-kuyok, the area that lies between the "actual" Chongjin and Ranam. Five *dong* emerged in the large area of Chongam-kuyok that lies north of the city center. In the 60s, especially the center became denser and the growth of the factory suburbs towards Ranam increased.

Apart from the dissolution of Puyun into six *dong*, new *dong* since 1970 mainly emerged in the northern Chongam-kuyok and especially in Ranam. Twelve of 19 *dong* in Ranam arose from 1970 on.

Chongjin	*Dong*-Formation	*Dong*-Splitting
1955 (34)		
1960 (42)	3	5
1963 (59)	-	17
1967 (62)	1	2
1970 (67)	-	(5)
1972 (70)	1	2
1973 (74)	4	-
1978 (79)	5	-
1985 (81)	2	-
1987 (85)	-	4
1991 (89)	1	3
1992 (92)	3	-
1993 (85)	-	(-6)
1994 (92)	-	(6)
1999 (93)	1	-

The numbers in parenthesis refer to the dissolution (1970, 1994) and respectively the re-formation (1993) of Puyun.

Chongjin—city of old industry with potential as traffic junction

Chongjin is an important industrial city and port in northeastern Korea. The most important factories were built in the 1930s. Especially iron smelting plays an important role. This puts Chongjin in a strong dependence of it. Chongjin is a twin city, which consists of the original Chongjin and the former city Ranam. Urban development processes were observed in the 1960s, afterwards only in Chongam and especially in the North of Ranam where the residential region Nam-Chongjin was built. Chongjin possesses a big potential for development due to its proximity to China, Russia and Japan.

IV.2.21. Hoeryong

Border city to China and birthplace of Kim Jong-il's mother

Hoeryong lies in the north of Hambuk Province on the Tumen, which is one of two border rivers of the DPR Korea to the People's Republic of China. Regarding the population it is one of the smallest, but is regarded as the area one of the largest cities of the DPR Korea. Therefore, Hoeryong has—referring to the whole urban space—the lowest population density of all North Korean cities.

Table Hoeryong-I. Basic data[83]

Population	153,532 (Rank 23)
Area	1,750 km² (Rank 3)
Population density	88 I./km² (Rank 27)
Administrative units	19 *dong*/28 *ri* (40%) (Rank 27)
"Urban" population/"rural" population	60.2%/38.8% (Rank 26)

At Hoeryong, the middle reach of the Tumen, the river is narrow and shallow. Thus, the city is situated at a place, which has been used as crossing ever since. When the Joson dynasty (1392-1910) was founded, the first ruler, King Taejo (r. 1392-1398), took measures, to get the area in the northeast to the Tumen, where the Jurchen people originally lived, under his control. But the Jurchen fought the Koreans temporarily back to Kyongsong. Therefore, King Sejong (r. 1418-1450) ordered the construction of six garrisons (Yukjin) in Jongsŏng, Onsong, Hoeryong, Kyongwon, Kyonghun and Puryong, in order to strengthen the northeastern border. Later Hoeryong became *tohobu*.

83 Population according to the Central Bureau of Statistics (2009), 18; area according to PSC-8 (2009, 627) and administrative units according to IPA-14 (2003, 224).

During the reign of the Qing dynasty (1644-1911) in China, Hoeryong increased trade with China. Hoeryong came under continental influence. Additionally, the proximity to Russia helped the city in becoming an early center of Christianity and the city relatively early came into contact with Western culture (Ko Thae-u 1992, 329).

The period of Japanese rule increased the trading activity in Hoeryong. In particular, after the Changchu-Tumen railway was opened in 1924, Hoeryong together with the city of Longjing, which lies on the Chinese side, developed into a trading center. Due to the abundance of coal and lime in this region mining was pushed forward. On the basis of harvested wood of the region Musan, a timber industry developed.

Longjing, which lies on the opposite side of Hoeryong in China, is a county-level city in the Yanbian Autonomous Prefecture of Koreans in the Jilin Province. Longjing has an area of 2,592 km^2 and has 250,000 inhabitants (2004). Longjing is divided into two sub districts, six towns and two townships. Opposite Hoeryong lies the township of Sanhe. A bridge connects the township with the about 5 km northwest situated city center of Hoeryong. For Chinese tourists a restaurant road was built between the Kim Jong-suk University of Education and the Hoeryong Coal Mining Machinery Factory (Yoo, Gwan-hee 2010), in which soft drink stands and restaurants serve special food, such as soup of entrails, rabbit, soup of uncurdled bean curd, maize food and chow mein (KCNA December 4, 2010).

City in the northwest of the Hamgyong mountain range

Hoeryong is located in the northwest of the Hamgyong mountain range and apart from the banks of the Tumen river in the north of the town, it is surrounded by them and by diverging mountains, so that a large basin has formed. The highest elevations in Hoeryong are the mountains Karaji-bong (1,418 m), Minsa-bong (1,428 m) and Obong-san (1,329 m). While the latter is located within the municipal area, the former marks the border with the Musan-kun and the second the border to Puryong-kun. The majority of the municipal area lies at an altitude of 500 m to 800 m.

Forest areas make up about 80% of the city (PSC-8 2009, 627). The rivers that flow through the city all flow into the Tumen. Among the most important rivers are the Hoeryŏng-chŏn, the Pharŭl-chŏn, the Poul-chŏn and the Ryongchŏn-chŏn.

Table Hoeryong-II. Climate values

Annual average	January temperature	August temperature	Precipitation
6.0℃ (26)	−11.4℃ (24)	21.0℃ (26)	497.3 mm (27)

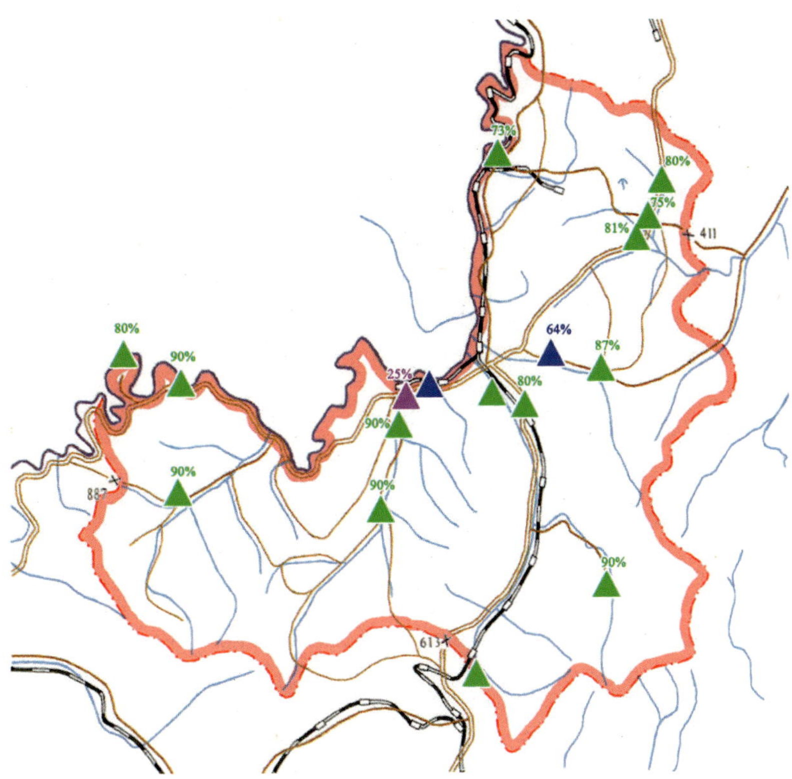

Figure Hoeryong-I. Forest area in the *ri*

As the city with the lowest precipitation and a city of low temperatures, Hoeryong is dominated by continental climatic factors. Only Hyesan is colder in the annual average value and in August temperatures than Hoeryong. In January—apart from Hyesan—Kanggye and Manpho are as well colder than Hoeryong.

Agricultural cultivable areas are found only in the vicinity of the basin around the city center of Hoeryong and west of it around Yusŏn. Apart from that forest areas predominate.

Food production and lignite mining

The municipal area is home to coal reserves and has rich forest resources. Important commercial farms are thus coal mines (Kungsim, Yusŏn, Hakpho) and paper manufacture.

In the north of Hambuk are many brown coal stockyards. In Hambuk are two coalfields: the northern and the southern coalfield. The northern coalfield reaches from Hoeryong to Aoji, embeds in tertiary layers on the river coast of the Tumen and is a large coal field, which occupies about 60% of the total reserves of North Korea. Some of these stockyards are located on the territory of the town of Hoeryong. The most important mines in Hoeryong are Hakbo, Kungsim and Yusŏn. The coal is used as a raw material for the chemical industry or as fuel for coal-fired power plants. After 1945, the engineering industry developed. There are also some industries that produce food (soy sauce, soybean paste, oil, etc.) and daily goods (shoes, soap, tooth paste, tools, kitchen appliances, sewing machines, medicines, etc.) (IPA-14, 2003, 230-232).

In 1960, mining was (with a share of the total production volume of the city of 30.1%) still the most important industry of the city. It was followed by the forest industry (17.8%) and the production of essential goods (13.1%). However, until 1984 the commercial structure of Hoeryong had greatly changed. In the meanwhile the most important industry was food production with 39.7% of the total production volume of the city, of which Hoeryong Cornstarch Factory had a large share. Mechanical engineering (16.3%) had grown into the second largest industry of the city, followed by the production of essential goods (14.6%). The importance of mining declined (11.3%) (KJY-29 1990, 746).

The North Korean homepage Naenara introduces in a book about Hoeryong the newly built Hoeryong Essential Foodstuff Factory, the Hoeryong Wood Processing Factory, the Hoeryong Shoemaking Factory, the Hoeryong Unha Export Clothing Factory and the Hoeryong Paper Mill as representative factories in the city, to stress the significance of light industry in the city.

Table Hoeryong-III. Ranking (in parenthesis: number of industrial companies or cultural institutions)

Hoeryong	KOFC	MOU	IPA	KCNA	KIET	Summary
Companies-total	11 (15)	17 (15)	5 (26)	20 (5)	18 (24)	15
Companies-important	22 (1)	25 (0)	10 (7)		23 (5)	17 (5)
Cultural institutions			19 (4)			

Compared to its population—Hoeryong ranks 23rd among the 27 cities of North Korea—there are relatively many companies. In Hoeryong are both companies of light industry and of heavy industry, as well as mines are located within it. The very high placement in the IPA is certainly due to the fact that Hoeryong has many administrative units (*dong* and *ri*), where the most important companies are listed in the respective administrative unit. However, there are not many companies in Hoeryong, which are regarded as especially important.

Table Hoeryong-IV. Ranking (total number of companies in relation to the population)

Hoeryong	KOFC	MOU	IPA	KCNA	KIET	Summary
Companies-total	1	10	2-3-16	18	7-22	2-11

Table Hoeryong-V. Specification (in parenthesis: number of industrial companies)

Hoeryong	Light Industry	Heavy Industry	Mining	Energy
KOFC	3 (7)	26 (3)	3 (5)	-
MOU	14 (9)	26 (1)	4 (5)	-
IPA	10 (14)	24 (5)	4 (7)	-
KCNA	5 (4)	20 (1)	-	-
KIET	2 (15)	27 (5)	4 (4)	-

The specialization on mining and light industry is clear. In contrast, the heavy industry plays a relatively minor role.

In chapter III.7.3., five important companies were determined for Hoeryong. These are —in three cases papermaking factories: Hoeryong Paper Production Complex, Hoeryong Paper Factory[84] and Hoeryong Craft Paper Factory—and the Hoeryong Cornstarch Factory and the Hoeryong Coal Mine Machine Factory.

In the Hoeryong Paper Factory, a variety of paper types are produced (copy paper, paper with patterns, writing paper, etc.). The factory was established as a small factory during the Japanese occupation period and was destroyed during the Korean War and then rebuilt (IPA-14 2003, 232). The Hoeryong Craft Paper Factory, which has been in operation since 1980, was constructed to meet the demand for cement bags in the DPR Korea (KJY-29 1990, 346).

The construction of the Hoeryong Cornstarch Factory began in 1954. At first mainly maize was processed. Over time, the range of products manufactured broadened. Among other things, they produce from biscuits, starch syrup, candy and oil to alcoholic beverages and cigarettes (IPA-14 2003, 232).[85]

When Kim Jong-il visited Hoeryong in December 2010, he visited, among other places, the following three companies of light industry: the Hoeryong Taesŏng Tobacco Factory, the newly built Hoeryong Foodstuff Processing Factory and the Hoeryong Koryo Medicine Factory (KCNA December 4, 2010).

One of the five important companies (as determined in chapter III.7.3) is the Hoeryong Coal Mine Machine Factory, which belongs to the heavy industry, and was founded in early 1960. Here, machines used in the mining industry are produced, such as drilling machines, conveyor belts etc. (IPA-14, 2003, 233).[86]

In the far west of the municipal area in Ryongchŏn-ri, the iron ore mine Oryung is

84 It is possible that the Hoeryong Paper Production Complex and the Hoeryong Paper Factory are different names of the same company.

85 For further information: KIET (1996, 58).

86 For further information: KIET (1996, 268-269).

located. It has been in operation since 2007. The ore is smelted in China (Choi, Kyung-soo 2010, 222). In 2006, a cooperation agreement with a company in Yanbian (China) has been completed (Choe Kyŏng-su 2011, 251).[87]

Through the center of the city runs the Hambuk railway line, thereby connecting Hoeryong with Rajin (335 km) and Chongjin (about 95 km). Branch terminal lines go from Hoeryong to Yusŏn, Kŭmsaeng to Kungsim and Sinhakpho to Sechŏn. There is a motorway between Chongjin and Hoeryong. From here to Chongjin it is 91 km.

The three beauties of Hoeryong

Hoeryong is known for its "Three Beauties." The first is the beauty of women, which is characterized by a pretty face, a virtuous way of life and a persevering character. The apricots from Hoeryong are the second beauty. Famous are the White Apricots, which have a pretty, charming and fragrant bloom and the fruits are much larger than normal apricots. The White apricots taste very sweet as well. The third beauty refers to the ground in the city. In Hoeryong white clay can be found, which is used for the production of high quality porcelain (Kim Pŏm-ju 2010, 204-205).

The White apricot blossom from Osan Hill

In North Korean literature it is especially emphasized that the mother of Kim Jong-il, Kim Jong-suk, was born on 24th December 1917 in Hoeryong and spent her childhood there. Her birth house, about 500 m south of the 800 m high Osan hill, is thus a touristic attraction and highlight for the Hoeryong visitors, as well as the bronze statue of Kim Jong-suk, which was established in 1969 on the occasion of the 20th anniversary of her death; and the Hoeryong revolutionary site, which opened in 1974, and where a large part of it is also dedicated to the first wife of Kim Il-sung (North Korea Online Travel Guide n.d.). The bond, which the North Korean propaganda wants to document between Kim Jong-suk and Hoeryong, shows in the term that KCNA has chosen for her: The White apricot blossom from Osan Hill.

A *kun* with seven *rodongjagu*

In 1991 Hoeryong-kun was appointed as a city (*si*). The *kun* in his former form originated

87 For further information: KOFC (2010, 480).

in 1974, when the Yusŏn-kun was integrated into Hoeryong-kun and Jongsŏng-kun was divided on Hoeryong-kun and Onsong-kun.

The following urbanized areas existed in Hoeryong-kun in 1974:

- Hoeryong-up
- Yusŏn-up, which now became a *rodongjagu*
- Mangyang-rodongjagu (founded in 1952)
- Sechŏn-rodongjagu (founded in 1954)
- Kungsim-rodongjagu (founded in 1961)
- Jungbong-rodongjagu (founded in 1967 in the Jongsŏng-kun)

In 1989 two additional *rodongjagu* (Nammun and Subuk) were established.

Foundation of the city in 1991, two development poles, coal mines in the Northeast

In July 1991 Hoeryong was designated as a city (*si*). Hoeryong-up and the *rodongjagu* become *dong* or were split into several *dong*. In the same year the *dong* of Kangan and Saemaŭl were formed, and in the south of the former *up* Jungdo-dong was created in December 1992, which is the southernmost *dong* of the city.

In Figure Hoeryong-II we see two development poles:

- the center, which consists of the former *up* of Hoeryong-kun, the former Mangyang-rodongjagu, which had been founded in 1952, the former *rodongjagu* of Nammun and Subuk of recent date (1989), as well as the *dong* of Kangan and Saemaŭl, both of which were created at the same time as the city founding in 1991.
- the former *up* of Yusŏn-kun in the west of the city.

In Mangyang the Manyang Mine Timber Manufacturing Plant is located. They produce blocks of wood that are used in the northern mines as pit-props (IPA-14 2003, 232). The Nammun-rodongjagu was split into the Nammun-dong and the Sanŏp-dong. In the latter, the Hoeryong Coal Mine Machine Factory is located.

The Yusŏn-rodongjagu was divided into three *dong* in 1991 (Yusŏn-dong, Kyerim-dong, Pŏul-dong). In Yusŏn-dong numerous factories are located: Hoeryong Foodstuff Factory, Hoeryong Furniture Factory, Hoeryong Cosmetics Factory, Hoeryong Clothing Factory, Hoeryong Weaving Factory, Hoeryong Instrument Factory, Hoeryong Building Materials Factory, Hoeryong Paper Production Complex, Yusŏn Refractory Plant (IPA-14 2003, 246-247). In the region of the former Yusŏn-rodongjagu, the Yusŏn Coal Mine is

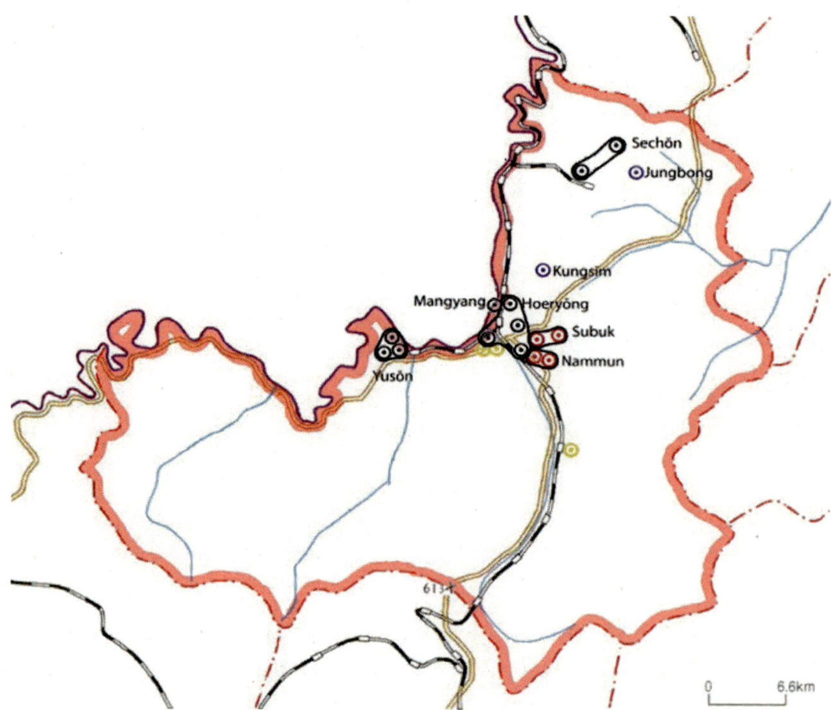

Figure Hoeryong-II. *Dong* and the former *up* and *rodongjagu*

located, which was built in 1900, and was called Kyerim Coal Mine before 1945 (KJY-29 1990, 746).

Another four *dong* are located in the northeast of the city

These *dong* emerged at the foundation of the city by converting the former *rodongjagu* of Sechŏn (established 1954, converted to Sechŏn-dong and Sinchon-dong in 1991), Kungsim (founded in 1961) and Jungbong (established in 1967).

Many coal mines are located in this region, such as the Kungsim Mine, Hakpho Mine in Sechon and the Jungbong Mine. Kungsim is about 8 km from the city center.

In the Jungbong Mine prisoners of the No. 22 Hoeryong (or Haengyŏng) Political Prisoners camp may have worked, which is located in this region, about 20 km from the city center. There are different reports on whether this camp actually exists.

In 1992, Jungdo-dong emerged in the south of the city center.

The IPA does not mention any change in the urban area after its founding in 1991. Except Jungdo-dong all *dong* were already formed at the time the town was founded.

Statistics

Urbanized areas prior to the city founding (*up* and *rodongjagu*)

1939-1949, 1952-1991 Hoeryong-up (1)
1952-1991 Yusŏn-up (since 1974 Yusŏn-rodongjagu)
1952-1991 Mangyang-rodongjagu
1954-1991 Sechŏn-rodongjagu
1961-1991 Kungsim-rodongjagu
1967-1991 Jungbong-rodongjagu
1989-1991 Nammun-rodongjagu
1989-1991 Subuk-rodongjagu

	Dong-Formation	*Dong*-Splitting
1991: (18)	2	(8)
1992: (19)	1	-

Hoeryong – Birthplace of Kim Jong-suk, mother of Kim Il-sung

According to North Korean history Hoeryong is the birthplace of Kim Jong-suk, the mother of Kim Jong-il, who also spent her childhood there. From all North Korean cities, is Hoeryong the one with the lowest population density. It is a border town to China with mostly small and medium companies. Hoeryong is known for its "Three Beauties" (beautiful women, beautiful apricots, beautiful earthenware). The quantitative analysis showed that compared to the population many industrial plants are located in Hoeryong. However, these are rather small and medium-sized companies. There are a low number of nationally significant assets. Hoeryong is shaped by the lignite reserves and rich forest resources, and has companies in the field of food processing, machinery and paper manufacturing.

IV.2.22. Kimchaek

One of the opened ports and base of Christian Mission

Kimchaek is located on the southern border of the Hambuk Province. In the North Kilju-kun and Hwadae-kun are located and in the West and the South Tanchon-si (Hamnam Province). In the East the city borders on the Korean East Sea. The municipal area has a North-South extent of 40 km and an east-west extent of 35 km. Kimchaek is famous for its steel industry and its shipyards. Kimchaek was called Sŏngjin until 1951, which had been appointed in 1939 as a city (*pu*), and thus was renamed after a military man and politician, Kim Chaek (1903-1951). Also in 1951, the adjacent Haksŏng-kun has been renamed Kimchaek-kun.

Table Kimchaek-I. Basic data

Population	207,299 (Rank 17)
Area	854 km² (Rank 7)
Population density	243 I./km² (Rank 23)
Administrative units	23 *dong*/19 *ri* (55%) (Rank 19)
"Urban" population/"rural" population	74.9%/25.1% (Rank 19)

For a long time only an abandoned fishing village existed in the neighborhood of current Kimchaek. Since it is a half-way station between Vladivostok and Wonsan, this region became an important strategic point at the end of the 19th century.

Thus in 1899, Sŏngjin, as Kimchaek was known before 1951, was one of eleven ports that were opened for trade with foreign countries.[88] Not only Japanese but other foreigners as well came to Sŏngjin and thus Christianity spread quickly. In 1901 the Canadian missionary Grierson arrived and the city became a base for Christianity on the northeast coast of Korea for the entire region. Not only churches but also Christian hospitals and schools were built, so that Sŏngjin was soon known as a city of religion.

At first, agricultural products, cowhide and fish products were exported through the port of Sŏngjin and slowly the city started to develop. Still, in 1910 less than 3,000 people lived there. A stronger development in Sŏngjin began only after 1915, when the Hamgyong railway line was built from Tanchon over Sŏngjin to Kilju. The railway and the abundance of sardines offshore led to a rapid growth of the urban area. Also, Sŏngjin was famous for its graphite, which was in great need during the First World War as it is a perfect material for molds of cannonballs. Then in May 1931, when the railway line was built from Hyesan to Kilju, Sŏngjin also developed into a port for export for products of the highland regions, especially for wood (Yun Jŏng-sŏp, 1987, 124-125).

Sŏngjin became the largest port between Hamhung and Chongjin. Since the construction of a steel plant in the 1930s, plants of all types developed and Sŏngjin became an industrial city.

88 From 1876 to 1910 eleven ports have been opened in Korea: Pusan (1876), Wonsan (1880), Inchon (1883), Nampho (1897), Mokpho (1897), Masan (1898), Kunsan (1899), Sŏngjin (1899), Ryongampho (1906), Chongjin (1908), Sinuiju (1910).

Change of name to honor General Kim Chaek

In 1951, during the Korean War, Sŏngjin was renamed Kimchaek, in order to honor General Kim Chaek (1903-1951), who was born in Sŏngjin. Not only the city of Kimchaek was named after Kim Chaek, but also the Kim Chaek Iron and Steel Complex in Chongjin and the Kim Chaek University of Technology in Pyongyang. On the other hand, the old name of the city was not completely erased and has been preserved for example in the Sŏngjin Steel Complex and the Sŏngjin Refractory Factory.

The Kimchaek Bay

There are numerous medium-sized and low mountains in the city. More than half of the urban area lie less than 300 m above sea level, 20% lie more than 800 m above sea level. From the Northwest the terrain flattens out towards the Southeast. In the West the Machŏnryŏng-mountain range forms a border to Tanchon. Here the highest mountains of the city are found, the Sobandŏk (1,664 m), the Tŏkman-san (1,506 m) and the Ryongyŏn-san (1,598 m). In the North, on the border to Kilju-kun, there are also some relatively high mountains such as Hangŏ-bong (1,278 m). In the East an important agricultural land is located: the Rimmyŏng plateau with its 60 km² is situated at the lower reaches of the Rimmyŏng-chŏn (57.2 km) and its tributaries Kalpha-chŏn and Ssangpho-chŏn. At the lower reaches of Kiljunamdae-chŏn, the Hakdong plane of 17 km² has developed.

The coast shows sections with a rocky coast, as well as sections with a sandy coast. East of Kimchaek a bay has formed through tectonic movements in the period between the end of the tertiary and the beginning of the quaternary, which is used as a base for fishing companies, which are primarily active in the field of deep-sea fishery. The bay favored the establishment of the Kimchaek port.

Important mineral resources in the urban area are graphite, limestone and marble. The forest accounts for 76% of the city area (IPA-14 2003, 157; PSC-8 2009, 626-627).

Kimchaek is the southernmost and warmest city of the province. The location near the East Sea brings mild winters. In summer, temperatures do not rise much and precipitation is less than in most other cities.

Table Kimchaek-II. Climate values

Annual average	January temperature	August temperature	Precipitation
8.9℃ (19)	-4.0℃ (6)	21.8℃ (23)	714,6 mm (23)

In Kimchaek the fishing industry is of great importance. The Kimchaek Taehung Fishery Enterprise concentrates on deep-sea fishing and the processing of sea products.

City of steel and Magnesia Clinker

Important industrial sectors that are represented in Kimchaek are the metal industry, the construction material industry, the machine construction and mining. Among them the metal industry has a nationwide significance. Steel and steel products that are important for engineering in the DPRK are manufactured in the Sŏngjin Steel Complex.

Significant construction material products of the city are magnesia clinker, firebrick and marble. The marble slabs produced in Janghyŏn-dong are a specialty of the city and can widely be used for monuments or housing construction.

Table Kimchaek-III. Ranking (in parenthesis: number of industrial companies and cultural institutions)

Kimchaek	KOFC	MOU	IPA	KCNA	KIET	Summary
Companies-total	18 (11)	22 (10)	19 (8)	23 (4)	17 (25)	21
Companies-important	10 (4)	8 (3)	20 (4)		20 (8)	21 (4)
Cultural institutions			16 (5)			

Table Kimchaek-IV. Ranking (Total number of companies in relation to population)

Kimchaek	KOFC	MOU	IPA	KCNA	KIET	Summary
Companies - total	13	21	20-15-15	23	14-17	22-21

The analysis shows that Kimchaek is in none of the five sources, concerning the number of industrial companies, better ranked than in terms of population, where the city came in 17th place.

Table Kimchaek-V. Specification (in parenthesis: number of industrial companies)

Kimchaek	Light Industry	Heavy Industry	Mining	Energy
KOFC	18 (2)	8 (8)	7 (1)	–
MOU	23 (4)	2 (5)	11 (1)	–
IPA	26 (1)	5 (5)	7 (1)	5 (1)
KCNA	–	1 (4)	–	–
KIET	27 (6)	5 (14)	3 (5)	–

A significant specialization of Kimchaek on heavy and chemical industry can be observed.

In chapter III.7.3. four companies were identified as important for Kimchaek: the Sŏngjin Steel Complex, the Sŏngjin Refractory Factory, the Kimchaek Ship Factory and the Ssangryong Phosphate Fertilizer Factory.

The Sŏngjin Steel Complex is directly located at the port of Kimchaek, is furthermore connected to the road network as well as to the Wŏlla railway line (Wonsan-Rason) and shows therefore favorable conditions for the transport of raw materials and goods. It employs about 25,000 workers. In 1934 the construction started, and from 1938 steel production began on the basis of iron ores of the Musan Mine and hydropower energy of Hŏchŏn-gang with the aim of steel production for the Japanese defense industry (KOFC 2010, 205-208; IPA-14 2003, 161-162).

The Sŏngjin Refractory Factory is, after the Tanchon Magnesia Factory, the second most important Refractory Factory of the DPR Korea. It manufactures mainly Magnesite Clinker and other firebricks and mainly supplies the Sŏngjin Steel Complex, but also other factories in the steel industry, the building material industry or machine construction. The Sŏngjin Magnesia Factory was a precursor of that factory which was built in 1936 (KOFC 2010, 445; IPA 14 2003, 161). In the Kimchaek Ship Factory cargo ships and fishing ships are built and repaired. It is located in Chonghak-dong and employs approximately 1,000 workers. This factory was already built in the period of the Japanese colonization, was destroyed during the Korean War and rebuilt between 1953-1954 (KOFC 2010, 327; IPA 14 2003, 160).

The Ssangryong Phosphate Fertilizer Factory is located in Unho-ri. In this factory lime fertilizer is produced. The construction started in 1981 (KOFC 2010, 385; IPA 14 2003, 162).

In Kimchaek there are a number of technical colleges and in Sechon-ri and Songhung-ri well known health resorts with hot springs are located.

Incorporations in 1952 and 1961, five *ri* outside the center became *dong*

As part of the regional rearrangement in 1952, six *ri* of Kimchaek-kun went to Kimchaek-si. Then Kimchaek-kun was incorporated into Kimchaek-si in February 1961. With the incorporation of Kimchaek-kun to Kimchaek-si, the administrative center of the *up*, Kimchaek-up, became Haksŏng-dong. Of the *ri*, which were incorporated to the city in 1952 and 1961, five were appointed to *dong*. These are the following (in parenthesis the year in which the *ri* became *dong*):

- Thanso-dong (1961), just north of Old Kimchaek
- Ŏbŏk-dong (1961), north of the urban area
- Kŭmchŏn-dong (1961), east of the northern part of Old Kimchaek
- Janghyŏng-dong (1961), southeast of Old Kimchaek
- Ssangryong-dong (1988), south of Old Kimchaek

Figure Kimchaek-I. New *dong* of Kimchaek (in the area of the former Kimchaek-kun)

Within Old-Kimchaek six new *dong* formed by separation

Another six new *dong* emerged by separating it from existing *dong*. Of these, only *dong* within Old-Kimchaek were affected.

Eight new *dong* from 1961 to 1965, afterwards only three new *dong*

In total Kimchaek consists of 22 *dong* (2002). In 1955, Kimchaek had ten *dong*. As another densely populated unit the *up* of Kimchaek-kun has to be mentioned, which became a *dong* (Haksŏng-dong) after being incorporated to Kimchaek-si. Eleven other *dong* came into existence between 1961-1993 by the upgrading of a *ri* or by splitting from other *dong*.

However, eight of these eleven *dong* were already formed between 1961-1965.

In 1972 Songryŏng-dong in the northwest corner of Old-Kimchaek was divided into two *dong* and in 1993 Ssangam-dong south of the station Jangphyŏng. In 1988 Ssangryong-ri became a *dong*.

Figure Kimchaek-II. New *dong* of Kimchaek city (in the down-town area)

Three centers of urban development and three new *dong* in the periphery

Let's take a look at the geographical distribution of the eleven *dong* that were formed between 1961 and 1993. In doing so, eight of these *dong* can be divided into three regions (encircled are the new *dong*):

1. the center around the Kimchaek train station; here two new *dong* were formed by separation in 1965.

Figure Kimchaek-III. Centers of development in Kimchaek

2. the area near the Sŏngjin Steel Complex: here two *dong* emerged in 1961, one by upgrading a *ri* (Thanso-dong, where the train station Jangphyŏng is situated), and one by separation. In 1993 another *dong* was formed by separation.

3. In 1961, in the northwest corner Kŭmchŏn-ri became a *dong* and Songryŏng-dong was formed by separation from two other *dong*. In 1972, Songryŏng was then split into two *dong*.

The other three *dong*, which were formed in 1961 and 1988 respectively, are situated at some distance from Old Kimchaek:

Ŏbok-dong is famous for its graphite mine (IPA-14 2003, 159) and Janghyŏn-dong for its marble (IPA 14 2003, 159). In Ssangryong-dong (*dong* since 1988) a large fertilizer factory is situated which construction began in 1981 and which started operation in 1985 (IPA-14 2003, 162).

Statistics

According to the IPA (2003), Kimchaek consists of 22 *dong* and 22 *ri*. In PSC-8 (2009, 626) 23 *dong* and 19 *ri* are indicated, with Songhŭng-ri, Phungnyŏn-ri and Hŭngphyŏng-ri no longer being listed. These three *ri* are all situated just north of the Songryŏng region.[89]

	Dong-Formation	*Dong*-Splitting
1955 (11)		
1961 (17)	4	2
1965 (19)	-	2
1972 (20)	-	1
1988 (21)	1	-
1993 (22)	-	1

Kimchaek–City in the shadow of Chongjin and Tanchon

Kimchaek consists of two centers which have developed at the East Sea coast and adjacent valleys. The actual city center is located in the south of the city; another center was formed in the North near the Sŏngjin Steel Complex.

The KCNA (May 13, 2008) reports a field guidance to units in Kilju county and Kimchaek City by Kim Jong-il. In Kimchaek there are two places he visited, the Kimchaek Taehung Fishery Company and the Pukkwandaechŏppi monument.[90] This is an indication that Kimchaek is not necessarily famous for its industrial plants, apart from the Sŏngjin Steel Complex, which however now has to use anthracite coal for smelting due to a shortage of coke which has to be imported, resulting in a reduction of quality of steel products.[91]

89 The names of the *dong* are not mentioned in the PSC-8 (2009).

90 KCNA (May 13, 2008) explains: „The monument in Rimmyong-ri, Kimchaek City, was erected in 1708 to commemorate the great victory Jong Mun Bu's volunteer corps won by decisively wiping out the Japanese aggression troops in Jangphyong, Rimmyong, Tanchon, Paekthap and other areas after their intrusion into Hamgyong Province during the Imjin Patriotic War (1592-98)."

91 In 1985 the metallurgy had accounted for 53.39% of the total production volume of the city Kimchaek, 14.53% accounted for the fishing industry, 10.88% for the construction material production and 10.26% for mechanical engineering. Following the slump in metallurgy the importance of fisheries is likely to have increased

Cooperation with China and Russia could spur the development of the city on the East Sea coast, however with the newly developed port in neighboring Tanchon a new competitor has emerged.

IV.2.23. Hamhung

Hometown of the Joson royal family

Hamhung is the largest city on the East Sea coast of the DPR Korea and is situated 344 km away from the capital Pyongyang. It is the cultural and economic center of Northeast Korea. Hamhung is considered to be the base of chemical industry of the country. The urban area was modified several times. The southern part of today's city area was a separate city under the name of Hungnam-si between 1949 and 1960 and 2001 and 2005, so one could speak of the twin cities Hamhung-Hungnam. After the Korean War, Hamhung was rebuilt with the help of the GDR.

Table Hamhung-I. Basic data[92]

Population	768,551 (Rank 3)
Area	556 km² (Rank 14)
Population density	1,382 I./km² (Rank 5)
Administrative units	101 *dong*/19 *ri* (84%) (Rank 6)
"Urban" population/"rural" population	91.6%/8.4% (Rank 4)

Hamhung is conveniently situated for public transport, because traffic routes that pass along the seaside of the East Sea intersect with streets that partly go through structural valleys and reach to the Kaema Highlands. Early on, it became a market place where agricultural products of the lowlands in Hamhung, fish and salt from the East Sea and special products as well as mineral resources from the highlands were merchandized. However, more important was the relevance of Hamhung as an administration center and military fortress against threats from the Northeast (Saitschikow 1958, 279).

Hamhung is considered to be "the hometown of the Joseon royal family" (National Museum of Korea). Yi Sŏng-gye (1335-1408), who founded the Joson period (1392-1910) as King Taejo (r. 1392-1398) spent his adolescence here and returned back to Hamhung, after he lost his position to his second son.[93] In Sonamu-dong the Hamhung Pon'gung (Hamhung

proportionally (KJY-26 1990, 525).

92 In Hamhung 99 *dong* and the *rodongjagu* of Choun and Raeil are located.

93 Also the time of the presence of Yi Sŏng-gye in Pon'gung probably refers to the proverbial term "Hamhung

Royal Villa) is located. It was constructed under Yi Sŏng-gye after his departure from the kingly office on the very spot, where the house of his ancestors was located.[94]

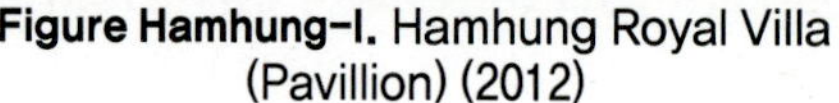

Figure Hamhung-I. Hamhung Royal Villa (Pavillion) (2012)

Figure Hamhung-II. Hamhung Royal Villa (2012)

Based on extensive hydro power sources of the rivers that run from the Kaema Highlands as well as due to local natural resources, Hamhung became an industrial city during the Japanese Occupation of Korea (Saitschikow 1958, 278). The urban image changed radically as well. The total population of approximately 10,000 at the end of the 19th century increased more than tenfold and neighborhoods with straight-lined, asphalted streets and multistoried buildings were created in the city center (Saitschikow 1958, 279). The Korean population lived in the southern part of the city. In the middle, the business district was situated from the train station to the West and in the Northeast to the Panryong-san (new name since 1977: Tonghŭng-san) the Japanese town developed (Lautensach 1945, 209). The Japanese colonial rulers built Hamhung because of its military strategic position on the Korean east coast as a starting point for the expansion towards China to an industrial center. (Speckmann 2010).

Hungnam grew from a fishing camp to a major location of chemical industry. Since 1927 the Noguchi fertilizer plant was built as one of the "largest fertilizer plants in the world in the early 1940s" (Armstrong 2005, 176) and completed in 1931 (KOFC 2010, 381). According to Saitschikow (1958, 278), its company grounds took up not less than half of the area of Hungnam.

messenger (Hamhung-chasa)," which means that a person who went away, who didn't return and nothing more had been heard from that person. Legend has it, that Yi Sŏng-gye killed or imprisoned those envoys that were sent from King Taejong (r. 1400-1418), the fifth son of Yi Sŏng-gye, in to appease him.

94 During the Hideyoshi invasions (1592-1598), it was destroyed in the end of the 16th century. In 1610, it was rebuilt but was repaired later; in the end of the 17th century it was again rebuilt. Also during the Korean War it was partly destroyed but then later restored (IPA-12 2003, 292-293).

Reconstruction of Hamhung and developments after 1945

After the Korean War many North Korean cities were in ruins, which especially applied to Hamhung. In November and December 1950, 80-90% of the city was destroyed by the USA when American troops beat their retreat due to the intervening Chinese (Speckmann 2010). Regarding the reconstruction of the cities after the war, the DPR Korea was supported by Eastern European states. The support of the GDR for the reconstruction of the city of Hamhung is especially highlighted in representations of "post-Korean War reconstruction of North Korea" (Armstrong 2005, 161-187). Kim Wŏn (1998, 244) lists the cities that received help for their reconstruction from the Eastern bloc.

Table Hamhung-II. Support for the reconstruction of North Korean cities by COMECON-states (according to Kim Wŏn 1998, 244)

City	Supporting countries	Planned timeframe
Pyongyang	Hungary, Bulgaria	1954-1957
Hamhung	GDR	1955-1964
Sunchon	Romania	1958-
Wonsan	Poland	1954-1966
Tokchon	Tchekoslovakia	1954-1956

However, the GDR quit offering their help two years earlier. Until 1962 around 450 East Germans should have stayed in Hamhung for a year (Speckmann 2010). During this time, the experts of the GDR built up with their Korean colleagues 5,236 apartments, many schools and kindergartens, one hospital, one concrete plant, one earthenware pipe factory and one construction and furniture joinery (Becker 1988, 42). Besides, a great number of professionals were educated. In total, the GDR invested according to Kang-Schmitz (2010, 128) 208 million rubles (218.4 million German mark) on the project.

In 1958 a plan for the reconstruction of the city was announced with the following focus areas:

1. Concentrated construction of apartments and cultural facilities in the center with Jungang-dong, Hoesang-dong, Wilhelm Pieck-Street[95] etc.
2. Measures, in order to use the support of GDR for the reconstruction of the city effectively
3. Construction of dikes and power plants to prevent the flooding caused by the Sŏngchŏn-gang.

95 One main road in Hamhung, in particular the street that connects at the bridge over the Sŏnchŏn-gang into the city was named after the GDR president, Wilhelm Pieck. However, it was later renamed into Jŏngsŏng-Street.

In June 1981 another plan was announced that discusses Hamhung not only as center for chemical industry, but aims to expand it as the largest international trading port in the northeast of Korea. In concrete terms the refurbishment of the Fertilizer Plant Hamhung, the 2.8. Vinalon Factory and the Ryongsŏng Machine Factory, the extension of the city area and the street network, the construction of an apartment tower complex in the Sapho area, the construction of day nurseries, kindergartens, leisure homes for children and youths and the enlargement of cropland for peanuts were planned (Kim Wŏn 1998, 247).

Figure Hamhung-III. Overlooking Jŏngsŏng-Street (2012)

Figure Hamhung-IV. Jŏngsŏng-Street (2012)

Location in the largest plain at the Northeast Korean East Sea Coast

Hamhung is located in the eastern part of the Hamhung Plain, which is also known as the Hamju-(100 Ri-)plain (IPA-12 2003, 37, 52). This plain lies in the reach of the lower course of the Sŏngchŏn-gang and the Kwangpho-gang and extends to the areas of Hamhung-si (including Hungnam) as well as Hamju-kun and Jongphyong-kun. It has a spread of 600 km^2 (IPA-12 2003, 52) and is for this reason the largest plain on the Northeast Korean East Sea coast. The Hamhung Plain, starting with the Sŏngchŏn-gang, is traversed by many large and small rivers and to a great extent the eastern part is fertile aggradation land and a sand beach coast developed as well (Kang Sŏk-o 1984, 344-345). The delta plain of the Sŏngchŏn-gang narrows due to the mountain spur of Tonghŭng-san (319 m) in the North, so that, seen from the East Sea, the first favorable transition possibility for streets and railroad arises here. The center of Hamhung developed at the bottom and slope of Tonghŭng-san which affords protection against flooding and it widened later to the Horŏng-chŏn in its flood-meadows (see Lautensach 1945, 209).

Figure Hamhung-V. Sŏngchŏn-gang (2012)

Figure Hamhung-VI. Center (view towards North) (2012)

At the border to Sinhung-kun are the Pakdal-bong (905 m) and the Kaejae-san (883 m), in the Northeast is the Hamgwanryŏng mountain range with the mountains Ponghwa-san (814 m) and Kalmi-bong (787 m). The Tonghŭng-san (319 m) is located in the Southwest.

In the northeast of Hungnam the Hamgyong mountain range spans to the sea. The Chŏnju-bong (561 m) is situated in it.

Table Hamhung-III. Climate values

Annual average	January temperature	August temperature	Precipitation
10.0℃ (9)	-4.2℃ (8)	22.8℃ (18)	822.3 mm (20)

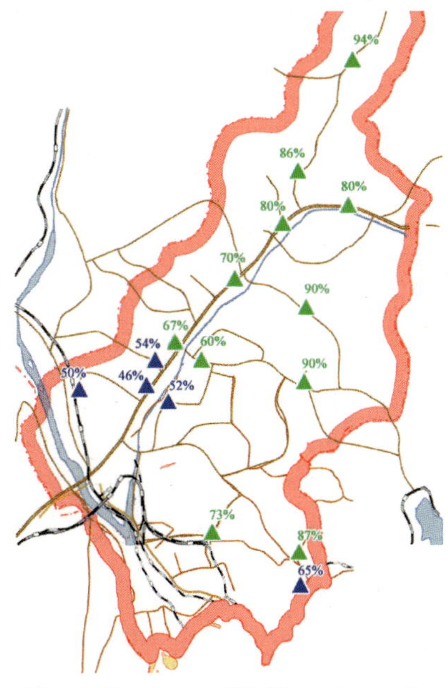

Figure Hamhung-VII. Forest area in the *ri*

A strong wind blows from the sea, except in winter.

Approximately 60% of the city region consists of woodland. Figure Hamhung-VII shows that the agricultural crop areas are almost limited to the southern parts of the municipal area. Important fishing companies of the city are the Sŏho Fishery Station and the Hŭngnam Fishery Station.

72 km away from the center of Hamhung, the Raeil-rodongjagu is located. It was built in August 2001 as an exclave of Hamhung-si out of Hamju-kun (Hamnam Province) and Taehung-kun (Phyongnam Province). 90% of the area consists of forests. An important establishment is the Goat Farm (IPA-12 2003, 66). The Hamhung

(City) Youth Goat Farm "is one of the largest stock-breeding bases in the DPRK" (KCNA December 7, 2009). "It is made up of tens of branch farms built along the 60 km-long ring-shape road of pasture" (KCNA July, 31 2002). Even though the Raeil-rodongjagu is only since 2001 an administrative part of Hamhung-si according to IPA-12 (2003, 48), its history as a goat farm region, in order to provide the people of Hamhung with food, is longer. According to a North Korean film documentation in 1992, 108 newlyweds were relocated into this region to cultivate a village for the keeping of domestic goats in order to ease the nutritional situation of Hamhung (Pak Hŭi-jin 2013, 336).

City of chemical industry

Hamhung was and still is famous for being an industrial city, especially as a city of chemical industry. The Hungnam Fertilizer Complex and the February 8 Vinalon Complex belong to the most important chemical companies of the country. Also machinery construction, first of all the Ryongsŏng Machine Complex, plays an important part. Further important industrial sectors of the city are the metal, material, and textile industry etc.

However, production decreased already in the second half of the 80s. The supply of primary products and other materials from the major providers China and Russia was almost aborted (Chosun Ilbo December 18, 1995). After the failure of Comecon, the situation turned dramatically and Hamhung was mocked as the „capital of the unemployed“ (Bauer 2005).

Table Hamhung-IV. Ranking (in parenthesis: number of industrial companies or cultural institutions)

Hamhung	KOFC	MOU	IPA	KCNA	KIET	Summary
Companies-total	3 (33)	3 (58)	3 (36)	2 (39)	2 (126)	3
Companies-important	5 (8)	4 (7)	4 (12)		2 (47)	3 (20)
Cultural institutions			3 (28)			

Table Hamhung-V. Ranking (Total number of companies in relation to population)

Hamhung	KOFC	MOU	IPA	KCNA	KIET	Summary
Companies-total	18	14	13-20-12	6	4-4	12-14

Nampho is ranked at second place in the ranking of industrial companies, according to three sources, although that rank belongs to Hamhung according to two other sources. The two latter sources are sources that directly stem from North Korea (KCNA) or are based on

North Korean sources (KIET is based on Rodong Sinmun). Companies from Hamhung are frequently mentioned in North Korean sources, since the city is often visited by high-level representatives of the state and many political events take place in Hamhung.[96] According to Ko Yu-hwan/Pak Hŭi-jin (2013, 109) Hamhung can be considered as "political city."

Table Hamhung-VI. Specification (in parenthesis: number of industrial companies)

Hamhung	Light Industry	Heavy Industry	Mining	Energy
KOFC	10 (9)	8 (24)	–	–
MOU	13 (36)	7 (22)	–	–
IPA	13 (18)	7 (18)	–	–
KCNA	16 (15)	4 (23)	–	16 (1)
KIET	19 (44)	2 (80)	–	14 (2)

All sources clearly indicate that the focus of the industry of Hamhung is on heavy industry. However, the result would be different if Hungnam would not be included in the calculation. At least the most important heavy industry plants are located in the northern part of the twin city Hamhung-Hungnam. Nevertheless, in "actual" Hungnam in the south many companies of the light industry are situated.

In chapter III.7.3. 20 companies were identified as important: Hungnam Fertilizer Complex, February 8 Vinalon Complex, Sinhŭng Chemical Complex, Hamhung Tire Factory, Hungnam Pharmaceutical Factory, Ryongsŏng Machine Complex, Hamhung Machine Tool Factory, Hamhung Trailed Farm Machine Factory, Sŏngchŏn'gang Electric Appliances Factory, Hungnam Smeltery, Smeltery July 27th, Hamhung Silicate Brick Factory, Hamhung Ceramic Constructional Goods Factory (Hamhung structural ceramics factory), Hamhung Wood Processing Factory, Hamhung Cornstarch Factory, Hamhung Woolen Mill, Hamhung Silk Mill, Hamhung Knitwear Factory, Sŏngchŏn'gang Garment Factory, Hamhung Disabled Soldiers' Essential Plastic Goods Factory.

Due to the electricity supply of the Jangjingang Power Station, the Pujŏngang Power Station and the Hŏchŏngang Power Station, the two most important chemical factories of the city are located in Hungnam, namely the Hungnam Fertilizer Complex and the February 8 Vinalon Complex. The Hungnam Fertilizer Complex is one of the major producers of chemical fertilizer in the DPR Korea. The factory was built between June 1927 and August 1931. After its destruction during the Korean War, it was rebuilt between 1953 and 1958 with Soviet help. From 2003 onwards, outdated parts of the factory were demolished and newly built. Recently, on the basis of coal gas fertilizer is produced. For that reason brown coal is used. The hard coal that is processed in this factory stems from

96 The February 8 Vinalon Complex, the Ryongsŏng Machine Complex and the Hungnam Fertilizer Complex belong to the companies that are mostly mentioned by the KCNA.

the Sudong Coal Mine, iron(ous) sulfate come from the Mandŏk Mine, apatite derives from the Tongam Mine and the Ssangyong Mine, and chalkstone comes from the Puraesan Mine. Industrial water either derives from the Sŏngchŏn-gang, which is sterilized in the Sapho sewage disposal facility, or from the sea (KOFC 2010, 381-384).

Figure Hamhung-VIII. Ryongsŏng Machine in the Hungnam Fertilizer Complex (2012)

Figure Hamhung-IX. February 8 Vinalon Complex (2012)

The February 8 Vinalon Complex is situated in Sapho-kuyok and has an area of 2,730,000 m². Different organic chemical products are made from vinalon and carbide. The factory was built between 1935 and 1936, destroyed in the Korean War and rebuilt in 1955 (KOFC 2010, 581-584). From 2004 onwards, outdated parts of the factory were demolished and rebuilt. The production of vinalon was cut off for 16 years, but recently resumed again (The Pyongyang Times February 11, 2013). Vinalon, which is also known as "Korean fiber," was, according to North Korean expositions, invented by Ri Sung Gi in the 1930s (1905-1996) and used as fiber after 1945. Raw materials are chalkstone and anthracite. The production of vinalon started on May 6th, 1961 (Jo, Am/An Chol Gang 2002, 142). The complex derives coal from Ŭn'gok Coal Mine, chalkstone from the Puraesan Mine, salt from the Phyongnam Province, industrial water is provided by Sŏngchŏn-gang. Vinalon and other synthetic fibers are delivered to textile factories in the DPR Korea (KOFC 2010, 581-584).

The Sinhŭng Chemical Complex produces agricultural pesticides and its construction was completed in September 1992 (KOFC 2010, 387).[97] The Hungnam Pharmaceutical Factory was founded in 1947. Its predecessor was the Pon'gung Chemical Factory which was established before 1945. It is the biggest producer of synthetic drugs and

97 According to NTI (Nuclear Threat Initiative), the plant has an area of 1.235.870 m² and produces chemical weapons; and it differs from the information in KOFC, as the information states that the plant is not located in Hamhung but in Sinhung-kun (NTI o.J. b).

pharmaceutical elements of the DPR Korea (IPA-12 2003, 291-292; KOFC 2010, 389). The in 1970 established Hamhung Tire Factory belongs to the most important tire factories of the country and is the most important one in the northeast of Korea. The Hamhung Factory Nr. 17 produces RDX (Research Department Explosive), fuel gas, dynamite and ammonium nitrate explosives. It was built in 1936. After an explosion accident in 1965 the production volume was further increased (KOFC 2010, 390).

The Ryongsŏng Machine Complex builds facilities for power plants, engine lathes, big tool machines, turbines, presses etc., which are used in mines, shipyards and other important establishments of the DPR Korea. The total complex area is 686,000 m². Approximately 10,000 people are employed here. The complex was built in 1938 as branch plant of the Hamhung Fertilizer Factory. After the destruction during the Korean War, it was rebuilt at first as Mine Machine Factory. Between 1957 and 1960 the factory was extended with the help of the Soviet Union and the product range was enlarged. Afterwards, further enlargements of the factory took place (IPA-12 2003, 289-290; KOFC 2010, 298-301).

Further important companies in the field of machine construction in Hamhung are amongst others the Hamhung Machine Tool Factory, the Hamhung Trailed Farm Machine Factory and the Sŏngchŏn'gang Electric Appliances Factory.

Also metallurgy is an important industrial sector of the city. The Hungnam Smeltery is located in Kŭmpich-dong, 600 m away from the port of Hungnam. It produces lead, copper, nickel and various types of metal alloys. Approximately 4,000 people are employed here. The smeltery was built in 1930, at the same time as the Hungnam Fertilizer Factory. During the Korean War the smeltery was badly damaged, but it was rebuilt again so that the work could resume from 1955 onwards. Copper ores are delivered by the Mandŏk and the Sangnong Mine, lead comes from the Kŏmdŏk Mine, the San'gok Mine, the Chŏnnam Mine, the Hamhŭng Mine and the Taehŭng Mine, nickel from the Punyun Mine (Chongjin), Samhae Mine (Rajin) and the Phangyo Mine (Kangwon Province) (IPA-12 2003, 291; KOFC 2013, 233). Electricity is delivered by the Jangjingang Power Station and the Pujŏngang Power Station.

The Smeltery July 27th (former name: Hungnam Nr. 2 Smeltery) is located in Songhŭng-dong (Haean-kuyok) with a total plant area of 150,000m² in a region that consists of 100 m high hills. In a circuit of 2 km around the plant, the Hungnam Fertilizer Complex, the February 8 Vinalon Complex and the Hungnam Smeltery are located. The Smeltery July 27th was built between 1981 and 1983 with the aim of gold production. Considerably high were the environmental problems that were caused by the smeltery. In 1990 the factory was closed (KOFC 2010, 235-237).

Also many other establishments of light industry are situated in this city. The most important foodstuff factory is the Hamhung Cornstarch Factory. It was built in 1974. Amongst others, confectionery products, oil and soy sauce are produced here. In 1980 the factory was restored and enlarged (IPA-12 2003, 54-55; KOFC 2010, 54-55).

The textile industry is represented by many establishments. The Hamhung Woolen Mill was built from 1964 onwards and with the help of the Soviet Union the construction was completed in 1967. It is situated in Hoesang3-dong and is considered to be the leading woolen mill in the DPR Korea. The total area of the company is 440,000 m² and approximately 5,000 people are employed here (IPA-12 2003, 55; KOFC 2010, 597-598). Other textile industry companies of Hamhung that are mentioned in many sources are the Hamhung Silk Mill, the Hamhung Knitwear Factory and the Sŏngchŏn'gang Garment Factory. One example for an establishment that produces essential goods is the Hamhung Disabled Soldiers' Essential Plastic Goods Factory.

It started in 1953 as a cooperative, when essential goods out of metal were produced to cover the postwar-needs. Since 1961 artificially produced resin is used as basic material in order to produce *inter alia* rainwear and bags (IPA-12 2003, 56).

The production of building materials has a great importance in Hamhung. The Hamhung Silicate Brick Factory was built since December 1986 and used sand from the banks of the Sŏngchŏn-gang (KOFC 2010, 447). The Hamhung Ceramic Constructional Goods Factory (Hamhung Architectural Ceramics Factory) was established in the context of the first Seven-Year Plan for the economy of the DPR Korea (1961-1970) and produces amongst others tiles (IPA-12 2003, 54; KOFC 2010, 54). The construction of the Hamhung Wood Processing Factory was started in 1958 and the factory went into operation in 1960. Here, furnishings and other timber products are produced. The total area of the factory is about 25,000 m² (IPA-12 2003, 55; KOFC 2010, 55).

The port of Hungnam is the third largest commercial port of the DPR Korea. Important export items are magnesite, cement, pig iron, graphite, steel ware, artificial fertilizer, machinery supplies etc. Important import items are chalkstone, mineral ores, salt, coal, and coke (KOFC 2010, 113).

Figure Hamhung-X. Majon Bathing Resort (2012)

Figure Hamhung-XI. Hungnam Port (2012)

In Hamhung are several universities with focus on Koryo Pharmacy, agriculture, education, politics, water technology, medicine, computer technology as well as various other aspects in the field of chemistry. There are also research institutions with focus on high polymer chemistry, analytical chemistry, organic chemistry, chemical engineering, disease prevention, surgery and clinical medicine, noble metals and agriculture. There are many cultural institutions in Hamhung as the city is a provincial capital and considered as the center of the northeastern part of Korea: an artist group that represents the Hamgyong Province, a daily newspaper, one stadium, museums, a broadcast station. Especially worth a mention is the Hamhung Grand Theater that was completed in 1984. Specialties of the city are acorn liquor and cold noodles that are for example offered in the restaurant Sinhŭnggwan on Jŏngsŏng street that was erected in 1976. The Majon Bathing Resort is situated 25 km southeast from the center of Hamhung. Of recent date the Majon Hotel was completed in 2009 with over 100 rooms (KCNA 28.7.2009).

Administrative Overview

Hamhung, the capital of the Hamnam Province was appointed to a city (*pu*) in 1930 and its municipal area was expanded several times. In 1938, together with Hungnam, it had 128,793 inhabitants (Lautensach 1945, 209). It developed on the eastern slope of the Sŏngchŏn'gang-plain.

In 1949 parts of Hamju-up were incorporated to Hamhung. Hungnam was designated as a city and thereby expanded. During the Korean War 80-90% of Hamhung was destroyed. The reconstruction in 1954/55 until 1962 was supported by technicians from the GDR.

In 1960 Hamhŭng became a *jikhalsi*. Hŭngnam-si, Thoejo-kun and parts of Hamju-kun as well as Oru-kun (in 1981 it was renamed Yŏnggwang-kun) were added. Also, Hamhung was divided into *kuyok*.

In 1970 Hamhung again became a normal city. During this process Thoeju-kuyok and Tŏksan-kuyok, which both consist out of regions that belonged to Thoeju-up, were again outsourced and became *kun*.

In 1974 Tŏksan-kun is included into the municipal area.

In 2001 Hungnam is rebuilt out of the *kuyok* of Hŭngnam, Hŭngdŏk, Haean and parts of Sapho-kuyok. The *kuyok*-system was abolished.

In 2005 Hungnam becomes again part of Hamhung-si.

Summarized, the following facts are considered as important administrative changes:

- Hamhung as province independent city: 1960-1970,
- existence of the city of Hungnam: 1949-1960 and 2001-2005,
- existence of the *kuyok*-system: 1960-2001 and since 2005.

Changes within the *kuyok*-system

Firstly, the most important changes of the *kuyok*-system are ascertained:

Due to the introduction of the *kuyok*-systems in 1960, nine *kuyok* were formed:

Thoejo, Tŏksan, Pon'gung, Panryong, Sapho, Sŏngchŏn, Hoesang, Ryongsŏng, Namhŭng.

In 1970 (7 *kuyok*): Thoejo and Tŏksan become again *kun* of the Hamgnam Province.

In 1974 (6 *kuyok*): Pon'gung-kuyok becomes part of Sapho-kuyok; Tŏksan-kun becomes part of Hoesang-kuyok.

In 1977 Panryong-kuyok is renamed to Tonghŭng-kuyok. In 1990 Sŏngchŏn-kuyok is renamed to Sŏngchŏn'gang-kuyok and Ryongsŏng-kuyok is renamed to Haean-kuyok.

In 1995 (7 *kuyok*): Hŭngdŏk-kuyok is split off from Sapho-kuyok. This involves the regions that formerly belonged to the in 1974 integrated Pon'gung-kuyok.

At the time of the abolishment of the *kuyok*-system seven *kuyok* existed in 2001. The *dong* and *ri* that belonged to *kuyok* of Sŏngchŏn'gang (Sŏngchŏn), Tonghŭng (Panryong),

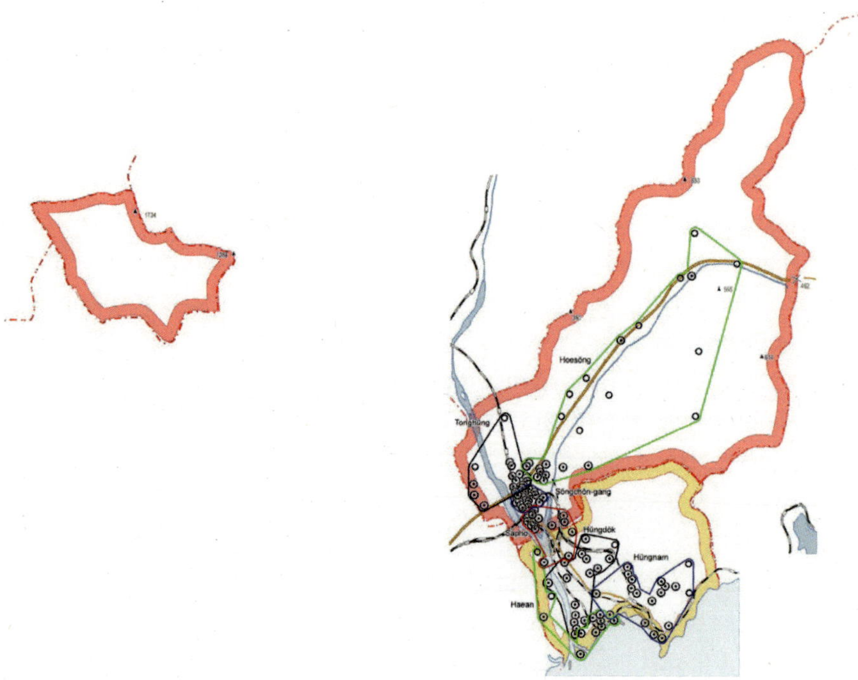

Figure Hamhung-XII. Districts and *dong* in Hamhung

Hoesang as well as parts of Sapho-kuyok remained with Hamhŭng-si.

Due to the rebuilding of Hŭngnam-si in 2001 the larger part of Sapho and the *kuyok* of Hŭngdŏk (Pon'gung, 1974-1995 part of Sapho), Haean (Ryongsŏng) and Hŭngnam became part of Hungnam-si.

After the reconstruction: Developments of the Sapho region

In the context of the reconstruction of Hamhŭng after the Korean War the city was divided into five *up*. According to Frank (1996, 22) those are: Center, P'alryong-san, Hoesang-ri, Sap'o-ri and Hamju.

The "Center" might be today's Sŏngchŏn'gang-kuyok. The other three refer to regions that are located in today's *kuyok* of Tonghŭng (formerly: Panryong), Sapho and Hoesang. The former Hamju-up (first in 1960, later again in 1974) was later included into Tonghŭng-kuyok.

The Sŏngchŏn'gang center is located at the train station. Tonghŭng adjoins in the West. In the Southwest is Old-Hamju (until 2001 also part of Tonghŭng-kuyok). In the East Sapho adjoins and in the South Hoesang is located, which consists of an urban part in the South and a rural part in the North. In the southern part of Sapho the Saegori1-4-area developed.

Hungdŏk adjoins to the former Hungnam-si at the southern part of Sapho, farther South the actual Hŭngnam is located and in the East is Haesan located (s. figure Hamhung-XII).

The development of each *kuyok* in regards to the reshuffle of *dong*:

Table Hamhung-VII. Number of *dong* in the *kuyok*

	1955	1956	1957	1960	1963	1965	1967	1970
Hamhung (Total number)	62	52	55	64	77	85	93	91
Hamhung (Total changes)		−10:−	−:−6/9	5:−1/5	4:9	2:6	−:8	1:−3
Sŏngchŏn	13 : −		− : 4	− : −1	− : 1		− : 1	
Tonghŭng	7 : −		− : 1	2 : 1	1 : 2		− : 2	−:(−3)
Hoesang	3 : −		− : 4	1 : −		2:1		1:−
Sapho	8 : −	−3 : −	− :−2/1	1 : −	2 : −	−:1	− : 1	
Hungnam	16 : −	−4 : −	− : −2	1 : 1	− : 1	−:1	− : 2	
Haean	7 : −		− : −2	− : 1	− : 2	−:2		
Hŭngdŏk	8 : −	−3 : −		− : 1	1 : 3	−:1	− : 2	

	1974	1982	1993	2001	Total	Population
	94	98	100	101		
Hamhung	–:3	(1):3	1:1	(1):–	99+(2)	768.551
Sŏngchŏn					18	127.102
Tonghŭng	– : (3)				16	120.559
Hoesang					12	156.608
Sapho		1 : 3	– : 1		13 +(1)	115.317
Hungnam					16	99.994
Haean			1 : –		11	80.878
Hŭngdŏk					13	68.093

Table Hamhung–VIII. Decrease of *dong* and formation of new *dong* in the *up*

	1950s	1960s		1950s	1960s	1970s	1980s	1990s
Hamhung (decrease of *dong*)	–16	–1	Hamhung (formation of new *dong*)	9	38	1	4	2
Sŏngchŏn		–1	Sŏngchŏn	4	2			
Tonghŭng			Tonghŭng	1	8			
Hoesang			Hoesang	4	4	1		
Sapho	–5		Sapho	1	5		4	1
Hungnam	–6		Hungnam		6			
Haean	–2		Haean		5			1
Hŭngdŏk	–3		Hŭngdŏk		8			

One can find that there were many *dong*-formations in the 1950s, but also several *dong*-mergers. Also, several *dong* were transformed again to *ri*. In the 1960s, as a result of the splitting or transformation of a *ri,* 39 new *dong* emerged in Hamhung (today's municipal area). After that time no major city developments in regards to *dong* is identifiable. Of the four new *dong* that emerged in the 1970s, three are the result of the re-splitting from the again incorporated (Old-) Hamju-up.

In the 1980s only four new *dong* emerged, in the 1990s two *dong* emerged as well the Raeil-rodongjagu that is located in an enclave. Five of the six new *dong* from the 1980s and 1990s are situated in Sapho, we are speaking about the Choun-dong, which emerged in 1982 and was converted into Choun-rodongjagu in 1984, and Saegŏri-dong 1 to 4. This data suggests that from the middle-end of the 1960s almost only Sapho (Saegŏri region) records new developments.

North Korean media were talking about a construction boom of apartments in multistoried buildings in the 1980s. The 20-storied circular Wŏnhyŏng-apartment tower in the Sapho region, for example, offers approximately 300 apartments (Ko Yu-hwan/Pak Hŭi-jin 2013, 110).

Figure Hamhung-XIII. Wŏnhyŏng-apartment tower (2012)

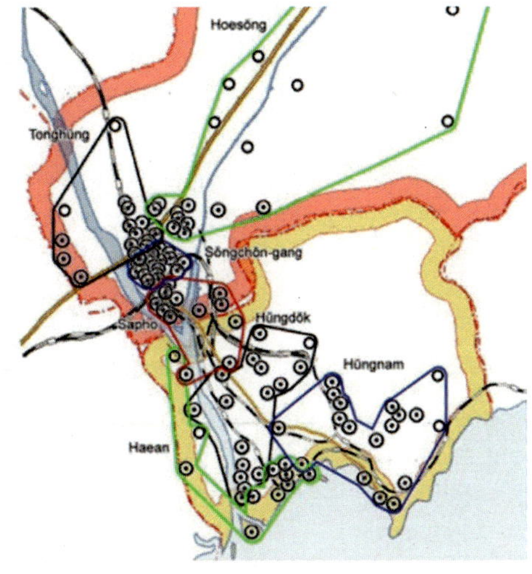

Figure Hamhung-XIV. *Dong* (Center)

Table Hamhung-IX. Increase of the number of *dong* (without *rodongjagu*)

	1955	Total	
Hamhŭng	62	99+(2)	60%
Sŏngchŏn	13	18	38%
Tonghŭng	7	16	129%
Hoesang	3	12	300%
Sapho	8	13 +(1)	63%
Hŭngnam	16	16	0%
Haean	7	11	57%
Hŭngdŏk	8	13	63%

	1955	1960	1970	1982	1993	2001
Hamhŭng	62	64	91	98	100	101
Sŏngchŏn	13	16	18	18	18	18
Tonghŭng	7	11	13	16	16	16
Hoesang	3	8	12	12	12	12
Sapho	8	5	9	13	14	14
Hŭngnam	16	12	16	16	16	16
Haean	7	6	10	10	11	11
Hŭngdŏk	8	6	13	13	13	13

	1955	1956	1957	1960	1963	1965	1967	1970
Hamhŭng	62	52	55	64	77	85	93	91
Sŏngchŏn	13	13	17	16	17	17	18	18
Tonghŭng	7	7	8	11	14	14	16	13
Hoesang	3	3	7	8	8	11	11	12
Sapho	8	5	4	5	7	8	9	9
Hŭngnam	16	12	10	12	13	14	16	16
Haean	7	7	5	6	8	10	10	10
Hŭngdŏk	8	5	5	6	10	11	13	13

	1974	1982	1993	2001	Total
Hamhŭng	94	98	100	101	99+(2)
Sŏngchŏn	18	18	18	18	18
Tonghŭng	16	16	16	16	16
Hoesang	12	12	12	12	12
Sapho	9	13	14	14	13 +(1)
Hŭngnam	16	16	16	16	16
Haean	10	10	11	11	11
Hŭngdŏk	13	13	13	13	13

Hamhung – center of Northeast Korea

Hamhung is the most important center in the northeastern part of Korea. In regards to the statistics about industrial companies, Hamhung is partly better ranked than Nampho, which might be due to the fact that Hamhung is a "political city," in which representatives of the state and the party show up frequently. A possible background might be the attempt to prevent or dam regionalism.

Hamhung, particularly Hungnam, is a city of chemistry. For this reason the absence of energy and raw materials was especially difficult for the city.

Hamhung was destroyed in the war and was rebuilt until the 1960s. The analysis of *dong* implies that there were not a lot of changes in the 1970s. The increase of development particularly in the Sapho region in the south of the city region in the direction of Hamhung only appeared in the 1980s.

IV.2.24. Tanchon

In the past as an intermediate stop before crossing the Machŏn-ryŏng

Tanchon is one of the most important mining and industrial cities of North Korea. There are several lead, zinc, magnesite and apatite mines in the city. Already in 1932, the lead and zinc mine Kŏmdŏk was built. In addition the Ryongyang Mine, from which magnesite was extracted, the Taehŭng Mine (magnesite) as well as the Tongam Mine (apatite) are one of the most important mines of North Korea.

Table Tanchon-I. Basic data[98]

Population	345,875 (Rank 7)
Area	2,172 km² (Rank 1)
Population density	159 I./km² (Rank 26)
Administrative units	40 *dong*/38 *ri* (51%) (Rank 21)
"Urban" population/"rural" population	69.6%/30.4% (Rank 24)

Tanchon was developed on the road along the east coast towards the Tumen river to an important intermediate stop before crossing the mountain pass Machŏn-ryŏng. At the time of the Japanese rule over Korea, railway lines were built, which came from the highlands of North Korea and run through Tanchon on to the route that runs along the coast of the East Sea, which underpinned the favorable traffic situation of the city. At first, the industrial development of Tanchon was closely linked with the agriculture and forestry (sawmill, linen weaving, dairy), but towards the end of the Japanese rule, more and more of the city became a location of processing local minerals, mainly obtained magnetite and table salt (Saitschikow 1945, 285). Since 1937, Tanchon got more and more urban traits and turned into an industrial region. The Japanese had planned much for Tanchon. In 1943, when the city had 164,241 inhabitants, plans were made to expand Tanchon into a city for 500,000 inhabitants. Towards the end of the Second World War the construction of the port was started, but only one third was completed. Then the defeat of the Japanese also finished their plans for the expansion of the port and the city (Yi Han-sun, 1991, 126).

In the north, east and west, the terrain is very steep. High mountains alternate with deep valleys. In the north, a basaltic plateau has formed. There the Turyu-san (2,309 m), the highest mountain of the city, is located. In the east are the Anban-tŏk (1,830 m) and the

98 In the IPA-12 (2003) 39 *dong* and 39 *ri* are listed. The PSC-8 (2009, 596) only lists the *ri*, but in case of the *dong* only the number is specified. The "missing" *ri* in PSC, compared to the IPA, is Tŏkju-ri, which lies in the south of the city, north of the former Tanchon-up.

Ryongyŏn-san (1,598 m). There are several mountains with a height of over 2,000 m in the West (Kŏmdŏk-san 2,151m, Manthap-san 2,012 m, Thaejo-bong 2,084 m).

Table Tanchon-II. Climate values

Annual average	January temperature	August temperature	Precipitation
9.2℃ (17)	−3.8℃ (5)	22℃ (22)	672.0 mm (24)

It is noticeable that Tanchon is one of the cities with relatively mild winters for North Korean circumstances, but in the summer the temperatures do not rise as much as in other parts of the country. Also, the city has relatively low precipitation.

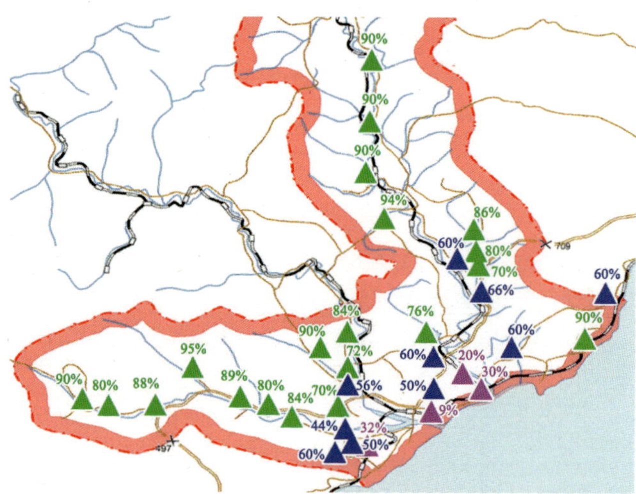

Figure Tanchon-I. Forest area in the *ri*

More than 80% of the city consists of forests, which are widespread in the North. Important forest species are, for example, pine, oak or aspen. The edible mushroom (pine mushroom) is very common. From the field acreage the rice fields account for 20%, and fruit growing makes up 10%. Main crops are rice plant, soybeans and corn. Important vegetables are cabbage, garlic, spinach and peppers. The livestock and poultry industry have an important function in the city.

Major rivers in the city are the Namdae-chŏn (176.3 km), Pukdae-chŏn (128.1 km) and the Pok-chŏn (50 km). At the lower section of the Namdae-chŏn and on the banks of Pok-chŏn, a 60 km² large Tanchon-level has formed, which represents the most important rice-growing area of the city.

The city has a 40 km long coastline. Thus, there are numerous fishing companies, whereupon the Tanchon Fishing Station is the most important one. They do both, deep-sea fishing as well as inshore fishing. Tanchon is famous for pollack fishing. Other important fish, which are fished in Tanchon are catfish, halibut, atka mackerel, trout, etc.

Mining Town

Tanchon is dominated by mining and by industries that process the extracted materials. Also the machinery and equipment that are required for the mining industry are produced in Tanchon. Additionally the energy industry is significant. Furthermore, there are regional companies in the textile industry and food industry.

Table Tanchon-III. Ranking (in parenthesis: number of industrial companies or cultural institutions)

Tanchon	KOFC	MOU	IPA	KCNA	KIET	Summary
Companies-total	17 (12)	8 (29)	14 (13)	13 (11)	10 (39)	11
Companies-important	6 (6)	5 (6)	15 (6)		11 (13)	12 (8)
Cultural institution			13 (7)			

Table Tanchon-IV. Ranking (Total number of companies in relation to population)

Tanchon	KOFC	MOU	IPA	KCNA	KIET	Summary
Companies-total	22	12	19-18-18	17	17-19	20-19

After evaluating all five sources, Tanchon has a lower rank in terms of numbers of industrial companies than in terms of population (Rank 7). According to the MOU source, Tanchon is stated with a lot of mines and according to KIET Tanchon has many factories in the heavy industry sector.

Table Tanchon-V. Specification (in parenthesis: number of industrial companies)

Tanchon	Light Industry	Heavy Industry	Mining	Energy
KOFC	22 (1)	20 (6)	4 (4)	6 (1)
MOU	26 (7)	16 (8)	2 (13)	8 (1)
IPA	24 (2)	16 (5)	2 (5)	6 (1)
KCNA	-	10 (5)	2 (5)	12 (1)
KIET	21 (13)	18 (18)	5 (6)	5 (2)

Compared with the population, there are not a lot of facilities in the field of higher education. There is no university in Tanchon, only colleges which focus on the subjects of mining, engineering and agriculture (Chosun Ilbo November 27, 1995).

Once again, the table Tanchon-V shows the embossing of Tanchon as a mining town. It is also clear that Tanchon is much more focused on heavy industry as on light industry, the latter of which only plays a minor role.

In chapter III.7.3. eight companies had been identified as important for Tanchon. These include the three most important mines, the Kŏmdŏk Mining Complex, the Taehŭng Youth Hero Mine and the Ryongyang Mine, as well as the Tanchon Magnesia Factory and Tanchon Smeltery for the further processing of raw materials. Also the Tanchon Mining Machine Plant is connected with the mining industry.

In Tanchon there is also the Tanchon Ship Repair Factory and as the only factory of light industry, the Kwangchŏn Foodstuff Factory, which was identified in chapter III.7.3. as one of the important companies of Tanchon. In the Kwangchŏn Foodstuff Factory puffed rice from corn, soy sauce and soybean paste are produced. The demand is not covered, but at least the taste is supposed to be fine (Chosun Ilbo November 27, 1995).

Mineral resources

Tanchon is a significant mining town in the DPR Korea. In the north of the city in the areas of Taehŭng, Kŏmdŏk, Ryongyang and Tongam significant mines are located. The Pukdae-chŏn, which flows through these regions, is an important domestic water supplier. The energy supply of most of the complexes is guaranteed through the Hŏchŏn-gang power plant over the Kŭmgŏl-network station.

Therefore, Tanchon became a potential candidate for investments from abroad and from the Republic of Korea. In the early stages of the Agreed Framework between the United States of America and the Democratic People's Republic of Korea, the DPR Korea proposed to the United States of America that it invest in two mines and a port in the Tanchon area (The Hankyoreh May 8, 2006). In 2006, Tanchon was in discussion as a "special joint resource development district" (The Hankyoreh May 8, 2006). In 2007, a South Korean delegation visited the regions of Taehŭng, Kŏmdŏk and Ryongyang, to investigate the areas in terms of joint projects between North and South Korea.

Located in Tanchon-si, Kŭmgol-dong, is the Kŏmdŏk Mining Complex, a leading mineral producer of the DPR Korea. In this region, numerous mineral resources are kept. At first, silver was mined on a small scale in Kŏmdŏk-valley. In 1932, the Kŏmdŏk Mine was put into operation. First, silver was mined, then lead and zinc (KCNA 6th April 2010). The Kŏmdŏk Mining Complex is one of the most important zinc mines in the world (KOFC 2010, 482). The mine is 98 km away from the port Kimchaek (Choe Kyŏng-su 2011, 245). Overall, the DPRK has a total of 8% of the world reserves of zinc. (SNKECSA (2011, 33). Among the eight major zinc mines, four are in the city of Tanchon.[99]

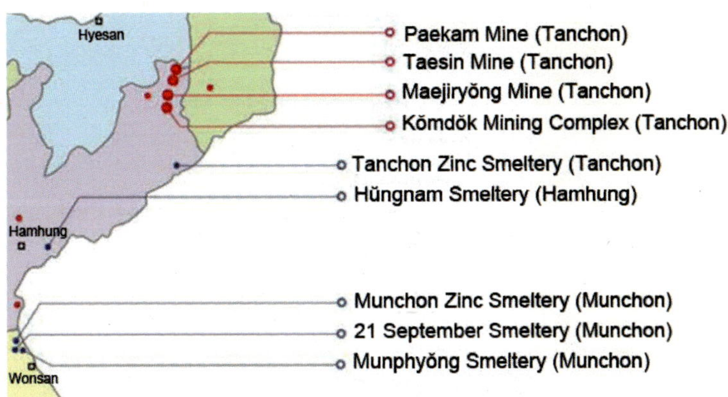

Figure Tanchon-II. Zinc mines and zinc smelteries in Northeast-Korea (source: SNKECSA (2011, 39).

The zinc ores, which are extracted in the Kŏmdŏk Mining Complex, are smelted in the Tanchon Smeltery, but also in the smelteries of Munchon and Hamhung. The Tanchon Zinc Smeltery is, after the Munpyŏng Smeltery, the one smeltery, which smelts the most zinc in the DPR Korea. Also gold is extracted in Kŏmdŏk, which is smelted in Munphyŏng (SNKECSA 2011, 56).

In Tanchon are the two most important magnesite mines in the DPR Korea, the Ryongyang Mine and the Taehŭng Youth Hero Mine. Magnesite is a mineral with high temperature resistance, which contains the metallic constituent magnesium. It is therefore used for the production of refractory bricks, with which, *inter alia*, smelting furnaces are lined. North Korea is after Russia and China the country with the most deposits of magnesite. According to estimates by the U.S. Geological Survey, these are 19% of the world reserves. However, the annual production is relatively low. This is connected with the fact that the further processing complexes are outdated, and that a large energy shortfall consists and the key markets are uncertain. In the 1980s, North Korea has produced over 2 million tons of magnesia per year at the Tanchon Magnesia Clinker Factory and sold to Eastern Europe. Meanwhile, the annual production dropped to only 120,000 tons. Also, it lacks the necessary cokes for the Magnesia Clinker production For the production of cokes, bituminous coal is needed, which does not exist in North Korea and has to be im-

99 The other four zinc mines are the Kyesaeng Mine (Jagang), the Sŏngchŏn Mine (Phyongnam), the Ŭnpha Mine (Hwangbuk) and the Rakyŏn Mine (Hwangnam).

ported. With the collapse of socialism in Eastern Europe and the economic crisis in North Korea the coke couldn't be imported anymore and thus the magnesia clinker - the production collapsed. With North Korean coal magnesia clinker of low quality was produced, which sold poorly. In recent years, a processing on commission is performed with Chinese institutions and Chinese capital (Choe Kyŏng-su 2011, 278-281).

All major magnesite mines in the DPR Korea are in Tanchon or its surroundings.

Figure Tanchon-III. Magnesite Mines and Magnisa Clinker Factories in Northeast Korea (source: SNKECSA 2011, 104)

The Ryongyang Mine has an annual capacity (concentrate) of 300,000 tons (2006). In 1988, it was still at 2.5 million tons. There are two ore processing plants. Ore dressing plant no. 1 was commissioned in 1988 and ore dressing plant no. 2 in 1983 (KOFC 2010, 486).[100] The Taehung Youth Hero Mine was developed in the 1980s (KOFC 2010, 487).[101] By train the distance from the mine to the port Kimchaek are 98 km (Ryongyang Mine) or 128 km (Taehung Youth Hero Mine) (Choe Kyŏng-su 2011, 280).

Magnesite is an important export good of the DPR Korea. Around 1993, magnesite was exported with a value of approximately USD $8 million to France, Japan and Romania (Chosun Ilbo November 27, 1995).

Not only the extraction of magnesite but also the production of magnesia products is maintained in Tanchon or its surroundings.

The Tanchon Magnesia Factory produces a wide range of goods made from magnesite. Originally, this plant was built in 1942 by the Japanese and heavily destroyed during the Korean War.

In July 1954, the reconstruction was completed and the operation was resumed. In 1980, facilities from the Federal Republic of Germany and of Austria were introduced in a

100 S. KCNA April 21, 2010.

101 S. KCNA June 1, 2012.

Table Tanchon-VI. Magnesia/Refractory Factories in the DPR Korea (source: SNKECSA 2011, 102)

Magnesia/Refractory Factory	Place	Mine, from which the raw material comes	Magnesite Clinker production capacity (year)
Tanchon Magnesia Factory	Tanchon Hanggu-dong	Taehŭng, Ryongyang	2,000,000 tons
Sŏngjin Refractory Factory	Kimchaek Chŏnghak-dong	Ssangryong, Namgye, Saengjang, Taehŭng, Ryongyang	300,000 tons
Taehŭng Magnesia Factory	Tanchon Taehŭng-dong	Taehŭng	100,000 tons
Chongjin Refractory Factory	Chongjin		50,000-100,000 tons
Ryongyang Magnesia Factory	Tanchon Tonsan-dong	Ryongyang	12,000 tons

value of 66 million dollars and an annual production capacity that is estimated at 2,000,000 tons was achieved (Chosun Ilbo November 27, 1995).

A large part of the production is exported to China in the meanwhile. In 2010, the DPR Korea exported over 130,000 tons of magnesite ore and clinker worth over 21.5 million U.S. dollars to the PR China (SNKECSA 2011, 105). The Tongam Mine is by far the largest apatite mine in the DPR Korea. In 1980, they began with their development. The mine supplies the Hungnam Fertilizer Factory and the Tanchon Phosphatic Fertilizer Factory. By train to Tanchon Fertilizer Factory it is about 40 km and to Kimchaek port 70 km. The Tongam station can be reached by truck or by cableway (Choe Kyŏng-su 2011, 284).[102]

Extension of the port

Until now, one was dependent on the port of Kimchaek concerning the supply of mines and factories in Tanchon with equipment from abroad as well as the removal of products by ship. In July 2009, the extension of the Tanchon port officially began. (Pyongyang Times February 26, 2011). In May 2012, the construction was officially completed.

The Japan-based North Korea-friendly Choson Sinbo made it clear that "Tanchon will become a key transit point in shipping goods to and from Russia's Siberia, the northeastern part of China and Mongolia" (Yonhap April 25, 2013) In particular, mineral resources (e.g. processed magnesite goods) are exported to China . It was predicted that the "areas will

102 S. SNKECSA (2011, 125-139).

become a new industrial zone with many new plants" (Yonhap April 25, 2013).

The importance of the construction of the harbor of Tanchon, was also made clear during the New Year speech of 2013 by Kim Jong-un, its completion particularly was mentioned next to the construction of the Huichon Power Station.

Development before the city designation in 1982

In 1982, Tanchon was designated as a city (*si*). Tanchon-kun, of which the city was formed, has been reduced during the process of the municipal reform in 1952, in favor of the newly formed Hŏchŏn-kun, which got one *myon*, and Kwangchŏn-kun, which got three *myon*, and also for the benefit of Paekam-kun (Ryanggang province), which got four *ri*. In 1974, Kwangchŏn-kun was again merged with the Tanchon-kun. Between 1952 and 1967, six *rodongjagu* had been created in Kwangchŏn-kun. Also in 1974, Tanchon had to award three *ri* to the Riwŏn-kun, of which two of them were returned in February 1981.

Before the city designation, Tanchon already had ten urbanized areas, Tanchon-up and nine *rodongjagu*.

1952-1982 Tanchon-up (1)
1952-1982 Kwangchŏn-up (since 1974 Kwangchŏn-rodongjagu) (2)
1952-1982 Sindŏk-rodongjagu (since 1972 Kŭmdŏk-rodongjagu (3)
1961-1982 Taehŭng-rodongjagu (4)
1961-1982 Ryongyang-rodongjagu (5)
1961-1982 Ryongdae-rodongjagu (6)
1961-1982 Tuŏn-rodongjagu (7)
1967-1982 Phogŏ-rodongjagu (8)
1967-1982 Tongam-rodongjagu (9)
1967-1982 Jikjŏl-rodongjagu (10)

From North to South, Tanchon's major urbanization centers reveal:

- former Taehŭng-rodongjagu with the Taehŭng Youth Hero Mine (magnesite)
- former Kŭmdŏk-rodongjagu with the Kŏmdŏk Mining Complex (lead, zinc)
- former Ryongyang-rodongjagu with the Ryongyang Mine (magnesite)
- former Tongam-rodongjagu with the Tongam Mine (apatite)
- former Kwangchon-up: here the provincial factories are crowded, food and consumer goods are produced to supply the population of Tanchon (Chosun Ilbo November 27, 1995), e.g. Kwangchŏng Foodstuff Factory
- former Tanchon-up (administrative center of the city, Tanchon Railway Station,

Tanchon Mining Factory)

- former Tuŏn-rodongjagu (Tanchon Smeltery, Tanchon Magnesia Factory, Tanchon Port)

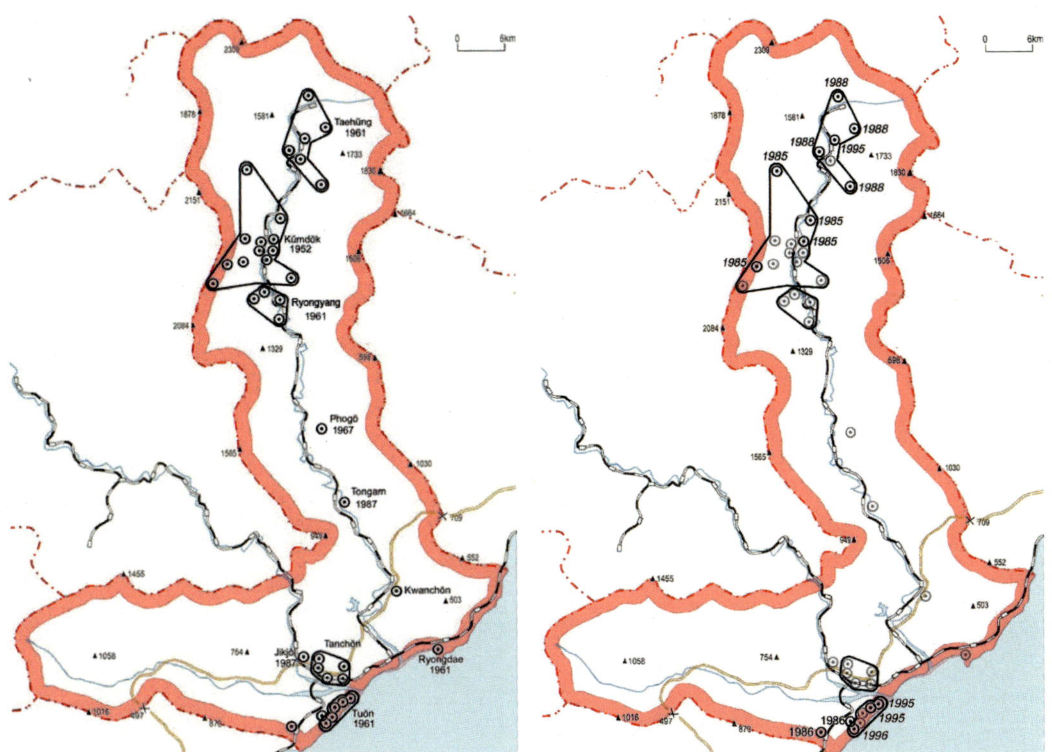

Figure Tanchon-IV. *Dong* and former *rodongjagu* in Tanchon

Figure Tanchon-V. New founded *dong* after designation of Tanchon as city

Developments after the city's designation in 1982

In 1982, when the city Tanchon was founded, the *up* and the *rodongjagu* were transformed into *dong* or divided into several *dong*. Consequentially a total of 25 *dong* were formed. Until 2002, further 14 *dong* came into being. Nine of these 14 new *dong* originated in the north of the city, five in the South.

In the North, the areas of the former Kŭmdŏk-rodongjagu (four new *dong*) and Taehŭng (five new *dong*) were affected. In 1985, four new *dong* were created by separating from existing *dong* in the area of the former Kŭmdŏk-rodongjagu. In the same way, the number of *dong* in the former Taehŭng-rodongjagu increased in 1988 by four *dong* and in 1995 by another dong.

In the early 1980s, a new city was built in the south of the city center towards the seashore. The area was called Sin-Tanchon ("New Tanchon") and resembles the dimensions of multi-storey estates in Seoul. There are high-rise buildings with 10-15 floors, these are, *inter alia*, accommodations for the workers of the neighboring Tanchon Smeltery, which was also built in the 1980s. However since a business network and further community facilities did not follow, the encouragement from the population was not particularly large (Chosun Ilbo November 27, 1995). In this context, two new *dong* were created from parts of Ryongyŏn-ri in 1986. In 1982, the Tuŏn-rodongjagu was split into the Tuŏn-dong and the Hanggu-dong (dockland area). In 1985, Tuŏn-dong was renamed in Haean-dong (coast district). In 1995, the Hanggu-dong was divided into three *dong* and in 1996 the Haean-dong into two *dong*, so that between 1995 and 1996 in the territory of the former Tuŏn-rodongjagu three new *dong* emerged. The expansion of mining in the north of the city became apparent particularly in the 1980s and to a lesser extent also in the 1990s, due to these formations of the *dong*,

Also in the 1980s, Sin-Tanchon has been developed. The 1990s mainly showed an expansion of the coastal region around the harbor.

Statistics

	Dong-Formation	*Dong*-Splitting
1982 (25)	-	(15)
1985 (29)	-	4
1986 (31)	2	-
1988 (35)	-	4
1995 (38)	-	3
1996 (39)	-	1

Tanchon – mining town with new port

Tanchon is dominated by mining and the raw materials processing industry. Particularly in the 1980s, Tanchon experienced an upsurge, when numerous mining products were exported. During this time, many plants were built or expanded. Tanchon became a city, thus new city districts were developed. However from the 1990s the production and the export fell. Now the DPR Korea is trying to develop mining and processing with the help from Chinese capital. An important indication for this is the completion of the renovation of the port in 2012.

IV.2.25. Sinpho

Most famous fishing harbor of North Korea

Sinpho has been known as a fishing port since ancient times. In October 1960 Sinpho-si was founded from a part of Sinpho-kun. In 1994 Sinpho came to public notice due to the "Agreed Framework between the United States of America and the Democratic People's Republic of Korea." Due to the agreement two 1000 MW light water reactors (LWR) power plants were to be built in the north-eastern part of Sinpho. In 2003 however, the project was cancelled. In this context, Kŭmho-jigu was outsourced from a part of Sinpho from the municipal area in September 1995.[103] The remaining part of the city is marked by fishing, fish processing and ship building.

Sinpho is a city with few inhabitants, and has a small area and a minor proportion of rural inhabitants.

Table Sinpho-I. Basic data

Population	152,759 (Rank 24)
Area	218 km² (Rank 23)
Population density	701 I./km² (Rank 12)
Administrative units	16 *dong*/6 *ri* (73%) (Rank 11)
"Urban" population/"rural" population	85.7%/14.3% (Rank 11)

The topographic structure of this city is very simple. The biggest part of the municipal area is occupied by a plain, which does not exceed the height of 100 m above sea level. When moving from the coast towards North and West, the terrain gradually increases. In the western border area of the city runs the Kŏdubong mountain range with the Jong-san (703 m), the highest mountain of the city in the Northwest. Here, the East Sea coast is relatively moved. The Yanghwa bay as well as the Sondo cape have formed here. The Sinpho port is protected by the Mayang island, which has a size of 8 km² and lies in front of the port (IPA-12 2003, 257-258).

Table Sinpho-II. Climate values

Annual average	January temperature	August temperature	Precipitation
9.7℃ (11)	−3.2℃ (3)	22.4℃ (21)	737 mm (22)

Due to maritime influence, the winter is mild and the summer is cool.

103 More to Sinpho Nuclear Power Plant see Lee, Jeong-sik (2000, 500-502).

Figure Sinpho-1. Forest area in the *ri*

The forest covers about 60% of the area and consists partly of pine trees or oaks.

This region was always known as a fishing grounds. Because of the rich fishing grounds numerous fisherman families lived for a long time especially in Sinpho bay and Yanghwa bay. Agriculture has developed on the banks of the Tongdae-chŏn, which flows at Phungŏ-dong in the West of the city into the East Sea (IPA-12 2003, 258-259).

As specialised crop, there is a mushroom farm in the city (KCNA June 12, 2007).

Sinpho area – a basis for the fishing industry

In Sinpho city there are not only the Sinpho Fishery Station and the Yanghwa Fishery Station as well as fishermen's cooperatives, culture farms and fishing sub-workteams, but also numerous fishery companies, which operate from various smaller and larger ports. The Sinpho Fishery Station is the biggest fishing base of the DPR Korea. At the end of the 19th century, a fishing village arose there and in 1936 first a fishery, where thousands of fishermen worked, was set up among the Japanese in order to exploit the Korean sea resources. After 1945 the business was further expanded. It also has a fish processing facility, which produces a wide product range (IPA-12 2003, 260-261). The Yanghwa Fishery Station was initially formed in 1947 as operational unit of a precursor of the Sinpho Fishery Station and is since 1952 an independent company. It is one of the largest of its kind of the DPR Korea. From 1968 docks were built, which enable bigger ships for deep-sea-fishing to land (IPA-12 2003, 261). Another Fishery Station is situated in Ryukdae1-dong (IPA-12 2003, 259 and 266). In Sinpho especially high sea fishery is carried out, since the "sea off Sinpho is Korea's leading Pollack fishing ground" (KCNA March 24, 1998). Fishing in Sinpho is possible throughout the year. Important products of the fish processing industry are "frozen fish, pickled fish, fish-powder and salted fish eggs" (KCNA March 24, 1998). Of major importance for the fish processing is the Sinpho Canned Fish Factory, which was built in 1953. From mackerel, trout, Yellowtail or flounders etc from the East Sea a huge variety of goods are produced. Also, in the bays of the city are breeding ponds, especially for seaweed and kelp (IPA-12 2003, 259-260). Furthermore in Sinpho there are a number of research institutes and educational establishments, which focus on the fishery industry. The Fishery Machine Research Institute explores methods for the mechanization of production in the area of the fishery industry. In 1969 it was officially opened. The Aquatic Products Processing Institute was originally a subdivision of the Tonghae (East Sea) Fishery Institute (founded in 1946), which is resident in Wonsan (s. KCNA July 14, 2008) and became independent in 1968. The Sinpho University of Fisheries was founded in 1979 and trains particularly employees of the fisheries undertakings, which are located in Sinpho, in fishery-specific technologies. The port Sinpho was expanded as fishing port as well as commercial port and is of regional significance.

Fish processing and shipbuilding

Fishing and the processing of fish, the construction and the repair of ships as well as the production of fishing equipment are the main industrial sectors of the city. In addition to that there are factories of local relevance, which produce food, goods for the daily need, medicine, chemical products, clothes, paper and building materials, in which the food processing is of particular importance. Besides seafood, also fruits and vegetables are processed (IPA-12 2003, 259).

Table Sinpho-III. Ranking (in parenthesis: number of industrial companies or cultural institutions)

Sinpho	KOFC	MOU	IPA	KCNA	KIET	Summary
Companies-total	22 (7)	27 (3)	27 (2)	27 (1)	26 (13)	26
Companies-important	16 (2)	24 (0)	26 (1)		27 (2)	27 (1)
Cultural institutions			14 (6)			

Table Sinpho-IV. Ranking (Total number of companies in relation to population)

Sinpho	KOFC	MOU	IPA	KCNA	KIET	Summary
Companies-total	17	27	27-26-10	27	25-27	27-26

In most of the sources Sinpho has a lower rank in industrial companies than in terms of population (rank 24).

Table Sinpho-V. Specification (in parenthesis: number of industrial companies)

Sinpho	Light Industry	Heavy Industry	Mining	Energy
KOFC	2 (4)	22 (3)	-	-
MOU	24 (1)	1 (2)	-	-
IPA	1 (2)	-	-	-
KCNA	1 (1)	-	-	-
KIET	1 (9)	26 (3)	8 (1)	-

Due to the low number of important companies in Sinpho, the fish processing companies and shipyards are very significant. Both define the city, so that there is no talk of an orientation to light or heavy industry and the sources depending on the orientation contradict. The naval repair yards of Sinpho are not mentioned especially in the North Korean sources.

In chapter III.7.3. only the Sinpho Canned Fish Factory was ascertained as an important company.

Sinpho – DPR Koreas Submarine Production Base

Sinpho has an important role not just for fishing, but also for shipbuilding, in particular the construction of submarines. The statements are however inconsistent regarding in which factories submarines are actually produced. On the one hand the Sinpho Shipyard is mentioned. It is located in Ryŏnho-dong and is said to be specialized in fishing boats as well as navy ships. Approximately 1,500 workers are employed there. From 1980 *inter alia* submarines, small undersea vehicles, air-cushion vehicles are produced there (An Yun-sŏk 2011). Also the Mayang-do Shipyard is considered a production site of submarines. The Mayang-do Naval Base on the north side of the island "provides operation and logistical support for submarines, antisubmarine craft, and patrol craft" (GlobalSecurity.com n.d.). On the other hand there are reports, according to which in Sinpho solely the Pongdae Boiler Factory, which is located in Ryukdae2-dong, produces submarines. The name of course is a cover. Its former name was Ryukdae-ri Shipyard. The annual production capacity is said to be four to five submarines per year. When on 26th March 2010 the Chŏnan, a Republic of Korea Navy warship, was sunk in the Yellow Sea, with 46 seamen being killed, there was speculation that the warship had been sunk by a North Korean torpedo fired by a midget submarine, which is said to have been produced in the Pongdae Boiler Factory (Ju Yong-jung/Yi Yong-su 2010).

City with numerous cultural institutions

Relatively high is the number of cultural institutions in Sinpho. In addition to numerous research and educational establishments relating to the fishing, especially the Kim Hyong Kwon University of Education is noteworthy. It is the college, where the teachers for the higher classes are trained in schools of the Hamnam Province. This college was founded in Hamhung in 1961, resettled in 1965 to the Sinhung-kun and in 1967 to Sinpho. In 1990, the name Hamnam University of Education Nr. 1 was changed to Kim Hyong Kwon University of Education, in memory of the anti-Japanese fighter Kim Hyong-kwon (1905-

1936), an uncle of Kim Il-sung[104] (IPA-12 2003, 261).

Structural Analysis

In October of 1960, the city Sinpho was founded from a part of Sinpho-kun. In January of 1974, eight *ri* of the Sinchang-kun were added to Sinpho-si, which then formed the Kŭmho-jigu in September 1995. In the same year, a further *ri* was added from Sinpho-si (Honam-ri) to Kŭmho-jigu.

Rodongjagu that existed before Sinpho became a city

In 1952 three *rodongjagu* were founded: Ryuktae, Tongho and Mayang. In 1953 Mayang-rodongjagu again became a *ri* and Ryŏnho became a *rodongjagu.*

At the founding of the city in 1960, the *up* was split up in four *dong* (Haeam, Ŏhang, Phohang, Haesan), Ryŏnho-rodongjagu in two (Ryŏnho-dong and Kwangbok-dong) and Sinhŭng-dong was formed from parts of the *up* and Ryŏnho-rodongjagu. The former *rodongjagu* Ryuktae and Tongho became *dong*, and Ryŏngmu-dong (in 1977 renamed Phungŏ-dong) was newly created.

After becoming a city, in 1971 a *rodong-jagu* again was founded (Mayang), which was trans- formed to a *dong* in 1974. Haeam-dong and Ryuktae-dong were split up in 1967, Kwangbok-dong and Tongho-dong in 1991. Yangji-dong was created in the same year by the splitting of Ryuktae1-dong.

The *rodongjagu* are located on the coast or on an island and seem to be for the most part associated with the fishing and the shipbuilding.

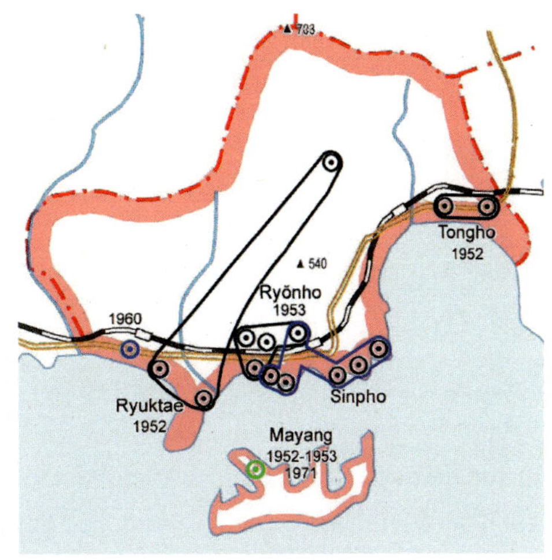

Figure Sinpho-II. *Dong* and the former *rodongjagu*

104 In the same year, also the Phungsan-kun (Ryanggang-do) was renamed Kimhonggwon-kun.

Structure

The center is the old *up* (Sinpho) and the former Ryŏnho-rodongjagu in the West. Further West and in the downtown is the area of the former Ryuktae-rodongjagu, whereas the former Tongho-rodongjagu is located on the eastern border of the city. The Mayang island was a *rodongjagu* between 1952 and 1953 and from 1971 until 1974 and is since that time a *dong*.

Urbanized areas before the city founding (*up* and *rodongjagu*)
1952-1960 Sinpho-up
1952-1960 Ruktae-rodongjagu
1952-1960 Tongho-rodongjagu
1952-1953 Mayang-rodongjagu
1953-1960 Ryŏnho-rodongjagu

Statistics

	Dong-Formation	*Dong*-Splitting
1960 (10)	1	(5)
1967 (12)	-	2
1971 (13)	1	-
1991 (16)	-	3

Sinpho – small town on the East Sea coast

Sinpho is an important fishing port on the East Sea coast. Moreover, there probably are submarine shipyards, which are however not mentioned in the North Korean press as well as in the depiction of the industry of North Korea and thus are not included in the statistics. In 1991 three new *dong* are created, but they are not adjoining the area, so that there can be no talk of a certain growth pole. The Kŭmho-jigu, famous for the initially planned assembling of light water reactors, was originally part of Sinpho-si, but has been separated from it.

IV.2.26. Wonsan

Capital of Kangwon Province (North)

Wonsan is the capital of the Kangwon Province of the DPR Korea. A province with the same name exists in South Korea as well. Wonsan, Munchon and their surroundings were originally parts of the Hamnam Province. Since 1946 though they belong to Kangwon.

Table Wonsan-I. Basic data

Population	363,127 (Rank 5)
Area	314 km² (Rank 19)
Population density	1156 I./km² (Rank 7)
Administrative units	45 *dong*/14 *ri* (76%) (Rank 9)
"Urban" population/"rural" population	90.5%/9.5% (Rank 5)

The built-up urban area of Wonsan borders on the hills of Jangdŏk-san and the Tongmyŏng-san[105] and has developed from South to North along the elongated coast. Originally Wonsan consisted of two parts.

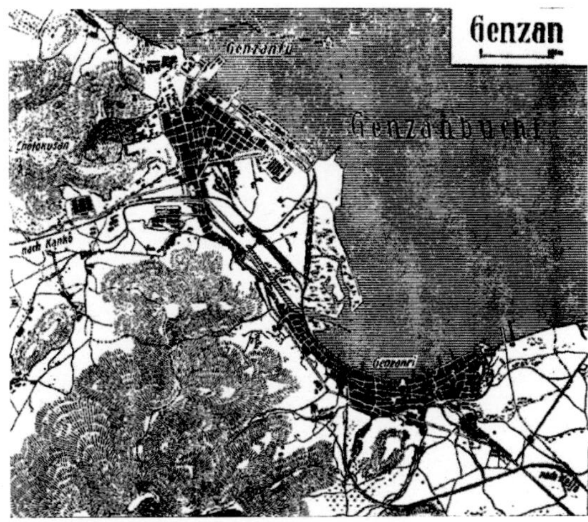

Figure Wonsan-I. Wonsan (according to an official plan); (Source: Lautensach 1945, 298)

Before the opening of the port by the Japanese, Wonsan consisted only of a poor fishing and farming village. In 1898 this village already counted 15,000 residents in 3,000 homes. It was a big village with a very large square in the center, on which every five days a market was held.

The concession area of the Japanese is about 6 km to the North. It was located in a reed field, which was drained after the opening of the port. In this part of the city the port Wonsan was built and it remained the center of the city until today. The port was

105 The mountain was originally named Pukmang-san and was renamed in January 1987 to Tongmyŏng-san. Tongmyŏng means "the East is bright." Written with Chinese characters, Pukmang is written with the character 邙, which has a harmless meaning and is used for mountain names. However, the character 亡 has the same pronunciation. And the meaning of this character is "spoil, go broke," so that Pukmang, without considering the correct Chinese character is not used since they are not in common use in North Korea, can be misinterpreted as "the North is broke."

opened on May 1st 1880 for trade with Japan, and on November 3rd 1883 for the entire international trade. Since the terrain was low and moist, many Japanese settlers suffered from malaria. In 1897 the number of Japanese residents amounted to 235. On January 1st 1900 there were already 1,560 Japanese living there. Next to the Japanese settlement, some Chinese traders lived in a small valley. In 1890 the quay was built, in 1910 the 27 m long Chan-bridge, in 1912 the long stone mole that protects against waves and drift ice from the North, in 1921 the harbor construction was completed after several additional buildings and until 1945 ships up to 20,000 tons could dock there.

Economically, the Japanese have not benefited much from the port and the concession area in Wonsan, but from the beginning Wonsan played a major role as military strategic points. The construction of the Japanese concession area blocked the advancement of Russia and during the Sino-Japanese War, Wonsan was, together with Pusan and Inchon, a base for the landing of Japanese troops (Yun Jŏng-sŏp 1987, 114).

In 1914 a railway line (223 km) was built through by Chugaryŏng tectonic valley; it connects Wonsan with Seoul. Before the Wŏlla railway line (Wonsan-Rajin) was opened in 1933, the port of Wonsan was the number 1 port of favor in Northeast Korea. After opening the Wŏlla line, it stagnated due to the reduction of the hinterland because of the rapid development of the port Chongjin. The establishment of industrial enterprises increased the population influx. In 1923 Wonsan counted 31,000 inhabitants, in 1936 it were 61,000, in 1940 it were 79,000 and in 1942, 122,000 (Saitschikow 1958, 277).

Wonsan Bay

Wonsan is situated in Wonsan Bay (also called Yŏnghŭng Bay), which is surrounded by the foothills and mountains of the Masikryŏng chain in the West. The bay is embraced in the North by the emerging 16 km long Hodo Peninsula and the protruding Kalma Peninsula in the South. About 20 large and small islands such as Modo, Thaedo, Sindo and Ryŏdo are located at the bay entrance. The bay is therefore protected by a natural breakwater against wind and waves.

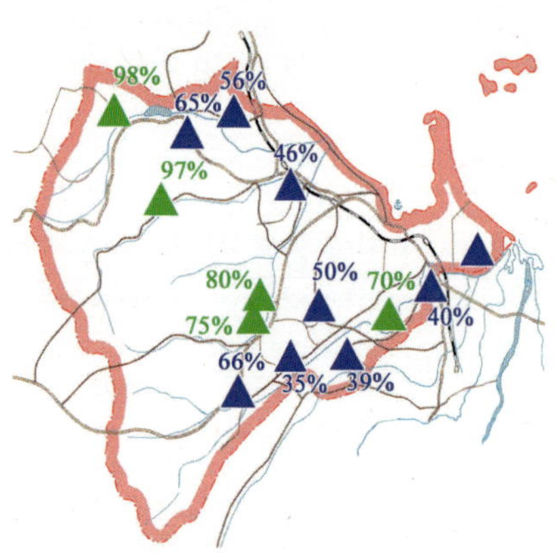

Figure Wonsan-II. Forest area in the *ri*

A characteristic feature of the climate of Wonsan's landscape are the frequent foehn winds, which fall mainly in spring and late autumn from the warm and dry passes of the main watershed into the Japanese Sea coast. They are of great importance for the growth and ripening of the crops. The winter of the Wonsan landscape is milder, summers are a bit cooler than at the coasts of Taedong-basin that are located the same latitude (Lautensach 1945, 300).

Table Wonsan-II. Climate values

Annual average	January temperature	August temperature	Precipitation
11°C (2)	−2.3°C (1)	23.2°C (16)	1,426.1 mm (2)

Walnuts – a special product of the city of Wonsan

Cultivation fields account for 18% of the total city area, on which rice, corn, vegetables, fruit and as important specialized crop, walnuts are grown. Figure Wonsan-III shows the rice development areas (dark blue) in the lowest lying areas. In the lowlands in the north of the municipal area both rice and corn are grown in greater quantities (light blue). In the southwest of the municipal area a region specialized in vegetable growing is located (red). Specialties of Wonsan are walnuts that are grown in the central areas of the city area (brown). In areas, in which rice cultivation is no longer possible without restriction, corn is the main crop (yellow).

The confluence of warm and cold ocean currents in front of Wonsan bay ensured favorable conditions for fishing. Until the early 1980s, the fishing companies of Wonsan boomed. They mainly caught flounder, sardines, Alaskan Pollack, herring and anchovies. Since the mid-1980s the situation for the fisheries has gotten worse. Accumulations of rivers opening into the East Sea, such as the Anbyon-Namdae-chŏn, affected the sea in the Wonsan bay to become flat, which had negative effects on the coastal fisheries particularly since the mid-1980s (Chosun Ilbo January 29, 1996).

Figure Wonsan-III. Agriculture in the *ri* of Wonsan city

Industrial zone of the second degree

Wonsan with its specialization on engineering and shipbuilding, Munchon with its non-ferrous metal smelting facilities and Chonnae-kun with its production of cement, form one of the industrial zones of North Korea. Important location factors for these industries are the mineral resources such as the coal field of Kowŏn, south of the Chonnae-kun, and limestone in Chonnae-ri; of great importance for the electric power supply are the hydropower plants of Kŭmgangsan and Jangjingang and for industrial water supply the Yŏnghŭng-gang. Relatively good transport connection provides the highway between Pyongyang-Wonsan, the Kangwon railway line and the port of Wonsan. (KOTRA 1995, 30) Since Wonsan also occupies the function of a city of tourism, culture and recreation, the industrial zone of Wonsan is classified by importance and extent as a second degree industrial zone. (KOTRA 1995, 28)

In Wonsan important companies in the field of railway carriages, shipbuilding, tractor production and chemistry are located. Important industrial sectors of the light industry are mainly the textile industry, the production of televisions, the food industry and the wood processing industry.

Table Wonsan-III. Ranking (in parenthesis: number of industrial companies or cultural institutions)

Wonsan	KOFC	MOU	IPA	KCNA	KIET	Summary
Companies-total	5 (27)	7 (31)	10 (19)	7 (15)	7 (46)	5
Companies-important	8 (5)	12 (3)	3 (13)		7 (20)	5 (12)
Cultural institutions			5 (19)			

Table Wonsan-IV. Ranking (Total number of companies in relation to population)

Wonsan	KOFC	MOU	IPA	KCNA	KIET	Summary
Companies – total	3	11	11-5-7	8	13-10	8-3

Table Wonsan-V. Specification (in parenthesis: number of industrial companies)

Wonsan	Light Industry	Heavy Industry	Mining	Energy
KOFC	11 (7)	19 (14)	11 (1)	3 (5)
MOU	6 (22)	13 (9)	–	–
IPA	17 (7)	4 (12)	–	–
KCNA	9 (8)	14 (5)	–	10 (2)
KIET	9 (21)	8 (25)	–	–

Although Wonsan is the city with the fifth-highest population of the DPR Korea, it ranks in the industrial companies ranking usually on the further lower ranked places. The focus of the city is on tourism so this will play a role here. In the city, both light and heavy industry companies are represented, so that Table-V Wonsan shows no clear specialization in one of the two industrial sectors.

In chapter III.7.3. twelve companies were identified as important: Wonsan Rolling Stock Complex, Wonsan Shipyard, Wonsan Ship Repair Factory, Wonsan Chungsŏng

Tractor Factory, Kŭmgang Motor Joint Venture Company, Wonsan Electro Cables Factory, Wonsan Chemical Factory, Wonsan Disabled Soldiers' Essential Plastic Goods Factory, Wonsan Shoes Factory, Wonsan Knitting Mill, Wonsan Export Garment Factory, Wonsan Disabled Soldiers' Bags Factory.

In the Wonsan Rolling Stock Complex (June 4th Rolling Stock Complex), situated in the city center in Kalmi-dong, mainly railway carriages and freight wagons are manufactured or repaired. The annual capacity of this complex is said to be about 200 railway carriages and 2,000 freight wagons. On a total area of 600,000 m² approximately 15,000 people are employed (Yun Ung 1995, 223). In the Korean War the company was evacuated to Hyesan and rebuilt after the war (IPA 11 2003, 113-114).

The Wonsan Shipyard in Haean-dong was built in 1939 and rebuilt in 1955 after the destruction of the Korean War. It is dedicated to both the construction and the repair of, inter alia, cargo ships, ships for net fishing, and all kinds of ships for the navy, and has a total area of 45,000 m² with 4,000 employees (KOFC 2010, 324-325).

In the Wonsan Chungsŏng Tractor Factory on a total area of 34,000 m² with approximately 1,000 employees tractors with 8PS are produced (KOFC 2010, 262-263). The Kŭmgang Motor Joint Venture Company is a company that is specialized on producing engines for agricultural equipment. It started its operations in 1959. Since 1993 it is operating as a joint venture enterprise with the Japanese company DIA-STAR CO., LTD., which a company that is run by Koreans living in Japan (IPA-11 2003, 113). The Wonsan Electro Cables Factory specializes in the production of cables for lamps (IPA-11 2003, 116).

The Wonsan Chemical Factory is located in Jangchon-dong and has a total area of 58,000 m². The Jangjingang Power Station supplies the plant with electricity. Industrial water is provided by the Namdae-chŏn. The plant was already built before 1945 and was dedicated to the production of crude oil. In 1958 the production was changed to manufacturing chromium salt products and photographic paper (KOFC 2010, 372). The Wonsan cement factory is in operation since 1990 and has a total area of 20,000m² (IPA-11 2003, 115). The Wonsan Glass Bottle Factory is frequently mentioned in the KCNA.

The Wonsan Disabled Soldiers' Essential Plastic Goods Factory was founded in 1952 and initially set up as a cooperative company for clothes manufacturing. Later it became a company that mainly produces kitchen appliances and toothbrushes in Namsan-dong (IPA 11 2003, 115-116). Further light industry enterprises are the Wonsan Shoes Factory that employs 720 persons (KOFC 2010, 610), the Wonsan Knitting Mill, that manufactures different yarns and supplies the textile factories in the Kangwon Province (IPA-11 2003, 115) and the Wonsan Export Garment Factory, which was built in 1974 and modernized in 1992 (IPA 2003-11, 115). Even televisions are assembled in Wonsan. The wood-processing industry is of importance too, which produces newsprint, cardboard and wrapping paper in Wonsan. The Wonsan Brewery was completed in 1986. Here, beer, soda and wine are produced (KOTRA 1995, 195). The Wonsan Cornstarch Factory has been in operation since 1978 (KOFC 2010, 567).

The Wonsan Youth Power Plant, which is located in Chilbong-ri, contributes significantly to the energy supply in Wonsan. Construction started in 2002. The inauguration ceremony took place in 2009 (KOFC 2010, 151).

Center of Transport and Culture

Wonsan has great potential in terms of traffic. The Chugaryŏng tectonic valley theoretically allows an easy access to Seoul, which is of course now interrupted by the DMZ. But a highway connects Wonsan with Pyongyang. There are connections from Wonsan railway station to Pyongyang and Rajin. After changing the routing, the Wonsan station was moved as well in 1945. Before 1945 the railway line grazed the southern edge of the former Japanese settlement, and a railway station was here as well: the railway line meandered between the Tongmyŏng-san in the South and the Chŏkdŏk-san in the North. This was straightened after 1945 by building a route through an approximately 2 km long tunnel at the foot of Tongmyŏng-san. The station is now about 1km northwest of the tunnel (Chosun Ilbo January 23, 1996).

Figure Wonsan-IV. Wonsan station (2012)

Figure Wonsan-V. Trolleybus Terminal (2012)

After the Korean War the port of Wonsan lost almost completely the function as a trading port, but survived as a fishing and military port.

Wonsan has four colleges of national importance with a total of 11,500 students, i.e. students from all over North Korea study here and the graduates can be employed nationwide. There are also five colleges of provincial importance with a total of 8,000 students, i.e. the students are all from Kangwon-do and the graduates are also appointed here (Chosun Ilbo January 23, 1996). The universities of the city are specialized in the areas of education, politics, agriculture, medicine, finance and engineering. There is also a research institute with the focus on marine technology. Wonsan has also a daily newspaper, a radio station, a zoo and museums.

Tourism Center Wonsan

When Koreans think of Wonsan, the seaside resorts of Myŏngsa-sibri and Songdowŏn come to mind. Myŏngsa-sibri is located about 10km from the city center at the end of Kalma Peninsula and is famous for its white sand beach and red wild roses. The pine trees in the background offer a cool-down in summer. The Kalma Peninsula extends in the east of Wonsan about 5 km into the southern part of the Wonsan Bay. Towards the end of the period of Japanese occupation this area became restricted due to an airport, which was built nearby. Even today, the area is not accessible for the population due to the military airport. But a recreation center for senior officers is located there. The airport is considered an important base for the North Korean Air Force. It is said that airplanes of the latest type are stationed here. The runway has a length of 10 km. It is about 5 km away from the center of Wonsan. Seoul would be able to be reached within 30 minutes.

The seaside resort of Songdowŏn (Song = pine; do = waves) is about 2-3 km far from the city center in northwestern direction. Songdowŏn is known for its many kilometers of white sandy beach and the pine grove, which was planted by the people here 700 years ago to hinder the sea winds and sand drifts. The width of the sandy beach is 40-100 m, not more than 1.5-2 m far from the sea coast the water depth is up to 100 m. There are several additional facilities including a Zoological Garden, an East Asian garden with an artificial lake that is a few acres large and walking trails at the neighboring mountain Jangdok-san. There are also games and sports courts in the area of the Songdowŏn seaside resort, a children's holiday home and recreation homes for the population. For the tourists, the eleven-storey hotel Songdowŏn (Category C-Hotel with 164 rooms) was built in Wonsan Phyŏngchŏn-dong on the northern city border right at the beach in 1963 (Chosun Ilbo January 23, 1996). Next to it the Tongmyŏng Hotel is located, which is opened for tourists too.

Above all Wonsan is an important starting point for trips to the Kŭmgang-san.

Compared with the dimensions of the city there are not many residents in Wonsan. The reason for this relatively small population is known to be the fact that Kim Il-sung, who visited this region in 1967, instructed to establish Wonsan as an international port city and a city of culture and recreation, and therefore to regulate the population to about 150,000. Because of this objective there are hardly any new larger industrial plants in Wonsan (Chosun Ilbo January 23, 1996). The plans were carried out on the occasion of

Kim Il-sung's visit in Wonsan in October 1978. He set the direction in which Wonsan should develop:

- to promote Wonsan as a starting point for the developing tourism in the Kŭmgangsan region,
- to establish Wonsan as the largest seaside resort city of the DPR Korea and
- to promote Wonsan as an international port city of culture.

Therefore, the following measures should be promoted

- reshaping of Yŏkjŏn Street, Haebang street and Haean Street,
- focus on developing an East Coast General Tourism Development Zone, which include the Songdowon, Songchondong Valley, eight landmarks of Kwandong and the Kŭmgangsan as well as
- the construction of a resort village, the upgrading of facilities of the beach resorts and the expansion of various utilities (Kim Wŏn 1998, 248-249).

Furthermore, when the South Korean President Roh Moo-hyun suggested at the inter-Korean summit in October 2007 to build an industrial park, such as the one in Kaesong, in Wonsan, his proposal was dismissed from the North Korean side with the remark that Wonsan is a "holiday destination" (Jeong, Yong-Soo 2013).

In 2013 a "General blueprint for the Wonsan District" emerged, which should further promote the development of Wonsan into a tourist destination.

For this purpose, aging factories, especially heavy industry factories such as automobile plants and shipyards, shall be closed and also the relocation of the military airport of the Kalma Peninsula to regions that are closer to the DMZ is planned. Concretely, three special districts in Wonsan are planned:

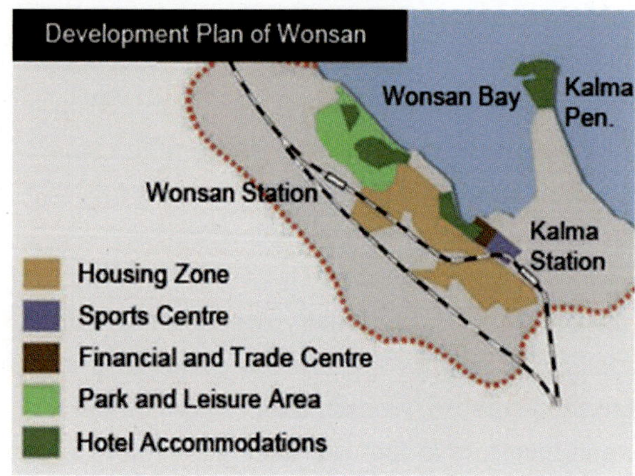

Figure Wonsan-VI. Development Plan; modified version of a figure in Jŏng Yong-su (2013)

Figure Wonsan-VII. Songdowon Hotel (2012)

- a financial district,
- an entertainment and sports area and
- a tourist destination.

Kim Jong-un is quoted that he plans to develop Songdowon Beach into a holiday destination for summers and a ski resort on Mount Masik for winter (Jeong Yong-Soo, 2013). He is talking about the 20 km far from the city center, just outside the city borders on a highway to Pyongyang situated ski resort, which is currently under construction and the first phase has already been completed. Since this is supposed to have happened with breathtaking speed, the North Korean propaganda talk about the "Masikryŏng Speed," which enabled this achievement.

Figure Wonsan-VIII. Urbanized areas (light blue) and industrial areas (dark blue) (In light green: Ski Resort Masikryong, blue green stripes: the underground "Thunderbirds runway" of the Air Force Base on the East Coast) (Source: Yi Sang-jun et. al. 2012, 99; modified)

The silhouette of Wonsan is characterized by approximately 20-storey skyscrapers that were built at the foot of Tongmyŏng-san. These shall also contribute to give Wonsan an atmosphere of an international port city a la Hong Kong. Construction work of the residential high-rise apartments started in 1984, in 1987 a part was finished, but due to lack of glass and other materials for the interior, however, the final completion was delayed (Chosun Ilbo January 23, 1996).

Figure Wonsan-IX. Skyline (2012)

Figure Wonsan-X. Mural in the International Youth Camp Songdowŏn (2012)

Changes in terms of the urban area

Wonsan was removed from the Tŏkwŏn-kun and appointed to a city (*pu*) in 1912.

Before the Korean War the city area was extended three times:

- In 1939 the urban area of Wonsan is increased by incorporations from the Tŏkwŏn-kun.
- In 1943 Tŏkwŏn-kun was dissolved, parts of the *kun* go to Wonsan-pu, other parts to Munchon-kun.
- In 1946 Wonsan is merged to Kangwon Province and becomes its capital. Parts of the newly formed Munchon-kun are included into the municipal area.

In 1952 three *ri* in the southeast of Wonsan are moved to Anbyon-kun.

Wonsan was extended from 1961 to 1976 by seven *ri* from the Munchon-kun:

- 1961 four *ri* from Munchon-kun were added to Wonsan
- 1972 Munchon-kun was dissolved, parts of the *kun* go to Wonsan. When in 1976 Munchon-kun was formed again, these areas were returned to the *kun* except three *ri*. In 1991 Munchon was declared as a city (*si*).

In 1984 four *ri* from Anbyon-kun go to Wonsan-si, which now make up the southwest part of the municipal area of Wonsan and build an important role for the vegetable supply of the city.

The in 1961 from Munchon incorporated parts are regions, which are situated in the valley of the Jangrim-chŏn and around the Tŏkwŏn station. These regions are now located,

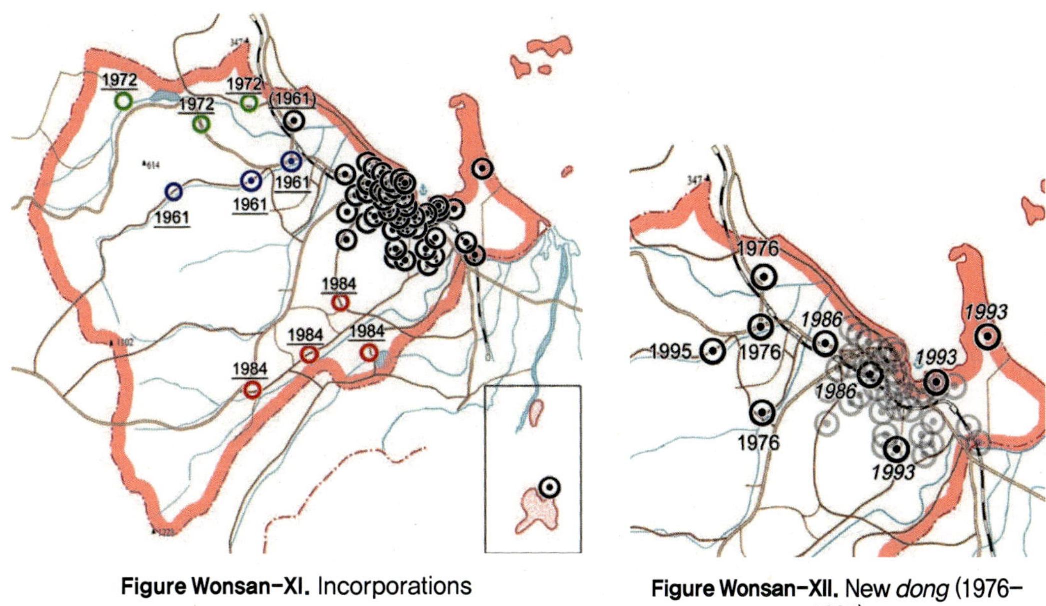

Figure Wonsan-XI. Incorporations

Figure Wonsan-XII. New *dong* (1976–1995)

where today Jangrim-ri, Sŏkhyŏn-dong, Segil-dong and parts of Songchŏn-dong located. The in 1972 incorporated parts from Munchon are three *ri* that are situated on the northern border of the city Wonsan.

Statistics

	Dong-Formation	*Dong*-Splitting
1955 (33)		
1957 (30)	-1	-3/1
1961 (35)	-	-2/7
1967 (36)	-	-1/2
1976 (39)	3	-
1986 (41)	-	2
1993 (44)	-	3
1995 (45)	1	-

Of the four newly created *dong*, which have been *ri*, two lie west of the city of Wonsan, and two in the North near the train station Tŏkwŏn.

Next to the main center of the city Wonsan in the North, separated by Jungphyŏng-ri, in which rice and vegetables for Wonsan's population are grown, lies the Tŏkwŏn region, in which German missionaries were before the Korean War, which can be seen as a smaller second development pole.

Wonsan – Great potential for tourism

Wonsan has very good requirements for further development as a tourist area. Additionally to the favorable climatic conditions, mountains and beaches are located here or nearby. Also Wonsan is easily accessible both by land and by sea.

In case of a reunification, Wonsan would also be easily accessible via the Chugaryŏng tectonic valley from Seoul.

IV.2.27. Munchon

Industrial city in the Basin of Wonsan

Munchon is considered a factory town, where steel and colors are manufactured. Especially famous is the non-ferrous metallurgy. Besides the Munphyŏng Smeltery, which is situated in the former Munphyŏng-rodongjagu, the 18th May Factory, the Munchon Zinc Smeltery, the Munchon Dye Factory and the Okphyŏng Porcelain Factory are located in Munchon. There is a building materials industry (timber) and a mechanical engineering industry, where valves, machine tools and machinery for food processing are produced. The ceramic arts and crafts in the former Okphyŏng-rodongjagu is praised as a well-known specialty. There is also a modern fishing industry in Munchon. There are mainly Alaska Pollack, cuttlefish, sand eel, flounder, herring and anchovies caught. Famous is the oyster rearing in Songjŏn Bay in the far north-east of the city area.

Among the cities of the DPR Korea only Manpho has fewer inhabitants than Munchon.

Table Munchon-I. Basic data

Population	122,934 (Rank 26)
Area	278 km² (Rank 20)
Population density	442 I./km² (Rank 16)
Administrative units	16 *dong*/14 *ri* (53%) (Rank 20)
"Urban" population/"rural" population	75.3%/24.7% (Rank 18)

The terrain is flat in comparison with other regions in the Kangwon Province. 63% of the urban area occupies surfaces, which are below the sea level of 200 m. In general, the area from Southwest to Northeast lowers gradually.

Figure Munchon-I. Landscape in the West (2012)

Figure Munchon-II. Downtown (2012)

The Masikryŏng-sanjulgi is located on the southwestern border of the urban area, which is divided in a north-eastern direction into the mountain chain of Sokko-sanjulgi and the Chŏnbul-sanjulgi and here are among others the Kulttuk-bong (772 m), Maebong-san (869 m), Sokko-san (734 m) mountains. The Masik-ryŏng, which literally means "the pass is difficult for horses to overcome, so they have to take a break" (IPA-11 2003, 177), has a height of 768m and is located between Pubang-ri (Munchon) and Jakdong-ri (Popdong-kun).

Table Munchon-II. Climate values

Annual average	January temperature	August temperature	Precipitation
10.6℃ (4)	−2.9℃ (2)	22.9℃ (17)	1,546.4 mm (1)

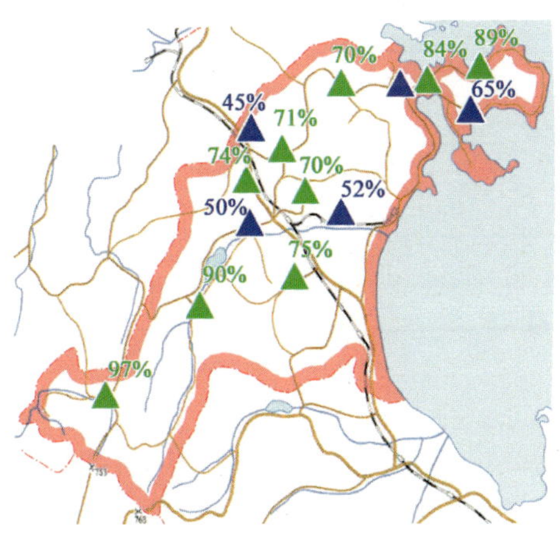

Figure Munchon-III. Forest area in the *ri*

The city has a mild oceanic climate and in the mountains in the southwest are certain features of the continental climate. The forest occupies 66% of the urban area and a large part consists of pine trees (oak and acacia). 34% of the agricultural area is occupied by wet rice cultivation, 51.2% by dry farming and 12.5% by orchards, on which 50% of the land consists of cultivated pear trees. In addition to two large Fishery establishments, there are four fishing cooperatives, aquaculture and processing facilities.

City of non-ferrous metallurgy

Three of the most important non-ferrous smelters of the DPR Korea are located in this city: the Munphyŏng Smeltery, the 21st September Smeltery and the Munchon Zinc Smeltery. Also of importance is still the fishing industry. Other important industries of the town are mechanical engineering, the chemical industry and the food industry and the production of goods for daily needs.

Table Munchon-III. Ranking (in parenthesis: number of industrial enterprises or cultural institutions)

Munchon	KOFC	MOU	IPA	KCNA	KIET	Summary
Companies-total	21 (8)	21 (10)	15 (12)	24 (3)	23 (16)	23
Companies-important	12 (3)	23 (0)	13 (6)		18 (8)	20 (4)
Cultural institutions			23 (2)			

Table Munchon-IV. Ranking (Total number of factories in relation to population)

Munchon	KOFC	MOU	IPA	KCNA	KIET	Summary
Companies – total	4	8	3-2-21	20	12-3	5-7

Munchon, especially the former Munphyŏng-rodongjagu, is an industrial city. It is therefore not surprising, that the city with the second fewest inhabitants of DPR Korea does well in the ranking of the total number of companies in proportion to the number of inhabitants. But Munchon achieved relatively poorer results in KCNA, which may suggest that the factories in Munchon are less successful lately.

Table Munchon-V. Specification (in parenthesis: number of industrial companies)

Munchon	Light Industry	Heavy Industry	Mining	Energy
KOFC	20 (1)	2 (7)	–	–
MOU	17 (5)	2 (5)	–	–
IPA	19 (4)	2 (8)	–	–
KCNA	–	1 (3)	–	–
KIET	11 (7)	4 (9)	–	–

It can be ascertained that there is a clear specialization on heavy and chemical industry regarding the industrial companies in Munchon.

In chapter III.7.3. four companies were identified as important for Munchon. In addition to the Munphyong Smeltery and the 21st September Smeltery, these are also the Munchon Dye Factory and the 18th May Factory.

The Munphyŏng Smeltery was founded in 1938 during the period of Japanese occupation after the name of Wonsan Steel Mill. During this time, they produced mainly crude copper (blister copper). The establishment was extended after the foundation of DPR Korea, so that various kinds of non-ferrous metals are now being produced. The raw materials come mainly from the mines Komdok (Tanchon) and Kaŭn (Munchon). Main products are galvanized lead and galvanized zinc. Besides melting gold and silver, fertilizer is produced here. The smeltery has about 7,300 employees (KOFC 2010, 229).

The 21st September Smeltery is right next to the Munphyŏng Smeltery, whose residue is processed by the smeltery. Construction of the plant was started in 1981. It employs about 2,500 people. Lead, zinc and gold are produced here mainly. It is considered as an establishment for the acquisition of valuta for the party, so that zinc and gold are exported to China and Japan. Factory facilities were imported from Japan in 1983 (KOFC 2010, 231-232).

The Munchon Zinc Smeltery is located 5 km north of Munphyŏng Smeltery and specializes in electro galvanizing. It consists of 15 buildings. It was built in 2004 (KOFC 2010, 240).

Colorants are produced in the Munchon Dye Factory for fabrics, for industrial use and for the coloring of houses. It was built in the 1960s (IPA-11 2003, 179-180; KJY-27 1990, 467). The 18th May Factory was built in the 1950s as the Munchon Machine Factory; later it was called Munchon Valve Factory and later it received its current name. It is a factory that specializes in valves and pipe components. (IPA 11 2003, 180; KJY-27 1990, 467).

Structural analysis Munchon

Munchon-si emerged from Munchon-kun. Munchon-kun itself had been disbanded in July 1972 and became, except for five *ri*,[106] part of Wonsan-si. In June 1976, Munchon-kun was then restored to its previous size.

At the time of dissolution of the *kun* in 1972, there were three *rodongjagu* in Munchon.

In 1952, the *rodongjagu* of Yathae (in 1958 renamed to Munphyŏng-rodongjagu) and Kaŭn[107] were established. In 1967, Okpyŏn-ri was transformed to *rodongjagu*. In the course of integration to Wonsan-si, the administrative center of the county, Munchon-up, was divided into two *rodongjagu* (Munchon and Sŏngmun). At the same time, Kaphyŏng-ri and Koam-ri became *rodongjagu*. In 1974, the latter *rodongjagu* were converted to *dong*. When

106 These five *ri* were first put into Chonnae-kun. Two of the *ri* were put in May 1974 into Wonsan-si.

107 Der Kaŭn-rodongjagu was downgraded in 1984 to Kaŭn-ri.

the Munchon-kun was then re-established in 1976, Munchon-up was formed again from Munchon-dong and Sŏngmun-dong and the other five *dong* were converted to *rodongjagu*.

The *up* and the *rodongjagu* were then reorganized into *dong* during the foundation of the city in 1991. Two *dong* were made from Sinan-ri: Sinan-dong and Pukhang-dong.

All *dong* thus arose at the foundation of the city in 1991, since then there were no other changes anymore.

Figure Munchon-IV. 18. May Factory (2012)

Figure Munchon-V. Central Street in Munchon (2012)

Figure Munchon-VI. *Dong* in Munchon

The *dong* can be divided genetically into the following units:

- the former *up* of the Munchon-kun in the Southeast
- the former *rodongjagu*

  Munphyŏng with its iron and steel mills,

  Okphyŏng, famous for its ceramic arts and its building materials factory, Koam (fishing base)

  Kaphyŏng (3 km from the former *up*). The Munchon Agar Factory is located there (KJY-27, 1990, 476).[108]
- the in 1991 emerged *dong* on the coast in the northeast of the municipal area

Figure Munchon-VII and VIII. View towards Munphyŏng (2012)

Figure Munchon-IX and X. Okphyon (2012)

108 According to the Nuclear Threat Initiative (NTI n.d. c), the Munchon Agar Factory was built after the visit of Kim Il-sung to East Germany in 1984. "During Kim's visit, he made an agreement with the East German government to acquire agar production equipment for bacterial cultures" (NTI n.d. c).

Statistics

According to the IPA, Munchon consists of 30 administrative units (16 *dong* and 14 *ri*). In PSC-8 only 27 (16 *dong* and 11 *ri*) administrative units are mentioned. Kaŭn-ri is missing in the very South, while Samdong-ri in the North and Songjuk-ri in the West find no mention in this source.

Urbanized areas before the city founding (*up* and *rodongjagu*)

1952-1991 Munchon-up (1972-1974 as Munchon-rodongjagu; 1974-1976 as Munchon-dong)
1972-1976 Sŏngmun-rodongjagu; (1974-1976 as Sŏngmun-dong); (result of the temporal division of Munchon-up into two *rodongjagu* of Wŏnsan-si)

1952-1991 Yathae-rodongjagu (from 1958 Munphyŏng-rodongjagu) (1974-1976 as Munphyŏng-dong)
1952-1984 Kaŭn-rodongjagu (1974-1976 as Kaŭn-dong)
1967-1991 Okypyŏng-rodongjagu (1974-1976 as Okyphyŏng-dong)
1972-1991 Kaphyŏng-rodongjagu (1974-1976 as Kaphyŏng-dong)
1972-1991 Koam-rodongjagu (1974-1976 as Koam-dong)

	Dong-Formation	*Dong*-Splitting
1991 (16)	2	(9)

Munchon – Small industrial city north of Wonsan

Munchon contains a basis of the North Korean non-ferrous metallurgy. Heavy industry companies characterize the city. There are also fishing companies and naval bases. Munchon is one of the smallest cities in the country and had been appointed in 1991 as a city. Temporarily it was part of the neighboring city of Wonsan.

V. Conclusion

V.1. The cities of North Korea – historical and socio-spatial aspects

The focus of the present work is an empirical study on industrial companies and on the internal structure of North Korea's cities. Furthermore, city descriptions were made taking into account not only economic and urban geography questions in the narrow sense, but also considering historical and socio-environmental factors.

When contemplating the North Korean urban system their imperialist character in the period of the Japanese rule and just before springs immediately to one's mind and this resulted in the fact that numerous cities of North Korea are situated on the coasts. On the other hand, new cities arose after the DPR Korea emerged, whereby non-costal locations were deliberately promoted. Of course administrative centers in the North of the peninsula existed even before the influence of the Japanese on the Korean urban system. The North Korean cities can therefore genetically be divided roughly into the three groups:

- traditional Korean cities,
- cities founded under Japanese influence and
- cities founded after the foundation of the DPR Korea.

Pyongyang has the image as one of the oldest cities in Korea. Numerous is the literature on the history of the city, which was since 427 the capital of the Koguryo dynasty (37 BC-668). Pyongyang is the undisputed historical center of the northern half of Korea. An administrative center in the northeast of the country is and was Hamhung. Hamhung is considered as the hometown of the Joson royal family (National Museum of Korea 2010). Yi Sŏng-gye (1335-1408), who had founded the Joson dynasty (1392-1910) as King Taejo (r. 1392-1398) spent his youth here and returned to this place after he lost his office to his second son. The Hamhung Royal Villa, which Yi Sŏng-gye built after leaving the kingly office at the place of the house of his ancestors, was rebuilt and restored after it had repeatedly been the victim of destruction. The Hamhung Royal Villa is now a tourist attraction for Hamhung visitors. Kaesong was in 919 capital of Koryo and is referred to as a "city of geomancy." There is hardly a Korean city, where there are so many discourses about a city's geomancy as about Kaesong (see Yoon, Hong-key 2006). Haeju is also a city that has held important administrative functions for a long time. When Korea was divided into 12 *mok* in 983, Haeju-mok was one of them. Other cities didn't have such a strong administrative function as the above mentioned cities, but since the border of Korea was temporarily south of the present border, numerous military camps were in the northern part of the country. Thus, the Koryo Kangdong Six (East of the River) Garrison Settlements were established in the reign of the Koryo King Kwangjong (r. 949-975) and one of these was Kuju, the current Kusong. The fortification of Kuju was built in 994 (Lee Ki-baik, 1984, 125), which still exists today in parts.

The modern urban development of Korea started after the opening of Korean ports and the construction of railway lines. From 1876 to 1910 eleven ports were opened, including six, which are in the area that is now part of the DPR Korea. Jinnampho, today's Nampho, Wonsan, Sŏngjin (today's Kimchaek) and Chongjin were small fishing villages before the First Sino-Japanese War (1894-1895). The seaport of Taedonggang Basin, Jinnampho, was established as a military supply base for the Japanese Army (Hŏ U-gung 2007, 102) since the First Sino-Japanese War. Jinnampho has been approved by the Korean government as an international treaty port in 1897. In Wonsan the Japanese built about six km north of the Korean village a concession area in a reed field, which was drained after the opening of the port. The port of Wonsan was built in this part of the city and it is still the center of the city. The port was opened on May 1st 1880 for the trade with Japan and on March 11th 1883 for the entire international trade. Economically, the Japanese did not benefit very much from Wonsan and the concession area of Wonsan, but Wonsan played an important role from the beginning from a military strategic point of view. Due to the construction of the Japanese concession area the way for the advance of Russia was blocked and Wonsan, with Pusan and Inchon, a base for the landing of Japanese troops was during the Sino-Japanese War (Yun Jŏng-sŏp 1987, 114). Sŏngjin (today's Kimchaek) was at the end of the 19th century as a half-way station between Vladivostok and Wonsan an important strategic point. After the opening of the port in 1899 not only many Japanese came to Sŏngjin. Also, several other foreigners came to Sŏngjin, so that the Christianity developed here rapidly. Chongjin was initially nothing more than a small fishing village, which developed on a foothill within the county of Puryong. When this was a landing place for military equipments of the Japanese in the Russo-Japanese War (1904-1905), the village had about 100 houses. Chongjin opened in 1908 for the international trade. During the Russo-Japanese War (1904-1905), the Japanese promoted as a supply route for its military a 90 km long railway line from Chongjin to Hoeryong, which was completed in 1906. Chongjin was an important port for the removal of timber and other products from the forest areas of North Korea and Manchuria, and for the transport of fishery products. The Japanese had also built in neighboring Ranam (now part of Chongjin-si) a large military base in 1907. In this regard, the port of Chongjin had become indispensable as a place of landing for any goods (Yun Jŏng-sŏp, 1987, 127-128). Sinuiju is located about 40 km above the mouth of the Yalu virtually in the north-western corner of the province directly on the Chinese border. Sinuiju developed in connection with the construction of a railway line by Japanese authorities, which should cross Korea from the Southeast to the Northwest. The most difficult problem was the question of the site for the construction of the bridge, which should cross the Yalu. A possible location was near the river crossing at the settlement Uiju, where there was an island in the Yalu River, and in this vicinity delegations between the Korean Joson dynasty and the Chinese Ch'ing Empire had already crossed the Yalu River. Another suggestion was to build the bridge over the Yalu River about 20 km downstream, where it meets on the Manchurian side on Antung County (Dandong City). In April 1905 it was opted to employ the latter proposal. On the flooded meadows of the Yalu River a new city was built as planned, which was called the "New Uiju," Sinuiju.

After the devastation of the Korean War, the cities were partially rebuilt with the assistance of the states of the real existing socialism. The most cited example in this context is the support of the GDR during the rising of the city of Hamhung. A main road in Hamhung was even named for a while after the GDR President Wilhelm Pieck.

An example of a North Korean city founding is the construction of the satellite town of Phyongsong north of the capital Pyongyang. After the Academy of Sciences found its place here, many other research institutes have been built under its auspices here. The main research and teaching facilities were in a special science district in the south of Phyongsong. In 1995 however, a separation of the southern part of Phyongsong followed, and this formed the Unjong-kuyok of the city of Pyongyang. Sunchon, which was agricultural before the Korean War, is one of the areas, which has been newly established as an industrial area. The change of Sunchon began immediately after the war. Based on rich limestone and coal reserves, large and small mines and factories were created. In particular, the production of cement has great significance for the city. Sunchon is a traffic junction and the establishment of the United Vinalon Complex started during the 1980s, which attracted many people from all parts and Sunchon got the face of a large city (Chosun Ilbo September 25, 1995). Vinalon is for some time now not produced in Suncheon anymore. Huichon, originally an important market as a gate to the plateau of the Jagang Province, where trading in products of agriculture of the surrounding areas and products of the high-plains region occurred, developed rapidly after the Korean War as an important location of machine construction. In each case, the largest machine tool factory and the largest precision machinery factory in North Korea are situated in this city.

Anju is an interesting city, because its urbanized regions can be divided into three regions, which can be assigned to each of the three groups described above genetically. The center of Anju goes back to an old fortified city. The meaning of Anju is also demonstrated by the province name Phyongan, which is composed of the initial syllables of the cities Pyongyang and Anju. However when, under Japanese rule, the railway line from Seoul to

Sinuiju was built, it ran west of the city of Anju. The "New Anju" Sinanju was developed on the railway line. The construction of the Namhŭng Youth Chemical Complex, one of the most important petrochemical factories in the western region of North Korea, in 1974 in the North of the present city of Anju marked the birth of the industrial region Anju. Around the chemical plant new districts have been created, so that the former center of Anju, Sinanju and Namhŭng represent three city regions with different roots, which are typical for the genesis of North Korean cities.

In the city descriptions the socio-spatial factors were also taken into account. These include, for example, prominent people, who come from that city or live in it. In addition, in the case of North Korea, certain political slogans here are consciously localized with certain companies or cities. Many of the socio-spatial factors can therefore be traced back to the product of deliberate measure of the North Korean state. Even the naming of administrative regional units is often made out of political considerations. When considering the names of the cities, we can note two cases, in which personal names were used for the name of a geographical unit. The first case is however very far ahead from the time of the existence of the DPRK and refers to the old name of the city of Songrim. In the 1880s, the Japanese military was looking for a landing site for the preparation of the Sino-Japanese War, which was then set up in today's Songrim, which was then named after the responsible commander Watanabe Kenji, Kenji-Port (Kenjiho, in Korean Kyŏmipho). Because the last name was too common, the first name was chosen. The second case of a personal name as a city name occurred during the Korean War. By renaming the port city on the East Sea, Sŏngjin to Kimchaek, General Kim Chaek (1903-1951), born in Sŏngjin, who was a comrade of Kim Il-sung from their days of the struggle against the Japanese occupation in Manchuria, was honored. Jongju was deemed already before 1945 as the home of pioneers. Born in Jongju or having attended the Christian Osan-school are among others the writers Yi Kwang-su (1892 - 1950) and Kim So-wŏl (1902-1934). But also the painter Yi Jungsŏp (1916-1956) and the philosopher Ham Sŏk-hŏn (1901-1989), the "Korean Ghandi," have among others attended the Osan-school. Moon Sun Myung (1920-2012), the founder of the Unification Church ("Moonies"), was born in Jongju. Moon has subsequently traveled to the DPR Korea and was received in 1991 by Kim Il-sung. Moon was able to acquire two large hotels in the capital Pyongyang. Furthermore, the government allowed the Unification Church to establish a place of pilgrimage for the Moon sect in Jongju. In North Korean sources, the importance of the city of Hoeryong as the birthplace of the mother of Kim Jong-il, Kim Jong-suk (1917-1949), and as the city where she spent her childhood, is particularly highlighted. Sariwon is especially honoring the general chief of staff Kang Kŏn (1918-1950), who had fallen in the Korean War. A statue was erected in 1968 in honor of him. One of the main streets of the city as well as a university was named after him. Also several slogans carry names of cities or are locatable within cities, in order to mobilize the population. Mobilization measures of the 1950 and 1960s like the Taean Work System, the Chongsanri-method and the Chollima-movement have names of places, which belong to the city of Nampho (its *kuyok* of Taean, Kangso and Chollima). In 1998, "the Kanggye spirit" was summoned, in 2001 the torch of Ranam was spread, and since 2009 North Koreans worked at "Huichon Speed." It is reported from the mountainous Jagang Province and the big industrial cities on the east coast, that they had to suffer particularly badly during the time of the famine in the 1990s. The cities of Kanggye and Huichon (both in Jagang Province) were therefore chosen intentionally for the North Korean propaganda slogans. Hamhung was designated the "Capital of the unemployed," because heavy industry especially was affected by the changes as a result of the collapse of Comecon (Bauer 2005). The novel "Nothing to Envy: Real Lives in North Korea" by Barbara Demick (2010) has probably contributed to the image of Chongjin as a city, which was particularly hard hit by the famine.

V.2. Evaluation of the quantitative studies of the number of industrial companies

V.2.1. Industrial structure of North Korean cities

In chapter III, five different sources are examined to ascertain the number of different industrial companies that are located in the cities of the DPR Korea.[1] Statistical studies, which only take into account the number of companies, are of course less meaningful than studies, which are based on numbers of employees and production yields of individual companies.

Due to the limited nature of the sources and information on the economy of North Korea, the present study is limited in its statistical approach to the number of industrial companies in the sources examined. To increase the validity of the results, the following measures were carried out:

Five different sources were investigated and the results of the studies of the five sources are shown separately from each other, in order to reflect the peculiarities of the sources

In chapter IV, the results of quantitative studies based on all sources are examined for each individual city and compiled separately, in order to allow a comparison of the results for the individual cities between the different sources

Chapter IV also gives information on the important companies of the individual cities.

1 It was also determined in the course of the investigations itself, how many industrial plants are located in the individual *kun* and in the provinces of the DPR Korea. But the present work is limited to an evaluation of the results for the cities.

In particular in the cases, where relevant information was available, data on the number of employees and the company size was given; whereby of course it should be noted, that these are neither objectively confirmed, nor stated, on which date these refer to. The descriptions and data can, however—as a complement to the statistical studies—give an impression, what significance the respective company in the city or the entire country has or had.

The present analysis now takes both into account: the results of the quantitative studies in chapter III as well as the results of the qualitative research on the industrial companies in chapter IV. It was clear in the description of the individual cities that some have a well-balanced versatile industrial structure, while in other cities a clear orientation of industry was noted on light industry, heavy industry or mining, or even a specialization in individual industries. There are also cities in the DPRK, where few or only one company exists, in which the majority of the industrial employees are employed. These observations certainly play a significant role in the interpretation of the statistical research. An extreme example is the city of Songrim, an industrial satellite city of Pyongyang. The industrial structure of the city is dominated by the Hwanghae Iron and Steel Complex, in which more than half of all industrial employees of the city are working and at the same time over 80% of the industrial production and industrial operations areas of the city fall upon according to North Korean figures in the late 1980s (KJY-26 1990, 444).

The probability that the industrial structure of a city is dominated by one or a few factories or industries is higher in smaller towns of course than in very large cities. Therefore, the population of the cities is taken into account in the following categorization and small, medium-sized and large cities are treated separately.

The goal of the examination is to ascertain whether the cities each accommodate a variety of different industrial sectors or whether one or a few companies, one or more industrial sectors dominate the industrial structure of the city, or whether a clear dominance of either the heavy or the light industry exists.

In three of the eleven small towns of the DPR Korea one company clearly dominates the industrial structure of the city. This is on the one hand, the already mentioned city of Songrim with the Hwanghae Iron and Steel Complex. However, the DPR Korea is looking for ways of diversifying the economic structure of the city, such as the 2013 published plan of the establishment of the Songrim Export Goods Processing Zone promises. Songrim enjoys quite a favorable location for economic developments outside of iron and steel, due to the proximity to Nampho and the capital Pyongyang and the port on the Taedong-gang. Also in the second city with a dominating factory, Jongju, the dominant company is a complex from the metallurgy industry, namely the Phyongbuk Smeltery. Besides this factory, there are only small companies in Jongju, which is an agricultural and fisheries economically dominated town. The location on the route between the North Korean-Chinese border at Sinuiju and the capital Pyongyang promises development possibilities. The third small town with a dominant company is Kusong, an intra-mountain center of machine construction that is dominated by the 3. April General Factory (Kusong Machine Tool Factory). The most important center of engineering of the DPR Korea is the small town Huichon. In each case, the largest machine tool factory, the Huichon Ryŏnha General Machinery Plant and the largest precision machinery factory in North Korea, the Precision Machinery Factory (Factory February 26), are located in this city. Like the economic structure of Huichon, the economic structure of Munchon is also largely dominated by one industry. In the Munphyŏng region of Munchon-si are with the Munphyŏng Smeltery, the 21 September Smeltery and the Munchon Zinc Smeltery three major factories of nonferrous metallurgy, although Munchon also has other industrial sectors (mechanical engineering, agar-factory). Sinpho is specialized on a sea-related industrial sector. Fishing and fish processing are the official stance of the city's economy. The Sinpho Shipyard and the Mayang-do Naval Base are known for their military use (submarines). Cities like Kimchaek and Manpho also each have a significant large-scale company, such as the Sŏngjin Steel Complex and the Aprokgang Tire Factory. However, there are in both cities several not insignificant other companies of the heavy industry (Kimchaek: Sŏngjin Refractory Factory, Kimchaek Ship Factory, Ssangryong Phosphate Fertilizer Factory; Manpho: Manpho Cement Factory, Manpho Chemical Factory), so that the dominance of the large company is not quite as overwhelming such as in Songrim. A mix of different industrial sectors (light industry, heavy industry and mining), are in the border towns to China, in Hoeryong and Hyesan. Rason has only one major establishment, the Sŭngri Petrochemical Complex, according to the analysis of the different sources. However, through the establishment of the special economic zone, various economic sectors have been added, so that Rason is classified as a city with various industries.

Haeju and Anju can be regarded among the twelve medium-sized cities as cities with a dominant company. Like in Songrim and Jongju, Haeju also has a metallurgy company, the Haeju October 13th Youth Smeltery. Anju became an industrial city thanks to the Namhŭng Youth Chemical Complex, built in the 1970s. Kaechon, Tanchon and Tokchon are typical mining towns. Tokchon had a special character due to the Sŭngri Motor Complex, which once had a great significance for the city's economy, but today produces only few vehicles. Sinuiju, Kanggye, Phyongsong and, according to the statistics, also Kanggye are regarded as cities of light industry. Kanggye is a center of the textile industry, however additionally well known as a major center of the defense industry of the DPR Korea. Also in Phyongsong a factory for military vehicles is situated. Various industrial sectors are located in Wonsan, Sariwon and Sunchon.

Chongjin, Hamhung and Nampho have, among the large cities, an emphasis on heavy industry, while the major focus in Pyongyang lies on the light industry.

V.2.2. Different production capacity in the industrial sectors in North Korea

In the interpretation of the data for the industrial companies in the cities of the DPR Korea, not only the size of the companies is important. Of importance is also the question whether all the companies concerned still produce, or if they were perhaps already demolished, how high the production capacity (rate of operation) is etc. In the description of the companies it has already been already mentioned in some cases, if the company mentioned in the source was demolished in the meantime, such as the Nampho General Smeltery and the Nampho Glass Complex. For other companies, there were reports of toll-processing procedure as for the Sŭngri Chemical Complex in Rason. In the country's media references about investments for the modernization of equipments are about prestige projects and companies of special importance for the economy of the DPR Korea. Otherwise, there are only vague conjectures on the utilization of North Korean companies. In the 1990s, a collapse of the North Korean industry has occurred, which practically covered all areas. The lack of raw materials and energy as well as outdated technologies have led to a dramatic reduction of the production capacity in the factories.

Observers of the North Korean economy however noted that the industry of the DPR Korea recovered in the 2000s partially, but the extent of recovery in the various industrial sectors is very unbalanced. In industries such as the electricity generation, coal mining and metal production, the recovery of production has set in first. A relatively large amount was invested in the building materials industry including the cement industry due to the need for the construction of power plants, large waterways (canals) and residential buildings, so that the recovery shaped up quickly. Also in the field of metallurgy, a recovery in production can be ascertained, but it is slower compared to the energy industry.

In machine construction, chemical industry, automobile manufacturing, shipyards, etc. a recovery of production on the other hand has almost never happened. Although the light industry is for example constantly emphasized during the New Year's speeches, the production recovery in these areas is not particularly large (Yi/Kim/Kim/Yang 2010, 15 and 124). More specifically, public investments were limited to hydroelectric power stations etc until the first half of the 2000s. Funds by the companies themselves or the mobilization of non-strategic areas, regions and the whole country played a significant role for other types of investment. The focus here was on the resumption of the establishment of factories or factory parts, investment for new construction were made for facilities of medium and small power plants or small and medium-sized coal mines.

The preference of the military and important sectors for the procurement of foreign currency in the investment by the North Korean state is mentioned as an important reason for the rapid development of certain industries. A research team from the Korea Institute for Industrial Economics & Trade interprets the meaning of the military for the unbalanced recovery of the North Korean economy as follows: the military has neither its own energy production sites, nor basic raw materials. When the North Korean economy collapsed, the energy sector and the raw materials industry, which is under the control of the cabinet, had to be first restored to supply the military with energy and raw materials. On the other hand, the military has its own production sites in the field of mechanical engineering as well as in the field of shipbuilding. Thus, from the perspective of the military, the recovery of civil engineering (machine tools, automotive, industrial equipment) under the control of the cabinet was of lower priority. The same applies to chemical industry. In the field of chemical industry, there are companies that are under the control of the military. This means that the need for further products of the chemical industry from civilian production in the military was relatively low (Yi/Kim/Kim/Yang 2010, 124).

The extension of the exploration of mineral resources, especially coal, but also iron ore, for public investment had a high priority due to the aim of obtaining foreign currency. Another factor contributing to a lack of uniformity in the degree of recovery of individual industrial sectors in North Korea is in the technical field.

Although the expansion of production of metallic raw materials is quite necessary, the recovery of the metal production is subject to limitations, because this necessitates a huge investment and the import of coking coal is needed. A try for a solution is to resort to the production of Juche steel, which is not manufactured using imported coke, but using domestic coal, but the chances of success seem to be not very big. Since the chemical industry is working in the form of large industrial plants, the necessary investment costs are huge here. The supply of energy and coal are also basic requirements for the operation. Therefore, greater state investment in the chemical industry can be identified only in the second half of the 2000s, after the shortage had eased somewhat in the area of electric power and coal.

V.3. Evaluation of the quantitative studies of the internal structure of the cities

V.3.1. Centers and sub-centers of the cities

One third of the 27 cities of the DPRK were founded before 1945 as a city (*pu*). Ten of the 27 cities received their appointments in the 13-year period between 1947 and 1969. The remaining eight cities were established in the thirteen years between 1982 and 1994. In the intervening twelve years, no new city was founded, which would still remain nowadays.[2] The same applies to the period after 1994.[3] A concern of the present research was to explore centers and sub-centers of each city. The cities that have emerged after 1945 have originated usually by converting a *kun* into a *si*. Within a *kun* exist *up*, *ri* and *rodongjagu*. In four of the eight cities, which had been founded between 1982 and 1994, the *kun*, which were converted into a *si*, had at the time of the city designation numerous *rodongjagu*.

Table Conclusion-I. Cities founded between 1982 and 1994 with more than five *rodongjagu*

Hoeryong (1991)	7 *rodongjagu*
Kaechon (1990)	10 *rodongjagu*
Tokchon (1986)	8 *rodongjagu*
Tanchon (1982)	9 *rodongjagu*

All of these cities that have more than five *rodongjagu* are mining towns. In the case of Hoeryong and Tanchon, the *kun*, from which the respective city later came into existence, was expanded with another *kun* in 1974 (Yusŏn-kun became part of Hoeryong-kun, Kwangchŏn-kun became part of Tanchon-kun) so that at the city designation in 1986 (Tanchon) and in 1991 (Hoeryong) the *kun* included a *rodongjagu*, which has previously been an *up* of the incorporated *kun*.

The other four *kun*, which had been designated to a city (*si*) between 1982 and 1994, had at the time of the designation, two to four *rodongjagu*, which had different functional orientations.

Table Conclusion-II. Cities founded between 1982 and 1994 with fewer than five *rodongjagu*

Jongju (1994)	3 *rodongjagu*
Munchon (1991)	4 *rodongjagu*
Anju (1987)	2 *rodongjagu*
Sunchon (1983)	3 *rodongjagu*

Until the appointment to a city, not too many *rodongjagu* had been formed in the older cities. Only in Sinpho-kun three *rodongjagu* existed at the time of the city designation. In the case of Rajin, there were two *rodongjagu* at the city designation in 1967. The incorporated Sonbong-kun in 1993 contained in addition to Sonbong-up also two *rodongjagu*. In some cities, a center and one or more sub-centers can be identified.

2 Taean-si, founded in 1978, was again dissolved in 1983.

3 Hungnam became a city (*si*) in 2001 and became part of Hamhung in 2004.

Table Conclusion-III. Centers and sub-centers in cities of the DPR Korea

	Centre	Sub-centers
Manpho	former *up*	1. former Haebang-rodongjagu (Aprokgang Tire Factory, Manpho Chemical Factory) 2. Munak-dong/Saemaŭl-dong (Manpho Cement Factory)
Huichon	former *up*	former Jŏnphyŏng-rodongjagu (Huichon Ryŏnha General Machine Factory)
Kusong	former *up*	1. former Chahŭng-rodongjagu, 2. former Panghyŏn-rodongjagu
Hyesan	former *up*	former Wiyŏnpho-rodongjagu
Songrim	river bank region (Hwanghae Iron and Steel Complex)	new city center
Kimchaek	former *up*	region around Sŏngjin Steel Complex
Haeju	city centre	1. Ryongdang-peninsula (harbor) 2. West-Haeju (Yŏnha-dong/Ŭppha-dong) 3. Hakhyŏn-dong/Yangji-dong
Kaesong	city centre	Kaesong Industrial Region
Hamhung	Hamhung-centre	Hungnam
Sinuiju	Old-Sinuiju	Nam-Sinuiju
Chongjin	Old-Chongjin	Old-Ranam
Nampho	Nampho-centre (Hanggu-kuyok, Waudo-kuyok)	Old-Taean (Taean-kuyok, Chollima-kuyok, Kangso-kuyok)

V.3.2. Disappearance of *dong*

565 new *dong* arose during the study period (1956-2009). But in 86 cases, existing *dong* were merged with other *dong* or became again a *ri*. This means that these *dong* have virtually disappeared. 11 of these 27 cities of North Korea are affected. In most cases, this phenomenon can be observed only in the years of building the cities until 1970.

Table Conclusion-IV. Vanished *dong* in nine cities of the DPR Korea

	Kanggye	Sinuiju	Sariwon	Kaesong	Haeju	Hyesan	Rason	Wonsan	Hamhung
1956									10
1957	3	2	3	1	2	1		4	6
1958				1					
1960									1
1961	2	7	1					2	
1967								1	8
1968							1		
1970									3
59	5	9	4	2	2	1	1	7	28

After 1970 *dong* were merged as well only in Songrim and Pyongyang.

Table Conclusion-V. Vanished *dong* in the regions of the DPR Korea as well as Songrim and Pyongyang[4]

	Region Northwest	Region Southwest	Kwanbuk	Songrim	Pyongyang	
1956			10			10
1957	5	6	11	7		29
1958		1		1		2
1959					1	1
1960			1		2	3
1961	9	1	2			12
1967			9			9
1968			1			1
1970			3			3
1972					3	3
1979					2	2
1981					3	3
1983					3	
1986					2	2
1988				1		1
1991					1	1
1992				1		1
	14	8	37	10	17	86

By far the most merging of *dong* happened in Hamhung. This can be interpreted as an indication that an intensive restructuring has taken place in this city during the period of reconstruction of the city after the destruction caused by the Korean War. This is followed by the capital Pyongyang, where the residential use in some parts of the city was displaced by the construction of prestigious squares, parks and buildings. In Songrim, the residential areas have been relocated due to the Hwanghae Iron and Steel Complex. In particular, in the years 1957 (29 *dong* in nine cities), 1961 (12 *dong* in four cities), 1956 (10 *dong* in Hamhung) and 1967 (9 *dong* in Hamhung and Wonsan) numerous *dong* vanished.

4 The Northwest region combines Kanggye and Sinuiju, the Southwest region Sariwon, Kaesong and Haeju and Kwanbuk Hyesan, Rason, Wonsan and Hamhung.

V.3.3. The emergence of new *dong*

In the following statistics only the new *dong*, which have been built after the founding of the city in question, are taken into account.

According to the information in IPA-1 (2003), 556 new *dong* emerged in conformity with the present evaluation between 1956 and 2002. Another nine emerged according to information from PSC-8 (2009) between 2002 and 2009.

The emergence of new *dong* could be considered as an indication of urbanization process and an increase in the population in urbanized regions. It is theoretically conceivable that whenever a certain population is exceeded in a *dong* or in an adjacent *dong*, one or more new *dong* are promptly established. On the other hand, there are probably conscious administrative reform measures that lead to a change in the number of *dong*. It should therefore be initially investigated, whether there are certain years, in which significantly more *dong* were established than in other years. In the years 1963 and 1967 more than 50 *dong* emerged in each year. This suggests that in these years were measures taken by some central organization of the DPR Korea, in order to change the internal structure of cities. In 1972 there were in the capital Pyongyang particularly numerous new *dong*.

Table Conclusion-VI. New *dong* in North Korean cities-divided by years and regions[5]

	Phyongbuk	Phyongnam	Pyongyang	Hwanghae	Hambuk	Hamnam	
1956				2			2
1957	3		7	1	1	10	22
1958				3			3
1959			3	2			5
1960		4	17		8	10	39
1961	10		1	15	12	7	45
1963		4	27	1	19	13	64
1965		8	13	8	4	8	41
1967	8	9	23	9	5	12	66
1969		12	2				14
1970						1	1
1971						1	1
1972	1		27	1	5		34
1973					7		7
1974			1			3	4
1976	3					3	6

5 Region Phyongbuk includes the province Jagang, region Phyongnam includes Nampho. Region Hambuk includes the province Ryanggang and Rason, region Hamnam includes the province Kangwon.

1977		1					1
1978					5		5
1979			7				7
1981	4	4		4	2		14
1982			9			4	13
1983			2	3			5
1984		2					2
1985	5				2	4	11
1986			1			4	5
1987					4		4
1988		1	7	4	1	4	17
1989	7	6	3				16
1990	3						3
1991		2	24	5	4		35
1992				1	4		5
1993		7	10	2	2	8	29
1994	5		2	1	1		9
1995	2	3	4			4	13
1996						1	1
1997		2					2
1999	1	1			1		3
2000					1		1
2001						1	1
after 2002	4	3			1	1	9
	56	69	190	62	89	99	565

V.3.4. Phases of the development of urbanization in the DPR Korea

Approximately 90% of South Korea's population lives in cities. Approximately half of the country is domiciled in the capital area (Seoul, Inchon, Kyonggi). In North Korea, the proportion of North Korea's population, who lives in cities, is much lower, with 46.4% (2008). In view of the possibilities of moving within the country, there are strong restrictions, which should *inter alia* prevent an increase in urbanization.

From the beginning in regard to the regulation of the territory the capitalist point of view, which considers a city and a country as a dualism, was considered as wrong by Kim Il-sung. His ideal of a socialist country development was that city and country form a unit and are thus to be developed in balance. It should not be the case that the countryside has a poor population and the city in contrast is wealthy, that workers live in the city and farmers in the rural area. And it should not be the case that the city population is the ruling class and that a worthy life on the countryside is not possible.

The task of urban planning under socialism is to overcome these contradictions. The difference in the quality of city and country should disappear and the provinces of North Korea are to develop in a balanced way, whereby the differences in terms of geography should be considered. On the other hand, as Kim Il-sung put it, Pyongyang should be the heart of the Korean people, the capital of the socialist fatherland and the origin of our revolution. (Verlag für Fremdsprachige Literatur 1995, 2).

The following should therefore examine the changes in the "urban" population over time and the regional development trends in the DPR Korea.

V.3.5. Changes in the "urban" population over time

It has already been pointed out that 46.4% (2008) of the North Korean population live in the 27 cities in the country. A lot has been said in the literature on North Korea about an "urbanization rate" or of "urban" population. It indicates the percentage or the number of people living in "urban" areas. These are according to the numbers of the "DPR Korea 2008 Population Census" about 60.6% of the North Korean population.

"Urban" are people, who live in *dong*, *up* and *rodongjagu*. "Rural" are people, who live in *ri*. This means that in cities (*si*) as well as in counties (*kun*) "rural" as well as "urban" live people, whereby of course the proportion of the "urban" population is greater in cities than in counties.

From this point, the numbers of the urbanization rate can be seen in the lower table. An increase in the rate of urbanization thus says nothing about whether this has come about an increase in the "urban" population in the cities or in the counties. Especially a lot of "urban" population have *kun* with many *rodongjagu*.

Table Conclusion-VII. Urban proportion and number of cities 1953–2008

Year	Total population	Urban proportion (%)	Number of cities
1953	8491	17.7	13
1956	9539	29.0	14
1960	10,789	40.6	14
1965	12,408	47.5	14
1970	14,619	54.2	18
1975	15,986	56.7	19
1980	17,298	56.9	20
1985	18,792	59.0	21
1993	20,522	60.9	26
2008	23,350	60.6	27

Source: Jo/Adler (2002, 208); DPR Korea 2008 Population Census (2009), own calculations.

A high level of urbanization can thus be stated for the period until the mid-1960s and the urbanization increased slightly until the mid 1980s. Since this date, stagnation has set in.

A decrease in the pace of urbanization says nothing about where this decline took place, which means that it is unclear whether the *dong* in the cities or whether the *rodongjagu* in counties are affected. It can be concluded however from the pace of the urbanization that the process of industrialization of North Korea, which runs parallel to the urbanization, has slowed down significantly in the 1970s and virtually stagnated in the 1980s.

The number of cities in North Korea stagnated, especially in the period of urbanization until 1967 and then increased rapidly. While the number of cities has almost doubled between 1967 and 2008, the growth of the urban population increased by just over 10% in the same period. The growth in the number of cities and the increase of the urban proportion thus were not parallel. The present study has dealt with the newly created *dong* within the 27 cities in the DPR Korea. Table Conclusion-VIII gives comprehensive information on how many new *dong* emerged in the cities of the individual regions of the DPR Korea and in which decade.

Table Conclusion-VIII. New *dong* in the cities of the DPR Korea – divided by decades and regions[6]

	Phyongbuk	Phyongnam	Pyongyang	Hwanghae	Hambuk	Hamnam	Total
1950s	3 (5.4%)	–	10 (5.3%)	8 (12.9%)	1 (1.1%)	10 (10.1%)	32 (5,7%)
1960s	18 (32.1%)	37 (53.6%)	83 (43.7%)	33 (53.2%)	48 (53.9%)	50 (50.5%)	269 (47.6%)
1970s	4 (7.1%)	1 (1.4%)	35 (18.4%)	1 (1.6)	17 (19.1%)	8 (8.1%)	66 (11.7%)
1980s	16(28.6%)	13 (18.8%)	22 (11.6%)	11 (17.7%)	9 (10.1%)	16 (16.2%)	87 (15.4%)
1990s	11 (19.6%)	15 (21.7%)	40 (21.1%)	9 (14.5%)	12 (13.5%)	13 (13.1%)	100 (17.7%)
2000s	4 (7.1%)	3 (4.3%)	–	–	2 (2.2%)	2 (2%)	11 (1.9%)
	56	69	190	62	89	99	565

It becomes clear, that over half of all new *dong* emerged in the period between the late 1950s and the 1960s. The relatively small number of the new *dong* from the 1970s reflects the trend of a low urbanization level of the DPR Korea during this period. Exceptions are Pyongyang and Chongjin (Hambuk). In the 1980s and 1990s the number of new *dong* only increases slightly, in many cities only to a significant extent, when special urban development projects were realized. In the 1980s for example, the construction of the new cities Nam-Sinuiju and Nam-Chongjin are conducted. In the 1990s, the number of *dong* increased especially in the capital, where the residential area Kwangbok and Thongil are constructed, and also in Nampho.

6 Region Phyongbuk includes the province Jagang, region Phyongnam Nampho. Region Hambuk also includes the province Ryanggang and Rason, Region Hamnam includes Kangwon.

V.4. Regional development trends in the DPR Korea

When summarizing in which decade and in each region the second most *dong* arose within the cities of the DPR Korea, we get the following picture:

- 1970s: Hambuk (including Ryanggang and Rason)
- 1980s: Phyongbuk (including Jagang), Hwanghae, Hamnam (including Kangwon)
- 1990s: Phyongnam (including Nampho), Pyongyang

It becomes clear, that from the 1980s, the urban development in the west of North Korea was greater than in the east of the country.

The following trends of regional development in North Korea can be roughly determined:

The colonialist Japan had established or expanded many North Korean cities on the coasts. To compensate this imbalance, but also for strategic reasons, inland cities of the DPR Korea were expanded particularly between 1945 and the late 1960s. The establishment of the mountain provinces of Jagang (1949) and Ryanggang (1954) in this period was supported. This is also the time, in which there is the most intense increase in the urban population and in the *dong* within cities.

The largest areas of the DPR Korea are taken from the areas, which belong to the former provinces of Phyongnam and Hamgyong. A balance of these two regions is a major concern of the North Korean government to prevent regionalist tendencies. From the 1960s until the mid-1980s, the cities Hamhung and Chongjin from the region Hamgyong were temporarily appointed *jikhalsi*. With the collapse of the economy of North Korea in the 1990s, these cities, which were in particular dominated by the heavy industry were drawn into a crisis.

There was a significant impetus for development of mining and industrial towns in the Phyongnam Province, south of Pyongyang, since the late 1960s, when the economic problems of the country were increasingly evident. Between 1983 and 1990, four cities were founded in Phyongnam.

The gap in the development of the capital Pyongyang and the other parts of the country was becoming more evident, which was reinforced by the crisis years in the 1990s. While new residential areas were built in Pyongyang, the development stagnated in other parts of the country. More than half of the new *dong* of the 1990s are located in the region Pyongyang/Nampho/Phyongnam.[7]

It can therefore be stated that North Korea has consciously pursued a policy of

7 Not taken into consideration in the investigations were special economic zones (Kaesong, Rason), as these have developed largely isolated from the rest of North Korea and developments have not yet had an impact on the present statistics, the industrial companies as well as the administrative units.

regional balance in regards economic development. However, the economic crisis and investment from outside have led to a weakening of these goals and the development of certain regions was given more preference. A reunification of Korea would clearly increase the differences in development between the regions with a great development potential and the other regions.

Especially the region of Pyongyang/Nampho would primarily benefit, which carries the best development opportunities based on the available labor, energy and infrastructure. That region is followed by the border regions in the northeast to China and also in the southwest to South Korea in regards to their high development potential.[8]

8 According to a report of the Chosun Ilbo (January 10, 2014), KIEP (Korea Institute for International Economic Policy) evaluated six North Korean city regions according to their development potential after the reunification with South Korea, whereby the region Pyongyang/Nampho with 9.5 points had the best record. This was followed by Chongjin (7.5 points), Haeju (7.0 points), Hamhung (6.8 points), Wonsan (6.3 points) and Sinuiju (6.0 points).

Bibliography

Sources:

DPR Korea 2008 Population Census

Central Bureau of Statistics (2009). *DPR Korea 2008 Population Census. National Report*. Pyongyang.

Han'guk-sanŏp-ŭnhaeng (2000)

The Korea Development Bank 韓國産業銀行 (2000). *The North Korean Industry* 北韓의 産業.

IPA (2003) - The Institute for Peace Affairs

Peace Research Institute science encyclopedia publisher (joint publication)

평화문제연구소 과학백과사전출판사 (공동편찬) (2003). *Encyclopedia of North Korean Geography and Culture; 20 volumes 조선향토대백과 20권*.

JC (2009)

Jido-chulphansa 지도출판사 (2009). *Road Atlas (Northern Korea) 도로지도첩 (공화국북반부)*. Pyongyang 평양.

Josŏn-jungang-thongsinsa (2005/2010/2011)

Korea Central News Agency 조선중앙통신사 (2005/2010/2011). *Korea Central Yearbook 조선중앙년감 2005/2010/2011*. Pyongyang 평양.

KCNA

Korean Central News Agency of DPRK (Democratic People's Republic of Korea) 조선통신. http://www.kcna.co.jp.

kdb (2005a,b)

The Korea Development Bank 산업은행(2005 a, b). *The North Korean industry* (new) (Part 1, Part 2) *新 북한의 산업* (上, 下).

KIET (1996) - Korea Institute for Industrial Economics & Trade

Yi Sang-jik, Choe Sin-rim, & Yi Sŏk-ki이상직, 최신림, 이석기 (1996). *Industry of North Korea – Mining and factory-based industry sector company manual-.北韓의 企業 – 광공업 부문 기업 편람*. Industrial Institute. Policy research material 96-43 産業研究院. 정책연구자료96-43. Seoul 서울.

KOFC (2010) (Korea Finance Corporation)

Korea Finance Corporation 한국정책금융공사 (2010). *The North Korean Industry 북한의 산업*.

KOTRA (1995)

Korea Trade Promotion Agency대한무역진흥공사 (1995). *The North Korean industry*

북한의 산업. 무공자료 95-23.

MOU (2012)

Ministry of Unification 통일부 (2012). *A Directory of leading members of important North Korean institutions and associations 북한 주요기관 · 단체 인명록 2012*.

PSC-8 (2009)

Paekkwa-sajŏn-chulphansa 백과사전출판사 (2009). *Kwangmyŏng Encyclopedia 8. Geography of Korea 광명백과사전 8. 조선의 지리*. Pyongyang 평양.

Yonhap News Agency (2011)

Yonhap News Agency 연합뉴스 (2011). *North Korea Yearbook 2011 북한연감 2011*. 서울.

Yonhap Yearbook (2012)

Yonhap Yearbook 2012 연합연감 2012.

Publications in asian languages:

An Yun-sŏk 안윤석. 2011. “The North Korean Hambuk Shipyard is building a 33m long submarine 北, 함북조선소 길이 33m 잠수함 건조 중.” *No Cut News 노컷뉴스*. http://m.nocutnews.co.kr/view.aspx?news=1719197 (29. 3. 2014).

Baidu (n.d.). The great bridge between Changbai and Hyesan 长惠大桥. http://baike.baidu.com/view/4692756.htm. (1. 5. 2013).

Chae Thae-hyŏng 채태형. 2010. *History of the Korean medieval urban development (revised edition) 조선중세도시발달사 (개정판)*. Pyongyang 평양: 사회과학출판사.

Choe Kyŏng-su 최경수. 2011. *New Report on underground resources of North Korea 새로운 지하자원의 보고 (寶庫) 북한*. 서울: 평화문제연구소 The Institute for Peace Affairs. IPA.

Choe Sŏn-yŏng 최선영. 2001. “The Sinuiju Enameled Ironware Factory in North Korea 북한 신의주법랑철기공장.” *TongilNews.com*. http://www.tongilnews.com/news/articleView.html?idxno=4983 (28. 3. 2014).

Choe Song-min 최송민. 2012. “North Korea, since 2003 planning to make Chongjin a Special Zone 北, 2003년부터 청진 특구화 계획 수립.” *Daily NK*. http://www.dailynk.com/korean/read_print.php?cataId=nk04500&num=96936&viewmode= (29. 3. 2014).

Choe Wan-kyu 최완규, ed. 2004a. *The Formation and Development of North Korea's Cities: Chongjin, Sinuiju, and Hyesan 북한 도시의 형성과 발전. 청진, 신의주, 혜산*. 한울아카데미.

______. 2004b. “Urbanization process of the province cities in the North Korea seen through changes in spatial structure 공간구조 변화를 통해 본 북한 지방대도시의 도시화 과정.” In *The Formation and Development of North Korea's Cities: Chongjin, Sinuiju, and Hyesan 북한 도시의 형성과 발전. 청진, 신의주, 혜산*. Choe Wan-kyu 최완규 (2004a), ed. 한울아

카데미.

______. 2006. *Crisis and change of North Korea's cities: Chongjin, Sinuiju, and Hyesan in the 1990s 북한 도시의 위기와 변화. 1990년대 청진, 신의주, 혜산*. 한울아카데미.

______. 2007. *The changing urban politics and prospects for North Korea's transformation: Chongjin, Sinuiju, and Hyesan in the early 2000s 북한의 도시정치의 발전과 체제변화: 2000년대 청진, 신의주, 혜산*. 한울아카데미.

Choe Yŏng-jae 崔寧宰 최영재. 1999. "Why attemps North Korea to get the waters around the five islands in the West Sea? 북한은 왜 서해 5도 수역 넘보나." *Sisa Journal 시사저널*, Nr. 505, 7. 1. 1999. http://www.sisapress.com/news/articleView.html?idxno=9875 (28. 3. 2014).

Corian Clio. 2012. "From Yŏn Kyŏng-je (36): the River Piryusu is the River Honha 연경재研經齋에서 (36): 비류수沸流水는 혼하渾河다." 고리아이, 24. 5. 2012. 01:15. http://blog.daum.net/coreai84/13388599 (28. 3. 2014). encykorea.aks.manphojin (n.d.). *Encyclopedia of Korean Culture 한국민족문화대백과사전*. Manpho-jin 만포진: Academy of Korean Studies 한국학중앙연구원. http://encykorea.aks.ac.kr/Contents/Contents?contents_id=E0017756 (29. 3. 2014).

Future Korea 미래한국. 2004. "Ryongchon explosion Syrians were on the scene." 10 Syrians bodies were repartriated 1 week after the accident [특종] "용천폭파 현장에 시리아인 있었다." 사고 1주일 후 시리아인 시체10구 송환." 10. 6. 2004. http://www.futurekorea.co.kr/news/articleView.html?idxno=5570 (18. 2. 2013).

Han'guk-munwŏn 한국문원. 1995. *50 Year of Division. Going to North Korea,* vol. 1-5 *분단 50년 북한을 가다* 1-5. Seoul 서울.

Hŏ U-kŭng 허우긍. 2007. "Growth process and development direction of North Korean Ports 북한 항만의 성장과정과 개발 방향." In *Strategies for the Industrial Development of North Korea: A Geographical Approach. 북한 산업개발 및 남북협력방안 지리적 접근*. Pak Sam-ok, Hŏ U-kŭng, Pak Ki-ho, & Pak Su-jin 박삼옥, 허우긍, 박기호, 박수진 (2007), 83-120. Seoul National University Press 서울대학교출판사.

Hwang Man-ik, & Yi Ki-sŏk황만익, 이기석. 2005. *Land Use Changes in Major Industrial Regions and New Open Areas for Foreign Investment in North Korea 북한 주요산업지역의 토지이용 변화와 개방지역에 관한 연구*. Seoul National University Press 서울대학교출판사.

IMHC (Institute for Military History Compilation) (n.d.). *Let's investigate the Korean War 6.25 전쟁 알아봅시다*. 국방부 군사편찬연구소. http://www.imhc.mil.kr/user/imhc/625/page.jsp?pgnum=42 (10. 10. 2013).

Im Tŏk-sun 任德淳. 1992. *Our National Land, Korea's geographical Generalities and Regions (II). The Regions 우리 國土 전체와 각 地域 (II). 각 地域의 理解*. 法文社.

Im Tong-u 임동우. 2011. *Pyongyang, and Pyongyang after _Urban Transformation in*

Program, Scale, Structure 평양 그리고 평양 이후. 평양 도시 공간에 대한 또 다른 시각: 1953-2011. Paju: Hyohyŏng Publication 파주: 효형출판.

Jang Se-hun 장세훈. 2006a. "Trends and prospects of the urbanization in North Korea in times of transition. Focusing on the changes in spatial structure of the provincial cities 전환기 북한 도시화의 추이와 전망. 지방 대도시의 공간구조 변화를 중심으로." in *Korean Sociology 40*th *collection 한국사회학*, Nr 4: 186-222.

_________. 2006b. "Urbanization process of big cities in North Korea: Focusing on the changes in the spatial structure of Chongjin, Sinuiju and Hyesan 북한 대도시의 도시화 과정: 청진, 신의주, 혜산의 공간 구조 변화를 중심으로." in *The Society of North Korea 북한의 사회*. Kyŏngin-munhwasa. The Korean Association of North Korean Studies 북한연구학회 (2006) (Hrsg.), 455-509. 景仁文化社.

Jŏng Yong-su 정용수. 2002. "Kaechon~Nampho Lake Thaesŏng waterway construction in Phyongan-namdo completed in 3 years 평안남도 개천~남포 태성호 수로공사 3년 만에 완공." *Jungan Ilbo*. 30. 10. 2002.

_________. 2013. "Kim Jong-un, making a special tourist zone in Wonsan 김정은, 원산에 관광특구 만든다." *Jungan Ilbo 중앙일보*. 26. 6. 2013. http://article.joins.com/news/article/article.asp?total_id=11904260 (29. 3. 2014).

Jŏng Jang-ho 鄭璋鎬. 1986. *Geography of Korea (revised edition). 韓國地理 (改訂版). 祐成文化史*.

Jŏng Thae-wŏn 정태원. 2007. ""Samsu Power Plant in Ryanggang-do used for controlling Chinese invasion" rumours going around "양강도 삼수발전소는 중국침공 견제용" 괴소문." *Daily NK*, 30. 11. 2007. 11:22. http://www.dailynk.com/korean/read.php?cataId=nk04500&num=50400 (2. 5. 2013).

Jŏng Ŭn-i 정은이. 2012. "Study on North Korea trading companies: focusing in the North Korean-Chines border area with a focus on the city Sinuiju 북한무역회사에 관한 연구: 북중 접경도시 '신의주'를 중심으로 [2012 통일부 신진연구자 정책과제]," 35.

Ju Yong-jung, & Yi Yong-su 유용중, 이용수. 2010. "North Korean torpedo factory at least 6 locations… submarine is made in Sinpho (Hamnam Bongdae boiler factory) 북한 어뢰공장 최소 6곳… 잠수함은 신포(함남 봉대 보일러 공장)서 만들어." 27. 5. 2010. *chosun.com*. http://issue.chosun.com/site/data/html_dir/2010/05/27/2010052700825.html (10. 10. 2013).

Kang Chŏl-hwan 강철환. 2011. "North Korea's second border town Hyesan, becoming the 2nd Berlin Wall 북한 제2의 국경도시 혜산, 제2의 베를린장벽 되나." *Weekly Chosun Nr. 2170 주간조선 [2170호]*, 22. 8. 2011. http://weekly.chosun.com/client/news/viw.asp?nNewsNumb=002170100002&ctcd=C06 (5. 4. 2013).

Kang Sŏk-o 姜錫午. 1984. *Revised New Geography of Korea* 改稿新韓國地理. 大學教材出版社.

Kim Chŏl-su 金哲洙. 2005. *The History of Urban Planning. Principles and Technics for space formation 都市計劃史 공강구성의 원리와 기법*. Seoul: Kimundang 서울: 技文堂.

Kim Hyŏn-su 김현수. 1994. "Study on North Korean urban planning 북한의 도시계획에 관한 연구." Seoul National University doctorate thesis 서울대학교 박사학위 논문.

Kim Ki-ho 김기호. 2006. "Urban Planning in North Korea 북한의 도시계획." In *A Comparative Study on Environmental Policy in South and North Koreas,* vol. 2 *남북한 환경정책 비교연구 2*. Kim Jŏng-uk et.al. 김정욱 외. 서울대학교 통일학 연구통서 5, 165-235. Seoul National University Press 서울대학교출판부.

Kim Pŏm-ju 김범주. 2010. *The meaning and origin of the vocabulary of our language 우리 말 어휘의 뜻과 유래*. Pyongyang: Kŭmsŏng Youth Press 평양: 금성청년출판사.

Kim Roi 로이 김. 2006. "Can Korea overcome the mistakes of the USA by themselves? 한국은 미국의 오류를 스스로 극복할까?" *ohmynews*. 16. 2. 2006. http://www.ohmynews.com/NWS_Web/View/at_pg.aspx?CNTN_CD=A0000304952 (22. 3. 2014)

Kim Ryŏn-ok 金蓮玉. 1991. "Nature of Jinnampho 진남포시 자연환경." In *Encyclopedia of Korean Folk Culture 한국만족문화대백과사전*. Academy of Korean Studies 한국정신문화연구원 (1991), 21: 405. Sŏngnam.

Kim Sŏk-jong 김석종. 2013. "The Unification Church shortly before the first anniversary of Mun Sŏng-myŏn's death… 2nd generation succession system rolled up, general director Han Hak-ja takes it all 문선명 1주기 앞둔 통일교… 2세 후계체제 접고 한학자 총재 전면에." *Kyŏnghyang Sinmun 경향신문*. 8. 8. 2013. http://news.khan.co.kr/kh_news/art_print.html?artid=201308082152435 (29. 3. 2014).

Kim Tu-hwan 김두환. 2003. "Sinuiju Cosmetics Factory in North Korea, construction facilities for utilities build 북 신의주화장품공장, 용기 생산시설 건설." *Yonhap News*. http://www.tongilnews.com/news/articleView.html?idxno=35334 (29. 3. 2014).

Kim Tu-sŏp, Choe Min-ja, Jŏn Kwang-hŭi, Yi Sam-sŏk, & Kim Hyŏng-sŏk 김두섭, 최민자, 전광희, 이섬식, 김형석. 2011. *North Korean population and population census 북한 인구와 인구센서스*. Taejon: Statistics Korea (KOSTAT) 대전: 통계청.

Kim Wŏn 김원. 1998. *Socialist urban planning 사회주의 도시계획*. 보성각.

Kim Yong-jae 김용재. 2004. "Kim Jong Il ruling system and power structure 김정일 통치체제와 권력구조." In *2004 Understanding North Korea 2004북한 이해*. Institute for Unification Education (Publ.) 통일부 통일교육원 (편), 18-64.

KJY. 1990. Kwahakwŏn Jirihak Yŏn'guso (Research Institute for Geography at the Academy of Science) 과학원 지리학 연구소 (1987-1990). *Complete Geography of Korean,* vol. 1-20 *조선 지리 전서 1-20*. Pyongyang 평양: 교육 도서 출판사.

Ko Thae-u 고태우. 1992. *The Northern Land already watched before reunification (revised edition) 통일 미리 가 본 북녘땅 (개정판)*. 우아당.

Ko Yu-hwan, & Pak Hŭi-jin 고유환, 박희진. 2013. *Explanation of Sources regarding the North Korean cities Hamhung and Phyongsong 북한도시 함흥 · 평성 자료해제집. 동국대북한학연구소총서*, 007.

Kondŭre Mandŭre 곤드레 만드레. 2005. "The Inner Wall of the City Wall of Anju, Phyongan-namdo 평안남도 안주성내성 북한문화재." http://roks821.egloos.com/8001331. (29. 3. 2014).

Ku Kap-u 구갑우 (et al.). 2008. *Private Sphere and People of Cities in North Korea 북한 도시 주민의 사적 영역 연구*. 북한대학원대학교 총서 7. 한울아카데미.

Kŭmsu-kangsan 금수강산. 2002. *Travel to Phyongan-namdo 평안남도기행 (1). 4호*, 36.

Mok Yong-jae 목용재. 2012. "What is the reason for the arising of a supersize propaganda slogan for Kim Jong-un in Samsu-kun? 김정은, 삼수군에 초대형 선전문구 새긴 이유는?" *Daily NK*, 22. 11. 2012. 16:39. http://www.dailynk.com/korean/read.php?cataId=nk05000&num=97750 (1. 5. 2013).

Nam Mun-hŭi 남문희. 2012. "North Korean rare earth element reserves, turns out to be the world's second largest. 북한 희토류 매장량, 알고 보니 세계 2위." 시사*IN Live*. 16. 11. 2012. http://www.sisainlive.com/news/articleView.html?idxno=14860 (29. 3. 2014).

National Museum of Korea 국립중앙박물관. 2010. *Hamheung, The Hometown of Joseon Royal Family 조선을 일으킨 땅, 함흥*.

NK Chosun.com. 2003. "Support for Learning Unification 통일교실 숙제 도우미." http://nk.chosun.com/board/read.php3?table=friend2&no=6384 (1. 10. 2011).

Pae Ki-chan 배기찬. 1994. *New Regional Geography of North Korea 신 북한 지리지*. 다나도서출판.

Pak Hŭi-jin 박희진. 2013. "Methods of reading while watching North Korean cities. The research of urban history and the utilizing of visual materials 북한 도시를 보면서 읽는 방법. 도시사 연구와 시각영상자료의 활용." In *An introduction to the research method of Socialist cities and North Korean cities 사회주의 도시와 북한도시사연구방법*. Pukhan-tosisa-yŏn'guthim 북한도시사연구팀 (2013), 306-340. 한울아카데미.

Pak In-ho 박인호. 2010. "New currency also hyperinflation phenomenon… the significance of administrated prices disappears 新화폐 역시 초인플레 현상… 국정가격 의미 사라져." *NK 지식인 연대 North Korea Intellectuals Solidarity* (3. 2. 2010). http://www.nkis.kr/board.php?board=kkknewsbuss&page=6&command=body&no=474 (1. 10. 2011).

Pak, Sam-ok 박삼옥. 2007. "An analysis of the North Korean industrial structure and industrial cluster 북한의 산업구조 및 산업집적지 분석." In *Strategies for the Industrial Development of North Korea: A Geographical Approach 북한 산업개발 및 남북협력방안 지리적 접근*. Pak Sam-ok, Hŏ U-kŭng, Pak Ki-ho, & Pak Su-jin 박삼옥, 허우긍, 박기호, 박수진 (2007), 121-175. Seoul National University Press 서울대학교출판사.

Panzercho. 2012. "Haeju-ŭp where the provincial office of Hwanghae-do has been. A journey through national defense by Panzer 황해도 감영이었던 해주읍성. 팬저의 국방여행." panzercho.egloos.com (28. 3. 2014).

Pukhan-tosisa-yŏn'guthim 북한도시사연구팀. 2013. *An introduction to the research method of Socialist cities and North Korean cities 사회주의 도시와 북한도시사연구방법*. 한울아카데미.

Sin Hyo-hŏn 신효헌. 2006. "The problem of the northern limit line between South and North Korea 남북한간의 북방한계선 (NLL) 문제." 외교 제 *78*호 (7. 2006), 17-22.

SNKECSA (South-North Korea Exchanges and Cooperation Support Association 남북교류협력지원협회). 2011. *The North Korean Mineral Resources 북한 광물자원 자료집*. Seoul 서울.

Taehan-thomok-hakhoe (Korean Society of Civil Engineers 대한토목학회), ed. 2009. *Urban and Regional Development in North Korea 북한의 도시 및 지역개발*. Seoul 서울: 보성각.

Yes24.com. 2007. "The Story of Lady Purang 부랑 이야기." http://ch.yes24.com/Article/View/13679 (29. 3. 2014).

Yi, Han-sun 李漢淳. 1991. "The ŭp and myŏn of Tanchon-kun. 단천군 읍 · 면." In *Encyclopedia of Korean Folk Culture 한국민족문화대백과사전*. Academy of Korean Studies 한국정신문화연구원 (1991), 6: 126-127. Sŏngnam.

Yi, Jŏng-hun. 이정훈 2001. "North Koreas "Hyesan Great Purge," 19 person publicly executed and 40000 person illegal arrested 북한의 "혜산 대숙청" 19명을 공개 총살하고 4000여명을 불법 연행." *Shindonga*. http://www.donga.com/docs/magazine/new_donga/200101/nd2001010180.html. (5. 4. 2013).

Yi, Ki-sŏk 이기석. 2001. "Research about the development of teaching materials primary and middle school teachers about the North Korean geography education. 북한 지리교육을 위한 초 · 중등학교 교수 · 학습자료 개발연구." *Education Policy Research 교육정책연구, 14. II*. 2001. Ministry of Education & Human Resources Development 교육인적자원부.

______. 2008. "North Korea Pyongyang-Nampo regional structure study of metropolitan area 북한 평양-남포 대도시권의 지역구조 연구. Report of research of Unification Studies 통일학연구보고서 03-17." Institute for Unification Studies Seoul National University 서울대통일연구소.

______. 2008. "Studies about the regional structures of the North Korean metropolis Pyongyang- Nampho 북한 평양-남포 대도시권의 지역구조 연구." Institute for Unification Studies Seoul National University. Report of Unification Studies 03/17. 서울대통일연구소 통일학연구보고서 03/17. 서울대통일연구소.

Yi, Ok-hŭi 이옥희. 2011. *North.China border area. Urban network of the North Korean-Chinese border area in times of transition 북 · 중 접경지역. 전환기 북 · 중 접경지역의 도시네트워크*. Seoul: Phurŭn kil 서울: 푸른길.

Yi, Sang-jun 이상준, 김천구, 박세훈, 신혜원 et. al. 2011. *Development issues of the growth centers in North Korea (I) (Preparing the reunification of the Korean Peninsula North Korea's development potential of major basis and policy issues.) 통일 한반도 시대에 대비한 북한 주요 거점의 개발잠재력과 정책과제 (I) 국토연 2011-50*. KRIHS (Korea Research Institute for Human Settlements) 국토연구원.

______. 2012. *Development issues of the growth centers in North Korea (II) (Preparing the reunification of the Korean Peninsula North Korea's development potential of major basis and policy issues.) 통일 한반도 시대에 대비한 북한 주요 거점의 개발잠재력과 정책과제 (II) 국토연 2012-2033*. KRIHS (Korea Research Institute for Human Settlements) 국토연구원.

Yi, Sang-jun, Kim, Chŏn-kyu, & Yi, Paek-jin 이상준, 김천규, 이백진. 2012. *A study on the 100 major inter-Korean cooperation issues focusing on spatial development for the Korean peninsula 북한 국토개발을 위한 남북협력 100대 과제와 추진방향. 국토연 2012-15*. KRIHS 국토연구원.

Yi, Sŏk-ki, Kim Sŏk-jin, Kim, Kye-hwan, & Yang, Mun-su 이석기, 김석진, 김계환, 양문수. 2010. *North Korean Industries and Firms in the 2000s: Recovery and Operation Mechanism 2000년대 북한의 산업과 기업 – 회복 실태와 작동 방식*. 서울: KIET 산업연구원.

Yi Wŏn-sun 李元淳. 1991. "History of Kaechon-kun 개천군 역사." *Encycolpaedy of Korean Folk Culture 한국민족문화대백과사전*. In Academy of Korean Studies 한국정신문화연구원 (1991), 1: 599-600. Sŏngnam.

Yi Yo-sep 이요셉. 2002. "각하는 어데로 Where is the Majesty?" http://www.donga.com/docs/magazine/new_donga/200101/nd2001010180.html (1. 10. 2010).

Yonhap News 연합뉴스. 2001. "April 3th factory 4월 3일 공장." http://100.daum.net/yearbook/view.do?id=46576. (1. 3. 2013).

Yonhap 연합. 2002. "Installation extensions of communication cable production line in North Korea 북, 통신케이블 생산라인 증설 (5. 7. 2002)." http://nk.chosun.com/news/news.html?ACT=detail&cat_id=12&page=8&res_id=20102 (29. 3. 2014).

Yun Jŏng-sŏp 尹定燮. 1987. "An Introduction to the History of Urban Planning 都市計劃史 概論." Seoul: Munundang 서울: 文運堂.

Yun Ung 윤웅. 1995. *A Journey through the Geography of North Korea 북한의 지리여행*. 서울: 문예산책.

Publications in western languages:

Armstrong, Charles K. 2005. "'Fraternal Socialism': The International Reconstruction of North Korea, 1953-1962." *Cold War History 5, no. 2* (May, 2005): 161-187. Routledge.

Bauer, Wolfgang. 2005. "Die letzte Stadt der DDR. Ein Besuch in Hamhung. (The last city of the GDR. A visit to Hamhung)." http://www.wolfgang-bauer.info/pages/reportagen/nordkorea/nordkorea.html (24. 5. 2010).

Becker, Anne-Katrein. 1988. *Länder der Erde. Korea (KDVR) (Countries of the world. DPRK)*. Kleine LdE Reihe. Verlag Die Wirtschaft. Berlin.

Bermudez Jr., Joseph S. 2001. *The Armed Forces of North Korea*. IB. Tauris. London. New York.

Choi Kyung-soo. 2010. "The Mining Industry of North Korea." In *The Korean Journal of*

Defense Analysis, 23, no. 2 (June 2011): 211-230.

Commie Travel: Korea/Anju. http://www.commietravel.nl/noordkorea/provinces/anju/anju.htm (14. 3. 2008).

Cronin, Patrick M. 2012. "Vital Venture. Economic Engagement of North Korea and the Kaeong Industrial Complex." Center for a New American Security.

Cumings, Bruce. 2004. "Consequences of the 'forgotten' war. Korea: forgotten nuclear threats." Le Monde diplomatique. English edition. December 2004. http://mondediplo.com/2004/12/08korea (29. 3. 2014).

Dege, Eckart. 1991. *Kleiner Reiseführer Nordkorea (Small travel guide North Korea).* Kiel.

Demick, Barbara. 2009. *Nothing to Envy: Ordinary Lives in North Korea.* Spiegel & Grau/ Random House. New York.

Dormels, Rainer. 1996. "Kangwŏn-do (Nord) - Potential und Perspektiven einer Provinz an der DMZ (North-Kangwŏn-do - Potential and perspectives of a province at the DMZ)." in *Zeitschrift der Koreanisch-Deutschen Gesellschaft für Sozialwissenschaften*, Bd. 6 (1996), S. 475-502. Seoul.

Eberstadt, Nicholas, and Banister, Nick. 1992. *The population of North Korea.* Institute of East Asian Studies, University of California, Center for Korean Studies. Berkely.

Frank, Rüdiger. 1996. *Die DDR und Nordkorea. Der Wiederaufbau der Stadt Hamhùng von 1954-1962. (The GDR and North Korea. The reconstruction of Hamhung-city from 1954-1962).* Shaker Verlag. Aachen. Master Thesis.

Grabowsky, Volker. 1985. "Eine Reise in das Land der Morgenfrische (A journey to the land of morning calm)." in *Blätter des iz3w*. Nr. 127 August 1985.

GlobalSecurity.com (n.d.). "Mayang Do Naval Base." http://www.globalsecurity.org/military/world/dprk/mayangdo.htm (29. 3. 2014).

Heineberg. Heinz. 2006. *Stadtgeographie (Urban Geography)*. Verlag UTB. Stuttgart.

Herl, Brandon K. 2004. "Urban Geography." In *North Korea. Geographic Perspectives.* Palka, Eugene J., & Galgano, Francis A. (2004), 75-85. The McGraw-Hill Companies.

Im, Jeong Jin. 2011. "Model Kim Chaek Complex in Dire Straits." *Daily NK.* http://www.dailynk.com/english/read.php?cataId=nk01500&num=7311 (29. 3. 2014).

Institute for Far East Studies. 2007. "2nd South-North Korean Summit Joint Statement." *NK Brief, no. 07-10-4-2.* http://www.nkeconwatch.com/category/economic-reform/special-administrative-regions/haeju/page/2 (18. 7. 2013).

Jeong, Yong-soo. 2013. "North is building ski, beach resorts in Wonsan." *Korea Joongang Daily.* 27. 6. 2013. http://koreajoongangdaily.joins.com/news/article/article.aspx?aid=2973720 (10. 10. 2013).

Jo Am, & An Chol Gang. 2002. *Korea im 20. Jahrhundert. 100 Tatsachen. (Korea in the 20th Century. 100 facts).* Verlag für Fremdsprachige Literatur. Pyongyang.

Jo, J. C., & S. Adler. 2002. "North Korean planning. Urban changes and regional balance." In *Cities, 19, no. 3*, 205-215.

Jong, Song Il. 2011. *DPR Korea Tour.* National Tourism Administration. Pyongyang.

Kang, Man-gil. 1982. "Merchants of Kaesong," 89-119. In *Economic Life in Korea.* The Si-sa-yong-o-sa Publishers, Inc. Seoul.

Kang-Schmitz,. Liana. 2010. *Nordkoreas Umgang mit Abhängigkeit und Sicherheitsrisiko: Am Beispiel der bilateralen Beziehungen zur DDR (North Korea dealing with dependency and safety risks: at the example of bilateral relations with the GDR)*. epubli GmbH. Berlin.

KBS World Radio. 2011. "Nordkorea beschließt Gesetz für Sonderwirtschaftszonen (North Korea adopts laws for special economic zones)." *Nordkorea a bis z.* http://world.kbs.co.kr/german/event/nkorea_nuclear/now_02_detail.htm?no=33823 (10. 10. 2013).

Kim, Kwang Jin. 2012. "2,500 Jobs Heading for Hyesan." *Daily NK* (23. 6. 2012. 11:42. http://www.dailynk.com/english/read.php?cataId=nk01500&num=9407 (5. 4. 2013).

Kim, Min Se. 2007. "A Scientific City Pyongsung Became a Distributors Haven for Goods." In *Daily NK* (9. 7. 2007). http://www.dailynk.com/english/read.php?cataId=nk00100&num=2342 (29. 3. 2014).

Kim, Mi-young. 2002. "The Struggling North Korean Automobile Industry." *Chosun Ilbo*. 5. 2. 2002. http://web.archive.org/web/20021205163459/http://english.chosun.com/w21data/html/news/200202/200202050269.html (29. 3. 2014).

Kindermann. 1994. *Der Aufstieg Koreas in der Weltpolitik. (The rise of Korea in world politics)*. Olzog Verlag. München.

Ko, Kyoung-tae. 2007. "Haeju in N.K. seem playing bigger roleHaeju in N.K. seem playing bigger role Tuesday." October 16th, 2007 Korea Herald. http://www.nkeconwatch.com/2007/10/16/haeju-in-nk-seem-playing-bigger-role/ (18. 7. 2013).

Kohn, Michael, & Humber, Yuriy. 2013. "Mongolia Taps North Korea Oil Potential to Ease Russian Grip (2)." *BloombergBusinessweek. 18. 6.* 2013. http://www.businessweek.com/news/2013-06-17/mongolia-taps-north-korean-oil-potential-to-ease-russia-reliance (29. 3. 2014). Yonhap News Agency. 2003. Korea Annual 2003. Seoul.

Lautensach, Hermann. 1945. *Korea. Eine Landeskunde aufgrund eigener Reisen und der Literatur*e *(Korea. A regional study trough journeys and literature)*. Leipzig.

Lee, Jeong-sik. 2000. "Opening of North Korea and the Tuman River Area Development Program." In *Korea. The Land and People*. The Organizing Committee of the 29th International Geographical Congress (2000), 483-506. Seoul: Kyohaksa.

Lee, Ki-baik. 1984. *A New History of Korea*. Edward W. Wagner with Edward J. Shultz trans. Harvard University Press.

Lim, Eul-chul. 2007. *Kaesong Industrial Complex. History, Pending Issues, and Outlook.* Seoul: Haenam Publishing Co.

McCune, Shannon. 1980. *Views of the Geography of Korea 1935-1960*. Published by The Korean Research Center. Seoul.

Mossman, Billy C. 1990. "EBB AND FLOW; NOVEMBER 1950 - JULY 1951." http://www.kmike.com/EbbAndFlow/EbbAndFlow.htm (1. 8. 2010).

Naenara. "Koreanische Handelsfirma Amnokgang" (Korean trading company Amnokgang). http://www.naenara.com.kp/de/realtrade/?company+5+4 (10. 10. 2013).

Newfocusintl. 2013. "Chongjin: North Korea's Fashion Capital." 14. 6. 2013. http://newfocusintl.com/all-roads-begin-at-chongjin.

NKEW. 2008. *Russian auto plant KamAZ in DPRK*.

North Korean Economic Watch. Archive for the 'Kamaz' Category. http://www.nkeconwatch.com/category/organizaitons/kamaz/ (10. 10. 2013).

North Korean Economy Watch. 2013 Market expansion: Sinuiju. http://www.nkeconwatch.com/2013/04/03/market-expansion-sinuiju/ (10. 10. 2013).

North Korea Online Travel Guide (n.d.). Osan Hill. http://www2.vnc.nl/korea/?City_Guide:Tuman:Osan_Hill (26. 2. 2013).

North Korea Leadership Watch. 2011. PRC-DPRK open Hyesan Mine. http://nkleadershipwatch.wordpress.com/2011/09/25/prc-dprk-open-hyesan-mine/ (1. 5. 2013).

NTI Nuclear Threat Initiative (n.d.a). No. 26 Factory. http://www.nti.org/facilities/266/ (15. 2. 2013).

NTI Nuclear Threat Initiative (n.d.b). Shinhŭng Chemical Complex. http://www.nti.org/facilities/615/ (10. 10. 2013).

NTI Nuclear Threat Initiative (n.d.c). Muncheon Agar Factory http://www.nti.org/facilities/564/ (10. 10. 2013).

Palka, Eugene J., & Galgano, Francis A. 2004. *North Korea. Geographic Perspectives*. The McGraw-Hill Companies. Guilfort.

Pews, Hans-Ulrich. 1987. *Korea-Land der Morgenfrische (Korea-Land of the morning calm)*. VEB Hermann Haack Geographisch-Kartographische Anstalt Gotha.

Quinones, C. Kenneth. 2002. *Paradise Lost - The International Response to North Korea's Agricultural Crisis*. American Research Center for Asia and the Pacific, Washington, DC.

Ramstadt, Evan. 2012. "End of the Road for North Korean Auto Maker?" *The Wall Street Journal*. 27. 11. 2012. http://blogs.wsj.com/korearealtime/2012/11/27/end-of-the-road-for-north-korean-auto-maker/tab/print/ (10. 10. 2013).

Stanislas Roussin, Stanislas, & Ducruet, César. 2010. "The Nampo-Pyongyang corridor." A strategic area for European investment in DPRK. Author manuscript, published in *Recent Changes in North Korea and the Role of the European Union (Institute of Unification. Studies & Hans Seidel Foundation, Seoul National University)*. Seoul: Korea, Republic Of (2007). Revised Version 25. 2. 2010. http://hal.archives-ouvertes.fr/docs/00/45/97/51/PDF/

Roussin_Ducruet_NPC_revised.pdf (10. 10. 2013).

Saitschikow, W. T. 1958. *Korea.* VEB Deutscher Verlag der Wissenschaften. Berlin. (In German).

Schinz, A., & E. Dege. 1990. "Pyongyang-Ancient and Modern-The Capital of North Korea." *Geo Journal 22: 1* (September 1990): 21-32.

Springer, Chris. 2003. *Pyongyang: The Hidden History of the North Korean Capital.* With photos by Eckart Dege 159 pages, 140 sites, 98 photos/illustrations, 7 maps. Published by Entente Bt.; First edition – 2003.

Schmidt-Lauber et al. (Schmidt-Lauber, Brigitta; Reinert, Wiebke; Wolfmayr, Georg; Ecker, Karin (n.d.)). Mittelstädtische Urbanitäten. Ethnographische Stadtforschung in Wels und Hildesheim (Middletown Urbanities. Ethnographic Urban Studies in Wels and Hildesheim). Forschungsprojekt, Institut für Europäische Ethnologie, Universität Wien. http://www.univie.ac.at/middletownurbanities/begriffliches (29. 3. 2014).

Speckmann, Thomas. 2010. Der erste deutsche Stellvertreterkrieg (German's frist proxy war). FAZ. http://www.faz.net/frankfurter-allgemeine-zeitung/bilder-und-zeiten/der-erste-deutsche-stellvertreterkrieg-1996284.html (29. 3. 2014).

The Chosunilbo. 2010. "How N. Korea Goes About Exporting Arms." Mar. 10, 2010. http://english.chosun.com/site/data/html_dir/2010/03/10/2010031000953.html (18. 2. 2013).

The Organizing Committee of the 29th International Geographical Congress. 2000. *Korea. The Land and People*. Seoul: Kyohaksa.

Tong. 2010. "Moves to enhance economic integration between Sino-Korean border." *Asia-Gazette*. http://www.asia-gazette.com/news/north-korea/41 (1. 10. 2011).

Unicef Österreich. 1997. "Hungertod von Kindern in Nordkorea (1. 4. 1997) (Children's death by starvation in North Korea)." http://www.unicef.at/131.html?&tx_ttnews%5Bpointer%5D=109&tx_ttnews%5Btt_news%5D=133&tx_ttnews%5BbackPid%5D=45&cHash=2d5119e23a (1. 10. 2011).

U.S. Government Printing Office. 1997. *North Korean Missile Proliferation. Hearing. First Session. October 21, 1997.* Washington. http://www.gpo.gov/fdsys/pkg/CHRG-105shrg44649/pdf/CHRG-105shrg44649.pdf (29. 3. 2014).

Verlag für Fremdsprachige Literatur. 1995. *Pyongyang stellt sich vor.* (Introducing Pyongyang). Pyongyang.

______. 2001. *Kim Jong Il Bibliographischer Abriss (Kim Jong Il Short Bibliography)*. Pyongyang.

VNC Asia Travel (n.d.). "North Korea Online Travel Guide." http://www2.vnc.nl/korea/?City_Guide:Paektusan:Hyesan (1. 5. 2013).

Wikimapia "7th Machine Industry Bureau Aircraft Parts Factory." http://wikimapia.org/13928842/7th-Machine-Industry-Bureau-Aircraft-Parts-Factory (10. 10. 2013).

Yoo, Cheong-mo. 2002. "Success in Sinuiju hinges on Gaesong project." in *Korea Herald*, 2. 10. 2002.

Yoo, Gwan Hee. 2010. "Food Avenue Finally Complete in Hoiryeong." *Daily NK* (19. 10. 2010). http://www.dailynk.com/english/read.php?cataId=nk01500&num=6920 (25. 2. 2013).

Yoon, Hong-key. 2006. *The culture of fengshui in Korea: an exploration of East Asian geomancy.* Lexington Books. Plymouth, UK.

Yoon, Suh-kyung. 2000. "Dollars and Sentiments." http://web.yonsei.kr/jgk/articles/CCG/Daewoo%20in%20NK%20NYT%20000622.doc. (10. 10. 2013).

Newspapers and Internet News etc.

Chosun Ilbo (Korean)

Daum Encyclopedia http://100.daum.net/top.index (Korean)

Foreign Trade (English)

Korea Herald (English)

Kukmin Ilbo (Korean)

NK Chosun.com (Korean)

Pyongyang Times (English)

RKI (Radio Korea International) (German)

The Hangyoreh (Korean)

Yonhap (Korean)

IV.2.1. Kanggye

Capital of the mountainous province of Jagang, which was founded in 1949; Already in the past: a city of great military importance; "World of rivers"; A center of textile and defense industries; Cultural center of the province; The "Spirit of Kanggye (Kanggye Spirit)"; Expansion of the urban area in the years 1952, 1963, 1967 and 1995 in a northern direction; Active development of the inner city until the 1960s and early 1980s, afterwards urbanization of the peripheral; Statistics; Kanggye – a symbol for "the spirit of defending socialism" in North Korean propaganda

IV.2.2. Huichon

Gate to the plateau of the province of Jagang; Urban development in typical basin area; Most important city of machine construction in the DPR Korea; "Huichon Speed"– The power plant construction as a symbol for the ascent to the great and powerful nation; The capitals of the northern neighbour-*kun* of Songwon and Tongsin were once part of Huichon-si; Three new *dong* in the mid 90s; Statistics; Huichon – City with two centers and two important companies

IV.2.3. Manpho

Settlement at the Korean-Chinese border; Lowlands at the middle reaches of the Yalu; From a Sawing Site to a Tire- and Rubber-Manufacturer; Rail junction at the northern border of DPR Korea; Since the city founding in 1967, there haven't been any new *dong* for about 40 years; Three urbanized regions of Manpho; Manpho – Economic development area for agriculture, tourism and trade

IV.2.4. Sinuiju

The "New Uiju"; City in flood-prone position; Important location for the light industry of DPR Korea; Sinuiju special economic zone; Center of education and culture in the northwest of the DPR Korea; The ten party members of Rakwŏn; Capital of the province of Phyongbuk; High population density in Old-Sinuiju; Old-Sinuiju, Nam-Sinuiju, Yŏnha: three urbanized areas; Incorporations in 1961, 1963 and 1989; Urbanization process in Sinuiju; The Development of Nam-Sinuiju since the end of the 1980s; Statistics; Sinuiju – Korea's Door to the Eurasian Mainland

IV.2.5. Kusong

One of the Kangdong Six Garrison Settlements from the Koryo era; Typical basin position; Mechanical Engineering and Textile Industry; Transport center in Phyongbuk; After the elevation to a city in 1967, there is no enlargement of the urban area; 1967, enlargement of central Kusong; 1976/1984: enlargement of the sub centers; One center and two sub centers; Statistics; Kusong – Traffic junction and location of machine construction in the mountainous country of Phyongbuk

IV.2.6. Jongju

Fortified city during the Joson period; Famous for rice but also for specialized crops such as chestnuts, fruits, tobacco; Phyongbuk Smeltery and numerous factories relevant to agriculture; Traffic center at the northern Yellow sea coast; Jongju Youth Gymnasium – a landmark of the city; Home of pioneers – from writers to cult founders; Internal structure such as the one in a rural county; Jongju – Agricultural center at the coastal flatland

IV.2.7. Phyongsong

Established as a city of science; Hilly land east of the Taedong-gang; Light industry and military vehicles; Training center for professionals in the region; Phyongsong as handling site for Chinese goods; Development of the city of Phyongsong and changes in the urban area; Two settlement guidelines; Statistics; Phyongsong – Provincial capital with educational institutions and little industry

IV.2.8. Anju

A city with a long tradition as an administrative and military center; Flood endangered downtown; Development into an industrial city after the construction of the Namhŭng Youth Chemical Complex in the 1970s; Three urbanized areas before the city founding in 1987; Changes after the city founding; Statistics; Anju – a city with different historical roots

IV.2.9. Kaechon

City with a tradition of craftmanship and trade; City between the rivers; A town specialized in mining; Transportation hub in northwestern Korea; Starting point for the Kaechon – Lake Thaesong Waterway; Between 1952 and 1969, ten *rodongjagu* developed, in 1990 Kaechon was appointed to city (*si*); From 1990, only four *dong* originated from *ri*; Structure of the urbanized areas of the city of Kaechon; Statistics; Kaechon – numerous former *rodongjagu* with its mining villages

IV.2.10. Tokchon

City of automobile industry and mining situated at a reservoir; Only 9% of agricultural land; Mining and the Sŭngri Motor Plant; Until the city founding eight *rodongjagu* existed; No changes after the designation as a city in 1986; Statistics; Tokchon – Many former working-class districts, a typical mining town with a car construction facility

IV.2.11. Sunchon

A new industrial city; Basin of the Taedong-gang in the central hilly terrain of Phyongnam; Significant cement production and a former Vinalon factory; Urban development at the Taedong-gang as well as mining and a cement factory in the east of the city; Reduction of the municipal area in favor of Unsan-kun and Ungok-jigu; Statistics; Sunchon – Industrial city with a variety of companies from different industrial sectors

IV.2.12. Pyongyang

IV.2.12.1. Overview

The historical center in the northwest of Korea; Largest industrial city of the DPRK; Changes of the bigger administrative regional units in Pyongyang

IV.2.12.2. Downtown districts west of the Taedong-gang

Jung-kuyok – the center of the capital; Phyongchon-kuyok – the *kuyok* with most of the industrial companies; Moranbong-kuyok – Parks and the Arch of Triumph; Pothonggang-kuyok - Ryugyong hotel and residential complex for the executive;

Sosong-kuyok – Location of Kim Jong Thae Electric Locomotive Complexes; Taesong-kuyok - urbanized West, Taesong-san in the East;

IV.2.12.3. Inner city districs east to the Taedong-gang

Taedonggang-kuyok – Munsu-Street and embassy area; Tongdaewon-kuyok – the *kuyok* east to the Juche Tower; Songyo-kuyok – Industrial area in East-Pyongyang;

IV.2.12.4. City suburbs west of the Taedong-gang

Samsok-kuyok – *Kuyok* with large agricultural companies; Unjong-kuyok – the science district; Ryongsong – kuyok at the foot of the Chŏngryong mountain range; Sunan-kuyok – *Kuyok* with the International Airport of Pyongyang; Hyongjesan-kuyok – *Kuyok* with the second highest increase in the rate of urbanization since 1986; Mangyongdae-kuyok – Kwangbok residental area and Chŏngchun Sport Village

IV.2.12.5. City suburbs east of the Taedong-gang

Sadong-kuyok – concentration of the population in the north of the *kuyok*; Ryokpho-kuyok - agricultural *kuyok* in the south of Pyongyang; Rakrang-kuyok – *Kuyok* with the latest high rise residential block neighborhood; Kangdong-kun - Location of significant coal mines; Kangnam-kun - rice producer for the capital's population

IV.2.12.6. Summary: Administrative changes in the *kuyok* and *kun* of Pyongyang

IV.2.13. Nampho

Port of Pyongyang – Second largest city of the DPR Korea; City on the lower reaches of the Taedong-gang; Major heavy industry companies in the Pyongyang-Nampho-Corridor; Largest port in the country and a good transport link to the neighbouring capital; Nampho–region of localization of political propaganda; The Twin Cities Nampho (from 1950)/Taean (1978-1983); 1963, 1974 and 1984 Enhancement of Old-Nampho; Phases of urban development in Old-Nampho; Statistics: Nampho Waudo-kuyok and Hanggu-kuyok (altogether 36 *dong*); Old-Taean; Development in the counties (*kun*); Nampho – a large potential for foreign investments after Korean Reunification

IV.2.14. Sariwon

Traffic center in Hwangbuk; Sariwon – endangered by drought; Center of the textile industry; Junction for the rail, road and water traffic – "City on the canal"; Provincial center for education, culture and health care; Tourism areas: Jŏngbang-san and Kyŏngam – "Folk Custom Street"; Newcomers with a "good reputation"; A statue for Kang Kŏn; International associations; "Residential buildings higher than the buildings of the administration"; Administrative, economic and cultural center of the province North-Hwanghae

City since 1947, since then incorporations (six times); Common administrative regrouping in the second half of the 50s; The 60s: Enhancement of the city center; 1981 and 1991: new *dong* also offside the municipal area; Structure of the city of Sariwon; Statistics; Sariwon – city on the way between Pyongyang and Seoul

IV.2.15. Songrim

Kyomipho – the port of Kenji; Songrim - the town of the Hwanghae Iron and Steel Complex; In 1947 city foundation, in 1954 slight reduction of the city's territory; 1957: Twelve *dong* on the Taedong-gang shore are combined into five *dong*; Industrial removal on the Taedong-gang shore in the 50s and in the 80s/90s; Removal of residential districts in the center of the city in the 1960s; From the 1960s and strengthened in 1988/92: "New life" in the East of the city; Statistics; Songrim – Industrial satellite town of Pyongyang

IV.2.16. Kaesong

Former capital of the Koryo dynasty; Dominance of light industry; The Kaesong industrial region; Unesco world heritage; Kaesong – once part of South Korea; 2002: Formation of the economic zone Kaesong; in 2003: Kaesong is incorporated into the Hwangbuk Province; Statistics; Structure; Kaesong - City in the middle of the Korean peninsula with big developing potential

IV.2.17. Haeju

An important city in the Koryo and Joson era; A city between sea and mountains; Smelters, cement factory and manufacture of agricultural machinery; The planned Haeju Special Economic Zone; Disputed maritime border between North and South Korea; Haeju as a touristic and cultural center; Developments of the city after 1945 and development centers; Statistics; Haeju – high potential for development after reunification

IV.2.18. Hyesan

Border town to China and gate to Paektusan; City of forestry; Situated in a basin on the upper Yalu; City with a high number of factories; Hyesan Youth Copper Mine as an example for the cooperation with China; The construction of the Samsu Hydroelectric Power Station; Provincial capital with appropriate cultural facilities; Border trade with China and its effects; Hyesan – the basis for the Paektusan tourism; 1954: city foundation – capital of Ryanggang Province; 1961 – Expansion of the city around the rural areas; Developments and structure; Statistics; Hyesan – border city with a considerable number of middle and small factories

IV.2.19. Rason

City in the northeast corner of the DPR Korea; Change in the economic structure by the construction of Sŭngri Chemical Complex; Rason Economic Special Zone; Rajin – City from 1936-1949; 1967-1993: Rajin-si, for a few months Unggi (Sonbong) is already part of the city; 1993 Rajin-Sonbong-jikhalsi; 2000 Rason-jikhalsi; 2010 Rason-thukbyolsi; Urban expansion, reductions; Structure; Statistics; Rason – Ports near the new Chinese economic development zones

IV.2.20. Chongjin

Port and industrial city established under Japanese rule; City development in the plain of Susŏng-chŏn; "City of Iron"; The second largest port of the DPR Korea – Investments from China and Russia; Cultural capital of Hambuk; Chongjin – "North Korea's Fashion Capital"; A city divided in *kuyok*; Developments in the individual *kuyok*; City center; Ranam; Puyun; Area between Chongjin center and Ranam; Chongam – the area between Chongjin center and Rason; Statistical Summary: from the 1970s on almost all new *dong* in Ranam and Chongam; Chongjin – city of old industry with potential as traffic junction

IV.2.21. Hoeryong

Border city to China and birthplace of Kim Jong-il's mother; City in the northwest of the Hamgyong mountain range; Food production and lignite mining; The three beauties of Hoeryong; The White apricot blossom from Osan Hill; A *kun* with seven *rodongjagu*; Foundation of the city in 1991, two development poles, coal mines in the Northeast; Statistics; Hoeryong – Birthplace of Kim Jong-suk, mother of Kim Il-sung

IV.2.22. Kimchaek

One of the opened ports and base of Christian Mission; Change of name to honor General Kim

Chaek; The Kimchaek Bay; City of steel and Magnesia Clinker; Incorporations in 1952 and 1961, five *ri* outside the center became *dong*; Within Old-Kimchaek six new *dong* formed by separation; Eight new *dong* from 1961 to 1965, afterwards only three new *dong*; Three centers of urban development and three new *dong* in the periphery; Statistics; Kimchaek – City in the shadow of Chongjin and Tanchon

IV.2.23. Hamhung

Hometown of the Joson royal family; Reconstruction of Hamhung and developments after 1945; Location in the largest plain at the Northeast Korean East Sea Coast; City of chemical industry; Administrative Overview; Changes within the *kuyok*-system; After the reconstruction: Developments of the Sapho region; Hamhung – center of Northeast Korea

IV.2.24. Tanchon

In the past as an intermediate stop before crossing the Machŏn-ryŏng; Mining Town; Mineral resources; Extension of the port; Development before the city designation in 1982; Developments after the city's designation in 1982; Statistics; Tanchon – mining town with new port

IV.2.25. Sinpho

Most famous fishing harbor of North Korea; Sinpho area – a basis for the fishing industry; Fish processing and shipbuilding; Sinpho – DPR Koreas Submarine Production Base; City with numerous cultural institutions; Structural Analysis; *Rodongjagu* that existed before Sinpho became a city; Structure; Statistics; Sinpho – small town on the East Sea coast

IV.2.26. Wonsan

Capital of Kangwon Province (North); Wonsan Bay; Walnuts – a special product of the city of Wonsan; Industrial zone of the second degree; Center of Transport and Culture; Tourism Center Wonsan; Changes in terms of the urban area; Statistics; Wonsan – Great potential for tourism

IV.2.27. Munchon

Industrial city in the Basin of Wonsan, City of non-ferrous metallurgy; Structural analysis Munchon; Statistics; Munchon – Small industrial city north of Wonsan

Appendix 2. List of industrial companies in DPR Korea (In Korean)

The following companies are listed by city in the same order as the cities appear in this volume. In the parenthesis the names of the province are provided.

Kanggye, Huichon, Manpho (Jagang);
Sinuiju, Kusong, Jongju (Phyongbuk);
Phyongsong, Anju, Kaechon, Tokchon, Sunchon (Phyongnam);
Pyongyang;
Nampho;
Sariwon, Songrim, Kaesong (Hwangbuk);
Haeju (Hwangnam);
Hyesan (Ryanggang);
Rason;
Chongjin, Hoeryong, Kimchaek (Hambuk);
Hamhung, Tanchon, Sinpho (Hamnam);
Wonsan, Munchon (Kangwon).
After the industrial companies are listed by city, the industrial companies of the counties (Kun) of the respective provinces are listed.
The numbers in the parenthesis behind the source indicate the number of industrial companies including the important factories. For example KOFC (14-1) defines 14 industrial companies which are listed in the source "KOFC" from which one is an important company. In the succeeding list, the companies which are referred to as important are therefore emphasized in bold.

Kanggye (Jagang Province)

KOFC (14-1)

경공업 (4-1)	식품 (2)	강계식료공장, 강계곡산공장
	섬유 (1)	**[강계방직공장 (9월방직공장)]**
	신발 (1)	강계신발공장
중화공업 (9)	금속 (1)	강계강철공장
	기계 (5)	강계자전거공장, 강계저울공장, 강계시계공장, 독로강공작기계공장, 강계뜨락또르공장
	전기/전자 (1)	강계제1통신기계공장
	건재 (2)	강계세멘트공장, 강계유리공장
전력 (1)	수력 (1)	강계청년발전소3호

MOU (23-1)

건재 (2)	강계목재가공공장, 강계시멘트공장
경공업 (18)	강계견방직공장, 강계고려약가공공장, 강계고려약공장, 강계기초식품공장, 강계리미액공장, 강계수출피복공장, 강계식료공장, 강계신발공장, 강계약공장, 강계연필공장, 강계영예군인피복공장, 강계은하피복공장, 강계종리공장, 강계편직공장, 강계포도술공장, 강계피복공장, 장자산종합식료공장, 9월방직공장
기계 (2-1)	**[강계정밀기계련합기업소]**; 강계기계공장
전력 (1)	흥주청년발전소

IPA (4-3)

공업 (3-3)	**[강계연필공장(江界鉛筆工場)]**, **[강계포도술공장]**, **[구월방직공장(九月紡織工場)]**;
전력 (1)	북천1호발전소

KCNA (22)

공업 (18)	강계기초식품공장, 강계식료공장, 장자산종합식료공장, 강계포도술공장, 9월방직공장, 강계견방적공장, 강계은하피복공장, 강계편직공장, 강계직물공장, 강계피복공장, 강계고려약가공공장, 강계기와공장, 강계목재가공공장, 강계연필공장, 강계뜨락또르종합공장, 강계애국복합미생물비료공장, 강계정밀기계련합기업소, 장자강공작기계공장
전력 (4)	강계청년발전소, 북천2호청년발전소, 의진발전소, 장자산발전소

KIET (29-7)

II. 음식료품, 담배 (2-1)	2) 곡물가공	강계곡산공장
	6) 음료	**[강계포도술공장]**
III. 섬유, 의복, 신발 (7-2)	1) 방직	**[9월방직공장]**
	3) 방적 등	강계방사공장
	5) 편직공장	강계편직공장
	6) 의류	강계피복공장, 강계영예군인피복공장
	8) 신발	**[강계신발공장]**
	10) 가죽 등	강계망사공장
IV. 목재, 펄프, 종이 (2)	1) 목재	강계목재가공공장

	3) 종이	강계종이공장
V. 화학 (3)	3) 비료	강계풍년비료공장
	8) 합성수지 등	강계수지일용품공장
	9) 제약	강계제약공장
VI. 시멘트, 유리 (2)	1) 시멘트	강계세멘트공장
	4) 유리	강계유리공장
VII. 1차 금속산업(2-1)	1) 제철, 제강	**[8호제강소]**, 강계철강공장
VIII. 조립금속, 기계장비 (6-3)	1) 종합기계	**[강계기계공장]**
	3b) 농업용	**[강계뜨락또르공장]**, 강계뜨락또르부속품공장
	3c) 기타	**[강계건설기계공장]**
	4) 정밀기계	강계실험기구공장, 강계정밀기계공장
X. 가구, 잡제품 (4)	2) 문방구 등	강계연필공장, 강계실험기구공장, 강계영예군인만년필공장
	3) 악기	강계선물악기공장
XI. 전력 (1)	1) 수력	흥주발전소

IMPORTANT (6)

공업 (6)	강계포도술공장, 9월방직공장, 강계신발공장, 강계연필공장, 강계뜨락또르(종합)공장, 강계정밀기계련합기업소

Huichon (Jagang Province)

KOFC (10-2)

중화공업 (8-2)	기계 (4-2)	**[희천련하기계종합공장 (구 희천공작기계종합공장)]**, **[희천정밀기계공장]**; 희천텔레비젼수상기조립공장, 희천영예군인자동화기구공장
	전기/전자 (2)	희천전구공장, 희천종합전자기기공장
	건재 (2)	희천세멘트공장, 희천경질유리그릇공장
전력 (2)	수력 (2)	유중발전소, 희천수력발전소

MOU (6-2)

경공업 (4-1)	**[희천시지방공업종합공장]**; 희천고려약공장, 희천제사공장, 희천철제일용품공장
기계 (2-1)	**[희천련하기계종합공장]**; 희천정밀기계공장 (2월26일공장)

IPA (3-1)

공업 (3-1)	**[희천공작기계공장 (熙川工作機械工場)]**; 희천제사공장, 희천정밀기계공장

KCNA (14)

공업 (11)	희천식료공장, 희천장공장, 희천경질유리그릇공장, 청년전기련합기업소, 희천도자기공장, 희천련하기계종합공장 (희천공작기계종합공장), 희천영예군인전자기구공장, 희천유리필수품공장, 희천정밀기계공장 (2월26일공장), 희천제사공장, 콩가공공장
전력 (3)	동문2호발전소, 희천발전소, 희천2호발전소

KIET (16-9)

I. 광업 (1)	1) 탄광	희천탄광
III. 섬유, 의복, 신발 (3-1)	3) 방적 등	**[희천제사공장]**
	2) 직물등	희천직물공장
	6) 의류	희천수출피복공장
VI. 시멘트, 유리 (2)	1) 시멘트	희천세멘트공장
	5) 도자기	희천도자기공장
VIII. 조립금속, 기계장비 (9-8)	1) 종합기계	희천기계수리공장
	2) 공작	**[희천고리끼합영회사], [희천공작기계종합공장]**
	4) 정밀	**[2월26일공장(희천정밀기계공장)]**
	5) 기계부품, 금속가공	**[희천철제일용품공장]**
	6a) 전기	**[희천전구공장]**
	6b) 전자등	**[희천전자관공장], [청년전기련합기업소]**
	6c) 통신	**[허민선동지가 일한 련합기업소]**
X. 가구, 잡제품 (1)	5) 기타	희천영예군인공장

IMPORTANT (3)

공업 (3)	희천제사공장, 희천련하기계종합공장(구희천공작기계공장), 희천정밀기계공장 (2월26일공장)

Manpho (Jagang Province)

KOFC (9-4)

경공업 (1)	신발 (1)	만포고무공장
중화공업 (6-3)	기계 (1)	만포림업기계공장
	화학 (3)	**[만포화학공장]**, **[압록강다이어공장]**, 만포13호공장
	건재 (2)	**[만포세멘트공장]**, 만포유리공장
전력 (2-1)	수력 (2)	**[장자강발전소]**, 연하발전소

MOU (11-1) 공업 (10) 전력 (1-1)

건재 (2)	8월2일시멘트공장, 차가평시멘트공장
경공업 (7)	압롱강다이야공장, 만포고개공장, 만포고치공장, 만포방사공장, 만포장유공장, 만포제약공장, 만포타올공장
기계 (1)	만포임업기계공장
전력 (1-1)	**[장자강발전소]**

IPA (25-4)

공업 (20-3)	**[만포세멘트공장]**, **[만포직물공장(滿浦織物工場)]**, **[압록강다이야공장]**; 만포편직공장, 만포모방사공장, 만포영예군인양말공장, 만포타올공장, 만포염색공장, 만포어린이옷공장, 만포피복공장, 만포림업기계공장, 만포정미기계공장, 만포재봉기공장, 만포어린이자전거공장, 만포기계수리공장, 만포농기구공장, 만포건재공장, 만포화학공장, 만포가성소다공장, 만포악기공장
광업 (0)	

전력 (5-1)	**[장자강발전소 (將子江發電所)]**; 등공1호발전소(登公一號發電所), 등공2호발전소(登公二號發電所), 송하발전소(松下發電所), 송학발전소(松鶴發電所)

KCNA (8)

공업 (5)	만포방사공장, 만포림업기계공장, 만포운화공장, 만포제련소, 압록강다이야공장
광업 (0)	
전력 (3)	송학발전소, 연하발전소, 장자강발전소

KIET (22- 4)

I. 광업 (1)	1) 탄광	만포탄광
II. 음식료품, 담배 (2)	3) 육류	만포시 남새 및 고기 가공공장
	4) 장류	만포장공장
III. 섬유, 의복, 신발 (4)	3) 방적 등	만포방사공장
	5) 편직공장	만포편직공장
	6) 의류	만포피복공장
	7) 양말 등	만포타올공장
V. 화학 (5-1)	3) 비료	7월4일공장
	5) 기초	만포가성소다공장, 만포화학공장
	7) 고무제품	**[압록강다이야공장]**, 만포고무제품공장
VI. 시멘트, 유리 (2-1)	1) 시멘트	**[8월2일세멘트공장]**
	4) 유리	만포유리공장
VIII. 조립금속, 기계장비 (3)	3c) 기타	만포림업기계공장, 만포재봉기공장
	5) 기계부품	만포어린이자전거공장
XI. 전력 (5-2)	1) 수력	**[독로강발전소]**, **[장자강발전소]**, 장자2호발전소, 장자3호발전소, 송학발전소

IMPORTANT (4)

공업 (3)	압록강다이야공장, 만포화학공장, 만포 (8월2일)세멘트공장
전력 (1)	장자강발전소

Kun (Jagang Province)

KOFC (30-4)

5	장강군 (1)
4	성간군 (1), 시중군, 화평군
3	룡림군
2	위원군 (1), 자성군 (1), 전천군, 초산군
1	고풍군, 우시군

중화공업 (13-1) 금속 (2), 기계 (2), 전기/전자 (1), 건재 (8)	**[성간제강소]**, 성간압연공장 (성간); 시중광산기계공장 (시중), 전천착암기공장 (전천); 성간통신기계수리공장 (성간); 고풍시멘트공장 (고풍), 룡림세멘트공장 (룡림), 성간시멘트공장 (성간), 시중시멘트공장, 시중유리공장 (시중), 장강시멘트공장 (장강), 전천세멘트공장 (전천), 초산시멘트공장 (초산)
재취 (4) 철 (1), 비 (3)	장강광산 (장강); 계생광산, 룡운광산 (룡림), 동방광산 (장강)
전력 (13-3) 수력 (3)	흥주청년발전소 3호 (시중), 하창청년발전소 2호 (우시), **[위원발전소]**, 고보청년발전소 (위원), **[운봉발전소]**, 귀인발전소 (자성), **[강계청년발전소 1-2호 (장강)]**, 초산읍발전소 (초산), 화평군발전소 1-3호, 화평읍발전소 1호 (화평)

MOU (45-1)

12	전천군 (1)
5	장강군
4	우시군
3	고풍군, 시중군, 위원군, 초산군
2	동신군, 랑림군, 성간군, 송원군, 중강군
1	자성군, 화평군

공업 (35) 광업 (8-1) 전력 (3)

건재 (2)	고풍시멘트공장 (고풍군), 위원시멘트공장 (위원군)
경공업 (29)	고풍식료공장(고풍군), 동신종이공장, 동착직물공장 (동신군), 랑림종이공장 (랑림군), 성간고기남새가공공장, 성간제약공장 (성간군), 송원장공장, 송원피복공장 (송원군), 시중유리공장, 시중종이공장 (시중군), 우시독공장, 우시식료공장 (우시군), 장강버섯공장, 장강사이다공장, 장강식료공장 (장강군), 전천고려약공장, 전천군독공장, 전천목재가공공장, 전천성냥공장, 전천수지일용품공장, 전천식료가공공장, 전천음료가공공장, 전천장공장, 전천편직공장 (전천군), 중강식료공장 (중강군), 초산고려약공장, 초산장공장, 초산직물공장 (초산군), 화평식료공장 (화평군)
기계 (2)	전천기계수리공장, 전천착암기공장 (전천군)
화학 (2)	우시화학공장 (우시군), 위원화학공장 (위원군)
광업 (8-1)	고풍탄광 (고풍군), 랑림광산 (랑림군), 시중광산 (시중군), 우시광산 (우시군), 연풍광산 (자성군), 장강광산 (장강군), **[전천탄광종합기업소 (전천군)]**, 3월5일청년광산 (중강군)
전력 (2)	위원발전소 (위원군), 강계청년발전소 (장강군)

IPA 195-27

고풍군 (10-1)

공업 (7-1)	**[고풍철제일용품공장 (古豊鐵製日用品工場)]**; 고풍도자기공장(古豊陶瓷器工場), 고풍건재공장, 고풍목재일용품공장(古豊木材日用品工場), 고풍제지공장, 고풍량곡가공공장, 고풍농기구공장
광업 (1)	고풍탄광
전력 (2)	룡대소형발전소, 삼평소형발전소

동신군 (20-2)

공업 (14-2)	**[동신남새가공공장]**, **[동창화학공장 (東倉化學工場)]**; 동신직물공장, 동창장공장, 동창직물공장, 동창종이공장, 동창목재일용품공장, 동신건재공장, 동신농기구공장, 동창피복공장, 동창철재공장, 생리교구비품공장, 랑림직물공장, 랑림남새공장
광업 (0)	
전력 (6)	문화발전소, 서양발전소(西陽發電所), 생리일호발전소(生里一號發電所), 생리이호발전소(生里二號發電所), 수전발전소(水田發電所), 온천발전소(溫泉發電所)

랑림군 (7-3)

공업 (7-3)	**[랑림목재가공공장 (狼林木材加功工場)]**, **[랑림식료공장 (狼林食料工場)]**, **[랑림제약공장 (狼林製藥工場)]**; 랑림종이공장, 랑림장공장, 랑림철제일용품공장;신원가성소다공장

룡림군 (15-2)

공업 (11-1)	**[룡림성냥공장]**; 룡림화학공장(龍林化學工場), 룡림장공장, 룡림직물공장, 룡림철제공장, 룡림제약공장, 룡림벽돌공장, 신장일용품공장, 신창농기구공장, 룡림벽돌공장, 룡림관공장
광업 (4-1)	**[고암탄광 (高岩炭鑛)]**; 온정탄광, 룡림탄광, 룡운광산

성간군 (9-1)

공업 (4-1)	**[성간목재가공공장 (城干木材加功工場)]**; 성간직물공장, 성간식료공장, 성간일용품공장
광업 (1)	부지흑연광산(富只黑鉛鑛山)
전력 (4)	성하발전소, 남리발전소(南里發電所), 무선발전소(舞仙發電所), 무채발전소(茂菜發電所)

송원군 (9-1)

공업 (8-1)	**[송원초물제품공장(松源草物製品工場)]**; 송원화학공장, 전창목재가공공장, 송원피복공장, 송원장공장, 송원일용품공장, 송원제약공장, 송원농기구공장
광업 (1)	송천발전소

시중군 (13-1)

공업 (12-1)	**[시중화학공장(時中化學工場)]**; 시중장공장, 시중기계수리공장, 시중유리공장, 시중직물공장, 시중광산기계수리공장, 시중독공장, 시중남새가공공장, 상청벽돌공장, 상청탐사기계공장, 상청배합먹이공장, 흥판세멘트공장
광업 (1)	시중광산

우시군 (15-2)

공업 (13-2)	**[우시식료공장(雩時食料場)]**, **[우시피복공장(雩時被服場)]**; 우시직물공장, 우시농기구공장, 우시철재일용품공장, 우시부식물가공공장, 우시장공장, 우시종이공장, 우시제약공장, 우시화학공장, 발은목재일용품가구공장, 발은종이공장, 발은석회공장
광업 (1)	발은광산
전력 (1)	평상발전소

위원군 (13-2)

공업 (12-1)	**[위원가구공장(渭原家具工場)]**; 위원식료공장, 위원장공장, 위원직물공장, 위원피복공장, 위원돼지공장, 위원배합사료공장, 위원초물공장, 위원종이공장, 룡연식료공장, 고성세멘트공장, 고성화학공장
전력 (1-1)	**[위원발전소(渭原發電所)]**;

자성군 (13-2)

공업 (10-1)	**[자성합판공장(慈城合板工場)]**; 자성장공장, 자성직물공장, 자성옷공장, 자성일용품공장, 자성가구공장, 자성제약공장, 운봉장공장, 운봉철제일용품공장, 상평배합먹이공장
광업 (0)	
전력 (3-1)	**[운봉발전소(雲峯發電所)]**; 대남발전소, 량덕발전소

장강군 (20-2)

공업 (12)	장강장공장, 장강직물공장, 장강옷공장, 장강목재일용품공장, 장강철제일용품공장, 장강화장품공장, 랑림가구공장, 오일식료공장, 오식재생섬유공장, 장평주철관공장, 종포사이다공장, 종포건재공장
광업 (3-1)	**[승방광산(勝芳鑛山)]**; 오일광산, 종포광산
전력 (5-1)	**[강계청년발전소(江界青年發電所)]**; 신성발전소, 종포발전소, 장강1호발전소, 장강3호군민청년발전소

전천군 (20-3)

공업 (19-2)	**[전천성냥공장]**, **[전천착암기공장(前川鑿巖機工場)]**; 전천식료공장, 전천직물공장, 전천일용품공장, 전천목재가공공장, 전천건재공장, 전천기계공장, 운송맥주공장, 운송사이다공장, 운송편직물공장, 운송직물공장, 운송철제일용품공장, 운송옷공장, 운송성냥공장, 전천배합먹이공장, 전천세멘트공장, 전천가구공장, 화암식료품공장
광업 (1-1)	**[전천탄광(前川炭鑛)]**

중강군 (9-1)

공업 (9-1)	**[중강식료공장(中江食料工場)]**; 중강방직공장, 중강피복공장, 중강화학공장, 중덕건재공장, 중상장공장, 중덕제약공장, 중상일용품공장, 중상농기구공장

초산군 (8-2)

공업 (7-2)	**[초산방직공장(楚山紡織場)]**, **[초산식료공장(楚山食料場)]**; 초산독공장, 초산기계공장, 초산피복공장, 초산건재공장, 초산화학공장
광업 (1)	초산탄광

화평군 (14-2)

공업 (13-2)	**[화평가구공장 (和坪家具工場)]**, **[화평영예군인악기공장(和坪榮譽軍人樂器工場)]**; 화평기계공장, 화평직물공장, 화평식료공장, 화평제약공장, 장백건재공장, 장백피복공장, 장백철제일용품공장, 중흥방직기재공장, 중흥연필공장
전력 (1)	부남청년발전소

KCNA (33)

7	장강군, 전천군
6	성간군
3	화평군
2	동신군, 중강군
1	송원군, 시중군, 우시군, 위원군, 자성군, 초산군

공업 (10)	동신갱목생산사업소 (동신군), 2월제강종합기업소 (성간군), 장강식료공장, 장강음료공장, 2.8기계종합공장 (장강군), 전천음료가공공장, 전천착암기공장 (전천군), 전천공업품상점, 전천목재가공공장, 전천성냥공장 (전천군)
광업 (3)	시중광산 (시중군), 전천탄광 (전천군), 3월5일청년광산 (중강군)
전력 (20)	동신2호발전소 (동신군), 성하발전소, 성간림산2호발전소, 성간성하3호발전소, 남리발전소, 외중발전소 (성간군), 송원언제발전소 (송원군), 하창청년발전소 (우시군), 위원발전소 (위원군), 귀인발전소 (자성군), 장강 1호발전소, 장강 2호발전소, 장강3호군민청년발전소, 장강5호발전소 (장강군), 전천탄광발전소 (전천군), 중상발전소 (중강군), 초산청년1호발전소 (초산군), 도안전국발전소, 부남청년발전소, 화평군민발전소 (화평군)

KIET 100-13

고풍군 (7)

I. 광업 (1)	1) 탄광	고풍탄광
II. 음식(1)	3) 육류	부식물가공공장
V. 화학 (2)	5) 기초	고풍화학공장
	9) 제약	고풍제약공장
VI. 시멘트 등(1)	5) 도자기	고풍도자기공장
VIII.조립금속, 기계장비(2)	1) 종합	고풍군기계수리공장
	5) 기계부품, 금속가공	고풍군철제일용품공장

동신군 (2)

III. 섬유 (1)	2) 직물	동신직물공장
X. 가구 등 (1)	1) 가구	동신교구비품공장

랑림 (5-1)

I. 광업 (1-1)	3) 비철	[랑림광산]
IV. 목재, 펄프, 종이 (1)	3) 종이	랑림종이공장
V. 화학 (1)	5) 기초	랑림가성소다공장
VIII. 조립금속등 (1)	5) 기계부품등	랑림철제일용품공장
X. 가구 등 (1)	1) 가구	랑림가구공장

룡림군 (11)

I. 광업 (5)	1) 탄광	고암탄광, 온정탄광
	2) 철광	계생광산, 룡운광산
	3) 비철	흑룡광산
II. 음식료품, 담배 (2)	3) 육류	룡림 남새 및 고기 가공공장
	4) 장류	룡림장공장
III. 섬유, 의복, 신발 (1)	6) 의류	룡림피복공장
IV. 목재, 펄프, 종이 (1)	1) 목재	룡림목기류공장
V. 화학 (1)	10) 화장품	룡림화학일용품공장
VI. 시멘트, 유리 (1)	1) 시멘트	룡림세멘트공장

성간군 (13-1)

I. 광업 (1)	1) 탄광	성간탄광
II. 음식료품, 담배 (3)	2) 곡물	성간군쌀기름공장
	3) 육류	고기 및 남새 가공공장
	6) 음료	성간맥주공장
III. 섬유, 의복, 신발 (2)	6) 의류	성간어린이옷공장, 성간피복공장
V. 화학 (1)	9) 제약	성간제약공장
VI. 시멘트, 유리 (1)	5) 도자기공장	성간독공장
VIII. 조립금속, 기계장비 (1-1)	5) 기계부품	[성간압형타공장]
X. 가구, 잡제품 (1)	1) 가구	성간가구공장
XI. 전력 (3)	2) 화력	무선발전소, 남리발전소, 무채발전소

송원군 (4)

II. 음식료품, 담배 (1)	4) 장류	송원피복공장
III. 섬유, 의복, 신발 (1)	6) 의류	송원피복공장
IV. 목재 (1)	1) 목재	송원목재가공공장
X. 가구, 잡제품 (1)	1) 가구	송원목재가구공장

시중군 (4-1)

I. 광업 (1)	4) 비금	시중광산
V. 화학 (1)	5) 기초	시중화학공장
VI. 시멘트, 유리 (1-1)	4) 유리	**[시중유리공장]**
VIII. 조립금속, 기계장비 (1)	3a) 탄광 등	시중탐사기계수리공장

우시군 (4-1)

I. 광업 (1)	4) 비금	우시광산
II. 음식료품, 담배 (2-1)	1) 일반	**[우시식료공장]**
	4) 장류	우시장공장
V. 화학 (1)	9) 화장품	우시제약공장

위원군 (1-1)

XI. 전력 (1-1)	1) 수력	**[위원발전소]**

자성군 (6-2)

I. 광업 (2)	4) 비금	연풍광산, 운봉광산
III. 섬유, 의복, 신발 (1)	6) 의류	자성피복공장
IV. 목재 (1-1)	1) 목재	**[자성합판공장]**
X. 가구, 잡제품 (1)	5) 기타	자성일용품공장
XI. 전력 (1-1)	1) 수력	**[운봉발전소]**

장강군 (8-2)

I. 광업 (2)	4) 비금	동방광산, 장강광산
II. 음식료품, 담배 (1-1)	6) 음료	**[장강사이다공장]**
V. 화학(1)	10) 화장품	장강화장품공장
VII.1차 금속산업(1)	3) 기타	장강주철관공장
X. 가구, 잡제품 (1)	5) 가구	장강가구공장
XI. 전력 (2-1)	1) 수력	**[강계청년발전소]**
	2) 화력	종포발전소

전천군 (16-3)

I. 광업 (1-1)	1) 탄광	**[전천탄광종합기업소]**
II. 음식료품, 담배 (2)	2) 곡물	전천기름공장
	4) 장류	전천장공장
III. 섬유, 의복, 신발 (4)	2) 직물	전천직물공장
	3) 방적 등	전천안감천공장
	5) 편직공장	전천편직물공장
	6) 의류	전천피복공장
IV. 목재 (1)	1) 목재	전천목재가공공장
V. 화학 (2)	5) 기초	전천가성소다공장
	8) 합성수지	전천수지일용품공장
VI. 시멘트, 유리 (2)	1) 시멘트	전천세멘트공장
	5) 도자기	전천독공장
VIII. 조립금속, 기계장비 (2-1)	3a) 탄광	**[전천착암기공장]**
	5) 기계부품	전천군손칼공장
X. 가구, 잡제품 (2-1)	3) 악기	고인악기용재공장
	5) 기타	**[전천성냥공장]**

중강군 (4-1)

I. 광업 (1-1)	3) 비철	[3월5일청년광산]
II. 음식료품, 담배 (1)	4) 장류	중강장공장
III. 섬유, 의복, 신발 (1)	6) 의류	중강피복공장
VIII. 조립금속, 기계장비 (1)	5) 기계부품, 금속가공	중강철제일용품공장

초산군 (10)

I) 광업 (1)	1) 탄광	초산탄광
II. 음식료품, 담배 (2)	4) 장류	초산장공장
	6) 음료	초산포도술공장
III. 섬유, 의복, 신발 (2)	2) 직물	초산군 직물공장
	5) 편직공장	초산편직물공장
V. 화학 (1)	5) 기초화학	초산가성소다공장
VI. 시멘트, 유리 (1)	3) 벽돌 등	초산군기와공장
VIII. 조립금속, 기계장비 (3)	1) 종합게계	초산군기계수리공장, 초산기계공장
	5) 기계부품, 금속가공	초산군철제일용품공장

화평군 (7)

I) 광업 (1)	1) 탄광	화평탄광
V. 화학(1)	9) 제약	화평제약공장
VIII. 조립금속, 기계장비 (2)	3c) 기타	화평방직기계공장
	5) 기계부품	화평방직기재공장
X. 가구, 잡제품 (1)	3) 악기	화평영예군인악기공장
XI. 전력 (2)	2) 화력	송덕발전소, 흑수발전소

IMPORTANT (9)

3	전천군
1	시중군, 우시군, 위원군 자성군, 장강군, 중강군

(9)

공업 (4)	시중유리공장 (시중군), 우시식료공장 (우시군). 전천착암기공장, 전천성냥공장(전천군),
광업 (2)	전천탄광(종합기업소) (전천군), 3월5일청년광산 (중강군)
전력 (3)	위원발전소 (위원군), 운봉발전소 (자성군), 강계청년발전소 (장강군)

Sinuiju (Phyongbuk Province)

KOFC (23-5)

경공업 (8-3)	섬유 (2)	**[신의주방직공장]**, **[신의주화학섬유련합기업소]**
	신발 (5)	**[신의주신발공장]**, 신의주신발부속품공장, 신의주구두신발공장, 신의주고무공장, 3월4일공장
	제지 (1)	신의주팔프공장
중화공업 (15-2)	기계 (8)	**[락원기계련합기업소]**, 신의주공작기계공장, 8월9일공장(신의주광산기계공장), 신의주방적기계공장, 신의주종합기계공장, 신의주저울공장, 신의주텔레비젼수상기공장, 신의주자동화기구공장
	철도차량 (1)	락원철도공장
	전기/전자 (1)	신의주건전지공장
	조선 (1)	**[신의주선박공장]**
	화학 (3)	신의주마이싱공장, 신의주타이어공장, 신의주화장품공장
	건재 (1)	신의주(판)유리공장

MOU (34-3) 공업 (33-3) 광업 (1)

건재 (1)	신의주유리공장
경공업 (23-1)	**[신의주방직공장]**; 백사피복공장, 신의주가정용품공장, 신의주고려약가공공장, 신의주구강재료공장, 신의주구두공장, 신의주기초식품공장, 신의주마이싱공장, 신의주모방직공장, 신의주수지일용품공장, 신의주수출피복공장, 신의주신발공장, 신의주신발부속품공장, 신의주영예군인학용품공장, 신의주은하타올공장, 신의주은하피복공장, 신의주제약공장, 신의주종이공장, 신의주체육기구공장, 신의주콩우유공장, 신의주타올공장, 신의주편직공장, 신의주화장품공장
기계 (6-1)	**[락원기계련합기업소]**; 신의주기계종합공장, 신의주뜨락또르다이아공장, 신의주방적기계공장, 신의주법랑철기공장, 3월4일공장
전자 (1)	신의주축전기공장
제철/조선 (1)	9월제철종합기업소
화학 (1-1)	**[신의주화학섬유련합기업소]**
광업 (1)	덕현광산

IPA (22-9)

공업 (22-9)	**[락원기계련합기업소(樂園機械聯合企業所)]**, **[신의주가정용품공장(新義州家庭用品工場)]**, **[신의주구두공장]**, **[신의주방직공장(新義州紡織工場)]**, **[신의주법랑철기공장(新義州琺瑯鐵器工場)]**, **[신의주신발공장]**, **[신의주화장품공장(新義州化粧品工場)]**, **[8월9일공장(신의주광산기계공장)]**, **[신의주화학섬유공장(新義州化學纖維工場)]**; 신의주마이싱공장, 신의주타올공장, 신의주기름공장, 신의주장공장, 신의주수지일용품공장, 신의주시계공장, 신의주악기공장, 신의주식료공장, 신의주모방직공장(新義州毛紡織工場), 신의주가죽구두공장, 기초식품공장, 압록강화학공장, 강안화학공장

KCNA (12)

공업 (12)	신의주기초식료품공장, 신의주방적기계공장, 신의주법랑철기공장, 신의주신발공장, 신의주전자기구공장,신의주콩우유공장, 신의주편직공장, 신의주화장품공장, 신의주방직공장, 9월제철종합기업소, 락원기계련합기업소, 락원산소분리기공장

KIET (36-19)

III. 섬유, 의복, 신발 (11-4)	1) 방적등	**[남신의주방직공장]**
	2) 직물공장	신의주직물공장
	5) 편직공장	신의주영예군인 편직공장, 신의주편직공장
	6) 의류	신의주수출피복공장, 신의주피복공장
	7) 양말 등	신의주타올공장
	8) 신발	**[신의주구두공장]**, **[신의주신발공장]**
	10) 가죽	**[신의주방직공장]**, 신의주어구공장
IV. 목재, 펄프, 종이 (3-2)	2) 펄프	**[신의주팔프공장]**
	3) 종이	**[신의주장식지공장]**, 신의주제지공장
V. 화학 (7-3)	4)화학섬유	**[신의주화학섬유련합기업소]**
	5) 기초화학	**[신의주가성소다공장]**, 신의주화학공장
	8) 합성수지, 수지제품	신의주수지일용품공장
	9) 제약	신의주제약공장, 신의주마이싱공장
	10) 화장품	**[신의주화장품공장]**
VI. 시멘트, 유리 (1-1)	4) 유리	**[신의주유리공장]**
VIII. 조립금속, 기계장비 (10-7)	1) 종합기계	**[락원기계련합기업소]**
	3a) 탄광, 광산용	**[8월9일공장(신의주광산기계공장)]**
	3c) 기타 산업용	**[신의주방적기계공장]**, **[신의주재봉기공장]**, 신의주제지기계공장
	4) 정밀	**[신의주영예군인시계공장]**
	5) 기계부품, 금속가공	**[신의주법랑철기공장]**, 신의주염색설비부속품공장
	6b) 전자, 자동화기기	**[신의주자동화기구공장]**, 신의주축전기공장
IX. 수송기계 (1-1)	1) 선박	**[신의주선박공장]**
X. 가구, 잡제품 (3-1)	2) 문방구, 완구, 체육기구	신의주영예군인학용품공장, 신의주원주필공장
	5) 기타	**[신의주가정용품공장]**

IMPORTANT (10)

공업 (10)	신의주구두공장, 신의주신발공장, 신의주방직공장, 신의주화학섬유(공장)련합기업소, 신의주화장품공장, 락원기계련합기업소, 8월9일공장(신의주광산기계공장), 신의주방적기계공장, 신의주법랑철기공장, 신의주가정용품공장

Kusong (Phyongbuk Province)

KOFC (4-3)

경공업 (1-1)	섬유 (1)	**[구성방직공장]**
중화공업 (3-2)	기계 (3)	**[4월3일종합공장(구성공작기계공장)]**, **[구성광산기계공장]**, 구성104공장

MOU (6-1)

경공업 (5)	구성일용품공장, 구성고려약공장, 구성방직공장, 구성식료공장, 구성영예군인주사약공장
기계 (1-1)	**[4월3일공작기계련합기업소 (구성공작기계공장)]**

IPA (7-4)

공업(7-4)	**[구성기계공장(龜城機械工場)]**, **[구성방직공장(龜城紡織工場)]**, **[구성제약공장(龜城製藥工場)]**, **[4월3일종합공장(四月三日綜合工場) (구성공작기계공장)]**; 구성벽돌공장, 대안붓공장, 조양독공장

KCNA (2)

공업 (2)	구성공작기계공장, 구성방직공장

KIET (16-8)

II. 음식료품, 담배 (2-1)	1) 일반	**[구성식료공장]**
	3) 육류	구성기 고기 및 남새 과실 가공공장
III. 섬유, 의복, 신발 (2-1)	1) 방적등	**[구성 방직공장]**
	6) 의류	구성피복공장
V. 화학 (4-2)	3)비료	구성제지공장
	8) 합성수지, 수지제품	구성영예군인수지일용품공장
	9) 제약	**[구성제약공장]**, **[구성영예군인주사약공장]**
VIII. 조립금속, 기계장비 (4-4)	2) 공작기계	**[구성104공장]**,**[4월3일종합공장]**
	3a) 탄광, 광산용	**[8월28일공장(구성광산기계공장)]**, **[구성기계공장]**
X. 가구, 잡제품 (4)	1) 가구	구성가구공장
	2) 문방구, 완구, 체육기구	구성샤프공장, 구성교구비품공장
	5) 기타	구성일용품공장

IMPORTANT (2)

공업 (2)	4월3일종합공장(구성공작기계공장), 구성방직공장

Jongju (Phyongbuk Province)

KOFC (5-1)

중화공업 (5-1)	금속 (2-1)	[평북제련소], 10월30일공장(정주베어링공장)
	기계 (2)	정주농기계공장, 정주뜨락또르부속품공장
	화학 (1)	25호공장

MOU (9) 공업 (8) 광업 (1)

경공업 (4)	정주가죽가공공장, 정주고치생산사업소, 정주과실가공공장, 정주수출피복공장
기계 (1)	정주뜨락또르부속품공장
제철/조선 (1)	평북제련소
화학 (2)	정주미량원소과린산석회비료공장, 정주시애국복합미생물비료공장
광업 (1)	정주탄광

IPA (7-6)

공업 (7-6)	**[10월30일공장(十月三十日工場)], [(정주베어링공장)], [정주뜨락또르부속품공장], [정주미량원소과린산석회비료공장(定州微量元素果鱗酸石灰肥料工場)], [정주수출피복공장(定州輸出被服工場)], [정주전진호뜨락또르조립공장], [평북제련소(平北製鍊所)]**; 정주농기계공장

KCNA (4)

공업 (4)	10월30일공장, 정주뜨락또르부속품공장, 정주피복공장, 평북제련소

KIET (20-5)

II. 음식료품, 담배 (4)	1) 일반	정주식료공장
	2) 곡물가공	정주쌀기름공장
	3) 육류	정주과실가공공장
	5) 사료	정주배합사료공장
III. 섬유, 의복, 신발 (5-1)	5) 편직공장	정주영예군인편직공장
	6) 의류	**[정주수출피복공장]**, 정주피복공장, 정주옷공장
	10) 가죽	정주가죽가공공장
IV. 목재, 펄프, 종이 (1)	1) 목재	정주건구공장
V. 화학 (4-1)	3) 비료	**[정주미량원소과린산석회비료공장]**
	5) 기초화학	정주가성소다공장
	9) 제약	정주가금생물약품공장, 정주제약공장
VI. 시멘트, 유리 (1)	3) 벽돌	정주건재공장
VII. 1차 금속산업 (1-1)	2) 제련	**[평북제련소]**
VIII. 조립금속, 기계장비 (4-2)	1) 종합기계	정주기계수리공장
	3b) 농업용	**[정주전진호뜨락또르조립공장]**, 정주뜨락또르부속품공장
	5) 기계부품, 금속가공	**[10월30일공장(정주베어링공장)]**

IMPORTANT (5)

공업 (5)	정주수출피복공장, 정주미량원소과린산석회비료공장, 평북제련소, 10월30일공장(정주베어링공장), 정주뜨락또르부속품공장

Kun (Phyongbuk Province)

KOFC (48-18)

9	구장군 (4)
6	룡천군 (3), 태천군 (1)
4	삭주군 (3), 의주군 (1)
3	동림군, 선천군
2	박천군 (1), 염주군, 운산군 (2), 피현군 (2)
1	곽산군, 녕변군 (1), 동창군, 창성군, 천마군

경공업 (4-1) 식품 (2), 섬유 (1), 신발 (1)	학소리 정제소금공장 (염주), 의주곡산공장 (의주); [**녕변견직공장** (녕변)]; 창성신방공장 (창성)
중화공업 (24-10) 금속공업 (2), 기계 (7), 철토차량 (1), 전기/전자 (6), 조선 (2), 화학 (3), 건재 (3)	[**룡암포제련소** (룡천)], [**덕현제철소 (舊 9월제철소)**] (의주); 곽산련결농기계공장 (곽산), 차령관광산기계공장 (8월28일공장) (동림), 룡암포기계공장 (룡천), 선천농기계공장 (선천), 염주정미기계공장 (염주), [**운산공구공장 (7월13일공장)** (운산)], [**량책베아링공장(10월30일)**] (피현); 구장철도공장 (구장); 동림전기공장, 동림세탁기공장 (동림), [**북중기계련합기업소**], 북중냉동기공장 (룡천), 박천통신기계공장 (박천), 선천영예군인통신기계공장 (선천); [**룡암포조선소** (룡천)], [**박천선박수리공장** (박천)]; [**청수화학공장** (삭주)], 선천타이어공장 (선천), [**봉화화학공장** (피현)]; [**구장세멘트공장** (구장)], 청선시멘트공장 (삭주), 의주세멘트공장 (의주)
재취 (12-4) 철 (1), 비 (1), 탄광 (9), 석회석 (1)	덕현광산 (의주); 대유동광산 (동창); [**구장지구탄광련합기업소**], [룡등탄광], [**룡문탄광**], 룡수탄광, 등립탄광, 구장탄광 (구장), 룡천탄광 (룡천), [**운산광산** (운산)], 태천탄광 (태천); 구장광산 (구장)
전력 (8-3) 수력 (8)	[**수풍발전소**], [**태평만발전소** (삭주)], 천마발전소 (천마), [**태천발전소** 1-5호 (태천)]

MOU (112-5) 공업 (90-3) 광업 (15-1) 전력 (7-1)

12	구장군 (2), 룡천군 (1)
10	동림군, 염주군 (1)
9	삭주군, 피현군
8	선천군, 태천군 (1)
4	곽산군, 박천군, 향산군
3	운산군, 운전군, 의주군, 천마군, 철산군
2	동창군, 벽동군, 녕병군
1	대관군

건재 (5−1)	**[구장시멘트공장** (구장군)**]**, 룡암포벽돌공장 (룡천군), 운전금속건재공장 (운전군), 피현내화물공장, 피현씨리카트벽돌공장 (피현군)
경공업 (66−1)	곽산종이공장 (곽산군), 구장수지일용품공장, 구장식료공장, 룡등수지일용품공장 (구장군), 팔원견직공장, 녕변견직공장 (녕병군), 대관수지가공공장 (대관군), 동림공업용천공장, 동림식료공장, 동림은하피복공장, 동림직물공장, 동림철제일용품공장 (동림군), 룡처피복공장, 룡천군화학일용품공장, 룡천도자기공장, 룡천양말공장, 룡천영예군인사출장화공장, 룡천영예군인신발공장, 룡천제약공장, 룡천종이공장 (룡천군), 박천견직공장, 박천식료공장, 박천종이공장 (박천군), 벽동식료공장, 벽동장공장 (벽동군), 삭주군수출피복공장, 삭주식료공장, 삭주어린이신발공장, 삭주직물공장, 창성식료공장, 창성직물공장, 수풍직물공장 (삭주군), 선천담배공장, 선천도자기공장, 선천시약공장, 선천식료공장, 선천군과일남새및고기가공공장, 선천기름공장 (선천군), **[염주군지방공업종합공장]**, 염주고려약공장, 염주그물공장, 염주수출피복공장, 염주식료공장, 염주식료화학공장, 염주영예군인수지일용품, 염주은하피복공장, 염주제약공장, 염주피복공장 (염주군), 운산공구공장, 운산식료공장 (우산군), 의주식료공장, 의주종이공장 (의주군), 천마식료공장, 천마영예군인제약공장 (천마군), 철산군피복공장, 철산식료공장, 철산영예군인제약공장 (철산군), 태천고려약공장, 태천철제일용품공장 (태천군), 피현위생자기공장, 피현은하피복공장, 피현피복공장, 피현화학일용품공장, 피현직물공장 (피현군), 묘향산의료기구공장, 향산종합식료공장 (향산군)
기계 (14−1)	곽산연력농기계공장, 청강기계화사업소 (곽산군), 탄광기계공장, 구장가마공장 (구장군), 동림광산기계공장, 8월1일철도공장, 8월28일공장(동림군), **[북중기계련합기업소]**, 룡천광산기계공장, 룡천기계수리공장 (룡천군), 선천영예군인통신기계공장 (선천군), 7월13일공장 (우산군), 운전군농기계공장(운전군), 량책베아링공장 (피현군)
전자 (1)	동림전기공장 (동림군)
화학 (4)	곽산애국복합미생물비료공장 (곽산군), 청수화학공장 (삭주군), 태천탄화규소공장 (태천군), 봉화화학공장 (피현군)
광업 (15−1)	**[구장지구탄광련합기업소]**; 구장탄광, 구장고회석광산, 룡등탄광, 룡수탄광, 룡문탄광 (구장군), 동림광산(동림군), 대유동광산, 동창광산 (동창군), 박천탄광 (박천군), 풍년광산 (삭주군), 선천광산 (선천군), 운전광산 (운전군), 옥강광산 (의주군), 천마광산 (천마군)
전력 (7−1)	**[태천(수력)발전(종합기업)소]**, 태천2호발전소, 태천3호발전소, 태천4호청년발전소, 태천5호발전소, 노현군민발전소, 향산갑문발전소 (향산군)

IPA 271−39

곽산군 (7−1)

공업 (7−1)	**[곽산련결농기계공장 (郭山連結農機械工場)]**; 곽산제약공장, 곽산가구공장, 곽산편직공장, 곽산종이공장, 곽산직물공장, 천대물고기가공공장

구장군 (19−1)

공업 (14−1)	**[구장세멘트공장]**; 구장가구공장, 룡등식료공장, 룡등편직물공장, 룡등철제일용품공장, 룡문타올공장, 룡문화학공장, 룡문가구공장, 룡문일용품공장, 수구식료가공공장, 수구교육실험기구공장, 수구가구공장, 운흥타올공장, 운흥운동구공장
광업 (4)	룡수탄광, 룡등탄광, 룡문탄광, 운흥고회석광산
전력 (1)	상초발전소

녕변군 (9-1)

공업 (8-1)	**[녕변견직공장(寧邊絹織工場)]**; 녕변종이공장, 녕변일용품공장, 녕변도자기공장, 녕변농기계공장, 팔원견직공장, 팔원농기구공장, 팔원배합먹이공장
광업 (1)	옥창광산

대관군 (9-1)

공업 (8-1)	**[대관식료공장(大館食料工場)]**; 대관옷공장, 대관가구공장, 대관제지공장, 대관편직물공장, 대관모피가공공장, 대관일용품공장, 대관양말공장
광업 (1)	신상광산

동림군 (18-1)

공업 (14-1)	**[8월28일공장(八月二十八日工場: 차련관광산기계공장)]**; 동림화학기계공장, 동림전기일용품공장, 동림화학일용품공장, 동림모피가공품공장, 신곡전동기공장, 신곡철제일용품공장, 오봉정밀기계공장, 오봉건설기계공장, 오봉과수기계공장, 오봉남새가공공장, 고군영배합사료공장, 고군영가구공장, 고군영초물제품공장
광업 (2)	신곡철산광산, 동창광산
전력 (2)	매봉발전소, 청강수력발전소

동창군 (13-3)

공업 (11-2)	**[동창식료공장(東倉食料工場)]**, **[동창직물공장(東倉織物工場)]**; 동창기계공장, 동창방직공장, 동창일용품공장, 동창종이공장, 동창건재공장, 동창제약공장, 대유피복공장, 대유철제일용품공장, 대유수지일용품공장
광업 (1-1)	**[대유동광산(大楡洞鑛山)]**
전력 (1)	동창청년1호발전소

룡천군 (22-2)

공업 (22-2)	**[룡암포조선소(龍巖浦造船所)]**, **[룡천광산기계공장(龍川鑛山機械工場)]**; 룡천신발공장, 룡천북중기계공장, 룡천기계공장, 룡천남새가공공장, 룡천양말공장, 룡천피복공장, 룡천가구공장, 룡천배합먹이공장, 룡암포기계공장, 룡암포랭동공장, 룡암포화학공장, 북중기계공장, 북중철제일용품공장, 북중식료품공장, 북중피복제품공장, 진흥중기계수리공장, 진흥선박수리공장, 동하기계공장, 신암축전지공장, 신암신발공장

박천군 (9-2)

공업 (9-2)	**[박천견직공장(博川絹織工場)]**, **[박천선박수리공장(博川船舶修理工場)]**; 봉성배합사료공장, 박천종이공장, 박천화학공장, 박천유리공장, 박천식료공장, 박천일용품공장, 중남기와공장

벽동군 (15-1)

공업 (13-1)	**[벽동가구공장(碧潼家具工場)]**; 벽동직물공장, 벽동농기구공장, 벽동장공장, 벽동식료공장, 벽동일용품공장, 벽동방직공장, 벽동종이공장, 벽동제약공장, 벽동기계공장, 송이세멘트공장, 송이제약공장, 송이독공장
광업 (1)	남하광산
전력 (1)	남천강발전소

삭주군 (26-5)

공업 (24-4)	**[삭주수출솔공장], [삭주식료공장(朔州食料工場)], [삭주직물공장(朔州織物工場)], [청수화학공장(青水化學工場)]**; 삭주어린이신발공장, 삭주가구공장, 삭주옷공장, 남사화학비료공장, 남사제약공장, 대대솔공장, 수풍전동기공장, 수풍옷공장, 수풍직물공장, 청성직물공장, 청성종이공장, 청성고기가공공장, 청성가구공장, 청성박제품공장, 청성제약공장, 청수세멘트공장, 청수일용품공장, 청수식료공장, 청수옷공장, 신서배합먹이공장
광업 (1-1)	**[풍년광산(豊年鑛山)]**
전력 (1)	수풍발전소

선천군 (10-3)

공업 (10-3)	**[선천농기계공장(宣川農機械工場)], [선천요업공장(宣川窯業工場)], [선천도자기공장]**; 선천식료공장(宣川食料工場), 선천견직공장(宣川絹織工場), 선천종이공장, 선천가구공장(宣川家具工場), 선천담배공장, 선천제약공장(宣川製藥工場), 선천일용품공장(宣川日用品工場)

신도군 (3-0)

공업 (3-0)	신도복장공장, 신도식료공장, 신도텍스판공장

염주군 (11-2)

공업 (11-2)	**[염주그물공장], [염주제염소(鹽州製鹽所)]**; 염주량곡기계공장, 염주화학일용품공장, 염주수지일용품공장, 염주성냥공장, 다사일용품공장, 염주식료공장, 염주가마니공장, 인광철제일용품공장, 남시제염소

운산군 (15-1)

공업 (14-1)	**[운산공구공장(雲山工具工場) (7월13일공장)]**; 운산기계공장, 운산식료품공장, 운산일용품공장, 운산종이공장, 북진식료품공장, 북진목재일용품공장, 상원농기구공장, 상원공구공장, 상원식료공장, 상원건재공장, 상원배합먹이공장, 운산식료공장, 운산군직물공장
광업 (1)	북진광산

운전군 (9-2)

공업 (8-2)	**[운전금속건재공장(雲田金屬建材工場)], [운전화학일용품공장(雲田化學日用品工場)]**; 운전식료공장, 운전직물공장, 운전옷공장, 운전종이공장, 운하정미공장, 운하금속건재공장
광업 (1)	운전광산

의주군 (14-3)

공업 (12-2)	**[의주건재공장(義州建材工場)], [의주곡산공장(義州穀産工場)]**; 의주기계공장, 의주제약공장, 의주종이공장, 의주방직공장, 의주피복공장, 의주식료공장(義州食料工場), 의주일용품공장(義州日用品工場), 덕현일용품공장, 옥돌공장, 의주세멘트공장
광업 (2-1)	**[덕현광산(德峴鑛山)]**; 옥강광산

창성군 (10-2)

공업 (10-2)	**[창성식료공장(昌城食料工場)]**, **[창성직물공장]**; 창성가구공장, 창성종이공장, 창성일용품공장, 창성마대공장, 창성화학공장, 창성제약공장, 창성기계수리공장, 창성농기구공장

천마군 (9)

공업 (9)	천마식료공장, 천마종이공장, 천마직물공장, 천마옷공장, 천마가구공장, 천마모피가공공장, 천마량곡가공공장, 천마건재공장, 천마농기구공장

철산군 (11-1)

공업 (10-1)	**[철산영예군인제약공장(鐵山榮譽軍人製藥工場)]**; 철산군식료공장, 철산군종이공장, 철산군직물공장, 철산군피복공장, 철신군일용품공장, 철산군가구공장, 가봉화학공장, 근천건재공장, 원세평배합사료공장
광업 (1)	철산광산

태천군 (17-3)

공업 (13-3)	**[태천철제일용품공장(泰川鐵製日用品工場)]**, **[태천초물제품공장(泰川草物製品工場)]**, **[태천옻공예품공장]**; 태천식료공장, 태천직물공장, 태천옷공장, 태천제약공장, 태천가구공장, 태천종이공장, 태천농기구공장, 송태가구공장, 송태철제일용품공장, 송태기계공장
광업 (2)	태천광산, 취흥광산
전력 (2)	태천수력발전소, 태천3호청년발전소

피현군 (11-2)

공업 (11-2)	**[룡계리씨리카트벽돌공장]**, **[피현벽돌공장]**; 피현식료공장, 피현고기가공공장, 피현직물공장, 피현옷공장, 피현화학일용품공장, 피현철제일용품공장, 봉화화학공장, 원유가공공장, 피현피복공장

향산군 (4-2)

공업 (4-2)	**[묘향산의료기구공장(妙香山醫療器具工場)]**, **[향산종합식료공장(香山綜合食料工場)]**; 향산기념품공장, 향산종이공장

KCNA (39)

6	태천군
5	삭주군
4	운산군, 창성군
3	구장군
2	녕변군, 대관군, 룡천군, 의주군, 피현군, 향산군
1	곽산군, 동창군, 박천군, 염주군, 천마군

공업 (23)	곽산련결농기계공장 (곽산군), 녕변견직공장 (녕변군), 대관메기공장, 대관유리공장 (대관군), 북중기계련합기업소, 북중전극공장 (룡천군), 박천견직공장 (박천군), 삭주식료공장, 수풍베아링공장, 압록강계기종합공장, 압록강일용품공장 (삭주군), 염주정제소금공장 (염주군), 운산군고려약공장, 운산메기공장, 운산옷공장, 운산공구공장 (운산군), 의주식료공장 (의주군), 창성식료공장, 창성종이공장, 창성직물공장 (창성군), 천마전기기계공장 (천마군), 량책베아링공장 (피현군), 향산기념품공장 (향산군)
광업 (5)	구장지구탄광련합기업소, 룡등탄광, 룡문탄광 (구장군), 대유동광산 (동창군), 덕현광산 (의주군)
전력 (11)	경수로발전소 (녕변군), 수풍발전소 (삭주군), 금야2호발전소 (창성군), 봉화화학공장화력발전소 (피현군), 태천(수력)발전(종합기업)소, 태천2호발전소, 태천3호청년발전소, 태천4호청년발전소, 태천5호발전소, 은흥청년발전소 (태천군), 로현군민발전소 (향산군)

KIET (173-51)

곽산군 (4-1)

II. 음식료품, 담배 (1)	3) 육류	곽산 남새 및 고기가공공장
V. 화학 (2)	9) 제약	곽산제약공장
	10) 화장품	곽산영예군인수지학용품공장
VIII. 조립금속, 기계장비 (1-1)	3b) 농업용	[곽산련결농기계공장]

구장 (10-3)

I. 광업 (4-2)	1) 탄광	**[구장지구탄광련합기업소]**, **[룡등탄광]**, 룡문탄광, 룡수탄광
II. 음식료품, 담배 (2)	1) 일반	구장식료공장
	3) 육류	구장군 남새 및 고기 가공공장
IV. 목재, 펄프, 종이 (1)	3) 종이	구장종이공장
V. 화학 (1)	8) 합성수지, 수지제품	구장수지일용품공장
VI. 시멘트, 유리 (2-1)	1) 시멘트	**[구장세멘트공장]**
	5) 도자기	구장도자기공장

녕변군 (9-2)

II. 음식료품, 담배 (1)	4) 장류	녕변장공장
III. 섬유, 의복, 신발 (5-2)	2) 직물공장	녕변직물공장
	4) 견직공장	[녕변견직공장], [팔원견직공장]
	6) 의류	녕변 여자 및 어린이옷 공장, 녕변피복공장
IV. 목재, 펄프, 종이 (1)	3) 종이	냥변종이공장
VIII. 조립금속, 기계장비 (1)	1) 종합기계	녕변기계수리공장
XI. 전력 (1)	2) 화력	녕변발전소

대관군 (5-1)

II. 음식료품, 담배 (1-1)	1) 일반	**[대관식료공장]**
IV. 목재, 펄프, 종이 (1)	3) 종이	대관군 종이공장
V. 화학(2)	6) 염료,도료,시약, 농약 등	대관식료화학공장
	8) 합성수지, 수지제품	대관수지가공공장
X. 가구, 잡제품(1)	1) 가구	대관가구공장

동림군 (12-3)

I. 광업 (1)	4) 비금속광물	동림광산
II. 음식료품, 담배 (1)	1) 일반	동림식료공장
III. 섬유, 의복, 신발 (3)	3) 방적, 제사, 직조	동림공업용천공장
	6) 의류	동림옷공장
	10) 가죽	동림모피공장
IV. 목재, 펄프, 종이 (1)	3) 종이	동림종이공장
VIII. 조립금속, 기계장비 (4-3)	3a) 탄광, 광산용	**[8월26일공장]**
	5) 기계부품등	**[동림철제일용품공장]**
	6a) 전기기기, 부품	**[동림전기공장]**
	6b) 전자등	동림세탁기공장
X. 가구, 잡제품 (2)	1) 가구	동림가구공장
	5) 기타	동림영예군인일용품공장

동창군 (7-3)

I. 광업 (2-1)	2) 철광	대유동광산
	3) 비철	**[동창광산]**
II. 음식료품, 담배 (1)	1) 일반	동창식료공장
III. 섬유, 의복, 신발 (1-1)	2) 직물공장	**[동창직물공장]**
IV. 목재, 펄프, 종이 (2)	3) 종이	동창종이공장
	1) 종합	동창목제품공장
X. 가구, 잡제품 (1-1)	5) 기타	**[동창일용품공장]**

룡천군 (16-6)

I. 광업 (1-1)	4) 비금속광물	**[장산광산]**
III. 섬유, 의복, 신발 (5-1)	6) 의류	룡천피복공장
	7) 양말 등	룡천양말공장
	8) 신발	**[룡천영예군인신발공장]**
	10) 화장품	룡천화학일용품공장
	3) 벽돌	룡암포벽돌공장
VI. 시멘트, 유리 (5-3)	1) 종합기계	**[룡암포기계공장]**, **[북중기계련합기업소]**
	3a) 탄광, 광산용	**[룡천광산기계공장]**, 룡천기계공장
	6b) 전자, 자동화기기	북중냉동기공장

Ⅸ. 수송기계 (2-1)	1) 선박	**[룡암포조선소]**, 진흥선박수리공장
Ⅹ. 가구, 잡제품 (2)	1) 가구	룡천가구공장
	4) 공예품, 장식품	진흥합영회사
Ⅺ. 전력 (1)	2) 화력	룡천발전소

박천군 (11-2)

Ⅱ. 음식료품, 담배 (1)	1)일반	박천식료공장
Ⅲ. 섬유, 의복, 신발 (3-1)	4) 견직공장	**[박천견직공장]**
	5) 편직공장	박천편직공장
	6) 의류	박천피복공장
Ⅳ. 목재, 펄프, 종이 (1)	3) 종이	박천종이공장
Ⅴ. 화학 (2)	5) 기초화학	박천화학공장
	9) 제약	박천제약공장
Ⅵ. 시멘트, 유리 (1)	4) 유리	박천유리공장
Ⅷ. 조립금속, 기계장비 (2-1)	5) 기계부품, 금속가공	박천군철제일용품공장
	6c) 통신기계	**[박천통신기계공장]**
Ⅹ. 가구, 잡제품 (1)	1) 가구	박천가구공장

벽동군 (2)

Ⅱ. 음식료품, 담배 (1)	1) 일반	벽동식료공장
Ⅲ. 섬유, 의복, 신발 (1)	2) 직물공장	벽동직물공장

삭주군 (20-6)

Ⅰ. 광업 (2)	1) 탄광	삭주탄광
	3) 비철	당목광산
Ⅱ. 음식료품, 담배 (9-2)	1) 일반	**[삭주식료공장]**, 청수식료공장
	6) 음료, 주류	삭주맥주공장
	2) 직물공장	**[삭주직물공장]**, 청성직물공장, 수풍직물공장
	5) 편직공장	청수피복공장
	6) 의류	수풍피복공장
	8) 신발	삭주어린이신발공장
Ⅴ. 화학 (5-1)	1) 종합	**[청수화학공장]**
	10) 화장품	삭주화학일용품공장, 청수화학일용품공장
	5) 도자기	삭주토기공장
	5) 기계부품, 금속가공	삭주철제일용품공장
Ⅹ. 가구, 잡제품 (2-1)	1) 가구	삭주가구공장
	5) 기타	**[삭주수출솔공장]**
Ⅺ. 전력 (2-2)	1) 수력	**[수풍발전소]**, **[태평만발전소]**

선천군 (12-4)

I. 광업 (2-1)	1) 탄광	선천탄광
	2) 철광	**[선천광산]**
II. 음식료품, 담배 (4-1)	2) 곡물가공	**[선천기름공장]**
	3) 육류	선천 남새 과일 및 고기 가공공장
	4) 장류	선천장공장
	7) 담배	선천담배공장
V. 화학 (2)	6) 염료,도료,시약, 농약 등	선천약공장
	10) 화장품	선천치약공장
VI. 시멘트, 유리 (1-1)	5) 도자기	**[선천도자기공장]**
VIII. 조립금속, 기계장비 (2-1)	3b) 농업용	선천농기계공장
	6c) 통신기계	**[선천영예군인통신기계공장]**
IX. 수송기계 (1)	3) 자동차	선천련결차공장

염주군 (12-3)

I. 광업 (1)	4) 비금속광물	남시제염소
II. 음식료품, 담배 (1-1)	1) 일반	**[염주식료공장]**
III. 섬유, 의복, 신발 (4-1)	2) 직물공장	염주직물공장
	5) 편직공장	염주편직공장
	6) 의류	염주수출피복공장
	10) 가죽	**[염주그물공장]**
V. 화학 (4-1)	5) 기초화학	염주화학공장
	6) 염료,도료,시약, 농약 등	**[염주식료화학공장]**
	8) 합성수지, 수지제품	염주영예군인수지일용품공장
	9) 제약	염주제약공장
VI. 시멘트, 유리 (1)	3) 벽돌	염주건재공장
VIII. 조립금속, 기계장비 (1)	1) 종합기계	염주기계수리공장

운산군 (4-1)

I. 광업 (1)	2) 철광	운산광산
II. 음식료품, 담배 (1)	1) 일반	운산식료공장
VI. 시멘트, 유리 (1)	3) 벽돌	운산건재공장
VIII. 조립금속, 기계장비 (1-1)	2) 공작기계	**[운산공구공장(7월13일공장)]**

운전군 (3-2)

II. 음식료품, 담배 (1)	1) 일반	운전식료공장
V. 화학 (1-1)	10) 화장품	**[운전화학일용품공장]**
VIII. 조립금속, 기계장비 (1-1)	5) 기계부품, 금속가공	**[운전금속건재공장]**

의주군 (9-3)

I. 광업 (1-1)	2) 철광	**[덕현광산]**
II. 음식료품, 담배 (3-1)	1) 일반	의주식료공장
	2) 곡물가공	**[의주곡산공장]**
	3) 육류	의주 고기 및 남새 가공공장
III. 섬유, 의복, 신발 (2-1)	3) 방적, 제사, 직조	**[의주제사공장]**
	6) 의류	의주피복공장
V. 화학 (2)	9) 제약	의주제약공장
	10) 화장품	의주군영예군인화학일용품공장
VIII. 조립금속, 기계장비 (1)	5) 기계부품, 금속가공	의주편직바늘공장

창성군 (14-2)

II. 음식료품, 담배 (1-1)	1) 일반	**[창성식료공장]**
III. 섬유, 의복, 신발 (3-1)	2) 직물공장	**[창성직물공장]**
	6) 의류	창성여자옷공장, 창성피복공장
IV. 목재, 펄프, 종이 (1)	3) 종이	창성공장
V. 화학 (3)	5) 기초화학	창성화학공장
	8) 합성수지, 수지제품	창성마대공장
	10) 화장품	창성화학일용품공장
VIII. 조립금속, 기계장비 (2)	1) 종합기계	창성기계수리공장
	5) 기계부품, 금속가공	창성철제일용품공장
X. 가구, 잡제품 (3)	1) 가구	창성가구공장
	2) 문방구, 완구, 체육기구	창성연필공장
	4) 공예품, 장식품	창성초물공장
XI. 전력 (1)	2) 화력	창성군 풍력발전소

천마군 (3-1)

I. 광업 (1-1)	3) 비철	**[천마광산]**
III. 섬유, 의복, 신발 (1)	2) 직물공장	천마직물공장
X. 가구, 잡제품 (1)	1) 가구	천마가구공장

철산군 (5-1)

I. 광업 (1)	4) 비금속광물	철산광산
II. 음식료품, 담배 (1)	1) 일반	철산식료공장
III. 섬유, 의복, 신발 (1)	6) 의류	철산피복공장
V. 화학 (1)	9) 제약	철산영예군인제약공장
VIII. 조립금속, 기계장비 (1-1)	6a) 전기기기, 부품	**[철산전기공장]**

태천군 (4-3)

II. 음식료품, 담배 (1-1)	2) 곡물가공	**[태천기름공장]**
VIII. 조립금속, 기계장비 (1-1)	5) 기계부품, 금속가공	**[태천철제일용품공장]**
X. 가구, 잡제품 (1)	4) 공예품, 장식품	태천옻공예품공장
XI. 전력 (1-1)	1) 수력	**[태천수력발전종합기업소]**

피현군 (8-2)

III. 섬유, 의복, 신발 (4)	2) 직물공장	피현직물공장
	5) 편직공장	피현영예군인편직공장
	6) 의류	피현군 옷공장, 피현수출피복공장
V. 화학 (1-1)	2) 정유	**[봉화화학공장]**
VI. 시멘트, 유리 (3-1)	2) 마그네사이트 크링커 및 내화물	피현내화물공장
	3) 벽돌	**[피현씨리카트벽돌공장]**, 피현흄관공장

향산군 (3-2)

II. 음식료품, 담배 (1-1)	1) 일반	**[향산종합식료공장]**
VIII. 조립금속, 기계장비 (1-1)	4) 정밀	**[묘향산의료기구공장]**
XI. 전력 (1)	1) 수력	향산발전소(수력)

IMPORTANT (38)

4	구장군, 룡천군, 삭주군
3	선천군
2	녕변군, 동림군, 동창군, 염주군, 의주군, 창성군, 태천군, 피현군, 향산군
1	곽산군, 박천군, 운산군, 운전군, 철산군

(38)

공업 (30)	곽산련결농기계공장 (곽산군), 구장세멘트공장 (구장군), 녕변견직공장, 팔원견직공장 (녕변군), 동림전기공장, 8월28일공장(차련관광산기계공장) (동림군), 룡암포기계공장, 북중기계련합기업소, 룡천광산기계공장, 룡암포조선소 (룡천군), 박천견직공장 (박천군), 삭주식료공장, 삭주직물공장, 청수화학공장 (삭주군), 선천도자기공장, 선천영예군인통신기계공장, 선천농기계공장 (선천군), 염주식료공장, 염주그물공장 (염주군), 운산공구공장(7월13일공장) (운산군), 운전금속건재공장 (운전군), 의주곡산공장(의주군), 창성식료공장, 창성직물공장 (창성군), 철산영예군인제약공장 (철산군), 태천철제일용품공장 (태천군), 봉화화학공장, 량책베아링공장(10월30일) (피현군), 향산종합식료공장, 묘향산의료기구공장 (향산군)
광업 (6)	구장지구탄광련합기업소, 룡등탄광, 룡문탄광 (구장군), 동창광산, 대유동광산 (동창군), 덕현광산 (의주군)
전력 (2)	수풍발전소 (삭주군), 태천발전소 (태천군)

Phyongsong (Phyongnam Province)

KOFC (7-1)

경공업 (1)	신발 (1)	평성합성가죽공장
중화공업 (6-1)	기계 (2)	평성텔레비젼수상기조립공장, 모란봉시계공장
	자동차 (1)	**[평성자동차공장]**
	전기/전자 (2)	평성축전지공장, 평성반도체공장
	건재 (1)	평성시멘트공장

MOU (19)

기계 (1)	평성농기계공장
경공업 (18)	평성고려약가공공장, 평성고무줄공장, 평성대동강피복공장, 평성대성편직공장, 평성대성피복공장, 평성시름공장, 평성식료가공공장, 평성옷공장, 평성은덕피복공장, 평성은하피복공장, 평성제약공장, 평성펄직수출품공장, 평성피복수출품공장, 평성합성가죽공장, 대동강수출피복공장, 모란봉시계공장, 백송종합식료공장, 봉학식료공장

IPA (16-5)

공업 (16-5)	**[평성고무줄공장]**, **[평성시계공장(平城時計工場)]**, **[평성식료품공장(平城食料品工場)]**, **[평성제약공장(平城製藥工場)]**, **[평성합성가죽공장(平城合成皮革工場)]**; 평성편직공장, 모란봉시계공장, 평성정미기계공장, 평성농기계공장, 평성일용품공장, 평성고순도공장, 대성피복공장, 평성화장품공장, 평성종이공장, 평성수예품공장, 보석공예창작사

KCNA (5)

공업 (5)	백송종합식료공장, 평성식료가공공장, 은덕피복공장, 평성합성가죽공장, 대동강수출피복공장

KIET (19-10)

II. 음식료품, 담배 (2-1)	1) 일반	[봉학식료종합공장]
	2) 곡물가공	평성기름공장
III. 섬유, 의복, 신발 (5-3)	5) 편직공장	평성편직수술품공장
	6) 의류	[평성옷공장], [평성은덕피복공장], 평성피복수출품공장
	9) 가방	[평성애국가방공장]
V. 화학 (2-1)	7) 고무제품	[평성고무줄공장]
	8) 합성수지, 수지제품	평성수지일용품공장
VIII. 조립금속, 기계장비 (6-4)	1) 종합기계	평성기계공장
	3b) 농업용	[평성농기계공장], [평성관개기계공장]
	4) 정밀	[모란봉시계공장]
	6b) 전자, 자동화기기	[평성반도체공장], 평성축전기공장
IX.수송기계 (2-1)	3) 자동차	[평성자동차공장], 평성자동차부속품공장,
X. 가구, 잡제품 (1)	4) 공예품, 장식품	평성수예품공장
XI. 전력 (1)	2) 화력	평성화력발전소

IMPORTANT (4)

공업 (4)	평성고무줄공장, 평성농기계공장, 모란봉시계공장, 평성합성가죽공장

Anju (Phyongnam Province)

KOFC (13-4)

경공업 (3-1)	식품 (1)	남흥애국곡산공장
	섬유 (1)	**[안주아닐론방적공장]**
	제지 (1)	121호공장 (안주제지공장)
중화공업 (8-3)	기계 (4)	남흥건설기계공장, 안주트랙터부속품공장, 신안주농기계공장(9월28일공장), 안주뽐프공장
	전기/전자 (1)	안주통신기계공장
	화학 (2)	**[남흥청년화학련합기업소]**, **[안주흙보산비료공장]**
	건재 (1)	**[안주씨리카트벽돌공장]**
채취 (1)	철 (1)	송암광산
전력 (1)	화력 (1)	청천강화력발전소

MOU (17-2) 공업 (16-1) 전력 (1-1)

경공업 (11)	9월28일공장, 안주절연물공장, 안주121호종이공장, 안주견직공장, 안주수출피복공장, 안주시청천강피복공장, 안주신발공장, 안주영예군인수지일용품공장, 안주장공장, 안주직물공장, 청천강피복공장
기계 (4)	안주뜨락또르부속품공장, 안주통신기계공장, 안주펌프공장, 1월18일기계종합공장
화학 (1-1)	**[남흥청년화학련합기업소]**
전력 (1-1)	**[청천강화력발전소]**

IPA (17-7)

공업 (14-7)	**[9월28일기계공장(九月二十八日機械工場) (구 안주련결농기계공장)]**, **[남흥청년화학련합기업소(南興青年化學聯合企業所)]**, **[신안주직물공장(新安州織物工場)]**, **[안주견직공장(安州絹織工場)]**, **[안주씨리카트벽돌공장]**, **[안주아닐론방적공장]**, **[121호공장 (안주제지공장)]**; 안주통신기계공장(安州通信機械工場), 안주뜨락또르부속품공장, 안주수출품피복공장(安州輸出品皮服工場), 청년수지마대공장, 룡계유리공장, 룡흥곡산공장, 룡흥씨리카트벽돌공장
광업 (2)	룡원광산(龍源鑛山), 안주탄광
전력 (1)	청천강화력발전소(淸川江火力發電所)

KCNA (9)

공업 (7)	9월28일공장, 안주견직공장, 안주뜨락또르부속품공장, 안주수출피복공장, 안주신발공장, 안주씨리카트벽돌공장, 안주절연물공장
전력 (2)	남흥청년화학련합기업소, 청천강화력발전소

KIET (32-14)

I. 광업 (2)	1) 탄광	운곡탄광
	4) 비금속광물	운곡광산
II. 음식료품, 담배 (2-1)	1) 일반	안주식료품공장
	4) 장류	**[안주장공장]**
III. 섬유, 의복, 신발 (6-3)	2) 직물공장	**[신안주직물공장]**, 안주직물공장
	3) 방적, 제사, 직조	**[안주아닐론방적공장]**
	4) 견직공장	**[안주견직공장]**
	5) 편직공장	안주편직물공장
	8) 신발	안주털신발공장
IV. 목재, 펄프, 종이 (3-1)	3) 종이	**[121호공장]**, 안주종이공장, 안주제지공장,
V. 화학 (6-3)	1) 종합	**[남흥청년화학련합기업소]**
	3) 비료	**[안주흙보산비료공장]**
	6) 염료,도료, 시약, 농약 등	**[안주절연물공장]**
	8) 합성수지, 수지제품	안주영예군인수지공장, 청년수지마대공장
	9) 제약	안주제약공장
VI. 시멘트, 유리 (2-1)	3) 벽돌	**[안주씨리카트벽돌공장]**
	4) 유리	안주유리병공장
VIII. 조립금속, 기계장비 (5-4)	3a) 탄광, 광산용	**[9월28일공장**(구 안주련결농기계공장)**]**
	3b) 농업용	안주뜨락또르부속품공장
	5) 기계부품, 금속가공	**[안주철제일용품공장]**
	6a) 전기기기, 부품	**[안주전선공장]**
	6c) 통신기계	**[안주통신기계공장]**
X. 가구, 잡제품 (3)	2) 문방구, 완구, 체육기구	안주영예군인학용품공장
	4) 공예품, 장식품	안주수예품공장
	5) 기타	안주영예군인공장
XI. 전력 (3-1)	2) 화력	**[청천강화력발전소]**, 안주화력발전소, 제2청천강화력발전소

IMPORTANT (8)

공업 (7)	안주아닐론방적공장, 안주견직공장, 121호공장 (안주제지공장), 남흥청년화학련합기업소, 안주씨리카트벽돌공장, 9월28일기계공장(九月二十八日機械工場) (구 안주련결농기계공장), 안주통신기계공장
전력 (1)	청천강화력발전소

Kaechon (Phyongnam Province)

KOFC (18-2)

경공업 (1)	제지 (1)	개천종이공장
중화공업 (3-1)	금속 (1)	개천선철공장
	철도차령 (1)	개천철도부속품공장
	건재 (1)	**[개천시멘트공장]**
채취 (14-1)	철 (3)	개천광산, 룡원광산, 천동광산
	비 (1)	승찬광산
	탄광 (10-1)	**[개천지구탄광련합기업소]**, 룡운탄광, 개천탄광, 봉천탄광, 조양탄광, 원리탄광, 신립탄광, 람전탄광, 신성탄광, 무진대청년탄광

MOU (24-1) 공업 (15) 광업 (9-1)

건재 (1)	개천시멘트공장
경공업 (11)	개천고무일용품공장, 개천기름공장, 개천기초식품공장, 개천도자기공장, 개천병공장, 개천수출피복공장, 개천식료가공공장, 개천식료공장, 개천영예군인악기공장, 개천은하피복공장, 개천직물공장
기계 (2)	개천탄광기계공장, 개천선철공장
전자 (1)	개천전구공장
광업 (9-1)	**[개천지구탄광련합기업소]**; 개천탄광, 개천철도탄광, 남전탄광, 신립탄광, 조양탄광, 원리탄광, 룡원광산, 무진대청년탄광

IPA (25-7)

공업 (13-5)	**[개천배합사료공장(价川配合飼料工場)]**, **[개천식료가공공장(价川食料工場)]**, **[개천영예군인악기공장(价川榮譽軍人樂器工場)]**, **[개천종이공장]**, **[개천수출피복공장(价川輸出被服工場)]**; 개천선철공장(价川銑鐵工場), 개천씰루민공장, 개천탐사기계수리공장(价川探査機械修理工場), 개천기계공장(价川機械工場), 개천서부지구탐사설비부속품공장 (价川西部地區探査設備附屬品工場), 외서벽돌공장, 준혁기름공장, 준혁철도부재공장
광업 (12-2)	**[조양탄광(朝陽炭鑛)]**, **[천동광산(泉洞鑛山)]**; 개천탄광(价川炭鑛), 원리광산(院里鑛山), 삼봉광산(三峯鑛山), 람전탄광(藍田炭鑛), 람전광산(藍田鑛山), 봉천탄광(鳳泉炭鑛), 신성탄광(新成炭鑛), 신립탄광(新立炭鑛), 무진대탄광(無盡臺炭鑛), 룡운탄광

KCNA (10)

공업 (4)	1월18일기계종합공장, 개천기초식품공장, 개천직물공장, 개천탄광기계공장
광업 (3)	개천지구탄광련합기업소, 무진대청년탄광, 봉천탄광
전력 (3)	평원1호발전소, 평원2호발전소, 평원3호발전소

KIET (41-12)

I. 광업 (17-6)	1) 탄광	**[개천지구탄광련합기업소]**, **[봉천탄광]**, **[조양탄광]**, **[개천탄광]**, 원리탄광, 선무덕탄광, 룡운탄광, 승창탄광, 신성탄광, 신립탄광, 무진대(청년)탄광, 람전탄광
	2) 철광	**[천동광산]**, **[룡원광산]**, 승창광산, 개천광산
	4) 비금속광물	람정광산
II. 음식료품, 담배 (4-1)	1) 일반	개천식료가공공사
	2) 곡물가공	**[개천기름공장]**
	4) 장류	개천장공장
	5) 사료	개천배합사료공장
III. 섬유, 의복, 신발 (6-1)	5) 편직공장	개천편직공장
	6) 의류	**[개천수출피복공장]**, 개천옷공장, 철도부 피복공장
	8) 신발	개천신발공장
	10) 가죽	개천모피가공공장
IV. 목재, 펄프, 종이 (1)	3) 종이	개천종이공장
V. 화학 (1)	9) 제약	개천제약공장
VI. 시멘트, 유리 (3)	4) 유리	개천병공장, 개천유리공장
	5) 도자기	개천도자기공장
VII. 1차 금속산엄(1-1)	1)제철, 제강	**[개천선철공장]**
VIII. 조립금속, 기계장비 (4-1)	1) 종합기계	개천기계공장
	5) 기계부품, 금속가공	**[개천법랑철기공장]**, 개천철제일용품공장
	6a) 전기	개천전등알공장
IX. 수송기계 (2-1)	2) 철도차량	**[개천철도부속품공장]**, 개천차량부속품공장
X. 가구, 잡제품 (2-1)	3) 악기	**[개천영예군인악기공장]**
	4) 공예품 등	개천초물공장

IMPORTANT (10)

공업 (4)	개천수출피복공장, 개천선철공장, 개천영예군인악기공장, 개천종이공장
광업 (6)	개천지구탄광련합기업소, 봉천탄광, 조양탄광, 개천탄광, 천동광산, 룡원광산

Tokchon (Phyongnam Province)

KOFC (15-3)

중화공업 (4-1)	기계 (2)	덕천자동차부속품공장, 덕천탄광기계공장
	화학 (1)	**[승리자동차련합기업소]**
	건재 (1)	덕천세멘트공장
재취 (10-1)	탄광 (10)	**[덕천지구탄광련합기업소]**, 덕천탄광, 덕성탄광, 제남탄광, 서창청년탄광, 형봉탄광, 월봉탄광, 남양탄광, 장안탄광, 남덕탄광
전력 (1-1)	수력 (1)	**[대동강발전소]**

MOU (13-3) 공업 (3-1) 광업 (9-1) 전력 (1-1)

경공업 (2)	덕천철제일용품공장, 덕천철제가정용품공장
기계 (1-1)	**[승리자동차련합기업소]**
광업 (9-1)	**[덕천지구탄광련합기업소]**; 남덕탄광, 서창청년탄광, 제남탄광, 덕천탄광, 월봉탄광, 형봉탄광, 덕성탄광, 남양탄광
전력 (1-1)	**[대동강발전소]**

IPA (6-3)

공업 (3-2)	**[승리자동차련합기업소(勝利自動車聯合企業所)], [덕천탄광기계련합기업소(德川炭鑛機械聯合企業所)]**; 무창벽돌공장
광업 (2-1)	**[덕천지구탄광련합기업소(德川地區炭鑛聯合企業所)]**, 운흥탄광
전력 (1)	대동강발전소

KCNA (11)

공업 (3)	덕천일반식료공장, 승리자동차련합기업소, 덕성기계공장
광업 (7)	덕천지구탄광련합기업소, 덕천탄광, 서창청년탄광, 형봉탄광, 남덕탄광, 남양탄광, 덕성탄광
전력 (1)	대동강발전소

KIET (21-10)

I. 광업 (8-5)	1) 탄광	**[덕천지구탄광련합기업소], [덕천탄광], [월봉탄광], [장안탄광], [제남탄광]**, 덕성탄광, 형봉탄광, 서창청년탄광
II. 음식료품, 담배 (3-1)	1) 일반	**[덕천일반식료공장]**
	3	덕천남새가공공장
	4) 장류	덕천장공장
III. 섬유, 의복, 신발 (3)	4) 경직	덕천견직공장
	5) 편직공장	덕천편직공장
	6) 의류	덕천수출피복공장
V. 화학 (1)	8) 합성수지 등	덕천수지일용품공장
VI. 시멘트, 유리 (1)	1) 제철등	덕천세멘트공장
VIII. 조립금속, 기계장비 (2-2)	3a) 탄광 등	**[덕천탄광기계공장]**
	5) 기계부품, 금속가공	**[덕천철제일용품공장]**
IX. 수송기계 (1-1)	3) 자동차	**[승리자동차종합공장]**
X. 가구, 잡제품 (1)	1) 가구	덕천가구공장
XI. 전력 (1-1)	1) 수력	**[대동강발전종합기업소]**

IMPORTANT (8)

공업 (2)	덕천탄광기계련합기업소, 승리자동차련합기업소
광업 (5)	덕천지구탄광련합기업소, 덕천탄광, 월봉탄광, 장안탄광, 제남탄광
전력 (1)	대동강발전소

Sunchon (Phyongnam Province)

KOFC (18-9)

경공업 (4-2)	섬유 (1)	**[순천비날론련합기업소]**
	신발 (2)	**[순천구두공장]**, 순천신발공장
	제지 (1)	순천(시)종이공장
중화공업 (10-4)	금속 (1)	**[부산알루미나공장]**
	기계 (2)	**[9월25일기계공장(순천뜨락또르공장)]**, 순천탄광기계공장
	전기/전자 (1)	순천자동화기구공장
	화학 (3)	**[순천석회질소비료공장]**, 순천제약공장, 순천타이어공장
	건재 (3)	**[순천시멘트련합기업소]**, 성산세멘트공장, 순천유리공장
채취 (3-2)	탄광 (2)	**[2.8직동청년탄광]**, **[순천지구탄광련합기업소]**
	석회석 (1)	성산광산
전력 (1-1)	화력 (1)	**[순천화력발전소]**

MOU (27-5) 공업 (18-3) 광업 (8-1) 전력 (1-1)

건재 (6-2)	**[순천시멘트련합기업소]**, **[성산시멘트공장]**; 순천건재품가공공장, 순천보온재공장, 순천건재공장, 부산리시멘트공장
경공업 (7)	순천피복공장, 순천구두공장, 순천담배공장, 순천식료가공공장, 순천아동신발공장, 순천제약공장, 순천직물공장
기계 (2)	소공구공장, 순천탄광기계공장
화학 (3-1)	**[순천비날론련합기업소]**; 순천석회질소비료종합공장, 순천애국복합미생물비료공장
광업 (8-1)	**[순천지구청년탄광련합기업소]**; 순천탄광, 천성청년탄광, 한령탄광, 칠리탄광, 2.8직동청년탄광, 5월4일광산, 점판암광산
전력 (1-1)	**[순천화력발전소]**

IPA (11-9)

공업 (9-9)	**[순천구두공장]**, **[순천세멘트련합기업소]**, **[순천아동신발공장(순천어린이신발공장)]**, **[순천제약공장(順川製藥工場)]**, **[순천직물공장(順川織物工場)]**, **[9월25일기계공장(순천뜨락또르공장)]**, **[순천세멘트공장]**, **[순천비날론공장(순천비날론련합기업소)]**, **[순천석회질소비료공장(順川石灰窒素肥料工長)]**
광업 (2)	직동탄광, 신리광산

KCNA (11)

공업 (5)	부품질석생산사업소, 순천구두공장, 순천비날론련합기업소, 순천세멘트련합기업소, 순천직물공장
광업 (4)	순천지구(청년)탄광련합기업소, 2.8직동청년탄광, 령대알탄련합기업소, 신창청년탄광
전력 (2)	순천갑문발전소, 순천화력발전소

KIET (60-25)

I. 광업 (8-6)	1) 탄광	**[순천지구탄광련합기업소]**, **[형태탄광]**, **[한룡탄광]**, **[2.8.직동청년탄광]**, 비날론탄광
	4) 비금속광물	**[5월4일광산]**, **[5월4일탄광]**, 성산광산
II.음식료품,담배 (8)	1) 일반	순천시 순천식료가공공장
	2) 곡물가공	련포기름공장, 순천기름공장
	4) 장류	순천식료가공공장
	6) 음료, 주류	순천맥주공장, 순천음료공장, 순천사이다공장
	7) 담배	순천담배공장
III. 섬유, 의복, 신발 (8-4)	2) 직물공장	**[순천직물공장]**
	3) 방적, 제사, 직조	**[순천조면공장]**, 순천타면공장
	5) 편직공장	순천편직공장
	6) 의류	수원피복공장
	8) 신발	**[순천구두공장]**, **[순천아동신방공장]**
	9) 가방	순천영예군인가방공장
IV. 목재, 펄프, 종이 (1)	3) 종이	순천(시)종이공장
V. 화학 (11-6)	1) 종합	**[순천비날론련합기업소]**
	3) 비료	**[순천석회질소비료공장]**
	5) 기초화학	**[령대알탄공장]**, 순천가성소다공장, 순천표백분공장
	6) 염료,도료,시약, 농약 등	**[순천시약공장]**
	7) 고무제품	순천다이야(재생)공장
	8) 합성수지, 수지제품	**[순천수지일용품공장]**
	9) 제약	**[순천제약공장]**, 순천동약공장
	10) 화장품	순천화학일용품공장
VI. 시멘트, 유리 (11-4)	1) 시멘트	**[부산리세멘트공장]**, **[순천세멘트련합기업소]**, 성산세멘트공장,
	3) 벽돌	**[순천보온재공장]**, 순천스레트공장, 순천벽돌공장
	4) 유리	련포유리병공장, 순천판유리공장
	5) 도자기	**[순천도자기공장]**, 순천독공장, 직동도자기공장
VIII. 조립금속, 기계장비 (8-4)	3a) 탄광, 광산용	**[순천탄광기계련합기업소]**
	3b) 농업용	**[9월25일기계공장 (순천뜨락또르공장)]**
	3c) 기타 산업용	**[9월25일지게차공장]**
	4) 정밀	순천실험기구공장
	5) 기계부품, 금속가공	순천군소공구공장, 순천시철제일용품공장
	6a) 전기기기, 부품	순천전기일용품공장
	6b) 전자, 자동화기기	**[순천자동화기구공장]**
X. 가구, 잡제품 (4)	1) 가구	순천가구공장
	2) 문방구, 완구, 체육기구	재동교구비품공장
	4) 공예품, 장식품	순천초물공장
	5) 기타	순천영예군인공장
XI. 전력 (1-1)	2) 화력	**[순천화력발전소]**

IMPORTANT (10)

공업 (7)	순천직물공장, 순천구두공장, 순천비날론련합기업소, 순천석회질소비료공장, 순천제약공장, 순천세멘트련합기업소, 9월25일기계공장(순천뜨락또르공장)
광업 (2)	순천지구탄광련합기업소, 2.8.직동청년탄광
전력 (1)	순천화력발전소

Kun (Phyongnam Province)

KOFC (43–9)

11	북창군 (3)
6	문덕군
5	성천군, 은산군 (3), 청남구 (3)
2	대흥군, 숙천군
1	득장구, 맹산군, 신양군, 양덕군, 영원군, 증산군, 회창군

경공업 (3) 식품 (2), 제지 (1)	북창곡산공장 (박창), 남양제염소 (숙천군); 신양제지공장 (신양)
중화공업 (13–1) 금속공업 (1), 기계 (3), 전기/전자 (1), 건재 (8)	**[북창알루미늄공장]**; 송남탄광기계공장 (북창), 장림탐사기계공장 (상천), 은산탄광설비부속품광장 (은산); 비류강전기공장 (성천); 맹산시멘트공장 (맹산), 덕판유리공장 (문덕), 북창시멘트공장 (북창), 성천시멘트공장 (성천), 양덕시멘트공장 (양덕), 은산세멘트공장 (은산), 증산시멘트공장 (증산), 청남구유리공장 (청남구)
재취 (22–7) 비 (3), 탄광 (19)	경수광산 (대흥), 성천광산 (성청), 성흥광산 (회창); 명학탄광 (득장구), 태향탄광, 룡림탄광, 서호탄광, 삼천포탄광, 서사탄광 (문덕군), 송남청년탄광, **[북창지구탄광련합기업소]**, 인포탄광, 회안탄광, 한령탄광 (북창), 칠리탄광 (숙천), **[신창탄광 (평남신창종합청년탄광)]**, **[천성청년탄광]**, **[령대탄광** (은산)**]**, **[안주지구탄광련합기업소]**, **[청남탄광]**, **[회풍탄광]**, 립석탄광 (청남구)
전력 (5–1) 수력 (4), 화력 (1)	대흥청년발전소 1호 (대흥), 대동강발전소 2호 (북창), 성천발전소 (성천) 영원발전소 (영원); **[북창화력발전련합기업소** (북창)**]**

MOU (82–7) 공업 (47–1) 광업 (32–5) 전력 (3–1)

24	북창군 (2)
9	청남구 (1), 성천군 (1)
7	은산군 (2)
4	득장구 (1), 문덕군, 신양군, 평원군
3	대흥군, 화창군
2	대동군, 맹산군, 숙천군, 양덕군
1	금야군, 녕원군, 증산군

건재 (2)	북창시멘트공장 (북창군), 양덕건재공업 (양덕군)
경공업 (40-1)	원평수산물가공공장 (금야군), 3월11일대흥가공사업소, 대흥장공장 (대흥군), 맹산식료공장, 맹산장공장 (맹산군), 문덕과실가공공장, 문덕기름공장, 문덕도자기공장 (문덕군), 북창가정용품공장, 북창고려약공장, 북창기초식품공장, 북창식료가공공장, 북창은하피복공장, 북창제약공장, 북창철제일용품공장, 송남철제일용품공장 (북창군), **[성천제사공장]**; 신성천콩크리트동발공장, 성천편직공장 (성천군), 숙천수출피복공장, 숙천진성피복공장 (숙천군), 신양고려약공장, 신양군장공장, 신양산과실가공공장, 신양수출피복공장 (신양군), 양덕군수출조물일용품공장 (양덕군), 은산군어린이식료공장, 은산군장공장 (은산군), 증산화장품공장 (증산군), 청남수출피복공장, 청남장공장, 청남직물공장, 청남탄부피복공장, 청남피복공장 (청남구), 평원수출피복공장, 평원은하피복공장, 평원피복공장 (평원군), 회창군산과실가공공장, 회창기초식품공장, 화창군기초식품공장 (화창군)
기계 (4)	득장탄광기계공장 (득장구), 송남탄광기계공장, 북창군농기구공장 (북창군), 장림탐사기계공장 (성천군)
화학 (1)	성천강화학공장 (성천군)
광업 (32-5)	삼신탄광, 장산광산 (대동군), 평화대흥광산 (대흥군), **[득장지구탄광련합기업소]**; 득장청년탄광, 명학탄광 (득장구), 룡림탄광 (문덕군), **[북창지구탄광련합기업소]**, 송남청년탄광, 인포탄광, 장안탄광, 채령탄광, 풍곡탄광, 룡산광산, 득장탄광, 인포탄광, 회안탄광, 봉창지구탄광, 봉천탄광 (북창군), 마전광산, 룡흥광산, 성천광산 (성천군), **[령대알탄련합기업소]**, **[천성청년탄광종합기업소]**; 령대탄광, 신창청년탄광, 성산광산 (은산군), **[안주지구탄광련합기업소]**; 입석탄광, 청남탄광, 화풍탄광 (청남구), 영유광산 (평원군)
전력 (3-1)	녕원발전소 (녕원군), **[북창화력발전련합기업소** (북창군)], 성천발전소 (성천군)

IPA (227-33)

녕원군 (11-4)

공업 (10-4)	**[녕원가구공장(寧遠家具工場)]**, **[녕원식료공장(寧遠食料工場)]**, **[녕원악기공장(寧遠樂器工場)]**, **[녕원제약공장(寧遠製藥工場)]**; 녕원일용품공장, 녕원직물공장, 녕원피복공장, 녕원건재공장, 문곡과실가공공장, 문곡농기구공장
광업 (1)	장산탄광

대동군 (24-1)

공업 (21-1)	**[대동내화물공장(大同耐火物工場)]**; 대동철제일용품공장(大同鐵製日用品工場), 대동수지일용품공장(大同樹脂日用品工場), 대동솔공장, 대동자동화기구공장(大同自動化器具工場), 대동저항기공장(大同抵抗器工場), 대동벽돌공장, 대동식료공장, 대동일용품공장(大同日用品工場),대동화학공장, 대동피복공장, 시정내화물공장, 시정전기기계공장, 시정식료공장, 시정일용품공장, 시정직물공장, 시정농기구공장, 성칠장공장, 성칠독공장, 원천종이공장, 팔청기와공장
광업 (3)	강서탄광, 대동탄광(大同炭鑛), 대동광산

대흥군 (11-2)

공업 (10-1)	**[대흥제약공장(大興製藥工場)]**; 대흥목재종합공장(大興木材綜合工場), 대흥목재품공장(大興木材品工場), 대흥장공장, 대흥식료가공공장(大興食料加工工場), 대흥목재가공공장, 대흥식료공장, 대흥일용품공장, 대흥피복공장, 산나물가공공장
광업 (1-1)	**[대흥청년광업종합기업소(大興青年鑛業綜合企業所)]**; 경수광산

맹산군 (9-1)

공업 (8-1)	**[맹산제약공장(孟山製藥工場)]**; 맹산장공장, 맹산식료공장, 맹산직물공장(孟山織物工場), 맹산피복공장(孟山被服工場), 맹산종이공장, 새마을식료공장, 새마을직물공장
광업 (1)	유승광산

문덕군 (16-2)

공업 (15-2)	**[문덕도자기공장(文德陶瓷器工場)]**, **[문덕전기자기공장(文德電氣瓷器工場)]**; 문덕화학공장, 문덕제지공장, 문덕건재공장, 문덕직물공장, 문덕옷공장, 문덕농기구공장, 문덕기계수리공장, 문덕과일가공공장, 문덕기름공장, 문덕장공장, 서호수산물가공공장, 흙보산비료를 생산하는 공장, 동발나무를 생산하는 만흥기업소
광업 (1)	룡림탄광

북창군/득장구 (31-5)

공업 (25-3)	**[북창가정용품공장(北倉家庭用品工場)]**, **[북창곡산공장(北倉穀産工場)]**, **[득장탄광기계공장(得將炭鑛機械工場)]**; 북창연재벽돌공장, 북창식료가공공장, 북창기름공장, 북창우산공장, 북창기계수리공장, 북창철제일용품공장, 북창옷공장, 관하농약공장, 북창배합먹이공장, 북창피복공장, 북창화학공장, 북창직물공장, 북창장공장, 북창모피가공공장, 북창농기구공장, 북창수지일용품공장, 송남탄광기계공장, 송남쇠동발공장, 송남일용품공장, 송남식료가공공장, 인포식료공장, 인포일용품공장
광업 (5-1)	**[송남청년탄광(松南靑年炭鑛)]**; 인포탄광, 풍곡탄광, 룡산탄광, 가창탄광(假倉炭鑛)
전력 (1-1)	**[북창화력발전련합기업소(北倉火力發展聯合企業所)]**;

성천군 (16-1)

공업 (13-1)	**[성천제사공장(成川製絲工場)]**; 성천식료공장, 성천일용품공장, 성천피복공장, 성천건재공장, 성천제약공장, 성천농기구공장, 신성천식료공장, 신성천화학공장, 장림탐사기계공장, 장림철제일용품공장, 장림마대공장, 덕암전기부속품공장
광업 (3)	은곡광산, 장림광산, 룡흥광산

숙천군 (10-1)

공업 (8-1)	**[숙천과일가공공장]**; 숙천식료공장, 숙천일용품공장, 숙천건재공장, 숙천피복공장, 숙천제약공장, 숙천도자기공장, 남양제염소
광업 (2)	창동탄광, 칠리탄광

신양군 (15-5)

공업 (14-4)	**[장성식료가공공장(長城食料加工工場)]**, **[신양제약공장(新陽製藥工場)]**, **[신양종이공장]**, **[신양초물제품공장(新陽草物製品工場)]**; 신양식료공장, 신양일용품공장, 신양피복공장, 신양건재공장, 신양농기구공장, 신양가죽공장, 인평식료공장, 인평일용품공장, 인평제약공장, 장산식료공장
광업 (1-1)	**[인평광산(仁坪鑛山)]**

양덕군 (12-1)

공업 (11-1)	**[동양술공장]**; 양덕식료가공공장(陽德食料加工工場), 양덕장공장(陽德醬工場), 양덕포도술공장(陽德葡萄酒工場), 양덕일용품공장(陽德日用品工場), 양덕목재품공장(陽德木材品工場), 양덕목재화학공장(陽德木材化學工場), 양덕종이공장, 양덕직물공장(陽德織物工場), 양덕피복공장(陽德被服工場), 온정목통공장
광업 (1)	운창광산

은산군 (28-4)

공업 (24-2)	**[은산탄광설비부속품공장(殷山炭鑛設備附屬品工場)**, 령대알탄공장]; 은산기계톱공장, 은산세멘트공장, 은산수지건재공장, 은산비료공장, 은산가성소다공장, 은산종이공장, 은산직물공장, 은산피복공장, 은산모피가공공장, 은산장공장, 은산식료공장, 은산철제일용품공장, 은산전기일용품공장, 은산목재일용품공장, 구봉수지건재공장, 구봉스레트공장, 구봉철제일용품공장, 구봉식료공장, 재동장공장, 재동일용품공장, 학산세멘트공장, 제현기계톱공장
광업 (4-2)	**[성산광산(聖山鑛山)], [신창탄광(新倉炭鑛)(평남신창종합청년탄광)]**; 령대탄광(靈臺炭鑛), 천성탄광(天聖炭鑛)

증산군 (9-1)

공업 (6-1)	**[림성종이공장]**; 증산화학공장, 증산군식료공장, 증산군피복공장, 소방기재공장, 랭동공장
광업 (3)	금송린회석광산(金宋燐灰石鑛山), 적송린회석광산, 심원광산

평원군 (18-2)

공업 (14-1)	**[평원식료공장(平原食料工場)]**; 평원장공장, 평원기름공장, 평원과일가공공장, 평원일용품공장, 평원직물공장, 평원피복공장, 평원농기구공장, 평원기계수리공장, 평원수출피복공장, 어파식료공장, 어파피복공장, 어파모피공장, 어파토기공장
광업 (4-1)	**[영유광산(永柔鑛山)]**; 어파광산, 룡상광산, 문흥절연물광산

회창군 (15-1)

공업 (8-1)	**[회창목재가구공장(檜倉木材家具工場)]**; 회창장공장; 염소젖가공공장; 산과실가공공장; 회창식료공장; 회창일용품공장; 회창피복공장; 문어종이공장
광업 (6)	성흥광산, 회창광산, 백령광산, 석항광산, 화전광산, 대곡광산
전력 (1)	회창1호청년발전소

청남구 (2-2)

공업 (1-1)	**[청남수출피복공장(淸南輸出被服工場)]**
광업 (1-1)	**[안주지구탄광련합기업소(安州地區炭鑛聯合企業所)]**

KCNA (24)

4	북창군
3	성천군, 숙천군, 은산군
2	녕원군, 대흥군, 청남구
1	대동군, 득장구, 문덕군, 신양군, 양덕군

공업 (8)	대흥고무공장 (대흥군), 북창기초식료품공장 (북창군), 남양정제소금공장, 남양제염소, 숙천진성피복공장 (숙천군), 신양산과실가공공장 (신양군), 동양샘물공장 (양덕군), 은산밀림기계톱공장 (은산군)
광업(10)	득장지구탄광련합기업소 (득장구), 안주지구탄광련합기업소, 화풍탄광 (청남구), 장산광산 (대동군), 북창지구탄광련합기업소, 인포탄광 (북창군), 룡흥광산 (성천군), 천성청년탄광, 령대탄광 (은산군), 태향탄광 (문덕군)
전력 (6)	성룡강청년1호발전소, 녕원발전소 (녕원군), 대흥청년발전소 (대흥군), 북창화력발전련합기업소 (북창), 신성천철도청년1호발전소, 신성천철도청년2호발전소 (성천군)

KIET (168-35)

녕원군 (8)

I. 광업 (2)	1) 탄광	녕원탄광
	4) 비금속광물	녕원인회암광산
II. 음식료품, 담배 (2)	3) 육류 등	녕원 산과실 가공공장
	4) 장류	녕원장공장
III. 섬유, 의복, 신발 (1)	6) 의류	녕원피복공장
IV. 목재, 펄프, 종이 (1)	3) 종이	녕원종이공장
X. 가구, 잡제품 (2)	3) 악기	녕원영예군인악기공장
	5) 기타	녕원일용품공장

대동군 (6-1)

I. 광업 (1-1)	4) 비금속광물	**[장산광산]**
II. 음식료품, 담배 (2)	1) 일반	대동식료공장
	4) 장류	대동장공장
III. 섬유, 의복, 신발 (1)	2) 직물	대동직물공장
VI. 시멘트, 유리 (1)	3) 벽돌 등	대동탄산화부재공장
XI. 전력 (1)	2) 화력	대보화력발전소

대흥군 (15-3)

I. 광업 (2-1)	2) 철광	경수광산
	4) 비금속광물	**[대흥청년광업종합기업소]**
II. 음식료품, 담배 (2)	1) 일반	대흥식료공장
	4) 장류	대흥군 장공장
III. 섬유, 의복, 신발 (2)	2) 직물	대흥직물공장
	6) 의류	대흥피복공장
IV. 목재, 펄프, 종이 (3-1)	1) 목재	**[대흥목재품공장]**, 대흥목재종합공장
	3) 종이	대흥종이공장
V. 화학 (2-1)	5) 기초	대흥화학공장
	9) 제약	**[대흥제약공장]**
VI. 시멘트, 유리 (1)	5) 도자기	대흥토기공장

VIII. 조립금속, 기계장비 (1)	1) 종합기계	대흥군기계수리공장
X. 가구, 잡제품 (2)	4) 공예품 등	대흥초물공장
	5) 기타	대흥일용품공장

맹산군 (6-1)

I. 광업 (1)	1) 탄광	맹산탄광
II. 음식료품, 담배 (2-1)	1) 일반	맹산식료가공공장
	4) 장류	**[맹산장공장]**
IV. 목재, 펄프, 종이 (1)	3) 종이	맹산종이공장
V. 화학 (2)	8) 합성수지	맹산수지일용품공장
	9) 제약	맹산영예군인제약공장

문덕군 (17-2)

I. 광업 (5)	1) 탄광	룡림탄광, 립석탄광 서호탄광, 태향탄광, 삼천포탄광
II. 음식료품, 담배 (5-1)	1) 일반	문덕어린이식료공장
	2) 곡물가공	문덕기름공장
	3) 육류	**[문덕과실가공공장]**
	4) 장류	문덕장공장, 청남장공장
III. 섬유, 의복, 신발 (1)	2) 직물	문덕직물공장
V. 화학 (1)	8) 합성	문덕영예군인수지일용품공장
VI. 시멘트, 유리 (3-1)	3) 벽돌	문덕건재공장
	5) 도자기	**[문덕도자기공장]**, 덕전기자기공장
VIII. 조립금속, 기계장비 (1)	5) 기계부품, 금속가공	문덕군철제일용품공장
X. 가구, 잡제품 (1)	5) 기타	문덕영예군인공장

득장구 (4-2)

I. 광업 (3-1)	1) 탄광	**[득장지구탄광련합기업소]**, 명학탄광, 득장청년탄광
VIII. 조립금속, 기계장비 (1-1)	3a) 탄광등	**[득장탄광기계공장]**

북창군 (22-10)

I. 광업 (7-3)	1) 탄광	**[북창지구탄광련합기업소]**, **[송남청년탄광]**, **[남양탄광]**, 회안탄광, 룡산탄광, 인포탄광, 회안탄광
II. 음식료품, 담배 (4-2)	1) 일반	**[북창식료가공공장]**
	2) 곡물가공	**[북창곡산공장]**, 북창기름공장
	4) 장류	북창장공장
III. 섬유, 의복, 신발 (3)	6) 의류	북창옷공장, 북창여자옷공장, 북창후방가족피복공장
V. 화학 (1)	9) 제약	북창군제약공장
VI. 시멘트, 유리 (1)	3) 벽돌	북창연재벽돌공장
VII. 1차 금속산엄(1-1)	3) 기타	**[북창알루미늄공장]**
VIII. 조립금속, 기계장비 (3-2)	3a) 탄광등	**[송남탄광기계공장]**, 송남철지주공장

	5) 기계부품, 금속가공	**[북창철제일용품공장]**
X. 가구, 잡제품 (1-1)	5) 기타	**[북창가정용품공장]**
XI. 전력 (1-1)	2) 화력	**[북창화력발전련합기업소]**

성천군 (10-5)

I. 광업 (5-3)	2) 철광	**[성천광산]**, **[신성청탄광]**, **[성천5.18광산]**, 장림광산
	4) 비금속광물	룡흥광산
III. 섬유, 의복, 신발 (3-1)	3) 방적등	**[성천제사공장]**
	6) 의류	성천군 뜨개옷공장
	7) 양말등	성천군 담요공장
VIII. 조립금속, 기계장비 (2-1)	3a) 탄광등	**[장림탐사기계공장]**
	6b) 전자등	비류강전자공장

숙천군 (8-1)

I. 광업 (2)	1) 탄광	창동탄광, 칠리탄광
II. 음식료품, 담배 (1)	4) 장류	숙천군 장공장
III. 섬유, 의복, 신발 (2)	6) 의류	숙천군 옷공장
	10) 가죽등	숙천모피가공공장
V. 화학 (1)	8) 합성수지, 수지제품	숙천영예군인수지일용품공장
VIII. 조립금속, 기계장비 (2-1)	3a) 탄광, 광산용	숙천탐사기계공장
	3b) 농업용	**[숙천군농기구공장]**

신양군 (13-3)

I. 광업 (2-1)	3) 비철	**[인평광산]**
	4) 비금속광물	인평청년광산
II. 음식료품, 담배 (2-1)	3) 육류	**[신양산과실가공공장]**
	4) 장류	신양장공장
III. 섬유, 의복, 신발 (1)	6) 의류	신양피복공장
IV. 목재, 펄프, 종이 (2)	1) 목재	신양목재일용품공장
	3) 종이	신양종이공장
V. 화학 (2-1)	5) 기초화학	신양화학공장
	9) 제약	**[신양제약공장]**
VI. 시멘트, 유리 (1)	5) 도자기	신양토기공장
VIII. 조립금속, 기계장비 (1)	5) 기계부품, 금속가공	신양군철제일용품공장
X. 가구, 잡제품 (2)	5) 기타	신양영예군인공장, 신양일용품공장

청남구 (8-2)

I. 광업 (3-1)	1) 탄광	**[안주지구탄광련합기업소]**, 신리탄광, 화풍탄광
III. 섬유, 의복, 신발 (3-1)	6) 의류	**[청남수출피복공장]**, 청남피복공장
	10) 가죽	청남어구공장
VI. 시멘트, 유리 (2)	4) 유리	청남유리공장, 청남거울공장

양덕군 (16-1)

II. 음식료품, 담배 (4)	1) 일반	양덕식료가공공장
	3) 육류	은하산과실고공공장
	4) 장류	양덕장공장
	6) 음료, 주류	양덕포도술공장
III. 섬유, 의복, 신발 (2)	2) 직물공장	양덕직물공장
	6) 의류	양덕피복공장
IV. 목재, 펄프, 종이 (2)	1) 목재	양덕목제품공장
	3) 종이	양덕종이공장
V. 화학 (1-1)	5) 기초화학	**[양덕가성소다공장]**
VI. 시멘트, 유리 (1)	5) 도자기	양덕독공장
VIII. 조립금속, 기계장비 (1)	1) 종합기계	양덕군기계수리공장
X. 가구, 잡제품 (3)	2) 문방구, 완구, 체육기구	양덕문방구공장
	4) 공예품, 장식품	양덕기념품공장, 양덕초물일용품공장
XI. 전력 (2)	2) 화력	은하리의 풍력발전소, 양덕발전소

은산군 (11-3)

I. 광업 (3-2)	1) 탄광	**[신창탄광]**, **[천성청년탄광]**, 령대탄광,
II. 음식료품, 담배 (2)	1) 일반	은산어린이식료품공장
	4) 장류	은산장공장
V. 화학 (1)	8) 합성수지, 수지제품	은산수지건재공장
VI. 시멘트, 유리 (1)	5) 도자기	은산도자기공장
VIII. 조립금속, 기계장비 (3-1)	3a) 탄광, 광산용	**[은산탄광설비부속품공장]**
	5) 기계부품, 금속가공	은산군철제일용품공장
	6a) 전기기기, 부품	은산군전기일용품공장
X. 가구, 잡제품 (1)	2) 문방구, 완구, 체육기구	은산교구비품공장

증산군 (7)

I. 광업 (1)	4) 비금속광물	증산광산
II. 음식료품, 담배(1)	4) 장류	증산장공장
IV. 목재, 펄프, 종이 (1)	3) 종이	증산종이공장
V. 화학 (2)	5) 기초화학	증산화학공장
	10) 화장품	증산화장품공장
VI. 시멘트, 유리 (1)	5) 도자기	증산토기공장
X. 가구, 잡제품(1)	1) 가구	증산목재가구공장

평원군 (12-1)

I. 광업 (2-1)	4) 비금속광물	**[영유광산]**, 남양제염소
II. 음식료품, 담배 (4)	2) 곡물가공	평원침출쌀기름공장
	3) 육류	평원 과실 공장, 평원젓갈품기공공장
	4) 장류	평원장공장
III. 섬유, 의복, 신발 (3)	2) 직물공장	평원직물공장
	6) 의류	평원수출피복공장, 평원피복공장
X. 가구, 잡제품 (3)	4) 공예품, 장식품	어파초물공장, 평원수출수예품공장, 평원초물공장

회창군 (5)

I. 광업 (1)	2) 철광	성흥광산
II. 음식료품, 담배 (2)	3) 육류	회창군 산과실가공공장
	4) 장류	회창군 장공장
III. 섬유, 의복, 신발 (1)	2) 직물공장	회창직물공장
VIII. 조립금속, 기계장비 (1)	3c) 기타 산업용	성흥건설기계공장

IMPORTANT (24)

9	북창군
4	은산군
3	성천군
2	득장구, 청남구
1	대동군, 맹산군, 문덕군, 평원군

공업 (11)	맹산장공장 (맹산군), 문덕도자기공장 (문덕군), 득장탄광기계공장 (득장구), 북창식료가공공장, 북창곡산공장, 송남탄광기계공장, 북창철제일용품공장, 북창가정용품공장 (북창군), 성천제사공장, 장림탐사기계공장 (성천군), 청남수출피복공장 (청남구)
광업 (12)	장산광산 (대동군), 득장지구탄광련합기업소(득장구), 북창지구탄광련합기업소, 송남청년탄광, 남양탄광 (북창군), 성천광산 (성천군), 안주지구탄광련합기업소 (청남구), 신창탄광, 천성청년탄광, 령대탄광, 성산광산 (은산군), 영유광산 (평원군)
전력 (1)	북창화력발전련합기업소(북창군)

Pyongyang

KOFC (118-22)

6	평천구역
2	강동군, 락랑구역, 만경대구역, 보통강구역, 선교구역
1	동대원구역, 력포구역, 룡성구역, 사동구역, 대동강구역, 서성구역

경공업 (6) 섬유 (2), 신발 (4)	(김정숙)평양(종합)방직공장 (선교), 김정숙평양제사공장 (평천); 평양신발공장 (동대원), 류원신발공장 (만경대), 보통강신발공장 (구 평양염화비닐신발공장 (보통강), 평양구두공장 (평천)

중화공업 (12) 금속공업 (1), 기계 (3), 자동차 (1), 전기/전자 (5), 건재 (2)	평양강철공장 (선교); 평양정밀기계공장 (3월25일공장) (룡성), 만경대공작기계공장(만경대), 평양탄광기계공장 (대동강); 평양무궤도전차공장 (舊 평양화물자동차수리공장) (서성); 보통강전기공장 (보통강), 대동강텔레비죤수상기공장 (사동), 3월26일공장, 대동강축전지공장, 10월5일자동화기구공장 (평천); 7월28일요업공장 (락랑), 평양건재공장 (력포)
재취 (1) 탄광 (1)	강동지구탄광련합기업소 (강동)
전력 (3) 수력 (1), 화력 (2)	남강발전소 (강동); 동평양화력발전소 (락랑), 평양화력발전련합기업소(평천)

경공업 (35-6)	식품 (22)	평양기초식품공장 (구 평양장공장, 평양장류공장), 룡성육류가공공장, 평양닭고기공장, 평양통조림공장, 평양요구르트공장, 모란봉김치공장, 광복거리김치공장, 대동강맥주공장, 평양냉천사이다공장, 평양청량음료공장, 대성담배공장, 룡성담배공장, 평양담배공장, 평양곡산공장, 평양밀가루종합가공공장, 룡성식료공장, 산흥식료공장, 만경대김치공장, 경련애국사이다공장, 대동강식료공장, 룡성맥주공장, 평양맥주공장
	섬유 (2)	**[(김정숙)평양(종합)방직공장]**, **[김정숙평양제사공장]**
	신빌 (9)	**[평양신발공장]**, **[류원신발공장]**, **[보통강신발공장 (구평양염화비닐신발공장)]**, **[평양구두공장]**, 평양신발형타공장, 평양가죽이김공장, 평천구두공장, 대성신발공장, 선교고무공장
	제지 (2)	락랑제지공장, 평천제지공장
중화공업 (70-12)	금속 (3)	**[평양강철공장]**, 10월9일강철공장, 평양비철금속공장 (평양유색공장);
	기계 (25)	**[평양정밀기계공장 (3월25일공장)]**, **[만경대공작기계공장]**, **[평양탄광기계공장]**, 평양승강기공장, 평양도시경영부속품공장, 평양금속건재공장, 동평양금속건구공장, 평양신발기계공장, 평천재봉기부속품공장, 평양박직기계공장, 평양편직바늘공장, 평양편직설비부속품공장, 동평양기계공장, 력포부속품공장, 대동강자동화기구공장, 평양관개기계공장, 평양공작기계공장, 룡성베어링공장 (9월18일공장), 서평양베아링공장, 평양측정계기공장, 만경대불도저공장, 평양건설기계공장 (85건설기계공장), 평양농기계공장, 9월19일(평성자동차)공장, 평양수지건재공장;
	자동차 (1)	**[평양무궤도전차공장 (舊 평양화물자동차수리공장)]**
	철도차량 (5)	김종태전기기관차공장, 평양디젤기관차공장, 평양철도차량부속품공장, 서포철도기계공장, 평양차량수리공장;
	전기/전자 (25)	**[보통강전기공장]**, **[대동강텔레비죤수상기공장]**, **[3월26일공장]**, **[대동강축전지공장]**, **[10월5일자동화기구공장]**, 평양전기기구합영회사, 룡성축전지공장, 조선반도체공장, 과학원 집적회로 시험공장, 새날전기공장, 평양조명기구종합공장, 평양소형원동기공장, 평양알루미니움제품공장, 모란봉자동화기구공장, 평양통신기계공장, 평양통신기계수리공장, 평양영예군인통신기계수리공장, 평양무선기구수리공장, 평양프로그람쎈터, 평양전구공장, 평양에나멜선공장, 평양영화기계공장, 평양도자기공장, 평양집적회로공장 (2극소자직장), 평양컴퓨터조립공장

	화학 (7)	만년제약공장, 애국예방약생산공장, 정성녹십자제약공장, 평양제약공장, 평스합영회사, 평양타이어공장, 평양화장품공장
	건재 (4)	**[7월28일요업공장]**, **[평양건재공장]**, 보통강유리기구공장, 대성요업공장
재취 (7-1)	탄광 (7)	**[강동지구탄광련합기업소]**, 강동청년탄광, 흑령탄광, 고비탄광, 덕산탄광, 심신탄광, 대리탄광
전력 (6-3)	수력 (4), 화력 (2)	**[남강발전소]**, 미림갑문발전소, 봉화(갑문)발전소, 봉화갑문발전소; **[동평양화력발전소]**, **[평양화력발전련합기업소]**

MOU (238-16)

건재 (11-2)	**[평양금속건재공장]**, **[평양목재공장]**; 평양목재가공공장, 대성요업공장, 미림블로크공장, 순안건재생산공장, 7월28일요업공장, 평양수지건재공장, 평양건재공장, 평양알루미늄공장, 강남건재공장
경공업 (175-3)	**[평양곡산공장]**, **[(김정숙)평양방직공장]**, **[평양제사공장]**; 락랑옷공장, 만경대제약공장, 만경대피복공장, 만경대후방가족우산공장, 보통강구역제약공장, 강동고려약공장, 강동군제약공장, 강동기초식품공장, 강동수지일용품공장, 강동쌀기름공장, 강동장공장, 릉라도수출피복공장, 릉라수출품가공공장, 대동강구역문수식료공장, 애국최종락피복공장, 대성구역용북종합식료공장, 동대원공예작물가공공장, 동대원식료품종합공장, 동대원애국편직공장, 동대원옷공장, 동대원은하피복공장, 동대원일용품고앙, 락랑봉화피복공장, 락랑수출피복공장, 락랑영예군인수지일용품공장, 락랑은하피복공장, 락랑종이공장, 봉화비누공장, 력포식료공장, 력포옷공장, 력포피복공장, 3월25일공장, 룡성가구공장, 룡성고기가공공장, 룡성구역고려약공장, 룡성식료공장, 룡성어구공장, 룡성영예군인사출장화공장, 룡성옷공장, 룡악선산샘물공장, 룡악식료공장, 금성식료공장, 만경대렌트겐공장, 만경대수출피복공장, 만경대스케이트신발공장, 만경대식료공장, 만경대애국늄창공장, 만경대영예군인만년필공장, 만경대옷공장, 만경대편직공장, 선흥식료공장, 모란봉구역제약공장, 모란봉은하피복공장, 모란식료공장, 모란피복공장, 애국모란피복공장, 문수옷공장, 보통강구역수출품가공공장, 보통강구역제약공장, 보통강신발공장(구평양염화비닐신발공장), 보통강철제일용품공장, 대동강맥주공장, 애국남새가공공장, 삼석피복공장, 삼석영예군인일용품공장, 삼석옷공장, 대동강과일종합가공공장, 대동강식료공장, 서성고려약공장, 서성구역제약공장, 서성은하피복공장, 선교가구공장, 선교도자기공장, 선교종합식료공장, 선교타면공장, 선교편직공장, 선교피복공장, 선봉피복공장, 순안오리털가공공장, 순안피복공장, 대흥은정목재가공공장, 중구고려약공장, 중구역제약공장, 중구피복공장, 창광수출품피복공장, 금컵체육인종합식료공장, 김정숙제사공장, 모란봉자동화기구공장, 평천고려약공장, 평천교육기재공장, 평천구역김치공장, 평천구역제약공장, 평천식료공장, 평천일용필수품공장, 형제산구역전기일용품공장, 형제산능라도피복공장, 서포옷공장, 하당은하피복공장, 경연애국사이다공장, 대동강그물공장, 대동강자라공장, 대동강주사기공장, 대동강타일공장, 대봉음료공장, 만년제약공장, 삼일포특산물공장, 영화필림복사공장, 유원신발공장, 평양8월풀가공공장, 평양가방공장, 평양가죽이김공장, 평양고무공장, 평양고무일용품공장, 평양과학실험기구공장, 평양구두공장, 평양기료품공장, 평양기초식품공장, 평양기포부재공장, 평양껌공장, 평양남새가공공장, 평양담배공장, 평양담배종이공장, 평양대성피복수출품공장, 평양대흥모피공장, 평양맛내기공장, 평양맥주공장, 평양모피수출품공장, 평양민족악기공장, 평양밀가루가공공장, 평양비누공장, 평양비단옷공장, 평양사기공구공장, 평양산기공구공장, 평양상표인쇄공장, 평양소주공장, 평양수지연필공장, 평양식료련합기업소, 평양식료품련합기업소, 평양식료품포장재공장, 평양신발공장, 평양신발형타공장, 평양실험기구공장, 평양악기공장, 평양애국편직공장, 평양양말공장, 평양어린이과자공장, 평양어린이옷공장, 평양어린이편직공장, 평양염료공장, 평양영예군인원주필공장, 평양영예군인통신기계공장, 평양예방약공장, 평양일영품공장, 평양일용형타공장, 평양전기일용품공장, 평양정미공장, 평양제약공장, 평양조명기구공장, 평양종이공장, 평양주단공장, 평양창광옷공장, 평양체육기구공장, 평양토성고려약수출품공장, 평양피복공장, 평양필림공장, 평양학습장공장, 평양학용품공장, 평양화장품공장, 12월7일공장, 대외식료공장, 강남영예군인피복공장, 강남요업공장

기계 (26-4)	**[김종태전기기관차련합기업소]**, **[만경대공작기계공장]**, **[10월5일자동화기구공장]**, **[평양탄광기계공장]**; 락랑구역농기구공장, 락랑농기계공장, 룡성베아링공장 (9월18일공장), 평천대경윤전기재공장, 대동강텔레비전수상기공장, 동평양기계공장, 서평양베아링공장, 애국천연색TV조립공장, 조선.(쿠바친선)평양방직기계공장, 평양건설기계공장, 평양뜨락또르부속품공장, 평양무궤도전차공장, 평양베아링공장, 평양신발기계공장, 평양영화기계공장, 평양자동차부속품공장, 평양자동화기구공장, 평양자전거부속품공장, 평양차량수리공장, 평양통신기계공장, 서포철도기계공장, 강남농기구공장
전자 (10-3)	**[평양집적회로공장]**, **[3대혁명붉은기 집적회로시험공장]**, **[아침-팬더콤퓨터합영회사]**; 평양빛섬유통신케이블공장, 새날전기공장, 대동강축전지공장, 10월5일전기공장, 보통강전기공장, 평양326전선공장, 평양전구공장
제철/조선 (4)	동평양금속건구공장, 평양강철공장, 평양유색금속관공장, 평양주철관공장
광업 (8-1)	**[강동지구탄광련합기업소 (강동탄광종합기업소)]**; 덕산탄광, 삼청광산, 평양규장석광산, 영남탄광, 강동탄광, 흑령탄광, 도골탄광
전력 (4-3)	**[동평양화력발전소]**, **[미림갑문발전소]**, **[평양화력발전(련합기업)소]**; 남강발전소;

IPA (139-89)

주요업체	[평양애국편직물공장(平壤愛國編織物工場)], [평양어린이옷공장], [평양종합인쇄공장(平壤綜合印刷工場)], [평양창광옷공장(平壤蒼光~工場) (Jung 4)], [대동강축전지공장(大同江蓄電池工場)], [만수대윈드아시아합작회사], [모란봉자동화기구공장(牡丹峰自動化器具工場)], [3월26일공장(三月二十六日工場)], [10월5일자동화기구공장(十月五日自動化器具工場)], [철도성콤퓨터공장], [평양구두공장], [평양기포부재공장], [평양남자옷공장], [평양어린이식료품공장], [평양제사공장(平壤製絲工場)], [평양화력발전소(平壤火力發電所) (Phyongchon 12: 11-0-1)], [모란봉종합식료공장(牡丹峰綜合食料工場)], [애국모란피복공장(愛國牡丹被服工場)], [평양모란영예군인악기공장(平壤牡丹榮譽軍人樂器工場) (Moranbong 3)], [보통강양해합영회사], [장수고려약수출품공장(長壽高麗藥輸出品工場)], [평양염화비닐신발공장 (Pothonggang 3)], [김종태전기기관차종합기업소(金宗泰電氣機關車綜合企業所)], [평양목재공장(平壤木材工場)], [평양수지건재공장 (Sosong 3)], [대성요업공장], [대성제약공장(大城製藥工場)], [룡북종합식료공장(龍北綜合食料工場)], [평양고등교육도서인쇄공장(平壤高等教育圖書印刷工場)], [평양화장품공장(平壤化粧品工場)], [대성산1호소형발전소(大城山一號小型發電所)], [대성산2호소형발전소(大城山二號小型發電所)], [대성산3호소형발전소(大城山三號小型發電所)], [대성산4호소형발전소(大城山四號小型發電所) (Taesong 9: 5-0-4)], [애국최종락피복공장], [조선만년보건총회사], [평양즉석국수공장 (Taedonggang 3)], [경련애국사이다공장], [교육도서인쇄공장(教育圖書印刷工場)], [동대원피복공장(東大院被服工場)], [모란봉합영회사,평양신발공장], [(Tongdaewon 5)], [평양강철공장(平壤鋼鐵工場)], [평양고무공장], [평양곡산공장(平壤穀産工場)], [평양기초식품공장(平壤基礎食品工場)], [(김정숙)평양방직공장(平壤紡織工場)], [평양방직기계공장(平壤紡織機械工場)], [평양방직기재공장(平壤紡織器材工場)], [평양선교편직공장(平壤船橋編織工場)], [평양승강기공장(平壤昇降機工場)], [평양일용품공장(平壤日用品工場)], [평양제약공장(平壤製藥工場)], [평양조명기구종합공장(平壤照明器具綜合工場), (Son'gyo 12)], [삼석8월풀정제공장 (Samsok 1)], [대흥은정목재가공공장, (Unjong 1)], [마람배합사료공장(馬嵐配合飼料工場)], [모란봉김치공장], [룡성고기가공공장 (Ryongsong 3)], [평양영화필림복사공장], [형제산수출편직공장(兄弟山輸出編織工場)], [(Hyongchesan 2)], [광복거리김치공장], [만경대공작기계공장(萬景臺工作機械工場)], [만경대렌트겐공장], [만경대영예군인만년필공장(萬景臺榮譽軍人萬年筆工場)], [평양밀가루종합가공공장], [평양알루미니움제품공장], [평양정미공장(平壤精米工場)], [평양필름공장 (Man'gyondae 8)], [대동강맥주공장(大同江麥酒工場)], [미림블로크공장], [사동종합식료공장(寺洞綜合食料工場)],

	[[평양대흥모피가공공장], [평양모피수출품가공공장(平壤毛皮輸出加工工場)], [대동강텔리비죤수상기공장 (Sadong 6)], [새날전기공장 (Ryokpho 1)], [락랑종이공장], [락연합작회사], [메아리음향사], [애국예방약생산공장(愛國豫防藥生産工場)], [7월28일요업공장(七月二十日窯業工場)], [평양가죽이김공장], [평양금속건재공장(平壤金屬建材工場)], [평양8월17일부재공장], [평양화학건재공장(平壤化學建材工場)], [동평양화력발전소(東平壤火力發電所) (Rakrang 10: 9-0-1)], [강동지구탄광련합기업소(江東地區炭鑛聯合企業所)], [흑령탄광(黑嶺炭鑛)], [남강발전소(南江發電所) (Kangdong 3: 0-1-2)]
공업(기타) 34	평양전구공장(平壤電具工場), 평양소형전동기공장(平壤小型電動機工場), 서평양베아링공장, 평양탄광기계공장(平壤炭鑛機械工場), 동평양기계공장(東平壤機械工場), 평양편직바늘공장, 평천재봉기부속품공장(平川裁縫機附屬品工場), 평양블로크공장, 평양목재건구공장(平壤木材建具工場), 평양석재공장(平壤石材工場), 평양가구공장(平壤家具工場), 평양시계공장, 보성인쇄화학공장, 력포부속품공장(力浦附屬品工場), 보통강전기공장(普通江電氣工場), 중성밥공장, 강동기계공장, 강동식료공장, 강동일용품공장, 강동피복공장, 강동건재공장, 고비건재공장, 고비화학공장, 고비벽돌공장, 대리화학일용품공장, 송가일용품공장, 하리목재일용품공장, 강남철제일용품공장, 강남옷공장, 강남농기구공장, 강남식료공장, 강남제약공장, 고읍자동차부속품공장, 강남세멘트공장
광업 (기타) (16)	덕산탄광(德山炭鑛), 장림탄광, 평산탄광, 하리광산,고비탄광, 대리탄광, 송가탄광, 강동탄광(江東炭鑛), 삼등탄광, 화강돌기와광산, 화강함수석광산, 함주석광산, 삼신탄광(三神炭鑛), 령남탄광(嶺南炭鑛), 룡흥탄광(龍興炭鑛), 석호고회석광산

KCNA 177

공업(163)	강동약전기구공장, 금성식료공장, 담배종이공장, 애국예방약생산공장, 애국최종락피복공장, 조선기계총회사, 문수식료공장, 전자제품개발회사, 대성요업공장, 조선금강원동기합영회사, 동대원공예작물가공공장, 동대원애국편직물공장, 동대원피복공장, 모란봉합영회사, 평양신발공장, 고려생명수기술쎈터, 락랑감자가공공장, 락랑기와공장, 락랑대성피복공장, 락랑봉화피복공장, 락랑영예군인수지일용품공장, (조선)락연합작회사, 발포수지공장, 봉화비누공장, 삼일포수출품가공공장, 진성합작회사, 평양껌공장, 평양화학건재공장, 새날전기공장, 마람배합사료공장, 3월25일공장, 룡성고기가공공장, 조선콤퓨터쎈터, 만경대공작기계공장, 만경대렌트겐공장, 만경대수지합영회사, 만경대애국늄창공장, 소백수련합회사, 수제악기제작사, 장훈식료합작회사, 련하기계회사, 류원신발공장, 선흥식료공장, 조선광명합작회사, 조선은하수기술합작회사, 조선부강제약회사, 보통강신발공장 (구평양염화비닐신발공장), 대동강맥주공장, 평양대흥모피가공공장, 대동강식료공장, 대동강과일종합가공공장, 대동강그물공장, 김종태전기기관차련합기업소, 평양건축장식품제작단, 평양수지건재공장, 선교편직공장, 평양곡산공장, 평양맛내기공장, 평양승강기공장, 평양조명기구(종합)공장, 평양포장재합영회사, 선교도자기공장, 너와나합작회사, 대흥은정목재가공공장, 릉라도수출피복공장, 애국편직물공장, 외성두부공장, 평양수지연필공장, 평양종합인쇄공장, 10월5일자동화기구공장, 3월26일공장 (평양326 전선공장), 모란봉자동화기구공장, 우선식료품가공공장, 평양구두공장, 평양기포부재공장, 평양피복공장, 평양화장품공장, 평천고려약공장, 평천김치공장, 평천일용필수품공장, 평천제약공장, 대동강축전지공장, 만수대윈드아시아(windasia co) 합작회사, 김정숙평양제사공장, 영광가구합영회사, 룡성영예군인사출장화공장, 룡악산샘물공장, 보통강양해합영회사, 천연건강식품회사, 통일거리김치공장, 평스제약합영회사, , 평양가죽이김공장, 평양건설기계공장, 평양기초식품공장, 평양대성다이야공장, 평양랭동공장, 평양맥주공장, 평양밀가루가공공장, 평양백산담배합영회사, 평양소주공장, 평양식료품포장재공장, 평양신발기계공장, 평양양말공장, 평양어린이식료품공장, 평양원종제약공장, 평양자전거합영공장, 평양전기기구합영회사, 평양조선옷공장, 평양집적회로공장, 평양한로식료품합작회사, 평양합성가죽공장, 보통강철제일용품공장, 애국남새가공공장, 평양건재공장, 대동강텔레비죤수상기공장, 석정장아찌공장, 구강종합병원 구강재료공장, 금컵체육인종합식료공장, 대동강과수종합농장 과일말린편공장, 룡성옷공장, 만경대구두회사, 만경대애국발효퇴비공장, 사동피복공장, 삼흥코스트합영회사, 애국모란피복공장, 장수고려약수출품공장, 조선승리합영회사, 중앙보석공예창작사, 태양열설비쎈터, 평양8월풀가공공장,

	평양강철공장, 평양금속건재공장, 평양기료품공장, 평양무궤도전차공장, 평양미림블로크공장, (김정숙)평양(종합)방직공장, 평양방직기계공장, 평양베아링공장, 평양비단회사, 평양빛섬유통신케블공장, 평양애국국수공장, 평양애국옥당공장, 평양어린이편직공장, 평양일용품공장, 평양자동화기구공장, 평양주단공장, 평양증착공구개발회사, 평양직접회로공장, 평양차량수리공장, 평양칠감공장, 평양피아노합영회사, 평양화력발전련합기업소, 평양학습장공장, 12월7일공장, 경련애국사이다공장, 대흥수의약품공장, 룡성베아링공장, 메이리음향사, 대동강제약공장, 평양악기공장, 평양고무공장, 5월11일공장, 과학원공업기술회사
광업 (3)	강동지구탄광련합기업소, 강동탄광, 상원탄광
전력 (11)	남강발전소, 금옥발전소, 대각청년발전소, 미림갑문발전소, 미성발전소, 봉화갑문발전소, 삼등발전소, 삼박골발전소, 성천갑문발전소, 향단발전소, 동평양화력발전소

KIET (283-136)

I. 광업 (14-6)	1) 탄광	**[강동지구탄광련합기업소]**, **[덕산탄광]**, **[강동탄광]**, **[령남탄광]**, **[평산탄광]**, 사동탄광, 삼신탄광, 8월26일탄광, 대리탄광, 송가탄광, 흑령탄광
	3) 비철	평양인곡광산
	4) 비금속광물	**[서포도자기원료광산]**, 린곡광산
II. 음식료품, 담배 (32-10)	1)일반	**[창광말린쌀밥공장]**, **[평양어린이식료품공장]**, **[룡북식료종합공장]**, **[사동종합식료공장]**, **[선교종합식료공장]**, 평양모란종합식료공장, 동대원구역김치공장, 강남종합식료공장
	2) 곡물가공	**[평양곡산공장]**, 평양정미공장, 평양어린이과자공장, 평양밀가루종합가공공장, 서성기름공장
	3)육류	평천김치공장, 공복거리김치공장, 통일거리김치공장, 서성김치공장, 애국남새가공공장, 평양남새가공공장, 평양김치공장, 룡성고기가공공장
	4) 장류	**[평양맛내기공장]**, 강동장공장, 평양애국간장공장
	5) 사료	**[마람배합사료공장]**, 룡성배합사료공장, 순안배합사료공장
	6) 음료, 주류	**[평양맥주공장]**, **[평양요그르트공장]**, 평양알콜공장, 경련애국사이다공장
	7) 담배	평양담배공장
III. 섬유, 의복, 신발 (67-28)	1)방적등	**[평양종합방직공장]**
	2) 직물공장	선교직물공장, 순안직물공장
	3) 방적, 제사, 직조	**[평양제사공장]**
	4) 견직공장	**[평양비단합영회사]**, **[평양수출비단옷공장]**, **[평양종합비단직물공장]**, 대동강견직공장
	5) 편직공장	**[애국편직공장]**, **[평양어린이편직공장]**, **[만경대편직공장]**, **[선교편직공장]**, 강동편직공장, 동대원애국편직물공장, 평양편직수출품공장, 형제산수출편직공장
	6) 의류	**[개선피복합작회사]**, **[옥류피복회사]**, **[평양창광옷공장]**, **[동대원피복공장]**, **[모란봉합영회사]**, **[만경대피복회사]**, **[애국모란피복공장]**, **[전진합영회사]**, **[평양피복공장]**, **[하당피복공장]**, **[선교피복공장]**, **[피복연구소의 피복수출공장]**, **[요원피복합영회사]**, 평양옷공장, 평양어린이옷공장, 문수피복회사, 외성고급피복공장, 창광수출품피복공장, 옥류피복공장, 강동피복공장, 대동강피복공장, 애국최종락피복공장,문수수출피복공장,력포옷공장,

		력포피복공장, 룡성옷공장, 룡성피복공장, 만경대피복공장, 삼석옷공장, 삼석피복공장, 보통강피복공장, 릉라도수출피복공장, 평천피복공장,순안 여자 및 어린이옷 공장, 순안피복공장
	7) 양말 등	평양모자공장, 평양양말공장
	8) 신발	**[평양신발형타공장]**, **[평양신발공장]**, **[평양염화비닐신발공장]**, **[평양구두공장]**, 류원신발수출품공장
	9) 가방	**[장산수출품공장]**, 평양영예군인가방공장, 평천가방공장
	10) 가죽	**[순안오리털가공공장]**, 평양모피가공공장, 평양모피수출품가공공장, 평양가죽이김공장, 룡성어구공장, 만경대가마니공장
Ⅳ. 목재, 펄프, 종이 (10-3)	1) 목재	**[평양목재건구공장]**, **[평양목재종합공장]**, 대성건구공장, 룡성목제일용품공장, 룡성목재가공공장
	3) 종이	**[평양포장재합영회사]**, 평양담배종이공장 , 평양종이공장, 락랑종이공장, 보통강종이공장
Ⅴ. 화학 (28-11)	3) 비료	풍년비료공장
	5) 기초화학	**[서성화학공장]**, 강남화학공장
	6) 염료,도료,시약, 농약 등	**[평양염료공장]**, 평양칠감공장, 대동강식료화학공장, 평양시약공장
	7) 고무제품	**[평양고무공장]**, **[강동다이야공장]**, 평양고무일용품공장, 평양다이야공장
	8) 합성수지, 수지제품	**[평양식료품포장재공장]**, **[평양수지건재공장]**, **[평양발포플라스틱공장]**, **[락랑영예군인수지일용품공장]**, **[만경대수지합영회사]**, 평양수지학용품공장, 평양애국의약품포장재공장, 평양필림공장, 평천영예군인수지가공공장
	9) 제약	**[평양제약공장]**, 통일거리 애국예방약공장, 대동강제약공장, 룡성제약공장, 모란봉구역제약공장, 보통강구역제약공장
	10) 화장품	**[평양화장품공장]**, 룡성화장품공장
Ⅵ. 시멘트, 유리 (22-10)	3)벽돌	**[평양시 건재공업총국]**, **[평양기포부재공장]**,**[평양블로크공장]**, **[평양연재기포블로크공장]**, **[대성요업공장]**, **[8월17일부재공장]**, **[7월28일요업공장]**, 석전주공장, 미림블로크공장, 평양석재공장, 강동건재공장, 락랑부재공장, 평양화학건재공장,보통강건재공장, 사동건재공장
	4) 유리	**[보통강유리병공장]**
	5) 도자기	평양사기공구공장, 평양도자기공장, 대동강도자기공장, 선교도자기공장
	6)기타 비금속광물 제품	**[평양연재분리공장]**, **[5월7일공장]**
Ⅶ. 1차 금속산업 (6-5)	1) 제철 제강	**[평양강철공장]**
	2) 제련	**[평양유색금속공장]**
	3) 기타 1차금속	**[평양도금공장]**, **[평양알루미늄제품공장]**, **[평양주철관공장]**, 평양종합주물공장
Ⅷ. 조립금속, 기계 장비 (65-43)	1) 종합기계	사동종합기계공장, 평천기계공장
	2) 공작기계	**[구성104공장]**, **[평양공장기계공장]**, **[만경대공작기계공장]**, 만경대공구공장,

	3a) 탄광, 광산용	**[평양탄광기계공장(3월30일공장)]**, **[동평양기계공장]**, **[평양측정계기공장]**
	3b) 농업용	**[평양관개부속품공장]**, **[평양량곡가공기계공장]**, **[평양뜨락또르부속품공장]**, 만경대뜨락또르부속품공장, 평양농기계부속품공장, 평양뜨락또르자동차부속품공장
	3c) 기타 산업용	**[평양건설기계공장]**, **[평양방직기계공장]**, **[평양승강기공장]**, **[평양영화기계공장]**, **[덕산건설기계합영회사]**, 만경대불도저공장, 평양신발기계공장, 평양편직기계공장,
	4) 정밀	**[평양의료기구공장]**, 평양도량형공장,만경대렌트겐공장
	5) 기계부품, 금속가공	**[평양베어링공장]**, **[평양금속건재공장]**, , **[평양편직바늘공장]**, **[평양법랑그릇공장]**, **[평양방직기재종합공장]**, **[동평양금속건구공장]**, **[서평양베어링공장]**, **[대동강철제일용품공장]**, **[금별합영회사]**, **[3월25일공장(평양정밀기계공장)]**, **[9월18일공장(룡성베어링공장)]**, **[만경대애국늪창공장]**, 모란철제일용품공장, 순안저울공장, 평양가금설비공장, 평양방직바늘공장, 력포분무기공장
	6a) 전기기기, 부품	**[새날전선공장(평양에나멜선공장)]**, **[새날전기공장]**, **[보통강전기공장]**, **[평양소형원동기공장]**, **[평양전구공장]**, **[3월26일공장(평양전선공장)]**, 평양영예군인직류전동기공장, 평양전기건재공장, 평양천리마전기공장
	6b) 전자, 자동화기기	**[옥류장동화기구공장]**, **[평양축전지공장]**, **[평양집적회로공장]**, **[10월5일자동화종합공장]**, **[평양컴퓨터공장]**, **[대동강축전지공장]**, **[대동강텔리비죤수상기공장]**, **[련하기계합영회사]**, **[모란봉자동화기구공장]**, 평양자동화기구공장, 룡성축전지공장
	6c) 통신기계	**[평양통신기계공장]**, 평양무선기구수리공장
IX. 수송기계 (10-7)	2) 철도차량	**[김종태전기기관차종합기업소]**, **[평양차량수리공장]**, , **[평양철도차량부속품공장]**, **[서포철도기계공장]**, 평양내연기관차공장,
	3) 자동차	**[평양화물자동차공장]**, **[평양무궤도자동차공장(구 평양화물자동차수리공장)]**, **[대동강자동차종합수리공장]**, 평양여객자동차수리공장, 평양영예군인자동차부속품공장
X. 가구, 잡제품 (23-10)	1) 가구	**[평양가구종합공장]**, 선교가구공장
	2) 문방구, 완구, 체육기구	**[평양영예군인원주필공장]**, **[만경대영예군인만년필공장]**, 평양학용품공장, 평양수지연필공장, 평양체육기구공장, 대동강놀이감공장
	3) 악기	**[평양피아노합영회사]**, **[모란영예군인악기공장]**, 평양옥류악기공장, 평양선물악기공장
	4) 공예품, 장식품	**[문수보석가공공장]**
	5) 기타	**[송신일용품공장]**, **[삼석영예군인일용품공장]**, **[평천일용품필수품공장]**, **[평천일용필수품공장]**, 평양일용품종합공장, 대동강영예군인공장, 대성6월4일합영공장, 동대원영예군인공장, 순안영예군인일용품공장, 순안일용품공장
XI. 전력 (6-3)	1) 수력	**[미림갑문발전소]**, 미림발전소, 맥전갑문 발전소, 봉화발전소
	2) 화력	**[평양화력발전련합기업소]**, **[동평양화력발전소]**

IMPORTANT (88)

공업 (80)	평양어린이식료품공장, 평양곡산공장, 평양맛내기공장, 마람배합사료공장, 평양맥주공장, (김정숙)평양(종합)방직공장, (김정숙)평양제사공장, (평양)애국(물)편직공장, 평양어린이편직공장, 선교편직공장, 평양창광옷공장, 동대원피복공장, 모란봉합영회사, 애국모란피복공장, 평양피복공장, 평양신발형타공장, 평양신발공장, 보통강신발공장 (구 평양염화비닐신발공장), 평양구두공장, 평양고무공장, 평양식료품포장재공장, 평양수지건재공장, 락랑영예군인수지일용품공장, 평양제약공장, 평양화장품공장, 평양기포부재공장, 대성요업공장, 7월28일요업공장, 평양강철공장, 만경대공작기계공장, 평양탄광기계공장(3월30일공장), 동평양기계공장, 평양건설기계공장, 평양방직기계공장, 평양승강기공장, 평양영화기계공장, 평양금속건재공장, 평양베어링공장, 서평양베어링공장, 평양편직바늘공장, 동평양금속건구공장, 3월25일공장(평양정밀기계공장), 9월18일공장(룡성베어링공장), 만경대애국늄창공장, 새날전기공장, 보통강전기공장, 평양전구공장, 3월26일공장(평양전선공장), 평양집적회로공장, 대동강축전지공장, 대동강텔리비죤수상기공장, 모란봉자동화기구공장, 평양통신기계공장, 평양차량수리공장, 서포철도기계공장, 만경대영예군인만년필공장, 평천일용필수품공장, 류원신발(수출품)공장, 평양건재공장, 평양무궤도전차공장 (舊 평양화물자동차수리공장), 애국최종락피복공장, 경련애국사이다공장, 락랑종이공장, 애국예방약생산공장, 평양가죽이김공장, 평양화학건재공장, 룡성고기가공공장, 만경대렌트겐공장, 평양밀가루종합가공공장, 평양정미공장, 대동강맥주공장, 미림블로크공장, 김종태전기기관차종합기업소, 평양기초식품공장, 평양조명기구종합공장, 대흥은정목재가공공장, 평양어린이옷공장, (평양)남새가공공장, 10월5일자동화기구공장, 평양일용품(종합)공장
광업 (4)	강동지구탄광련합기업소, 덕산탄광, 강동탄광, 흑령탄광
전력 (4)	미림갑문발전소, 평양화력발전련합기업소, 동평양화력발전소, 남강발전소

Nampho

KOFC (35-15)

	경	중화	재취	전력
강서구역 (6-1)	3	3-1		
대안구역 (5-2)		4-2		1
와우도구역 (4-1)	2	2-1		
전리마구역 (7-5)		6-4		1-1
항구구역 (10-6)		10-6		
룡강 (1)		1		
온천 (2)	2			
35-15	7	26-14		2-1

강서구역 (6-1)

경공업 (3)	식품 (2)	강서약수가공공장, 강서부식물가공공장
	신빌 (1)	강서신발공장
중화공업 (3-1)	기계 (2)	**[금성트랙터종합공장 (구 기양트랙터공장)]**, 강서스리브공장
	화학 (1)	강서화학공장

대안구역 (5-2)

중화공업 (4-2)	기계 (1)	대안스리브공장
	전기/전자 (2)	**[대안중기계련합기업소]**, 대동강전기공장
	건재 (1)	**[대안친선유리공장]**
전력 (1)	조력 (1)	대안조력발전소

와우도구역 (4-1)

경공업 (2)	식품 (2)	남포식료공장, 광량만정제소금공장
중화공업 (2-1)	조선 (2)	**[령남배수리공장]**, 서해선박수리공장

천리마구역 (7-5)

중화공업 (6-4)	금속공업 (2)	**[천리마제강련합기업소]**, **[4월13일제철소]**
	전기/전자 (1)	강선자동화기구공장
	화학 (1)	**[천리마타이어공장]**
	건재 (2)	**[대동강타일공장]**, 강선제강시멘트공장
전력 (1-1)	화력 (1)	**[12월화력발전소]**

항구구역 (10-6)

중화공업 (10-6)	금속 (2)	**[남포제련종합기업소(철거)]**, **[211호제련소 (철거)]**
	기계 (1)	남포선박수리공장
	자동차 (1)	평화자동차종합공장
	전기/전자 (1)	**[남포통신기계공장]**
	조선 (3)	**[남포조선소련합기업소]**, **[9월10일배수리공장]**, 남포선박공장
	화학 (1)	남포어린이약공장
	건재 (1)	**[남포유리공장 (철거)]**

군 (3)

경공업 (2) 식품(1) 신빌 (1)	온천맥주공장, 온천구두공장 (온천)
중화광업 (1) 전기/전자 (1)	룡강축전지공장 (룡강)

MOU (71-8) 공업 62-7

건재 (2-1)	**[대안친선유라공장]**; 대동강타일공장
경공업 (42)	남포기초식품공장, 남포봉화칠감공장, 남포봉화피복공장, 남포수출솜편공장, 남포수출전자가공공장, 남포수출전자기구종합공장, 남포염료공장, 남포유리병공장, 남포의료기구공장, 남포제분공장, 강서도자기공장, 강서봉화피복공장, 강서분무기공장, 강서비누공장, 강서신발공장, 강서약수공장, 강서은하피복공장, 강서장공장, 강서제사공장, 강서편직공장, 강서화장품공장, 기양모피가공공장, 대동강가구공장, 대안수출피복공장, 대안장공장, 룡강고치생산사업소, 룡강군수지일용품공장, 룡강옷공장, 남포경공업공장, 온천대성식료공장, 온천제약공장, 온천직물공장, 와우도봉화피복공장, 와우도제약공장, 남흥피복공장, 5월18일대형단조공장, 천리마구역기름공장, 천리마구역장공장, 남포영예군인신발공장, 항구식료공장, 남포유리공장, 남포어린이약공장

기계 (10-2)	**[금성뜨락또르공장]**, **[대안중기계련합기업소]**; 남포상업기계공장, 남포수출전가기구공장, 강서기관부속품공장, 대안유리섬유공장, 룡강전기기계공장, 룡강전동기공장, 와우도분공장, 9월10일 (룡남)배수리공장
전자 (3)	대안전기공장, 대동강전기공장, 남포전극공장
제철/조선 (5-4)	**[천리마제강련합기업소]**, **[남포선박공장]**, **[남포제련종합기업소]**, **[남포조선련합기업소]**; 보산제철소
광업 (8-1)	**[강서지구탄광종합기업소]**; 섬록암광산, 강서도자기원료공산, 대보탄광, 강서탄광, 룡강오석산화강석광산, 룡강화강석광산, 온천화강석광산
전력 (1)	12월화력발전소

IPA (81-26)

공업 (74-26)	**[강서신발공장]**, **[금성뜨락또르종합공장]**, **[강서편직공장(江西編織工場)]**, **[남포전기기계공장(南浦電氣機械工場)]**, **[대동강전기공장(大同江電氣工場)]**, **[대안중기계련합기업소(大安重機械聯合企業所)]**, **[남포식료공장(南浦食料工場)]**, **[남포제염소(南浦製鹽所)]**, **[5월18일대형단조공장(五月十八日大型鍛造工場)]**, **[4월13일제철소(四月十三日製鐵所)]**, **[천리마제강련합기업소(千里馬製鋼聯合企業所)]**; **[남포편직공장(南浦編織工場)]**, **[남포통신기계공장(南浦通信機械工場)]**, **[남포제련종합기업소(南浦製鋼綜合企業所)]**, **[남포조선소련합기업소(南浦造船所聯合企業所)]**, **[남포제련종합기업소비료분공장(南浦製鋼綜合企業所肥料分工場)]**, **[남포조명기구공장(南浦照明器具工場)]**, **[남포어린이약공장]**, **[남포유리련합회사(南浦琉璃聯合會社)]**, **[남포전극공장]**, **[남포선박공장(南浦船舶工場)]**, **[남포선박수리공장(南浦船舶修理工場)]**, **[룡강농기계공장(龍岡農機械工場)]**, **[룡강전기기계공장(龍岡電氣機械工場)]**, **[룡강화강석광산(龍岡花鋼石鑛山)]**, **[고려신덕산샘물공장]**, **[광량만제염소(廣梁灣製鹽所)]**; 남포염료공장(南浦染料工場), 강서제사공장, 강서약수가공공장, 잠진사기제품공장, 태성전기공장(台城電氣工場), 태성맥주공장, 강서제약공장(江西製藥工場), 강서양말공장, 기양유리일용품공장, 대안중기계종합공장, 남포피복공장, 유리옷공장, 서해선박수리공장(西海船舶修理工場), 와우도제약공장(臥牛島製藥工場), 와우도전등알공장, 령남제염소, 강선자동화기구공장(降仙自動化器具工場), 강선수예품공장(降仙手藝品工場), 립석소석회공장, 룡강곡산공장, 룡강철제일용품공장, 룡강가구공장, 룡강종이공장, 룡강제약공장(龍岡製藥工場), 룡강수지일용품공장, 룡강초물제품공장, 영평청량음료공장, 애원축전지공장, 룡강전동기공장(龍岡電動機工場), 룡강통신기계공장(龍岡通信機械工場), 온천기름공장, 온천모피공장, 온천벽돌공장, 온천식료가공공장, 온천장공장, 온천종이공장, 온천직물공장, 온천타일공장, 온천편직공장, 온천피복공장, 귀성탄산소다공장, 마영건재공장, 보림수지일용품공장, 보림벽돌공장, 보림토기공장, 금성제염소(金城製鹽所), 운하제염소(雲霞製鹽所), 귀성제염소(貴城製鹽所)
광업 (7)	남포섬록암광산(南浦閃綠巖鑛山), 룡강화강석광산(龍岡花鋼石鑛山), 룡호광산, 후산광산, 룡강돌광산, 마영화강석광산, 룡월화강석광산

KCNA (27)

공업 (24)	남포영예군인신발공장, 남포제련종합기업소, 남포조선소련합기업소, 평화자동차종합공장, 남포유리련합회사 (한구구역), 정제소금공장, 남포유리병공장, 령남배수리공장 (9월10일배수리공장) (와우도구역), 강서약수(가공)공장, 강서신발공장, 강서제사공장, 강서편직공장, 강서도자기공장, 금성뜨락또르공장, 대동강가구공장 (강서구역), 대안친선유리공장, 대안중기계련합기업소(대안구역), 천리마제강련합기업소, 대동강타일공장, 천리마고려약공장 (천리마구역), 온천신덕샘물공장, 온천청년제염소, 온천화강석공장 (온천군), 남포기초식료품공장 (?)
광업 (1)	강서탄광 (강서군)
전력 (2)	서해갑문발전소 (와우도구역), 12월화력발전소 (대안구역)

KIET (115-45)

I. 광업 (11-2)	1) 탄광	**[강서지구탄광종합기업소]**, 강서탄광, 대보탄광, 룡정탄광
	4) 비금속광물	**[대대리광산]**, 비류강광산, 남포제염소, 룡강화강석광산, 귀성제염소, 금성제염소, 광량만제염소
II. 음식료품, 담배 (14-4)	1) 일반	**[대성식료공장]**, 온천식료가공공장, 천리마구역식료공장, 항구구역식료종합공장
	2) 곡물가공	**[남포제분공장]**, 룡강군쌀기름공장, 온천기름공장, 기양기름공장,
	3) 육류	룡강고기가공공장, 항구고기고공품공장
	4) 장류	**[룡강장광장]**, 온천장공장
	6) 음료, 주류	**[신덕샘물공장]**, 룡강음료공장,
III. 섬유, 의복, 신발 (17-5)	2) 직물공장	온천직물공장
	3) 방적, 제사, 직조	**[대성제사공장]**
	4) 견직공장	남포견직공장
	5) 편직공장	**[강서편직공장]**, 남포편직공장, 천편직공장
	6) 의류	강서피복공장, 와우도피복공장, 항구피복공장, 와우도구역옷공장, 온천피복공장
	8) 신발	**[남포영예군인신발공장]**, **[강서신발공장]**
	10) 가죽	**[강서모피가공공장]**, 기양모피가공공장, 룡강모피가공공장, 온천모피공장
IV. 목재, 펄프, 종이 (2)	3) 종이	룡강제지공장, 온천종이공장
V. 화학 (13-4)	5) 기초화학	**[남포화학공장]**, 강서화학공장, 룡강소석회공장, 룡강화학공장,
	6) 염료, 도료, 시약, 농약 등	**[남포염료공장]**
	8) 합성수지, 수지제품	**[룡강수지일용품공장]**, 천리마구역영예군인수지일용품공장, 강서수지일용품공장, 남포수지일용품공장, 와우도수지일용품공장
	9) 제약	남포어린이약공장, 남포제약공장
	10) 화장품	**[강서화장품공장]**
VI. 시멘트, 유리 (10-3)	1) 시멘트	강서세멘트공장
	3) 벽돌	온천타일공장, 온천벽돌공장, 강서건설자기공장, 남포부재공장
	4) 유리	**[남포유리련합회사]**, **[남포유리제품수출공장]**, **[대안유리섬유공장]**
	5) 도자기	강서도자기공장
	6) 염료, 도료, 시약, 농약 등	룡강절연물공장
VII. 1차 금속산업 (5-4)	1) 제철 제강	**[천리마제강련합기업소]**, **[4월13일제철소]**, 강선압연공장,
	2) 제련	**[남포제련종합기업소]**, **[남포유색금속공장]**
VIII. 조립금속, 기계장비 (28-17)	1) 종합기계	**[대안중기계련합기업소]**
	3b) 농업용	**[금성뜨락또르종합공장]**, 남포농기계공장, 항구농기구공장
	3c) 기타 산업용	**[남포상업기계공장]**

	5) 기계부품, 금속가공	**[남포용접봉공장]**, **[강선금속건구공장]**, **[기양스리브공장]**, 남포규격품공장, 대안스리브공장, 강서스리브공장, 강서의식기재공장, 강선철제일용품공장
	6) 전기, 전자	**[대동강전기공장]**
	6a) 전기기기, 부품	**[남포전선공장]**, **[남포전극공장, 룡강전기기계공장]**, **[룡강전동기공장]**, 남포전기기계공장, 남포전기공장
	6b) 전자, 자동화기기	**[남포수출전자기구공장]**, **[강선자동화기구공장]**, **[룡강축전지공장]**, 성자동화기구공장, 강텔레비죤조립공장
	6c) 통신기계	**[남포통신기계공장]**, **[룡강통신기계공장]**, **[3월14일공장]**
IX. 수송기계 (7-4)	1) 선박	**[남포선박공장]**, **[남포조선소련합기업소]**, **[서해선박수리공장]**, **[9월10일배수리공장]**, 남포선박수리공장, 남포해운선박공장, 서해항만건설사업소,
X. 가구, 잡제품 (5-1)	3) 악기	항구악기공장
	4) 공예품, 장식품	강서초물공장, 기양초물공장
	5) 기타	**[항구가정용품공장]**, 강선생활필수품공장
XI. 전력 (3-1)	2) 화력	**[12월화력발전소]**, 남포화력발전소, 대안조력발전소

IMPORTANT (27)

공업 (25)	강서편직공장, 강서신발공장, 남포영예군인신발공장, 남포염료공장, 남포유리련합회사, 천리마제강련합기업소, 남포제련종합기업소, 금성뜨락또르종합공장, 대동강전기공장, 남포전극공장, 룡강전기기계공장, 룡강전동기공장, 강선자동화기구공장, 남포통신기계공장, 남포선박공장, 남포조선소련합기업소, 서해선박수리공장, 대동강타일공장, 남포어린이약공장, 남포선박수리공장, 4월13일제철소, 9월10일배수리공장, 대안중기계련합기업소, 신덕샘물공장, 대안친선유리공장
광업 (1)	룡강화강석광산
전력 (1)	12월화력발전소

Sariwon (Hwangbuk Province)

KOFC (16-1)

경공업 (4-1)	식품 (2)	사리원육류가공공장, 사리원곡산공장
	섬유 (1)	**[사리원방직공장]**
	신발 (1)	사리원신발공장
중화공업 (12)	금속 (2)	2월10일공장, 사리원압연공장
	기계 (7)	사리원탄광기계공장, 사리원트랙터공장, 사리원기계공장, 사리원전기공장, 사리원건설기계공장, 사리원광산기계공장, 사리원뜨락또르부속품공장
	화학 (1)	사리원타이어공장
	건재 (2)	사리원시멘트공장, 사리원판유리공장

MOU (28-3) 공업 (26-3) 광업 (2)

경공업 (18-2)	**[사리원곡산공장]**, **[사리원방직공장]**; 사리원기초식품공장, 사리원담배공장, 사리원대성타올공장, 사리원수출피복공장, 사리원신발공장, 사리원애국수지일용품공장, 사리원어린이식료품공장, 사리원영예군인재봉사공장, 사리원은하피복공장, 사리원장공장, 사리원제약공장, 사리원타올수출품공장, 사리원편직공장, 사리원포도술공장, 경암산은하피복공장, 정방산종합식료공장
기계 (3)	사리원광산기계공장, 사리원기계공장, 사리원뜨락또르부속품공장
전자 (1)	사리원전기공장
제철/조선 (3)	사리원종합주물공장, 사리원강철공장, 사리원금속공장
화학 (1-1)	**[사리원카리비료련합기업소]**
광업 (2)	사리원탄광, 사리원화강석광산

IPA (10-4)

공업 (10-4)	**[사리원곡산공장(沙里院谷産工場)]**, **[사리원담배공장]**, **[사리원방직공장(沙里院紡織工場)]**, **[사리원타올수출품공장]**; 사리원기계공장, 사리원농기계공장, 사리원광산기계공장, 사리원카리비료공장, 사리원편직공장(沙里院編織工場), 경암산피복공장(景岩山被服工場)

KCNA (11)

공업 (11)	사리원방직기계공장, 경암산수출피복공장, 사리원기초식품공장, 사리원뜨락또르부속품공장, 사리원방직공장, 사리원수출피복공장, 사리원신발공장, 사리원타올수출품공장, 사리원편직공장, 사리원포도술공장, 정방산종합식료공장

KIET (32-18)

I. 광업 (2)	1) 탄광	경암탄광, 사리원탄광
II. 음식료품, 담배 (4)	2) 곡물가공	사리원과자공장, 사리원곡산공장
	4) 장류	사리원장공장
	7) 담배	사리원담배공장
III. 섬유, 의복, 신발 (8-4)	3) 방적, 제사, 직조	사리원영예군인재봉사공장
	5) 편직공장	**[사리원편직공장]**
	6) 의류	경암산수출피복공장, 사리원수출피복공장, 사리원피복공장
	7) 양말 등	**[사리원타올수출품공장]**
	8) 신발	**[사리원신발공장]**
	10) 가죽	**[사리원방직공장]**
V. 화학 (2-2)	3) 비료	**[사리원카리비료련합기업소]**
	8) 합성수지, 수지제품	**[사리원애국수지일용품공장]**
VII. 1차 금속산업 (3-3)	1) 제철 제강	**[사리원강철공장, 2월10일공장]**
	3) 기타	**[사리원종합주물공장]**
VIII. 조립금속, 기계장비 (11-7)	3a) 탄광, 광산용	**[사리원광산기계공장]**, 사리원탐사기계수리공장
	3b) 농업용	**[사리원뜨락또르부속품공장]**, 사리원련결농기계공장
	3c) 기타 산업용	**[사리원방적기계공장]**, **[사리원방직기계공장]**
	5) 기계부품, 금속가공	**[사리원기계공장]**
	6a) 전기기기, 부품	**[사리원전기공장]**, 사리원전등알공장

	6b) 전자, 자동화기기	**[사리원축전지공장]**, 사리원텔레비죤수상기조립공장
IX. 수송기계 (1-1)	3) 자동차	**[사리원자동차부속품공장]**
X. 가구, 잡제품 (1-1)	5) 기타	**[길성포합작회사]**

IMPORTANT (11)

공업 (11)	사리원편직공장, 사리원타올수출품공장, 사리원신발공장, 사리원방직공장, 사리원광산기계공장, 사리원뜨락또르부속품공장, 사리원기계공장, 사리원전기공장, 사리원곡산공장, 사리원담배공장, 사리원카리비료련합기업소

Songrim (Hwangbuk Province)

KOFC (3-1)

중화공업 (2-1)	금속 (1)	[황해제철련합기업소]
	건재 (1)	송림판유리공장
재취 (1)	철 (1)	송림광산

MOU (4-1) 공업 (3-1) 광업 (1)

경공업 (2)	송림종이공장, 송림피복공장
제철/조선 (1-1)	**[황해제철련합기업소]**
광업 (1)	송림광산

IPA (4-1)

공업 (4-1)	**[황해제철련합기업소(黃海製鐵聯合企業所)]**; 애국편직공장(愛國編織工場), 당산랭동공장, 당산식료공장

KCNA (2)

공업 (1)	황해제철련합기업소
전력 (1)	황해제철소발전소

KIET (11-3)

II. 음식료품, 담배 (2)	1) 일반	송림식료공장
	2) 곡물가공	송림밀가루종합가공공장
III. 섬유, 의복, 신발 (2)	5) 편직공장	송림애국편직공장
	6) 의류	송림피복공장
V. 화학 (2-1)	5) 기초화학	**[송림화학공장]**
	9) 제약	송림제약공장
VII. 1차금속산업 (1-1)	1) 제철 제강	**[황해제철련합기업소]**
VIII. 조립금속, 기계장비 (3-1)	5) 기계부품, 금속가공	**[송림금속설비부속품공장]**, 송림시철제일용품공장, 송림시자전거공장
X. 가구, 잡제품 (1)	5) 기타	송림일용품공장

IMPORTANT (1)

공업 (1)	황해제철련합기업소

Kaesong (Hwangbuk Province)

KOFC (13-1)

경공업 (8-1)	식품 (4)	개성기름가공공장, 개성식료품공장, 개성고려인삼주공장, 개성육류가공공장
	섬유 (1)	**[개성방직공장]**
	신발 (1)	개성구두신발공장
	제지 (2)	개성제지공장, 개풍제지공장
중화공업 (5)	기계 (2)	개성련결농기계공장, 개성시계공장
	전기/전자 (1)	개성축전지공장
	건재 (2)	개성유리공장, 려현건재공장

MOU (33-1)

건재 (1)	개풍요현세멘트공장 (개풍군)
경공업 (29-1)	**[개성방직공장]**; 개성기초식품공장, 개성도자기공장, 개성돌가공공장, 개성선물악기공장, 개성송도피복공장, 개성송악산피복공장, 개성수예수출품공장, 개성수지일용품공장, 개성신발공장, 개성악기공장, 개성애국피복공장, 개성어린이식료품공장, 개성영예군인의료기구공장, 개성영예군인제약공장; 개성인삼가공공장, 개성재봉사공장, 개성편직공장, 개성피복공장, 송도피복공장, 고려식료가공공장, 개성9월14일피복공장, 개성방직공장, 판문배합먹이공장, 판문직물공장, 판문피복공장, 개풍식료공장, 개풍피복공장, 개풍철제일용품공장
기계 (2)	개성기계공장, 개성뜨락또르부속품공장
제철/조선 (1)	개성금속제품공장

IPA (27-10)

공업 (25-9)	**[개성고려인삼주공장(開城高麗人蔘酒工場)]**, **[개성수지일용품공장(開城樹脂日用品工場])**, **[개성종합식료공장(開城綜合食料工場)]**, **[개성방직공장(開城紡織工場)]**, **[개성사기제품공장(開城砂器製品工場)]**, **[자남산수출피복공장(子男山輸出被服工場)]**, **[판문인삼가공공장(板門人蔘加工工場)]**, **[판문초물제품공장(板門草物製品工場)]**, **[개풍초물공장(開豊草物工場)]**; 개성고려약가공공장(開城高麗藥加工工場), 개성재봉사공장(開城裁縫絲工場), 개성타올공장, 판문직물공장(板門織物工場), 개성피복공장(開城被服工場), 9월14일피복공장(九月十四日被服工場), 개성인삼가공공장(開城人蔘加工工場), 개성녀자옷공장, 판문제약공장, 판문식료공장, 진봉소석회공장, 개풍식료공장, 개풍제약공장, 개풍직물공장(開豊織物工場), 개풍벽돌공장, 해선화강석공장
광업 (2-1)	**[개풍규석광산(開豊硅石鑛山)]**; 해선석회석광산

KCNA (7)

공업 (7)	개성고려인삼술공장, 개성기초식료품공장, 개성방직공장, 개성보석공예창작사, 개성애국피복공장, 개성인삼가공공장, 개성편직공장

KIET (72-24)

I. 광업 (3)	1) 탄광	개성탄광
	4) 비금속광물	개풍광산, 개풍규석광산
II. 음식료품, 담배 (10-2)	1) 일반	개성송도식료공장, 개풍식료공장
	2) 곡물가공	**[개성기름가공공장]**, 개성과자공장, 개성쌀기름공장
	3) 육류	개성인삼가공공장, 개성고기남새가공공장
	4) 장류	**[고려고추장공장]**, 개성장공장
	6) 음료, 주류	개성강포도술광장
III. 섬유, 의복, 신발 (17-7)	1) 방적등	**[개성방직공장]**
	2) 직물공장	판문군 판문직물공장, 개풍직물공장
	3) 방적, 제사, 직조	**[개성재봉사공장]**, 개성제섬공장
	5) 편직공장	**[개성편직공장]**
	6) 의류	**[개성피복공장]**, **[개성애국피복공장]**, 개성송도피복공장, 자남산수출피복공장, 9월14일피복공장, 개풍피복공장
	7) 양말, 타월, 모자	**[개성타올공장]**
	8) 신발	**[개성신발공장]**, 개성구두공장
	10) 가죽	판문모피화학공장, 개풍모피공장
IV. 목재, 펄프, 종이 (3)	1) 목재	판문목재일용품공장, 개풍목재일용품공장
	3) 종이	개풍종이공장
V. 화학 (6-2)	5) 기초화학	개성화학공장, 려현화학공장
	8) 합성수지, 수지제품	**[개성수지일용품공장]**
	9) 제약	**[개성영예군인제약공장]**, 판문제약공장
	10) 화장품	개성화장품공장
VI. 시멘트, 유리 (6-1)	1) 시멘트	려현세멘트공장
	3) 벽돌	판문기와공장
	4) 유리	**[개성유리공장]**
	5) 도자기	개성도자기공장, 판문토기공장, 개풍토기공장
VII. 1차 금속산업 (2-1)	1) 제철 제강	**[개성선철공장]**
	3) 기타 1차금속	개성금속공장
VIII. 조립금속, 기계장비 (14-10)	1) 종합기계	**[개성기계공장]**, **[개풍기계수리공장]**
	3b) 농업용	**[개성뜨락또르부속품공장]**, **[개풍농기구공장]**, 개성농기계종합공장
	3c) 기타 산업용	개성건설기계공장, 개성편직기계공장
	4) 정밀	**[개성영예군인의료기구공장]**
	5) 기계부품, 금속가공	**[개성금속제품공장]**, **[판문군 철제일용품공장]**, **[개풍철제일용품공장]**
	6b) 전자, 자동화기기	**[개성축전지공장]**, 개성텔레비죤조립공장
	6c) 통신기계	**[개성통신기계부속품공장]**
X. 가구, 잡제품 (9-1)	2) 문방구, 완구, 체육기구	개성생물표본공장, 개성영예군인문방구공장
	3) 악기	**[개성선물악기공장]**

	4) 공예품, 장식품	개성수예수출품공장, 개성고려수예품공장, 개성만월수예품공장, 개성초물공장, 개풍초물공장
	5) 기타	려현일용품공장
XI. 전력 (2)	2) 화력	선적발전소, 송도1호발전소

IMPORTANT (6)

공업 (6)	개성방직공장, 개성재봉사공장, 개성편직공장, 개성피복공장, 개성애국피복공장, 개성수지일용품공장

Kun (Hwangbuk Province)

KOFC (22-4)

4	봉산군 (1)
3	연산군 (1)
2	서흥군, 수안군, 승호군 (8), 신평군, 토산군, 황주군
1	배천군, 상원군 (1), 은파군

경공업 (1) 식품 (1)	황주과일가공공장 (황주)
중화공업 (7-3) 기계 (1), 건재 (6)	봉산련결농기계공장 (종산); [2.8**세멘트련합기업소** (봉산)], [**상원세멘트련합기업소** (상원)], 서흥시멘트공장, 문무시멘트공장 (서흥), [**승호리세멘트공장** (승호)], 은파세멘트공장 (은파)
채취 (9-1) 철 (2), 비 (4), 석회석 (3)	연산광산 (연산), 황주광산 (황주); 수안광산 (수안), 멱미광산, 백년광산 (신평), [**홀동광산** (연산)]; 마동광산, 청룡광산 (봉산), 승호광산 (승호)
전력 (5) 수력 (5)	예성강6호발전소 (백천), 수안청년2호발전소 (수안), 연산군민발전소 (연산), 예성강청년발전소 1-2호 (토산)

MOU군 (56-4) 공업 (37-4) 광업 (16) 전력 (3)

8	봉산군 (1)
6	연산군
5	상원군 (1), 승호군 (1), 은파군
4	연탄군, 평산군
3	수안군, 황주군
2	서흥군, 신계군, 신평군, 장풍군, 토산군 (1)
1	곡산군, 금천군, 중화군

건재 (5-3)	[2.8**시멘트련합기업소 (봉산군)**], [**상원시멘트련합기업소**], 상원석회석광산 (상원군), [**승호리시멘트공장**], 승호콘크리트침목공장 (승호군)
경공업 (26-1)	곡산식료공장 (곡산군), 금천영예군인일용품공장 (금천군), 봉산피복공장, 봉산식료공장, 봉산영예군인고려약공장, 봉산영예군인제약공장, 봉산은한피복공장 (봉산군), 서흥군공예사업소 (서흥군), 승호제약공장, 승호피복공장 (승호군), 신계군기름공장 (신계군), 연산군식료공장, 연산군피복공장, 연산영예군인고려약공장 (연산군), 연탄시멘트공장, 연탄식료공장, 연탄장공장,

	연탄피복공장 (연탄군), 은파장공장 (은파군), 장풍군식료공장, 장풍제약공장 (장풍군), 중화군공예품가공사업소 (중화군), [황해북도토산군지방공업종합공장] (토산군), 평산직물공장 (평산군), 황주영예군인수지일용품공장, 황주직물공장 (황주군)
기계 (3)	은파군농기구공장, 은파주름판지공장 (은판군), 황주기계공장 (황주군)
화학 (3)	서흥화학공장 (서흥군), 신계화학공장 (신계군), 평산군화학공장 (평산군)
광업 (16)	마동광산, 마동탄광 (봉산군), 화천탄광, 상원탄광 (상원군), 대각광산, 금화광산, 남정광산 (수안군), 만년광산, 신평광산 (신평군), 오봉광산, 홀동광산, 연산군3월8일광산 (연산군), 11월8일광산, 은파광산 (은파군), 평산대리석광산, 평산탄광 (평산군)
전력 (3)	상원군민발전소 (상원군), 승호철도청년발전소 (승호군), 예성강발전소 (토산군)

IPA (174-36)

곡산군 (4-1)

공업 (4-1)	**[곡산식료공장(谷山食料工場)]**; 곡산직물공장, 곡산일용품공장, 청송금속건구공장

금천군 (8-2)

공업 (8-2)	**[금천식료공장(金川食料工場)]**, **[금천일용품공장(金川日用品工場)]**; 금천피복공장, 금천방직공장, 금천화학공장, 금천종이공장, 금천가구공장, 원명토기공장

린산군 (4-1)

공업 (4-1)	**[린산수지일용품공장(麟山樹脂日用品工場)]**, **[린산식료품가공공장(麟山食料品加工工場)]**, **[린산제약공장(麟山製藥工場)]**; 린산종이공장

봉산군 (17-4)

공업 (15-3)	**[봉산게사니공장]**, **[봉산배합사료공장(鳳山配合飼料工場)]**, **[2.8세멘트련합기업소]**; 봉산선박기계공장, 봉산자동화기구공장, 봉산자전거공장, 봉산화학공장, 봉산피복공장, 봉산벽돌공장, 봉산제지공장, 봉산제약공장, 관정도자기공장, 흥수도자기공장, 구연식료가공공장, 토성농기구공장
광업 (2-1)	**[마동광산(馬洞鑛山)]**, **[청룡광산(靑龍鑛山)]**; 토성탄광

서흥군 (7-2)

공업 (5-1)	**[서흥영예군인제약공장(瑞興榮譽軍人製藥工場)]**; 서흥식료공장, 서흥기계공장, 서흥장공장, 봉하화학공장
광업 (2-1)	[문무리광산(文武里鑛山)]; 운흥광산

수안군 (13-2)

공업 (10-2)	**[수안모피공장(遂安毛皮工場)]**, **[수안제약공장(遂安製藥工場)]**; 수안식료공장(遂安食料工場), 수안기계수리공장(遂安機械修理工場), 수안직물공장(遂安織物工場), 수안옷공장(遂安衣服工場), 수안종이공장, 남정식료공장, 남정기계수리공장, 석담독공장
광업 (3)	금화광산, 대각광산(大角鑛山), 남정광산

신계군 (14-2)

공업 (13-2)	**[신계영예군인공장(新溪榮譽軍人工場)]**, **[신계편직물공장(新溪編織物工場)]**; 신계식료공장, 신계기계수리공장, 신계기름공장, 신계고기가공공장, 신계화학공장, 신계초물공장, 신계종이공장, 신계가구공장, 지석오리공장, 해포돼지공장, 해포차수리공장
광업 (1)	가무리광산(歌舞里鑛山)

신평군 (12-2)

공업 (10-2)	**[신평식료가공공장(新坪食料加工工場)]**, **[신평일용품공장(新坪日用品工場)]**; 신평가구공장(新坪家具工場), 신평식료공장, 신평직물공장, 신평화학공장, 만년장공장, 만년편직공장, 만년피복공장, 멱미성냥공장
광업 (2)	만년광산(萬年鑛山), 멱미광산(覓美鑛山)

연산군 (15-4)

공업 (11-2)	**[연산곡산공장(延山谷産工場)]**, **[연산종이공장]**; 연산식료공장, 연산건재공장, 연산일용품공장, 연산편직물공장, 연산화학공장, 홀동식료공장, 홀동직물공장, 홀동일용품공장, 홀동옷공장
광업 (4-2)	**[대평광산(大坪鑛山)]**, **[홀동광산(笏洞鑛山)]**; 연산광산(延山鑛山), 반천옥돌광산

연탄군 (10-2)

공업 (9-2)	**[연탄식료가공공장(燕灘食料加工工場)]**, **[연탄화학공장(燕灘化學工場)]**; 연탄직물공장, 연탄종이공장, 연탄피복공장, 연탄철제일용품공장, 연탄모피가공공장, 연탄고기및물고기가공공장, 연탄제약공장
광업 (1)	스레트광산

은파군 (4-2)

공업 (3-2)	**[은파식료공장(銀波食料工場)]**, **[은파주름판지공장]**; 은파일용품공장
광업 (1)	구련광산

토산군 (4-2)

공업 (4-2)	**[토산식료가공공장(兎山食料加工工場)]**, **[토산종이공장]**; 토산일용품공장, 토산제약공장

평산군 (20-2)

공업 (12-1)	**[평산식료공장(平山食料工場)]**; 평산직물공장, 평산피복공장, 평산마대공장, 평산만년필공장, 평산유리공장, 평산화학공장, 평산토기공장, 평산제약공장, 청학세멘트공장, 봉천리오리공장, 와현일용품공장
광업 (8-1)	**[와현스레트광산]**; 평산광산(平山鑛山), 남천광산(南川鑛山), 평산화강석광산, 상암대리석광산, 청수대리석광산, 해월대리석광산, 평산대리석광산(平山大理石鑛山)

황주군 (6-1)

공업 (6-1)	**[황주식료공장(黃州食料工場)]**; 황주옥돌가공공장, 황주과일가공공장, 황주직물공장, 황주고기가공공장, 황주피복공장

승호군 (10-1)

공업 (8-1)	**[승호리세멘트공장]**; 광정소석회공장, 금옥세멘트공장, 리천채소가공공장, 리천일용품공장, 만달식료공장, 만달화학공장, 만달섬유공장
광업 (2)	금옥탄광(金玉炭鑛), 도골탄광

상원군 (9-2)

공업 (8-1)	**[상원세멘트련합기업소]**; 대동채석공장, 상원식료공장(祥原食料工場), 상원일용품공장(祥原日用品工場), 상원피복공장(祥原被服工場), 상원전기공장(祥原電氣工場), 상원제약공장(祥原製藥工場), 상원농기구공장(祥原農器具工場)
전력 (1-1)	**[상원군민발전소]**

중화군 (7-2)

공업 (7-2)	**[중화전동기공장(中和電動機工場)]**, **[중화제약공장(中和製藥工場)]**; 중화식료공장, 중화일용품공장, 중화농기구공장, 중화설비부속품공장, 중화건재공장

장풍군 (10-2)

공업 (10-2)	**[장풍식료가공공장(長豊食料加工工場)]**, **[장풍직물공장(長豊織物工場)]**; 장풍피복가공공장, 장풍토기공장, 장풍일용품공장, 장풍종이공장, 장풍농기계공장, 장풍초물제품공장, 고읍석회공장, 고읍세멘트공장

KCNA (16)

4	상원군
2	수안군, 토산군
1	금천군, 린산군, 봉산군, 서흥군, 승호군, 연산군, 연탄군, 황주군

공업 (5)	전승업동무가 일하는 공장 (린산군), 상원세멘트련합기업소 (상원군), 승호리세멘트공장 (승호군), 토산종이공장 (토산군), 황주직물공장 (황주군)
광업 (4)	봉산탄광 (봉산군), 삼청광산, 상원석회석광산 (상원군), 수안규조토광산 (수안군)
전력 (7)	례성강6호발전소 (금천군), 상원군민발전소 (상원군), 범안발전소 (서흥군), 수안청년2호반전소 (수안군), 연산군민발전소 (연산군), 연탄1호발전소 (연탄군), 례성강발전소 (토산군)

KIET (134-24)

장풍군 (14-2)

II. 음식료품, 담배 (2-1)	1) 일반	**[장풍식료공장]**
	3) 육류	장풍과일남새고기가공공장
III. 섬유, 의복, 신발 (2-1)	2) 직물공장	**[장풍직물공장]**
	10) 가죽	장풍모피공장
IV. 목재, 펄프, 종이 (1)	3) 종이	장풍종이공장
V. 화학 (1)	9) 제약	장풍제약공장
VI. 시멘트, 유리 (1)	5) 도자기	장풍토기공장

VIII. 조립금속, 기계장비 (3)	1) 종합기계	장풍기계수리공장
	3b) 농업용	장풍농기구공장
	5) 기계부품, 금속가공	장풍철제일용품공장
X. 가구, 잡제품 (4)	1) 가구	장풍가구공장
	4) 공예품, 장식품	장풍초물공장
	5) 기타	장풍마산일용품공장, 장풍문화일용품공장

곡산군 (6)

I. 광업 (2)	1) 탄광	곡산탄광
	3) 비철	기주광산
II. 음식료품, 담배 (1)	4) 장류	곡산장공장
V. 화학 (2)	5) 기초화학	곡산화학공장
	9) 제약	곡산영예군인제약공장
VI. 시멘트, 유리 (1)	1) 시멘트	곡산세멘트공장

금천군 (7-1)

I. 광업 (1)	1) 탄광	금천탄광
II. 음식료품, 담배 (1)	1) 일반	금천식료공장
V. 화학 (3)	5) 기초화학	금천화학공장
	8) 합성수지, 수지제품	금천영예군인수지일용품공장
	9) 제약	금천제약공장
VIII. 조립금속, 기계장비 (1)	1) 종합기계	금천기계수리공장
X. 가구, 잡제품 (1-1)	5) 기타	**[금천영예군인일용품공장]**

린산군 (2-1)

I. 광업 (1)	1) 탄광	린산탄광
V. 화학 (1-1)	9) 제약	[린산영예군인제약공장]

봉산군 (14-1)

I. 광업 (3)	1) 탄광	마동탄광, 봉산탄광
	4) 비금속광물	마동광산
II. 음식료품, 담배 (3)	1) 일반	봉산식료공장, 흥수식료공장
	4) 장류	봉산장공장
III. 섬유, 의복, 신발 (3)	6) 의류	봉산수출피복공장, 봉산피복공장
	10) 가죽	봉산모피가공공장
IV. 목재, 펄프, 종이 (1)	3) 종이	봉산종이공장
V. 화학 (1)	5) 기초화학	봉산화학공장
VI. 시멘트, 유리 (3-1)	1) 시멘트	**[2.8세멘트련합기업소]**
	5) 도자기	봉산도자기공장, 봉산토기공장

서흥군 (4)

II. 음식료품, 담배 (1)	1) 일반	서흥식료공장
V. 화학 (3)	5) 기초화학	서흥화학공장
	9) 제약	서흥제약공장, 서흥영예군인제약공장

수안군 (4-1)

I. 광업 (2-1)	3) 비철	**[대각광산]**, 수안광산
III. 섬유, 의복, 신발 (2)	2) 직물공장	수안직물공장
	10) 가죽	수안모피가공공장

신계군 (5-1)

I. 광업 (1)	1) 탄광	신계탄광
V. 화학 (2-1)	9) 제약	**[신계영예군인제약공장]**, 신계제약공장
VI. 시멘트, 유리 (1)	3) 벽돌	신계위생자기공장
VIII. 조립금속, 기계장비 (1)	5) 기계부품, 금속가공	신계철제일용품공장

신평군 (7-1)

I. 광업 (3-1)	2) 철광	멱미광산
	3) 비철	**[만년광산]**
	4) 금속광물	신평광산
II. 음식료품, 담배 (1)	1) 일반	신평식료공장
IV. 목재, 펄프, 종이 (1)	3) 종이	신평종이공장
V. 화학 (1)	9) 제약	신평영예군인제약공장
X. 가구, 잡제품 (1)	1) 가구	신평가구공장

연산군 (8-1)

I. 광업 (4-1)	2) 철광	**[흘동광산]**, 연산탄광
	3) 비철	물동광산
	4) 금속광물	연산광산
III. 섬유, 의복, 신발 (1)	6) 의류	연산피복공장
V. 화학 (1)	9) 제약	연산제약공장
VIII. 조립금속, 기계장비 (1)	1) 종합기계	연산기계수리공장
X. 가구, 잡제품 (1)	5) 기타	연산영예군인일용품공장

연탄 (3-1)

I. 광업 (1)	3) 비철	연탄스레트광산
II. 음식료품, 담배 (1-1)	4) 장류	**[연탄장공장]**
III. 섬유, 의복, 신발 (1)	6) 의류	연탄피복공장

은파군 (16-2)

I. 광업 (4-2)	1) 탄광	**[은파탄광]**, 묵천탄광
	3) 비철	**[11월8일광산]**, 은파광산
II. 음식료품, 담배 (2)	1) 일반	은파식료공장
	4) 장류	은파군 장공장
III. 섬유, 의복, 신발 (2)	2) 직물공장	은파직물공장
	6) 의류	은파피복공장
IV. 목재, 펄프, 종이 (2)	3) 종이	은파주름판지공장, 은파종이공장
V. 화학 (1)	8) 합성수지, 수지제품	은파수지일용품공장
VI. 시멘트, 유리 (3)	1) 시멘트	은파세멘트공장
	3) 벽돌	은파벽돌공장
	5) 도자기	은파도자기공장
X. 가구, 잡제품 (2)	1) 가구	은파가구공장
	5) 기타	은파일용품공장

토산군 (2)

I. 광업 (1)	1) 탄광	토산탄광
IV. 목재, 펄프, 종이 (1)	3) 종이	토산종이공장

평산군 (18-4)

I. 광업 (3)	3) 비철	평산광산
	4) 금속광물	평산화강석광산, 남천광산
II. 음식료품, 담배 (4-2)	1) 일반	평산식료공장
	2) 곡물가공	**[평산곡산공장]**
	3) 육류	평산고기고공공장
	4) 장류	**[평산장공장]**
III. 섬유, 의복, 신발 (1-1)	2) 직물공장	**[평산직물공장]**
IV. 목재, 펄프, 종이 (1)	3) 종이	평산종이공장
V. 화학 (4-1)	5) 기초화학	평산화학공장
	8) 합성수지, 수지제품	평산영예군인수지일용품공장
	9) 제약	**[평산제약공장]**, 평산영예군인제약공장
VI. 시멘트, 유리 (3)	1) 시멘트	평산세멘트공장
	4) 유리	평산유리공장
	5) 도자기	평산토기공장
X. 가구, 잡제품 (2)	2) 문방구, 완구, 체육기구	평산만년필공장
	5) 기타	평산일용품공장

황주군 (6-2)

II. 음식료품, 담배 (2-1)	3) 육류	**[황주과실(가공)공장]**
	4) 장류	황주장공장
III. 섬유, 의복, 신발 (1-1)	2) 직물공장	**[황주직물공장]**
V. 화학 (2)	8) 합성수지, 수지제품	황주영예군인수지일용품공장
	9) 제약	황주제약공장
VIII. 조립금속, 기계장비 (1)	1) 종합기계	황주기계공장

상원 (5-2)

I. 광업 (1)	1) 탄광	화천탄광
IV. 목재, 펄프, 종이 (1)	3) 종이	상원종이공장
V. 화학 (1-1)	9) 제약	**[상원만년제약공장]**
VI. 시멘트, 유리 (2-1)	1) 시멘트	**[상원세멘트련합기업소]**
	2) 마그네사이트 등	상원세멘트련합기업소의 내화물공장

승호군 (7-3)

I. 광업 (1)	1) 탄광	도골탄광
II. 음식료품, 담배 (1-1)	1) 일반	**[승호종합식료공장]**
III. 섬유, 의복, 신발 (3)	2) 직물공장	승호직물공장
	6) 의류	승호옷공장, 승호피복공장
VI. 시멘트, 유리 (2-2)	1) 시멘트	**[승호리세멘트공장]**
	3) 벽돌	**[승호리콩크리트침목공장]**

중화군 (6-1)

II. 음식료품, 담배 (1)	1) 일반	중화종합긱료공장
III. 섬유, 의복, 신발 (1)	2) 직물공장	중화직물공장
V. 화학 (2-1)	6) 염료,도료,시약, 농약 등	중화군 생물비료 및 농약공장
	8) 합성수지, 수지제품	**[중화테프공장]**
VI. 시멘트, 유리 (1)	1) 시멘트	중화세멘트공장
VIII. 조립금속, 기계장비 (1)	3c) 기타 산업용	중화기계공장

IMPORTANT (12)

2	봉산군, 상원군
1	수안군, 신평군, 승호군, 연산군, 은파군, 토산군, 평산군, 황주군

공업 (7)	2.8세멘트련합기업소 (봉산군), 상원세멘트련합기업소 (상원군), 승호리세멘트공장 (승호군), 은파주름판지공장 (은파군), 토산종이공장 (토산군), 평산직물공장 (평산군), 황주직물공장 (황주군)
광업 (4)	마동광산 (봉산군), 대각광산 (수안군), 만년광산 (신평군), 홀동광산 (연산군)
전력 (1)	상원군민발전소 (상원군)

Haeju (Hwangnam Province)

KOFC (17-2)

경공업 (6)	식품 (2)	해주곡산공장, 해주제분공장
	신발 (2)	해주신발공장, 해주구두공장
	제지 (2)	해주종이(련합기업소)공장, 해주주름판지공장
중화공업 (10-2)	금속 (2)	**[해주제련소]**, 해주강철공장
	기계 (5)	해주트랙터부속품공장, 해주전기공장, 해주자전거공장, 해주농기계공장, 해주련결농기계공장
	화학 (1)	해주화약공장
	건재 (2)	**[해주세멘트공장]**, 해주판유리공장
전력 (1)	기타 (1)	해주조력발전소

MOU (25-2)

건재 (1-1)	**[해주시멘트공장]**
경공업 (16)	수양산종합식료공장, 해주구두공장, 해주기초식품공장, 해주도자기공장, 해주맥주공장, 해주수양산수출피복공장, 해주시제품공장, 해주시직물공장, 해주신발공장, 해주영예군인만년필공장, 해주일용품화학공장, 해주포장재공장, 행주옷공장. 행주일용품종합공장, 행주제분공장. 행주편직공장
기계 (3-1)	**[해주종합기계공장]**; 해주뜨락똘르부속품공장, 해주연련결농기계공장
제철/조선 (4)	해주제련소, 10월13일청년제련소, 해주강철공장, 해주금강청년제련소
화학 (1)	해주화학공장

IPA (16-5)

공업 (15-5)	**[해주련결농기계공장(海州連結農機械工場)]**, **[해주10월13일청년제련소(海州十月十三日青年製錬所)]**, **[해주세멘트공장]**, **[해주제련소(海州製錬所)]**, **[해주판유리공장]**; 해주흄관공장, 해주편직공장(海州編織工場), 해주뜨락또르부속품공장, 해주농기계공장(海州農機械工場), 해주구두공장, 해주곡산공장(海州谷産工場), 해주린비료공장, 해주주철관공장, 해주위생자기공장, 해주천신발공장
광업 (1)	내호광산(内湖鑛山)

KCNA (9)

공업 (9)	10월13일청년제련소, 수양산종합식료공장, 해주1월10일기계공장, 해주기초식(료)품공장, 해주련결농기계공장, 해주직물공장, 해주편직공장, 흙보산비료공장, 해주세멘트공장

KIET (43-12)

I. 광업 (1)	4) 비금속광물	내호리광산, 영양광산
II. 음식료품, 담배 (2-1)	2) 곡물가공	**[해주제분공장]**, 해주곡산공장
III. 섬유, 의복, 신발 (7-2)	5) 편직공장	**[해주편직공장]**
	6) 의류	수양산피복공장, 해주수출피복공장, 해주옷공장
	8) 신발	**[해주신발공장]**, 해주구두공장
	10) 가죽	해주어구공장

IV. 목재, 펄프, 종이 (2-1)	3) 종이	**[해주종이련합기업소]**, 해주주름판지공장
V. 화학 (5-1)	3) 비료	**[해주중화석공장]**
	5) 기초화학	해주탄산소다공장, 해주화학공장
	10) 화장품	해주화장품공장, 해주화학일용품공장
VI. 시멘트, 유리 (5-1)	1) 시멘트	**[해주세멘트공장]**
	3) 벽돌	해주부재공장, 해주흄관공장
	4) 유리	해주판유리공장
	5) 도자기	해주도자기공장
VII. 1차 금속산업 (2-2)	2) 제련	**[해주제련소]**, **[10월13일청년제련소]**
VIII. 조립금속, 기계장비 (11-3)	1) 종합기계	해주1월10일기계공장, 해주종합기계공장
	3b) 농업용	**[해주련결농기계공장]**, **[해주관개기계종합공장]**, 해주농기계공장, 해주뜨락또르부속품공장
	5) 기계부품, 금속가공	해주남비공장, 해주자전거공장
	6a) 전기기기, 부품	해주전기공장
	6b) 전자, 자동화기기	**[해주전자자기공장]**, 해주텔레비죤조립공장
IX. 수송기계 (2)	1) 선박	해주선박수리공장
	3) 자동차	해주자동차수리공장
X. 가구, 잡제품 (4-1)	2) 문방구, 완구, 체육기구	해주영예군인만년필공장
	3) 악기	해주선물악기공장, 해주영예군인선물악기공장
	5) 기타	**[해주일용품종합공장]**
XI. 전력 (2)	2) 화력	해주시멘트공장 화력발전소, 해주화력발전소

IMPORTANT (7)

공업 (7)	해주편직공장, 해주신발공장, 해주세멘트공장, 해주제련소, 10월13일청년제련소, 해주련결농기계공장, 해주판유리공장

Kun (Hwangnam Province)

KOFC (30-5)

5	신원군 (1)
3	신천군, 연안군 (2), 은률군 (1), 재령군 (1)
2	은천군 청단군
1	강령군, 과일군, 배천군, 벽성군, 삼천군, 안악군, 옹진군, 장연군, 태탄군

경공업 (4) 식품 (3), 제지 (1)	풍천과일가공공장 (과일), 연안 정제소금공장 (연안), 황남청년제염소 (청단); 배천제지공장 (배천)
중화공업 (13-1) 기계 (8), 화학 (2), 건재 (3)	신원기계공장, 신원련결농기계공장 (신원), 신천기계공장, 신천공작기계공장, 신천군련결농기계공장 (신천), 은천제염기계공장 (은천), 재령광산설비 및 부속품공장, 재령탄광기계공장 (재령); 수교광산 (삼천), **[하성타이어공장 (신원)]**; 신원세멘트공장 (신원), 은천시멘트공장 (은천), 청단시멘트공장 (청단)

재취 (9-4) 철 (4), 비 (1), 탄광 (4)	하성광산 (신원), 안악광산 (안악), 서해리광산 (은률), 태탄광산 (태탄); 락연광산 (장연); **[룡호광산]**, **[정촌광산 (연안)]**, **[은률광산 (은률)]**, **[재령광산 (재령)]**
전력 (4) 기타 (4)	청수도 2호 조력발전소 (강령), 취야조력발전소 (벽성), 옹진1호조력발전소 (옹진), 조력발전소 (중단) (은률)

MOU 군 (55) 공업 (47) 광업 (8)

10	신천군
7	옹진군, 재령군
4	안악군, 연안군, 장연군, 청단군
2	과일군, 배천군, 벽성군, 산천군, 신원군, 은률군
1	가령군, 송화군, 은천군

경공업 (43)	강령영예군인식료공장 (강령군), 풍천과일가공공장, 과일말린편공장 (과일군), 배천영예군인식료공장 (배천군), 벽성군종합식료공장, 벽성장공장 (벽상군), 삼천장공장 (삼천군), 신천견직공장, 신천고려약공장, 신천군벼짚가공공장, 신천담배공장, 신천영예군인식료공장, 신천옷공장, 신천장공장, 신천제약공장 (신천군), 안악봉화피복공장, 안악영예군인수지일용품공장, 안악장공장, 안악직물공장 (안악군), 연안영예군인수지일용품공장, 연안장공장, 연안종이공장 (연안군), 옹진건재공장, 옹진고려약공장, 옹진군영예군인장공장, 옹진군지방종합공장, 옹진영예군인식료공장, 옹진편직바늘공장 (옹진군), 은률장공장 (은률군), 은천소석회공장 (은천군), 장연도자기공장, 장연식료공장, 장연영예군인제약공장, 장연직물공장 (장연군), 재령군남지공장, 재령봉화피복공장, 재령수출피복공장, 재령영예군인수지일용품공장, 재령직물공장, 재령초물공장 (재령군), 청단군장공장, 청단옷공장, 흥상담배공장 (청단군)
기계 (2)	송화군농기계공장 (송화군), 신원군농기구공장 (신원군)
제철/조선 (1)	선군주철공장 (청단군)
화학 (1)	삼천화학공장 (삼천군)
광업 (8)	배천광산 (배천군), 신덕광산 (신원군), 신천광산, 신천탄광 (신천군), 룡호광산 (연안군), 옹진광산 (옹진군), 은률광산 (은률군), 재령광산 (재령군)

IPA (176-40)

강령군 (9-4)

공업 (9-4)	**[강령고구마가공공장]**, **[강령기류품공장(康翎杞柳品工場)]**, **[강령식료공장(康翎食料工場)]**, **[강령직물공장(康翎織物工場)]**; 강령다시마가공공장, 부포녀자옷공장, 부포다시마가공공장, 부포어린이식료공장, 부민소석회공장

과일군 (6-1)

공업 (6-1)	**[풍천과일가공공장]**; 과일식료공장, 과일물고기가공공장, 과일화학공장, 과일고무공장, 과일편직공장

룡연군 (6-0)

공업 (6)	룡연고기가공공장, 룡연피복공장, 룡연화학공장, 석교세멘트공장, 석교소석회공장, 룡연세멘트공장

배천군 (7-2)

공업 (6-1)	**[배천식료공장(白川食料工場)]**; 배천직물공장, 배천일용품공장, 봉량화학공장(鳳兩化學工場), 봉량편직공장(鳳兩編織工場), 봉량도자기공장(鳳兩陶瓷器工場)
광업 (1-1)	**[봉량광산(鳳兩鑛山)]**

벽성군 (4-2)

공업 (4-2)	**[벽성영예군인식료공장(碧城榮譽軍人食料工場)]**, **[벽성일용품공장(碧城日用品工場)]**; 벽성곡산공장, 벽성기계공장

봉천군 (11-3)

공업 (11-3)	**[봉천장공장(鳳泉醬工場)]**, **[봉천제약공장(鳳泉製藥工場)]**, **[봉천종이공장]**; 봉천고기가공공장, 봉천식료공장(鳳泉食料工場), 봉천초물공장(鳳泉草物工場), 봉천도자기공장(鳳泉陶瓷器工場), 봉천화학공장(鳳泉化學工場), 봉천가구공장(鳳泉家具工場), 죽동소석회공장(竹洞消石灰工場), 한정세멘트공장

삼천군 (8-2)

공업 (8-2)	**[삼천식료공장(三泉食料工場)]**, **[삼천일용품공장(三泉日用品工場)]**; 삼천과일채소가공공장, 삼천기름공장, 삼천성냥공장, 삼천모피가공공장, 삼천편직물공장, 삼천직물공장

송화군 (4-3)

공업 (4-3)	**[송화과실가공공장(松禾果實加工工場)]**, **[송화식료가공공장(松禾食料加工工場)]**, **[송화제약공장(松禾製藥工場)]**; 송화화학공장

신원군 (13-2)

공업 (11-1)	**[신원제약공장(新院製藥工場)]**; 신원기계공장(新院機械工場), 신원세멘트공장, 신원소석회공장, 신원석회석광산, 신원의료기구공장, 신원장공장, 신원일용화학공장, 신원채소및고기가공공장, 신원종이공장, 하성다이야공장
광업 (2-1)	**[신덕광산(新德鑛山)]**; 석회석광산

신천군 (14-4)

공업 (14-4)	**[신천기계공장(信川機械工場)]**, **[신천담배공장]**, **[신천식료공장(信川食料工場)]**, **[신천일용품공장(信川日用品工場)]**; 신천과수기계공장, 신천장공장, 신천영예군인과자공장, 신천고기공장, 신천과일가공공장, 신천견직공장, 신천마대공장, 신천제약공장, 신천차수리공장, 반정사기공장

안악군 (10-2)

공업 (10-2)	**[안악식료공장(安岳食料工場)]**, **[안악초물공장(安岳草物工場)]**; 안악가구일용품공장, 안악철제일용품공장, 안악직물공장, 안악기름공장, 안악과실 및 남새가공공장, 안악제약공장, 판룩기와공장, 판룩고기가공공장

연안군 (8-2)

공업 (8-2)	**[연안식료공장(延安食料工場)], [연백제염소(延白製鹽所)]**; 연안견직공장, 연안편직물공장, 연안방직공장, 연안옷공장, 연안수지일용품공장, 연안도자기공장

옹진군 (20-2)

공업 (17-2)	**[옹진초물수출일용품공장(甕津草物輸出日用品工場)], [옹진제염사업소(甕津製鹽事業所)]**; 옹진식료공장, 옹진화학공장, 옹진철제일용품공장, 옹진옷공장, 옹진부채공장, 옹진편직물공장, 옹진건재공장, 옹진선박수리공장, 옹진종이공장, 옹진영예군인시계공장, 옹진직물공장, 옹진도자기공장, 옹진화학공장, 옹진도자기공장, 원사벽돌공장
광업 (3)	구곡광산(九谷鑛山), 원사백토광산, 원사소석회광산

은률군 (11-1)

공업 (9)	은률식료가공공장, 은률일용품공장, 은률방직공장, 은률피복가공공장, 은률화학공장, 은률기계공장, 금산포식료공장, 금산포솔공장, 금산포옷공장
광업 (2-1)	**[은률광산(殷栗鑛山)]**; 락천동광산, 서해리광산(西海里鑛山)

은천군 (7-3)

공업 (7-3)	**[은천식료공장(銀泉食料工場)], [은천일용품공장(銀泉日用品工場)], [은천직물공장(銀泉織物工場)]**; 은천건재공장, 은천화학공장, 은천제약공장, 제도소석회공장

장연군 (18-2)

공업 (16-2)	**[장연일용품공장(長淵日用品工場)], [화원종이공장]**; 장연세멘트공장, 장연식료공장, 장연기계공장, 락연편직물공장, 락연피복공장, 락연채소가공공장, 락연맥주공장, 눌산세멘트공장, 눌산소석회공장, 화원안경공장, 화원철제일용품공장, 화원영예군인제약공장, 화원농기구공장, 화원화학공장
광업 (2)	락연광산, 산수광산

재령군 (7-2)

공업 (6-2)	**[재령탄광기계공장(載寧炭鑛機械工場)], [재령식료공장(載寧食料工場)]**; 고산피복공장, 석탄사기공장, 천마종이공장, 천마장공장
광업 (1)	재령광산

청단군 (7-2)

공업 (4-1)	**[청단일용품공장(青丹日用品工場)]**; 청단식료공장, 청단영예군인제약공장, 금학토기공장
광업 (3-1)	**[삼정광산(三井鑛山)]**; 흥산흑연광산(興山黑鉛鑛山), 청단광산

태탄군 (6-1)

공업 (5)	태탄식료공장, 태탄화학공장, 태탄일용품공장, 태탄직물공장, 태탄제약공장
광업 (1-1)	**[태탄광산(苔灘鑛山)]**

KCNA 군 (8)

2	벽성군, 연안군, 재령군
1	옹진군, 은률군

공업 (5)	벽성식료공장, 벽성장공장 (벽성군), 연백제염소 (연안군), 옹진편직바늘공장 (옹진군), 재령식료공장 (재령군)
광업 (3)	정촌천연흑연광산 (연안군), 은률광산 (은률군), 재령광산 (재령군)

KIET (136-21)

강령군 (4-1)

I. 광업 (1-1)	4) 비금속광물	**[2월광산]**
II. 음식료품, 담배 (1)	1) 일반	강령영예군인식료공장
III. 섬유, 의복, 신발 (1)	6) 의류	강령뜨개옷공장
IV. 목재, 펄프, 종이 (1)	3) 종이	강령종이공장

과일군 (2-1)

II. 음식료품, 담배 (1-1)	3) 육류	**[풍천과일가공공장]**
X. 가구, 잡제품 (1)	4) 공예품, 장식품	과일군 초물공장

배천군 (7)

II. 음식료품, 담배 (1)	1) 일반	배천영예군인식료공장
III. 섬유, 의복, 신발 (2)	5) 편직공장	배천편직공장
	6) 의류	배천군 옷공장
IV. 목재, 펄프, 종이 (1)	3) 종이	배천종이공장
V. 화학 (3)	5) 기초화학	배천화학공장
	8) 합성수지, 수지제품	배천수지일용품공장
	9) 제약	배천제약공장

벽성군 (4)

II. 음식료품, 담배 (1)	1) 일반	벽성영예군인식료공장
V. 화학 (2)	5) 기초화학	벽성화학공장
	8) 합성수지, 수지제품	벽성수지일용품공장
X. 가구, 잡제품 (1)	1) 가구	벽성가구일용품공장

봉천군 (1-1)

V. 화학 (1-1)	5) 기초화학	**[봉천화학공장]**

삼천군 (3-1)

V. 화학 (1)	5) 기초화학	삼천화학공장
VIII. 조립금속, 기계장비 (1-1)	3b) 농업용	**[삼천군농기구공장]**
X. 가구, 잡제품 (1)	1) 가구	삼천가구일용품공장

송화군 (5-1)

II. 음식료품, 담배 (2-1)	3) 육류	송화과실공장
	4) 장류	**[송화장공장]**
III. 섬유, 의복, 신발 (1)	5) 편직공장	송화편직공장
V. 화학 (1)	5) 기초화학	송화화학공장
X. 가구, 잡제품 (1)	1) 가구	송화가구공장

신원군 (21-2)

I. 광업 (4)	1) 탄광	신원탄광
	2) 철광	하성광산, 신원광산
	4) 비금속광물	하성석회석광산
II. 음식료품, 담배 (4)	1) 일반	신원영예군인식료공장
	3) 육류	신원남새고기가공공장, 신원군남새가공공장
	4) 장류	신원장공장
III. 섬유, 의복, 신발 (2)	2) 직물공장	신원직물공장
	6) 의류	신원옷공장
IV. 목재, 펄프, 종이 (2)	1) 목재	신원목통공장
	3) 종이	신원종이공장
V. 화학 (5-1)	5) 기초화학	신원화학공장, 신원카바이드공장, 신원탄산소다공장
	7) 고무제품	**[하성다이야공장]**
	10) 화장품	신원일용화학공장
VI. 시멘트, 유리 (2)	1) 시멘트	신원세멘트공장
	5) 도자기	신원토기공장
VIII. 조립금속, 기계장비 (1-1)	3b) 농업용	**[신원기계공장]**
X. 가구, 잡제품 (1)	5) 기타	신원영예군인일용품공장

신천군 (11-2)

I. 광업 (2)	1) 탄광	신천탄광
	4) 비금속광물	신천광산
II. 음식료품, 담배 (3)	1) 일반	신천영예군인식료공장
	2) 곡물가공	신천영예군인과자공장
	7) 담배	신천담배공장
III. 섬유, 의복, 신발 (2)	4) 견직공장	신천견직공장
	6) 의류	신천옷공장
V. 화학 (1)	5) 기초화학	신천제지공장
VIII. 조립금속, 기계장비 (2-2)	1) 종합기계	**[신천기계공장]**
	3b) 농업용	**[신천군련결농기계공장]**
X. 가구, 잡제품 (1)	5) 기타	신천일용품공장

안악군 (2)

IV. 목재, 펄프, 종이 (1)	3) 종이	안악종이공장
V. 화학 (1)	5) 기초화학	안악화학공장

연안군 (5-1)

I. 광업 (1)	4) 비금속광물	연백재염소
II. 음식료품, 담배 (1)	4) 장류	연안장공장
III. 섬유, 의복, 신발 (1)	3) 방적, 제사, 직조	연안직조공장
V. 화학 (1-1)	8) 합성수지, 수지제품	**[연안영예군인수지일용품공장]**
VII. 1차 금속산업 (1)	3)기타 1차금속	연백제련소

옹진군 (7)

I. 광업 (2)	3) 비철	은동광산
	4) 비금속광물	구곡광산
II. 음식료품, 담배 (1)	1) 일반	옹진영예군인식료공장
V. 화학 (1)	8) 합성수지, 수지제품	옹진영예군인수지일용품공장
VIII. 조립금속, 기계장비 (1)	4) 정밀	옹진영예군인시계공장
X. 가구, 잡제품 (1)	1) 가구	옹진가구공장
XI. 전력 (1)	2) 화력	은동발전소

은률군 (9-2)

I. 광업 (2-1)	2) 철광	**[은률갈철광]**
	4) 비금속광물	서해리광산
III. 섬유, 의복, 신발 (4)	2) 직물공장	은률직물공장
	5) 편직공장	은률영예군인편직공장
	6) 의류	은률영예군인피복공장, 은률옷공장
IV. 목재, 펄프, 종이 (1)	3) 종이	은률종이공장
V. 화학 (1-1)	5) 기초화학	**[은률화학공장]**
VI. 시멘트, 유리 (1)	5) 도자기	은률도자기공장

은천군 (4)

II. 음식료품, 담배 (1)	1) 일반	은천영예군인식료공장
V. 화학 (1)	5) 기초화학	은천화학공장
X. 가구, 잡제품 (1)	4) 공예품, 장식품	은천벼짚가공공장
XI. 전력 (1)	2) 화력	은천군의 풍력발전소

장연군 (11-4)

I. 광업 (2-1)	2) 철광	**[락연광산]**
	4) 비금속광물	장연광산
III. 섬유, 의복, 신발 (1-1)	2) 직물공장	**[장연직물공장]**
V. 화학 (1-1)	9) 제약	**[장연영예군인제약공장]**
VI. 시멘트, 유리 (1)	5) 도자기	장연도자기공장
VIII. 조립금속, 기계장비 (3)	1) 종합기계	장연군기계공장
	3a) 탄광, 광산용	장연광산기계부속품공장
	5) 기계부품, 금속가공	장연군철제일용품공장
X. 가구, 잡제품 (3-1)	1) 가구	장연가구일용품공장
	4) 공예품, 장식품	장연초물공장
	5) 기타	**[락연광산일용품공장]**

재령군 (14-2)

II. 음식료품, 담배 (1)	1) 일반	재령식료공장
III. 섬유, 의복, 신발 (2)	6) 의류	재령수출피복공장, 재령피복공장
IV. 목재, 펄프, 종이 (2)	1) 목재	재령목재일용품공장
	3) 종이	재령종이공장
V. 화학 (4-1)	5) 기초화학	재령화학공장
	6) 염료,도료,시약, 농약 등	재령직관자제공장
	8) 합성수지, 수지제품	**[재령영예군인수지일용품공장]**
	9) 제약	재령제약공장
VIII. 조립금속, 기계장비 (4-1)	3a) 탄광, 광산용	**[재령탐사기계수리공장]**, 재령광산설비부속품공장, 재령탐사기계공장
	5) 기계부품, 금속가공	재령선물직관자재공장
X. 가구, 잡제품 (1)	4) 공예품, 장식품	재령초물공장

청단군 (13-3)

I. 광업 (3-2)	2) 철광	**[홍산광산]**
	4) 비금속광물	**[홍상광산]**, 청단광산
II. 음식료품, 담배 (2)	4) 장류	청단장공장
	7) 담배	흥상담배공장
III. 섬유, 의복, 신발 (2)	5) 편직공장	청단편직공장
	6) 의류	청단옷공장
IV. 목재, 펄프, 종이 (1)	3) 종이	청단종이공장
V. 화학 (2-1)	5) 기초화학	청단화학공장
	8) 합성수지, 수지제품	**[청단수지일용품공장]**
VI. 시멘트, 유리 (1)	5) 도자기	청단도자기공장
VIII. 조립금속, 기계장비 (2)	5) 기계부품, 금속가공	청단철제일용품공장
	6a) 전기기기, 부품	흥상전동기공장

태탄군 (13)

I. 광업 (1)	2) 철광	태탄광산
II. 음식료품, 담배 (3)	1) 일반	태탄식료공장
	4) 장류	태탄장공장
	6) 음료, 주류	태탄맥주공장
III. 섬유, 의복, 신발 (2)	5) 편직공장	태탄편직공장
	6) 의류	태탄옷공장
IV. 목재, 펄프, 종이 (2)	1) 목재	태탄목재가공공장
	3) 종이	태탄종이공장
VI. 시멘트, 유리 (3)	1) 시멘트	태탄세멘트공장
	5) 도자기	태탄도자기공장, 태탄토기공장
VIII. 조립금속, 기계장비 (1)	5) 기계부품, 금속가공	태탄군철제일용품공장
IX. 수송기계 (1)	1) 선박	성남선박수리공장

IMPORTANT (10)

2	신원군, 신천군, 재령군
1	과일군, 은률군, 장연군, 태탄군

공업 (6)	풍천과일가공공장 (과일군), 신원기계공장, 하성다이야공장 (신원군), 신천기계공장, 신천담배공장 (신천군), 재령식료공장 (재령군)
광업 (4)	은률광산 (은률군), 락연광산 (장연군), 재령광산 (재령군), 태탄광산 (태탄군)

Hyesan (Ryanggang Province)

KOFC (12-2)

경공업 (5-1)	식품 (2)	혜산가공주공장, 혜산맥주공장
	섬유 (1)	**[혜산방직공장]**
	신발 (1)	혜산신발공장
	제지 (1)	혜산제지련합기업소
중화공업 (5)	금속 (1)	혜산강철공장
	기계 (2)	혜산트랙터부속품공장, 5월8일(혜산)림업기계공장
	건재 (2)	혜산세멘트공장, 혜산유리공장
재취 (1-1)	비 (1)	**[혜산청년광산]**
전력 (1)	수력 (1)	삼수발전소

MOU (22-3) 공업 (17-1) 광업 (5-2)

건재 (3)	위연제재공장, 혜산건재공장, 혜산시멘트공장
경공업 (10-1)	**[혜산방직공장]**; 백두산들쭉가공공장, 청봉종합식료공장, 혜산기초식품공장, 혜산목재일용품공장, 혜산병원맥주공장, 혜산신발공장, 혜산어린이식료공장, 혜산편직공장, 혜산피복공장
기계 (3)	혜산연결농기계공장, 혜산임업기계공장, 5월8일임업기계공장
제철/조선 (1)	혜산강철공장
광업 (5-2)	**[혜산지구광업련합기업소]**, **[량강도광업련합기업소]**; 대봉광산, 혜산청년광산, 혜산청년탄광

IPA (9-9)

공업 (8-8)	**[5월8일림업기계공장 (五月八日林業機械工場)]**, **[위연제재공장 (渭淵製材才工場)]**, **[혜산들쭉가공공장]**, **[혜산방직공장 (惠山紡織工場)]**, **[혜산신발공장]**, **[혜산철제일용품공장 (惠山鐵製日用品工場)]**, **[혜산흄관공장]**, **[혜산종이공장]**
광업 (1-1)	**[혜산청년광산 (惠山青年鑛山)]**

KCNA (17)

공업 (12)	혜산기초식료품공장, 청봉종합식료공장, 혜산들쭉가공공장, 혜산방직공장, 혜산신발공장, 혜산영예군인일용품공장, 혜산제지공장, 5월8일림업기계공장, 연림목재합영회사, 위연제재공장, 혜산강철공장, 혜산세멘트공장
광업 (3)	량강도광업련합기업소, 혜산청년광산, 혜산청년탄광
전력 (2)	운총강3호발전소, 삼수발전소

KIET (29-11)

I. 광업 (2-1)	1) 탄광	혜산(청년)탄광
	3) 비철금석	**[혜산청년광산]**
II. 음식료품, 담배 (3-1)	1) 일반	**[혜산식료련합회사]**
	2) 곡물가공	혜산쌀기름공장
	3) 육료	혜산들쭉가공공장
III. 섬유, 의복, 신발 (4-2)	1) 방직	**[혜산방직종합공장]**
	5) 편직공장	혜산편직공장
	6) 의류	혜산옷공장
	8) 신발	**[혜산신발공장]**
IV. 목재, 펄프, 종이 (2-2)	1) 목재	**[위연제재공장]**
	3) 종이	**[혜산제지(련합기업소)공장]**
V. 화학 (4)	3) 비료	혜산카리비료공장
	5) 기초화학	혜산화학공장
	9) 제약	혜산제약공장
	10) 와장품 등	혜산화장품공장
VI. 시멘트, 유리 (3-1)	1) 시멘트	혜산세멘트공장
	3) 벽돌 등	**[혜산흄관공장]**
	5) 도자기	혜산도자기공장
VII. 1차 금속산업 (1-1)	1) 제철, 제강	**[혜산철강공장]**

VIII. 조립금속, 기계장비 (6-2)	1) 종합기계	혜산종합기계공장
	3a) 탄광, 광산용	혜산탐사기계수리공장
	3b) 농업용	혜산련결농기계공장
	3c) 기타	**[5월8일림업기계공장]**
	5) 기계부품, 금속가공	**[혜산철제일용품공장]**, 혜산금속건구공장,
IX. 수송기계 (1-1)	3) 자동차	**[혜산자동차수리공장]**
X. 가구, 잡제품 (3)	3)악기	혜산악기공장
	5) 기타	혜산솔공장, 혜산영예군인일용품공장

IMPORTANT (7)

공업 (6)	혜산신발공장, 위연제재공장, 5월8일림업기계공장, 혜산제지(련합기업소)공장, 혜산방직공장, 혜산들쭉가공공장
광업 (1)	혜산청년광산

Kun (Ryanggang Province)

KOFC 군 (10-1)

4	운흥군 (1)
2	백안군
1	갑산군, 김형권군, 김형직군, 삼수군

중화공업 (5-1) 금속공업 (1), 기계(1) 건재 (3)	**[운흥제련소 (은흥)]**; 운흥광산기계공장 (은흥); 백암루마시멘트공장 (백암), 운흥광산시멘트공장, 운흥유리공장 (은흥)
재취 (2) 철 (1), 비 (1)	풍산광산 (김형권); 갑산광산 (갑산)
전력 (3) 수력 (3)	내중리발전소 (김형직), 백두산선군청년발전소 (백안), 삼수발전소 (삼수)

MOU 군 (11)

3	김정숙군,
2	대홍단군, 풍서군
1	갑산군, 백암군, 삼지연군, 운흥군

공업 (10) 광업 (1)

건재 (1)	풍서건재공장 (풍서군)
경공업 (6)	갑산영예군인수지일영품공장 (갑산군), 김정숙군고려약공장, 신파제약공장 (김정숙군), 대홍단감자가공공장 (대홍단군), 량강도감자조직배양공장 (백암군), 삼지연장공장 (삼지연군)
기계 (1)	풍서농기구공장 (풍서군)
광업 (2)	량강(신파)광산 (김정숙군), 운흥광산 (운흥군)
전력 (1)	서두수발전소 (대홍단군)

IPA (145-19)

갑산군 (15-1)

공업 (8)	갑산목재일용품공장, 갑산가죽가공공장, 갑산식료공장, 갑산아마섬유공장, 동점식료공장, 동점피복공장, 동점종이공장, 사장소석회공장
광업 (6-1)	**[갑산광산 (甲山鑛山)]**; 삼일광산, 오일광산, 사장탄광, 양흥탄광, 8월광산
전력 (1)	금풍소형발전소

김정숙군 (7-1)

공업 (5-1)	**[김정숙식료공장 (金正淑食料工場)]**; 김정숙기계공장, 김정숙피복공장, 김정숙직물공장, 룡하교구비품공장
광업 (2)	룡하광산, 상대소석회광산

김형권군 (5-1)

공업 (5-1)	**[풍산식료공장(豊山食料工場)]**; 김형권아마공장, 김형권직물공장, 김형권목재일용품공장, 하지경유리공장

김형직군 (9-2)

공업 (8-2)	**[김형직기념품공장 (金亨稷紀念品工場)]**, **[김형직방직기재공장 (金亨稷紡織器材工場)]**; 김형직성냥공장, 김형직식료공장, 김형직일용품공장, 록림식료공장, 연포합판공장, 월탄화학공장
광업 (1)	록림광산

대홍단군 (10-1)

공업 (9-1)	**[대홍단식료공장 (大紅湍食料工場)]**; 대홍단농기계수리공장, 대홍단고기 및 채소가공공장, 대홍단량곡가공공장, 대홍단목재일용품공장, 대홍단종이공장, 유곡제재공장, 유곡목제품공장, 유곡림철수리공장
전력 (1)	대홍단5호발전소 (大紅湍五號發電所)

백암군 (34-3)

공업 (29-1)	**[연암식료공장 (延岩食料工場)]**; 연암제재공장, 백암직물공장, 백암제약공장, 백암피복공장, 백암학용품공장, 백암기계수리공장, 백암목재일용품공장, 백암식료공장, 백암종이공장, 굴송가구공장, 동계목재가공공장, 연암맛내기공장, 연암일용품공장, 연암문화용품공장, 연암주름판기와공장, 연암유리공장, 연암오지공장, 연암털가죽공장, 산양림업기계수리공장, 산양목재가공공장, 양흥공예품공장, 원봉교구비품공장, 유평제재공장, 유평목재가구공장, 유평일용품공장, 천수식료공장, 천수가구공장, 천수토기공장
광업 (5-2)	**[백암탄광(白岩炭鑛)]**, **[남계광산(南溪鑛山)]**; 북계수탄광, 연암고회석광산, 양흥광산

보천군 (5-1)

공업 (5-1)	**[보천기념품공장(普天紀念品工場)]**; 보천식료공장, 보천일용품공장, 보천농기계공장, 대평교구비품공장

삼수군 (11-1)

공업 (11-1)	**[삼수식료공장 (三水食料工場)]**; 삼수방직공장, 삼수목재일용품공장, 삼수종이공장, 삼수화학공장, 삼수토기공장, 삼수기계공장, 광생석회공장, 광생세멘트공장, 중평장기와공장, 중평장가구공장

삼지연군 (11-3)

공업 (11-3)	**[혜산들쭉가공공장삼지연분공장]**, **[포태화학공장]**, **[포태농기계수리공장]**; 12월13일기념품공장 (十二月十三日紀念品工場), 삼지연목재일용품공장, 삼지연식료공장, 삼지연옷공장, 삼지연교구비품공장, 삼지연기계수리공장, 리명수목재가공공장, 무봉색소공장

운흥군 (25-5)

공업 (19-3)	**[운흥식료공장 (雲興食料工場)]**, **[운흥초물공장 (雲興草物工場)]**, **[운흥제련소 (雲興製鍊所)]**; 운흥피복공장, 운흥가죽공장, 운흥목재일용품공장, 운흥종이공장, 운흥건재공장, 남중제지공장, 대동세멘트공장, 대동장공장, 대오시천방사공장, 대오시천영예군인공장, 대오시천식료공장, 생장제재공장, 생장목재품공장, 일건광산기계공장, 일건화학공장, 일건염산공장
광업 (6-2)	**[일건광산 (日建鑛山)]**, **[운흥광산 (雲興鑛山)]**; 대덕광산, 대동광산, 령하광산, 룡암광산

풍서군 (13-0)

공업 (13)	풍서농기구공장 (豊西農器具工場), 풍서토기공장 (豊西土器工場), 풍서직물공장 (豊西織物工場), 풍서가죽공장 (豊西皮革工場), 풍서화학공장 (豊西化學工場), 풍서종이공장, 풍서식료공장 (豊西食料工場), 풍서일용품공장 (豊西日用品工場), 풍서피복공장 (豊西被服工場), 풍서건재공장 (豊西建材工場), 풍서제약공장 (豊西製藥工場), 풍서농기계공장, 합포기계수리공장 (合浦機械修理工場)

KCNA 군 (17)

5	대홍단군, 삼지연군
2	김정숙군, 김형직군
1	백암군, 삼수군, 운흥군

공업 (3)	대홍단감자가공공장 (대홍단군), 백두산청년들쭉사업소, 삼지연장공장 (삼지연군)
광업 (3)	룡암광산, 신파청년광산 (김정숙군), 운흥광산 (운흥군)
전력 (11)	제410호군민발전소, 남사강발전소 (김형직군), 대홍단1호발전소, 대홍단2호발전소, 대홍단4호청년발전소, 대홍단5호발전소 (대홍단군), 백두산선군청년발전소 (백암군), 삼수발전소 (삼수군), 무봉청년발전소, 포태3호발전소, 618발전소 (삼지연군)

KIET (57-6)

갑산군 (6-2)

I. 광업 (2-1)	1) 탄광	갑산탄광
	3) 비철	**[갑산광산]**
II. 음식 (1)	1) 일반	동점식료공장
III. 섬유 등 (1)	6) 의류	갑산피복공장
IV. 목제 등 (1)	1) 목제	갑산목재일용품공장
V. 화학 (1-1)	5)기초화학	**[갑산화학공장]**

김정숙군 (10-2)

I. 광업 (2-1)	2) 철광	신파광산
	3) 비철금속	**[신파청년광산]**
II. 음식 (2)	1) 일반	김정숙식료공장, 신파식료공장
III.성유 (2)	2) 직물	신파직물공장, 김정숙군 직물공장
IV. 목재 (2)	1) 목재	신파목재일용품공장
	3) 종이	신파종이공장
VI. 시멘트 등 (1)	3) 벽돌	신파건재공장
VIII.조립금속, 기계장비 (1-1)	1) 종합	**[신파기계수리공장]**

김현권군 (1)

IV. 목재 (1)	1) 목재	신파목재일용품공장

김형직군 (4)

IV. 목재 (1)	1) 목재	후창목재일용품공장
VI. 시멘트 등 (2)	3) 벽돌	후창건재공장
	5) 도자기	후창토기공장
X. 가구 (1)	5) 기타	후창성냥공장

대흥단군 (3)

II. 음식 (2)	3) 육류	대흥단고기가공공장, 대흥단사탕무우가공공장
XI. 전력 (1)	2) 화력	대흥단군 제5호발전소

백암군 (14-1)

I. 광업 (2)	1) 탄광	백암탄광, 북계수탄광
II. 음식 (2)	3) 육류	연암고기가공공장
	4) 장류	백암맛내기공장
III. 성유 (1)	2) 직물	연암직물공장
IV. 목재 (2)	1) 목재	백암목재일용품공장, 연암목재일용품공장
VI. 시멘트 등 (3-1)	3) 벽돌	**[백암마그네샤지붕판공장]**

	4) 유리	백암유리제품공장
	5) 도자기	백암오지공장
VIII. 조립금속, 기계장비 (1)	1) 종합	백암군기계수리공장
X. 가구 등 (3)	1) 가구	백암굴송가구공장, 상담가구공장
	2) 문방구, 완구 등	연암학용품공장

보천군 (2)

III. 섬유 등 (1)	6) 의류	보천피복공장
X. 가구 등 (1)	2) 문방구 등	보천학용품공장

삼수군 (5)

I. 광업 (2)	1) 탄광	삼수탄광
	4) 비금속광물	삼수광산
III. 섬유 등 (1)	2) 직물	삼수직물공장
IV. 목제 등 (1)	1) 목제	삼수목재일용품공장
V. 화학 (1)	9) 제약	삼수제약공장

삼지연군 (3-1)

II. 음식 (1-1)	6) 음료	[삼지연청량음료공장]
IV. 목제 등 (1)	1) 목제	삼지연목재일용품공장
X. 가구 (1)	4) 공예품	12월13일기념품공장

운흥군(6)

I. 광업 (2)	3) 철광	운흥광산
	4) 비금속광물	령하광산
V. 화학 (2)	5) 기초화학	운흥염산공장, 운흥화학공장
X. 가구 (2)	4) 공예품	운흥수예품공장
	5) 기타	운흥영예군인일용품공장

풍서군(3)

I. 광업 (1)	4) 비금속광물	풍서광산
IV. 목제 등 (1)	1) 목제	풍서목재일용품공장
X. 가구 (1)	기타	풍서영예군인일용품공장

IMPORTANT 군 (2)

1	갑산군, 운흥군

전력 (2)	갑산광산 (갑산군), 운흥광산 (운흥군)

Rason

KOFC (6-3)

경공업 (2)	식품 (2)	선봉랭동공장, 수산물가공센터 물고기종합가공공장
중화공업 (3-2)	조선 (1)	**[라진조선소]**
	화학 (1)	**[승리화학련합기업소]**
	건재 (1)	선봉세멘트공장
전력 (1-1)	화력 (1)	**[6.16화력발전소]**

MOU (12-1)

건재 (2)	선봉시멘트공장, 라진세멘트공장
경공업 (5)	라선식료가공공장, 라선종합식료공장, 라선편직물공장, 라진장공장, 라진피복공장
화학 (1)	승리화학공장
광업 (2)	선봉탄광, 라선탄광
전력 (2-1)	**[6월16일화력발전소]**; 선봉화력발전소

IPA (4-3)

공업 (3-2)	**[두만강침목제재공장(豆滿江枕木製材工場)]**, **[승리화학련합기업소(勝利化學聯合企業所)]**; 선봉랭동공장
전력 (1-1)	**[6.16화력발전소(六.一六火力發電所)]**

KCNA (7)

공업 (6)	라선기초식품공장, 라선대흥무역회사 수산물종합가공공장, 라진음료공장, 라진피복공장, 라선가구조립회사, 라선백석합영회사
광업 (0)	
전력 (1)	라선청년2호발전소

KIET (29-6)

I) 광업 (2)	3) 비철	락산광산, 부해광산
II. 음식료품, 담배 (2-1)	3) 육류등	라진물고기가공공장
	4) 장류	**[라진장공장]**
III. 섬유, 의복, 신발 (6)	1) 목재	라진직물공장
	3) 방적, 제사, 직조	라진직조공장
	6) 의류	선봉피복공장, 선봉옷공장
	10) 가죽등	라진모피공장, 선봉가죽가공공장
IV. 목재, 펄프, 종이 (2)	1) 목재	두만강침목제재공장
	3) 종이	라진제지공장
V. 화학 (7-2)	2) 정유	**[승리화학련합기업소]**
	5) 기초화학	선봉화학공장, 선봉탄산소다공장
	8) 합성수지, 수지제품	**[선봉영예군인수지일용품공장]**, 라진수지일용품공장
	9) 제약	라진제약공장

	10) 화장품	라진-선봉시 라지화학일용품공장
VI. 시멘트, 유리 (2)	1) 시멘트	선봉세멘트공장
	4) 유리	라진유리공장
VIII. 조립금속, 기계장비 (2-1)	5) 기계부품, 금속가공	라진철제일용수출품공장
	6b) 전자, 자동화기기	**[선봉합영회사]**
IX. 수송기계 (3-1)	1) 선박	**[라진조선소]**, 선봉선박수리공장, 라진선박수리공장
X. 가구, 잡제품 (1)	5) 기타	선봉영예군인공장
XI. 전력 (2-1)	2) 화력	**[선봉6월16일화력발전소]**, 선봉군의 풍력발전소

IMPORTANT (2)

공업 (1)	승리화학련합기업소
전력 (1)	6.16화력발전소

Chongjin (Hambuk Province)

KOFC (32-9)

경공업 (6-1)	식품 (3)	청진기름공장, 청진냉동공장, 충성의청진정제소금공장
	섬유 (1)	**[청진화학섬유공장]**
	신발 (2)	청진구두공장, 청잔산발공장
중화공업 (21-6)	금속 (3)	**[김책제철련합기업소]**, **[청진제강소]**, 청진강재공장
	기계 (7)	**[라남탄광기계련합기업소]**, 청진트랙터공장, 청진자동화기구공장, 청진련결농기계공장, 관모탄광기계공장, 라남탐사부속품공장, 청진공작기계공장
	자동차 (1)	**[청진뻐스공장]**
	철도차량 (1)	청진철도공장
	전기/전자 (3)	청진철도신호기공장, 청진전기공장, 청진텔레비죤수상기공장
	조선 (1)	**[함북조선소련합기업소 (청진조선소)]**
	화학 (1)	라남제약공장
	건재 (4)	**[강덕내화물공장]**, 청진세멘트공장, 청진유리공장, 청진내화물공장
채취 (1)	비 (1)	부윤광산
전력 (4-2)	수력 (3)	**[3월17일발전소 1-3호]**
	화력 (1)	**[청진화력발전소]**

MOU (33-7) 공업 (31-5) 전력 (2-2)

건재 (3)	청진수지관공장, 청진스레트공장, 청진내화물공장
경공업 (17)	청진수출품가공사업소, 6월7일공장, 5월31일사기그릇공장, 라남모피가공공장, 라남제약공장, 수성천종합식료공장, 신암구역문화일용품공장, 청진시초식품공장, 청진신발공장, 청진알루미늄그릇공장, 청진옷공장, 청진유리공장, 청진철도칠감공장, 청진편직공장, 청진화장품공장, 신암고려약공장, 청암고려약공장
기계 (7-2)	**[라남탄광기계련합기업소]**, **[청진뜨락또르부속품공장]**; 청진건설기계공장, 청진농기계공장, 청진버스공장, 청진차량부속품공장, 청진철도공장
제철/조선 (3-2)	**[김책제철련합기업소]**, **[청진제강련합기업소]**; 청진강재공장
화학 (1-1)	**[청진화학섬유련합기업소]**
전력 (2-2)	**[3월17일수력발전종합기업소]**, **[청진화력발전련합기업소]**

IPA (26-10)

공업 (23-7)	**[김책제철련합기업소 (金策製鐵聯合企業所)]**, **[라남제약공장 (羅南製藥工場)]**, **[라남탄광기계련합기업소 (羅南炭鑛機械聯合基業所)]**, **[청진공작기계공장 (淸津工作機械工場)]**, **[청진빠스공장]**, **[청진화학섬유공장 (淸津化學纖維工場)]**, **[함북조선소련합기업소 (咸北造船所聯合企業所)]**, **[(청진조선소)]**; 청진철도공장 (淸津鐵道工場), 강덕내화물공장 (康德耐火物工場), 청진장공장, 청진기름공장, 라남기계공장, 라남탐사설비공장, 라남포장재공장, 라남자전거공장, 라남식료공장, 라남일용품공장, 라남성냥공장, 라남견직공장, 라남시계공장, 라남옷공장, 송곡뜨락또르부속품공장, 청진영예군인수지일용품공장
광업 (1-1)	**[라남탄광 (羅南炭鑛)]**
전력 (2-2)	**[3월17일발전소 (三月十七日發電所)]**, **[청진화력발전소 (淸津火力發電所)]**

KCNA (21)

공업 (17)	관모봉기계공장, 라남탄광기계련합기업소, 수성천종합식료공장, 청진금속합작회사, 청진기초식품공장, 청진뜨락또르부속품공장, 청진빠스공장, 청진수지관공장, 청진스레트공장, 청진시기초식료품공장, 청진정제소금공장, 청진제강소, 청진철도공장, 청진화학섬유공장, 청진신발공장, 천수동샘물공장, 함북조선소련합기업소
전력 (4)	3월17일발전소, 김철발전소, 서두수발전소, 청진화력발전소

KIET(93-35)

I. 광업 (4)	1) 탄광	라남탄광
	2) 철광	부윤광산
	3) 비철	련천광산, 청진광산
II. 음식료품, 담배 (13-3)	1) 일반	**[부윤식료공장]**, **[신임식료공장]**, 수성식료공장, 청암식료공장, 청진어린이식료공장
	2) 곡물가공	**[청진기름공장]**, 청진과자공장, 청진제분공장
	3) 육류	청진김치가공공장, 청진수산물가공공장
	4) 장류	청진장공장
	5) 사료	청진배합사료공장
	6) 음료, 주류	청진음료공장
III. 섬유, 의복, 신발 (16-5)	2) 직물공장	**[청진직물공장]**
	3) 방적, 제사, 직조	**[청천강합영회사]**, 부윤직조공장, 청진방사공장, 포항직조공장

	4) 견직공장	라남견직공장
	5) 편직공장	청진편직공장
	6) 의류	라남옷공장, 송평비복공장, 청암피복공장, 청진옷공장, 청진피복공장
	7) 양말 등	**[청진양말공장]**
	8) 신발	**[청진신발공장]**, **[청진구두공장]**
	10) 가죽	청진그물공장
IV. 목재, 펄프, 종이 (1)	3) 종이	라남수출품장재공장
V. 화학 (9-4)	4) 화학섬유	**[청진화학섬유공장]**
	5) 기초화학	송평영예군인화학공장, 청진화학공장
	8) 합성수지, 수지제품	라남영예군인수지일용품공장, 송평수지일용품공장, 청진영예군인수지일용품공장
	9) 제약	**[신암제약공장]**, **[라남제약공장]**
	10) 화장품	**[청진화장품공장]**
VI. 시멘트, 유리 (5-1)	1) 시멘트	청진세멘트공장
	2) 마그네사이트 크링커 및 내화물	강덕내화물공장
	3) 벽돌	청진스레트공장
	4) 유리	청진유리공장
	5) 도자기	**[5월31일사기그릇공장]**
VII. 1차 금속산업 (8-5)	1) 제철 제강	**[청진강재공장]**, **[김책제철련합기업소]**, **[청진제강소]**, 10월30일공장
	2) 제련	**[부령합금철련합기업소]**
	3) 기타 1차금속	[청진도금공장], 청진알루미니움공장, 송편압연공장
VIII. 조립금속, 기계장비 (20-10)	2) 공작기계	**[청진공작기계공장]**, **[6월7일공장]**
	3a) 탄광, 광산용	**[라남탄광기계(5월10일)련합기업소]**, 청진내화물공장
	3b) 농업용	**[청진뜨락또르부속품공장]**, **[청진련결농기계공장]**, 청진종합기계공장, 청진량곡가공기계공장,
	4) 정밀	나남시계공장, 청진시계공장
	5) 기계부품, 금속가공	**[청진저울공장]**, **[청진침함공장]**, **[청진법랑철기공장]**, **[청진알루미니움그릇공장]**, 청진압연공장, 청진금속건구공장
	6a) 전기기기, 부품	라남전기일용품공장
	6b) 전자, 자동화기기	**[청진저항기공장]**, **[청진전기공장]**, 청진철도신호기계공장, 청진자동화기구공장
IX. 수송기계 (7-4)	1) 선박	**[방진선박수리공장]**, **[함북조선소련합기업소(청진조선소)]**, 청진선박수리공장, 6 · 2항만건설사업소
	2) 철도차량	**[청진철도공장]**
	3) 자동차	**[청진빠스공장]**, 청진자동차수리공장
X. 가구, 잡제품 (6)	2) 문방구, 완구, 체육기구	청진연필공장
	3) 악기	청진악기공장

	4) 공예품, 장식품	청진공예품공장
	5) 기타	청진성냥공장, 청암일용품공장, 라남영예군인공장
XI. 전력 (4-3)	1) 수력	**[서두수발전소]**, **[3월17일수력발전종합기업소]**
	2) 화력	**[청진화력발전소]**, 김책화력발전소

IMPORTANT(16)

공업 (14)	청진기름공장, 청진신발공장, 청진화학섬유공장, 라남제약공장, 청진강재공장, 김책제철련합기업소, 청진제강소, 청진공작기계공장, 라남탄광기계련합기업소, 청진뜨락또르부속품공장, 함북조선소련합기업소(청진조선소), 청진철도공장, 청진뻐스공장, 강덕내화물공장
전력 (2)	3월17일수력발전소, 청진화력발전소

Hoeryong (Hambuk Province)

KOFC (15-1)

경공업 (7)	식품 (3)	회령제당공장, 회령담배공장, 회령곡산공장
	신발 (1)	회령구두공장
	제지 (3)	회령종이(공장)련합기엽소, 회령크라프트지공장, 회령제지공장
중화공업 (3)	기계 (1)	회령탄광기계공장
	건재 (2)	회령유리공장, 유선내화물공장
재취 (5-1)	탄광 (4)	**[오룡광산]**, 학포탄광, 회령탄광, 유선탄광
	석회석 (1)	중도광산

MOU (15) 공업 (10) 광업 (5)

경공업 (9)	회령고려약공장, 회령구두공장, 회령기초식품공장, 회령대성담배공장, 회령백살구가공공장, 회령식료가공공장, 회령은하피복공장, 회령종이공장, 회령화학일용품공장
기계 (1)	회령탄광기계공장
광업 (5)	회령5호광산, 회령대흥광산, 상화청년탄광, 유선탄광, 학포탄광

IPA (26-7)

공업 (19-4)	**[회령곡산공장(會寧谷産工場)]**, **[회령제지공장 (會寧製紙工場)]**, **[회령크라프트지공장]**, **[회령탄광기계공장 (會寧炭鑛機械工場)]**; 회령악기공장, 회령피복공장, 회령일용품공장, 망양종이공장, 망양건재공장, 회령식료공장, 회령가구공장, 회령화장품공장, 회령피복공장, 회령직조공장, 회령건재공장, 회령종이공장, 유선내화물공장 (遊仙耐火物工場), 중도세멘트공장, 중도모피가공공장
광업 (7-3)	**[궁심탄광 (弓心炭鑛)]**, **[유선탄광 (遊仙炭鑛)]**, **[학포탄광 (鶴浦炭鑛)]**; 계림탄광, 회령탄광, 중도광산, 성북탄광
전력 (0)	창효발전소

KCNA (5)

공업 (5)	회령고려약공장, 회령기초식품공장, 회령대성담배공장, 회령목재가공공장, 회령식료가공공장

KIET (24-5)

I. 광업 (4)	1) 탄광	유선탄광, 궁심탄광, 학포탄광
	4) 비금속광물	중봉광산
II. 음식료품, 담배 (7-2)	1) 일반	**[회령식료련합회사]**
	2) 곡물가공	**[회령곡산공장]**, 회령제당공장
	3) 육류	회령백살구가공공장
	4) 장류	회령장공장, 유선장공장
	7) 담배	회령담배공장
III. 섬유, 의복, 신발 (3-1)	6) 의류	**[진달래합영회사]**, 회령피복공장
	8) 신발	회령구두공장
IV. 목재, 펄프, 종이 (4-1)	3) 종이	**[회령종이련합기업소]**, 회령크라프트지공장, 회령제지공장
	9) 제약	회령제약공장
VI. 시멘트, 유리 (1)	1) 시멘트	회령세멘트공장
VIII. 조립금속, 기계장비 (4-1)	1) 종합기계	회령시기계수리공장
	3a) 탄광, 광산용	**[회령탄광기계공장]**
	3c) 기타 산업용	진달래재봉기공장
	6a) 전기기기, 부품	회령전동기공장
X. 가구, 잡제품 (1)	2) 문방구, 완구, 체육기구	회령영예군인학용품공장

IMPORTANT (5)

공업 (5)	회령곡산공장, 회령종이(공장)련합기엽소, 회령탄광기계공장, 회령제지공장, 회령크라프트지공장

Kimchaek (Hambuk Province)

KOFC (11-4)

경공업 (2)	식품 (2)	김책수산물가공공장, 김책냉동공장
중화공업 (8-4)	금속 (1)	**[성진제강련합기업소]**
	기계 (2)	김책공구공장, 김책착암기공장
	전기/전자 (1)	김책전기공장
	조선 (1)	**[김책선박공장]**
	화학 (1)	**[쌍룡린비료공장]**
	건재 (2)	**[성진내화물공장]**, 김책유리공장
재취 (1)	비	업억광산

MOU (10-3) 공업 (9-3) 광업 (1)

건재 (2-1)	**[김책시멘트련합기업소]**; 성진내화물공장
경공업 (4)	김책기초식품공장, 김책대흥가공사업소, 김책장공장, 김책편직공장
기계 (1)	김책착암기공장
제철/조선 (2-2)	**[김책선박공장]**, **[성진제강련합기업소]**
광업 (1)	쌍룡광산

IPA (8-4)

공업 (6-4)	[김책선박공장 (金策船舶工場)], [성진내화물공장 (城津耐火物工場)], [성진제강련합기업소 (城津製鋼聯合企業所)], [쌍룡린비료공장 (雙龍磷肥料工場)]; 김책대리석가공공장 (金策大理石加工工場), 5월24일수출품수산사업소 (五月二十四日輸出品水産事業所)
광업 (1)	학동탄광
전력 (1)	송흥발전소

KCNA (4)

공업 (4)	김책제철련합기업소, 박제품공장, 성진내화물공장, 성진제강련합기업소

KIET (25-8)

I. 광업 (5-2)	1) 탄광	학동탄광
	2) 철광	업억광산
	4) 비금속광물	**[쌍룡광산]**, **[풍년광산]**, 중도광산
II. 음식료품, 담배 (3-1)	1) 일반	김책식료공장
	3) 육류	**[5월24일 수출품수산사업소]**, 김책수산물가공공장
III. 섬유, 의복, 신발 (2)	5) 편직공장	김책편직공장
	6) 의류	김책옷공장
V. 화학 (3)	3) 비료	쌍룡린비료공장
	5) 기초화학	김책화학공장
	9) 제약	김책제약공장
VI. 시멘트, 유리 (2-1)	2) 마그네사이트 크링커 및 내화물	**[성진내화물공장]**
	4) 유리	김책유리일용품공장
VII. 1차 금속산업 (1-1)	1) 제철 제강	**[성진제강련합기업소]**
VIII. 조립금속, 기계장비 (7-2)	2) 공작기계	김책공조기계공장, 김책공구공장
	3a) 탄광, 광산용	**[4월25일기계공장]**
	5) 기계부품, 금속가공	**[장평금속건구공장]**, 김책금속건구공장, 김책철제일용품공장
	6a) 전기기기, 부품	김책전기공장
IX. 수송기계 (1-1)	1) 선박	**[김책선박공장]**
X. 가구, 잡제품 (1)	3) 악기	김책선물악기공장

IMPORTANT (4)

공업 (4)	성진내화물공장, 김책선박공장, 성진제강련합기업소, 쌍룡린비료공장

Kun (Hambuk Province)

KOFC 군 (51-8)

9	온성군
8	부령군 (3)
6	경흥군 (1)
5	화성군 (1)
4	경원군, 길주군, 명천군, 어랑군 (1)
3	경성군 (1), 무산군 (1)
1	화대군

경공업 (3) 식품 (2), 제지 (1)	8월1일청년제염소(어대진제염소) (화성), 어대진수산사업소 (어랑); 길주펄프종합공장 (길주)
중화공업 (11-6) 금속 (1), 기계 (1), 전기/전자 (2), 조선 (1), 화학 (2), 건재 (4)	**[부령야금공장** (부령)]; 경성기계공장; **[주을전기공장** (경성)], 5월7일통신기계공장(길주); **[어대진선박수리공장** (어랑)]; **[7월7일련합기업소** (경흥)] **[화성화학공장** (화성)], 박충건설자기공장 (경성), 무산시멘트공장 (무산), **[고무산세멘트공장** (부령)], 온성세멘트공장 (온성)
재취 (30-1) 비 (1), 탄광 (27), 석회석 (2)	주원강철공장 (온성); 경원지구탄광련힙기업소, 고건원탄광, 룡북청년탄광, 하면탄광 (경원), 6월13일탄광, 경흥탄광, 오봉탄광, 경흥지구탄광련합기업소, 룡연탄광 (경흥), 일신탄광, 덕신탄광 (길주), 명천탄광, 양정탄광, 고참탄광, 명천지구탄광련합기업소 (명천), **[무산광산련합기업소** (무산]), 온성탄광, 강안탄광, 상화청년탄광, 주원탄광, 풍인탄광, 동포탄광, 온성지구탄광련합기업소 (온성), 석성틴광 (화대), 명간탄광, 화성탄광, 극동탄광 (화성); 고무산광산, 무수광산 (부령)
전력 (7-1) 수력 (7)	흥암청년발전소 (무산), **[부령발전소** 1-4호 (부령)], 어랑천발전소1-2호 (어랑)

MOU 군 (52-6) 공업 (30-1) 광업 (20-5) 전력 (2)

9	경성군 (1)
7	길주군, 명천군 (1)
6	경흥군 (1)
5	무산군 (1), 부령군
4	화성군
3	경원군 (1),온성군 (1)
2	화대군
1	어령군

건재 (4)	길주시멘트공장, 길주침목방부공장, 길주합판공장 (길주군), 고무산시멘트공장 (부령군)
경공업 (20-1)	**[경성도자기련합기업소]**; 경성영예군인주사약공장, 경성은하피복공장, 경성종합식료공장, 경성화학일용품공장 (경성군), 은덕영예군인제약공장, 은덕피복공장 (경흥군), 길주제지공장, 길주펄프공장, 길주화학일용품공장 (길주군), 명천영예군인식료공장, 명천장공장, 명천피복공장 (명천군), 무산기초식품공장, 무산식료공장, 무산장공장 (무산군), 함경북도어구공장 (어령군), 온성옷공장 (온성군), 화대군장공장 (화대군), 화성제약공장 (화성군)

기계 (1)	무산림업기계공장 (무산군)
전자 (2)	6월5일전기종합공장, 경성애자공장 (경성군)
제철/조선 (1)	부령치금공장 (부령군)
화학 (2)	**[7월7일련합기업소 (경흥군)]**, 화성화학공장 (화성군)
광업 (20-5)	생기령광산, 경성탄광 (경성군), **[경원지구탄광련합기업소]**; 룡북청년탄광, 고건원탄광 (경원군), 6월13일탄광, 오봉탄광, 은성탄광 (경흥군), 일신탄광 (길주군), **[명천지구탄광련합기업소]**, 명천탄광, 량정탄광, 고참탄광 (명천군), 무산광산련합기업소 (무산군)], 부령탄광 (부령군), **[온성지구탄광련합기업소]**, 강안탄광 (온성군), 화대광산 (화대군), 명간탄광, 화성탄광 (화성군)
전력 (2)	금강3호발전소, 부령발전소 (부령군)

IPA (200-40)

경성군 (16-5)

공업 (10-5)	**[경성도자기공장 (鏡城陶瓷器工場)]**, **[박충건설자기공장 (朴忠建設瓷器工場)]**, **[3월13일공장 (三月十三日工場)]**, **[생기령요업공장 (生氣嶺窯業工場)]**, **[6월5일전기종합공장 (六月五日電氣綜合工場)]**; 경성식료품공장, 경성일용품공장, 경성피복공장, 경성제약공장, 룡천아마공장
광업 (4)	생기령고령토광산, 생기령와목점토광산, 생기령석탄광산, 룡현탄광
전력 (2)	온포3호발전소, 온포4호발전소

경원군 (14-3)

공업 (14-3)	**[고건원탄광 (古乾原炭鑛)]**, **[룡북청년탄광 (龍北靑年炭鑛)]**, **[하면탄광 (下面炭鑛)]**; 새별식료공장, 새별피복공장, 새별직물공장, 고건원식료공장, 고건원도자기공장, 고건원옷공장, 고건원유리공장, 고건원가구공장, 룡북식료공장, 안원세멘트공장, 안원소석회공장

경흥군 (14-5)

공업 (10-2)	**[오봉도자기공장 (梧鳳陶瓷器工場)]**, **[은덕화학공장 (銀德化學工場)]**; 은덕식료품공장, 은덕천공장, 은덕옷공장, 은덕물고기가공품공장, 은덕화학일용품공장, 귀락쌀기름공장, 귀락배합먹이공장, 귀락소석회공장
광업 (4-3)	**[오봉탄광 (梧鳳炭鑛)]**, **[6월13일탄광 (六月十三日炭鑛)]**, **[은덕탄광 (恩德炭鑛)]**; 학송탄광

길주군 (25-4)

공업 (20-3)	**[길주식료공장 (吉州食料工場)]**, **[길주팔프공장]**, **[길주합판공장 (吉州合板工場)]**; 길주2월26일공장, 길주방부제공장, 길주종이공장, 길주경판지공장, 룡담전기기계공장, 룡담전기기구공장, 길주팔프공장, 길주제지공장, 길주방부제공장, 일신벽돌공장, 일신부재공장, 일신세멘트공장, 길주절연물광산 분공장, 길주소석회공장, 길주털가죽공장, 금천보온재공장, 남양보온재료공장, 5월7일통신기계공장
광업 (3-1)	**[룡담운모광산 (龍潭雲母鑛山)]**; 일신탄광, 로동탄광
전력 (2)	신동발전소, 풍계발전소

명천군 (14-3)

공업 (10)	명천방직공장, 명천가구공장, 명천옷공장, 명천식료품공장, 명천일용품공장, 룡암식료공장, 황곡오지공장, 황곡종이공장, 황곡벽돌공장, 황곡농기구공장
광업 (4-3)	**[고참탄광 (古站炭鑛)], [명천탄광 (明川炭鑛)], [양정탄광 (楊亭炭鑛)]**; 독포탄광

무산군 (24-2)

공업 (22-1)	**[무산제재공장 (茂山製材工場)]**; 무산림업기계공장 (茂山林業機械工場), 무산건재공장 (茂山建材工場), 무산직물공장, 무산피복공장, 무산모피공장, 무산맥주공장, 무산기계수리공장, 무산버섯공장, 무산농기구공장, 무산화학공장, 무산식료공장, 무산연필공장, 무산악기공장, 무산오지공장, 무산제약공장, 삼봉제재공장, 삼봉목재가공공장, 삼봉화학공장, 삼봉연필공장, 삼봉악기공장, 삼봉오지공장
광업 (2-1)	**[무산광산련합기업소 (茂山鑛山聯合企業所)]**; 무산광산

부령군 (18-4)

공업 (13-1)	**[고무산세멘트공장]**; 부령야금공장, 부령식료공장, 부령종이공장, 부령일용품공장, 부령모피공장, 부령피복공장, 부령제약공장, 부령농기구공장, 부령건재공장, 고무산식료공장, 고무산일용품공장, 금강부재공장
광업 (4-2)	**[고무산광산 (古茂山鑛山)], [무수광산 (舞袖鑛山)]**; 석막광산, 창평회중석광산
전력 (1-1)	**[부령발전소 (富寧發電所)]**

어랑군 (12-4)

공업 (9-4)	**[어대진선박수리공장 (漁大津船舶修理工場)], [어대진어구공장 (漁大津漁具工場)], [어랑식료공장(漁郎食料工場)], [어랑종이공장]**; 어랑농기계공장, 어랑고려약공장, 어랑인견천공장, 어랑옷공장, 어랑일용품공장
광업 (3)	룡연탄광, 삼향탄광, 봉강점토광산

연사군 (4-2)

공업 (4-2)	**[연사가구공장 (延社家具工場)], [연사식료품공장 (延社食料品工場)]**; 연사화학공장, 연사초물제품공장

온성군 (33-5)

공업 (21-1)	**[온성식료품공장 (穩城食料品工場)]**; 온성철제일용품공장, 온성수지일용품공장, 온성천공장, 온성편직물공장, 온성가구공장, 남양직물공장, 남양옷공장, 남양제약공장, 남양가구공장, 산성모피공장, 삼봉차량부속품공장, 상화피복공장, 종성식료공장, 종성가구공장, 종성직물공장, 종성피복공장, 종성농기구공장, 종성저울부속품공장, 종성배합먹이공장, 풍리옷공장
광업 (12-4)	**[상화청년탄광 (上和青年炭鑛)], [온성탄광 (穩城炭鑛)], [주원탄광 (周原炭鑛)], [풍인탄광 (豊仁炭鑛)]**; 석수탄광, 강안탄광, 산성광산, 삼봉석회석광산, 석수탄광, 창평탄광, 수산탄광, 룡남탄광

화대군 (9-1)

공업 (8-1)	**[화대식료공장 (花臺食料工場)]**; 화대일용품공장, 화대옷공장, 화대직물공장, 화대가구공장, 화대기계수리공장, 화대건재공장, 토원선박수리공장
광업 (1)	금성유연탄광

화성군 (17-2)

공업 (8-1)	**[화성화학공장 (化成化學工場)]**; 화성일용품공장, 화성수지일용품공장, 극동탄광기계수리공장, 극동농기계공장, 룡반오지공장, 룡반가구공장, 화성모피가공공장
광업 (9-1)	**[부화광산 (富禾鑛山)]**; 화성탄광, 극동탄광, 룡반규산염광산, 근동탄광 근동광산, 룡덕광산, 화성규산염광산, 부화고령토광산, 신양광산

KCNA군 (31)

7	경성군
4	길주군
3	경원군, 무산군, 부령군, 어랑군, 온성군
2	명천군
1	연사군, 경흥군, 화대군

공업(14)	경성도자기련합기업소, 경성애자공장, 생기령요업공장, 6월5일전기종합공장 (경성군), 길주팔프공장 (길주군), 명천메기공장 (명천군), 무산광산련합기업소, 무산림업기계공장, 무산식료공장 (무산군), 고무산세멘트공장, 부령합금철공장 (부령군), 8월1일청년제염소 (어랑군), 연사가구공장 (연사군), 7월7일련합기업소 (경흥군)
광업 (9)	생기령광산 (경성군), 경원지구탄광련합기업소, 고건원탄광, 룡북청년탄광 (경원군), 명천지구탄광련합기업소 (명천군), 온성지구탄광련합기업소, 풍인탄광, 상화청년탄광 (온성군), 석성탄광 (화대군)
전력 (8)	온포3호발전소, 온포4호발전소 (경성군), 남대천1호발전소, 남대천2호발전소, 남대천3호발전소 (길주군), 금강5호발전소 (부령군), 어랑천 (1호)발전소, 어랑천2호발전소 (어랑군)

KIET (138-38)

경성군(13-6)

I. 광업 (1-1)	4) 비금속광물	**[생기령광산]**
III. 섬유, 의복, 신발 (3)	4) 견직공장	경성견직공장, 주을견직공장
	6) 의류	경성옷공장
V. 화학 (1-1)	9) 제약	**[경성영예군인주사약공장]**
VI. 시멘트, 유리 (5-2)	3) 벽돌	박충건설자기공장
	5) 도자기	**[경성도자기련합회사]**, **[7월6일도자기공장]**, 생기령요업공장, 승암도자기공장
VIII. 조립금속, 기계장비 (3-2)	3c) 기타 산업용	**[3월13일수산기계공장]**
	6a) 전기기기, 부품	**[6월5일전기종합공장 (주을전기공장)]**
	6b) 전자, 자동화기기	경성자동화기구공장

경원군(7-3)

I. 광업 (6-3)	1) 탄광	**[새별지구탄광련합기업소]**, **[고건원탄공]**, **[하면탄광]**, 룡북(청년)탄광, 덕흥탄광, 룡북탄광,
VI. 시멘트, 유리 (1)	1) 시멘트	새별세멘트공장

길주군 (16-4)

I. 광업 (3)	1) 탄광	**[일신탄광]**, 덕신탄광
	4) 비금속광물	**[포수광산]**
II. 음식료품, 담배 (1)	1) 일반	길주식료공장
III. 섬유, 의복, 신발 (1)	2) 직물공장	길주직물공장
IV. 목재, 펄프, 종이 (3-2)	1) 목재	**[길주합판공장]**
	2) 펄프	**[길주팔프종합공장]**
	3) 종이	길주경판지스레트공장
V. 화학 (3)	5) 기초화학	길주가성소다공장
	8) 합성수지, 수지제품	길주수지일용품공장
	10) 화장품	길주화학일용품공장
VI. 시멘트, 유리 (1)	1) 시멘트	길주세멘트공장
VIII. 조립금속, 기계장비 (4-2)	3b) 농업용	길주농기구공장
	4) 정밀	**[길주2월26일공장]**
	6c) 통신기계	**[5월7일영예군인통신기계공장]**, 길주통신기계공장

명천군 (10-3)

I. 광업 (4-2)	1) 탄광	**[명천지구탄광련합기업소]**, **[고참탄광]**, 명천탄광, 양정탄광
II. 음식료품, 담배 (2-1)	1) 일반	**[명천영예군인식료공장]**
	4) 장류	명천장공장
III. 섬유, 의복, 신발 (1)	3) 방적, 제사, 직조	명천직조공장
V. 화학 (1)	8) 합성수지, 수지제품	명천수지일용품공장
VI. 시멘트, 유리 (1)	1) 시멘트	명천세멘트공장
X. 가구, 잡제품 (1)	5) 기타	명천일용품공장

무산군 (11-3)

I. 광업 (1-1)	2) 철광	**[무산자철광]**
II. 음식료품, 담배 (4-1)	1) 일반	무산식료공장
	3) 육류	남새가공공장
	4) 장류	무산장공장
	6) 음료, 주류	문산맥주공장
III. 섬유, 의복, 신발 (1)	6) 의류	무산피복공장
IV. 목재, 펄프, 종이 (1-1)	1) 목재	**[무산제재공장]**
V. 화학 (1)	5) 기초화학	무산화학공장
VIII. 조립금속, 기계장비 (2)	1) 종합기계	무산기계수리공장
	3c) 기타 산업용	무산림업기계공장
X. 가구, 잡제품 (1)	2) 문방구, 완구, 체육기구	무산연필공장

부령군 (6-3)

I. 광업 (1)	4) 비금속광물	고무산광산
III. 섬유, 의복, 신발 (1)	4) 견직공장	고무산견직공장
IV. 목재, 펄프, 종이 (1-1)	3) 종이	**[부령제지공장]**
VI. 시멘트, 유리 (2-1)	1) 시멘트	**[고무산세멘트공장]**
	3) 벽돌	고무산블로크공장
XI. 전력 (1-1)	1) 수력	**[부령발전소]**

어랑군 (7-2)

II. 음식료품, 담배 (1)	4) 장류	어랑장공장
III. 섬유, 의복, 신발 (4)	4) 견직공장	어랑견직공장
	6) 의류	어랑피복공장, 어랑수출피복공장
	10) 가죽	어랑영예군인어구공장
VIII. 조립금속, 기계장비 (1-1)	3b) 농업용	**[어랑련결농기계공장]**
IX. 수송기계 (1-1)	1) 선박	**[어대진선박수리공장]**

연사군 (9-1)

II. 음식료품, 담배 (2)	1) 일반	연사식료공장
	4) 장류	연사장공장
III. 섬유, 의복, 신발 (1)	6) 의류	연사피복공장
V. 화학 (2-1)	5) 기초화학	**[연사화학공장]**
	9) 제약	연사제약공장
VI. 시멘트, 유리 (2)	3) 벽돌	연사건재공장
	5) 도자기	연사오지공장
X. 가구, 잡제품 (2)	2) 문방구, 완구, 체육기구	연사운동기구공장 연사학용품공장

온성군 (17-4)

I. 광업 (8-2)	1) 탄광	**[온성지구탄광련합기업소]**, **[풍인탄광]**, 창평탄광, 강안탄광, 주원탄광, 온성탄광, 상화청탄광, 동포탄광
II. 음식료품, 담배 (2)	1) 일반	종성종합식료공장
	4) 장류	온성장공장
III. 섬유, 의복, 신발 (1)	2) 직물공장	종성직물공장
V. 화학 (2)	8) 합성수지, 수지제품	온성영예군인수지일용품공장
	9) 제약	온성제약공장
VI. 시멘트, 유리 (2-1)	1) 시멘트	온성세멘트공장
	5) 도자기	**[온성도자기공장]**
X. 가구, 잡제품 (2-1)	1) 가구	종성가구공장
	5) 기타	**[온성일용품공장]**

경흥군 (23-6)

I. 광업 (5-1)	1) 탄광	**[6월13일 탄광]**, 룡연탄광, 오봉탄광, 은덕탄광, 아오지탄광
II. 음식료품, 담배 (3-2)	1) 일반	**[은덕식료공장]**
	2) 곡물가공	은덕쌀기름공장
	4) 장류	**[은덕장공장]**
III. 섬유, 의복, 신발 (6)	2) 직물공장	은덕직물공장
	3) 방적, 제사, 직조	은덕직조공장
	5) 편직공장	은덕옷공장
	6) 의류	은덕피복공장, 은산피복공장
	10) 가죽	은덕모피공장
IV. 목재, 펄프, 종이 (1)	3) 종이	은덕제지공장
V. 화학 (5-3)	1) 종합	**[7월7일련합기업소]**
	8) 합성수지, 수지제품	은덕수지일용품공장
	9) 제약	**[은덕영예군인제약공장]**, 은덕제약공장
	10) 화장품	**[은덕화학일용품공장]**
VI. 시멘트, 유리 (1)	5) 도자기	은덕도자기공장
VIII. 조립금속, 기계장비 (2)	3b) 농업용	은덕군농기구공장
	5) 기계부품, 금속가공	은덕군철제일용품공장

화대군 (8)

I. 광업 (1)	4) 비금속광물	남대천광산
II. 음식료품, 담배 (2)	1) 일반	화대식료공장
	4) 장류	화대장공장
III. 섬유, 의복, 신발 (2)	3) 방적, 제사, 직조	화대직조공장
	6) 의류	화대피복공장
VIII. 조립금속, 기계장비 (1)	3b) 농업용	화대농기구공장
X. 가구, 잡제품 (2)	1) 가구	화대가구공장
	5) 기타	화대일용품공장

화성군 (11-3)

I. 광업 (3-1)	1) 탄광	**[화성탄광]**, 명간탄광
	4) 비금속광물	화성규산염광산
II. 음식료품, 담배 (1)	4) 장류	화성장공장
III. 섬유, 의복, 신발 (1)	10) 가죽	화성모피공장
V. 화학 (3-1)	1) 종합	**[화성화학공장]**
	8) 합성수지, 수지제품	화성수지일용품공장
	9) 제약	화성제약공장
VI. 시멘트, 유리 (1)	1) 시멘트	화성세멘트공장
X. 가구, 잡제품 (2-1)	5) 기타	**[명간일용품공장]**, 화성일용품공장

IMPORTANT (30)

5	경성군, 온성군
4	길주군, 명천군
3	경흥군, 부령군
2	경원군, 화성군
1	어랑군, 무산군

공업 (11)	경성도자기(련합회사)공장, 박충건설자기공장, 생기령요업공장, 6월5일전기종합공장 (경성군), 7월7일련합기업소 (경흥군), 길주합판공장, 길주펄프종합공장, 5월7일영예군인통신기계공장, (길주군), 고무산세멘트공장 (부령군), 어대진선박수리공장 (어랑군), 화성화학공장 (화성군)
광업 (18)	생기령광산 (경성군), 경원지구탄광련합기업소, 하면탄광 (경원군), 오봉탄광, 6월13일 탄광 (경흥군), 일신탄광 (길주군), 명천지구탄광련합기업소, 고참탄광, 명천탄광, 양정탄광 (명천군), 무산광산련합기업소 (무산군), 고무산광산 (부령군), 온성지구탄광련합기업소, 풍인탄광, 상화청년탄광, 온성탄광, 주원탄광 (온성군), 화성탄광 (화성군)]
전력 (1)	부령발전소 (부령군)

Hamhung (Hamnam Province)

KOFC (33-8)

경공업 (9-2)	식품 (4)	함흥냉동공장, 함흥육류가공공장, 함흥정제소금공장, 함흥곡산공장
	섬유 (2)	**[함흥모방직공장]**, **[2.8비날론련합기업소]**
	신발 (2)	흥남구두공장, 항흥염화비닐신발공장
	제지 (1)	함흥제1제지공장
중화공업 (24-6)	금속 (3)	**[7월27일제련소(舊 흥남제2제련소)]**, 흥남제련소, 함흥강철공장
	기계 (5)	신흥기계공장, 함흥트랙터부속품공장, 함흥공작기계공장, 함흥련결농기계공장, 6월1일전기기구공장
	자동차 (1)	함남련결차공장
	철도차량 (1)	함흥철도종합공장
	전기/전자 (5)	**[함흥전기기구종합공장]**, **[룡성기계련합기업소]**, 본궁전기공장, 성천강전기공장, 함흥세탁기공장
	화학 (5)	**[흥남비료련합기업소]**, 신흥화학련합기업소, 함흥제약공장, 함흥17호공장, 함흥타이어공장
	건재 (4)	**[함흥씨리카트벽돌공장]**, 본궁규산염화학공장, 함흥유리병공장, 함흥건설자기공장

MOU (58-7)

건재 (5-2)	**[함흥목재종합공장]**, **[함흥씨리카트벽돌공장]**; 함흥건재공장, 함흥시멘트공장, 동흥산건재공장
경공업 (36)	함흥향료공장, 함흥구두공장, 함흥기초식품공장, 함흥다이야공장, 함흥대외봉사수출품공장, 함흥동흥산피복공장, 함흥모방직공장, 함흥목재가공공장, 함흥목제품공장, 함흥성천강피복공장, 함흥수예품공장, 함흥수지지우개공장, 함흥알루미늄가정용품공장, 함흥영예군인교정기구공장, 함흥영예군인수지일용품공장, 함흥영예군인의료기구공장, 함흥영예군인일용품공장, 함흥유리실험기구공장, 함흥일용품공장, 함흥제분공장, 함흥제사공장, 함흥종이공장, 함흥편직공장, 함흥후방가족피복공장, 흥남타올공장, 흥남시해안수출피복공장, 흥남장공장, 흥남제약공장, 5월20일대성공장, 동흥산수출피복공장, 동흥산은하피복공장, 동흥산직물공장, 동흥산화학일용품공장, 백운산종합식료공장, 해안구역식료공장, 흥남구두공장
기계 (3-1)	**[룡성기계련합기업소]**; 함흠대형공작기계공장, 함흥대외봉사수출품공장
전자 (6-1)	**[함흥반도체재료공장]**; 함흥발전설비부속품공장, 함흥청년전기기구공장, 흥남전극공장, 6월1일청년전기기구공장, 성천강전기공장
제철/조선 (4)	함흥강철공장, 선군주철공장, 727호제련소, 흥남제련소
화학 (4-3)	**[2.8비날론련합기업소]**, **[흥남비료련합기업소]**; **[신흥화학련합기업소]**, 함흥규산염화학공장

IPA (36-12)

공업 (36-12)	**[함흥건설자기공장 (咸興建設瓷器工場)]**, **[함흥곡산공장 (咸興穀産工場)]**, **[함흥모방직공장 (咸興毛紡織工場)]**, **[함흥목재가공공장 (咸興木材加工工場)]**, **[함흥씨리카트벽돌공장]**, **[함흥염화비닐신발공장]**, **[함흥영예군인수지일용품공장 (咸興榮譽軍人樹脂日用品工場)]**, **[룡성기계련합총국 (龍城機械聯合總局)]**, **[2.8비날론련합기업소]**, **[흥남비료련합기업소 (興南肥料聯合企業所)]**, **[흥남제련소 (興南製錬所)]**, **[흥남제약공장 (興南製藥工場)]**; 흥남타올공장, 흥남전극공장 (興南電極工場), 새마을피복공장, 흥남규산염화물공장 (興南硅酸鹽化物工場), 함흥건재공장 (咸興建材工場), 함흥위생자기공장 (咸興衛生瓷器工場), 함흥접착제공장, 함흥과자공장, 흥남판지공장 (興南板紙工場), 함흥비닐신발공장, 흥남구두공장, 함흥블로크공장, 함흥흄관공장, 함흥금속건재공장 (咸興金屬建材工場), 함흥화학건재공장 (咸興化學建材工場), 함흥편직공장 (咸興編織工場), 함흥제사공장 (咸興製絲工場), 함흥신발공장, 함흥구두공장, 함흥가구공장 (咸興家具工場), 함흥목제품공장 (咸興木製品工場), 함흥강철공장 (咸興鋼鐵工場), 함흥고기가공공장, 함흥일용품종합공장

KCNA (39)

공업(38)	2.8비날론련합기업소, 룡성기계련합기업소, 룡성식료공장, 선군주철공장, 성천강전기공장, 신흥산화학공장, 함흥규격품공장, 함흥목재가공공장, 함흥성천강피복공장, 함흥신발공장, 함흥영예군인수지일용품공장, 함흥영예군인원주필공장, 함흥피복공장, 흥남구두공장, 흥남비료련합기업소, 흥남전극공장, 흥남제약공장, 흥남제약기계공장, 5월20일대성공장, 함흥건설기계공장, 함흥기초식품공장, 함흥대형공작기계공장, 함흥련결농기계공장, 함흥목제품공장, 함흥씨리카트벽돌공장, 함흥제사공장, 백운산종합식료공장, 신흥화학련합기업소, 함흥강철공장, 함흥공작기계공장, 함흥구두공장, 함흥반도체재료공장, 함흥시원료기지공장, 함흥압축기공장, 함흥향료공장, 신흥기계공장, 함흥모방직공장, 흥남제련소
전력 (1)	함흥청년발전소

KIET (126-47)

II. 음식료품, 담배 (13-1)	1) 일반	덕산식료공장, 룡성식료공장, 류정식료공장, 사포식료공장, 천기식료공장, 해안식료공장, 함흥어린이식료품공장
	2) 곡물가공	**[함흥곡산공장]**
	3) 육류	서호수산물가공공장, 함흥고기가공공장
	4) 장류	흥남장공장
	5) 사료	함흥배합사료공장
	6) 음료, 주류	함흥사이다공장
III. 섬유, 의복, 신발 (16-5)	1) 방적등	**[함흥모방직공장]**
	2) 직물공장	동흥산직물공장
	3) 방적, 제사, 직조	**[함흥제사공장]**
	5) 편직공장	**[함흥편직공장]**, 동흥산편직공장
	6) 의류	**[성천강피복공장]**, 동흥산피복공장, 함흥수산피복공장, 함흥피복공장, 함흥후방가족피복공장, 흥남수출피복공장
	7) 양말 등	흥남타올공장
	8) 신발	함흥신발공장, 함흥염화비닐신발공장, 흥남구두공장
	10) 가죽	**[함흥어구 및 피복공장]**
IV. 목재, 펄프, 종이 (5-2)	1) 목재	**[밀림단일합영회사]**, **[함흥목재가공공장]**
	3) 종이	동흥산종이공장,사포종이공장, 흥남제지공장
V. 화학 (25-11)	1) 종합	**[신흥화학련합기업소]**, **[2.8비날론련합기업소]**
	3) 비료	**[흥남비료련합기업소]**
	5) 기초화학	**[성천강화학공장]**, **[함흥화학합영공장]**, 룡성화학공장, 본궁규산염화학공장
	6) 염료,도료,시약, 농약 등	**[과학원 함흥분원 애국접착제직장]**, **[함흥살초제공장]**, 사포도금시약공장, 사포물감공장, 흥남시약공장
	7) 고무제품	**[함흥다이야공장]**, 고무운동구공장, 함흥합성고무공장
	8) 합성수지, 수지제품	**[함흥영예군인수지일용품공장]**, 흥남영예군인수지포장용품공장 흥남영예군인수지일용품공장
	9) 제약	**[흥남제약공장]**, 함흥제약공장,
	10) 화장품	**[동흥산화학일용품공장]**, 사포화학일용품공장 성천강화학일용품공장, 회상화학일용품공장, 성천향료공장,
VI. 시멘트, 유리 (7-4)	2) 마그네사이트 크링커 및 내화물	**[함흥규산염화학공장]**
	3) 벽돌	**[함흥흄관공장]**, **[함흥씨리카트벽돌공장]**, **[함흥건설자기공장]**, 동흥산건재공장
	4) 유리	사포거울공장
	6)기타 비금속광물 제품	함흥희토분리공장

VII. 1차 금속산업(4-1)	1) 제철 제강	함흥강철공장
	2) 제련	**[727호제련소]**
	3) 기타 1차금속	사포철선공장, 함흥규격품공장(규격강재 생산)
VIII. 조립금속, 기계장비 (38-19)	1) 종합기계	**[룡성기계련합총국]**, 함흥압축기공장,
	2) 공작기계	**[성천강기계공장]**, **[함흥대형공작기계공장]**, **[12월5일공장]**, **[함흥공작기계공장]**
	3a) 탄광, 광산용	**[함흥물리탐사계기공장]**
	3b) 농업용	**[함흥뜨락또르부속품공장]**, **[함흥련결농기계공장]**
	3c) 기타 산업용	**[함흥건설기계공장]**, [함흥재봉기공장], 함흥상업설비공장,
	4) 정밀	**[함흥과학실험기구종합공장]**, 함흥분석기계공장, 함흥수출품시계공장, 함흥영예군인의료기구공장
	5) 기계부품, 금속가공	**[함흥금속건재공장]**, **[함흥발브공장]**, **[함흥전력설비부속품공장]**, 함흥자전거공장, 함흥형타공장, 함흥방직설비부속품공장, 사포철제학용품공장, 함흥철선.아연도금공장
	6a) 전기기기, 부품	**[본궁전기공장]**, **[성천강전기공장]**, **[6월1일청년전기기구종합공장]**, 함흥전구공장, 흥덕전기공장, 사포전기실험기구공장, 함흥영예군인전기일용품공장, 함흥전기기구공장
	6b) 전자, 자동화기기	**[함흥자동화기구공장]**, **[마동자동화기구공장]**, 사포자동화기구공장, 함흥가정용냉동기공장, 함흥세탁기공장
	6c) 통신기계	함흥통신기계공장
IX. 수송기계 (6)	1) 선박	서호선박수리공장, 흥남배부속품공장
	2) 철도차량	함흥차량부속품공장, 함흥철도종합공장
	3) 자동차	함흥자동차부속품공장, 흥남련결차공장
X. 가구, 잡제품 (10-3)	2) 문방구, 완구, 체육기구	**[함흥영예군인원주필공장]**, 함흥체육기구공장 함흥학용품공장
	3) 악기	함흥선물악기공장
	4) 공예품, 장식품	**[함흥수예품공장]**
	5) 기타	**[함흥일용품종합공장]**, 동흥산영예군인공장, 성천강영예군인공장, 함흥문화용품공장, 함흥문화일용품공장
XI. 전력 (2-1)	2) 화력	**[함흥발전소련합기업소]**, 흥남비료공장 화력발전소

IMPORTANT (20)

공업 (20)	함흥곡산공장, 함흥모방직공장, 함흥제사공장, 함흥편직공장, 성천강피복공장, 신흥화학련합기업소, 2.8비날론련합기업소, 흥남비료련합기업소, 함흥다이야공장, 함흥영예군인수지일용품공장, 흥남제약공장, 함흥씨리카트벽돌공장, 함흥건설자기공장, 함흥공작기계공장, 함흥련결농기계공장, 성천강전기공장, 흥남제련소, 727호제련소, 룡성기계련합기업소, 함흥목재가공공장

Tanchon (Hamnam Province)

KOFC (12-6)

경공업 (1)	제지 (1)	단천종이공장
중화공업 (6-3)	금속 (1)	**[단천제련소]**
	기계 (2)	**[단천광산기계공장(4월28일공장)]**, 단천공작기계공장
	조선 (1)	단천선박수리공장
	건재 (2)	**[단천마그네샤종합공장]**, 대흥광산마그네샤크링커공장
채취 (4-3)	철 (1)	단천광산
	탄광 (3)	**[검덕광업련합기업소]**, **[룡양광산]**, **[대흥청년영웅광산 (전 대흥청년광업종합기업소)]**
전력 (1)	수력 (1)	허천강발전소 4호

MOU (29-6) 공업 (15-4), 광업 (13-2) 전력 (1)

건재 (4-1)	**[단천마그네샤공장]**; 단천시멘트공장, 대흥마그네샤크링카분공장, 단천내화물공장
경공업 (7)	단천시약공장, 단천장공장, 단천초물공장, 단천포장제공장, 단천고려약공장, 광천식료공장, 광천영예군인수지일용품공장
기계 (1)	단천광산기계공장
전자 (1-1)	**[단천영예군인반도체공장]**
제철/조선 (2-2)	**[단천선박수리공장]**, **[단천제련소]**
광업 (13-2)	**[검덕광업련합기업소]**, **[대흥청년광업종합기업소 (대흥청년(영웅)광산)]**; 검덕광산, 단천대리석광산, 공무분공장, 남풍광산, 백바위광산, 북대천광산, 광천광산, 용양광산, 남풍광산, 로은광산, 금골광산
전렬 (1)	허천강4호발전소

IPA (13-6)

공업 (7-3)	**[단천가죽일용품공장]**, **[단천마그네샤공장]**, **[단천제련소(端川製鍊所)]**; 단천수지건재공장 (端川樹脂建材工場), 단천옥돌가공공장, 광천석재가공공장 (廣泉石材加工工場), 광천식료공장 (廣泉食料工場)
광업 (5-2)	**[검덕광업련합기업소 (檢德鑛業聯合企業所)]**, **[룡양광산(龍陽鑛山)]**; 석면광산(石綿鑛山), 로천광산(露天鑛山), 대흥광산(大興鑛山)
전력 (1-1)	**[허천강발전소 4호발전소]**; 양평발전소

KCNA (11)

공업 (5)	단천갱목생산사업소, 단천광산기계공장, 단천내화물공장, 단천마그네샤공장, 단천제련소
광업 (5)	검덕광업련합기업소, 대흥청년영웅광산 (대흥광업종합기업소), 룡양광산, 남풍광산, 제남탄광
전력 (1)	단천청년발전소

KIET (39-13)

I. 광업 (6-3)	2) 철광	**[검덕광업련합기업소]**
	3) 비철	북대천광산
	4) 비금속광물	**[룡양광산]**, **[동암광산]**, 광천노동자구 광천광산, 단천대리석광산
II. 음식료품, 담배 (5-1)	1) 일반	**[광천식료공장]**, 룡양식료공장
	3) 육류	단천시 남새공장
	4) 장류	단천장공장, 검덕노동자구 검덕장공장
III. 섬유, 의복, 신발 (4)	4) 견직공장	단천견직공장
	6) 의류	광천옷공장, 단천피복공장
	7) 양말 등	룡양양말공장
IV. 목재, 펄프, 종이 (3)	1) 목재	단천목제품공장
	3) 종이	단천공장, 단천종이공장
V. 화학 (8-4)	3) 비료	**[단천린안바료공장]**
	5) 기초화학	광천노동자구 광천화학공장, 단천가성소다공장, 단천탄산소다공장
	6) 염료,도료,시약, 농약 등	**[단천시약공장]**
	8) 합성수지, 수지제품	**[광천영예군인수지일용품공장]**, 단천포장재공장
	10) 화장품	**[단천화학일용품공장]**
VI. 시멘트, 유리 (4-1)	1) 시멘트	단천세멘트공장
	2) 마그네사이트 크링거 및 내화물	**[단천마그네샤종합공장]**
	4) 유리	단천유리일용품공장
	5) 도자기	덕주오지공장
VII. 1차 금속산업(1)	2) 제련	단천제련소
VIII. 조립금속, 기계장비 (4-2)	3a) 탄광, 광산용	**[단천광산기계공장(4월28일공장)]**, **[단천탐사기계공장]**
	6b) 전자, 자동화기기	단천영예군인반도체공장, 단천영예군인텔리비존공장
IX. 수송기계 (1-1)	1) 선박	**[단천선박수리공장]**
X. 가구, 잡제품 (1)	5) 기타	광천영예군인공장
XI. 전력 (2-1)	1) 수력	**[상술령청년발전소]**
	2) 화력	광천발전소

IMPORTANT (8)

공업 (5)	광천식료공장, 단천마그네샤(종합)공장, 단천광산기계공장, 단천선박수리공장, 단천제련소
광업 (3)	검덕광업련합기업소, 대흥청년영웅광산 (전 대흥청년광업종합기업소), 룡양광산

Sinpho (Hamnam Province)

KOFC (7-2)

경공업 (4)	식품 (4)	신포어류통조림공장, 신포냉동공장, 신포정제소금공장, 신포통조림공장
중화공업 (3-2)	조선 (2)	**[룩대조선소]**, **[신포조선소]**
	건재 (1)	신포세멘트공장

MOU (3)

건재 (1)	신포시멘트공장
경공업 (1)	신포물고기통조림공장
기계 (1)	신포향주철직장

IPA (2-1)

공업 (2-1)	[신포물고기통졸임공장]; 신포통졸임공장

KCNA (1)

공업 (1)	신포정제소금공장

KIET (13-2)

I. 광업 (1)	1) 탄광	신포탄광
II. 음식료품, 담배 (5-1)	1) 일반	신포식료공장, 신포어린이식료공장
	3) 육류	**[신포물고기통조림공장]**, 신포포도가공공장
	4) 장류	신포장공장
III. 섬유, 의복, 신발 (2)	2) 직물공장	신포직물공장
	6) 의류	신포옷공장
IV. 목재, 펄프, 종이 (1)	3) 종이	신포종이공장
V. 화학 (1)	8) 합성수지, 수지제품	신포영예군인수지일용품공장
VI. 시멘트, 유리 (1)	1) 시멘트	신포세멘트공장
IX. 수송기계 (1-1)	1) 선박	**[신포조선소]**
X. 가구, 잡제품 (1)	5) 기타	신포영예군인공장

IMPORTANT (1)

공업 (1)	신포물고기통졸임공장

Kun (Hamnam Province)

KOFC. 군, 지구 (60-7)

10	수동구 (1)
9	북청군
8	신흥군 (1), 허천군 (2)
5	영광군 (1)
4	리원군 (1)
3	정평군
2	고원군 (1), 금야군, 덕성군, 락원군
1	그호지구, 요덕군, 장연군, 함주군, 홍원군

경공업 (4) 식품 (3), 신발 (1)	광명성제염소 (금야), 락원대흥수산사업소 정제소금분공장 (락원), 북청과일가공공장; 북청신발공장 (북청)
중화공업 (10-2) 기계 (3), 철도차량 (1), 전기/전자 (1), 조선 (1), 건재 (4)	락원수지건재경장 (락원), 정평트랙터부속품공장, 금진강기계공장 (정평); 7월6일철도공장 (라흥철도차량공장); (리원); 흥상전기기구공장 (요덕); **[리원선박수리공장 (리원)]**; **[부래산세멘트공장] (고원)]**, 리원유리공장 (리원), 신흥세멘트공장 (신흥), 운포과일가공공장 (홍원)
재취 (14-2) 철 (4), 비 (1), 탄광 (8), 석회석 (1)	덕성광산 (덕성), 리원광산 (리원), 룡원광산, 허천광산; 만덕광산 (허천); **[함남지구탄광련합기업소]**, 고원탄광, 12월16일탄광, 운곡탄광, 수동탄광, 둔전탄광, 성내탄광 (수동구), **[상농광업련합기업소 (허천)]**; 부래산광산
전력 (32-3) 수력 (31), 기타 (1)	금야강군민발전소 (금야), 장흥청년발전소 (덕성), 북청강발전소 7-12, 라흥천발전소 (북천), 덕지강발전소 2호, 10-11호 (수동구), [부전강발전소 1-6호], 성천강15호발전소 (신흥), **[장진강발전소 1-5호 (영광)]**, 장연군민발전소 (장연), 구창(금진강4호)발전소 (정평), 추상(금진강3호)발전소 (함주), **[허천강발전소 1-3호]**, 황곡7호발전소 (허천); 경수로발전소 (중단) (금호지구)

MOU 군 (57-6) 공업 (38-1) 광업 (14-2) 전력 (5-3)

8	금야군
7	고원군, 리원군, 수동구(1), 허천군 (2)
5	정평군 (1)
3	락원군, 신흥군 (1), 영광군 (1)
2	함주군 (1), 홍원군
1	부전군, 북청군, 요덕군

건재 (6)	부래산시멘트공장 (고원군), 금야시멘트공장 (금야군), 락원건제공장, 락원관개수리공장 (락원군), 정평건재공장 (정평군), 허천시멘트공장 (허천군)
경공업 (25)	고원식료공장, 고원양말공장, 고원옷공장, 고원장공장 (고원군), 금야견식공장, 금야군식료공장, 금야기초식품공장, 금야은하피복공장, 금야장공장, 금야제약공장 (금야군), 락원일용품공장 (락원군), 리원공예품공장, 리원군종이공장, 리원장공장 (리원군), 부전감자전분공장 (부전군), 북청신발공장 (북청군), 신흥수출피복공장 (신흥군), 영광유리일용품공장, 영광장공장 (영광군), 요덕비날론인견직공장 (요덕군), 정평초물공장, 정평군직물공장 (정평군), 함주군장공장 (함주군), 허천종이공장 (허천군), 홍원철제일용품공장 (홍원군)

기계 (5-1)	고원광산기계공장, 고원농기구공장 (고원군), 7월6일철도공장 (리원군), **[정평농기계부속품공장 (정평군)]**, 허천군농기구공장 (허천군)
화학 (2)	리원화학공장 (리원군), 정평군애국복합미생물비료공장 (정평군)
광업 (14-2)	금야청년탄광 (금야군), 리원광산, 증산광산 (리원군), **[함남지구탄광련합기업소]**; 고원탄광, 수동탄광, 12월16일탄광, 둔전탄광, 운곡탄광 (수동구), 신흥광산 (신흥군), **[상농광업련합기업소]**; 만덕광산, 상농광산 (허천군), 홍원탄광 (홍원군)
전력 (5-3)	덕지강발전소 (수동구), 부전강발전소 (신흥군), **[장진강발전소 (영광군)]**, **[금진강흥봉청년발전소 (함주군)]**, **[허천강발전소 (허천군)]**

IPA (233-44)

고원군 (14-4)

공업 (10-3)	**[고원양말공장]**, **[고원나무그릇공장]**, **[부래산세멘트공장]**; 고원식료공장, 고원일용품공장, 고원종이공장, 고원기계공장, 상산토기공장(上山土器工場), 군내식료공장(郡內食料工場), 황송건재공장
광업 (4-1)	**[부래산석회석광산 (浮來山石灰石鑛山)]**; 부래산광산, 남흥니탄광산, 풍남광산(豊南鑛山)

금야군 (28-4)

공업 (24-2)	**[광명성제염소 (光明星製鹽所)]**, **[비단견직공장 (緋緞絹織工場)]**; 금야화강석공장 (金野花剛石工場), 금야장공장(金野醬工場), 금야과실가공공장 (金野果實加工工場), 금야수산물가공공장 (金野水産物加工工場), 금야고기가공공장, 금야포장용기공장 (金野包裝容器工場), 금야식료공장, 금야일용품공장 (金野日用品工場), 금야화학공장 (金野化學工場), 금야종이공장, 금야농기구공장, 금야피복공장, 금야건재공장, 금야제약공장, 가진병졸임공장, 인흥식료공장, 인흥옷공장, 인흥철제일용품공장, 인흥종이공장, 금사도자기공장, 금야견직공장, 청동화강석공장
광업 (4-2)	**[금야청년탄광 (金野青年炭鑛)]**, **[동흥팽윤토광산 (東興澎潤土鑛山)]**; 백산팽윤토광산, 신성탄광

덕성군 (12-2)

공업 (10-1)	**[덕성과일가공공장]**; 덕성장공장, 덕성철제일용품공장, 덕성전동기공장, 덕성직물공장, 덕성피복공장, 덕성소다공장, 덕성농기계공장, 덕성종이공장, 덕성제약공장
광업 (2-1)	**[덕성광산 (德城鑛山)]**; 철산광산

락원군 (16-3)

공업 (16-3)	**[락원건재공장 (樂園建材工場)]**, **[락원식료공장 (樂園食料工場)]**, **[락원직물공장 (樂園織物工場)]**; 락원주철관공장 (樂園鑄鐵管工場), 락원수지공장 (樂園樹脂工場), 락원랭동공장, 락원선박수리공장, 락원수산물가공공장, 락원수지건재공장, 락원기계공장, 락원세멘트공장, 락원종이공장, 락원일용품공장, 락원장공장, 사동건재공장, 사동농기구공장

리원군 (20-7)

공업 (17-6)	**[리원공예품공장 (利原工藝品工場)]**, **[리원선박수리공장 (利原船泊修理工場)]**, **[리원식료공장 (利原食料工場)]**, **[리원종이공장]**, **[리원직물공장 (利原織物工場)]**, **[리원철도공장 (利原鐵道工場)]**; 리원장공장, 리원피복공장, 리원가구공장, 리원유리공장, 리원물고기가공공장, 라흥철도공장, 라흥철도침목공장, 라흥세탁기공장, 라흥식료품공장, 구읍소석회공장, 염성내화물공장
광업 (3-1)	**[리원광산 (利原鑛山)]**; 라흥규석광산, 기암광산

부전군 (14-0)

공업 (14-0)	부전직물공장, 부전식료공장, 부전일용품공장, 부전기계수리공장, 부전종이공장, 부전목제품공장, 부전성냥공장, 부전옷공장, 부전가성소다공장, 부전토기공장, 부전제약공장, 부전농기구공장, 호반목재일용품공장, 릉구일용품공장

북청군 (24-2)

공업 (24-2)	**[북청과수기계공장 (北靑果樹機械工場)], [북청량곡기계공장 (北靑糧穀機械工場)]**; 북청과일가공공장, 북청신발공장, 북청일용품공장, 북청과실가공공장, 북청옷공장, 북청방사공장, 북청성냥공장, 북청제약공장, 북청건재공장, 북청식료공장, 신창식료공장, 신창피복공장, 신창종이공장, 신창화학공장, 신창철제일용품공장, 신창수산물가공공장, 룡전과일가공공장, 서리성냥공장, 서리과수기계공장, 서리장공장, 청흥직물공장, 북청직물공장 (北靑織物工場)

신흥군 (10-3)

공업 (8-2)	**[신흥제약공장 (新興製藥工場)], [신흥화학일용품공장 (新興化學日用品工場)]**; 신흥식료공장, 신흥일용품공장, 신흥직물공장, 신흥옷공장, 신흥화학공장, 발전전기일용품공장
전력 (2-1)	[부전강발전소 (赴戰江發電所)]; 하원천발전소

영광군 (13-3)

공업 (8-1)	**[영광전주공장 (榮光電柱工場)]**; 영광식료공장, 영광일용품공장, 영광건재공장, 영광벽돌공장, 영광종이공장, 수전전기일용품공장, 수전옷공장
광업 (1-1)	**[천불산광산 (千佛山鑛山)]**
전력 (4-1)	**[장진강발전소 (長津江發電所)]**; 성천강29호발전소 (城川江二十九號發電所), 성천강30호발전소 (城川江三十號發電所), 성천강32호발전소 (城川江三十二號發電所)

요덕군 (12-2)

공업 (8-2)	**[요덕제약공장 (曜德製藥工場)], [요덕종이공장]**; 요덕식료공장, 요덕화학일용품공장, 요덕직물공장, 구읍박제품공장, 구읍화학공장, 구읍제약공장
전력 (4)	금야강발전소 (金野江發電所), 요덕발전소 (耀德發電所), 미삼발전소 (美三發電所), 평원발전소 (坪原發電所)

장진군 (9-2)

공업 (9-2)	**[장진목재가공공장 (長津木材加工工場)], [장진합판공장 (長津合板工場)]**; 장진종이공장, 장진식료공장, 장진직물공장, 장진제약공장, 장진가죽공장, 만풍식료공장, 황초목재가공공장

정평군 (21-0)

공업 (17)	정평내화물공장 (定坪耐火物工場), 정평도자기공장, 정평직물공장, 정평피복공장, 정평식료공장 정평일용품공장, 정평벽돌공장, 정평종이공장, 신상식료공장, 신상일용품공장, 신상편직공장, 신상목재가공공장, 신상장판지공장, 신상전동기공장, 신상기계공장, 신상라이타공장, 동천과일가공공장, 부평배합먹이공장, 부평벽돌공장
광업 (4)	정평광산, 신상탄광, 정평탄광. 서흥니탄광산

함주군 (6-1)

공업 (6-1)	**[흥상요업공장 (興上窯業工場)]**; 함주담배공장, 함주건재공장, 수흥요업공장, 신경기와공장, 신성련결농기계공장

허천군 (13-5)

공업 (5-1)	**[허천식료공장 (虛川食料工場)]**; 허천일용품공장, 허천전등알공장, 허천직물공장, 룡원식료공장
광업 (4-3)	**[만덕광산 (萬德鑛山)]**, **[상농광산 (上農鑛山)]**, **[허천청년광산 (虛川靑年鑛山)]**; 화장광산
전력 (4-1)	**[허천강수력발전소 (虛川江水力發電所)]**; 금창발전소 (金倉發電所), 은흥발전소 (殷興發電所), 황곡발전소 (黃谷發電所)

홍원군 (13-4)

공업 (10-3)	**[홍원일용품공장 (洪原日用品工場)]**, **[운포세멘트공장]**, **[운포과일가공공장]**; 홍원식료공장, 홍원피복공장, 홍원종이공장, 홍원가구공장, 경포화학공장, 남산토기공장, 남산어린이식료품공장
광업 (1-1)	**[운포광산 (雲浦鑛山)]**
전력 (2)	룡삼발전소, 원덕발전소

소동구 (8-2)

공업 (1)	룡평피복공장
광업 (7-2)	**[고원탄광 (高原炭鑛)]**, **[운곡탄광 (雲谷炭鑛)]**; 성남탄광, 성내탄광, 수산탄광, 장량탄광, 천을탄광

KCNA. 군 (27)

4	영광군, 정평군
3	고원군, 리원군, 수동구, 함주군
2	금야군, 허천군
1	부전군, 신흥군, 홍원군

공업 (9)	고원양말공장, 고원옷공장 (고원군), 광명성제염소 (금야군), 7월6일철도공장, 라흥콩크리트침목공장 (리원군), 부전감자전분공장 (부전군), 금진강기계공장 (정평군), 함주림업기계공장 (함주군), 홍원자동화기구공장 (홍원군)
광업 (5)	고원광산 (고원군), 리원광산 (리원군), 함남지구탄광련합기업소, 운곡탄광 (수동구), 허천청년광산 (허천군)
전력 (13)	금야강군민발전소 (금야군), 덕지강청년발전소 (수동구), 부전강발전소 (신흥군), 장진강발전소, 성천강29호발전소, 성천강30호발전소, 성천강32호발전소 (영광군), 금진강발전소, 금진강구창청년발전소, 금진강제6호청년발전소 (정평군), 금진강흥봉청년발전소, 흥봉발전소 (함주군), 허천강발전소 (허천군)

KIET (186-43)

고원군 (19-6)

I. 광업 (1)	4) 비금속광물	부래산광산
II. 음식료품, 담배 (1)	1) 일반	고원식료공장
III. 섬유, 의복, 신발 (7-2)	4) 견직공장	고원장공장
	5) 편직공장	고원배합사료공장
	6) 의류	**[고원옷공장]**, 고원수출피복공장, 고원여자옷공장
	7) 양말 등	**[고원양말공장]**
	10) 가죽	고원모피가공공장
V. 화학 (2)	8) 합성수지, 수지제품	고원영예군인수지일용품공장
	10) 화장품	고원화학일용품공장
VI. 시멘트, 유리 (1-1)	1) 시멘트	**[부래산세멘트공장]**
VIII. 조립금속, 기계장비 (1-1)	3a) 탄광, 광산용	**[고원광산기계공장]**
IX. 수송기계 (1)	2) 철도차량	고원철도영예군인공장
X. 가구, 잡제품 (4-2)	2) 문방구, 완구, 체육기구	**[고원어린이자전거공장]**
	4) 공예품, 장식품	광명공예품공장
	5) 기타	**[고원영예군인일용품공장]**, 고원일용품공장
XI. 전력 (1)	2) 화력	고원군발전소

금야군 (16-5)

I. 광업 (3-1)	1) 탄광	**[금야청년탄광]**
	3) 비철	금야청년광산
	4) 비금속광물	금야화강석광산
II. 음식료품, 담배 (4)	1) 일반	인흥과일공장
	3) 육류	원평수산물가공공장
	4) 장류	금야장공장, 인흥장공장
III. 섬유, 의복, 신발 (3-1)	4) 견직공장	**[금야견직공장]**
	5) 편직공장	금야편직물공장
	6) 의류	금야수출피복공장
V. 화학 (3-2)	3) 비료	금야흙보산비료공장
	9) 제약	**[금야제약공장]**
	10) 화장품	**[금야화학일용품공장]**
VI. 시멘트, 유리 (1)	4) 유리	인흥유리공장
VIII. 조립금속, 기계장비 (1)	5) 기계부품, 금속가공	인흥철제일용품공장
X. 가구, 잡제품 (1-1)	5) 기타	**[금야영예군인일용품공장]**

덕성군 (7-3)

I. 광업 (1-1)	2) 철광	**[덕성광산]**
II. 음식료품, 담배 (1-1)	3) 육류	**[덕성과실가공공장]**
V. 화학 (2)	5) 기초화학	덕성가성소다공장
	9) 제약	덕성제약공장
X. 가구, 잡제품 (1-1)	5) 기타	**[덕성영예탄부공장]**
XI. 전력 (2)	2) 화력	락원1, 2호발전소

락원군 (5)

II. 음식료품, 담배 (1)	1) 일반	삼호식료공장
IV. 목재, 펄프, 종이 (1)	3) 종이	락원종이공장
V. 화학 (2)	8) 합성수지, 수지제품	락원수지건재공장
	9) 제약	락원제약공장
X. 가구, 잡제품 (1)	5) 기타	락원일용품공장

리원군 (15-3)

I. 광업 (4)	1) 탄광	리원탄광
	2) 철광	리원 일원 적철광, 리원광산
	4) 비금속광물	라흥규석광산
II. 음식료품, 담배 (1)	1) 일반	리원식료공장
III. 섬유, 의복, 신발 (1)	6) 의류	리원수출피복공장
IV. 목재, 펄프, 종이 (1)	3) 종이	리원종이공장
V. 화학 (3-1)	5) 기초화학	리원학공장
	9) 제약	**[리원영예군인제약공장]**
	10) 화장품	리원화학일용품공장
VI. 시멘트, 유리 (1-1)	3) 벽돌	**[라흥콩크리트침목공장]**
VIII. 조립금속, 기계장비 (1)	6b) 전자, 자동화기기	리원세탁기공장
X. 가구, 잡제품 (2-1)	2) 문방구, 완구, 체육기구	**[7월6일철도공장(라흥철도공장)]**
	5) 기타	리원일용품공장
XI. 전력 (1)	2) 화력	문암1, 2, 3호발전소

부전군 (7)

II. 음식료품, 담배 (1)	1) 일반	부전식료공장
III. 섬유, 의복, 신발 (2)	2) 직물공장	부전직물공장
	6) 의류	부전피복공장
IV. 목재, 펄프, 종이 (2)	1) 목재	부전목제품공장
	3) 종이	부전제지공장
VIII. 조립금속, 기계장비 (1)	1) 종합기계	부전군기계수리공장
XI. 전력 (1)	2) 화력	부전군의 소형발전소

북청군 (16-6)

I. 광업 (1)	1) 탄광	북청탄광
II. 음식료품, 담배 (4-1)	1) 일반	**[풍천과일가공공장]**
	3) 육류	대덕수산합영회사, 과실가공공장 고기 및 물고기 가공공장
III. 섬유, 의복, 신발 (3)	2) 직물공장	북청직물공장
	3) 방적, 제사, 직조	북청방사공장
	8) 신발	북청신발공장
V. 화학 (1-1)	8) 합성수지, 수지제품	**[북청수지일용품공장]**
VI. 시멘트, 유리 (1)	5) 도자기	북청도자기공장
VIII. 조립금속, 기계장비 (6-4)	1) 종합기계	**[북청기계공장]**, 신창기계수리공장
	3b) 농업용	북청농기계공장
	3c) 기타 산업용	**[북청과수기계공장]**, **[신북청철길기계공장]**
	5) 기계부품, 금속가공	**[북청철제일용품공장]**

수동구 (12-4)

I. 광업 (7-2)	1) 탄광	**[함남지구탄광련합기업소]**, **[고원탄광]**, 성내탄광, 둔전탄광, 운곡탄광, 12월16일탄광, 수동(청년)탄광
II. 음식료품, 담배 (2-1)	1) 일반	수동식료공장
	4) 장류	**[수동장공장]**
V. 화학 (2)	10) 화장품	고원화학일용품공장, 수동화학일용품공장
VI. 시멘트, 유리 (1-1)	5) 도자기	**[수동토기공장]**

신흥군 (19-3)

I. 광업 (2)	1) 탄광	신흥탄광
	4) 비금속광물	신흥광산
II. 음식료품, 담배 (1)	1) 일반	신흥식료공장
III. 섬유, 의복, 신발 (3-1)	2) 직물공장	**[신흥직물공장]**
	5) 편직공장	신흥편직공장
	8) 신발	신흥신발공장
IV. 목재, 펄프, 종이 (2)	1) 목재	신흥목제품공장
	3) 종이	신흥종이공장
V. 화학 (4)	5) 기초화학	신흥가성소다공장
	9) 제약	신흥제약공장
	10)화장품	신흥치약공장, 신흥화학일용품공장
VI. 시멘트, 유리 (2-1)	1) 시멘트	신흥세멘트공장
	3) 벽돌	**[길봉애국인도블로크공장]**
VIII. 조립금속, 기계장비 (1)	6a) 전기기기, 부품	신흥전기일용품공장
X. 가구, 잡제품 (2)	4) 공예품, 장식품	신흥영예군인공예품공장
	5) 기타	신흥문화일용품공장
XI. 전력 (2-1)	1) 수력	**[부전강발전소]**
	2) 화력	성천강1호발전소

영광군 (9-2)

II. 음식료품, 담배 (1)	4) 장류	영광장공장
III. 섬유, 의복, 신발 (2)	3) 방적, 제사, 직조	영광직조공장
	6) 의류	영광피복공장
VIII. 조립금속, 기계장비 (3-1)	3c) 기타 산업용	기상수문기계공장
	5) 기계부품, 금속가공	영광군철제일용품공장
	6a) 전기기기, 부품	**[영광전기공장]**
X. 가구, 잡제품 (1)	5) 기타	영광영예군인공장
XI. 전력 (2-1)	1) 수력	**[장진강발전소]**
	2) 화력	영광1호발전소

요덕군 (10-1)

II. 음식료품, 담배 (1)	1) 일반	요덕식료공장
III. 섬유, 의복, 신발 (3-1)	2) 직물공장	요덕직물공장
	3) 방적, 제사, 직조	**[요덕비날론인견사공장]**
	6) 의류	요덕피복공장
IV. 목재, 펄프, 종이 (1)	3) 종이	요덕종이공장
VIII. 조립금속, 기계장비 (1)	1) 종합기계	요덕군기계수리공장
X. 가구, 잡제품 (4)	1) 가구	요덕가구공장
	3) 악기	요덕악기공장
	4) 공예품, 장식품	요덕박제품공장
	5) 기타	요덕영예군인공장

장진군 (2)

I. 광업 (1)	4) 비금속광물	중흥광산
V. 화학 (1)	5) 기초화학	장진가성소다공장

정평군 (15-2)

I. 광업 (1-1)	3) 비철	**[정평광산]**
II. 음식료품, 담배 (3-1)	1) 일반	정평식료공장
	3) 육류	**[신상과일가공공장]**
	5) 사료	정평배합사료공장
III. 섬유, 의복, 신발 (2)	5) 편직공장	신상편직공장
	10) 가죽	광포합영회사
IV. 목재, 펄프, 종이 (3)	1) 목재	신상목재공장
	3) 종이	신상장판공장, 정평종이공장
VI. 시멘트, 유리 (3)	2) 마그네사이트 크링커 및 내화물	정평내화물공장
	3) 벽돌	신성천탄광콘크리트동발공장
	5) 도자기	정평도자기공장

VIII. 조립금속, 기계장비 (2)	3b) 농업용	정평농기계부속품공장
	6b) 전자, 자동화기기	신상영예군인자동화기구공장
XI. 전력 (1)	2) 화력	금진강발전소

함주군 (10-4)

I. 광업 (1)	1) 탄광	함주탄광
II. 음식료품, 담배 (1)	2) 곡물가공	함주기름공장
III. 섬유, 의복, 신발 (1-1)	5) 편직공장	**[함주편직공장]**
V. 화학 (1-1)	10) 화장품	**[함주화학일용품공장]**
VI. 시멘트, 유리 (2-1)	3) 벽돌	**[흥상요업공장]**, 함주화학건재공장,
VIII. 조립금속, 기계장비 (3-1)	3c) 기타 산업용	함주림업기계공장
	5) 기계부품, 금속가공	**[함주영예군인철제일용품공장]**
	6b) 전자, 자동화기기	함주자동화기구공장
X. 가구, 잡제품 (1)	5) 기타	함주영예군인일용품공장

허천군 (15-3)

I. 광업 (5-2)	1) 탄광	허천탄광, 만덕광산
	2) 철광	**[룡원광산]**, 허천청년광산
	3) 비철	**[상농광업련합기업소]**
II. 음식료품, 담배 (1)	1)일반	허천식료공장
III. 섬유, 의복, 신발 (1)	6) 의류	허천피복공장
V. 화학 (1)	10) 화장품	허천화학일용품공장
VI. 시멘트, 유리 (2)	1) 시멘트	허천세멘트공장
	5) 도자기	허천토기공장
VIII. 조립금속, 기계장비 (1)	6a) 전기기기, 부품	허천군전등알공장
X. 가구, 잡제품 (1)	4) 공예품, 장식품	허천초물공장
XI. 전력 (3-1)	1) 수력	**[허천강발전소]**
	2) 화력	내종발전소, 황곡2호발전소

홍원군 (9-1)

I. 광업 (1)	4) 비금속광물	운포광산
III. 섬유, 의복, 신발 (1)	4) 견직공장	홍원견직공장
VIII. 조립금속, 기계장비 (1)	6b) 전자, 자동화기기	홍원자동화기구공장
IX. 수송기계 (1-1)	1) 선박	**[홍원조선소]**
X. 가구, 잡제품 (3)	1) 가구	홍원가구공장
	5) 기타	홍원영예군인공장,홍원일용품공장
XI. 전력 (2)	2) 화력	룡삼발전소, 원덕발전소

IMPORTANT (19)

4	허천군
3	고원군, 금야군, 수동구
2	리원군
1	덕성군, 신흥군, 영광군, 요덕군

공업 (6)	고원옷공장, 고원양말공장, 부래산세멘트공장 (고원군), 금야제약공장, 광명성제염소 (금야군), 7월6일철도공장(라흥철도공장) (리원군)
광업 (9)	금야청년탄광 (금야군), 덕성광산 (덕성군), 리원광산 (리원군), 함남지구탄광련합기업소, 고원탄광, 운곡탄광 (수동구), 상농광업련합기업소, 만덕광산, 허천청년광산 (허천군)
전력 (4)	부전강발전소 (신흥군), 장진강발전소 (영광군), 금야강 (국민)발전소 (요덕군), 허천강발전소 (허천군)

Wonsan (Kangwon Province)

KOFC (27-5)

경공업 (7-1)	식품 (5)	원산수산물가공공장, 원산랭공장, 원산맥주공장, 원산곡산공장, 원산담배공장
	신빌 (2)	**[원산구두공장]**, 원산신발공장
중화공업 (14-4)	금속 (1)	**[원산금제련소]**
	기계 (3)	**[원산충성호트랙터공장]**, 원산뜨락또르부속품공장, 원산원동기공장
	철도차량 (2)	갈마철도차량공장, 원산철도차량공장 (6월4일차량공장)
	전기/전자 (2)	원산전선공장, 원산축전지공장
	조선 (2)	**[원산조선소]**, 원산선박수리공장
	화학 (1)	**[원산화학공장]**
	건재 (3)	원산판유리공장, 원산전등알공장, 원산유리병공장
재취 (1)	비 (1)	원산강철공장
전력 (5)	수력 (5)	원산청년발전소 1-4호, 원산군민발전소

MOU (31-3)

경공업 (22)	봉춘식료가공공장, 송동원은하피복공장, 송동원종합식료공장, 원산가구공장, 원산갈마옷공장, 원산고기가공공장, 원산구두공장, 원산방적공장, 원산봉화피복공장, 원산수출피복공장, 원산신발공장, 원산영예군인가방공장, 원산영예군인수지가공공장, 원산영예군인수지일용품공장, 원산유리병공장, 원산은하피복공장, 원산장공장, 원산충성남자옷공장, 원산통신케블공장, 원산편직공장, 원산화장품공장, 부운식료공장
기계(7-2)	**[6월4일차량공장 (원산철도차량련합기업소)]**, **[충성호뜨락또르공장]**; 원산기계공장, 원산뜨락또르부속품공장, 원산원동기공장, 원산자동차수리공장, 송도기계공장
제철/조선 (1)	원산선박수리공장
화학 (1-1)	[원산화학공장]

IPA (19-13)

공업 (19-13)	**[금강원동합영회사(金剛原動合營會社)]**, **[6월4일차량종합기업소(六月四日車輛綜合企業所)]**, **[원산가성소다공장]**, **[원산방적공장(元山紡績工場)**, **[원산세멘트공장]**, **[원산수출피복공장(元山輸出被服工場)]**, **[원산영예군인가방공장]**, **[원산전선공장(元山電線工場)]**, **[원산조선소]**, **[원산철제일용품공장(元山鐵製日用品工場)]**, **[원산칠감공장]**, **[원산화학공장(元山化學工場)]**, **[충성호뜨락또르공장]**; 원산뜨락또르부속품공장, 원산편직공장(元山編織工場), 원산선박수리공장, 원산원동기공장, 산영예군인수지일용품공장(元山榮譽軍人樹脂日用品工場), 원산부재공장(元山部材工場)

KCNA (15)

공업 (13)	원산기초식품공장, 송도원종합식료공장, 원산만제염소, 원산제염소, 원산방적공장, 원산수출피복공장, 원산구두공장, 6월4일차량종합기업소, 금강원동기공장, 원산유리병공장, 원산전등알공장, 원산철도차량련합기업소, 원산화학공장
전력 (2)	원산군민발전소, 원산청년발전소

KIET (46-20)

II. 음식료품, 담배 (8-5)	1) 일반	**[봉춘식료가공공장]**, **[송도원식료공장]**
	2) 곡물가공	**[원산곡산공장]**, 원산과자공장, 원산밀가루종합가공공장
	4) 장류	**[원산장공장]**
	6) 음료, 주류	**[원산맥주공장]**
	7) 담배	원산담배공장
III. 섬유, 의복, 신발 (9-2)	3) 방적, 제사, 직조	원산직조공장,
	4) 견직공장	원산견직공장
	5) 편직공장	원산편직공장
	6) 의류	**[원산수출피복공장]**, 송도원수출피복공장, 갈마옷공장, 원산피복공장
	9) 가방	**[원산영예군인가방공장]**, 원산가방공장
IV. 목재, 펄프, 종이 (1)	1) 목재	원산목재일용품공장
V. 화학 (7-4)	5) 기초화학	**[원산가성소다공장]**, **[원산화학공장]**, 갈마화학공장, 삼봉화학공장
	6) 염료,도료,시약, 농약 등	**[원산 칠감공장]**
	8) 합성수지, 수지제품	**[원산영예군인수지일용품공장]**, 원산수지일용품공장
VI. 시멘트, 유리 (2-1)	1) 시멘트	**[원산세멘트공장]**
	4) 유리	원산유리병공장
VIII. 조립금속, 기계장비 (13-5)	1) 종합기계	**[원산기계공장]**
	3a) 탄광, 광산용	**[금강원동합영회사]**
	3c) 기타 산업용	**[송도기계공장]**, 충성호뜨락또르공장, 원산뜨락또르부속품공장,
	5) 기계부품, 금속가공	**[원산철제일용품공장]**, 원산관풍기계공장, 원산형타공장
	6a) 전기기기, 부품	**[원산전선공장]**, 원산전기일용품공장, 원산전동기공장,

	6b) 전자, 자동화기기	원산텔레비죤조립공장
	6c) 통신기계	원산통신기계공장
IX. 수송기계 (3-3)	1) 선박	**[원산선박수리공장], [원산시 원산조선소]**
	2) 철도차량	**[원산철도차량공장]**
X. 가구, 잡제품 (3)	2) 문방구, 완구, 체육기구	원산만년필공장
	4) 공예품, 장식품	원산기념품공장, 원산건축장식품공장

IMPORTANT (12)

공업 (12)	원산수출피복공장, 원산영예군인가방공장, 원산화학공장, 원산영예군인수지일용품공장, 금강원동합영회사, 원산전선공장, 원산선박수리공장, 원산조선소, 6월4일차량종합기업소 (원산철도차량공장), 원산구두공장, 원산충성호트랙터공장, 원산방적공장

Munchon (Kangwon Province)

KOFC (8-3)

경공업 (1)	식품 (1)	문천냉동공장
중화공업 (7-3)	금속 (5)	**[문천아연제련소], [문평제련소], [9월21일제련소]**, 문천베어링공장, 문천강철공장
	기계 (1)	5월18일(문천기계)공장
	건재 (1)	문평세멘트공장

MOU (10)

건재 (1)	문천벽돌공장
경공업 (5)	5월18일공장, 문천봉화피복공장, 문천식료공장, 문천염료공장, 문천한천공장
제철/조선 (4)	9월21일제련소, 문천강철공장, 문천금강제련소, 문평제련소

IPA (12-6)

공업 (12-6)	**[9월21일제련소(九月二十一日製鍊所)], [문천물감공장], [문천염료공장(文川染料工場)], [문천영예군인전기일용품공장(文川榮譽軍人電氣日用品工場)], [문평제련소(文坪製鍊所)], [5월18일공장(五月十八日工場)]**; 문천련결농기계공장(文川連結農機械工場), 문천농기구공장(文川農器具工場), 문천식료기계공장(文川食料機械工場), 문천강철공장(文川鋼鐵工場), 남창음료공장, 남창일용품공장

KCNA (3)

공업 (3)	9월21일제련소, 문천금강제련소, 5월18일공장 (문천기계공장, 문천발브공장)

KIET (16-8)

II. 음식료품 (5-1)	1) 일반	문천식료공장
	3) 육류, 어류, 채소	**[문천한천공장]**, 문천문고기가공공장
	4) 장류	문천물고기양념공장, 문천장공장
III. 섬유, 의복, 신발 (2)	4) 견직공장	문천견직공장
	10) 가죽	문천모피공장
V. 화학 (1-1)	6) 염료,도료,시약, 농약 등	**[문천염료공장]**
VI. 시멘트 등 (1-1)	5) 도자기공장	**[옥평도자기공장]**
VII. 1차 금속산업 (4-3)	1) 제철 제강	**[문천베어링강공장]**, 문천강철공장
	2) 제련	**[9월21일제련소]**, **[문평제련소]**
VIII. 조립금속, 기계장비 (3-2)	5) 기계부품	**[5월18일공장]**, **[문천영예군인전기일용품공장]**, 문천금속건구공장

IMPORTANT (4)

공업 (4)	문천염료공장, 9월21일제련소, 문평제련소, 5월18일공장

Kun (Kangwon Province)

KOFC 군 (17-4)

5	천내군 (2), 통천군
3	안변군 (1)
1	고산군 (1), 고성군, 이천군, 평강군

경고업 (3) 식품 (3)	원산만제염소, 천내소금공장 (천내), 통천냉동공장 (통천)
중화공업 (7-3) 기계 (1), 건재 (6)	고성공작기계공장 (고성); [고산세멘트공장 (고산)], 안변판유리공장 (안변), 이천세멘트공장 (이천), [천내리세멘트공장], [룡담세멘트공장], (천내), 평강세멘트공장 (평강)
재취 (1)	천내리광산 (천내)
전력 (6-1) 수력 (6)	[안변청년발전소 1-2호 (안변)], 통천발전소 1-4호 (통천)

MOU 군 (30-2)

7	천내군 (2)
6	안변군
4	고산군
3	철원군
2	금강군, 김화군, 세포군
1	고성군, 법동군, 이천군, 통천군

공업 (21-1) 광업 (7-1) 전력 (2)

건재 (4-1)	김화시멘트공장 (김화군), 안변요업공장 (안변군), [천내리시멘트련합기업소 (천내군)], 철원시멘트공장 (철원군)
경공업 (15)	고산시초식품공장, 고산종이공장, 고산항생소공장 (고산군), 고성공예생산협동조합 (고성군), 금강군식료가공공장 (금강군), 세포남자옷공장, 세포직조공장 (세포군), 안변대성영예군인피복공장, 안변버섯공장, 안변일용품공장, 안변직조공장 (안변군), 이천제약공장 (이천군), 천내식료공장, 천내장공장 (천내군), 철원장공장 (철원군)
기계 (2)	고산과수비닐공장 (고산군), 금강농기계공장 (금강군)
광업 (7-1)	창도광산 (김화군), 상서청년광산 (법동군), [천내지구탄광련합기업소], 문천탄광, 천내탄광, 삼천탄광 (천내군), 철원스레트광산 (철원군)
전력 (2)	안변청년2호발전소 (안변군), 통천발전소 (통천군)

IPA (205-36)

고산군 (15-1)

공업 (13-1)	**[고산과일가공공장]**; 고산기계수리공장(高山機械修理工場), 고산농기구공장(高山農器具工場), 고산자동차수리공장(高山自動車修理工場), 고산련결차공장(高山連結車工場), 고산기계공장, 고산식료공장(高山食料工場), 고산방직공장, 고산일용품공장, 고산제지공장, 고산제약공장, 룡지원건재공장, 연호도자기공장
광업 (2)	대령광산(大嶺鑛山), 고산광산(高山鑛山)

고성군 (7-2)

공업 (7-2)	**[고성참대일용품공장], [고성식료공장 (高城食料工場)]**; 고성장공장, 고성과자공장, 고성기계공장, 고성직조공장, 고성가구공장

금강군 (15-3)

공업(15-3)	**[금강식료공장(金剛食料工場)], [금강직물공장(金剛織物工場)], [금강초물제품공장(金剛草物製品工場)]**; 금강장공장, 금강량곡가공공장, 금강피복공장, 금강독공장, 금강기계수리공장, 금강농기구공장, 금강제약공장, 금강종이공장, 금강일용품공장, 금강방직공장, 금강기계공장, 단풍가구공장

김화군 (9-2)

공업 (8-1)	**[김화제약공장(金化製藥工場)]**; 구봉장공장(九峯醬工場), 김화목재일용품공장(金化日用品工場), 김화기계수리공장(金化機械修理工場), 김화화학공장(金化化學工場), 김화식료공장(金化食料工場), 학방식료공장(鶴芳食料工場), 학방화학공장
광업 (1-1)	**[창도광산(昌道鑛山)]**

법동군 (9-4)

공업 (7-4)	**[법동가구공장(法洞家具工場)], [법동식료공장(法洞食料工場)], [법동종이공장], [법동성냥공장]**; 법동옷공장, 률동세멘트공장, 마전연필공장
광업 (2-0)	법동광산, 상서광산

세포군 (14-3)

공업 (11-3)	**[세포가죽공장]**, **[세포식료공장(洗浦食料工場)]**, **[세포초물공장(洗浦草物工場)]**; 장촌장공장, 세포일용품공장, 세포기계공장, 세포피복공장, 세포제지공장, 삼방목재일용품공장, 삼방제약공장, 신생건재공장
광업 (1)	신풍린회석광산
전력 (2)	삼방청년발전소, 중평소형수력발전소

안변군 (27-3)

공업 (24-2)	**[안변식료공장(安邊食料工場)]**, **[안변요업공장(安邊窯業工場)]**; 안변영예군인공장, 안변소석회공장(安邊消石灰工場), 안변세멘트공장, 안변벽돌공장, 안변기계공장, 안변방직공장, 안변일용품공장, 안변제지공장, 안변제약공장, 앞강요업공장, 앞강벽돌공장, 앞강주름판지공장, 앞강독공장, 앞강기와공장, 미현세멘트공장, 미현소석회공장, 배화초물공장, 배화제약공장, 영예군인제약공장, 옥리가구공장, 옥리철제일용품공장, 옥리과일남새가공공장
광업 (2-0)	룡대광산, 남계탄광
전력 (1-1)	**[안변청년발전소(安邊靑年發電所)]**

이천군 (15-2)

공업 (14-2)	**[이천목재일용품공장(伊川木材日用品工場)]**, **[이천식료가공공장(伊川食料加工工場)]**; 이천고기가공공장, 이천일용품공장, 이천방직공장, 이천피복공장, 이천종이공장, 이천화학공장, 이천기계공장, 이천제약공장, 이천장공장, 산참세멘트공장, 산참소석회공장, 희유금속광물생산기지
광업 (1)	문동광산

창도군 (10-3)

공업 (9-3)	**[창도식료품공장(昌道食料品工場)]**, **[창도일용품공장(昌道日用品工場)]**, **[창도제약공장(昌道製藥工場)]**; 창도장공장, 창도방직공장, 창도옷공장, 대백고회석공장, 지석배합먹이공장, 구룡건재공장
광업 (1)	구룡탄광

천내군 (19-2)

공업 (14-2)	**[천내리세멘트공장]**, **[천내식료공장(川内食料工場)]**; 천내일용품공장, 천내기계공장, 룡담세멘트공장, 룡담소석회공장, 룡담옷공장, 룡담토기공장, 신산피복공장, 화라실험기구공장, 화라목재일용품공장, 신흥소석회공장, 신흥세멘트공장, 신흥토기공장
광업 (5)	천내탄광(川内炭鑛), 문천탄광(文川炭鑛), 철산탄광, 신풍리탄광(新豊里炭鑛), 화라탄광

철원군 (13-2)

공업 (11-2)	**[철원종이공장]**, **[철원초물제품공장(鐵原草物製品工場)]**; 철원가구공장, 철원직물공장, 철원피복공장, 철원기계공장, 철원식료품공장, 류대포벽돌공장, 립석독공장, 반석소석회공장, 립석소석회공장
광업 (2)	철원탄광, 부압스레트광산

통천군 (20-3)

공업 (17-1)	**[통천식료공장(通川食料工場)]**; 통천기계공장, 통천화학공장, 통천건재공장, 통천종이공장, 통천제약공장, 통천선박수리공장, 구읍도자기공장, 미평리가성소다공장, 미평종이공장, 미평건재공장, 미평화학일용품공장, 방포기와공장, 봉호전분공장, 송전기념품공장, 장진세멘트공장, 장진대리석공장
광업 (1-1)	**[통천탄광(通川炭鑛)]**
전력 (2-1)	**[금강산발전소(金剛山發電所)]**; 통천발전소(通川發電所)

판교군 (11-1)

공업 (11-1)	**[판교식료공장(板橋食料工場)]**; 판교방직공장, 판교일용품공장, 판교기계공장, 판교화학공장, 판교종이공장, 판교제약공장, 구봉제약공장, 지하토기공장, 천암세멘트공장, 천암소석회공장

평강군 (14-3)

공업 (14-3)	**[평강식료공장(平康食料工場)]**, **[평강제약공장(平康製藥工場)]**, **[평강뜨락또르수리공장]**; 평강무우가공공장, 평강기계공장, 평강피복공장, 평강일용품공장, 복계수지일용품공장, 복계세멘트공장, 복계가구공장, 상갑종이공장, 상갑토기공장, 상갑벽돌공장, 해방음료공장

회양군 (7-2)

공업 (6-2)	**[회양식료공장(淮陽食料工場)]**, **[회양일용품공장(淮陽日用品工場)]**; 회양피복공장, 회양기계공장, 광전토기공장, 소풍세멘트공장
광업 (1-0)	회양탄광

KCNA 군 (9)

4	천내군
2	세포군, 안변군
1	고성군

공업 (3)	천내장공장, 천내정제소금공장, 천내리세멘트공장 (천내군)
광업 (1)	천내지구탄광련합기업소 (천내군)
전력 (5)	월비산발전소 (고성군), 내평발전소, 내평2호군민발전소, (세포군), 안변청년발전소, 안변청년2호발전소 (안변군)

KIET (78-14)

고산군 (6)

I. 관업 (1)	3) 비철	봉련광산
II. 음식료품 (2)	3) 육류, 어류, 채소	고산과일가공공장
	4) 장류	고산군장공장
V. 화학 (1)	8) 합성수지 등	고산비닐관공장
VIII. 조립금속, 기계장비 (1)	3b) 농업 기계	광명련결차공장
X. 가구 (1)	3) 악기	고산영예군인선물악기공장

고성군 (5)

I. 광업 (1)	3) 비철금속	대봉광산
II. 음식료품 (2)	1) 일반	고성식료공장
	4) 장류	고성장공장
III. 섬유 등 (1)	6) 의류	고성군 여자 및 어린이옷 공장
X. 가구 (1)	1) 가구	고성가구공장

금강군 (4)

I. 광업 (2)	1) 탄광	금강탄광
	4) 비금속광물	금강광산
III. 섬유 (1)	3) 방적 등	금강직조공장
X. 가구 (1)	4) 공예품	금강초물공장

김화군 (5)

I. 광업 (2)	1) 탄광	김화탄광
	4) 비금속광물	신풍린회석광산
III. 섬유 등 (1)	6) 의류	김화옷공장
IV. 목제 등 (1)	3) 종이	김화군 제지공장
V. 화학 (1)	9) 제약	김화제약공장

법동군 (6-1)

I. 광업 (3)	1) 탄광	법동탄광
	3) 비철금속	상서청년광산
	4) 비금속광물	법동광산
II. 음식료품 (1-1)	1) 일반	**[법동식료공장]**
III. 섬유 등 (1)	6) 의류	법동옷공장
XI. 전력 (1)	2) 화력	법동발전소

세포군 (8-2)

II. 음식료품 (3)	3) 육류응	삼방련합합영공사, 세포고기가공공장
	5) 사료	세포배합사료공장
III. 섬유 등 (2-2)	3) 방적, 제사, 등	**[세포직조공장]**
	10) 가죽, 모피 등	**[세포모피가공공장]**
IV. 목재 등 (1)	1) 복재	세포목재일용품공장
VIII. 조립금속, 기계장비 (2)	1) 종합	세포군 직조기계수리공장, 세포기계수리공장

안변군 (7-4)

I. 광업 (1-1)	4) 비금속광물	**[안변화강석광산]**
II. 음식 (1-1)	3) 육료, 어류 등	**[안변남새과일가공공장]**
V. 화학 (1)	9) 제약공장	배화리 배화영예군인제약공장
VI. 시멘트 등 (2-1)	3) 벽돌, 타일 등	**[안변요업공장]**, 안변화강석공장,
X. 가구 (2-1)	5) 기타	**[안변일용품공장]**, 안변영예군인우산공장

창도군 (4-1)

I. 광업 (2-1)	1) 탄광	**[창도탄광]**
	4) 비금속광물	창도광산
II. 음식 (1)	4) 장류	창도장공장
X. 가구 (1)	1) 가구	창도가구공장

천내군 (10-2)

I. 광업 (5-1)	1) 탄광	**[천내지구탄광련합기업소]**, 철산탄광, 문천탄광, 천내탄광, 화라탄광
II. 음식 (1)	4) 장류	천내장공장
III. 섬유 (1)	3) 방적	천내직조공장
VI. 시멘트 등 (1-1)	1) 시멘트	**[천내리세멘트공장]**
VIII.조립금속, 기계장비 (1)	5) 기계부품	천내철제일용품공장
X. 가구 (1)	2) 문방구, 완구등	청암원주필공장

철원군 (4-1)

I. 광업 (2-1)	1) 탄광	철원탄광
	4) 비금속광물	**[철원군스레트광산]**
II. 음식 (1)	4) 장류	철원군 장공장
X. 가구 (1)	4) 공예품	철원초물공장

통천군 (7-2)

I. 광업 (1)	1) 탄광	통천탄광
II. 음식료품 (2)	1)일반	통천식료공장
	3) 육류 등	통천수출품수산사업소
III. 섬유, 의복등 (1-1)	6) 의료	**[통천옷공장]**
IX. 수송기계 (1)	1) 선박	통천선박수리공장
XI. 전력 (2-1)	1) 수력	**[금강산발전소 (안변청년)]**
	2) 화력	통천발전소

판교군 (3)

II. 음식료품 (1)	1) 일반	판교식료가공공장
III. 섬유 등(1)	3) 방적, 제사, 직조 등	판교직조공장
V. 화학(1)	9) 제약	판교영예군인제약공장

평강군 (4)

II. 음식료품 (2)	3) 육료 등	평강과일남새가공공장
	6) 음료 등	평강영예군인음료공장
III. 섬유 등 (1)	6) 의류	평강남자옷공장
V. 화학 (1)	9) 제약	평강제약공장

회양군 (5-1)

I. 광업 (1-1)	1) 탄광	**[회양탄광]**
II. 음식료품 (1)	4) 장류	회양장공장
III. 섬유 등 (2)	3) 방적등	회양직조공장
	6) 의류	회양 여자 및 어린이옷 공장
V. 화학 (1)	9) 제약	회양제약공장

IMPORTANT (6)

3	안변군
2	천내군
1	통천군

공업 (3)	천내리세멘트공장 (천내군), 안변요업공장, 안변일용품공장 (안변군)
광업 (1)	천내지구탄광련합기업소 (천내군)
전력 (2)	안변청년발전소 (안변군), 금강산발전소 (통천군)

저자소개: Rainer Dormels

독일 쾰른대학교 대학원 졸업 (지리학, 신학)
서울대학교 대학원 졸업 (국어학)
독일 함부르크대학교 한국학 박사학위 취득
독일 보쿰대학교 교수자격시험 합격
(교수자격논문: 대한민국 장관 충원과 정치문화)
2003년부터 비엔나대학교 동아시아학연구소 한국학과 교수

북한의 도시들: 산업인프라, 내부구조와 특징 가격 75,000원

2014년 6월 30일 1판 1쇄

저 자	Rainer Dormels
발행인	임 삼 규
발행처	**지 문 당**
주 소	413-756 경기도 파주시 광인사길 85(본사) 110-360 서울시 종로구 돈화문로 82(서울사무소)
등 록	1997. 12. 30. 제406-2003-000038호
영업부	(02)743-3192~3 팩스(02)742-4657
전자우편	sale@jimoon.co.kr
편집부	(02)743-3096 팩스(02)743-0227
전자우편	edit@jimoon.co.kr
홈페이지	www.jimoon.co.kr

ISBN 978-89-6297-167-5